# Narrative
## of a Child
# Analysis

*The Writings of Melanie Klein*

THE PSYCHO-ANALYSIS OF CHILDREN

NARRATIVE OF A CHILD ANALYSIS

LOVE, GUILT AND REPARATION
AND OTHER WORKS

ENVY AND GRATITUDE AND OTHER WORKS

# MELANIE KLEIN

# Narrative of a Child Analysis

THE CONDUCT OF
THE PSYCHO-ANALYSIS OF CHILDREN
AS SEEN IN THE TREATMENT OF
A TEN-YEAR-OLD BOY

**With a Foreword by ELLIOTT JAQUES**

"... come de vray il faut noter que
les jeux des enfants ne sont pas
jeux, et faut juger en eux comme
leurs plus serieuses actions."
> MONTAIGNE'S *Essays*:
> Bk. 1  Chapter XXIII

DELACORTE PRESS / SEYMOUR LAWRENCE

# FOREWORD

The *Narrative of a Child Analysis* occupies a unique position in the body of Mrs. Klein's work.

It is a daily account of the analysis of a child of ten, which lasted four months. Each session is followed by notes in which Mrs. Klein evaluates her technique and the patient's material in terms of her later theories. These notes, being much fuller and, of course, more authoritative than any other editorial comment could be, such comments are not included in this volume.

I had the unusual opportunity to know Mrs. Klein's attitude to this work through the good fortune of having been invited by her to help with the editing of the material and the preparation of the notes in many hours of discussion extending over some years. I know that it had long been her ambition to write a full case study of a child's analysis, based on daily detailed notes which she had always kept, session by session, for all her child patients. But the problem of scale in giving a satisfactory account of a total analysis seemed insurmountable.

Then the war threw up a circumstance which suddenly offered a possible solution. An analysis was arranged for Richard. There was a limited and known amount of time available—four months. This limit was known equally to the analyst and the patient from the beginning. So Mrs. Klein found herself with case notes of a short analysis, which could be encompassed in a single volume. She did not contend that it was in no way different from an analysis of normal duration. She felt particularly the lack of the opportunity to work through particular anxieties and then to encounter them in other forms and work through them again in greater depth. In this process, other types of anxieties, other psychic processes, would have been uncovered. But notwithstanding the shortcomings, she thought that the essential elements of a full analysis were all present, sufficiently to illustrate both the patient's personality and her work.

Some fifteen years later she decided to work seriously on the book. She went through the case notes for each session, carefully editing in style, but not in content, so as to leave intact the picture of how the work had gone at the time. Then she subjected each session in her mind to self-criticism and evaluation. These new thoughts about the sessions and the changes in her way of thinking are recorded in detailed notes which she prepared, going through each session, association by association, interpretation by interpretation, so as to be able to explain her work as fully as she could.

# FOREWORD

She probably devoted more intense care to the *Narrative of a Child Analysis* than to any other of her works. Indeed, in the hospital, a few days before her death, she was still going through the proofs and index of the book. She wanted to leave as faithful an account as she could of both her practical and theoretical work. In this, I think, she succeeded. The book is a living thing. It presents Mrs. Klein at work as no other paper does. It gives a faithful picture of her technique and, through the notes, an insight into how her mind worked. It shows her theoretical concepts at the time of the analysis. A great many of her formulations in the paper "The Oedipus Complex in the Light of Early Anxieties" (1945, *Writings*, 1) are based on Richard's material, but it also reveals new ideas at the point of their emergence, ideas intuitively conceived, but not yet developed or conceptualised. This, her last work, is a fitting monument of her creativity.

Elliott Jaques

### Note About the References

References in the text and footnotes to other works by Melanie Klein have, in most cases, been changed to indicate the volume number in *The Writings of Melanie Klein* in which they may be found. (For this purpose, the abbreviation *Writings* has been used throughout.)

In the case of *The Psycho-Analysis of Children* (*Writings*, 2) only the page references have been changed, to conform with the *Writings* edition.

# CONTENTS

# CONTENTS

## CONTENTS

# CONTENTS

*Illustrations follow page 288*

## AUTHOR'S NOTE

The illustrations are photographs of Richard's original drawings, some in pencil and some in crayon. They have been photographed and slightly reduced in size : all originally measured approximately 7 inches by $4\frac{1}{2}$ inches. The only alterations that have been made were to emphasise details such as names where the originals had faded, the insertion of letters, viz. (*a*), where I needed to refer to parts of a drawing in the text, and the blacking-out of certain names.                    M. K.

# PREFACE

In presenting the following case-history, I have several aims in view. I wish first of all to illustrate my technique in greater detail than I have done formerly. The extensive notes I made enable the reader to observe how interpretations find confirmation in the material following them. The day-to-day movement in the analysis, and the continuity running through it, thus become perceptible. Furthermore, the details of this analysis clarify and support my concepts. The reader will find all my comments about theory and technique at the end of each session.

In *The Psycho-Analysis of Children* I was only able to give extracts of my observations and interpretations; and since in that book I was mainly concerned with putting forward a number of hypotheses regarding previously undiscovered anxiety contents and defences, I could not give at the time an all-round picture of my technique; in particular, the fact that I made consistent use of transference interpretations was not sufficiently evident. However, in my view the main principles put forward in *The Psycho-Analysis of Children* remain valid.

Though the analysis I am describing here lasted only ninety-three sessions, extending over about four months, the unusual co-operativeness of the child enabled me to penetrate to great depths.

I took fairly extensive notes, but I could of course not always be sure of the sequence, nor quote literally the patient's associations and my interpretations. This difficulty is one of a general nature in reporting on case material. To give verbatim accounts could only be done if the analyst were to take notes during the session; this would disturb the patient considerably and break the unhindered flow of associations, as well as divert the analyst's attention from the course of the analysis. Another possibility of obtaining literal accounts is the use of a recording machine, either visible or hidden —a measure which, in my view, is absolutely against the fundamental principles on which psycho-analysis rests, namely the exclusion of any audience during an analytic session. Not only do I believe that the patient, if he had any reason to suspect that a machine was being used (and the unconscious is very perspicacious), would not speak and behave in the way he does when he is alone with the analyst; but I am also convinced that the analyst, speaking to an audience which the machine implies, would not interpret in the same natural and intuitive way as he does when alone with his patient.

For all these reasons I am sure that notes taken as soon as possible after each session provide the best picture of the day-to-day happenings in the analysis, and therefore of the course of the analysis. Hence I believe that—allowing for all the limitations I have enumerated—I am giving in this book a true account of my technique and of the material.

It has to be kept in mind that the evidence which the analyst can present differs essentially from that which is required in physical science, because the whole nature of psycho-analysis is different. In my view, endeavours to provide comparable exact data result in a pseudo-scientific approach, because the workings of the unconscious mind, and the response of the psycho-analyst to them, cannot be submitted to measurement nor classified into rigid categories. For instance, a machine could only reproduce the actual words spoken, without their accompaniment of facial expressions and movements. These intangible factors play an important part in an analysis, as does the intuition of the analyst.

Nevertheless, since certain working hypotheses are put forward and tested in the material which the patient produces, psychoanalysis is a scientific procedure and its technique embodies scientific principles. The assessment and interpretation of the patient's material by the analyst are based on a coherent framework of theory. It is the task of the analyst, however, to combine his theoretical knowledge with insight into the individual variations presented by each patient. At any given moment we are confronted with one dominant trend of anxieties, emotions, and object-relations, and the symbolic content of the patient's material has a precise and exact meaning in connection with this dominant theme.

This book is intended to illustrate the psycho-analytic procedure, which consists in selecting the most urgent aspects of the material and interpreting them with precision. The patient's reactions and subsequent associations amount to further material, which again has to be analysed on the same principles.

Working-through was one of the essential demands that Freud made on an analysis. The necessity to work through is again and again proved in our day-to-day experience : for instance, we see that patients, who at some stage have gained insight, repudiate this very insight in the following sessions and sometimes even seem to have forgotten that they had ever accepted it. It is only by drawing our conclusions from the material as it reappears in different contexts, and is interpreted accordingly, that we gradually help the patient to acquire insight in a more lasting way. The process of adequately working-through includes bringing about changes in the character and strength of the manifold splitting processes which we meet with even in neurotic patients, as well as the consistent analysis of paranoid and depressive anxieties. Ultimately this leads to greater integration.

The analysis I am presenting, though it remained unfinished, was illuminating in various ways. As my account shows, I could penetrate into very deep layers of the mind, thus enabling the patient to free much of his phantasy life and to become conscious of some of his anxieties and defences; but adequate working-through was not possible.

In spite of the difficulties inherent in the shortness of this analysis, I was determined not to modify my technique and to interpret in the usual way even deep anxiety situations as they came up and the corresponding defences. If such interpretations are to some extent understood by the patient, even though not adequately worked through, the analysis has in fact not been without value. Although splitting processes and repression are bound to set in again, some lasting alterations have taken place in fundamental regions of the mind.

Nevertheless, I remain fully convinced that however much we improve our technique in the future, this progress will not lead to shorter analyses. On the contrary, my experience points to the conclusion that the more time was have at our disposal for carrying out our treatment, the better we can diminish persecutory and depressive anxiety and help the patient to achieve integration.

# ACKNOWLEDGEMENTS

My thanks are first and foremost due to my patient. His unusual cooperativeness and insight allowed me to gather a wealth of material within a few months, and made it possible to present a consecutive day-by-day account of an analysis without making the book too long. In spite of the shortness of the treatment, the patient's insight allowed me to explore even the deeper layers of his mind and thus enabled me to confirm a number of my theoretical conclusions.

Again, as on former occasions, I wish to thank my friend Lola Brook for her assistance in compiling this volume. Her indefatigable patience, her willingness to help, and her deep understanding of my work, acquired in the course of seventeen years of cooperation, have proved invaluable.

I am much indebted to Dr Elliott Jaques for taking the great trouble to go carefully through the whole manuscript. He has made a number of helpful suggestions as well as some comments which I found very stimulating.

Finally, I wish to express my thanks to Mrs Matilda Harris who, with the assistance of Mrs Maureen Brook, did a great deal of work on the index.

# INTRODUCTION

Richard was ten years old when I began his analysis.[1] His symptoms had developed to such an extent that it had become impossible for him to attend school after the age of eight, when the outbreak of the war in 1939 had increased his anxieties. He was very frightened of other children and this contributed to an increasing avoidance of going out by himself. Moreover, since about the age of four or five, a progressive inhibition of his faculties and interests had been causing great concern to his parents. In addition to these symptoms, he was very hypochondriacal and frequently subject to depressed moods. These difficulties showed themselves in his appearance, for he looked very worried and unhappy. At times, however —and this became striking during analytic sessions—his depression lifted, and then suddenly life and sparkle came into his eyes, completely transforming his face.

Richard was in many ways a precocious and gifted child. He was very musical and showed this at an early age. His love of nature was pronounced, though in its pleasant aspects only. His artistic gifts could be seen, for instance, in the way in which he chose his words and in a feeling for the dramatic which enlivened his conversation. He could not get on with children and was at his best with adults, particularly with women. He tried to impress them by his conversational gifts and to ingratiate himself in a rather precocious way.

Breast-feeding had been unsatisfactory and probably continued only for several weeks.[2] He had always been delicate and had suffered from colds and illnesses from infancy onwards.. His mother reported two operations (circumcision at three years and tonsillectomy in his sixth year). Richard was the younger of two children, his brother being about eight years older. His mother, though not ill in a clinical sense, was inclined towards depression. She was very worried about any illness in Richard, and her attitude had some effect on his hypochondriacal fears. There was no doubt that Richard was rather a disappointment to her and that, although she

[1] The details of the patient's background given here are largely identical with the introductory passages of my paper, 'The Oedipus Complex in the Light of Early Anxieties' (1945, *Writings*, 1) in which I illustrated my conclusions with material drawn from the analysis of the same patient.

[2] The mother's report on this point and on others was rather vague, and therefore there is a number of details of Richard's early history which I should have liked to know more about but was unable to find out.

tried not to show it, she preferred the elder brother, who had been a great success at school and had never caused her any worry. Though Richard was devoted to her, he was an extremely difficult child to live with; he had no hobbies to occupy him, was over-anxious and over-affectionate towards his mother and, since he could not bear to be away from her, clung to her in a persistent and exhausting way; his hypochondriacal fears related to her health as well as his own.

Much care was lavished on him by his mother and in some ways she pampered him, but she did not seem to realize his great inherent capacity for love and kindness and had little confidence in his future development. At the same time she was very patient; for instance, she did not attempt to press the company of other children on him or to force him to attend school.

Richard's father was fond of him and very kind, but he seemed to leave the responsibility for the boy's upbringing predominantly to the mother. Although his brother was friendly with Richard, the two boys had little in common. The family life was on the whole peaceful.

The outbreak of the war had greatly increased Richard's difficulties. His parents moved to the country, and his brother was sent away with his school. For purposes of the analysis, arrangements were made for Richard and his mother to stay in a hotel in 'X', the Welsh village where I was living at the time, not very far from the place where they had settled for the duration of the war, which I shall call 'Y'. On Saturdays he went home for the weekend. Leaving his home town, which I shall call 'Z', upset Richard a good deal. Moreover, the war stirred up all his anxieties, and he was particularly frightened of air-raids and bombs. He followed the news closely and took a great interest in the changes in the war situation, and this preoccupation came up again and again during the course of his analysis.

I was renting a playroom for my child patients, since my lodgings, where I treated my adult patients, were unsuitable for analysing children. This playroom was a large place with two doors and an adjoining kitchen and lavatory. Richard identified the playroom with me and with the analysis, and in consequence had almost a personal relation to it. However, it had some drawbacks: it was used at other times by Girl Guides, and I was unable to remove a number of books, pictures, maps, and so on. Another drawback was the absence of a waiting-room and the fact that there was nobody to answer the door. I collected the key and unlocked and locked up the house before and after each session with a child patient. If Richard was early, he occasionally came a little way to meet me.

Since I left the house when the session was over, Richard waited for me until I had locked up and then went a short distance with me to the corner of the road (which was only a hundred yards or so from the playroom), except on those occasions when I had to go to the village to do some shopping; then Richard walked with me a little farther. When this happened, though I could not refuse to have some conversation with the boy, I was averse from giving any interpretations or entering into any intimate details. In fact, I kept as closely as I could to the arranged length of the session, which was fifty minutes as with adults.

In the course of his treatment Richard produced a series of drawings. The way he made them was significant: he did not start out with any deliberate plan and was often surprised to see the finished picture. I provided various sorts of play material; in addition, the pencils and crayons with which he made his drawings also figured in his play as people, and he brought his own set of toy ships. When Richard wanted to take the drawings home, I pointed out to him that it would be useful for the analysis to keep them with the toys; for we might sometimes wish to have a look at them again. I was quite aware, and found it repeatedly confirmed in the course of the analysis, that he understood that these drawings had some value for me and that in a sense he was giving me a present. He derived some reassurance from having these 'gifts' accepted and valued, and felt this as a means of making reparation—all of which I analysed. This reassuring effect of the analyst's intention to keep drawings is a problem with which the child analyst is often confronted. Our adult patients frequently experience the wish to make themselves useful to the analyst outside the analytic situation. There is a similarity between such desires and the child's wish to give the analyst a present; and I have found that the only way of dealing with these feelings is to analyse them.

Although I endeavoured on the whole to put down detailed notes after each session, the amount of detail recorded varied from one hour to another and, particularly at the beginning, a few sessions were incompletely recorded. Except for some of the patient's remarks, which are indicated by inverted commas, I could not reproduce his associations or my interpretations verbatim, nor could they all be noted down. There were also hours in which the boy's anxiety made him silent for long periods and he produced less material. It was impossible to describe the nuances of behaviour, gesture, facial expression, and the length of pauses between associations, all of which, as we know, are of particular significance during the analytic work.

In my interpretations I tried, as always, to avoid (as I would with adults as well as with children) introducing any similes, metaphors, or quotations to illustrate my point. For the sake of brevity I occasionally use technical terms in this report when referring back to details from previous sessions. In practice, even when reminding a patient of former material, I never use technical terms, and this again applies not only to children but also to adults. I make a point of using whenever possible the words that the patient has used, and I find that this has the effect both of diminishing resistance and of bringing fully back into his mind the material I am referring to. With Richard I had to introduce in the course of the analysis certain terms which were unknown to him, such as 'genital', 'potent', 'sexual relations', or 'sexual intercourse'. From one point onwards Richard referred to the analysis as 'the work'. While I was always concerned to word my interpretations as nearly as I could in Richard's own language, in writing them down I have been able to give only a summary approximation. Moreover, I have sometimes brought together what were in fact several interpretations separated by some play or comment of the child, which may give the impression that the interpretations were longer than they actually were.

I thought it would be helpful to define certain points in the material and in my interpretations in the same terms as I use in my theoretical writings. Of course, I did not use these formulations in speaking to the child, but have added them in square brackets in the text.

As far as details of the patient's background are concerned, some slight alterations have been made for reasons of discretion; and in publishing this report I have, therefore, to avoid various references to people and to external circumstances. In spite of all these qualifications, however, I feel confident, as I have said earlier, that I am giving an essentially true picture of this child's psycho-analysis and of my technique.

I knew from the beginning that it would not be possible to prolong the analysis beyond four months. After careful consideration I undertook it nevertheless, since the impression the child gave me led me to assume that, although I could only expect a partial result, I might be able to produce some improvement in him. He was very much aware of his great difficulties and so strongly wished to be helped that I had no reason to doubt that he would be very cooperative. I also knew that for years to come he would have no other opportunity to be analysed. His eagerness to be treated by me was increased by the fact that a much older boy whom he knew well was a patient of mine.

Although I have, even to the last hour, kept in all essentials to my usual techniques, I found in re-reading my notes that I had answered more questions than in my other child cases. Richard knew from the beginning that his analysis would last only four months. But as the treatment went on he fully understood that he needed much more analysis, and the nearer we came to the end the more pathetic was his fear of being left without it. I was aware of my positive counter-transference but, being on my guard, I was able to keep to the fundamental principle of analysing consistently the negative as well as the positive transference and the deep anxieties which I encountered. I was convinced that, however difficult the actual situation was, the analysis of the anxieties stirred up by his fears of the war [1] was the only means of helping him as much as possible. I believe that I have avoided the pitfalls which great sympathy with the suffering of the patient and a positive counter-transference can lead to.

The result of this analysis was, as I expected, only a partial one, but it had in fact an influence on his further development. He was able to go to school for a time; later on he was taught privately and eventually went successfully through a University Course. His relation to his contemporaries improved and his dependence on his mother diminished. He has developed scientific interests and there are some real possibilities of a career for him. I have seen him on several occasions since the end of the war, but there has been no chance so far of continuing his analysis.

# FIRST SESSION (Monday)

(The first two sessions are based on incomplete notes)

*Mrs K.* had prepared some little toys and a writing-pad, pencils, and chalks on a table, with two chairs by it. When she sat down, Richard also sat down, paying no attention to the toys and looking at her in an expectant and eager way, obviously waiting for her to say something. She suggested that he knew why he was coming to her : he had some difficulties with which he wanted to be helped.

Richard agreed and at once began to talk about his worries (Note I). He was afraid of boys he met in the street and of going out by himself, and this fear had been getting worse and worse. It had made him hate school. He also thought much about the war. Of course he knew the Allies were going to win and was not worried, but was it not awful what Hitler did to people, particularly the terrible things he did to the Poles? Did he mean to do the same over

Cf. 'On the Theory of Anxiety and Guilt' (1948, *Writings*, 3).

here? But he, Richard, felt confident that Hitler would be beaten. (When speaking about Hitler, he went to have a look at a large map hanging on the wall.) . . . Mrs K. was Austrian, wasn't she? Hitler had been awful to the Austrians though he was Austrian himself. . . . Richard also told of a bomb that had fallen near their garden at their old home (in 'Z'). Poor Cook had been in the house all by herself. He gave a dramatic description of what had happened. The actual damage had not been great; only some windows were blown in and the greenhouse in the garden collapsed. Poor Cook must have been terrified; she went to neighbours to sleep. Richard thought the canaries in their cages must have been shaken and very frightened. . . . He again spoke of Hitler's cruel treatment of conquered countries. . . . After that he tried to remember whether he had any worries he had not yet mentioned. Oh yes, he often wondered what he was like inside and what other people's insides were like. He was puzzled about the way blood flowed. If one stood for a long time on one's head and all the blood went down into it, wouldn't one die?

*Mrs K.* asked whether he also worried about his mother sometimes.[1]

Richard said that he often felt frightened at night, and until four or five years ago he used to be actually terrified. Lately, too, he often felt 'lonely and deserted' before going to sleep. He was frequently worried about Mummy's health : she was sometimes not well. Once she had been brought home on a stretcher after an accident : she had been run over. This had happened before he was born; he had only been told about it, but he often thought about it. . . . In the evenings he often feared that a nasty man—a kind of tramp—would come and kidnap Mummy during the night. He then pictured how he, Richard, would go to her help, would scald the tramp with hot water and make him unconscious; and if he, Richard, were to be killed, he would not mind—no, he would mind very much—but this would not stop him from going to Mummy's rescue.

*Mrs K.* asked how he thought the tramp would get into Mummy's room.

Richard said (after some resistance) that he might get in through the window : perhaps he would break in.

[1] I had been told by his mother that he was very worried as soon as there was anything wrong with her. Such information cannot be used often and should become part of interpretations only if it fits very closely into the material. It is safer to rely only on the material given by the child, because otherwise his suspicion might be aroused that the analyst is in close touch with the parents. But in this particular case I felt that the boy was exceptionally ready to talk about all his worries.

*Mrs K.* asked if he also wondered whether the tramp would hurt Mummy.

Richard (reluctantly) answered that he thought the man might hurt her, but he, Richard, would go to her rescue.

*Mrs K.* suggested that the tramp who would hurt Mummy at night seemed to him very much like Hitler who frightened Cook in the air-raid and ill-treated the Austrians. Richard knew that Mrs K. was Austrian, and so she too would be ill-treated. At night he might have been afraid that when his parents went to bed something could happen between them with their genitals that would injure Mummy (Note II).

Richard looked surprised and frightened. He did not seem to understand what the word 'genital' meant.[1] Up to this point he had obviously understood and had listened with mixed feelings.

*Mrs K.* asked whether he knew what she meant by 'genital'.

Richard first said no, then admitted that he thought he knew. Mummy had told him that babies grew inside her, that she had little eggs there and Daddy put some kind of fluid into her which made them grow. (Consciously he seemed to have no conception of sexual intercourse, nor a name for the genitals.)[2] He went on to say that Daddy was very nice, very kind, he wouldn't do anything to Mummy.

*Mrs K.* interpreted that he might have contradictory thoughts about Daddy. Although Richard knew that Daddy was a kind man, at night, when he was frightened, he might fear that Daddy was doing some harm to Mummy. When he thought of the tramp, he did not remember that Daddy, who was in the bedroom with Mummy, would protect her; and that was, Mrs K. suggested, because he felt that it was Daddy himself who might hurt Mummy. (At that moment Richard looked impressed and evidently accepted the interpretation.) In day-time he thought Daddy was nice, but at

---

[1] Cf. Introduction.

[2] I had asked Richard's mother about the expression he used for his genital and was told that he had none for it and never referred to it. He seemed to have no name for urination and defæcation either; but when I introduced the words 'big job' and 'little job', and sometime later 'fæces', he had no difficulty in understanding these expressions.

In a case where repression, encouraged by the environment, has gone so far that no name for the genital or for bodily functions exist, the analyst has to introduce words for them. Doubtless the child knows that he has a genital, as he knows that he produces urine and fæces, and the words introduced will bring up the association with this knowledge, as was shown in this case. Similarly, the expression for sexual intercourse had to be introduced to begin with by describing what he actually unconsciously expected his parents were doing at night. Gradually I used the expression 'sexual relations', and later also 'sexual intercourse'.

night when he, Richard, could not see his parents and did not know what they were doing in bed, he might have felt that Daddy was bad and dangerous and that all the terrible things which happened to Cook, and the shaking and breaking of windows, were happening to Mummy [Splitting of the father figure into good and bad]. Such thoughts might be in his mind though he was not at all aware of them. Just now he had spoken of the terrible things the Austrian Hitler did to the Austrians. By this he meant that Hitler was in a way ill-treating his own people, including Mrs K., just as the bad Daddy would ill-treat Mummy.

Richard, though he did not say so, appeared to accept this interpretation (Note III). From the beginning of the session he seemed extremely keen to tell all about himself, as if he had been waiting for this chance for a long time. Though he repeatedly showed anxiety and surprise, and rejected some of the interpretations, his whole attitude towards the end of the hour had altered and he was less tense. He said he had noticed the toys, the pad, and pencils on the table, but he did not like toys, he liked talking and thinking. He was very friendly and satisfied when he left Mrs K. and said he was glad to come again next day (Note IV).

*Notes to First Session:*

I. It is not unusual for a child in the latency period to ask why he is coming to analysis. Most likely he has already put this question at home, and it is useful to discuss this point with the mother or parents beforehand. If there are any difficulties that the child himself recognizes, then the answer is simple : the analyst would reply that it is because of these difficulties that the child is sent to him for treatment. With Richard I opened the question myself; I have found this useful in some cases where the child, though obviously desiring information, would not put the question himself. Otherwise it might take a number of sessions until the analyst has an opportunity to explain the reasons for the treatment. There are, however, children with whom we might first have to trace in the unconscious material the child's wish to know about his relation to the analyst and his realization that he needs the analysis and that it is helpful. (I have given instances of the beginning of a latency analysis in *The Psycho-Analysis of Children*, Chapter IV.)

II. Views among analysts differ about the point in the transference at which the material should be interpreted. Whereas I believe that there should be no session without any transference interpretation, my experience has shown me that it is not always at the beginning of the interpretation that the transference should be gone into. When the patient is deeply engrossed in his relation with his father or mother, brother or sister, with his experiences in the past or even in the present, it is necessary to give him every opportunity to enlarge on these subjects. The reference to the analyst then has to come later. On other occasions the analyst might feel that, whatever the patient is speaking about, the whole emotional emphasis lies on his relation to the analyst. In this case, the interpretation would first refer to the transference. Needless to say, a transference interpretation always means referring back the emotions experienced towards the analyst to earlier objects. Otherwise it will not fulfil its purpose sufficiently. This technique of transference interpretation was discovered by Freud in the early days of psycho-analysis and retains its full significance. The intuition of the analyst must guide him in recognizing the transference in material in which he may not have been mentioned directly.

III. In the course of this report I indicate at various places Richard's reply to my interpretations : sometimes these replies were negative, even expressing strong objection; sometimes they expressed a definite agreement; and sometimes his attention wandered and he did not appear to hear me. Even when his attention wandered, however, it would be wrong to assume that he did not respond at all. But often I did not or could not record the fleeting effect the interpretation made on him. The child would seldom have been sitting silently. while I was speaking. He might get up, pick up a toy or a pencil or pad. He might interject something which was a further association or a doubt. Therefore my interpretations may frequently appear more lengthy and consecutive than they in fact were.

IV. It is unusual for a child in the latency period to bring in the first hours the kind of material that Richard produced, and therefore the interpretations given in other cases would also be different. The content of interpretations and the moment at which they are given vary from patient to patient, according to the material presented and the emotional situation prevailing. (Cf. *The Psycho-Analysis of Children*, Chapter IV.)

## SECOND SESSION (Tuesday)

Richard arrived a few minutes early and waited for Mrs K. on the doorstep. He seemed eager to start. He said he remembered something else he often worried about, but added that it was very different from the things he had talked about yesterday, altogether far away. He feared there might be a collision between the sun and the earth and the sun might burn up the earth ; Jupiter and the other planets would be pulverized ; and the earth, the one planet

with living people on it, was so important and precious. . . . He
again looked at the map and commented how awful it was what
Hitler did to the world, the misery he caused. He thought Hitler
was probably gloating in his room because others were suffering and
would enjoy having people whipped. . . . He pointed at Switzerland
on the map, saying it was a small neutral country that was 'encircled' by the huge Germany. There was also little Portugal, a
friend. (He had mentioned, by the way, that he read three newspapers every day and listened to all the news on the wireless.) Brave
little Switzerland had dared to shoot down planes, German or
British, which flew over her territory.

*Mrs K.* interpreted that the 'precious earth' was Mummy, the
living people her children, whom he wanted as allies and friends;
hence his references to Portugal, the small country, and to the
planets. The sun and earth in collision stood for something happening between his parents. 'Far away' meant near by, in the parents'
bedroom. The pulverized planets stood for himself (Jupiter), and
Mummy's other children, if they came between the parents. After
speaking about the collision, he had again referred to Hitler destroying Europe and the world. The little countries, such as Switzerland,
also represented himself. Mrs K. reminded him of yesterday's
material : how he would attack the tramp who kidnapped Mummy,
would scald him, make him unconscious, and how he, Richard,
might be killed. This had the same meaning as Jupiter—himself—
being pulverized between the colliding earth and sun—his parents.

Richard agreed to part of the interpretation. He said he had
often thought in connection with the tramp that he might be killed
while defending Mummy, but would rather die than not put up a
fight. He agreed, too, with Mrs K.'s interpretation that the earth,
precious because of the living people, meant Mummy. He had
heard the saying 'Mother Earth'. . . . He mentioned that he had
asked Mummy when had she been run over by a car and brought
home on a stretcher. Mummy said he had been two years old at
the time. He had thought that it had happened before he was born.
. . . He said he hated Hitler and would like to hurt him, also
Goebbels and Ribbentrop who had dared to say Britain was the
aggressor.

*Mrs K.* referred to yesterday's material about his attacking the
tramp and suggested that when he was in bed at night, he not only
feared that Daddy would hurt Mummy, but sometimes he might
also think that his parents were enjoying themselves [1] ; therefore he

---

[1] This is an instance of the difficulty arising from the incompleteness of my
notes. The record of this interpretation is misleading, for I would never have
given such an interpretation without some material to base it on.

would be jealous and angry with them for leaving him 'lonely and deserted'. If he wished to hurt them because he was jealous, he would feel very guilty. He had told Mrs K. that he often thought about Mummy's accident but assumed that it had happened before he was born; this error could be due to his feeling of guilt. He had to convince himself that he had nothing to do with this accident and that it was not his fault. His fear lest the tramp-father should injure his mother, and that sun and earth would collide, might have been connected with his having hostile feelings against his parents.

Richard at first strongly denied that he had such thoughts when he was sent to bed, and said he only felt frightened and unhappy. But he went on to say that he could argue with his parents until they were quite exhausted and could not stand it any longer—and that he enjoyed doing this. He also said he felt jealous when Paul, his brother, came home on leave [1] and he thought Paul was Mummy's favourite. Mummy sometimes sent him chocolates, which Richard resented, though he thought she was right to do so.

*Mrs K.* referred to his indignation at Ribbentrop's lies about Britain being the aggressor. She said that his anger about these lies might be all the stronger because he felt the accusation applied to himself. If he experienced jealousy and anger, and also wanted to make trouble between his parents, he would be the aggressor.

Richard remained silent, obviously thinking over the interpretation, and then smiled. When asked why he smiled, he answered that it was because he liked thinking; he had been thinking about what Mrs K. had said and thought she was right. . . . (The interpretation about his aggressiveness had obviously, after some resistance, produced relief.) He spoke about his relation with Paul who some years before used to tease and chase him. He often hated Paul, but also liked him. Sometimes they were allies against Nurse and teased her [2] (Note I). Sometimes Nurse helped him against Paul. He also spoke of a fight he recently had with his cousin Peter whom he usually liked but who hurt him on this occasion. He mentioned how huge his cousin was in comparison with himself.

*Mrs K.* pointed out that when Peter was rough in a fight, Richard felt him to be a mixture of the nice father and of the bad Hitler—or tramp—father. It was easy for Richard to hate Hitler but painful when he hated his Daddy whom he also loved [Ambivalence].

[1] By then Paul, who had turned nineteen, was in the army.

[2] Nurse had been with the family from the time Richard was born or soon after. She was much loved by him and seems to have been very understanding and kind to him. She had left the family and, since her marriage, did not live far from 'X'.

Richard again spoke with resentment of the welcome Mummy gave Paul when he came home on leave. Then he mentioned Bobby, his spaniel, who always gave Richard a welcome and loved him more than it loved anybody else in the family. (His eyes shone when he said this.) He had been given Bobby as a puppy, and it still jumped on to his lap. He described with evident amusement how, when Daddy got up from his chair, Bobby took his place and Daddy had to sit on the edge. They had had another dog which fell ill when it was eleven years old, and had to be destroyed. Richard had been very sad but got over it. . . . He also mentioned his granny, of whom he had been very fond and who had died some years before.

*Mrs K.* interpreted his jealousy in connection with what he had said about Mummy's love for Paul; immediately after this he had spoken of Bobby welcoming him and jumping on his lap. It seemed that Bobby stood for his child and that he, Richard, overcame his jealousy and resentment by putting himself in the place of Mummy. But when Bobby welcomed and loved him best of all, he, Richard, was the child who was loved by Mummy, and Bobby stood for Mummy. He had mentioned the death of his granny after he had spoken of the old dog which had to be destroyed. This seemed to show that she, too, had been destroyed, possibly he felt—as with Mummy's accident—through some fault of his. Granny, of whom he was fond, might also stand for Mrs K. and perhaps he feared that some harm would happen to her through him.

(My notes here are particularly incomplete. I am quite certain that Richard must have responded to this interpretation, probably rejecting it; also I have no indication how this session finished. But if my memory is correct, there was no refusal to come on the following day (Note II).)

*Notes to Second Session:*

I. Generally speaking, a nurse, an aunt or uncle, or a grandparent are of great importance in the young child's life. The conflict which is always aroused up to a point in the relation to parents does not apply so much to these figures who are removed from the direct impact of the Œdipus situation. The same applies to brothers and sisters. These loved objects also strengthen the good aspect of the mother or father. The memory of such relations becomes important because additional good objects have been introjected.

II. In the first of these two sessions I have clearly aimed at analysing the conscious and unconscious anxiety about harm done to his mother by the 'bad' and sexual father. In the second hour I was concerned with the part which his own aggression played in these anxieties. This would suggest that my first aim in analysing a child—and I have repeatedly pointed this out—is to analyse the anxieties that are activated. However, this needs qualification. For it is impossible to analyse anxieties without recognizing the defences which operate against them and which in turn must be analysed.

To return to my present material: Richard was aware of his fear that the tramp would kidnap and harm his mother. He was not conscious of the fact that this fear was a derivative of the anxieties relating to the parents' sexual intercourse. When I interpreted that specific anxiety content, I also stressed that it was too painful for him to think of his father as a bad man, and that therefore he had turned his fear and suspicion against the tramp and Hitler. This implies analysing a defence as well.

In the second session his anger against Ribbentrop, because he had called Britain an aggressor, was interpreted as representing (as well as hate of the actual Ribbentrop) his revulsion against himself for being aggressive. There, too, I analysed not only the anxiety but also the defence against it, as can be seen if the details of the session and interpretations are considered.

I have pointed out in *The Psycho-Analysis of Children* (Chapter V) that each interpretation should follow to a certain extent the role of the super-ego, id, and ego. This implies that the various parts of the mind and their functions are systematically explored in an adequate interpretation.

There are analysts who take the view (and I am referring particularly to Anna Freud's writings) that the analysis of anxieties should be left for a later stage and that defences (either against anxiety or against instinctual urges) should primarily be analysed. I have made it clear in other connections that I do not agree with this view. (Cf. 'Symposium on Child Analysis', 1927, *Writings*, 1.)

## THIRD SESSION (Wednesday)

Richard was on time. He soon turned to the map and expressed his fears about the British battleships being blockaded in the Mediterranean if Gibraltar were taken by the Germans. They could not get through Suez. He also spoke of injured soldiers and showed some anxiety about their fate. He wondered how the British troops could be rescued from Greece. What would Hitler do to the Greeks; would he enslave them? Looking at the map, he said with concern that Portugal was a very small country compared with big Germany, and would be overcome by Hitler. He mentioned Norway, about whose attitude he was doubtful, though it might not prove to be a bad ally after all.

*Mrs K.* interpreted that he also worried unconsciously about what might happen to Daddy when he put his genital into Mummy. Daddy might not be able to get out of Mummy's inside and would be caught there, like the ships in the Mediterranean. This also applied to the troops which had to be retrieved from Greece. She referred to what he had said in the first session about a person standing on his head and dying because his blood flowed down. This was what he thought might happen to Daddy when at night he put his genital into Mummy. He was also afraid that Mummy would be hurt by the tramp-Daddy. Thus he felt anxious about *both* parents and guilty because of his aggressive wishes against them. His dog Bobby stood for himself wanting to take his father's place with Mummy (the armchair standing for the bed), and whenever he felt jealous and angry, he hated and attacked Daddy in his thoughts (Note I). This made him also feel sorry and guilty [Œdipus situation].

Richard smiled agreement at Mrs K.'s saying that the dog stood for himself, but disagreed emphatically with the other part of the interpretation, because he would never *do* such a thing.

*Mrs K.* explained that the feeling that he would not really carry out such an attack was a great relief to him, but pointed out that he might have felt that hostile wishes could be so powerful that if he wished Daddy to die, he would actually die [Omnipotence of thought]. (At this point Richard appeared to agree.) Mrs K. also connected Richard's anxiety about Britain's allies with his brother, who he felt was not a reliable ally against the hostile united parents (in the material, Germany and Hitler).

Richard said that it was likely that his parents were angry with him when he had been in a bad temper and worried them, and that a good ally would be a help. He expressed his great admiration for Churchill who would help Britain through, and spoke about this at great length.

*Mrs K.* interpreted that Churchill and Britain represented another aspect of the parents: the good Daddy who protected Mummy, the wonderful parents, more admired than the real ones (Richard agreed to this), while Germany and Hitler stood for the bad parents when they were angry with him [Splitting of both parents into good and bad, and projection].

Richard seemed deeply interested in this interpretation. He remained silent, evidently thinking about it. His gratification over this new insight was very striking. Then he commented on how difficult it was with so many kinds of parents in his mind.

*Mrs K.* pointed out that it was the contradiction in his feelings that was so difficult, actually painful. He loved his parents, but felt he hurt them by his hatred and hostile wishes, and then felt guilty about the injuries he thought he had done to them. She connected this with the material about the accident to his mother when he had been two years old. He might have felt at that time that the car, standing for the bad tramp-father, had injured Mummy because he, Richard, had been angry with her and had wished it. . . .

Richard said that he liked to go for walks with Bobby. One evening he was out with him till ten, having been to visit various people, and he mentioned one lady in particular. Bobby would like to have a wife and babies, but Mummy did not want two dogs in the house.

*Mrs K.* interpreted that Bobby stood for himself : it was he who wanted to be independent, have a wife and babies, and then he would not be frustrated and feel hate and guilt.

Richard then spoke of the happiest day he had had that year. They had been out with their sledges in the snow. Some friends who were with them came down on their sledge so badly that the man's nose was cut and his wife fell on top of him. He, Richard, had also fallen from his sledge, but had not hurt himself and it had all been great fun.

*Mrs K.* suggested that the couple who had the accident stood for his parents. She had just interpreted to him his hostile impulses towards them, particularly relating to their sexual intercourse (Note II). The incident he mentioned had come up in his mind because it stood for the sexual intercourse of the parents. He therefore felt guilty about the accident, but it had turned out not to be serious after all. The man cutting his nose and Richard being so amused about it meant that Father had injured his genital and that Richard had wished him to do so. Yet it turned out not to be serious, and this was why Richard enjoyed it and the day had been a happy one.

Richard said : 'I have discovered that there is no happiness without tragedy', and went on to speak of another happy day he had two years previously when he went with his parents to London. They visited the zoo, where he fed monkeys behind bars. A mandrill looked 'awfully nasty'. A little monkey jumped at Richard, knocked off his cap, and tried to grab the nuts out of his hand. Such a greedy little monkey—and he was feeding the monkeys, anyway.

*Mrs K.* pointed out that the greedy little monkey stood for himself as a greedy baby; but when Richard was feeding the monkeys he stood for Father and Mother feeding their children. The baby (the monkey and Richard) was greedy, ungrateful, and tore off the father's genital (Richard's cap). Therefore the father mandrill looked nasty and dangerous [Projection of aggressive impulses on to the object] (Note III).

Richard (looking worried) asked where Mrs K.'s clock was, which she usually kept in her bag.[1] He said it was a nice clock and he liked to look at it.

*Mrs K.* took the clock out of her bag. She pointed out that he felt worried and suggested that his reason for wanting to see the clock was that he wished to leave.

Richard said no, he did not want to go, but he did wish to make sure that he would leave on time because he was going for a walk with Mummy. Also he liked the look of the clock.

*Mrs K.* interpreted that he was anxious to see that Mummy was all right, not injured by his greedy attacks, and still loving him. Looking at the clock (which was a folding travelling clock) was like looking into Mrs K. : he was afraid that he had attacked her as the little monkey had attacked him, and that she was now injured or angry with him. Mrs K. asked whether the monkey incident had been the tragedy on the happy day.

Richard answered no, that incident had been quite amusing. Nothing serious had happened. But later on there had been a storm, and he had caught a cold and had earache. . . . He looked at the map and expressed his worries about the war situation. He wanted Mrs K. to look with him, comparing the sizes of Germany and France. He said he hated Darlan, who helped the Germans and was a traitor.

*Mrs K.* interpreted that he felt himself to be a traitor if he was greedy, aggressive, and ungrateful. Therefore it was actually the incident with the monkey that had been the 'tragedy'—though it was also amusing—because the greedy little monkey stood for himself.

Richard again showed signs of anxiety. He kept his eyes on the clock and got up from his chair as soon as the time was up. His behaviour towards Mrs K., however, remained friendly. He said he liked staying fifty minutes, but after that he wanted to go to Mummy. It was quite obvious that his resistance had increased and that he was most anxious to leave, but at the same time wanted to remain friendly with Mrs K.

[1] I had used this clock in the first session because my watch had stopped.

*Notes to Third Session:*

I. As the continuation of the analysis will show, Richard's phantasied attacks on his father were directed against him as an external *and* internal object. However, I confined my interpretation at this stage to his thoughts about the relation to the external object. I do not interpret in terms of internal objects and relationships until I have explicit material showing phantasies of internalizing the object in concrete and physical terms.

II. It is characteristic that Richard could allow himself to express his enjoyment of the accident which happened to this couple. This was not only because the accident did not take a serious form but also because the people concerned were not his parents.

III. There is another aspect of the attempted projection expressed in this material. By projecting his destructive impulses on to the monkey, Richard was also trying to split off a part of himself so as to keep good feelings safely apart from the hostile ones. This also showed when Richard, after my interpretation, wanted to look at my clock which he praised and said he liked. He was in this way attempting to preserve the good relation to the analyst, standing for the mother. I would add that the 'tragedy' to which Richard referred, and which he endeavoured to explain by the cold he caught on that day, was the danger that, had he not projected his aggression, he would have felt he had injured his parents and therefore would have become prey to depression and guilt.


# FOURTH SESSION (Thursday)

Richard again talked about the war, particularly about Russia's uncertain attitude, which would make trouble for herself in the end. He also returned to the previous day's material about his experience at the Zoo; no accident had actually happened to him, the tragedy was that he caught a cold and had earache. (By implication he showed his resistance against Mrs K.'s interpretation of the previous day about the actual meaning of the tragedy in that context). He questioned Mrs K. about the way she spent her time and about her family. He wanted to know about Mr K. and how many children they had, how old the children were and what their professions were. Then, looking at the various pictures hanging in the room, he pointed with interest at a picture of two dogs together, also at another showing a puppy between two big dogs. He said the puppy was very sweet.

*Mrs K.* gave him briefly the personal information he asked for.[1]

Richard was obviously taken aback by the fact that Mr K. was dead (though he knew this before he started his analysis), but he was pleased by the information about her son.

*Mrs K.* then interpreted his wish to receive more love and attention from her, as well as his jealousy of her other patients and of her children; and that this derived from his jealousy about Daddy and Paul in relation to Mummy. She added that he was curious about what Mrs K. did at night, just as he was about Mummy. The two dogs stood for Mrs K. and Mr K.[2]—also for Mummy and Daddy —and he wished to be the little dog (the baby) coming between the parents, as well as enjoying them both. He also wished to restore Mr K. to Mrs K.

Richard showed great interest in Mrs K.'s clock and said it was a 'nice clock'. He asked to see how it opened and shut, and while playing with it he said he was happy; the weather was nice, the sun was shining. He agreed that the puppy in the picture was like a baby.

*Mrs K.* suggested that he might have wished Mummy to have babies, though he would also have been jealous.

Richard replied with conviction that he had often said to Mummy she should have babies. She always answered that she was too old, but that was nonsense, of course she could have 'plenty of babies'. (He was still handling the clock.)

*Mrs K.* interpreted that his pleasure and interest in the 'nice' clock (standing for Mrs K.) was connected with his satisfaction in finding out something about Mrs K.'s family and her life. His enjoyment of the sunshine linked with the 'good' Mummy and with his wish that she should have babies to make her happy. In the same way he was also pleased that Mrs K. had a son and a grandson.

Richard again looked at the map and expressed his uncertainty

---

[1] When treating children I answer, though briefly, some of the personal questions when they first come up, before I proceed to analyse them. This is different from the technique I use with adults, when questions are as a rule not answered, but only analysed. But, as I said in the Introduction, I answered more of Richard's questions than I did in other child cases. On looking back, I do not think that the analysis was furthered by giving him this reassurance. In general I have found that whenever I have—for whatever reason—overstepped the boundaries of the purely psycho-analytic technique, I afterwards have grounds to regret it.

[2] As will appear in the course of the analysis, Richard's attitude to Mr K. persistently implied that he was still alive.

about Russia's attitude. He also asked on whose side Austria had been in the last war (though he obviously knew the answer). Then he asked Mrs K. which countries on the Continent she knew.

*Mrs K.* mentioned a few countries she had visited. She interpreted that his doubts about Austria expressed his uncertainty about her, and that his suspicion of Russia related to her as well as to his mother [The 'bad' mother]. He had doubts whether Mrs K. and Mummy were his allies against the 'bad' father (the Austrian Hitler).

Richard spoke about Bobby, who was actually his dog though he shared him with Mummy. Bobby loved him very much. It was mischievous and often naughty; it would eat coal, and would also bite when teased; it had even bitten Richard. He again said that when Daddy got out of his chair by the fire Bobby would jump into it and take up so much room that there was only a tiny bit left for Daddy.

*Mrs K.* reminded him of her interpretation that Bobby jumping into Daddy's chair stood for Richard when he felt jealous and wanted to take Daddy's place. Richard, too, might have wished to bite when angry and jealous. His interest in the dog eating coal, she suggested, linked with Richard's interest in 'big job' in the past and possibly his wish to taste it.

Richard said emphatically that he would do no such thing, though he might have thought of it when he was little. He admitted that he was aware of his tendency to bite; when he felt angry he often wanted to bite, and made biting movments with his jaws, particularly when making faces. As a little boy he had bitten his nurse. When he had a fight with his dog, he bit it if it bit him. Then he asked about Mrs K.'s other patients, particularly about John Wilson,[1] and wanted to know whether they too came to this room for treatment.

*Mrs K.* interpreted that he wished to know this because he felt ashamed of being one of the children using the playroom, since being a child meant being uncontrolled—playing with 'big job' and biting like a dog. Also that he was jealous of John just as he was of Paul, who was no longer a 'bad' child. (Again, since Richard often met John and no doubt got some information from him, he knew quite well that John was not being treated in the playroom, in the same way as he had known that Mr K. was dead. His need to get this information from Mrs K. had various causes, among them the wish to find out whether she told him the truth.)

[1] John Wilson was the patient referred to in the Introduction whom Richard knew and frequently met. He was some years older than Richard and was therefore not treated in the playroom.

## FIFTH SESSION (Friday)

Richard began by saying that he felt very happy. The sun was shining. He had made friends with a little boy about seven years old and they played in the sand together, building canals. He said how much he liked the playroom and how nice it was. There were so many pictures of dogs on the walls. He was looking forward to going home for the weekend. The garden there was very nice but, when they first moved in, 'one could have died' when one saw the weeds. He commented on Lord Beaverbrook's change of job and wondered if his successor would be as good.

*Mrs K.* interpreted that the playroom was 'nice' because of his feelings about her, the room also standing for her. The new friend represented a younger brother. This was bound up with his wish for a strong father who would give Mummy many babies (the many dogs). She also interpreted his concern that, if he pushed Daddy out (as Bobby did), he would take Daddy's place but would be unable to make babies and hold the family together. He was also happy because he was going home and, in order to keep the family life friendly, he wished to inhibit his desire to take Daddy's place. The weeds stood for himself when he upset the family peace by his jealousy and competition with his father. He had used the expression 'one could have died' when referring to the weeds, because they represented something dangerous.

Richard sneezed and became very worried.[1] He wondered whether he was starting a cold and said, half to himself : 'He knows his blows', meaning to say, 'He blows his nose', and was very amused when Mrs K. drew his attention to this slip of the tongue.

*Mrs K.* went on to interpret his fear of a cold as something bad inside him, hence the blows.

Richard again looked at the map and asked which countries remained neutral. Sweden was one of them, but this might not last long. Then he bent down and looked at the map upside-down and commented what a 'funny' shape Europe had when looked at that way. He said it was 'not proper' and seemed 'muddled and mixed up'.

*Mrs K.* linked this with his parents, 'muddled and mixed up' in sexual intercourse so that he could not make out who was who when he thought of them in this situation. She also interpreted his

[1] As mentioned before, he was very hypochondriacal. This was partly due to the fact that his mother, who often had colds, fussed a good deal over him when he caught one.

fear that in sexual intercourse the parents became so mixed up that the bad Hitler-penis inside Mummy remained in her [Combined parent figure]. This was what he meant by 'not proper', 'funny'; and he actually felt it to be bad and dangerous.

Richard showed anxiety. He got up from his chair and looked round the room. He explored various corners, had a look at the piano, opened and tried it. On a side-table he discovered a china shoe he had not noticed before, with an india-rubber inside it, which he took out and put back again. Richard said he thought it was a nice room and he liked it very much. . . . He picked up Mrs K's clock and wanted to know where and when she had got it. This led to questions similar to those he had previously asked about her husband.

*Mrs K.* interpreted that this exploring the room stood for the wish to explore her inside—due to his anxiety to find out whether there was a Hitler-penis in it or a good one. Therefore he again asked about Mr K. All this linked with Mummy and with the 'mixed-up' parents. His uncertainty about Mummy's inside was connected with his fears about his own inside and his fear of colds and inner blows. At the same time he was also comforting himself that the room was nice, that he liked it, and this was felt to be proof that Mummy and Mrs K. were all right and that they did not contain the bad Hitler-father [Manic Defence].

Richard continued to explore the room and found a postcard stuck inside a screen, in the angle formed by two sides. He admired the picture and said it was a charming little robin; he would like to be a robin himself, he always liked them.

*Mrs K.* interpreted that the robin stood for the good penis, also for a baby, and that he wished to make babies and to replace Mr K. and Daddy. His interest in the angle of the screen (with the two sides opening like legs) stood for his desire for sexual intercourse with Mrs K. and Mummy.

Richard made no reply to most of these interpretations. He only said that he once had a robin and fed it, but it flew away and did not return. Then he looked at the clock and wanted to know if his time was up.[1]

*Mrs K.* interpreted his wish to go and never to return, and linked this with his fears stirred up by the interpretations of sexual intercourse with her. The robin also stood for his genital, which he was afraid of losing or of having lost.

---

[1] Richard's not replying to my interpretations and soon asking whether his time was up were some of the signs of resistance which came up again and again. At the same time, he was very keen to keep up his friendly relation with me.

Richard was at first reluctant to admit that he wanted to go, and tried to be polite. Then he said, yes, he did wish that the time were up but he did not want to go before the end of the hour. (When the session was finished he left by himself, without waiting for Mrs K.)

## SIXTH SESSION (Saturday)

Richard's mother had brought him to the house [1] because he was too frightened of children to come by himself. He told Mrs K. this, and then there was a long silence.

*Mrs K.* referred to her interpretation of yesterday's material (Note I), when the robin had stood for his genital which he wished to put into her genital; but he had been very frightened of this wish, particularly because he had become afraid of being attacked by the tramp-father. His fear of being alone with Mrs K. in what he felt to be a dangerous situation was the reason why his fear of hostile children on the way to Mrs K. had so much increased; having his mother bring him to the playroom was also a reassurance that nothing wrong would happen between him and Mrs K. Since he was going home for the weekend after this session, he felt that his wishes towards his mother might lead to his father attacking him. He needed a good mother all the more to protect him against the hostile children and the hostile Daddy. But in so far as she (now represented by Mrs K.) roused his desires, she was also dangerous.

Richard had been looking at the map. He spoke of 'lonely Rumania' and enlarged on the disruption in other countries.

*Mrs K.* interpreted Richard's concern about the disruption in his family if his desires to have Mummy all to himself were to be satisfied. This would make him afraid of both Daddy and Paul, which was shown by his increased fear of the children on the road. Also, if Mummy loved him best and he displaced Daddy, Daddy would be lonely and unhappy.

Richard, looking pained and worried, said he did not wish to hear such unpleasant things. After a silence he asked about John: he was not all right yet, was he? When would he be all right?

*Mrs K.* interpreted Richard's doubts in her and in analysis; could it be helpful since it brought up such unpleasant and frightening thoughts? He also feared that if he had sexual desires he must be very bad indeed and could not be helped. This also stirred up his doubts in Mummy because he felt that she was the cause of these

[1] Usually his mother brought him only part of the way.

wishes (Note II); and if she was not to be trusted, she would not help him against Daddy or help him to control himself so that he should not attack or displace Daddy.

Richard then spoke at some length about a 'tragedy' which happened on the previous day: when playing in the sand he lost his trowel and could not find it again.

*Mrs K.* interpreted his fear of losing his penis (trowel) as a consequence of his wishes towards Mrs K. and Mummy; she also mentioned that his mother had told her about the operation on his genital which had frightened him a good deal (Note III).

Richard was very interested to hear about the talk between Mrs K. and his mother; he was obviously quite aware that when his mother arranged with Mrs K. for his treatment, she had talked about him, but he had not referred to this previously. Now he asked what else his mother had told Mrs K.

*Mrs K.* gave a short report: Mummy had mentioned his being often worried, his fear of children, and his other difficulties. She had also told Mrs K. about him as a young child, including his operations.

Richard was very pleased with this report, but it was clear that he was still doubtful and suspicious. He at once took up the story of his operations in great detail. He remembered something of his circumcision which took place when he was about three. He had no pain, but it was awful being given ether. He had been told beforehand that he would be given some kind of perfume to smell and was promised that nothing else would be done to him (this tallied with his mother's account). He took with him a bottle of perfume and wanted them to use this instead of their perfume. When this was not allowed, he wanted to throw the bottle at the doctor, and even now he would like to fight him. He had hated the doctor ever since. He hated the smell of ether and was still afraid of it. Suddenly he said, referring to the moment when the ether was given: 'It was as if hundreds or thousands of people were there.' But he felt that his nurse was there with him and that she would protect him.[1]

*Mrs K.* interpreted the strength of his feelings of persecution: he had said he felt surrounded by hundreds and thousands of enemies,

---

[1] At the time his castration fear had become quite conscious: according to his mother, on the day after the operation he pointed towards his genital and said that it had 'all gone'. There is no doubt about the influence of this experience on his castration fears. But, as the further course of the analysis proved, his early destructive impulses, both against the mother's breast and against the father's penis, were a fundamental cause for his fear of retaliation, in particular for his fear of being castrated by his father. The operation no doubt intensified these anxieties.

and quite powerless. He had only one friend to protect him, the nurse standing for the good Mummy. But there was also in his mind the bad Mummy, his mother who had told him a lie and therefore, he felt, had joined up with his enemies. The 'bad' doctor whom he wanted to fight stood for the bad father who would make him helpless and cut off his penis.

Richard agreed to this. He went on talking about having his tonsils out when he was five. Again the awful thing was the ether he had been given. He said he was quite ill for a long time after that operation. Then he spoke about his 'third operation' when he was seven and a half: he had several teeth out and was again given ether. (Richard spoke very dramatically: he obviously enjoyed giving this report. No doubt it was a great relief to complain, to express his feelings and anxieties, and to know that Mrs K. was listening with sympathy and interest).

Richard had again been exploring the room and focused his attention on the 'nice' little robin on the postcard stuck into the screen. He asked whether Mrs K. liked it. Then he found another postcard with a robin, but said it was not so nice.

*Mrs K.* pointed out that the first robin, which he preferred, was holding its head erect and stood for Richard's uninjured penis, while the second robin was hanging its head down and represented Richard's injured penis. Richard wanted to show his penis to Mrs K., who stood for the good nurse who loved and protected him, and wanted her to like it; this he felt would also convince him that it was not injured.

Richard mentioned his two canaries, of which he was very fond. He told Mrs K. that they often spoke angrily to each other and he was quite sure they quarrelled. . . . He discovered a picture of two dogs and was interested to see that although they were of the same breed, they were different in some ways. Then he pointed at the picture of three dogs together, which he had previously liked (fourth session) and again admired the puppy in the middle.

*Mrs K.* interpreted his interest in the difference between his parents and between their genitals. The puppy in the middle represented himself wishing to separate the parents when they were in bed together, partly because he was jealous, and partly because he was afraid of their uniting against him, as he might have felt on the occasion of the operation and when Mrs K. and his mother were discussing him. He seemed very much afraid of their quarrelling and he wondered what they were quarrelling about; he might perhaps feel that he was the cause of their quarrels.

(For this session, again, I have no notes about the end of the hour.)

*Notes to Sixth Session:*

I. As a rule the analyst would base his first interpretation on fresh material coming up in that session; but if anxiety is so acute that the patient cannot express it, an interpretation referring to the material of the previous session (or sessions) is required. In this instance, the increase of anxiety shown by Richard's insistence on his mother accompanying him to the playroom as well as by his unusually long silence was the clue to the anxiety prevailing at the moment.

II. The accusation against the mother that, by causing sexual desires towards her, she is guilty not only of having aroused them but of having seduced the child, appears frequently in analysis. This accusation is rooted in the actual experience of having been physically cared for by the mother in infancy, which involves the genital being touched and thereby stimulated. In some cases a certain amount of unconscious or even conscious seduction actually enters into the relation of the mother towards the child. Nevertheless, I think it is very important to take account of and analyse the projection of the child's own sexual desires on to the mother, and of his wish to seduce her.

III. This raises a vital point of technique in child analysis. I have referred here to an important piece of information which Richard's mother had given me. In doing so I was sure that Richard knew that I had discussed him with his mother. In fact, though he had been too frightened to ask, he had obviously been wondering what his mother and I had been talking about and was suspicious about our conversation. It was a noticeable relief to him when I told him about this talk, although his doubts relating to my contacts with his mother were obviously not completely allayed. (This could not be expected with such a suspicious child, and probably not with anyone.) We can take it for granted that a child for whom treatment is arranged by his parents is aware that some information has been given and it is advisable to refer to this fact at an opportune moment. On the preceding day, castration anxiety had come to the fore, and in this session it was very acute. Therefore the castration fears aroused by the operation and the suspicion of the mother formed part of the material, and it seemed essential to bring this fact up at this point.

While there are times when some information given by the parents —for instance about an illness or other important event—can be referred to by the analyst as having been given by one of the parents, this should be an exception in the analysis. The analyst has to find his own material from the child, although it might help him sometimes to interpret more fully if he has been in contact with the mother and been informed about changes in the child or given other relevant data. If, however, he refers too often to conversations with the parents, this will arouse the child's persecutory feelings.

## SEVENTH SESSION (Monday)

Richard was very pleased to see Mrs K. He mentioned that the weekend seemed quite short; it was as if he had only just left her. She was 'about'; it was as if he had been seeing a picture of her (obviously meaning that she had been much in his mind).[1] He told her in great detail all that had happened while he was away (Note I). He said he had had a very happy weekend. There was one tragedy: on the way to Mrs K., when he was going down the steps of the hotel, he twisted his ankle. . . . He asked Mrs K. to look at his new suit. Didn't the colour of the socks go well with it? He was in a communicative mood and went on to say that there was one thing that often worried him: he was afraid he might turn out to be a dunce, no good at all.

*Mrs K.* interpreted that his twisting his ankle on the way to her was an expression of his fear that he would injure his genital if he fulfilled his desire to be a man and put his genital into Mrs K's genital. When he pointed out his new suit to her and wished her to admire his socks, he also showed the wish for her to admire his genital. But that was followed by his fear that he was no good at all (his turning out to be a dunce), that he would never have the adult and effective genital that he wanted.

Richard asked a little later whether the electric fire belonged to Mrs K. He noticed now for the first time that one of the bars was broken. . . . He told Mrs. K. that the first person to greet him when he arrived home was Bobby, who gave him a great welcome. No, actually it was Daddy who greeted him first. Daddy was surprised —no, Richard had not meant to say that—Daddy seemed glad to see him. The canaries were not well. They seemed to have an illness and were going bald. When Richard was playing with his bow and arrows, an arrow happened to hit Daddy lightly on the head, but Daddy was not hurt and was not angry either.

[1] It is characteristic of my technique and my whole approach that analysing anxiety when it is most acute, either manifest or latent, has the effect of alleviating it. For instance, between the previous session and the present one, the interpretation of castration fear and its underlying causes had been followed by a strong increase in positive transference and an obvious relief of anxiety.

*Mrs K.* interpreted his fears and suspicions about Daddy's love because Richard wished to shoot him. Therefore, although he meant to say that Daddy *was* glad, he said something else, he said that Daddy was surprised to see him, as if Daddy had not been expecting him. Actually the 'surprise' stood for a much stronger feeling. Richard thought that his father did not want him to come. For Richard knew unconsciously that he had hostile impulses against him. Referring to the canaries going bald, Mrs K. asked Richard whether his father was going bald.

Richard said yes.

*Mrs K.* interpreted that when he mentioned the canaries, Richard felt that he had made Daddy ill, had injured his genital as well as his head because he was jealous of him and wanted to take his place with Mummy. Therefore Richard was so afraid of Daddy retaliating; in the previous session the fear of the bad doctor hurting his genital, or destroying it, or taking it away, expressed his fear of what his father would do to him. The broken bar in the fire, which he had only noticed today, stood for his genital, the fire for Mrs K.'s or Mummy's genital. His need for Mrs K. to admire his suit and socks—altogether for her to like him—was increased by the fear of his father punishing and attacking him if he discovered his desires towards Mummy, or rather his genital inside Mummy's genital.

Richard was looking at the map. He said that the war news was good; many German bombers had been brought down. What a funny shape Rumania was! It was a 'lonely' country. Richard looked at the map upside-down (bending down to do so). He 'could not make anything out'. He again said that it did not look proper, it looked muddled. Looking up he pointed at Brest and said Daddy had make a joke about Brest : he said something about the Germans going on to attack the legs now they had started with the breast. Richard pointed out various continental towns. Then he looked round the room and was thrilled to discover some things he had not noticed before, such as the second door, many more photos and picture postcards, and a number of little stools (Note II). He again looked at the china shoe and also found a picture calendar. He admired one of the photographs, particularly the two mountains on it. He next expressed dislike of a picture but skipped over that.

*Mrs K.* asked him why he disliked that picture.

Richard (with some hesitation) said he disliked the brown colour of the picture (it was in sepia), which made the country look ugly. He picked up Mrs K.'s travelling clock, which was of brown leather, moved it about, turned it with its back to him and Mrs K., and laughed heartily; he said it looked so funny.

*Mrs K.* interpreted that he was laughing about the brown back of the clock because it connected with 'big job'. She suggested that he did not like the picture where everything was brown because it made Mrs K., or rather Mummy (the country), all dirty and ugly. Yet at the same time he also felt it was funny and was amused about 'big job' and Mrs K.'s bottom.

Richard at once agreed about the back of the clock standing for Mrs K.'s bottom.

*Mrs K.* interpreted Richard's desire to explore her inside as well as Mummy's. The lonely Rumania, attacked and in trouble, and the subjugated towns on the Continent now represented Mrs K. and the injured Mummy. Daddy, who made the joke about Brest, stood for the bad tramp—and the Germans—attacking Mummy's breast and body. Richard's admiration for the two mountains expressed his love for Mummy's breasts and his wish to keep them undamaged. His finding so many new things in the playroom was due to his becoming more aware of his wish to put his genital into Mummy and explore her inside with it. At the same time he objected to the brown colour which made the country look ugly, and this showed his anxiety about the 'big job' inside Mrs K.—the back of the clock—although he was also amused about her bottom.

Richard then spoke about some poems, particularly Wordsworth's 'The Daffodils'; he admired another picture which represented a big tower in a landscape, with the sun shining on it.

*Mrs K.* interpreted the tower in the landscape as standing for his father's genital inside mother. Admiring this sunny picture showed his desire for the parents to be happily united (Note III). (The manic element in Richard's excitement when admiring beauty in nature was marked.)

Richard asked Mrs K. whether she was again going down to the village [1] (which meant that he would be able to go with her a little way), and admitted that he wanted her to protect him against the children he might meet on the road.

*Mrs K.* interpreted that the children of whom he was afraid were now standing for Daddy, or for Daddy's dangerous genital, and Richard wished Mummy to protect him against Daddy.

Richard appeared worried and did not seem to listen. He looked at Mrs K.'s clock.

*Mrs K.* asked whether this meant that he wished to go.

Richard agreed but said he would not go before his time was up. He went to urinate.

---

[1] Though I have no record of it, at the end of one of the preceding sessions I must have been going to the village.

*Mrs K.* interpreted, when he came back, his fear of the dangers of sexual relations with her. His urinating was also to make sure that his genital was still there.

Richard had again been looking round and found a photograph of a man and woman in uniform and thought that they were important. He seemed pleased and interested.

*Mrs K.* interpreted his desire to preserve the happiness and authority of his parents. He wished to leave Mrs K. when he became frightened of his own desires towards her. At the same time he had asked her to protect him against the bad attacking Daddy, or his genital. He was therefore alternating between the wish to be with Mrs K. and the wish to leave her.

*Notes to Seventh Session:*

I. This is one of the ways in which patients express their unconscious feeling of having internalized the analyst. These feelings find expression in different forms. For instance, a patient said he felt during a break as if I were hovering over him. It seems contradictory that the same patient might give detailed descriptions of all he had been doing and experiencing during a break (or from one session to another). But it is in this way that the patient attempts to correlate an internal situation with an external one, i.e. the analyst as an internal figure with the analyst as an external one. In so far as the analyst is so strongly felt to be an internal part of the patient, he or she shares the patient's life and therefore should know each of his thoughts and experiences. But on meeting the analyst again and recognizing that he is an external figure, the patient feels the discrepancy between what he wished and what is real, and by his detailed report he tries to bring together the internal and external situations.

II. Both in child and adult analyses it is a sign of progress and of the strengthening of the transference when the patient begins to see more details, previously unnoticed, in the consulting-room and in the analyst's appearance. The analyst is often able to analyse the emotional reasons why these particular objects had escaped the patient's attention. Such incapacity to see at times even quite large and obvious things illustrates the inhibition of perception for unconscious reasons.

III. Here we see a change from the sessions in which the active wish to castrate the father and the fear of being castrated by him—implying the fear of a bad father's genital, dangerous to him and to mother —had been experienced and interpreted. The analysis of such fears is very often followed by the opposite feeling coming to the fore : the admiration for the father's genital and potency; the wish for mother and father to be united. By analysing the suspicions and the anxieties attaching to the parents, and in particular to their sexual intercourse, repression of the positive feelings—the wish to make reparation and for the parents to be happy and united—can be lifted.


## EIGHTH SESSION (Tuesday)

Richard was very worried about the children passing the house, but said he felt protected by Mrs K. He had nearly bumped into a boy at the corner of the road—the boy looked very unfriendly. Richard had also hurt his leg on the way to Mrs K. and it bled a little. He seemed continually on the alert and very tense, watching the road. He showed Mrs K. a horse's head at the turning of the road. (A horse and cart were standing there but the horse's body was hidden.) Richard looked again and again at this head and seemed frightened of it; from time to time he turned his attention to the map on the wall. He asked Mrs K. which country they could talk about. How very small Portugal was. He again looked at the map upside-down. He would like the shape of Europe if Turkey and Russia were not there. They seemed so 'out of place'; they 'bulged out' and were too big. Also they were so uncertain; one did not know what they were going to do, particularly Russia.

*Mrs K.* interpreted the bulging Turkey, the horse's head at the turn of the road, and the hostile boy whom he also met at a corner, as standing for Daddy's frightening big genital inside Mummy. Yesterday he had referred to the map as a woman's body, mentioning his father's joke about the attack on the breast leading to the attack on the legs. In that way Daddy was dangerous to Mummy in sexual relations; he was attacking her. When they were together, muddled up, not proper—which meant that Mummy was mixed up with Daddy's genital—he also could not be sure whether Mummy would remain friendly towards himself or would join up with Daddy against him. This was expressed by uncertain Russia.

Richard tried to find out where Mrs K.'s head would be on the map. He had clearly accepted her interpretation about the map representing her body and his mother's. He suddenly wondered where he had put his cap, found it on a shelf, and held it tight. He asked if he could look at the clock, opened it and made the alarm go. When he put the clock back on the table, he laid his cap, which he had held on his knees while inspecting the clock, on top of it— accidentally he said. He remarked that he liked the clock, picked it up and touched it swiftly with his lips. He again looked at the map upside-down and said that he could not 'make it out' that way at all.

*Mrs K.* interpreted Richard's desire and love for her (the clock), his wish to inspect her inside and to put his cap, standing for his genital, into her genital. But there was the fear of the bulging Turkey on the map, which represented Mr K. in sexual relations with Mrs K. (Daddy with Mummy) and Richard's feeling that he could not understand what sexual relations were, how Mummy and Daddy got mixed up and what happened to the penis inside the woman.

Richard asked if they were stuck together like Siamese twins. It must be terrible for those twins if they could never get away from each other.

*Mrs K.* interpreted this anxiety in connection with the parents' sexual relations as well as with danger to himself if he were to put his genital into her. He might never get it out again. This was why he had wished to run away yesterday.

Richard decided that he was now going to talk about Britain. He was taking a trip on the map to London, which he thought beautiful; then he went along the map on a cruise in the Mediterranean to Gibraltar and Suez, which must be lovely. (Here again his mood became manic, as always when his appreciation of beauty was aroused. The depression underneath the manic element was quite clear.)

*Mrs K.* interpreted the 'lovely' cruise as an exploration of Mrs K.'s and Mummy's inside. But the 'lovely' cruise involved countries which were seriously endangered by the war. In this way Richard was denying the fear of these dangers, as well as of the thrilling but dangerous sexual relations.[1]

Richard interrupted to ask Mrs K. whether she would mind if he put his feet on the bar of her chair.

*Mrs K.* interpreted that the chair stood for the genital, Richard's feet for his penis. Her permission to put his feet on the bar also meant for him permission to have sexual desires, even though they could not be carried out (Note I).

Richard again referred to Turkey and asked if he could pick up the china shoe. He took out the india-rubber and put it back again. Then he explored the room further. On a shelf he found some envelopes containing photographs which he counted; he said there were lots of them.

[1] It is worth remembering that in the third session Richard had taken a sudden interest in the ships which would be blockaded in the Mediterranean if Gibraltar were taken. I interpreted this as his fear about the danger to his father in sexual intercourse with mother.

*Mrs K.* interpreted that, when Richard was exploring the room, it stood for her, and the many photos he found represented the many babies she contained.

Richard went into the kitchen and had a look at the oven. He decided that it was not clean. He smelt a bottle of ink and said it was very 'smelly stuff'. Back in the room he looked at the clock and repeated that he liked it very much. He turned its back to him, laughed, and said it looked funny.

*Mrs K.* linked his dislike of the 'smelly stuff' with his dislike of the 'big job' inside her, which he thought was there as well as the babies. She reminded him that on the previous day he had not wished to look at one picture in the calendar because the country was spoilt by the brown colour, also that the back of the leather clock had made him think of Mrs K.'s bottom.

Richard seemed worried and looked to see what the time was. To Mrs K.'s suggestion that he did so because he wanted to leave, Richard agreed but said he would not run away. He thought the work was doing him good.[1] He had felt much less frightened over the weekend. He went to urinate and, when he came back, asked Mrs K. how long the treatment would last.

*Mrs K.* interpreted his fears about her bottom, her 'big job', as something bad and dangerous, and that he also felt worried about his own urine and faeces as bad things. This was why he had gone to urinate at that moment. Mrs K. reminded him of his fears, strongly shown in the previous sessions, that something would happen to his genital if he was alone with her and wished to have sexual relations with her. His penis might be injured and the bad man he connected with Mrs K.—the tramp-father—would attack him.

Richard now put a great many questions to Mrs K.: how many patients had she; how many used she to have; what was their trouble; what was John's trouble? Meanwhile he kept turning the electric fire on and off.

*Mrs K.* replied that she could not discuss other patients with him any more than she would discuss him with other people. (Richard evidently saw the point of this, but was clearly dissatisfied.) Mrs K. interpreted his jealousy and fear of her other patients, standing for her husband and children. She referred to the boy at the corner of the road, the horse's head, bulging Turkey, and suggested that all this showed his fear of the father's bad genital inside Mummy (Mr K.'s inside Mrs K.) and his wish to destroy Daddy because of fear

---

[1] Richard here speaks of the analysis as 'the work'. I can no longer recall whether this expression, which he used throughout his analysis, derived from anything I had said.

as well as jealousy. This bad Daddy inside Mummy either injured Mummy or made her bad too. If he (Richard) attacked Daddy inside Mummy, which he expressed by turning off the fire, then she would die; this was why he went on turning the fire off and on, not feeling sure what to do. All these anxieties and doubts contributed to his doubts about Mrs K.'s work.

(During some of Mrs K.'s interpretations, particularly those of castration fear, Richard looked pained and frightened and did not seem to listen. This was similar to his behaviour on the previous day. But it was clear that every such interpretation was followed by further exploration of the room and by an evident diminution of anxiety. For instance, soon after Mrs K.'s interpretation about the horse's head at the corner, he looked in that direction again, said that the cart had moved, the horse was nearer, and its head looked quite nice.)

*Note to Eighth Session:*

I. On other occasions, too, although not always specifically referred to, Richard obtained marked relief through the lessening of the repression of his phantasies, and the ensuing increase in capacity to express them symbolically. In ordinary play, where the child remains largely unconscious of the content of his incestuous and aggressive phantasies and impulses, he nevertheless experiences relief through the very fact that he expresses them symbolically; and this is one of the factors which make play so important for the child's development. In analysis we should aim at getting access to deeply repressed phantasies and desires and thus helping the child to become conscious of them. It is important that the analyst should be able to convey to the child the meaning of his phantasies—whether they are deeply repressed or nearer consciousness—and to verbalize them. My experience has shown me that in doing so we meet closely the child's unconscious needs. I believe it to be a fallacy that there could be any harm to the child or to his relation to his parents from translating, as it were, his unconscious incestuous and aggressive desires and his criticism into concrete words.

## NINTH SESSION (Wednesday)

Richard and Mrs K. met on the road near the house. Unexpectedly Mrs K. had been unable to get the key on her way, and she and Richard went back to fetch it. Richard was obviously dis-

turbed and worried about this, though he did not say so. He commented, however, on the noise the crows were making, remarking
that they 'sounded frightened'. He also asked if Mrs K. would make
up the time lost in going to fetch the key.

*Mrs K.* interpreted [1] that the crows stood for himself and that he
felt frightened, not only because he had lost some time, which Mrs
K. was willing to make up, but also because he no longer felt sure
that he would always find the playroom and Mrs K. ready for him.

Richard said that he had an 'important question' which he was
going to put to Mrs K. when they were back in the playroom. But
then he asked it straightaway : could she help him not to have
dreams?

*Mrs K.* asked him why he did not want to have dreams, and
why he did not want to tell her this now.

Richard explained that his dreams were always frightening or
unpleasant. He also said that he was afraid of being overheard,
particularly by any children they might meet. All the time he had
been speaking in whispers, although there was hardly anyone on
the road. . . .

Back in the playroom Richard mentioned some dreams. One had
to do with being given ether by the Queen in *Alice in Wonderland*;
another with a German troop-carrier which came down quite close
to him ; this dream reminded him of something which he had
dreamt a long time ago. A car, looking 'old, black, and deserted',
with lots of numberplates, came towards him and stopped at his
feet. (While talking about the dreams he was turning the electric
fire on and off.)

*Mrs K.* interpreted that the fire looked black when it was turned
off and then might appear dead to him. In the dream the old, black,
and deserted car seemed dead too.

Richard pointed out that when the fire was turned on, something
red moved in it. (He was referring to a vibration behind the metal
shield.)

*Mrs K.* interpreted that the fire stood for Mummy, who he
thought contained something moving inside her which Richard
wanted to stop. If he attacked it—which he felt he did by turning
off the fire—then Mummy too would be old, black, and deserted,
i.e. dead like the car in the dream ; and now he felt the same fear
about Mrs K. Mrs K. also suggested that the troop-carrier containing enemies stood for her and for Mummy containing the bad
Hitler-father. The Queen in *Alice in Wonderland*, who, in his
dream, had given him ether, also represented the bad Mummy and

[1] On this occasion, since the unexpected walk took up a good deal of time,
I deviated from my usual rule not to interpret when he walked with me.

Daddy. When he was operated on, Mummy turned bad because she had not told him the truth, and he felt she had united with the bad doctor (Note I). The Queen in *Alice in Wonderland* had people's heads cut off and therefore she stood for the dangerous parents cutting his genital off after he had been made unconscious by ether. When Richard wanted to turn off the fire, he meant to attack or destroy the bad man inside Mrs K., the bad Daddy inside Mummy. He had told Mrs K. about the many enemies who he thought were present during his operation, and this had helped him to be less frightened. Mrs K., therefore, stood also for Nurse whom he believed was the only person who would protect him at the time (See Sixth Session).

Richard chose a country on the map to speak about; this time Germany. He said he wanted to whack Hitler and to attack Germany. Then he decided to 'choose' France instead. He spoke about France, which betrayed Britain but might not have been able to help it, and he was sorry for France.

*Mrs K.* pointed out that there were various kinds of Mummy in his mind : the bad Mummy, Germany, whom he wanted to attack in order to destroy Hitler inside her; the injured and not-so-good Mummy whom he still loved, represented by France; when they came together in his mind, he could not bear to attack Germany, and rather turned to France for whom he could allow himself to feel sorry. Germany (or rather Austria) also stood for Mrs K., who had been invaded by Hitler (Note II) [Synthesis of the split-off aspects of the object, and corresponding guilt and depressive anxiety].

Richard again investigated the room as on the preceding days. He picked up some books but without interest and seemed lost in thought. . . . He mentioned an ugly little girl with protruding teeth who lived in the hotel and said he hated her. He looked worried and depressed.

*Mrs K.* interpreted that he hated the little girl because she stood for himself when he felt the wish to attack by biting. He had spoken (cf. Fourth Session) of his biting nurse and Bobby and grinding his teeth when he was angry. He was afraid that in exploring Mummy's inside, for which the room also stood, he would bite and eat both her and what he felt she contained : babies and Daddy's genital. But the room now also stood for Mrs K., whom he wished to explore and attack in a similar way. . . .[1]

*Mrs K.* referred back to his wish for Mummy to have 'plenty of babies' (Fourth and Fifth Sessions), but at the same time it had

[1] It is evident that some material that Richard brought at this stage is missing from my notes.

appeared how jealous he was of his brother Paul. When he felt jealous of the babies which would come out of Mummy, he wished to attack them as well as her. Then she would change into the black fire where nothing was moving and into the 'old, black, and deserted' car, with the many numberplates representing dead babies. This would change the 'plenty of babies', which had made the room nice (the pictures of the dogs), into dead babies. He had mentioned (First Session) that he often felt 'deserted' at night, just as he had spoken of the car as being 'deserted'. If the car, standing for Mummy, would die, then he, too, would be deserted and dead. Because these anxieties had come up so strongly he took no pleasure today in exploring the room.

Richard again asked if Mrs K. would keep him longer because they had started later.

*Mrs K.* repeated that she would do so, but interpreted that from the beginning of the session his fear of losing some of his time with her had been due to the anxiety about Mrs K. and Mummy dying because he had destroyed them or might do so through his greed and jealousy.

Richard again began to inspect the room, particularly the little stools standing there. He said they were dusty and began to beat them in order to get the dust out. He fetched a broom and set about sweeping the room.

*Mrs K.* interpreted that Richard was trying to make the babies inside Mummy (the stools inside the room) better [1]; that he might have been afraid of Mummy containing dirty and greedy babies, as greedy as he felt himself to be. These babies inside Mummy were also represented by the hostile children on the street, of whom he was so afraid. Beating the stools meant attacking the bad babies as well.

Richard went to urinate. He said he wanted (for some trivial reason) to leave punctually, although Mrs K. was prepared to keep him longer. However, he made her promise that she would give him this extra time some other day.

*Mrs K.* interpreted that Richard did not want to take too much of her time because of his fear of eating her up greedily.

Richard went out into the garden, asking Mrs K. to come with him, and thoroughly enjoyed the sunshine and the 'lovely country'; he said he felt happy (Note III).

*Mrs K.* suggested that he now seemed to feel less frightened of bad babies inside Mummy and Mrs K., and could therefore take

[1] The change of mood following these interpretations is significant. Depression had diminished and the wish to restore (the tendency to make reparation) had come to the fore.

pleasure in the good side of Mummy, now represented by the 'lovely' country; but that he enjoyed looking at the beautiful surroundings all the more because he felt this as a help against his fear about all that was bad and dangerous inside her [Manic defence].

*Notes to Ninth Session:*

I. The question whether or not in an analysis the child's criticism of his parents, either repressed or consciously held back, should be brought into the open has often been discussed. I have very early on in my work found that it is important to allow criticism, whether justified or not, to come up. The reasons for this can easily be understood. The lifting of repression of hostile feelings is necessary for the analysis; also a relation based on idealization is insecure; when the parents are actually seen, and admitted to be seen, in a more realistic light, idealization is diminished and tolerance can come about. Unconsciously criticism leads to phantastic exaggerations, such as those seen when the lie which Richard's mother told him gave rise to the phantasy of the Queen in *Alice in Wonderland*, who not only gave him ether but, as the story implies, ordered people's heads to be cut off. One cannot fully analyse such phantasies without also allowing the actual grievances against the parents to come up. In fact, I found that the relation to the parents improved considerably when both criticism of them and phantasies bound up with these grievances had been analysed.

II. The conflict between the impulses to attack and to keep alive a loved person, expressed here by the feelings relating to the countries on the map (and by turning the fire on and off), lies at the root of the infantile depressive position. Such anxieties first arise in the baby in relation to the mother (her breast) as an external and internalized object and have many ramifications. There is, for instance, the infant's urge to destroy the bad object inside the good one, partly for the sake of the object, partly for the sake of the subject; but by such attacks the good object is felt to be endangered. (Cf. my 'Contribution to the Psychogenesis of Manic-Depressive States', 1935, *Writings*, 1.)

III. As a sequel to the anxiety coming up during this session and the interpretations of it, Richard's mood had completely changed. Such changes during one session are, in my experience, not at all unusual. They are due to the fact that the manic defence against depression comes up. However, as a result of the working through and of the interpretations, actual relief of anxiety, diminution of depression, and the desire to make reparation also become operative. There is, therefore, a distinction to be drawn between the familiar fluctuations from depressive to manic states and *vice versa* on the one hand, and the manic defence, which comes about as a step in the ego's greater capacity to deal with depression. Such steps are inherent in normal development, when the infant goes through the depressive position and by various means deals with it, and are, in the course of an analysis, initiated by the analytic procedure.

## TENTH SESSION (Thursday)

Richard arrived a few minutes late and was very upset. He told Mrs K. he had been home and that instead of going straight from the bus to her, he had first gone with his mother to the hotel; this had made him late. (Mrs K. gathered that he was afraid of a conflict between his mother and her.[1]) He said he had been very frightened of children on the road. One little evacuee girl with red hair had asked him whether he was Italian (there were a number of Italians in 'X') and this frightened and worried him; he thought the Italians, being Hitler's friends, were treacherous and bad.

*Mrs K.* interpreted his worry about a possible conflict between Mummy and herself, and that he might have felt that way about trouble between his parents.

Richard said that Daddy and Mummy never quarrelled, but there was much trouble between Nurse and Cook. (His mother had mentioned to me that the quarrels between the nurse and the cook, which led to the nurse leaving, had very much upset Richard and that in fact he had never forgiven the cook, who was still with them.) . . . He again chose a country; at first he said he would choose Estonia, but then decided that because Estonia was hostile to the Poles, he did not want it and chose 'little Latvia' instead.[2] Meanwhile he again turned the electric fire on and off, looked at the little stools in the room, and beat them to get the dust out.

*Mrs K.* interpreted that although Richard thought there never was a quarrel between his parents, he may nonetheless have been much concerned about the possibility of disagreement between them. This fear would increase his wish to have a younger sister or brother (little Latvia) to turn to and to be his ally, both because he

[1] Actual conflicts between parents or people who play an important part in the child's life (such as nurse, maid, or teacher) cause much anxiety in children at any age. This is, however, particularly strong during the latency period. (Cf. *Psycho-Analysis of Children*, Chapter IV.)

[2] At this stage he no longer chose a country to talk about but chose it as a possession.

felt frightened of the quarrelling parents and because he needed help in bringing the parents together again. But he was also afraid of hostile brothers or sisters who would accuse him of treachery (the red-haired girl who thought he was Italian) either towards them or towards the parents because of his aggressive and jealous feelings; he was also afraid that Mummy's babies would be dirty and harmful to her (the dusty stools).

Richard, a little later, told Mrs K. about a school he went to at the beginning of the war. There were rats there, and there were also rats in a laundry in 'X'. Rats were hateful and made food poisonous. He went on to talk of Bobby who sometimes bit him, and again said that if Bobby bit him, he bit back; he also spoke of 'dive-bombing' Bobby. . . . He asked Mrs K. about her other patients, and said he wanted to know all her secrets. He wanted to know what she was thinking and to 'burrow' his mind 'into Mrs K.'s mind'.

*Mrs K.* repeated that she could not discuss her other patients with him. She interpreted that he wanted to burrow himself with his teeth—which was why he was worried by the little girl with protruding teeth—into Mrs K. (and Mummy) and find there all the secret babies (Mrs K.'s other patients); that this wish was increased by the fear that babies might be bad—like rats—and would chew up Mrs K. (and Mummy) and poison her. As a baby he might have wished to burrow himself into Mummy's breast and devour it. She also suggested that in his mind the rat stood for Daddy's genital as well, which, he thought, burrowed itself into Mummy and remained inside her. If he attacked the father and babies inside Mummy, they might turn on him and devour him. With Bobby he could bite in a playful, which meant harmless, way and get away from the guilt about attacking the little brothers (Mummy's babies) for whom Bobby stood.

Richard picked up a picture calendar and looked at the pages. He very much liked the picture of a battleship and associated a captain whom he admired, a friend of his parents. Suddenly he bit the edge of the picture and also picked up his cap and bit it.

*Mrs K.* interpreted that Richard thought so highly of the captain partly because he stood for Daddy taking care of Mummy, the battleship; he admired him so much at this moment because he did not wish to think of the dangerous rat-father and because thinking of a good father comforted him when he was afraid of the rat-father [Manic defence]. She also suggested that when he admired Daddy's strong and potent [1] genital, this meant that Richard had not injured

---

[1] The word 'potent' had entered into my interpretations after my having explained to Richard what I meant by it.

it, also that the strong father could protect and help Mummy. Yet Richard also felt jealous and envious of this potent genital and wanted to bite it off, and this was why he had at that moment bitten the edge of the picture and his cap.

Richard had become very affectionate towards Mrs K.; he said he was 'terribly fond' of her and that she was 'sweet'. Obviously the interpretations had given him relief; he asked if he could again wait for her to walk as far as the corner of the road with her and repeatedly said goodbye to her on parting.

## ELEVENTH SESSION (Friday)

Richard was very worried about some children whom he could see on the road while he sat near the window with Mrs K. He said (looking very unhappy, as if he now realized how persecuted he felt) that he was all the time on his 'guard', even when he was with Mrs K., whom he obviously felt as a protective figure. He asked her whether she, too, had had such fears as a child. He had heard it said that all children do. He watched the electric fire while he turned it on and off. Then he picked up Mrs K.'s clock, wound it, opened it, and for a moment rubbed his face against it caressingly. . . . He spoke of the success of the British bombers on the previous night, also of the German fleet and of the wiping out of the battle-ships at Brest. He wondered how Hitler had managed to make Germany into a Nazi country; now one could not get rid of Hitler without attacking Germany.

*Mrs K.* interpreted his fear that if he wanted to destroy the bad Daddy and bad babies inside Mummy, he would have to attack Mummy herself and might injure her (Germany which had now to be attacked because of the bad Hitler). She also suggested that when he investigated her clock, it was really her inside, her genital, and the bad Mr K. (Hitler-father) inside her that he wanted to find out about. As to the electric fire which he kept turning on and off, Mrs K. referred back to her previous interpretation (Ninth Session) about his wish to destroy the bad father and babies inside Mummy; but then he became frightened that this might kill Mummy. When he caressed the clock, this stood for caressing Mrs K., partly because he was sorry for her being injured by the bad Mr K. and babies inside her—the bad Hitler inside Germany.

Richard went on playing with the fire, and then turned back to the clock. He wanted to know why the alarm was set for such an early hour and asked what Mrs K. had been doing at that time. . . . Then he announced that he was 'choosing' Austria on the map. He said Hitler was Austrian, wasn't he? But he quickly added that Mozart had been Austrian as well, and said that he loved Mozart very much.

*Mrs K.* interpreted that Richard was suspicious about her connections with men; this was also why he wanted to know what she had been doing at that early hour of the morning; the 'Austrian' Hitler, who made Germany into a Nazi country, stood for the bad Mr K. making Mrs K. bad. The loved Mozart represented the good Mr K. and the thought of him was a comfort against the fear of the bad Hitler-Mr K. With Mummy, too, Richard tried to avoid feeling that the bad Daddy was inside her and would make her bad.

Richard was very listless during these interpretations and appeared not to hear them. He again explored the room and remarked on the dirty stools. As before, he beat the dust out of them. Then he opened the door and admired the view, particularly commenting on the hills.

*Mrs K.* interpreted that the lovely countryside was a proof that there was a beautiful, good, external world; therefore he could hope that the internal world, particularly his mother's, was good too. This made him also less suspicious about Mrs K.'s (and Mummy's) relations to bad men. Mrs K. referred to his fear of children he met in the road and suggested that they stood for the bad, dirty rat-children inside Mummy whom he wanted to attack, and that this was why he was afraid that they would attack him on the road. She pointed out that at the beginning of this session he had realized how very frightened he was of them.

Richard now showed less resistance to Mrs K.'s interpretations. He looked very serious and was obviously more conscious of his persecutory fears and concerned about them.[1]

---

[1] This session is very short not only because my notes might have been incomplete but because over the last few sessions—together with deeper anxieties coming up—Richard actually had begun to speak much less and the analysis had become more difficult. All this links with footnote 1 to the next session, p. 56.

# TWELFTH SESSION (Saturday)

*Mrs K.* had brought pencils, crayons, and a pad of writing-paper, and put them on the table.[1]

Richard asked eagerly what they were for, whether he could use them for writing or drawing.

*Mrs K.* said he could do whatever he liked with them.

Richard had hardly begun the first drawing when he repeatedly asked whether Mrs K. minded that he was drawing.

*Mrs K.* interpreted that he seemed to be afraid that by drawing he was doing something harmful to her.

Richard, when he had finished Drawing 1, repeated his questions and suddenly noticed that he had made marks on the second page of the pad.

*Mrs K.* interpreted that he was worried about the pencil marks because he was afraid that he was doing something destructive when he was drawing, and connected this with the fact that the drawing indicated a battle.

Richard stopped when he had finished the first two drawings.[2]

*Mrs K.* asked him what they were about.

Richard said there was an attack going on, but he did not know who would attack first, *Salmon* or the U-boat. He pointed at U 102 and said that 10 was his own age; and to U 16 he associated the

---

[1] In the first session, as mentioned earlier, I had prepared toys, paper, pencils, etc., on a table, but Richard took no interest in them and said he did not want to play, he only liked to think and to talk. During the last few sessions, however, he had talked much less and, together with his experiencing deeper anxieties, his need to play and to act out had become evident. This was shown by his looking more frequently at the map, 'choosing' a country, playing with the clock, looking into it and caressing it, turning the fire on and off, exploring the room more closely, inspecting the pictures and the postcards on the screen, and beating the little stools.

As the room was also used for other purposes, I had not been able to follow my ordinary procedure of keeping the toys and other articles in a place accessible to the child—in an unlocked drawer or on a table—thus leaving it to him whether and in what way he would make use of them. (The analyst should refrain from directing the child's play or other activities, and this corresponds to the principle of 'free association' in the analysis of adults.) Nor could I prepare these things before each session, for if Richard was early, I should have had to do so in his presence. However, it had now become clear that Richard urgently required a more appropriate medium for expressing his unconscious, and I therefore decided to bring back paper, pencils, and crayons, but not yet the toys, and see how he would respond to this.

[2] U 2 at the bottom of Drawing 1 was added two sessions later.

age of John Wilson. He was very surprised when he realized the unconscious meaning of these numbers and extremely interested to find that drawing could be a means of expressing unconscious thoughts.

*Mrs K.* pointed out that the numbers also indicated that he and John were represented by German U-boats, and were therefore hostile and dangerous to the British.

Richard was very much taken aback and disturbed by this inter-pretation, but after a silence he agreed that it must be right. He said, though, that he surely could not wish to attack the British, for he was very 'patriotic'.

*Mrs K.* interpreted that the British represented his own family and that he had already recognized that he not only loved and wished to protect but also wished to attack them [Split in the ego]; this appeared from the drawing where he was allied with John, who also partly stood for his brother. But since John was being analysed by Mrs K., he appeared as an ally against her whenever Richard felt towards her the same hostility as he experienced to-wards his family. Mrs K. reminded him how upset he had been when the little girl had taken him for an Italian (Tenth Session) and that she had interpreted that he felt so strongly about that because it meant being treacherous towards the British—his parents. The British *Truant* and *Sunfish* represented his parents whom he, together with John (standing for Paul), attacked.

Richard then enlarged on U 72 being on the right-hand side of *Truant* and *Sunfish*. He said he liked the number 2 because 'it was a nice even number'; 7 was uneven and he did not like uneven numbers. . . . He told a story about two people shooting rabbits and wondered how they would divide seven rabbits between them.

*Mrs K.* interpreted that the two people shooting and dividing the rabbits appeared to be himself and John. Now it seemed that his parents (who had been attacked by the U-boats) were the rabbits which were to be shot, divided, and devoured. The 7 in 72 stood for the devoured parents, the 2 for himself and John who was his ally, as Paul might have been his ally when he felt angry with Daddy and Mummy. At present John was also an ally against Mrs K., and then she, too, was represented by the rabbits who were shot and divided. She also reminded Richard that the 2 was part of 102 which he had recognized as standing for himself. But now 72 also represented himself (Note I). Going back to U 102, Mrs K. pointed out that he was here much bigger than the attacked British ships, and this showed his wish to be stronger and more powerful than his parents and therefore able to control them; he wished this all the more because he was afraid of their counter-attacks [Projection of aggression and fear of retaliation].

Richard, referring to Mrs K.'s interpretation, spoke about his brother being sometimes an ally, particularly against Nurse, but sometimes hostile to him, as, for instance, when he was teasing Richard.

*Mrs K.* interpreted that when Richard allied himself with John against Mrs K., she also stood for Nurse. Then she pointed out that on top of Drawing 1, *Salmon* and the U-boat also represented Paul and himself, and that he had said that he did not know who was going to attack whom.

Richard pointed out to Mrs K. that on Drawing 1 the periscope of *Sunfish* went through *Truant*.

*Mrs K.* interpreted that he was showing that the parents, too, were fighting, and that the periscope, standing for the father's genital, was a piercing and dangerous thing, injuring Mummy; that if Richard felt jealous about his parents having pleasure in sexual relations, he wished Daddy to attack Mummy (the tramp, Hitler), which meant that he himself was attacking her, though indirectly. Therefore he was terrified of the harm they were doing one another. The shooting and dividing of the rabbits also implied his direct attack on the parents, and now—also helped by John—directly attacking Mrs K.

Richard, looking at Drawing 2, pointed at U 19 and said with surprise that this was his brother's age. He was again much impressed by this and had now clearly become more convinced that Paul, John, and himself were represented by the hostile U-boats which were dangerous to the parents and to Mrs K. He also said that U 10 (in the lower half of Drawing 2) was himself; that he was bigger than Paul and on top of both parents; but he pointed out that they had put their periscopes through him.

*Mrs K.* interpreted Richard's wish to be on top of everybody; he was the smallest and weakest, and wished to be the strongest and most important member of the family. But his being such a big and dangerous U-boat implied that his attacks on his parents would destroy them, and he was afraid of this. They were also dangerous to him, because they had put their periscope genitals into him, and this meant that he had a sexual relation with both, but one in which they were stronger than he was. (While she was explaining this, Richard drew a swastika and showed her how easily it could be changed into a Union Jack.) Mrs K. said that this showed that he hoped he could change his hostile and aggressive U-boat self into a British one—and that meant a good one.

Richard, during these interpretations, had begun Drawing 3 and said that he wanted to make a 'lovely ship'. When drawing the line beneath the ship, he remarked that the lower half of the picture was 'under water' and had 'nothing to do with the upper part'. Under water there was a hungry starfish which liked the plant. He did not know what the U-boat near by would do, probably it would attack the ship. The fish was swimming quietly and peacefully. He added : 'This is Mummy, and the starfish is a baby.'

*Mrs K.* interpreted that his making a 'lovely ship' was meant to put the parents right, both parents being represented by the ship.

Richard asked : 'Are they the funnels?'

*Mrs K.* showed him that the smoke went up in a straight line from one funnel and that might represent his father's genital. The other funnel was a little thinner and the smoke line was crooked. This was meant to be Mummy's genital.

Richard said Mummy was thinner than Daddy, but he said he had never seen a woman's genital. He felt less sure, though, that he might not have seen a little girl's genital.

*Mrs K.* also interpreted that the hungry starfish, the baby, was himself ; the plant, Mummy's breast which he wished to feed from. When he felt like a greedy baby, who wanted his mother all to himself and could not have her, he became angry and jealous and felt he attacked both parents. This was represented by the U-boat, which would 'probably' attack the ship. He was also very jealous of John because, as Mrs K.'s patient, he received time and attention from her. The analysis stood now for being fed. He had said that everything which went on under water had nothing to do with the upper part. This meant that greed, jealousy, and aggression were not known to one part of his mind, they were kept unconscious. In the top part of the drawing, divided off from the lower half, he expressed his wish to unite his parents and to have them happily together. These feelings, of which he was quite aware, were experienced in what he felt to be the upper part of his mind [The unconscious split off from the conscious and subsequently repressed].

Richard had followed this interpretation with great interest and attention, and clearly felt relief (Note II). (Soon after he had begun to make the drawings, he asked whether he could take them home. Mrs K. suggested that she would rather keep them so that they could be looked at whenever Richard felt like it. Richard was obviously flattered by this suggestion and also took a special interest in the fact that Mrs K. was dating the drawings. It was clear that he realized she wished to keep them. His feeling that he was giving her a present in this way entered into the material at different points.) H told Mrs K. on leaving that he was greatly looking forward to going home for the weekend.

*Notes to Twelfth Session:*

I. Further conclusions (not interpreted) emerge from this material : Richard felt he had devoured the parents (rabbits) and they had become part of his self; they were the 7 in U 72. The greedy, destructive aspect of himself was expressed by U (the dangerous hostile U-boat), the 'good' aspect by the 2 (the 'nice even number' he liked). The 2 stood for himself as well, allied with John, and this implied that he had also internalized him (and Paul) in his bad (greedy) as well as helpful aspect (the ally). The 'nice even' part of himself, the 2, therefore, was not only the good part of himself in contrast to the U-boat part; since it was allied with the bad brother, it was also felt to be dangerous. The 'nice even' had moreover the particular meaning of being hypocritical, seemingly smooth. This point was fully confirmed by Richard's whole character formation. As will be seen in later material, there was a strong tendency in him, which he himself deeply distrusted, to be pleasant, flattering, and so on. The U 72, with the associations gained in this session as well as in the light of former and later material, was most revealing of Richard's ego structure and included the various split-off aspects of his self, namely, the greedy and destructive impulses, the reparative and loving tendencies, the appeasing and hypocritical ones, and some of his internalized figures : the shot, cut-up, and devoured parents who had turned into injured, hostile, retaliating, and devouring objects in his inner world. (See, for instance, the devouring bird-figure which the internalized mother represented in the Forty-fourth Session.) Two sessions later, at a moment when Richard had become aware of his greed and jealousy, he quickly added U 2 to that drawing and said afterwards that it was himself. He explained that he put his periscope so violently through U 102 and U 16 because he was very cross with them. I interpreted that one part of himself hated another one—the hostile, greedy U-boat part. This punishing part (the Super-ego), although it was felt to be doing the right thing, was also angry and aggressive and therefore also represented by a U-boat. But because it was both good and bad, the swastika of U 2 had come out indistinctly—it seemed a mixture of swastika and Union Jack.

I am choosing here one instance out of many to illustrate and substantiate my contention that the ego builds itself up from the beginning of post-natal life by its internalized objects; and that splitting processes of the ego are bound up with split-off aspects of the object. The shooting and dividing of the rabbits came up after Richard had said that he would wish to burrow himself into my mind—the rat material (Tenth Session). I had interpreted that as burrowing into his mother's inside, biting her, and eating the contents of her body. This took us back to the earliest internalization processes, the devouring of the mother's breast and the origin of injured and devouring internal objects. In other words, Richard's ego structure could be traced back to quite early material, some of it pre-verbal. Such processes can be found not only in a child of ten but also in adults (who would, of course, present the material differently from the child) if the analysis is carried into deep layers of the mind.

II. Although Richard had welcomed the paper and pencils and at once started to use them, he was, to begin with, inhibited in expressing his unconscious thoughts. He first drew *Salmon* and the U-boat on top of Drawing 1. He crossed out the next three ships, and it was only after he had drawn *Truant*, *Sunfish*, and U 72 that his U-boats became much bigger. By then I had already interpreted his anxiety lest his drawing should be harmful to me. This interpretation I could link, when he had finished Drawing 1, with his pointing out to me the pencil marks on the empty page underneath. He expressed himself more freely in Drawing 2 and in the associations to it; and the interpretations of Drawings 1 and 2 led to the rich material of Drawing 3. This illustrates my experience that the approach to the patient's associations and the unconscious material they contain—i.e. the analysis of the specific unconscious meaning of the patient's attitude, behaviour, and associations, and the timely interpretation of all this— influences the quantity and nature of the material which can be obtained and fundamentally affects the course the analysis takes.


## THIRTEENTH SESSION (Monday)

Richard was subdued and sad. He told Mrs K. that his mother had been ill over the weekend and could not come to 'X' with him; she had eaten a piece of salmon which did not agree with her. Everyone else ate it without being upset. He said with tears in his eyes that he was very unhappy about leaving home, his parents, and everything he liked.[1] Though he had not told this to his mother, he had not wanted to return to analysis. He had been wondering whether Mrs K. would bring his drawings and paper and pencils— he had not thought she would. (He spoke very listlessly, his words interspersed with silences.)

*Mrs K.* interpreted his fear that the drawings he made in the

[1] Sometimes Richard's mother stayed with him at the hotel, at other times the cook, or his former nurse who lived in the neighbourhood.

previous session were harmful to her. They might have injured or even killed her, or she might have become hostile towards him and 'bad'. Therefore he had not expected her to bring his drawings and the writing material. His great worry about Mummy's sickness, too, connected with his feelings that he had injured her through the attacks expressed in his drawings. In two of them the submarine *Salmon* had played an important role, and Mummy had now in fact been harmed by a salmon. This reinforced his unconscious feeling that he was responsible for Mummy's indisposition.

Richard thereupon began to draw. Looking again and again at Drawing 3, he said he wanted to make an exact copy of it and give it to his mother. When he had finished it (Drawing 4), he was very surprised to find that it was quite different from the original. In fact, he at once decided not to give it to his mother. While making this drawing he spoke of a tragedy : his canaries were going bald.

*Mrs K.* pointed out that in the copy (Drawing 4) the starfish, which represented the greedy baby and was himself, was farther away from the plant that stood for his mother's breasts; that his fear of harming her through his greed had caused him to put himself farther away from her; however, there were now two U-boats instead of the one in Drawing 3 which had represented himself torpedoing (or possibly torpedoing) the 'lovely ship', the two parents.

Richard showed Mrs K. that in Drawing 4 the torpedo was not going in the direction of the ship and therefore could not harm it. He added that there were now two fishes : they were Daddy and Mummy watching the U-boat carefully and preventing it from doing harm.

*Mrs K.* interpreted that Richard's wish to make an exact copy to give to his mother also expressed his feeling that he ought not to prefer Mrs K. to Mummy. He seemed to have felt that way about Mummy and Nurse, for whom Mrs K. now stood. Since he thought of the drawing with the 'lovely ship' as a present, guilt about having given it to Mrs K. was much increased by his mother's sickness and by his wish to make her well again—which he felt the 'lovely ship' might do; as he could not make an exact copy, he did not care to give it to his mother. His fear of having injured his parents had been the cause of the difference between the two drawings (3 and 4). In Drawing 4 he was both preventing himself from doing harm and being prevented by the watchful parents. This was the same as when in his analysis Mrs K. found out his aggressive wishes and he thought she would thereby help him to control them. Mrs K. asked him whom the second U-boat represented.

Richard said it was Paul. Then he realized with surprise his 'mistake' in colouring the ship in Drawing 4; for the colour was different from that in Drawing 3.

*Mrs K.* interpreted that Daddy and Mummy, who had in the former drawing been represented by the funnels, were now red, probably because he felt they were injured. Also he had made the right-hand funnel a little fatter, and both funnels, which had been standing for the parents' genitals, now had the same smoke line. This expressed his wish to make them equal so that there should be no trouble between them (Note I). Mrs K. reminded him of the canaries which were going bald and interpreted that they were the same as the red funnels—the injured parents.

Richard said that Daddy was going bald and was often unwell, but he was nice and Richard was very fond of him. . . . He added with strong feeling that there was 'something good' about Daddy not being so fit—he had been exempt in the last war. . . .

*Mrs K.* pointed out how strong his struggle between love and hatred was, and that his feelings of guilt increased his worry.

Richard was much less sad when leaving. He asked Mrs K. to bring the drawings and also the toys which he had seen in the first hour; he might now like to play with them. During Mrs K.'s interpretations his attention wandered, but once or twice he looked at her in a very interested and understanding way, particularly when she interpreted the conflict between love and hatred, his fear that he could not control his destructive impulses, and his wish to make reparation. At the end of the hour Richard made Drawing 5 and told Mrs K. that the outline in the bottom left-hand corner, on which he had put down the score of British and German planes shot down, was also a hangar at Dover. (This drawing is analysed in the Sixteenth Session.)

*Note to Thirteenth Session:*

I. I would conclude that Richard's own envy—both of mother's fertility and father's potency—led him to project it on to his parents. By making them equal, mother need not envy father nor father envy mother.

## FOURTEENTH SESSION (Tuesday)

*Mrs K.* had brought the toys[1] and put them on the table. Richard was very interested and at once began to play. He first picked up the two little swings, put them side by side, made them swing, and then laid them down beside each other, saying : 'They are having fun.' He filled one truck of the train which he called the 'goods train' with small figures, and said 'the children' were off on a pleasure trip to Dover. He added a slightly larger toy woman in a pink dress, whom he at once called 'Mummy'. (In all his subsequent play she figured as Mummy (Note I).) He said that Mummy, too, was going on the pleasure trip with the children. He added one of the bigger men, whom he called 'the minister' because he was wearing a hat, but soon took him out of the truck, sat him on the roof of a house, added the pink woman, and they both tumbled down. He put them by themselves in a truck facing one another and said : 'Mummy and Daddy are making love.' He had taken out the small figures from the first truck and put one of them in the second truck, turned towards the couple in the first one.

*Mrs K.* interpreted that the swings represented his parents ; laying them down side by side and saying that they were having fun meant their being in bed together, and the movement of the swings indicated their sexual relations. When the pink woman (whom he called 'Mummy) was to go away with the children on a pleasure trip, this meant that the parents should not be together. He would also allow Mrs K. to be with him and the other children (Paul, John, and so on) but not with any man who stood for Mr K. Feeling guilty and sorry about having separated the parents, Richard brought back Daddy, now represented by the 'minister'. Then again, as with the swings, he allowed them to be together and have

[1] The toys consisted of: little wooden figures, some of them dressed as men, others as women, some small, some larger. The 'pink woman' and 'minister' were sitting figures; two swings with a person on each seat; two trains, one with two closed carriages which he called the 'electric' or 'express' train, often referring to its closed carriages as 'passenger cars', the other with open trucks, which he declared to be a 'goods' train—he kept to these names for them throughout. Both trains had engines. The electric train was bigger than the goods train. These trains had no mechanism, and when they are described as running, it was always Richard who made them move. There were also little animals, houses in two different sizes, a coal lorry and a lorry with timber, some fences and trees. (I have said repeatedly that I avoided any specific toy which would give too direct a lead, but, for some reason I cannot recall any more, the two lorries were among my collection of toys at the time.)

sexual relations by placing them together on the roof. When they fell, which meant that they were injured, he put them by themselves in a truck, and the 'child' in the second truck stood for himself watching the parents 'making love', but in a friendly relation with them. (From now on this combination of three figures, sometimes represented by animals, expressed his good relation with his parents (Note II).)

Richard made various groups of the little figures: there were two men together, then a cow and a horse in the first truck, and a sheep in the second. Then he arranged the little houses to form a 'village and a station'. He made the train run round and into the station. As he had left too little space, the train knocked over the houses, and he put them up again. He pushed the other train (which he called an 'electric' train) and a collision ensued. He became very upset and made the 'electric' train run over everything. The toys piled up and he spoke of it as a 'mess' and a 'disaster'. In the end only the 'electric' train was left standing up (Note III).

*Mrs K.* interpreted that the children's pleasure trip to Dover meant that they, too, wanted to do something sexual as the parents did; that when he took them to Dover, which had in fact been so badly damaged recently (and to which he had referred in Drawing 5), this meant that the parents' sexual intercourse was dangerous. This danger was also expressed by putting the minister-father and Mummy on the roof, from which they fell down. In the end it all finished in 'disaster'. Mrs K. also interpreted his fear that the analysis might finish in disaster and that it would be his fault, in the same way as he felt he had done harm to Mummy. She reminded him as well of the dog which had to be destroyed and of his mentioning his granny's death (cf. Second Session).

Richard was extremely impressed by Mrs K.'s interpretation. He expressed his surprise that his thoughts and feelings could be shown in his play.

*Mrs K.* interpreted that his recognizing that his play expressed his feelings also meant that Mrs K. made what went on in him clear to him. This proved to him that the analysis and Mrs K. were good and helpful. She now represented the good mother who would help him after all, in spite of the 'disaster' which he took to be his own fault.

Richard asked Mrs K. if what happened in the end meant that the 'electric' train was himself and that he was the strongest of all.

*Mrs K.* reminded him that he had been the biggest and most powerful of the family when he was represented by the big U-boat in Drawing 2.

Richard, after a pause, pushed the toys aside and said he was 'tired' of them. He began to draw very elaborately and with great zest (Drawing 6).[1] He said there were lots of babies, starfishes, there: they were in a 'blazing fury' and very hungry. They wanted to be near the plant (which he had not yet drawn), so they tore the octopus out from there. Richard then decided to make port-holes on the *Nelson*.

*Mrs K.* interpreted that the port-holes also represented babies, as did the starfishes and the numberplates on the black car (Ninth Session). He wanted Mummy to have many babies to make her better. When they tore out the bad octopus, this meant that he and Paul were tearing father's bad genital out of Mummy, and that he and John tore the Hitler-penis out of Mrs K. The salmon which made Mummy ill over the weekend was also Daddy's bad genital. The port-holes meant having easier access to Mummy's body so that there would be no need to tear things out of her. The plant to which the babies wanted to be near stood for Mummy's breast, her genital, and her inside. The babies wished to be near Mummy and feed from her as well as to make their way into Mummy's inside. They were also feeding from Mrs K.—the analysis being felt as a feeding. They tore out the octopus, not only because it was harmful to Mummy but because they were in a 'blazing fury', being jealous of it, and felt greedy and wanted to take its place. Mrs K. reminded him of her earlier interpretations that his jealous and angry wish for Daddy to injure Mummy had caused his fear of the 'bad' Daddy (the tramp in the first session, and now the octopus). In his play he had been wavering between jealousy (taking Mummy, the little pink figure, away from Daddy, the minister) and the wish to bring them together (allowing them to make love). In this play the parents had not actually appeared to be bad but to have sexual pleasure together, and Richard felt in a 'blazing fury' of jealousy.

Richard said, 'Yes, the babies want to be there [meaning near the plant]. They do not want the nasty octopus to be there.' But it appeared that he had also to some extent accepted Mrs K.'s interpretation of the attacks on the father caused by his own jealousy, and not only by his feeling that the father's genital—the 'nasty octopus'—was bad. . . . Richard again looked at the drawings and he quickly added U 2 to Drawing 1 (Twelfth Session) and said afterwards that it was himself. He said he must have put his periscope through U 102 and U 16 because he was so cross with them.

*Mrs K.* interpreted that he had already indicated (Twelfth Session) that one part of himself hated another one, represented by the hostile U-boat. The part of himself which attacked his U-boat self—and the bad John (and Paul)—although it was felt to be

[1] A number of details were added in the next session.

restraining and punishing his own hostile tendencies, did this in an angry and aggressive way, and was, therefore, also represented by a U-boat [the dreaded Super-ego]. But since he felt that this part of himself was doing the *right* thing, the swastika of U 2 had come out very indistinctly—it seemed to be a mixture of Union Jack and swastika, i.e. a mixture of what he felt to be his good and his bad self (Note IV).

*Notes to Fourteenth Session:*

I. Some of the toys kept their symbolic meaning throughout the analysis, such as the 'goods train' and the 'minister'. Others changed roles, which is an interesting point, suggesting that symbols have not always the same meaning.

II. The desire for the parents to be united but watched by him had many sources. There was, of course, sexual curiosity, the wish to control the parents, but also the security which the observation that they were not doing harm to one another but actually 'making love' would give him. In the Introduction I have referred to Richard's strong capacity for love. It found expression, together with the wish to make reparation, throughout his analysis. These factors, which allowed depressive features to dominate over the schizoid ones, also explain why Richard was such a cooperative patient and made it possible for even this very short analysis to become fruitful.

III. One of the advantages of the play technique—particularly with small toys—is that in expressing by these means a variety of emotions and situations the child comes nearest to showing us the happenings in his inner world. To some extent this is also expressed in drawings and in other forms of play, and in dreams. But it is when the child plays with the small toys that we can see the expression of opposing emotions most distinctly. The fact that Richard straight away produced so much important material recalls the well-known experience that patients often in the first dream they bring in analysis reveal much of their unconscious; as can be observed, such dreams often foreshadow the material that will play an important role in the analysis.

IV. It is interesting that, although strong resistance came up following the interpretation of Richard's play, and he had therefore stopped playing, he nevertheless drew with zest and thereby gave material which went back to even more fundamental emotions : his oral anxieties regarding himself and his father and the plotting with his brother against the father. The conclusion is that on the one hand resistance was stirred up and led to giving up his play, and on the other hand the interpretations had to some extent been accepted and produced further material. Although the need to express his unconscious has not been diminished, the medium by which it was expressed

—the toys—had at that moment become bad and therefore he went on to drawing. We find in adults too that a line of association might be discontinued owing to resistance, but that we get the same and even further material by a dream following such a session or even by the sudden remembering of a dream that had not previously been told to the analyst.

## FIFTEENTH SESSION (Wednesday)

Richard said that he had expected Mummy, but she did not come because of a sore throat; he was disappointed, but what he was mainly upset about was that Mummy was ill. He began to play. Many details were similar to those described in the previous session. He moved the swings, making different groups, returning again and again to the arrangement in which two figures (sometimes represented by animals) were together in one truck and a third in the next truck. Then suddenly a little toy dog jumped into one of the trucks and threw out the 'minister' (Note I). Richard then put him on the roof. The children were going for pleasure trips by themselves in both trains, then decided to take the pink mother with them. He said the trains would go through the station safely, but the figures began to fall down, and in the end the 'electric' train ran over everything and was the only survivor (Note II). As in the preceding session, he pushed the toys aside after the 'disaster' and said he did not like playing. Richard eagerly began to draw and became more lively and less depressed. . . .[1] He first finished Drawing 6, adding a few details and pointing them out to Mrs K.: he coloured the octopus red, and gave it a mouth. He told Mrs K. that the two fishes were whispering. They were teasing the octopus because it tickled them with its tentacles. The octopus was very hungry and wanted food. Richard said, while colouring the starfishes, that now he was going to 'make the babies alive';[2] so far they had only been 'jelly'. The two tiny ones between the plants were not yet quite

[1] I have no note about the interpretation given regarding the new features in the play, such as the direct assault on the father by the dog, nor about his turning away from the toys because of the 'disaster'. But I have no doubt that I did interpret this.

[2] It was clear from the context that by colouring the drawing the people represented in it had come to life. This seems similar to the experience of one or two adult patients who during the analysis began to dream in colour and felt this as a great progress. It meant to them that they could revive their objects.

alive. Now, while colouring the starfishes, he added the plants. He explained that the two fishes whispering were he and Paul annoying Daddy. He added that Mummy was not in that picture.

*Mrs K.* interpreted that Mummy was there, represented by the plant standing for her breast, genital, and inside. It was because the fight over Mummy was bound to destroy her that he did not wish to admit that she was in the picture, but giving Mummy so many babies (the starfishes and the port-holes) was felt to revive her and make her better. Mrs K. was not to be there either, because she was to be saved from his and John's greedy attacks. As had been seen in the previous session, Mummy was felt to be ill because the greedy octopus-Daddy was eating her; but when the hungry babies in a 'blazing fury' tore him out, they, too, injured her; moreover, they, too, wanted to devour her. Richard and Paul plotting against the octopus-Daddy also meant starving Daddy, as Richard had said that the octopus was so hungry. Mrs K. suggested that the two fishes were also Daddy and Mummy whispering about what the children were doing (as well as Mrs K. and the suspect Mr K.), i.e. that Richard would feel that his parents had found him out and plotted against him as he wanted to plot with Paul against them [Persecutory anxiety and fear of retaliation]. Mrs K. was now finding out his secrets and therefore was also suspected of being in a plot against him.

Richard pointed out to Mrs K. that Mummy was also there in another form because she was the ship *Nelson* and Daddy the submarine *Salmon*. He said again that Mummy had become sick through eating salmon. (It was clear that he had now linked her illness with the unconscious meaning of the drawing.)

*Mrs K.* interpreted that the small fish by itself between *Nelson* and *Salmon* represented Richard, who wished to separate the parents in order to prevent the dangerous Daddy from injuring Mummy (and the dangerous Hitler from destroying Mrs K.). But he was also separating them out of jealousy.

Richard then drew another picture of a fight between aeroplanes, and said the ugly big plane which was crossed out (i.e. shot down) was Paul, but at once contradicted himself and said that it was his uncle Tony, whom he did not like.

*Mrs K.* asked who shot Paul or his uncle (the ugly plane).

Richard answered without hesitation, 'I did.'

*Mrs K.* asked where he had got the anti-aircraft gun from.

Richard laughed and said, 'I pinched it from Uncle Tony who is a gunner.' He was highly amused about this. He then explained that the British plane—the nice one—was Mummy. He, Richard, was protecting Mummy with his big gun against the nasty Daddy, Paul, and Uncle, and he killed them all.

*Mrs K.* interpreted that Uncle Tony, whom he did not like, stood for the bad Daddy, that he felt he had stolen his penis (the gun) and was both attacking him with it and saving Mummy in that way.

Richard then made Drawing 7 and explained it to Mrs K. The starfishes were babies, the fish was Mummy who had put her head above the periscope so that the U-boat should not see the British ship. It would be deceived because it saw nothing but yellow. Richard did not know whether the submarine or the U-boat would be destroyed. The fat fish on top was also Mummy. She had eaten a starfish, which was now breaking through with its edges and hurting her. The U-boat at the bottom was lazy. It slept instead of helping the other U-boat. Richard said laughingly, 'It is snoring,' and then added : 'But Paul actually snores.'

*Mrs K.* interpreted that the upper U-boat which was attacking the submarine represented Richard attacking Daddy. The lower, 'snoring' U-boat was obviously Paul, who had deserted him and was a bad ally. Again he and John were also attacking Mr K. but he could not rely on John. Mummy, who was protecting the British and trying to deceive the U-boat which stood for Richard, was on Daddy's side (Note III) and had also deserted Richard. Richard wanted to punish the Hitler-Daddy for having put such a dangerous starfish genital into Mummy—the fat fish on top—which injured her inside. But Mummy, too, was felt to be greedy because she ate father's starfish-genital—the actual salmon which had made her ill. The starfish inside the fat Mummy-fish was also a baby, and she was fat because it grew inside her. This was shown in the previous session (Drawing 6) when he spoke of the babies which were still jelly and not yet alive and were meant to be the babies growing inside Mummy. Mrs K. also interpreted that the two torpedoes represented Daddy's salmon, and Richard's U-boat genitals, and were red because they were eating each other up.

Richard had listened with great interest, though sometimes he was obviously reluctant to accept Mrs K.'s interpretations. He was much happier and more friendly when he left. In some ways the situation in this session was similar to that in the previous one. Resistance set in after the play, but there was a wealth of associations and material in the drawings that followed. Towards the end of the session his mood was much more depressed, the feeling that he could not make reparation and of being deserted by both his mother and his brother stirred up loneliness and anxiety. In Drawing 7 there are a number of uncoloured starfishes, which means unborn ones he could not make alive. This mood was influenced by his mother still being unwell, which meant to him an awful illness or the delivery of a dangerous baby. In contrast to his ill mother, Mrs K. represented the mother who was well (I would think the healthy nurse in contrast to the ill mother). This fact in the transference enabled him to express both his attacks and his anxieties relating to the ill mother.

*Notes to Fifteenth Session:*

I. It frequently happens that material, both in child and adult analyses, looks very similar. All the more attention has to be paid to any new details—sometimes apparently insignificant ones—because they may introduce a new aspect of the material. In this particular instance, the attack on the father, though of course symbolically represented, appeared more directly and distinctly.

If material—and this again applies both to adults and to children— is obsessionally repeated over and over again, there are two possibilities. The one is that the analyst has not noticed slight alterations which should have been interpreted; or the obsessional attitude of the patient has not yet been diminished and needs further exploration.

II. It is well known that young children's attempts at constructive activities are often hampered by their lack of skill. For instance, when children begin to paint, they are likely to make a mess. They tend to take this as evidence that their destructive impulses predominate over their constructive and reparative ones. It can often be observed that when their efforts go wrong, they tear up the paper, or make an even bigger mess. One of the deepest causes for this attitude is that distrust of themselves and despair reinforce their destructive tendencies.

With Richard there was an intense unconscious anxiety lest his play —which, as we have seen, expressed such fundamental desires and processes—should finish in 'disaster', as well as a very strong determination to avoid it. The small toys were easily overturned, and when that happened Richard was filled with despair and hatred of himself. For this proved to him that he was unable to control his aggressive impulses and could not make reparation. As a consequence his feelings of persecution and destructive impulses were reinforced—the mess, the pile of destroyed objects, had turned hostile in his mind and should all the more be destroyed. Therefore the play finished with the dangerous part of himself—e.g. the 'electric' train—surviving, and as a further consequence he felt overwhelmed by loneliness, anxiety, and guilt which were in turn to be denied.

III. When Richard showed that his mother—the fish—was protecting his father against the hostile sons, he was upset about being deserted by her and by the parents uniting against him. But he was also satisfied because his mother was protecting his father against Richard's destructive impulses. This illustrates an important feature in the child's emotional situation, particularly in the latency period. The child feels that the parents should be in harmony with one another, and it is a source of great conflict and insecurity if he believes that he has succeeded in making trouble between them and in allying himself with one against the other. I have already referred to the fact that, particularly in the latency period, the child feels insecure if the parents or other people in authority do not agree with one another. This goes side by side with the opposite desire that one of the parents should become an ally against the other one.

## SIXTEENTH SESSION (Thursday)

Richard seemed particularly pleased to see Mrs K. He said he was 'terribly fond' of her and that she was 'sweet'. He told Mrs K. that his mother had not come; he did not mind that so much but he was sorry that she was still not well. (Obviously he was trying to be reasonable about it but his mood was serious and downcast.) He at once began to play, making groups as before : some children to-gether; the minister alone on the roof; the minister and the pink woman together; groups of animals—two in one truck (cow and horse) looking at each other, and in the next truck a sheep looking towards them. A new detail was that the minister fell off the roof because he was pushed over by a little man; this was followed by the same action as on the previous day : the dog jumped into a truck and threw a man out of it. Richard again put up the 'station' (the same house that he had previously used for this) and said that there were slums at the back of the station. At this point he looked worried and was reluctant to answer Mrs K.'s question about what the slums looked like. But he remarked that there were dirty chil-dren there and diseases. When saying this he put aside a few figures that had some small defects, and said he did not want them. He set both trains going and the goods train collided with the electric train. Suddenly Richard bit the tower of a house (which he called a 'church'). Then the dog bit somebody and disaster followed. Every-thing collapsed and the dog was the only survivor. Richard again put the toys aside, as he had done after the previous disasters, and said that he was 'tired' of them. He looked worried when he said so. He got up, looked round the room and went out of the door; he cheered up as he gazed (with genuine admiration) at the countryside, remarking on its beauty. Coming back he began to draw, saying that he was making 'a wild picture' (Drawing 8). To Mrs K.'s question, 'Why wild?', he replied that he did not know; he just *felt* like that. After having done part of the drawing Richard explained that the starfishes were 'very greedy'; they were all round the sunk *Emden* and wanted to attack her. They hated her and wanted to help the British. He pointed out that the fish was about to touch the flag, but both the fish and the starfishes were 'in the way' of the submarine *Salmon* which wanted to salvage the sunk *Emden*. Then Richard decided that the fish was not in the way, it was helping the *Salmon*.

*Mrs K.* interpreted that Richard's need to make a 'wild' picture was expressed by the starfishes having so many more jagged edges than in former drawings and, since Richard said that they were 'very greedy', Mrs K. suggested that these edges represented the teeth of the greedy babies. They came so close to the *Emden* because they attacked her breasts (the two funnels). The sunk *Emden* stood for Mummy who died because she was eaten and destroyed by the children (and for Mrs K. who had been destroyed by Richard's and John's greed). Daddy appeared here as good, for he was trying to save Mummy (the submarine *Salmon* salvaging the sunk *Emden*), and the bad children (the starfishes) were trying to prevent him (Note I). In the upper half of the picture a different situation was presented. Mummy (the fish) was alive, close to Daddy (about to touch the flag), and Richard (the submarine *Severn*) was on good terms with them. Mrs K. suggested that the British plane might stand for Paul, who was included in the happy family situation. In his play the slums had stood for the injured mother, who had been made ill (the diseases). This meant, as had been seen formerly, that the bad father's genital—in Drawing 7 the salmon-genital and the big starfish which she ate [1]—had made her ill. (This fear was stimulated by his mother's sore throat.) He might be afraid that the greedy starfishes (he and John) would also make Mrs K. ill. She pointed out, moreover, that when playing with the

---

[1] Richard's suspicions of himself as destructive (the greedy baby), which extended to the other children (here John and Paul), co-existed with the suspicions of the bad father. Their greed was predominantly felt to be a danger to mother. With the children (starfishes) the destructive impulses and phantasies expressed themselves by biting and devouring; with the father the weapon of destruction was the greedy, biting, poisonous genital. Richard's guilt, as we had seen in the material, related not only to his own destructiveness but also to the father's, for he felt the father's destructive impulses to be a result of his own hostile wishes, stirred up by jealousy. In the play the disaster was basically due to his attacking his father or both parents because of his jealousy.

toys he had again directly attacked Daddy. Richard had been first represented by the little man pushing the minister (Daddy) off the roof, and then by the dog which threw the man out of the truck (Note II).

Richard had been looking at some of the earlier pictures, particularly at Drawing 5, which had not been analysed at the time it was drawn.

*Mrs K.* asked him what he thought it meant. Richard was unwilling to reply. She interpreted that the four British planes might represent the family.

Richard became interested and cooperative and said that the crossed-out German bomber on the right also represented himself. Suddenly he became restless, stood up, and said (after an obvious inner struggle) that he had a secret which he could not tell Mrs K. But then he told it almost at once : he had dirtied his trousers last night and Cook had washed them. Richard added shamefacedly that this hardly ever happened, but sometimes he thought he could hold his 'big job' and then couldn't after all.

*Mrs K.* interpreted that the thought about the 'secret' had occurred at the moment when he had recognized that in the drawing he was the bad German bomber, and she added that his 'big job' was felt to be the bombs. His fear lest he might bomb his family with his fæces might have been the cause of his dirtying his trousers last night, for in that way he could confess his fears, test whether his 'big job' was dangerous, and also get rid of these secret fæces which he felt he contained. Mrs K. also pointed out that the bombs on the drawing were falling on the anti-aircraft gun and on one of the British planes (which he had therefore crossed out). He had recently said that he had stolen the anti-aircraft gun from his uncle and attacked him, Daddy and Paul; but in the drawing the ack-ack gun had destroyed the German bomber, which represented the bad part of himself which had stolen Daddy's genital (the gun) and attacked Daddy with it. Richard therefore felt that he should be punished and destroyed.[1]

Richard pointed out the little man looking at the bomb-crater.

*Mrs K.* suggested that the little man was also Richard, concerned about the damage; the bomb-crater was Mummy's breast, and since the ack-ack gun was Daddy's (and Uncle's) genital, Richard's bomb-fæces were aimed at both parents; furthermore, the hangar also represented Mummy, and Richard (the little man) had in that way, too, put himself between the parents.

[1] We see here for the first time that Richard's destructiveness, through fear of retaliation, engendered the fear of his death. The need for punishment is also unmistakable.

Richard pointed out that he, Mummy, and Paul were still alive, for they were the three undamaged British planes. The one that was shot down was Daddy. Of the German planes Richard said that the 'ugly one' in the top left-hand corner was Paul; the one next to it, himself; and the third (intact) one, Mummy.

*Mrs K.* interpreted that the German alive plane also stood for her. The shot-down British plane represented the destroyed Daddy. At the bottom of the drawing, however, Daddy was still alive, represented by the ack-ack gun, and together with Mummy (the hangar).

Richard said that he himself was alive, on the top of the drawing, because the three German planes which were shot down were also Daddy, Mummy, and Paul; and here he, Richard, was the only survivor.

*Mrs K.* again interpreted that when his feelings fluctuated between hatred, fear, guilt, and the wish to make reparation, people (including himself) and situations changed in his mind. Then they were bad or destroyed or good or dead or alive.

*Mrs K.* had to cut short this session by a few minutes and pointed this out to Richard, suggesting that she would make up for this next day.

Richard asked whether she had to see John earlier.

### Notes to Sixteenth Session:

I. By that time oral desires and phantasies, which together with anal material had already played a prominent part in his analysis, were expressed in full force. The sunk *Emden*, in Drawing 8, devoured by the greedy starfish babies represented his mother eaten up again and again internally and therefore felt to be dead and an enemy. It is of interest that from Drawing 3 onwards Richard drew a dividing line, which according to him meant that what happened above it had nothing to do with what happened underneath it. The interpretation that he was separating his unconscious from his conscious mind was fully substantiated. I believe, considering in particular Drawing 8, that the dividing line also expressed divisions between an internal situation and an external one, as well as between love and hate and the situations to which these conflicting emotions would give rise. The depressive position had come to the fore. An essential aspect of this position is based on the dangers threatening the internal object; and the sunk *Emden* which could not be saved represented the internal mother hopelessly injured by Richard's greed. (His mother's illness, though in fact not serious, had strongly stirred up anxiety and guilt.) At the same time feelings of love and reparative tendencies, bound up with the depressive position, are expressed by the happenings on top of the dividing line as well as in the middle of the drawing.

The ship and the British plane hovering above represent the good and united parents and the good Paul, who would attempt to control Richard's destructive impulses and thus prevent disaster to the family, including himself. The mother fish almost touching the flag, representing the father, and the *Salmon* trying to salvage the sunk *Emden,* are also an expression of the good relation between the parents. His ambivalent feelings about that relation were shown by his first saying that the fish was in the way and allied with the greedy starfishes and then correcting himself and saying that it was not in the way. The fact that the fish-mother was in the first association meant to stop the *Salmon* from saving the sunk *Emden* has several determinants. It is a denial that the sunk *Emden* is the internal destroyed mother. It also means dividing the external situation from an internal one; and it means that the external and internal mothers differ from each other, the external one being allied with the son, the internal one being devoured and therefore hostile and dangerous. The greedy starfishes devouring the mother and preventing the *Salmon*-father from saving her express the destructive impulses in full force.

The fact that these divided aspects could be revealed in the drawing as operating simultaneously was due to the analysis of splitting processes and projection, bound up with anal- and oral-sadistic impulses and phantasies, which made it possible for the depressive position to be to some extent experienced.

I have mentioned that some steps towards synthesis were shown in the Ninth Session. In that session Richard felt uneasy about his hate of Germany—his mother who had been made bad by Hitler (the bad father)—and he chose France instead, for whom he felt sympathy although she had, as he said, 'betrayed' the British. This meant that the good and bad mother had come closer together in his mind and that he was more able to love his object, in spite of its imperfections. Drawing 8 leads us farther still. For a pre-condition for synthesis arising with the depressive position is the growing unconscious awareness of internal reality, of the contrasting and split-off aspects of his emotions and desires, which are shown in this drawing.

II. Richard had thus expressed in his play and in the drawing a variety of aspects, not only of people (parents, brother, and himself) but also of the situations that in his mind came about or could come about as a result of the interrelations of these people. Mother touching the flag—i.e. on good terms with Father; Father saving Mother; he and Paul on friendly terms with the ship (parents). What he felt about these various situations was strongly influenced by his own desires, emotions, and anxieties prevalent at the time and attributed to his family. It is an essential part of psycho-analytic therapy (and this applies to children and adults) that the patient should be enabled by the analyst's interpretations to integrate the split-off and contrasting aspects of his self; this implies also the synthesis of the split-off aspects of other people and of situations. Such progress in synthesis and integration during an analysis, while giving relief, also brings up anxiety. For the patient is bound to experience the persecutory and depressive anxieties which were largely responsible for the tendency to split, splitting being one of the fundamental defences against persecutory and depressive anxiety.

## SEVENTEENTH SESSION (Friday)

Richard looked depressed and told Mrs K. that he had been expecting Mummy and Paul, who was home on leave, but they had not come. Possibly they would arrive tomorrow. He was very sorry to miss most of his brother's leave. If he saw Paul tomorrow, it would only be for a few hours. Richard had asked Cook (who was still staying with him in the hotel) what she thought the family might be doing; the description she gave of Daddy and Mummy sitting by the fire with Paul and Bobby made Richard feel so miserable and lonely that he could hardly bear it. He said listlessly that he would not draw but would like to play with the toys. But he soon left off playing and said he did not want to play, or draw, or talk, or even think. After a little while, however, he took up the toys, noticed that a little woman had come off her stand, and threw her aside, saying that he did not like her. Then he told Mrs K. that he had sent Mummy a drawing similar to the one he had made yesterday (Drawing 8).

*Mrs K.* suggested that Richard, by making this drawing for his mother, felt that he was not only giving her a present and in this way making her feel better, but had also confessed to her his guilt about having injured her, which he expressed on the drawing by the sunk *Emden*. Moreover, he was guilty about rejecting the injured Mummy (the little woman who had come off her stand), feeling that he was the cause of her illness or injury. By sending Mummy a drawing similar to that which he had made for Mrs K., he also expressed his wish not to reject his mother (who was ill, and to him very injured) and not to prefer Mrs K., who was now felt to be the uninjured Mummy, also the nurse (Note I).

Richard again took up the toys and made various groups: two

little girls together (two of the smaller women figures); two women; the man and the woman on the roof; two boys; then again two animals (cow and horse) in one truck looking at each other and in the next truck a sheep watching them. Richard said that they were all happy. He arranged two stations, one for the goods train carrying animals, and the other for the express (or electric) train. He left a good deal of space and also arranged the various groups so that the trains could pass safely. He said emphatically, 'All is going well, there will be no disaster today.' Then, more dubiously, 'At least I hope not.' He moved the dog about repeatedly from one group to another and finally put it near the little girls, saying that it was wagging its tail at them. While doing that he swiftly set one of the swings going (setting the swings going had represented the parents' sexual intercourse from the Fourteenth Session onwards). Then he pushed the truck towards the girls and the dog, and made it knock over all three of them. Suddenly the coal lorry broke through the station and knocked down the houses, including the one which was supposed on the previous day to have the slum at its back. The express train (which in the Fourteenth Session stood for himself when he was biggest and strongest, and now stood for the parents) knocked over the rest of the toys. As in the previous session, he gave up playing at this point and began to draw.

*Mrs K.* interpreted that at first he did not wish to play because of his fear that he would produce a disaster in the family, having felt so lonely and envious of the others who were at home and happy together. When after her interpretation he had become more hopeful that he might after all manage not to attack them, he began to play and insisted that everybody was happy. But he could not carry this through because he was so jealous of the family being together. The two animals in the first truck, with the other one alone in the second, had repeatedly expressed the solution by which he allowed his parents to make love to one another and remained friendly towards them if he could be near them. But then there should be only three of them together, and Paul was left out. Another way by which he tried to keep the peace in his play was by putting together the two boys, representing Paul and himself (a group which he had not arranged previously), thus expressing his wish to turn away from the parents in order not to harm them and to join up with Paul instead.

Richard said it made him particularly angry to think that Bobby was now welcoming Paul instead of him.

*Mrs K.* reminded him that Bobby stood for a friend, brother, baby, and also for Richard himself. In the play the dog had repeatedly thrown the minister-Daddy out of the truck (which represented Mummy). Bobby actually often took Daddy's place in the armchair, which meant to Richard his taking Daddy's place with Mummy. When Richard felt disappointed with both parents and Paul, he might have wished to have little girls—sisters—to play with; he might also have wanted to do something to them with his genital (in his play the dog wagging his tail towards the little girls), but that seemed dangerous, and finished in disaster. The coal lorry breaking up the station meant his attacking Mummy with his 'big job' (bombs), and the express train knocking everything over stood for the parents discovering all the things he had done and punishing and even killing him.

Richard then started drawing a picture similar to his first submarine drawings, but soon gave it up and tore the page. Then he drew a large starfish (Drawing 9). As soon as he noticed the many sharp edges of the starfish, he said that he wanted to make a nice drawing and coloured it in with the crayons; then he drew a circle round it, filled in the space with red, and remarked, 'It looks lovely.'

*Mrs K.* reminded him that two days ago (in the Fifteenth Session, Drawing 7) a starfish had represented Daddy's devouring genital which the fish-Mummy had eaten, and he drew that at the time when Mummy had a sore throat. In that drawing the fish was very fat, containing the starfish, which also meant the genital of the father devoured by Mummy and the baby growing inside her. In today's drawing the big starfish also seemed to represent Daddy's devoured genital which made her bleed because it ate her inside; this was shown by the red border round the starfish. The starfish also stood for the greedy and frustrated baby—himself—injuring and eating Mummy's inside when he wanted her and she did not come. This was revived when Mummy had disappointed him and stayed with Daddy and Paul. Mrs K. reminded him that on the previous day she had to send him away a few minutes early and that he had then asked whether she would see John Wilson earlier. Richard had felt jealous of Paul and John and frustrated by both Mrs K. and Mummy; so he attacked them directly by wishing to eat Mummy's and Mrs K.'s inside and indirectly by putting Daddy's dangerous genital into them.

Richard said hesitantly and in a low voice that when Mummy had a headache or felt sick she often said that it was his fault because he had been naughty.

*Mrs K.* replied that when Mummy said this, it confirmed his fears about his being dangerous and destructive to her.

Richard got up, walked about the room, and found a duster with which he dusted the shelves and other things. He said that he wished to clean Mummy and make her better. Then he opened the door and showed Mrs K. the lovely scenery and said the air was 'fresh and clean'. He jumped down from the steps, just missing a flower-bed, and asked Mrs K. whether he had 'killed the plantation'.

*Mrs K.* interpreted that he again found comfort in looking at the uninjured beautiful external mother, represented by the hills, because this made him feel that she was not destroyed, or dirty, or eaten up from within. He moreover wished to put her right and to make her as healthy and nice as the countryside (the clean fresh air); he had also expressed this by dusting the shelves.

Richard showed some anxiety. He was concerned about noises outside on the road, and particularly whether children—his enemies —were passing by. Then he looked round the room again and took a football off a shelf. He blew it up, saying that he was filling it with his own air and now he had none left. When he let the air out of the football, he said it sounded like the wind in the 'Everest' film (which meant it sounded uncanny). He added, 'Like somebody crying.'

*Mrs K.* referred to today's drawing (9) and linked Mummy's bleeding inside on the drawing with the football.

Richard replied that by blowing up the ball he was reviving Mummy.

*Mrs K.* reminded him of yesterday's material: the dirty room meant the same as the slums with diseased and dirty children; and he had felt that his fæces, which were to him the same as bombs, had poisoned and injured Mummy, who was also eaten up from inside by the bad children. Therefore she was represented by the sunk *Emden* (Sixteenth Session). Mrs K. also referred to the black car with many numberplates (Ninth Session) and to his efforts to restore and revive Mummy (the electric fire).

Richard was lying on top of the inflated football and squeezing the air out of it; he said, 'Now Mummy is empty again and dying.'

*Mrs K.* suggested that the greedy starfish baby—Richard himself—was also felt to squeeze her and her breast dry; that when he was a baby he had been afraid of losing Mummy through his greed and was therefore sad and worried. If he tried to restore her by filling her with everything good he contained, he thought he would be exhausted and die. Then he felt greedier and again wished to squeeze her dry in order to keep himself alive; but this would make her die. The same applied to Mrs K. He had asked if she would keep him longer tomorrow to make up for last week's short session (Ninth) as she was doing today to make up for the time missed the previous session. This showed his wish to get as much as possible from her; but his fear of exhausting her and making her die was one of the reasons why he usually did not want to stay any longer than fifty minutes.

Richard's mood during this session had been at times persecuted, when he watched the road, but predominantly depressed, though in the course of the session depression became less strong than on previous days.

*Note to Seventeenth Session:*

I. I suggested that in Drawing 8 Richard attempted to split off the external from the internal situation. I was kept as the healthy mother who could also be helpful; the actual mother, though ill, was still loved, and he tried to make reparation to her. But the little woman, whom he discarded, showed the ambivalent attitude towards the ill mother and also stood for the injured internal mother who aroused too much anxiety in him. It is the relation to the internal mother which seems to underlie peace and security and—if she is felt to be injured or persecutory—becomes a fundamental cause of mental disturbance.

## EIGHTEENTH SESSION (Saturday)

Richard was very subdued. His parents and Paul had come to see him but they had gone back a day earlier than they had intended. He said he did not want the toys and did not feel like drawing. He had hated leaving Mrs K. yesterday, he was so fond of her. He then spoke about the news and said he was glad about Sollum being captured; but he still felt doubts about the situation in general. Would the Allies be able to beat the Germans on so many fronts? (He said this earnestly and with concern.) Then he reported what he called a 'funny dream'.

*He was in Berlin. A German boy about his own age was 'bellowing' at him in German, saying something insulting to him about his being British and having no right to be there. Richard bellowed back so loudly that the boy was terrified and ran away. There were also a few other boys there, nice ones who spoke English like English boys. Richard talked to Mr Matsuoka, blaming him for his policy. Matsuoka was at first friendly, but then 'turned nasty' because Richard teased him by threatening to break his 'billy-glass' (monocle). Then suddenly Mummy was also there and spoke to Matsuoka as if he were an old acquaintance, but she took no notice of Richard. Then Matsuoka was not there any more, he seemed to have been frightened away by Richard.*

At this point Richard remembered the beginning of the dream : *He was in an armoured car, with six guns, five cannons, and one machine-gun. German troops had driven him out of Berlin, but he 'wheeled round and spat fire' at them; they turned round and ran away as quickly as they could. There were two armoured cars full of troops. Probably each German car had six guns but not as good ones as his.* Here Richard became uncertain and looked anxious. He remarked on the idea that he could frighten everyone, seemed amused by this and said, 'The silly things one can dream.' He thought he might have 'added a few bits' to the dream, but they 'seemed to belong to it'. His amusement soon gave way to depression. While reporting the dream he had begun a drawing again representing a large starfish which he coloured in with different crayons. When he was speaking about the two German armoured cars, he held two pencils together (forming an acute angle) and put them into his mouth. He also set one of the swings moving.

*Mrs K.* interpreted[1] that his dreaming about being in Berlin expressed his feeling that he was surrounded and overwhelmed by enemies. He himself had commented how funny it was that he should be so terrifying and powerful, frightening away the German boy, Matsuoka, and the German troops in the armoured cars. In this way he managed in the dream to deny his fears, but in fact he would have been completely powerless in that situation [Manic defence]. Matsuoka 'turned nasty' because Richard teased him. Earlier (Fifteenth Session) he had told Mrs K. that the two fishes, standing for Paul and himself (Drawing 6), were teasing the octopus-father. Matsuoka's 'billy-glass' stood for Daddy's genital which Richard threatened to destroy, and he felt that the Matsuoka-father would attack and destroy Richard's genital in retaliation. Paul as an ally was represented by the nice boys who spoke English, while the hostile Paul was the 'bellowing' German boy. The way Mummy came into the dream expressed his attempt to have her as his ally. Nevertheless, she seemed to join up with Matsuoka and ignored Richard. His need for the good and helpful Mummy was shown by his turning to Mrs K. and telling her how fond he was of her. But in the dream situation Mummy had deserted him. The anxiety in the dream that he was surrounded by enemies was linked with his having felt deserted by his parents and Paul when they left him on the previous day. During the preceding days he had been

[1] This again is an interpretation which, though presented here consecutively, was no doubt interrupted by some response or material.

very jealous about their being together and had felt deserted and lonely, but the dream showed that in his mind they had turned into enemies, were uniting against him, and going to attack him. The cars contained troops and this meant that not only the parents, but the whole family, were combining against him. Mrs K. also suggested that the two pencils held together, which he had put into his mouth, represented the parents whom he had eaten, the rabbits which were divided between him and Paul (Twelfth Session). In the dream the parents were represented by the two armoured cars and they were also, Mrs K. suggested, eaten up and taken in by him [Internalization of the object]. They were dangerous and united against him—Mummy joining up with Matsuoka.

Richard told Mrs K. that something pleasant had happened yesterday. He was at the railway station and an engine-driver asked him to come on the engine and have a look round. When his parents came to see him later on, he saw the same goods train at the station.

*Mrs K.* interpreted that Richard mentioned the incident of the engine-driver when she had spoken of the hostile armoured-car parents. At that moment he wished to express his feeling that he had taken into himself the nice father (the engine-driver); the goods train, which he allowed Richard to inspect, standing for Mummy. This meant that Richard felt he also had the good parents inside him. In the dream there were nice boys too in Germany, who stood for good and helpful brothers. However, this good side did not seem to help him sufficiently against his fears that he had swallowed and therefore contained the whole family who had combined against him in a hostile way, and this made him full of enemies [Relation to internal objects].

Richard seemed to have been far away in his thoughts during these interpretations. He became very restless and looked at the drawings, particularly at the one he had just made.

*Mrs K.* asked him what he thought about it.

Richard said it was a big starfish but he had changed it into a nice design.

*Mrs K.* reminded him that on the previous day the big starfish (Drawing 9), which he changed into a nice design, had injured Mummy's inside and made it bleed. In today's drawing the starfish also had many teeth and this expressed his attacks by biting. These attacks seemed to link with his armoured car shooting and spitting fire in the dream. Such fears entered also into yesterday's play when he had wished to keep the family happy but could not carry it through. These fears drove him to destroy the family in various ways.

In his play a few days previously he had bitten the church tower (Sixteenth Session) and agreed to Mrs K.'s interpretation that this meant eating what the tower stood for, i.e. Daddy's genital. In the previous day's play the dog, which was the only survivor, represented himself; but this meant that he (the dog) had eaten up the family.

Richard had been listening more attentively and now seemed relieved and lively. He pointed at the 'brown-coloured teeth' and said yes, these were guns. He then opened the door and again expressed his delight about the countryside. Then he picked some grass in the garden and, back in the room, put the grass to his mouth and then threw it away. He explored the room and the little kitchen next door, found a broom there, and began to clean the place thoroughly. Throughout this activity, however, he was listless and subdued. After sweeping, he fetched the football he had played with in the previous session, blew it up, and squeezed it empty by holding it against his body. He listened to the noise of the escaping air and remarked, 'It is like talking.'

*Mrs K.* asked him who was talking.

Richard replied without hesitation, 'Mummy and Daddy.'

*Mrs K.* interpreted that the football with the rubber tube represented the parents and their two genitals, and that he felt they were secretly talking to one another.

Richard had gone on blowing up the ball and squeezing out the air. He again listened to the noise of the escaping air and said, 'She is crying. Daddy squeezes her and they are fighting.'

*Mrs K.* pointed out that by squeezing the football-parents against his tummy he had again expressed his feeling that he had taken the parents into himself, either fighting each other or uniting against him—the two armoured cars in the dream—Matsuoka and Mummy; that he also contained the injured or dead Mummy, for Daddy squeezed her. Because of this fear about his containing fighting parents, parents plotting against him, the ill Mummy with the bad Daddy injuring her, he had found it so difficult yesterday to leave Mrs K., particularly as his parents and Paul had left him. This not only meant that he was deserted but that they were joining up against him inside him as well. The external parents, Paul, and Mrs K. were so strongly needed because of his fear of containing them as dangerous and injured people. His feeling of being lonely, deserted, and frightened had much to do with his fears about his inside (Note I).

Richard had again been listening more attentively and seemed to have understood the last interpretation. Before leaving he quickly made Drawings 10 and 11.

*Note to Eighteenth Session:*

I. This material illustrates the fact that various aspects of the sexual relationship between the parents, as the infant phantasies them (i.e. that they are fighting one another; or that they are allied in a hostile way against the infant; or that one of them—or both—is injured or destroyed), become internalized. With the young infant these situations are thus transferred into the internal world, where they are re-enacted. The infant experiences every detail of such fights and injuries as happening inside him, and these phantasies may therefore become the source of hypochondriacal complaints of various kinds. It is, however, not only the phantasies of the sexual relation of the parents but also other aspects of their relation (phantasied as well as observed) which are internalized and fundamentally influence both the ego and the super-ego development of the child.

I wish to draw attention to the concreteness which in this session characterizes the phantasies of oral incorporation, e.g. the two pencils which he held together and put into his mouth when he was speaking of the armoured cars. This material also throws light on the different types of relation to internalized objects, and on the variety of identifications.

Another point illustrated by this material is the close connection between internal danger situations and the corresponding insecurity about the internal and external worlds. This insecurity, essentially the fear of being exposed to internal persecutors and deprived of a good and helpful object, is in my experience one of the deepest causes of loneliness.

# NINETEENTH SESSION (Monday)

Richard said he was much happier. He had had a happy weekend; he had also seen Paul for a few hours. Mummy had come to 'X' with him and was staying on. Richard brought some toys of his own, a small fleet of warships,[1] and began to play with them. He put some destroyers on one side and said they were German. On the other side battleships, cruisers, destroyers, and submarines represented the British fleet. (Richard was excited and elated.) The two battleships were attacking the destroyers; one blew up, the others

[1] The fleet consisted of 2 battleships, 3 cruisers, 5 destroyers, 5 submarines: 15 pieces in all. The submarines were the smallest. Although the ships in each group were equal in size, Richard in his play often referred to one of them being larger or smaller than the others in the same category. I use quotes to indicate where he differentiates their size in accordance with his phantasies.

were scuttled and sunk. While Richard moved the ships, he made sounds that were supposed to come from the ships and were most expressive and varied, something between the noise of engines running and human voices, clearly indicating whether the ships felt happy, friendly, angry, etc. When two or three ships were together this sounded like a conversation, although no words were used. (Richard was even more conscious than usual of noises outside and of children passing the house. He repeatedly jumped up to look out.)

*Mrs K.* interpreted that the German destroyers stood for Mummy's babies, whom he felt he had attacked because he was jealous and hated them, and therefore he expected them to be hostile to him. While he was playing with the destroyers, he was afraid and suspicious of children passing by; he had been listening to noises, being 'on guard'. All children in the world had come to stand for Mummy's babies and therefore he would expect to find enemies wherever he met children.

Richard opened the door and asked Mrs K. to look at the lovely view. He pointed out that there were many butterflies. They looked nice but were destructive, eating cabbages and other vegetables; last year he had destroyed sixty of them in one day. He came back into the playroom.

*Mrs K.* interpreted that the butterflies were to him the same as the starfishes—that is, greedy babies, just as he felt that he himself was greedy; they should all be destroyed in order to save Mummy. Mrs K., too, should be saved from him when he became jealous of her other patients and wanted to get as much as possible from her: attention, time, ultimately her exclusive love. But while one reason for attacking the children was to preserve Mummy, there was also his fear of them, and of what they would do to him—the children on the road, the hostile destroyers. This fear drove him to attack them.

Richard now put the whole fleet on one side and said that they were all British; they were one happy family. He pointed out to Mrs K. that the two battleships were the parents, the cruisers were the cook, maid, and Paul, and the destroyers were babies which were still inside Mummy. Richard now began to play with the other toys. He arranged a town with people beside a railway line and said that nothing would move, not even the trains (which were standing one behind the other). He told a little girl figure not to go on to the railway line because it was dangerous. He made various groups, including the three animals in two trucks, but put aside the pink woman and a few other figures which he had frequently used in earlier play. The dog was supposed to be wagging its tail but otherwise to be motionless. Then Richard said that the whole family was now happy. Suddenly, however, he moved both trains, made them collide, and everything was knocked over. Richard said that the trains had begun to quarrel; one said to the other that he was the more important, and the other answered that *he* was, and then they began to fight and made a mess of everything.

*Mrs K.* interpreted his longing for the whole family to be happily united and his wish to have only friendly feelings towards them, but his jealousy of Paul—in the play the collision of the two trains— produced disaster. At the weekend and on the preceding days, when Paul had been at home and Richard in 'X', he had felt extremely jealous of Paul. Paul, having come home on leave, received much attention and Richard felt that Paul was admired and considered to be so much more important than himself. The fighting trains also represented the parents in sexual intercourse. In the previous hour he had felt they were inside him. Therefore only by keeping them all, including himself, motionless and under control could he hope to remain friendly and the family happy, for controlling [1] them also implied keeping his feelings in check. He had, moreover, pointed out to the little girl, standing for himself, that she should not go near the parents in sexual intercourse (the trains), which meant that she should keep away from any fight.

Richard told Mrs K. a secret. He sometimes took Bobby with him to bed and they 'had much fun' together, but Mummy should not know that. When Richard had left off playing, he looked out of the window, as so often before, and noticed a boy standing there. He watched him for a little while and called out rather loudly— although he could not be heard outside the room—'Go away!' From the beginning of the session he was excited, but during the play, when he made the trains fight, this excitement increased, and he was clearly in a manic state when he tried to control the boy on the road. Then Richard gave the Hitler salute and asked Mrs K. whether people had to do this in Austria, and said how very silly it was.

*Mrs K.* interpreted that the boy on the road, whom he wanted to get rid of, stood for the bad Hitler-father-penis which he felt he had taken in. He attempted to control this internal enemy, but was afraid that he was controlled by him and therefore had to salute him. He had mentioned during this hour that he had eaten salmon —standing for the attractive genital of the father and brother—and

---

[1] The need to control internal objects can express itself in rigid postures as well as in many other phenomena. In its extreme forms it is, in my view, one of the deepest causes of catatonia. (See *Psycho-Analysis of Children*, Chapter VIII.)

that it did not do him any harm (his mother had some days previously been sick after eating salmon—Thirteenth Session), but he seemed to feel that it had turned inside him into a nasty, bullying father and brother whom he had to keep still and under control.

Richard had again begun to play. He rebuilt the town and said that it was Hamburg and that his fleet was shelling it.

*Mrs K.* pointed out that, as before, the family which he felt he had attacked (earlier in the session the German destroyers, now Hamburg) had turned hostile and then he had to keep on attacking them.

Richard got up; he dusted the room, stamped hard on the little stools, kicked a ball about, which he had taken out of a cupboard, saying he did not want it to be there. He shut the cupboard door, saying that he did not want the ball to jump into the cupboard; it might get lost in there and he would not be able to get it out again. Then he threw another ball at the first one and said that they were 'having fun'.

*Mrs K.* interpreted that Richard had shown that he wanted to take the father's genital, represented by the ball, out of Mrs K. and Mummy (the cupboard) and to play with it himself. This was expressed by the two balls 'having fun'; he had used the same expression for what he was doing secretly with Bobby in his bed, which meant doing something with the dog's genital. Mummy was not to know about this, not only because she would in any case object to it, but also because he felt that Bobby stood for Daddy and Paul and therefore Mummy would feel that Richard was robbing her of them. The fear that the bad Hitler-penis inside him would control and destroy him made him want to throw it out of himself (as well as out of Mummy). This increased his wish to take in Daddy's 'good' genital, which would give him pleasure as well as reassure him against the fear of the bad penis. But he feared that he would in this way deprive Mummy, who he felt also contained a 'good' Daddy genital (Note I).

Richard suddenly asked whether, if he went to school in the autumn, the big boys would 'hurt' him. While saying this he bent his head so that it touched the mast of one of the battleships; he fingered it to see whether it pricked.

*Mrs K.* said that he had just shown how he felt about these big boys who would hurt him, particularly by injuring or destroying his genital. At the same time he wished to play with their genitals, partly to find out how dangerous they were. Mrs K. also linked this with Richard's great interest in her patients, particularly John with whom he would like to make love, taking him away from Mrs K.

It seemed as if he had felt that way about Paul whom he both desired and feared.

Richard had become very restless. He kept on watching the road for children, stamping about the room, and talking very quickly. He seemed hardly to have listened to the last interpretations, and he interrupted Mrs K. repeatedly. At the end of the session, mentioning that he was now going to meet Mummy, he hit two houses together.

*Mrs K.* interpreted that being now alone with his mother, since his father and brother were away, he wished to have sexual intercourse with Mummy (hitting the two houses together), but that he was afraid of what Daddy and Paul would do to him, as well as of losing his genital inside Mummy (the ball in the cupboard).

*Note to Nineteenth Session:*
I. The fear of the internalized dangerous penis is a strong incentive for testing out this fear in external reality and strengthens homosexual desires. If anxiety about the internalized dangerous penis is very strong, such reassurance is of course not obtained, and this may lead to an obsessional increase in homosexuality. (Cf. *Psycho-Analysis of Children,* Chapter XII.)

TWENTIETH SESSION (Tuesday)

The playroom was not available that day, so Mrs K. met Richard outside and took him to the house where she was living.

Richard was very thrilled to see Mrs K.'s lodgings at last, all the more as he knew that he was one of the few patients whom she did not treat there. On the way he was in a happy, somewhat elated mood, pointed out a house with flowers in the front garden, and said it was 'exquisite and lovely'; he hoped that no bomb would ever fall there. He also remarked that it was a pity that he could not have the playroom that day and said with feeling that he still liked it and that it had 'always been loyal to us' (meaning himself and Mrs K.). On entering the house he said, 'Mrs K., I am terribly fond of you.' He looked round in the room and asked questions about Mrs K.'s other patients, particularly in which room she was seeing John. (Since Richard knew that Mrs K.'s lodgings consisted of two rooms, his question implied that she might see John in her bedroom.) Richard then put further questions: how many patients had Mrs K.?; was he the last yesterday? (He had come in the afternoon, which was unusual.) A little later he asked Mrs K. what she had done on the previous evening.[1]

*Mrs K.* interpreted his jealousy concerning her sexual relations with men, particularly her patients (John), and linked this with his jealousy of Paul and Daddy in relation to Mummy, feelings which were reinforced through Paul's recent visit.

Richard had put his battle-fleet on the table, pointing out that one destroyer had lost its mast. He said they were now all British, prepared against the enemy and happy together. While talking about Mrs K.'s patients, he had arranged the fleet in columns, according to size, on the corner of the table nearest to Mrs K.

*Mrs K.* interpreted that the ships represented her patients and also his family arranged in order of age; first father, brother, Richard himself, and then the babies who might still come. They should all share Mrs K., just as his family should share Mummy.

Richard agreed, counted the ships, and said that Mrs K. had fifteen patients, but they would all have their turn. Then he went on playing with the fleet on the carpet, saying he needed more room for operations. He picked up one of the submarines and said it was the smallest of all but the straightest, called it *Salmon* and declared that it was himself. He put all the ships on the floor in one line, again emphasizing that they were happy together, no enemy was in sight. Then he looked round the room, went to the bookshelf, asked Mrs K. if he could take out a book, pointing at the largest volume. He looked into it and read a little but soon put it back, saying it was too grown-up for him and he did not like it. Then he asked Mrs K. to read a few words in 'Austrian' from one of the German books. (He always spoke of 'Austrian', wishing to ignore the fact that Mrs K.'s language was German.) He listened with interest, but said it was difficult and returned to his fleet play. One destroyer was going on patrol quite near to Mrs K. *Rodney*, the battleship which he had just said was Mummy, followed. *Nelson* (Daddy) came between the destroyer and *Rodney*. Richard moved some other destroyers and submarines nearer to these ships, but *Nelson, Rodney*, and the first destroyer remained in a group by themselves. Richard said, 'Daddy is inspecting his wife and children.' *Nelson* was moved slowly and carefully alongside *Rodney*, just touching her, and Richard said, 'Daddy courts Mummy very gently'; he moved the first destroyer away a little. *Nelson* followed,

---

[1] Since 'X' was a village, it was easy for Richard, who was extremely inquisitive, to get personal information about me. He knew a certain amount about some of my patients, my landlady, and the other lodger in the same house. Also, when I went out, I often met Richard in the street. All this entered, as will be seen, into his analysis.

touching this destroyer lightly. Richard explained, 'Now Daddy loves *me*. I was awfully fond of Daddy over the weekend,' and he added that he hugged and kissed him a lot. Meanwhile Richard made *Nelson* push *Rodney* away and brought him back alongside the destroyer which, as he had just shown, represented himself. Richard commented, 'We don't want Mummy; she can go away,' but very soon he made *Nelson* go back to *Rodney* and 'court her gently', and another destroyer joined up with the Richard-destroyer.

*Mrs K.* interpreted that Richard first decided to be the smallest but the straightest, which expressed his thought that it was safer to remain a child with a small but undamaged genital. Then he wished to explore Mrs K. (and Mummy) represented by the big book. 'Too grown-up' for him meant not only that it was too advanced but also that Mrs K. (and Mummy) was too big; that he was not capable of putting his small penis into such a vast genital. Just as in the previous session he had been afraid of the ball getting lost in the cupboard, he was afraid of losing his penis inside the grown-up Mrs K. and Mummy. His wish to find out about Mrs K.'s foreign and therefore secret language meant finding out about her (and his mother's) mysterious genital and inside. There was also the fear that he might find in her the dangerous octopus- or Hitler-penis, which would attack him. Therefore he again felt (as with the smallest submarine) that he would much rather remain a child. Soon, however, Richard became the leading destroyer and was close to *Rodney* (Mummy). Being guilty and afraid that he was again taking Mummy away, he felt that Daddy should separate him from Mummy. As long as he could keep the fleet still, he could control the family and himself, and thus keep the peace, as in the previous hour's play when the town and trains were kept motionless. Also, if Daddy would only court Mummy 'gently'—that is to say, have no sexual intercourse with her—Richard might be able to control himself and not interfere. The 'inspecting' had meant that Richard wished to be controlled by Daddy and prevented from taking Mummy away and having sexual intercourse with her. Thus he had shown in his play with the fleet that the wish to take Mummy away was connected with guilt towards Daddy, and therefore the need to restore her to him; in turn he wished to have Daddy to himself, to replace Mummy in the sexual relation with him, and so pushed Mummy away; this, however, meant that Mummy was alone and deserted, therefore he repented and joined the parents together in gentle courting; this, too, did not last and he resorted to the sexual relation with Paul. This again showed that Bobby had been standing for Paul.

During these interpretations, to which Richard had been listening attentively, he restored the earlier order according to size, obviously in a renewed attempt to avoid conflict, but suddenly he declared that he was tired of playing and stopped. He began to draw, and first finished Drawing 10 begun in the Eighteenth Session. While filling in *Truant* with black, he spoke about Oliver, a boy in his home town, a next-door neighbour whom he disliked. The boy did not know this and even thought that Richard liked him. But Richard wanted to kick him away so hard that he would go round the world; Richard never wanted to see him again. Then Richard pointed out with surprise and interest that there were three of everything in the drawing: three planes, three starfishes, three submarines, and even three bullets coming out from the middle fighter's gun; he asked why this should be so.

*Mrs K.* referred to the Eighteenth Session when Richard had been very depressed and lonely, his parents having gone off with Paul the day before. In the drawings that he had made on that day, the three of everything represented Daddy, Mummy, and Richard; Paul, of whom he was so jealous at the time, was left out. What Richard said about the boy next door, which implied his unconscious wish that the boy should die, seemed to refer to Paul. This was the significance of the three throughout that drawing (10). Richard had said that the boy thought that Richard liked him; here too Richard seemed to refer to Paul, who did not realize how much Richard hated him when he was jealous, while also admiring him and showing his love for him at other times. This made Richard feel very insincere.

Richard protested strongly and said he liked Paul and would *not* want him to die.

*Mrs K.* interpreted his conflict between love and hatred.

Richard then pointed out that there was only one fish on the drawing and asked whether this fish was Mrs K.

*Mrs K.* agreed, and suggested that the fish was also Mummy who was placed between the smaller submarine (Richard in the play with the fleet) and the larger submarine (Daddy). So here again the three of them, the parents and Richard, were together. The same would apply to Mrs K. who was between Richard (the smaller submarine) and John (standing for Mr K.) represented by the larger submarine.

Richard said that she (the fish) was sniffing at Daddy's periscope and wagging her tail.

*Mrs K.* reminded him that in an earlier drawing the fish had been almost touching the flag (Drawing 8). This drawing represented Mummy taking Daddy's genital into her mouth; it also meant that the tail she wagged (as the dog wagged its tail) stood for a penis which he attributed to her.

Richard remarked that though he was the smallest submarine, he did not have the smallest flag.

*Mrs K.* replied that in fact his flag was longer than the others and that this expressed his wish to have the biggest genital after all.

Richard agreed that his flag was the longest, but he said that it was not as good as the flags of the other submarines, meaning that it was rather narrow. Then he again mentioned that the fish was sniffing at the periscope and said that dogs did that and would get on the back of other dogs. Once when he was bending over Bobby, a dog tried to get on his back.

*Mrs K.* suggested that since he had compared the dogs with the fish sniffing at the periscope, it seemed that the fish was not only standing for Mummy but also for Daddy and for himself. He had told her about the fun he secretly had with Bobby in his bed, and it seemed that he actually had played with the dog's genital and allowed Bobby to sniff and lick him; but that he might also have had such experiences (as he described about the fish and the periscope) with another boy; he might have taken the boy's penis into his mouth. Perhaps this had happened in the past with his brother.

Richard replied after a silence that he often went to bed with Paul, but quickly added that they were not in the same bed, only in the same room. Mummy and Daddy did not sleep in one bed either, but in the same room.

*Mrs K.* interpreted that what he had just said would mean that Paul and he had done something sexual together as he thought that Mummy and Daddy did. Though they, too, slept in different beds, he assumed that at times they were together in one bed.


TWENTY-FIRST SESSION (Wednesday)

Richard met Mrs K. on the way to the playroom. He was delighted to find that she had the key to the house. It now appeared that yesterday's incident meant to him that the playroom might never again be available. He said with feeling, 'Good old room, I am very fond of it and glad to see it again.' He asked Mrs K. how long he had been with her.

*Mrs K.* replied that it was three and a half weeks.

Richard was very surprised. He said it seemed so much longer; it seemed to have been going on for a very long time. He settled down contentedly to play with the fleet and said that he was happy.

*Mrs K.* interpreted his fear of losing the 'old playroom' as the fear of losing Mrs K. through death. She referred to the time (Ninth Session) when she and Richard had to fetch the key; after that he had told her his dreams about the black and deserted car, and switched the electric fire on and off which, as Mrs K. had pointed out, expressed his fear of Mrs K. and Mummy dying. The fear of losing the *old* room also expressed his grief about the death of his granny. Regaining the room meant to him that Mrs K. would remain alive and that Granny was revived.

Richard interrupted his play with the fleet and looked straight at Mrs K., saying quietly and with deep conviction, 'There is one thing I know and that is that you will be a lifelong friend of mine.' He added that Mrs K. was very kind, that he liked her very much, and that he knew that what she was doing with him was good for him, though sometimes it was very unpleasant. He could not say how he knew it was doing him good but he felt it.

*Mrs K.* interpreted that her explaining to him his fear of her death and his sorrow for his granny gave him the feeling that his granny was still alive in his mind—a lifelong friend of his—and that Mrs K., too, would remain alive for ever in this way, because he would contain her in his mind (Note I).

Richard went back to playing with the fleet, drawing it up on one side: the ships representing the parents were now among the children; *Rodney* went out alone on patrol, making friendly sounds. Richard remarked that she was well and happy. The other ships were still together. He pointed out that today one of the destroyers was himself and a submarine was Paul.

*Mrs K.* interpreted that this showed his wish to be older than Paul, thus making him the younger brother.

Richard agreed laughingly and continued his play. *Nelson* came close to the Richard-destroyer, nearly touching him, but Richard suddenly made *Nelson* join *Rodney*. He moved them on together but not quite touching one another. Other ships followed. Richard said that they were all happy together. *Nelson* came close to *Rodney*, while the Richard-destroyer was put on the other side of the table, followed by another destroyer. Then he made sounds which were supposed to come from *Rodney* and *Nelson*. The sounds became loud and worried and were just like the cackling of a hen. Richard remarked that a hen had her neck wrung and laid an egg.

*Mrs K.* interpreted his renewed attempts to stop his parents' sexual intercourse in order to prevent himself from being jealous and therefore attacking them; and also because of his great fear that his father would harm his mother. This fear he had expressed in connection with the tramp, collisions between trains, the minister and the pink woman falling off the roof, the football-mother calling for help. Not only did he believe that sexual intercourse was dangerous to his mother, but also that for her to have a baby would be so painful that it would kill her (the hen's neck being wrung).

Richard replied that he knew that women cried when giving birth to a child and that it was very painful. Mummy had told him so.

Mrs K. interpreted that his fears were not only due to having been told this; but since he felt that his father's genital was dangerous and bad, he was bound to feel that sexual intercourse and childbirth were bad and dangerous. This belief was also connected with his jealousy and his wish that sexual intercourse should be painful. Mrs K. also reminded him of the greedy baby inside Mummy who would eat her up, as shown in the drawing of the starfish (Drawing 7).

Richard made various changes in the arrangement of the ships. The whole fleet was steaming out. One submarine remained behind and tried to go between two long pencils which Richard had put together with their sharpened ends touching at an acute angle.

Mrs K. reminded him that the pencils stood as before (Eighteenth Session) for his parents [1] and that the small submarine represented Richard as a small child trying to separate the parents and prevent them from having sexual intercourse.

Richard during this interpretation took first one pencil and then the other into his mouth.

Mrs K. interpreted that he had again felt he had taken his parents (particularly Eighteenth Session) into himself, with anger and jealousy.

Richard took out the crayons and made a barrier of them, saying that the submarine could not get through because they would not let him, although he wanted to go back to the other ships, that being his home.

Mrs K. asked him who 'they' were.

Richard said they were the starfishes, the other babies. He emptied the crayon box and pushed the submarine in and out of it.

Mrs K. interpreted that Richard, the submarine, felt barred both by the parents and by the babies inside Mummy from penetrating into her, but in the end he managed to do so and also succeeded in

[1] The two long pencils from then onwards in his play represented the parents, and the crayons, which were shorter, the children. But at certain times some of the crayons (according to colours) also represented the parents.

getting out again, which implied that if Richard put his genital into Mummy's or Mrs K.'s genital, it would not get lost there.

Richard did not reply, but put all the crayons back into the box, closed it, and put it aside. Meanwhile he had been inquiring about Mrs K.'s family. He had heard that she had a grandchild, and he asked what his name was and how old he was.

*Mrs K.* replied briefly to these questions. She then interpreted that when he took the crayons out, this not only implied getting rid of his rivals who would fight inside Mummy, but also taking the babies away from Mummy because he would like to have them himself. The questions to Mrs K. meant that he would like to have her grandchild. Mrs K. pointed out that he had put one or two crayons to his mouth and this also meant taking the babies into himself (Note II).

Richard strongly objected—boys could not have babies and he wanted to be a man.

*Mrs K.* interpreted that he certainly was afraid of losing his genital and of not being a man, but nevertheless he was envious of Mummy's body and of her being able to have babies inside her and to feed them. He very much wanted Daddy or Paul to give him a baby. She referred to the previous day's play with the fleet when Mummy was to be sent away and he and Daddy were to make love to one another, and also to what he had said yesterday about Drawing 10, the Mummy-fish sniffing at Daddy's periscope as dogs wished to do with Richard, and his remarks about dogs.

Richard had been looking at the toys and Drawing (10) and remained silent.

*Mrs K.* analysed this drawing further.

Richard was at first very reluctant to speak about it, but soon commented again that there were three of everything and that all three submarines had periscopes.

*Mrs K.* drew his attention to the one in the middle which stood for Richard, and interpreted that he was telling her that he had a genital like Daddy and Paul.

Richard replied hesitantly that he was not the smallest, he was now the biggest at the bottom of the drawing, and he also had the best flag.

*Mrs K.* reminded him that he had told her yesterday that the submarine at the bottom was Daddy and that his flag was not as good as the one in the middle which yesterday had represented Richard. Now he seemed to have the best flag—that is to say, father's genital—by biting it off when he sniffed at it as the Mummy-fish did (which meant taking Daddy's genital into her mouth). Mrs K. also pointed out that while she was speaking to him, Richard had repeatedly put the big pencil to his mouth.

Richard asked why there were three starfish babies. Then he added that he thought the one which was on top of the Mummy-fish would like to be on his own but he had nowhere to go.

*Mrs K.* interpreted that this was himself : yesterday and today the destroyer which went off alone soon wanted to go back home and then the starfish-babies barred his way. She suggested, moreover, that his being on top of Mummy also meant that he would make babies with her; the other two starfishes would be their two children, as Mummy and Daddy had two children, Paul and himself.

Richard wondered why there was only one fish.

*Mrs K.* suggested that this question seemed to show that he did not believe that the fish could only represent Mummy because Daddy, too, was very important to him. She suggested that the fish was either Mummy or Daddy, and that there was only one of each. Yesterday he had pointed out that the fish was wagging its tail and that also indicated that the fish represented Daddy with his genital (the dog which had been wagging its tail). The fish was in the middle of the page and represented the most important, the central, thing in his life. He both desired Daddy, with whom he wanted to take Mummy's place, and Mummy, with whom he wanted to take Daddy's place, but he was afraid of the dangers in both these situations.

Richard arranged the toys in a way similar to that of the preceding session, but now it was not an enemy town (Hamburg) but an English one. People admired the fleet opposite, the coast was made by two long pencils. Various incidents happened at great speed :[1]

(i) The dog stood among friendly people and was growling. Richard took him off the table and put him on the window-sill, but soon put him back.

(ii) A little girl had come too near the two trains which he had also put out, the electric train behind the goods train, and he again warned her not to be run over.

(iii) A few people were put aside on the corner of the table, among them were some of the slightly damaged figures, also the pink woman. Richard said it was a hospital and covered them up with little buckets, saying that they were ill. For a little while he took no notice of them, but then made the trains pass by, saying

---

[1] At this point I found the following remarks in my notes: there was such a multitude of constantly altering details in Richard's play, such a wealth of material, that I was only able to interpret some of it and could keep only to what I thought were the main points.

that they were carrying food and bandages for the ill people, and were showing them that 'life still goes on'.

(iv) The trains were again arranged, the electric one behind the goods train. Then Richard moved the electric train and made the trains bump together a few times. Suddenly Richard called out loudly to the goods train which had the three animals grouped as described previously, 'Move on, move on !'

*Mrs K.* interpreted (i) as representing the growling and biting Richard who was threatening to make trouble within his family and within Mrs K.'s family, although Richard had so much wished that there should be no hostility—a wish he had expressed by the whole arrangement; for the people and the children had been admiring the fleet and everything seemed happy. Therefore Richard removed the growling, dissatisfied dog, standing for a part of himself. For the same reason the starfish-Richard should have left home and been on his own, because he would destroy the peace of the family; but Richard could not stand being by himself and quickly returned.

She interpreted to (ii) that the little girl was standing for Richard, as previously in the same play arrangement, and he was warning himself not to interfere with the parents' sexual intercourse lest he would be destroyed (run over).

She interpreted to (iii) that here the trouble had already arisen ; the ill people were the parents and Paul, and Richard covered them up wishing to cover up the situation in his mind as well [Denial]— that is to say, not to know about the harm he felt he had done. But he could not forget them and was trying to revive them, hence the trains would bring food and bandages ; he also wished to encourage them by showing them that 'life went on'.

*Mrs K.* interpreted to (iv) that he had been suddenly overwhelmed by anger because the two trains together again represented Daddy having sexual intercourse with Mummy, and possessing Mummy and the children.

Meanwhile Richard had made the trains push over everything ; the disaster had set in and the electric train was the only survivor. Richard suddenly exclaimed that he had eaten the biggest dinner of his life yesterday, mentioning various dishes and also four pieces of toast.

*Mrs K.* interpreted that the disaster did not only happen externally but by his eating up everybody—the growling dog, too, had been devouring—he felt that the hospital, the illness, and the disaster also happened inside ; he was represented here by the electric train which controlled everything, including the two parents inside himself.

Richard took a little figure dressed in red into his mouth for a moment and bit her.

*Mrs K.* interpreted that this figure represented herself, who was wearing a red coat that day, and meant that she was included in, the disaster, being eaten up and destroyed.[1]

Richard asked whether she was going to the village now and what she was going to do in the afternoon.

*Mrs K.* interpreted that at that moment he needed a proof that she was still alive and existing externally, and he needed such proofs continually about Mummy when he strongly feared that he had destroyed her by taking her in greedily. Therefore he clung to Mummy so persistently.

Richard had been listening attentively; then he got up and went out, admiring the countryside and obviously wishing Mrs K. to appreciate it too. He was greatly enjoying himself, but while jumping about in front of the door he suddenly looked into the room at the toys which were still lying as he had left them.

*Mrs K.* interpreted that his admiration of the external world was also felt by him to dispel his fear about the disaster inside him, and this was why he suddenly remembered the internal disaster represented by the toys lying on the table, and looked at them; but that his very great enjoyment today seemed also to show that he was in fact less frightened and therefore more able to enjoy the external world.

*Notes to Twenty-first Session:*

I. This expresses, as I see it, the feeling that he has always possessed me—in other words, a strong feeling of having internalized me. This reminds me of another patient who, having been in analysis with me as a young child, saw me when he was nearly grown up. I asked him what he remembered of his analysis, and he mentioned that he once tied me to a chair, and also that he always had a feeling as if he had known me very well. I do not doubt that this represented his having strongly internalized me and that he had kept alive the feeling that I was a good internal object.

This is an instance of the relief obtained from the interpretation of very frightening and painful material. The fact that, by making unconscious material conscious through interpretation, anxiety is somewhat diminished (which does not prevent its return), is in keeping with a well-established principle of technique. Nevertheless, I have often heard doubt expressed whether it is advisable to interpret and make

---

[1] It is interesting that only at this stage of the analysis did references to me appear more distinctly in the unconscious material and I was differentiated from the figure of his mother.

manifest to children (and for that matter to adults) anxieties of such a deep and particularly painful nature. I therefore wish to draw attention to this instance.

It is in fact striking that very painful interpretations—and I am particularly thinking of the interpretations referring to death and to dead internalized objects, which is a psychotic anxiety—could have the effect of reviving hope and making the patient feel more alive. My explanation for this would be that bringing a very deep anxiety nearer to consciousness, in itself produces relief. But I also believe that the very fact that the analysis gets into contact with deep-lying unconscious anxieties gives the patient a feeling of being understood and therefore revives hope. I have often met in adult patients the strong desire to have been analysed as a child. This was not only because of the obvious advantages of child analysis, but in retrospect the deep longing for having one's unconscious understood had come to the fore. Very understanding and sympathetic parents—and that can also apply to other people—are in contact with the child's unconscious, but there is still a difference between this and the understanding of the unconscious implied in psycho-analysis.

II. This is the first time in Richard's analysis that I saw clearly his feminine identification and the envy of the mother producing babies. According to my present views this envy is a deep-rooted feature in both the boy's and the girl's development and first of all refers to the feeding breast. (Cf. my *Envy and Gratitude*, 1957, *Writings*, 3.)

## T WENTY-SECOND SESSION (Thursday)

Richard had arrived early and was waiting for Mrs K. outside the playroom. He was very silent and serious, looking paler than usual, but was friendly. His mood was very different from that of the previous day when he had strongly expressed his love for Mrs K. and his trust in her. He put the battle-fleet out. *Rodney* was steaming out by herself, but *Nelson* soon followed. *Nelson* seemed uncertain whether to come quite close to *Rodney*, which meant courting her, or not. Then Richard pointed out a destroyer with a bent mast, saying that it was Paul. Richard's play was hesitant and listless. He asked Mrs K. haltingly whether she had heard the news today. (On the previous days he had ignored the attempted invasion of Crete, which was striking, since he took such a lively interest in every detail of the war situation. For instance, he had previously expressed his dismay about Vichy.)

*Mrs K.* asked him whether his question about the news referred to Crete.

Richard, looking worried, agreed. He got up, stopped playing, and told Mrs K. that last night he had not intended to go to the cinema but went by himself after all. He ran out after five minutes because he felt sick, and went home. The sing-song had got on his nerves and he could not stand the noise. Then he again attempted to play. *Nelson* came alongside the submarine which Richard had earlier said was himself. Richard once more left off playing and, as before, asked Mrs K. about John's analysis. He said he knew, because Mrs K. had told him so, that she could not speak to him about John any more than she would tell John about Richard's analysis; but he would like to know whether she would be 'allowed' to talk about her patients to Mr K., and whether she would talk about him, Richard, to Mr K.

*Mrs K.* asked him by whom she would be allowed to speak to Mr K.

Richard answered, by herself, by her own mind.

*Mrs K.* repeated what she had already told him earlier (Fourth Session) in reply to his questions about her family, that Mr K. was dead.

Richard said he had forgotten this. He wanted to find out which side Mr K. was on in the last war. He added that he really knew that he must have been on the other side. (In fact Richard knew all these details, having, as mentioned previously, received a good deal of information about Mrs K.)

*Mrs K.* interpreted that he had forgotten that Mr K. was dead because this had stirred up the fear of his father's death; also his distrust of Mr K. being an enemy brought him rather near to Hitler; in his mind Mr K. still existed and was felt to be inside Mrs K. Richard was afraid of Mrs K. uniting with the bad Hitler-father (Mr K.) against himself. . . .

Richard spoke again about John and asked what he told Mrs K. about his feelings towards her, or about Richard. John had told him something about Mrs K. which Richard hated to repeat because he was afraid of hurting her, but he had thought about it a great deal. Then he told her that when she was in London (before Richard's analysis had begun), John had said he wished she were already in her grave, then he need not come to analysis any more. (All the time Richard was watching Mrs K.'s reactions most anxiously.)

*Mrs K.* referred to yesterday's play when he put aside the little pink woman and covered her up saying she was in hospital, which had expressed his wish not only to forget and do away with the injured Mummy but also with the injured Mrs K. Therefore he felt that he was doing to Mrs K. what John had said he wished should happen to her. In yesterday's play it was not clear who had injured the pink woman; but previously, when they had discussed Drawing 9 (Seventeenth Session), and on other occasions, it had become clear not only that the bad Hitler was injuring Mrs K., but that Richard wished him to do so. He was very much afraid that this wish would actually hurt her, and this fear was even worse than the unpleasantness of having to tell her about John's remark.

During this last interpretation Richard got up, went to the door, and stepped outside. It was drizzling. (Richard hated rain and was depressed by it, whereas sunshine very much cheered him up.) . . . He came back into the room and went on playing with the fleet. But he soon left off and, obviously having come to a decision, told Mrs K. that he had had a nightmare. *He was invited by fishes to have dinner with them in the water. Richard refused and the leader of the fishes told him that in that case great dangers were ahead of him. Richard replied that he did not care, he would go to Munich. On his way there he met his parents and his cousin who joined him. They were all on bicycles and so was Richard. He had his mackintosh on because it was raining. An engine ran off the rails and came close to him: it was on fire, and the fire chased Richard. It was awful. He fled as quickly as he could, saved himself but deserted his parents.* He woke up with a great fright and went on 'awake with the dream'. (He clearly felt that he had actually been able to continue the dream and undo the harm.) *He fetched many buckets of water, put out the fire and helped the ground, which had been very much dried up by the fire, to become fertile: he felt practically sure that his parents also had saved themselves.*

*Mrs K.* asked why he did not want to have dinner with the fishes?

Richard, without hesitation, said that he was sure they would eat fried octopus and he would hate that.

*Mrs K.* asked what he thought the leader of the fishes meant by 'great dangers' if Richard refused the dinner invitation.

Richard only replied that if he did not eat the dinner he would be in great danger. (He associated reluctantly, but seemed to find it much easier when he accompanied his words by playing with the fleet. Resistance became very strong when Mrs K. asked what he thought about going to Munich instead. Richard looked anxious and did not reply.)

*Mrs K.* reminded him that he had spoken about Munich as the headquarters of the Nazis and about the Brown House as a particularly dangerous place.

Richard agreed and said he would be frightened and therefore could not see why he should have gone there at all.

*Mrs K.* pointed out that the disaster in yesterday's play was felt by him not only as an external but as an internal disaster, because he had been the 'growling dog' who devoured everybody. Since his fears about his inside had been much aroused, he had felt that the singing and the noise at the cinema were going on inside him and he could not stand it. Also he was terrified of having devoured Mrs K. and therefore she would not help him with his anxieties. He had shown this by taking the little red woman (standing for Mrs K.) into his mouth and biting her—the last thing he had done in the play in the previous session.

Richard said that he also heard some children's voices during the sing-song at the cinema and was afraid that when he came out of the cinema they would all turn on him.

*Mrs K.* pointed out his fear that Mummy's babies, whom he wished to attack and to devour, would turn on him and attack him both internally and in the outside world. The fried octopus that the leader of the fishes would give him to eat represented both his father, whom Richard would wish to attack and eat up, and himself, who in retaliation would be devoured by his father. But the leader was Hitler invading Crete, which stood for Britain, for Mummy, for himself. Richard was very doubtful whether even if he obeyed the leader he would be out of danger, because the leader, being Hitler, was lying and deceiving. Going to Munich, therefore, meant going right into the midst of danger. But this was felt to be an external danger, while the fried octopus and the leader of the fishes stood for the bad Hitler-father (Mr K. in the earlier material) inside himself [Flight to external danger as a defence against internal dangers].

Richard agreed with conviction that it would be much easier to fight Hitler in Munich than in his inside.

*Mrs K.* said that when in the dream he met his parents and his cousin (also standing for Paul) he wished that they and his brother would help him. But he was worried whether he could rely on them as helpers. His suspicion was shown by his wondering whether Mrs K. would tell Mr K. about him; also whether Mr K. had been an enemy in the last war. His previous reference to Vichy and France in general expressed his doubts whether Paul was a reliable ally. But in this very session he had told Mrs K. about John's remarks about her and therefore felt he had given John away. So he doubted his own value as an ally for his brother. Since he knew that Mr K. was dead, his suspicion related to Mr K. inside Mrs K., as if he lived on inside her. She also reminded him that in yesterday's 'disaster' in his play, when the trains had pushed everything over, he had suddenly thought of the large meal he had eaten. That meant that he had also eaten up the parents in sexual intercourse. The fire from the engine which was pursuing him in the dream was felt to be inside him where he was afraid it would burn the good parents and the babies. He had not wished to see the injured or dead Mummy, he had covered her up (Twenty-first Session); but in his mind she was inside him. His hope was to save them with good fertilizing water which, Mrs K. suggested, was his good urine, while the bad fiery stuff coming out of Daddy's engine was felt to be dangerous urine which would burn Mummy and him.

Richard, who at the beginning of the session had been disturbed and listless, had become more lively and responsive during these interpretations. He had listened while continuing to play with the fleet. *Rodney* had come alongside *Nelson*, *Nelson* alongside the Richard-destroyer. *Nelson* was attacking *Rodney*, which was now a German battleship, and was blowing her up. Then *Nelson* was German and *Rodney* British, and *Nelson* was blown up by *Rodney*. Towards the end of Mrs K.'s interpretation, Richard fetched the football, blew it up, and squeezed the air out by lying on it, saying that Mummy was again empty and crying. . . . He fetched the broom, swept the room, and said that it was cleaner now.

*Mrs K.* interpreted his attempts to improve his internal Mummy. She also asked him what he had for dinner last night.

Richard replied that it was fish, but he liked it. He suddenly looked very surprised and interested and said, 'But then I dreamed that the fishes had asked *me* to dinner.' He left Mrs K. in a serious and thoughtful mood, but friendly and not unhappy (Note I).

*Note to Twenty-second Session:*

I. I remarked in Note I to the Twenty-first Session on the striking fact that interpretations of very frightening emotions and situations often produce relief even in the same session. The very fact that Richard could at last confess to me something which clearly had been very much on his mind (John's hostile remarks about me) shows that the interpretations of the previous session had had the effect of increasing his trust in me. I would also take it as progress that he was able to have this particular nightmare, to keep it in mind, and to report it to me. From the present material one would also conclude that the anxieties interpreted in the previous session—while to some extent relieved—had nevertheless been active in the intervening period. One of the reasons why this was the case may be that the anxieties relating to internalization had been activated in great strength and also coincided with anxieties aroused by external circumstances. In order to get away from this combined pressure of internal and external danger situations, Richard attempted to concentrate on the external ones; thus to his own surprise he escaped from the fish-danger to Munich. In general I would say that externalization is one of the main defences against internal danger situations, though it often miscarries. The material shows clearly how Richard was trying in his dream to find relief from internal anxieties by turning to external ones, and he himself said that it would be easier to fight Hitler outside than inside. We must remember that this defence was used under circumstances in which the fear of external dangers was very strongly activated, because the fear that Britain might be occupied by Hitler was a very potent factor in his mental state.

It is of interest that in his attempts to deal with the internal situation he used some of the methods that he would also apply to external dangers, such as processes of denial, splitting, pacifying the internal object, plotting against it with another object. The analysis of the interaction of internal and external situations, and the way in which they coincide and differ, is in my experience of great importance.

## TWENTY-THIRD SESSION (Friday)

Richard was a little late and therefore had run all the way; he was very concerned about losing two minutes of his session. He said that he had not brought the fleet; he had decided that he did not want it. After a pause he added that he did not want it to get wet in the rain. . . . A little later he said how much he disliked rainy weather. There was again a silence.

*Mrs K.* reminded him that in the previous day's dream he had a mackintosh on because it rained.

Richard in the meantime had begun to draw, more deliberately and carefully than usual. He said that it was not so much because of the rain that he had put on a mackintosh, but that at the beginning of the dream he had been in the water with the fishes. (At this point he showed resistance but did reply to a few questions about the dream.) He said the leader of the fishes was not the same as any fish represented in his drawings; it might have been a trout. He had also been very friendly and sweet to Richard.

*Mrs K.* suggested that Richard did not trust the fish, as he had agreed yesterday, and that this was shown by his preferring to go to Munich.

Here Richard again showed anxiety and resistance. He first

denied that he distrusted the fish, but then reluctantly said, no, he did not trust it, or the meal.

*Mrs K.* pointed out that a fish that was peaceful and friendly had in his drawings repeatedly represented Mummy. Although he often said that she was so sweet, he might not always trust her. Two sessions before he had spoken of Mrs K. as being 'sweet' and of his loving her very much, but in the last session he had been afraid that she would report him to Mr K., who represented an enemy.

Richard strongly objected; scrutinizing Mrs K.'s face he said, no, he thought she was very nice.

*Mrs K.* interpreted that nevertheless his suspicion was roused when she was felt to combine internally with the suspect Mr K.

Richard said thoughtfully that this could not be true because he did not know Mr K. and would never know him; but he was sure that Mrs K. was nice and therefore Mr K. must have been nice too. He added that he could not really distrust Mummy. Then he showed Mrs K. what he had been drawing. He stressed that there were two of everything on the picture and was again impressed that this had happened without any deliberate intention on his part.[1] He showed Mrs K. that there were two funnels on *Nelson*, two ships on the page, and two people, namely the big and the small fish. Then he discovered that the smoke coming out of *Nelson*'s funnels finished in a figure that was actually a 2.

*Mrs K.* suggested that the baby fish, swimming happily with Mummy, was himself; they were swimming away from the submarine *Salmon*, standing for Daddy, but for the bad Daddy, the octopus-Daddy, who in Richard's mind was so dangerous inside Mrs K. and inside Mummy. His distrust of Mrs K. containing the unknown and suspect Mr K., and of Mummy containing the bad father, implied that they were in a hostile union against Richard, and that this hostile union was bound up with their sexual intercourse; or that Mummy was endangered by having eaten the octopus-Daddy.

Richard then pointed out that there was only one starfish while there were two of everything else (by then he had drawn only one starfish at the bottom) and said this was Paul, who was furious and jealous because Richard was swimming with Mummy. While saying this, Richard drew some other starfishes and also put in the names of his brother and the maid, as well as the words 'yell and shriek'. Paul shrieked and yelled so loudly that the maid and cook

---

[1] Although Richard began by drawing deliberately and carefully, being clearly in a state of anxiety and strong resistance, it turned out that he nevertheless had expressed unconscious material. I am not publishing this drawing because it contains several names, such as the brother's and the maid's.

as well as Daddy came to attack him and to hold him back (the three new starfishes.)

*Mrs K.* interpreted that on the upper part of the drawing he had allowed Daddy and Mummy to be together; for he had given *Nelson* two funnels and also gave Mummy and Daddy equal shares of everything: two guns on each side, which represented two breasts, two babies, and the same kind of genital; each had also got a penis (same smoke line). He had brought the parents together in this way, yet when he swam under the dividing line with Mummy, he showed that he wished to have her all to himself. Also, when he turned away from Daddy, represented by *Salmon*, it was supposed to be the bad Daddy, the one who made Mummy sick. Above the mother and baby fish was the starfish yelling and shrieking, representing the jealous Paul. Daddy, represented by one of the starfishes (which he had named Daddy), as well as Cook and the maid, were protecting Richard by holding Paul back (Note I).

Richard had again begun to draw during Mrs K.'s interpretations. (He made this drawing in the usual way, quite spontaneously.) There was first a row of letters beginning with A (about six or seven of them) which were covered up, while at the bottom right-hand corner they were still visible. These letters were linked with each other by scribbles. All this was done very quickly and was at once scribbled over, though not yet as thoroughly as in the final version.

*Mrs K.* pointed out that the first drawing had been made clearly and deliberately, while in this one the letters were mixed up and covered with black scribbles. She suggested that in the first drawing he turned to his external relations and expressed his fears about them, in order to get away from the much more frightening 'inside' (his own, Mrs K.'s, and Mummy's), full of dangerous and injured people all mixed up and blackened by his own 'big job'.

Richard meanwhile had begun Drawing 12. It started off as the usual big starfish shape, which he filled in with colours. He said that this was an empire and the various colours represented different countries. There was no fighting. 'They come in but the smaller countries don't mind being taken.'

*Mrs K.* asked who 'they' were.

Richard did not reply but said that the black people were horrid and nasty. The light blue and the red were very nice people and were the ones the smaller countries did not mind having there.

*Mrs K.* suggested, referring back to the first drawing in this session, that this empire again represented the family.

Richard at once agreed. He said that the nasty black was Paul, the light blue was Mummy, the purple was the maid (Bessie) and the cook. The very small area of heliotrope blue in the centre was himself, and the red was Daddy. Suddenly he said, 'And the whole is a greedy starfish full of big teeth.' Meanwhile he had begun on the same page Drawing 13. He said that now Paul was very nice—and he often was. Now Paul was the red, and the nasty black was Daddy. The heliotrope was Mummy, and the tiny black section in the centre was himself.

*Mrs K.* pointed out his uncertainty about both Daddy and Paul. He felt them sometimes to be nice and sometimes bad, and he therefore could not rely on them. However, in the second drawing (13) the black in the centre represented himself and was the same colour as the bad Paul in Drawing 12 and Daddy in 13. His suspicion that Paul and Daddy were bad and unreliable was therefore connected with his feeling that he himself was bad and unreliable. In the previous sessions it had been understood—particularly from the dream about the fishes—that he was afraid that he had devoured his family and therefore the empire, the 'greedy starfish' representing himself. The 'big teeth' of the starfish and his 'big job'—the black in the centre—were the weapons with which he felt he had destroyed everyone. But then it turned out that 'they'—his father and brother—had penetrated into small countries and this meant that he felt his inside was invaded, so much so that there was nothing left of him but the little black section.[1] Mrs K. next referred to the fire from the engine chasing him in the dream and suggested that this also meant that inside him his fæces were endangering him.

Richard fetched the football, filled it with air and lay on top of it to squeeze the air out. Suddenly he said angrily under his breath—obviously addressing the football—'You wicked brute !'

*Mrs K.* interpreted that Richard had been deeply distrustful in the previous session of her connection with Mr K., and that he feared that Mummy containing Daddy was either injured or hostile towards himself. Today he had strongly maintained that both Mummy and Mrs K. were good but that Daddy was bad. But Mrs K. thought that he was trying hard to keep Mummy good and to make Daddy black because it was too painful and frightening to distrust Mummy. Mrs K. suggested that Richard denied his anger about his mother going to bed with his father and—so Richard felt

---

[1] The little black section which proved to be Richard's bad self had various meanings. Richard was the centre from which danger might spread all round, for, however small he was, he played a dominant role. Also, the fear of his being invaded by the bad black father corresponded to his, Richard's, own impulses and phantasies to invade all the others with his fæces [Projective identification]. Cf. my 'Notes on Some Schizoid Mechanisms' (1946, *Writings*, 3.)

—taking his father into herself and uniting with him against Richard. In his attempts to keep Mummy good he denied that he hated as well as loved her and transferred his hatred of her on to his father. Richard also resented that Mummy harmed herself by taking the dangerous octopus- and tramp-father into her inside. Mrs K. suggested, therefore, that the 'wicked brute' was meant to be Daddy, but it was also meant to be Mummy and Mrs K.

Richard strongly objected. He would not call Mrs K. or Mummy such names, for he loved them both.

*Mrs K.* interpreted the strength of his conflict when he felt he hated Mummy who was the person he loved most. She also reminded him that he had (Twenty-first Session) buried the pink woman, who had represented Mummy throughout his play, because he wanted to get rid of the injured Mummy.

Richard said, with evident pain, 'Don't say this, it makes me unhappy!'

*Mrs K.* interpreted that because her interpretations were often painful, he felt that she was a 'brute'.

Richard had been sharpening a pencil with his penkife and for a moment put the blade to the football, but without cutting it. Instead of this he violently blackened the second drawing he had made during this session and pricked it all over with his pencil. He walked up and down the room, stamping his feet, discovered a Union Jack on a shelf and unfolded it. He sang 'God save the King' noisily, looked at the map (which he had not done for some days [1]), and asked if he could shade in all the countries which Germany had already taken (the map on the wall dated from the beginning of the war), but he did not do so when Mrs K. reminded him that it was not her map. He had become very restless and said he wished to go, but waited till his time was exactly up and then ran towards the door.

*Mrs K.* interpreted his fear of actually attacking and damaging her (putting the knife to the football and blackening and pricking the drawing), behaving like Hitler and the black Daddy when they conquered the countries (standing for Mummy and Mrs K.).

Richard turned back on the doorstep and asked Mrs K. whether she, too, was going to the village and then walked with her to the corner of the road. He said that yesterday she had left the window open, which should be closed, shouldn't it? By then he was very friendly but obviously relieved to be out of the house. In the course of this session he had told Mrs K. that he had been to the cinema the previous evening; when he went in, he saw a boy of whom he

[1] This was in keeping with his not having spoken about the war news which had been very bad at that time.

was afraid, but he went in nevertheless and stayed there for the performance (Note II).

*Notes to Twenty-third Session:*

I. These constant attempts to avoid conflict in internal and external situations are fundamental defences and a characteristic feature of mental life. They apply particularly to young children in their struggle to achieve stability and a good relation with the external world. Richard had rarely, if ever, experienced periods of emotional stability of any length and this had influenced his whole development. I have referred to these attempts at compromise in my paper, 'The Œdipus Complex in the light of Early Anxieties' (1945, *Writings*, 1), and in Chapter VI, 'On Neurosis in Children', of the *Psycho-Analysis of Children*.

II. While manic defences were quite prominent in this session, Richard was at the same time more able to face his anxieties. His manic attitude showed itself in stamping up and down and being so noisy that at times he drowned my voice. Again, he did not mention the war and avoided any reference to the invasion of Crete. On the other hand, he had been able to go to the cinema, and his drawing of the empire invaded by hostile forces had an indirect link with the war. Over and above this, he realized and himself interpreted that the empire drawing represented a greedy starfish with big teeth, namely himself; he expressed his conflicts and anxieties about the bad father and the whole family in a much clearer way. This combination of denial and manic defence simultaneously with increasing insight and capacity to face anxiety is characteristic of those steps in analysis (or in the course of development) in which changes in defences come about. Denial referred to some aspects (the external war situation), whereas there was greater insight as regards internal reality.

# TWENTY-FOURTH SESSION (Saturday)

Richard was again a little late.[1] He said he had forgotten to look at the clock and then had run all the way. He was silent, looking frightened and unhappy.

*Mrs K.* interpreted that his forgetting about the time meant much the same as his wish to run away from the playroom the day before.

[1] It is of interest that, together with the changes indicated in Note II to the Twenty-third Session, his resistance was shown by his coming late; at the same time, his running all the way was evidence of a contrary feeling.

In the previous session she had interpreted to him his doubts of Mummy and herself (the 'wicked brute'). Yesterday, on leaving the playroom, he had said that on the previous day she had left the window open and it should have been shut. This remark also expressed his grievance against the wicked brute-mother and Mrs K. They should not have left the window—standing for the genital—open, which allowed the brute-octopus, the bad father, to have sexual intercourse and to get inside.

Richard repeated that he could not possibly wish to attack and abuse Mrs K. and Mummy; it made him unhappy even to think that he could wish to do that. He began to draw (Drawing 14), speaking at the same time of the possibility of an invasion by Germany; he had thought of it this very morning. If the invasion began, would Mrs K. be able to see him? How would he get to 'X'? He had been drawing the usual big starfish and then divided it into sections. He said Daddy was coming, made the black pencil march towards the drawing, at the same time humming a marching tune which was meant to be sinister,[1] and he filled in some sections with black.[2] Next the red pencil was moved quickly, and he accompanied this with a lively tune; as he was about to fill in the red sections, he announced, 'This is me, and you will see what a large part of the empire I get.' Then he coloured some sections light blue, and while doing so he looked up at Mrs K. and said, 'I feel happy.' (He actually looked happy and also appeared to be in close contact with Mrs K.) A moment later, having finished the blue sections, he said, 'Can you see how Mummy has spread herself. She has got much more of the empire.' While filling in some sections with purple, he said, 'Paul is nice, he is helping me.' He had left a few sections near the centre blank and now filled them in with black, saying that Daddy was squeezed in, surrounded by Paul, Mummy, and Richard. When he had finished, he paused, looked at Mrs K., and asked, 'Do I really think this of all of you? I don't know if I do. How can you really know what I think?'

*Mrs K.* replied that from his play, drawings, and what he was saying and doing she gathered some of his unconscious thoughts; but he had just expressed his doubts whether she was right and could be trusted. These doubts, Mrs K. interpreted, had come up together with his general distrust of her and Mummy, which had

---

[1] I have already remarked on Richard's capacity to produce a great variety of sounds most expressive of the emotional situation he wanted to convey. Such sounds accompanied, e.g., the fleet play, bouncing the ball, moving the pencils. He was able at times to convey the impression that these sounds came from deep within himself.

[2] From this session onwards, black always stood for his father, light blue for his mother (and Mrs K.), and red for himself.

been more marked in the last few days, though he still liked to refer to them as 'sweet'. He had expressed his suspicion that Mrs K. would give him away to Mr K., whom he rather thought of as an enemy. In the dream two days before (Twenty-second Session) the leader of the fishes was the treacherous Hitler-father, but in his drawing the fish had usually represented Mummy. This was why he called Mrs K. and Mummy—represented by the football—'wicked brute'. Nevertheless he was also happy because the light blue—the good Mummy—and Mrs K., who had recently been wearing a light-blue cardigan, was felt to spread over the empire. The empire, as he had said on the previous day, was a greedy starfish, with big teeth; it represented himself swallowing everybody: he would get more and more of the good Mummy into himself, because she was spread over the empire, but she would not resent this if she were the good Mummy who would *wish* to be inside him and protect him there against the bad father and against his own greed and hatred. Recently he had unconsciously expressed his death wishes towards Mummy and Mrs K., and found it very painful and frightening when Mrs K. interpreted this. But he felt relieved and happier afterwards. It seemed, therefore, that he experienced both trust and distrust more strongly.

Richard seemed to be thinking over what Mrs K. had said. He expressed surprise at the suggestion, which he, however, appeared to accept, that to know more about the reasons for feeling unhappy could subsequently have made him feel happier and more confident. He then drew an oblong outline round the 'empire' and filled it in with red.

*Mrs K.* asked him whether it represented himself, as the red had stood for himself in the empire.

Richard said no, this was something different; it did not belong to the empire at all. He just made it red because it looked brighter. While drawing he again began to talk about Hitler (not with reference to Crete—a topic which he still avoided). He said that Hitler was very wicked, making the whole world unhappy, but he was very clever, wasn't he? Was he often drunk? Richard then reflected on Hitler's talents, of which, it appeared, he thought highly. Then he laughed at the thought that we had some tanks on Crete while Hitler had none. 'Just think,' he said; 'for once Hitler has not got tanks.'

*Mrs K.* pointed out that he had now for the first time referred spontaneously to Crete, partly because he was less frightened of the internal Hitler and also because Hitler's lack of tanks raised some hope in Richard, while previously he seemed to have despaired of the situation (Note I). But this also meant to Richard that it was possible to deprive the bad father of his dangerous penis and thus to preserve the loved Mummy and Mrs K.—Britain. He had now surrounded the starfish empire (himself) by a red area which he felt did not stand for himself. Red had previously also represented blood, and when he coloured the area red, he had been speaking of wicked Hitler making the whole world suffer. Red represented Mummy's blood which the bad Hitler-father (whom, in Richard's mind, she contained) had shed. Mummy was the world suffering through the bad father and containing him as well [Projective identification] (Note II). She was also injured by Richard himself, the greedy starfish baby, entering her and making her bleed.

Richard fetched the football and played with it in the way previously described. He drew Mrs K.'s attention to the noise 'she' was making, which had formerly meant Mummy crying or dying or calling for help; but now he also made noises like a cock and a hen. Then he threw the football away. He hesitantly put a question to Mrs K., prefacing it by the remark that he would hate to hurt her feelings. Was she a foreigner or not? He at once replied himself that in a way she was not; she was a British subject, having been a long time in England; but her English, though 'very good', was not like that of an English person, and she had not been born in England. In the last war, when she was on the other side, was she glad about English defeats? Richard said all this with great difficulty and embarrassment, and without waiting for an answer went on to say, 'Anyhow, now you are on the side of the British, aren't you? Now you are quite on our side.'

*Mrs K.* pointed out that his distrust of the parents plotting against him, experienced now in relation to Mrs K. and Mr K., seemed to have been a source of great anxiety to him. Every time he felt he was guilty, or when his parents were together without him, particularly at night, he seemed to have been deeply worried by such suspicions. He could not find out what actually went on in his parents' minds, and Mummy (and now Mrs K.) represented the foreigner, possibly hostile to him; nor could he discover whether she contained the good or the bad father. Whenever he felt less suspicious of Mummy (now of Mrs K.), this meant that he had more of the protective good Mummy inside him; that he now trusted Mrs K. more was shown by his being able to express his doubts and criticism.

Richard agreed that he was afraid of hurting Mummy, but that he often made her exhausted by arguing with her, bothering her with questions, and making her do what he wanted. He then said he was looking forward to the weekend and told Mrs K. that he had bought an ashtray with a cock on it as a present for Daddy.

*Mrs K.* interpreted that he had put the cock—father's penis—back into mother and this meant also restoring the good father's penis; but at the same time there was his anxiety that the cock might also be the octopus-father who made Mummy cry and die, as he had shown when the football represented a hen whose neck was wrung. . . .

Richard had in the meantime been all round the room, exploring, looking into books, and finding things on the shelves. He repeatedly touched Mrs K.'s bag, obviously wishing to open and examine it. He squeezed a little ball between his feet and then began to do the goose-step, saying what a silly way of marching it was.

*Mrs K.* interpreted that the little ball represented the world; Mummy and Mrs K., squeezed by German boots—the goose-step. In doing this Richard expressed his feeling that he not only contained the good Mummy but also the Hitler-father, and was destroying Mummy as the bad father did.

Richard strongly objected, saying that he was not like Hitler, but he seemed to understand that the goose-stepping and the squeezing feet represented this. It was nearly time to go and Richard had become very friendly and affectionate. Turning off the electric fire he said, 'Poor old radiator will have a rest.' He carefully put the crayons according to sizes into the box and closed it, and helped Mrs K. to put the toys away in her bag. At the end of the session he reminded Mrs K. to be sure to bring all the drawings next time. (In fact, she always brought them.) He asked her to be quite silent, held his breath, and said, 'Poor old room, so silent.' Then he asked Mrs K. what she was going to do over the weekend.

*Mrs K.* interpreted his fear that she might die at the weekend—the poor old silent room. That was why he had to make sure about her bringing the drawings; this also expressed his wish to help in the analysis, and thus to put Mrs K. right and preserve her. This was why he wished for Mrs K.—the poor old radiator—to have a rest, not to be exhausted by her patients, particularly by him.

*Notes to Twenty-fourth Session:*

I. This illustrates the fact that denial is one of the ways of dealing with despair stirred up by internal or external danger situations and happenings. In this instance the internal danger situation consisted of the good mother being attacked and destroyed by his hatred, and this gave rise to depression and despair. The analysis reduced his anxiety, diminished denial, and increased his hope that he could preserve the internal mother as well as the external one (the light-blue Mummy would spread herself inside him). This in turn had the effect that denial relating to external dangers—the war situation, the invasion of Crete, and the danger of Britain being invaded—was reduced and that this anxiety could be faced better and expressed. It must also be remembered that the external situation had, in Richard's view, improved.

II. In the same hour Richard had expressed his greedily internalizing the mother, myself, in fact everybody, by the starfish-empire drawing. Now the red border represented the process of projective identification (cf. 'Notes on Some Schizoid Mechanisms, 1946, *Writings*, 3). The greedy part of himself—the starfish—had invaded the mother; and Richard's anxiety, feelings of guilt, and sympathy related to his mother's suffering both through his intrusion and through the bad father damaging and controlling her internally. In my view the processes of internalization and projective identification are complementary and operate from the beginning of post-natal life; they vitally determine object-relations. The mother can be felt to be taken in with all her internalized objects; the subject, too, which has entered another person, may be felt to take with him his objects (and his relations with them). The further exploration of the vicissitudes of internalized object-relations, which are at every step bound up with projective processes, should—in my view—throw much light on the development of the personality and of object-relations.

## TWENTY-FIFTH SESSION (Monday)

Richard was a few minutes late and looked very worried. He inquired whether Mrs K. had brought the drawings (he had particularly asked for them in the previous session). He looked through them and said he did not want to see the last drawing (14). He also disliked Drawing 8, but decided to put it aside to be completed. . . . He said he had been thinking quite a lot about Mrs K. on Sunday when he was playing in the garden. It would have been very nice if she had walked by, come in, and seen him play. He also told her some of the family news. Paul was coming home on leave for a week and Mummy was going home on Thursday, but Nurse would come and stay with him in 'X'. As he was telling this, he looked angry and worried. He drew an empire (Drawing 15) and said that Daddy (black) was quite near Mummy (blue); but he, Richard, was also near by. There was very little of Paul (purple). . . . On his way to Mrs K. a tragedy had happened. He looked upset and sad as he said so. A woman who had three noisy, talkative children with her was sick in the bus and she was still sick when she got out. Richard was so sorry for her and felt that it had been the children's fault.

*Mrs K.* interpreted his guilt. He felt that he was noisy and talkative and that he exhausted Mummy (as he had told Mrs K. repeatedly), and had done the same to Mrs K. in the last session. He could not protect them either from the black Hitler-father or from his own attacks and greed.

Richard was very restless, got up, walked about, stamped his feet. He was listening intently to noises, wondering whether any children were passing outside. He stood at a little distance from Mrs K. and looked white with anxiety. He asked whether, if he became very frightened and wanted to run away—say after ten or twenty minutes—Mrs K. would let him go. (When he asked this, twenty minutes had just passed, but he had not been looking at the clock.)

*Mrs K.* said that she would let him go.

Richard then said that he was very worried about Mrs K.—did she really have to go back to London? [1]

*Mrs K.* interpreted that his fear about the dangers she would be exposed to in London was much increased by other fears. She reminded him that when he had mentioned that Mummy was going home to stay with Daddy and Paul, he had looked very angry and worried; he might be afraid of attacking and harming his mother because of his anger and jealousy. He felt the same about Mrs K., who was going to London to stay with her family, and she, too, was in danger of being attacked by him. This guilt was also why he felt so strongly about the noisy children in the bus who had made their mother ill.

Richard asked what Mrs K. did on Sundays. How old was her son? Was he an Austrian?

*Mrs K.* in her interpretation reminded him of his repeated curiosity about her secrets, which was increased by jealousy about her son and his fears about the unknown and internal Mr K. Richard was wondering whether they were like Hitler, injuring Mrs K., or whether she was uniting with them against Richard. He was experiencing the same fears and suspicions now that his mother was going to stay with Daddy and Paul without him. . . .

Richard had been drawing (15). While doing so, he spoke about the blowing up of the *Hood*, and looked very worried. He said it was terrible and it had made him jump when he heard about it. He spoke at some length about this.

*Mrs K.* referred back to his fleet play (Twenty-second Session)

[1] I was planning a visit to London at that time and had already mentioned this to Richard.

when the Daddy- and Mummy-ships had been blowing each other up, each being the enemy ship in turn. In the same way Richard felt that he could not protect either Mummy or Britain or Mrs K. from the bad Hitler-father and from himself.

Richard said he was very worried about the invasion and he could not stop thinking about it.

*Mrs K.* asked him what he thought would happen then.

Richard said he was afraid of being shot and of Mummy being shot.

*Mrs K.* reminded him of his fear, expressed in the previous session, that if there were an invasion he would not be able to come and see her; but before leaving her to go home for the weekend he had also shown his fear lest she might be injured or killed by the bad Hitler-father, the 'wicked brute' she contained.

Richard had become thoughtful and serious. Then he said he would not wish to die before he saw the world nice and peaceful again.

*Mrs K.* linked his wish to see the world at peace with his need to restore peace in the family and to be able to keep his internal parents safe—particularly to feel that his mother was out of danger. If he could bring all this about, death would not be felt as an internal disaster, as a fight in which his parents and he himself would be destroyed.

Richard had been sharpening crayons, throwing the shavings about, and called a broken point a 'dead body'. He also, as he said 'unintentionally', threw some of the shavings at Mrs K. He showed her a crayon which he had sharpened at both ends, saying that this was himself, and tried the point on Mrs K.'s hand, asking her whether it hurt her. Then he sharpened two long pencils, made them very pointed, and took them alternately to his mouth and bit them. He held them with their points against each other, saying that they were fighting.

*Mrs K.* asked who they were.

Richard pointed first at the yellow pencil, saying that this was Daddy, and then at the green one, which he said was Mummy. Then he said it was the other way round, and again that he did not know himself which was which. He showed Mrs K. that both had marks on them.

*Mrs K.* pointed out that he had just been biting them and this was what had made the marks. (Richard was surprised: he had obviously not noticed that he had been biting the pencils.) Mrs K. interpreted that he had expressed his fear of having injured as well as eaten up his parents, who were also fighting with one another. He therefore feared that he too would die, because they continued this fight inside him [The internalized parents in fighting sexual intercourse]. He also felt them to be so mixed up with one another that he could not distinguish between them [Combined parent figure] (Note I).

Richard had tried to make the two pencils stand up and he was angry when they fell down. He made them again fight with each other, and crayons and other pencils join in the fight; then he left them in a heap. In between this battle he had been scribbling and writing on the back of the last drawing (16).

*Mrs K.* suggested that again, as with the toys, a disaster had happened; not only were the parents fighting and could not be repaired (his attempts to make the pencils stand up), but also the brothers (represented by the crayons) were fighting and attacking each other's genitals. The knowledge that Paul was coming home had increased these fears.

Richard repeatedly got up, walking about noisily with an angry expression. He again mentioned the *Hood,* went to the map, and—looking very worried—speculated about Britain's 'naval strength'. Suddenly he murmured, 'Richard, Richard, Richard,' as if it were a call for help.

*Mrs K.* asked whether anybody was crying out for him to help.

Richard said yes.

*Mrs K.* suggested they were the sailors from the *Hood.*

Richard agreed and said they were drowning and calling him. Then he murmured in the same sad tone, 'Daddy, Daddy, Daddy.'

*Mrs K.* interpreted that when the blown-up *Hood* represented Mummy who was attacked by him, the sailors calling for help represented the babies inside her. They were calling him as well as Daddy to help them. . . . Mrs K. asked what he thought about when he had just been writing and scribbling, and Richard replied he did not want to speak about it. He only mentioned that in one corner he had drawn a full moon and a quarter moon.

During the entire session he had been alternately angry and worried, and at times in despair. He became a little quieter towards the end of the session.

*Note to Twenty-fifth Session:*

I. These two concepts express not so much two different situations in the child's unconscious as two stages of the same phantasy. One of the earliest phantasies relating to the sexuality of the parents is, I believe, built round part-objects : the father's penis intruding into the mother's breast. This may very soon lead to the feeling that the parents' genitals are always mingled. A further development of the 'combined parent figure' is the phantasy that the parents as whole persons are felt to be in a fighting sexual intercourse. When these anxieties are experienced, the infant has already developed a greater reality sense, a clearer perception of the external world, and a relation to whole objects. However, he is still under the sway of early unconscious phantasies (which, indeed, are never completely given up), of destructive impulses, greed, and possessiveness. All this explains why the sexual intercourse of the parents is felt to be so destructive.

When the child's stability increases, the internal parents are felt to be in a more peaceful relation which, however, does not include a peaceful sexual intercourse. By contrast, as far as the external parents are concerned, we frequently find that even very young children desire that mother or father should not be sexually frustrated and wish at certain moments that they should satisfy each other genitally. This is only one of the instances of relations to external objects differing from those to internal ones, though there is always some connection between the internal and external situations (cf. *Psycho-Analysis of Children*, Chapter IX).

I have more recently described the earliest stage of the relation to the mother and to her breast as crucial for happiness and security. The length and intensity of this phase seems to vary greatly, partly owing to external factors, and these variations are of considerable importance for the whole of development. The phantasies of the combined parent figure—such as the penis of the father entering the mother's breast—are already a consequence of this early relation being disturbed. The longing to keep an undisturbed possession of the mother is, of course, influenced by a variety of factors, such as anxiety, greed, and possessiveness. On the other hand, only if envy is not too strong, can such a relation have any permanence. In any case, the intrusion of another object increases all conflicts, stirs up hate and distrust of both parents, and these feelings influence the strength of the combined parent figure in its different variations and colour the early stages of the Œdipus complex.

# TWENTY-SIXTH SESSION (Tuesday)

Richard arrived punctually and was much less worried. He was eager to show Mrs K. what was in his attaché case : the fleet and a pair of new slippers which his mother wanted him to change into from his rubber boots. He admired his slippers, told Mrs K. what they had cost, asked her to touch them and feel how soft and nice they were. Then he put out the fleet. He told Mrs K. that his mother was in bed. She had a sore throat and he was very concerned. He said he was looking after her, so he was doing his 'bit', wasn't he? He had also told his mother about the question he had put to Mrs K. yesterday—whether she would let him go earlier if he were frightened and wanted to run away. Mummy said that this was a silly idea and Richard thought so himself; for he had no reason to run away, because Mrs K. was very nice.

*Mrs K.* interpreted that three sessions previously he had been frightened of her because she represented the 'wicked brute' (the football) containing the foreign son and husband, the brute-father. He was also afraid that she was injured by the Hitler-father inside her. This linked with his fear of the united fighting parents inside him, the two long sharp pencils that were so mixed up that he did not know which was father or mother.

Richard, as so often, had been listening to noises on the road, asking Mrs K. to be silent so that he could hear. He was again 'on guard' against the hostile children who were passing. (In fact, Richard was scarcely ever without this fear, as he repeatedly admitted, even when he felt protected by Mrs K.)

*Mrs K.* drew his attention to this constant anxiety.

Richard agreed and told her that recently, when he was travelling by bus with Mummy, a boy of his own age had come in and Richard at once felt frightened; he looked fiercely at the boy and the boy looked at him. Richard added that he did not wish to attack the boy, but he felt he might have to attack him to prevent an attack on himself. Then he reflected that quite often when he met children and thought they would fight him, they ignored him and he felt relieved. Would he be very unhappy if he went back to school? Would he go on all his life being afraid of children, or perhaps later on of grown-ups? Did his mother want him to do this work with Mrs K. because she thought that he would not get on at school? He would like to go to the university as his brother was planning to do.

*Mrs K.* agreed that his mother had these fears in mind when she came to arrange treatment for him.

Richard asked what else his mother had discussed with her.

*Mrs K.* repeated that Mummy had mentioned that Richard was at times very moody and that she thought he might be unhappy.

Richard listened thoughtfully and looked serious. He said, 'It is very good for me to have this work and I think you are very nice.'

*Mrs K.* interpreted his satisfaction that she and Mummy were on good terms and that both cared for him, just as he had often felt about Mummy and Nurse. At other times, however, he was afraid of conflict between them. Moreover, Mrs K. and Mummy agreeing seemed to reinforce his belief in the good Mummy whom Mrs K. also represented. Nevertheless, he was very much afraid of the hostile children who stood for the unborn babies inside Mummy whom he felt he had attacked and was still attacking. . . .

Richard had been putting out the fleet; he said they were only on manœuvres and there was no battle. He told Mrs K. that he was a small destroyer, Paul a cruiser. But then he changed them so that Richard became the big ship and Paul the smaller one. They were very friendly together. *Nelson* (Daddy) was with the children but he soon followed *Rodney* (Mummy). *Nelson* touched *Rodney,* but only slightly, and the same happened to Richard and Paul. Thus everyone received fairly equal attention. He also put out in a row some smaller craft which he said were Cook and Bessie and, after a pause, he added, 'Mummy's babies inside her.' Twice during this play he looked up and said, 'I am very happy.' He also referred again, while playing with the fleet, to the slippers, saying that he liked them because they were so comfortable.

*Mrs K.* interpreted that he seemed very grateful to Mummy for buying them and also for sending him to Mrs K. for analysis; both meant to him signs of Mummy's love.

Richard confirmed this and repeated that the slippers were very nice and added with feeling : 'I like to have them beside me, they are Daddy and Mummy.'

*Mrs K.* pointed out that he now felt not only that Mummy was helpful but that Daddy was too; and that Mummy allowed him to have the good father; also that both parents inside him could be peaceful with one another and helpful to him. He still felt he was controlling them, but they were all on good terms with one another. Mrs K. further interpreted that he could only achieve a peaceful relation between his parents, himself, and his brother if they received equal shares of everything. In the play Paul had first been the bigger ship, then Richard had changed roles with him. Another condition for peace seemed to be that the parents should not have sexual intercourse; they should not give more sexual gratification and affection to each other than they gave to each child (*Nelson* only slightly touching *Rodney* and the same happening to the Richard and Paul ships). He had made Mummy's unborn babies come to life and this meant that he would have no enemies; therefore he felt so happy. Mrs K. seemed to stand here for the good Daddy who would unite with Mummy in loving Richard, while she also represented his nurse being on good terms with Mummy.

Richard said that in some ways he preferred being the younger because then he would live longer than Paul. A fortune-teller had once told him that he had a long life-line and that he would live to be eighty. He asked to see Mrs K.'s palm and looked worried because her life-line was not so long. But then he decided that it was long enough : she might live up to seventy or perhaps even to eighty. . . . Richard had a quick look at the previous hour's drawing (16). He said he did not like the roughly scribbled circle. He had at once crossed out the head he drew near it, and now said that it was Hitler's head.

*Mrs K.* asked him about the moon in the corner of the page.

Richard said he liked the moon. While saying this he drew the phases of the moon again and finished up with the circle filled in with black. Then he made the black line in the centre of the rough circle and, turning the page over, he made a mark on the other side as if the pencil line had gone through the paper. He pressed hard with his pencil but restrained himself from tearing the paper.

*Mrs K.* interpreted that he did not like the circle in the middle of the page because he had drawn it yesterday when he had been angry with her and afraid of her. It stood for the football, the 'wicked brute'; near the circle was Hitler's head which he had crossed out at once. But in the middle of the circle he had made a little black line which expressed his feeling that Mrs K. and Mummy contained the black Hitler-father. On the previous day he had first scribbled the circle, then the Hitler head, and then the phases of the moon. Mrs K. now reminded him of the order in which he had drawn this and suggested that the quarter moon near the full moon represented his father's penis near mother's breast and tummy, and that he had just now finished another version of the phases of the moon with a circle filled in with black, because he felt that the Hitler-father was blackening Mummy, as Richard would do if he were angry and hated her.

Richard half-heartedly denied that he could hate, blacken, and abuse Mrs K. and Mummy, and pointed out that he had written at the bottom of the page in large letters that Mrs K. was very sweet.

*Mrs K.* reminded him that he had paused after writing 'very' and might have wished to write something nasty instead, but had decided to remain friendly and was also much too frightened of Mrs K. to insult her.

Richard now agreed. During these last interpretations he had been making cock and hen noises, which at first seemed fairly peaceful. He said that they were happy. But then the noises became more and more angry and distressed.

*Mrs K.* asked what was happening to the cock and hen now.

Richard, without a moment's hesitation, said that this time it was the cock who had his neck wrung and not the hen.

*Mrs K.* interpreted that he believed that Mummy was also dangerous in sexual intercourse to Daddy, that she injured or cut off his penis. He had just shown how doubtful he was about Mrs K.'s being sweet.[1]

Richard said that the cock and hen were biting each other. . . . He said he remembered last night's nightmares: *he had three operations. He was not frightened, or rather he was not very frightened, because though he was given ether, he did not smell it.*

*Mrs K.* asked his thoughts about the number three.

Richard said: 'Daddy, Mummy, Paul.'

*Mrs K.* asked whether he knew what kind of operations they were.

Richard said very definitely: 'The throat.'

*Mrs K.* pointed out that this meant his throat had been operated on three times.

Richard said he did not know why.

*Mrs K.* reminded him that he had actually in the past undergone three operations, one on the genital, one on the throat, and one on his mouth (teeth): but in the dream they were all happening to his throat.

Richard was interested in this unconscious link and added that he was three years old when his genital was operated on.

*Mrs K.* interpreted that he was very worried just now about his mother's sore throat. He felt that Mummy too, and not only he himself, had her genital cut off by the Hitler-Daddy. Also that he, Richard, had eaten up everybody (as quite recent material had shown) and he therefore felt that all the 'three'—Daddy, Mummy, and Paul—were operated on inside him.[2] She pointed out that though he said he did not feel very frightened in the dream, he knew it was a frightening dream and had therefore called it a nightmare. Yet he had managed to get some reassurance by not smelling the ether.

Richard began Drawing 17. While colouring it, he sang the German anthem in a sinister voice. When filling in the two pointed top sections with black, he said this was Daddy. Then, singing the British anthem in a lively way, he coloured some sections with red, saying this was himself. As he filled in the blue sections, he sang the Greek national anthem, saying this was Mummy and Mrs K. He

[1] It is noteworthy that this clear expression of his suspicions about the dangerous mother followed my interpretation of the material in which the distrust and anger about myself and his mother had still been unconscious.

[2] A further conclusion would be that the operation on his throat must have also meant to him that the devoured people were now taken out of him.

said the purple sections were Paul, and sang the Belgian anthem. He made various remarks while drawing : at one point he said that he, Richard, was getting quickly into this country before Daddy could get there ; then he said : 'Paul has just cut off Daddy from Mummy's country' ; and, 'Now I am grabbing this one.'

*Mrs K.* asked him where the whole empire was situated, and Richard said it was in Europe. Mrs K. interpreted that Greece— since fighting was going on in Crete at that time—was the invaded and injured Mummy and Mrs K. But Richard too was 'grabbing', like Hitler. All the three men—Daddy, Paul, and Richard—were grabbing, devouring Mummy and injuring her with their genitals. She was injured inside and this was what he felt about her present illness.

Richard strongly objected to Mrs K. saying he was like Hitler.

*Mrs K.* referred to former material about his devouring Mummy, but this wish was concurrent with his desire to protect Mummy against the bad Daddy and the bad part of himself.

Richard thereupon pointed out that he—the red—was on both sides of the light-blue Mummy.

*Mrs K.* reminded him that he had said, when he drew the light blue, that this was Mummy and Mrs K.

Richard said that Paul, too, protected Mummy against Daddy. Then he made Drawing 18. He only sang the Norwegian anthem while drawing, and said the blue sections now represented Mrs K. It was a smaller empire and he had no idea where it was.

*Mrs K.* interpreted that (17) represented Europe. Mummy's big inside, invaded, robbed, as well as protected; (18), the completely unknown, represented his own inside, the Norwegian national anthem indicating that he was only small. Mrs K. linked this with his great fear of invasion, expressed in the previous session, and with the fear of being shot as well as with the nightmare in which the operations meant having his genital cut off and being invaded by the hostile family. Instead of Mummy, the light blue now represented Mrs K. because she stood for the good nurse (the good Mummy) who, together with Paul, would protect him. The brown sections stood for his fæces, and the whole battle against Mummy would be felt to go on inside him, since he had in his mind taken in both the protecting and the hostile members of the family.

Richard said at the end of the session that he would bring the slippers again. He put his fleet away into a cardboard box which, as he showed Mrs K., was labelled 'sweets', and said he wished there were sweets in the box instead of the fleet.

*Mrs K.* interpreted that he also wished that the whole internal family, including the hostile babies and fighting parents, were nice and sweet inside him.[1]

## TWENTY-SEVENTH SESSION (Wednesday)

Richard looked frightened and worried. It was raining (which always depressed him), and while putting his raincoat down to dry he expressed his dislike of the rain. Then he murmured 'drowned rat', but quickly put out the fleet and was unwilling to say what he meant. (This way of murmuring a few words and then quickly trying to change the subject had by then turned out to mean that he could not help expressing something important and yet wished to deny it.)

*Mrs K.* drew his attention to what this behaviour meant and reminded him of his feelings when the *Hood* was blown up (Twenty-fifth Session). The sailors had been calling out 'Richard, Richard, Richard,' and he had also been murmuring in the same way then.

Richard said that he knew this. They were calling him to save them. But even if he had been there, he could have saved only a few of them. Or could he have saved any? . . . At the same time he was 'on guard' against the children outside. He also mentioned that he had met some children as he came along and had been afraid of them.

*Mrs K.* interpreted his desire to attack the babies inside Mummy and to blow her up with his 'big job', and reminded him of yesterday's blackened circle and the brown section of the empire representing himself. The sailors then stood for the babies inside Mummy whom he would drown with urine. But at the same time he wished to save them and despaired of his capacity to do so because he could not control his hate (Note I). He was also afraid

---

[1] Richard had twice mentioned that the war situation was improving. The Allies were hunting the *Bismarck* and might destroy her. Crete was still holding out. This improvement in the external situation had to some extent lessened his anxiety. He was also reassured because his mother explicitly supported the analysis (her remark that it would be silly to run away from me). But the main decrease of anxiety derived, I think, from the analysis of the previous session. This could be seen in the way in which Richard could consciously express some anxiety, showed more insight, less denial, and had an increased urge for reparation. There was more sadness and at the same time more trust and hope.

of these attacked children, who would retaliate. Mrs K. reminded him of the dinner invitation by the fishes (Twenty-second Session). As he had said, he needed his mackintosh because he was in the water. He did not trust the fishes, and was afraid that he, too, would be drowned like the babies; his wish to save and revive them was linked with the fear of what would be done to him. His expression 'drowned *rat*' showed, however, that he also felt he deserved it because he was bad.

Richard, while Mrs K. was interpreting this material, had played that the submarine *Salmon*—standing for himself—had attacked *Rodney*, which was now meant to be the *Bismarck*, and had blown her up.

*Mrs K.* drew his attention to what he was doing and pointed out that *Rodney*—now *Bismarck*—which he had just blown up had always represented Mummy (Note II). Mrs K. also reminded him of his feelings when the *Hood* was sunk and that she had interpreted this in connection with the sunk *Emden* in Drawing 8, which represented the dead Mummy who had been attacked and devoured by her children, the starfishes.

Richard objected to Mrs K.'s interpretation of his blowing up and sinking Mummy, and said that it was the nasty Daddy who was doing that.

*Mrs K.* agreed that he felt the bad tramp- and Hitler-Daddy would kill Mummy; but when he was blowing up the *Bismarck* (*Rodney*) it was he himself who had attacked the bad Mummy. She had become bad because he not only loved but also hated her, and because she contained the bad Daddy and the retaliating dangerous babies who would all come back because he attacked them. However, when he sank the *Emden*-Mummy, she was not felt to be only the bad Mummy, but she was also the good Mummy, devoured and killed by the greedy babies standing for himself.

Richard went on with the fleet play, reproducing the sinking of the *Bismarck* as described in the newspapers. She was blown up into the air, circling round, and in the end she lay down on one side and was finished. Richard now mentioned the *Thetis* disaster, and spoke at some length with strong feelings about how awful it was that the men had been suffocated inside.

*Mrs K.* linked this with her former interpretations about babies dying inside Mummy, babies who had never been born.

Richard said, 'Dead people can't come back, can they, and attack one?'

*Mrs K.* interpreted his fear of the retaliating and injured dead Mummy and babies—these were the ghosts of whom he was afraid; he also felt that the unborn babies would come back from being dead and they were the hostile children in the street. He felt that they had been born after all, but as enemies.

Richard meanwhile had gone on playing with the fleet and made various arrangements. At the moment when Mrs K. was interpreting the dead and hostile babies, he had put all the small ships in one line and one larger ship by itself, which he said was himself.

*Mrs K.* interpreted that the hostile babies were lined up against him.

Richard said he had some unpleasant dreams but had forgotten them. . . . He asked Mrs K. about her lodgings. He had heard that there was another lodger there. Did Mrs K. and he have meals together, or did they have separate sitting-rooms? While talking about this he had moved *Rodney* away by herself to the other end of the table.

*Mrs K.* interpreted that *Rodney* alone represented Mrs K. by herself, and that Richard felt worried lest she might be lonely at her lodgings, and he therefore wished her to have company. But he had shown by moving *Rodney* away that he also had opposite feelings.

Richard meanwhile made first one of the destroyers, then *Nelson* and the small ships, follow *Rodney*.

*Mrs K.* interpreted that he had just restored the family not only to Mummy but also to Mrs K., *Rodney* also standing for Mrs K.

Richard said yes, her son and other members of her family had come to see her. He then asked more questions about Mrs K.'s son and whether she would tell him about Richard. Then he wanted to know whether she and her son spoke Austrian together. . . .

*Mrs K.* referred to her former answers to these questions and also interpreted that she and her son speaking Austrian meant that Richard did not wish to think of the German language because it would at once make him realize that he distrusted them as foreigners and even as spies. She further interpreted his fear that not only would she give him away to her son, but also that Mummy would ally herself with Paul and Daddy in his absence.

Richard objected to this interpretation but without conviction. He spoke about fifth columnists and said he hoped that there were not many of them, or what would Mrs K. think?

*Mrs K.* replied that this was what one would hope.

Richard asked very distrustfully what was it she hoped—that there were or were not many?

*Mrs K.* interpreted that he had now clearly shown how much he distrusted her and her son as foreigners and potential spies. They also stood for the unknown Mummy and Daddy, the parents who had secrets, particularly sexual ones, and he felt he could not know whether Mummy contained the Hitler-Daddy. When he was not with his parents, he often distrusted them and he thought that Mummy would give him away to Daddy. Paul, too, at times seemed spying and unreliable. But all that linked with his feelings that he himself was trying to spy on Paul and on his parents and could not be relied upon.

Richard at once agreed that he often spied and so did Paul, but he would never suspect his mother. Suddenly and with determination he said that he wanted to tell Mrs K. something which was worrying him very much. He was afraid of being poisoned by Cook or Bessie. They would do this because he was often horrid or cheeky to them. From time to time he had a good look at the food to find out whether it was poisoned. He looked into bottles in the kitchen to see what they contained; they might have poison in them which Cook would mix with his food. Sometimes he thought that Bessie, the maid, was a German spy. He occasionally listened at the key-hole to find out whether Cook and Bessie were speaking German together. (Both Cook and Bessie were British and did not know a word of German, as I subsequently ascertained.) He obviously forced himself to tell all this, looking tortured and worried. He had got up, went to the window away from Mrs K., and repeatedly looked exhausted when anxiety increased. He said that these fears made him very unhappy and asked if Mrs K. could help him with them (Note III).

*Mrs K.* said she agreed the work might help him, but that he also hoped to keep the helpful light-blue Mummy who was to protect him against the bad parents and the bad part of himself.

Richard was at this point obviously incapable of saying anything more. He kept on looking out of the window to see whether children were passing. He ran out into the garden, pointed at some wild flowers in the grass and wondered who had spoiled them because they looked 'awful' (which was not so in fact). He came back into the room and said, 'Please, let us play.' The submarine *Salmon* was first made to shoot at *Rodney*, which again represented the *Bismarck*; but then everything became mixed up. For *Salmon*, which intended to shoot at a German destroyer, fired by mistake on *Rodney*, which was now supposed to be British. Richard said that *Salmon* had the 'silliest commander'—how could he make such a mistake?

*Mrs K.* interpreted that he distrusted not only Cook and Bessie but also his parents because he wished to blow them up with his 'big job' as well as to poison them with his urine, both of which were felt to be poisonous when he hated his parents. Therefore he expected them to do the same to him. The bottle that he was trying to examine also stood for his father's penis and for his mother's breast. This fear had something to do with his fear of rain—the rain coming from above represented his parents urinating on top of him as he had wished to do on top of them when he was jealous and angry about their being in bed together. He said he was afraid that Cook and Bessie would retaliate because he had been nasty to them. But he had also admitted that he felt he was often very difficult with his parents, and exhausted his mother by his arguments. He knew, moreover, that he wanted to spy on them and therefore he was afraid they would spy on him. But his main fear and guilt came from his unconscious desires to attack them with urine and fæces, to devour and kill them. The 'silly commander' of *Salmon* stood for a part of himself. He blamed himself for having attacked and therefore made his parents (his own battleship) hostile, and for thus having himself caused all the dreaded persecution, external and internal.

Richard had somewhat calmed down towards the end of the session. He was relieved that the rain had stopped. But although a little less tense at the end of the hour, he looked worried and unhappy. It only came out then that his mother was still ill and even a little worse. Mrs K. pointed out that this had contributed to all the fears and unhappiness that he had felt during this session. Before leaving Mrs K., Richard put together the two chairs, as he frequently did, and remarked that he and she (their chairs) were friends.

*Notes to Twenty-seventh Session:*

I. Such despair is an inherent part of depression and is first experienced during the depressive position. Since early destructive impulses are felt to be omnipotent, they are in a sense felt to be irreparable. When they are revived at any stage of life, they retain some of the omnipotent character of infancy. Furthermore, the feeling that destructive impulses cannot be sufficiently controlled increases this revival of primary anxieties.

II. The fleet play, the drawings, and the play with toys, together with his associations to each of them, sometimes expressed the same material in different ways, thus corroborating each other; at other times his various activities brought up new material which allowed insight into different aspects of his phantasies and emotional situations. In my report I am not always able to show in sufficient detail how Richard's unconscious material, expressed for instance by the fleet play, was amplified and corroborated by the other media of expression. It repeatedly happened that, having become 'tired' of playing with the toys, for example, or having protested against some interpretations of his play, Richard took up another form of activity which turned out to substantiate my interpretations. It is a characteristic feature of child analysis that the various activities of the child allow the analyst to see how resistance interacts with growing insight and the great need of the unconscious to express itself.

III. Richard had from the beginning of his analysis, in spite of the resistance that inevitably came up, attempted to reveal his thoughts and feelings fully. Yet he had not been able to tell me certain *conscious* anxieties, such as his fear of being poisoned. He became able to tell me about this, though even then not without difficulty, only after some analysis of his unconscious material, particularly of inner persecution and of his destructive impulses. It can be assumed that Richard felt particularly badly about the fear of being poisoned because he thought of it as irrational and abnormal and therefore tried to keep it secret. This links with the general observation that even severe paranoics often manage to deceive their environment about the strength of their persecutory anxieties to such an extent that, should they commit suicide or a murder, this would come as a surprise even to people closely in touch with them.

## TWENTY-EIGHTH SESSION (Thursday)

Richard asked Mrs K. to take the fleet out of his overcoat pocket because he was watching out for children on the road and did not wish to miss anything. Some children passed on their way to school, and the red-haired girl was running ahead of the others. Richard said, 'There she is, my enemy, running for her life,' and stated that the others were pursuing her. If he could, he would also chase her.

*Mrs K.* interpreted that he felt that the girl was threatened by him who wished to kill her, and that he had attributed to the other children his wish to chase and kill her. (This was the girl who had asked him whether he was Italian : see Tenth Session.) Mrs K. interpreted that he also feared and hated this girl because she stood for himself who was afraid of foreigners and spies; in the previous session these had turned out to be poisoners as well.

Richard agreed that he was frightened of spies and foreigners, but stoutly affirmed that he was not frightened of Mrs K. At that moment he made sure that the door was properly shut.

*Mrs K.* interpreted that he was making certain that neither children nor spies should intrude.

Richard said that Paul was arriving the same day and Mummy was going back home either that day or the following one. But he did not mind because his old nurse, whom he liked, was coming to stay with him. While saying this, he arranged most of the fleet on one side and one cruiser and four destroyers on the other, all in battle position.

*Mrs K.* interpreted his suspicion about Mummy going home. The battle fleet represented the parents, Paul, the maids—all united against him.[1]

Richard pointed out that he was not alone, either, because he had some helpers.

*Mrs K.* interpreted that the four destroyers—his helpers—represented his old nurse or Mrs K., his canaries, and his dog. Sometimes he felt that Mummy or Cook were on his side. Mrs K. had appeared to him as a reliable ally against spies and intruders at the beginning of the session. His jealousy and anger about Paul were increased by the fear that Paul allied himself with the parents against Richard. Mrs K. reminded him that Paul had often teased him in the past, and sometimes did so even now, and that then Nurse often sided with him. Because Nurse was coming to stay with him, he felt that she was his ally.

Richard then reversed the situation with the fleet. Now the cruiser represented Paul and all the other ships were against him. Here Richard picked up the doorkeys and asked Mrs K. whether, if he went out and shut the door, he would be locked out.

*Mrs K.* interpreted that his wish to find out whether she would lock him out of the playroom might express an early fear of his lest he should be thrown out of his home. He might also wish to lock Mrs K. in.

Richard laughed at this suggestion and said that it would be nice to lock her in because then she would have to stay there until he came next day.

*Mrs K.* interpreted his wish to keep her from seeing John and other patients, and to make sure that she would be there for Richard. (He heartily agreed.) He also wished to lock Mummy in at the hotel so that she could not go home to love Paul and Daddy.

Richard took up the fleet. The submarine *Salmon* was now left by itself and attacked *Rodney*. Richard then carried out similar activities as with the sinking of the *Bismarck*. The *Rodney* was sunk, and a great battle followed, involving other ships. Richard

[1] This is an instance of the phenomenon that we can frequently observe, that jealousy and loneliness are reinforced by persecutory fear.

said something about carcasses being in the way and having to be removed.

*Mrs K.* asked where they would be removed to.

Richard said they would be removed to graveyards and buried there, and then they would be safe. While *Rodney* was being sunk he made 'cock and hen' noises, the hen calling out more and more desperately. Richard said that her neck was being wrung, that she was killed by the cock. He suddenly pulled the curtains, asking Mrs K. to help him darken the room. He was very thrilled and looked at the fleet which, he said, had become quite indistinct; he could not see what was going on. He asked if Mrs K. was crying— a question which he repeated a little later. Then he again made the 'cock and hen' noises, more and more desperately (Note I).

*Mrs K.* interpreted that at night he might have been in terror, expecting Mummy to cry because she was injured and perhaps killed by the tramp-Daddy. But from what he had said and showed Mrs K., he not only feared that Daddy would kill Mummy but also that he himself might do so. He had shown his jealousy and fear of Mummy joining up with Daddy and Paul; and *Salmon*, standing for himself, had suddenly blown up *Rodney*.

Richard said hesitantly that the *Rodney* was British. Then he corrected himself and said, 'No, I meant German. No. . . . I don't know. . . .'

*Mrs K.* pointed out that he (*Salmon*) had blown up the British *Rodney*—that is to say, the loved mother—because he hated her when he was jealous and suspicious.

Richard said that the battle of Cape Matapan must have been terrible. They could not see what they were doing and the Italians were attacking each other.

*Mrs K.* added that at night he became very frightened that Mummy was going to be destroyed by the bad Daddy and by his own attacks. She reminded him of the way in which he had reproduced the *Hood* catastrophe, when his 'big job' represented explosives; his blowing up the ship, standing for mother, also implied the destruction of the babies (Twenty-fifth Session). For the sailors had been calling out for Richard and Daddy. His wish that the dead should be buried and thus safe also expressed his fear of the dead babies coming back and attacking him, represented by the children on the road or by ghosts (see previous session).

Richard fully agreed that the sailors were the children.

*Mrs K.* interpreted that by darkening the room Richard had shown how he felt when he was afraid at night. He could not see what actually happened to his parents and therefore did not know whether his hostile wishes had been fulfilled. There was also his uncertainty as to whether he was attacking the loved or the hated mother, whether the good Daddy or the bad Daddy was with Mummy, and who was shooting and attacking whom [Confusion]. All this uncertainty and fear were expressed by his mentioning the battle of Cape Matapan, the situation in darkness when he could not tell whether Mrs K. was crying, and his not knowing whether it was the *Rodney* or the *Bismarck* which was being destroyed.

Richard, while Mrs K. was interpreting, switched on the light and expressed great pleasure at seeing the room lit up. He said how very nice it all looked, and that it had been awful before. He again switched off the light. He then said how terrified he used to be at night. Nurse had to sit at his bedside until he went to sleep. He used to wake up in terror and yell until people came. This was four or five years ago. He added that it was not so nowadays, but he did not sound at all convinced (Note II).

*Mrs K.* interpreted his relief when he switched on the light in the playroom ; the fears, which he had re-experienced, were lessened because Mrs K. was there with him and because he could turn on the light when he wanted to, as well as discuss all his fears with her. Mrs K. therefore represented Nurse or Mummy at their best, as he would have wished them to be at night when he was alone. But it was not only in the past that he had felt these fears ; they were still active ; he had shown this in his play and in what he said.

Richard mentioned that his mother was better today than she had been yesterday.

*Mrs K.* interpreted that yesterday he had felt that Mummy's bad throat meant that she, too, was poisoned, since so much of the material in that session had to do with his great fear of being poisoned and of being poisonous.

Richard agreed that he might have felt this, but at once added, 'But poisoned by Bessie.'

*Mrs K.* reminded him that he had said he was looking after Mummy but had not said how he did it.

Richard was very hesitant. Then he said he had bought something for her from the chemist's. It was something to sniff up her nose, and he added : probably some poisonous stuff.

*Mrs K.* asked whether it was in a bottle.

Richard said yes.

*Mrs K.* interpreted that because he felt poisonous when he was angry and jealous he did not feel that he was able to help his mother, even when he wished to do so. The bottle he brought from the chemist turned to poison in his mind.

Richard became very restless, walked up and down, and said he did not want to hear this. He was sick of what Mrs K. was saying.

*Mrs K.* pointed out that he had used the word 'sick' because he felt that Mrs K.'s words were now the same as the poisonous food which the maids—actually Mummy—would put into him as a punishment for his poisoning them and, in the previous session, poisoning Mrs K.

Richard, after a little pause, became much less restless. He pulled open the curtains and asked whether Mrs K. was not hurt when patients thought and said such nasty things to her.

*Mrs K.* interpreted that he was afraid of hurting her as he had already been afraid of hurting Mummy, not only by his words but by his unconscious attacks. Mrs K. added that it was part of her work to wish to know everything a patient thought and felt.

Richard said that the day before he had thought of Mrs K. as a wicked brute, and not only when she had spoken so much about his wish to be poisonous. He wondered what Mrs K. would do if he threw things at her or attacked her in some other way. He wanted to know whether John had actually tried to hurt her.

*Mrs K.* replied that she would not allow him, nor any other patient, to attack her physically. (Here Richard looked pleased and reassured.) She suggested that he was afraid that he might be carried away by his hostile feelings, and because he felt them to be so dangerous, he wondered how she would protect herself. Richard had always been afraid, as the analysis had shown, that his mother could not protect herself from the attacks by the tramp-father or Hitler-father. His wish to attack Mrs K. physically had become clearer to him when he was stamping on the football and called it 'wicked brute'.

Richard again made 'cock and hen' noises, first sounding desperate; then the hen made cheerful gurgling noises. Richard explained that now the hen was quite happy, she had just laid an egg, she was going to have a baby. That was why she first cried. He said that their next-door neighbour, Mrs A., had two hens which had been expected to have thirteen chicks, but they had only had two.

*Mrs K.* asked him what he thought had caused this.

Richard said reluctantly that he did not know. He thought the eggs must have been bad. He knelt down at the table (which was unusual) and played with his fleet. *Rodney* was again attacked by a destroyer. Then he discovered that he had dirtied his knees by kneeling and went to wash them at the sink. He called out that the water he had used looked awful.

*Mrs K.* interpreted that he felt that the water from the tap had turned awful because he had dirtied it with his knees; all this had followed the sinking of the *Rodney* (Mummy). In his mind he was poisoning Mummy with his urine and 'big job', and his dirty knees stood for his bottom. Kneeling also meant asking forgiveness for the attacks on Mrs K. He had told her about the hens who had only two chicks, although they were expected to have many more; they stood for Mummy who, he felt, would have had many more children if he had not poisoned them. He thought he had poisoned the eggs and made them bad.

Richard ran the dirty water out and began to play at the sink, filling it, emptying it, and speaking about flooding.

*Mrs K.* interpreted his fear of rain which he so much hated, partly because it represented the poisonous and flooding urine of his father.

Richard went outside to watch the water run away and then returned and filled the sink again. He appeared calmer and said that now the water looked quite nice, he could in fact put a goldfish into it.

*Mrs K.* interpreted that he was less frightened about poisoning and flooding her and Mummy, and more capable of cleaning them and repairing the damage by giving Mummy and Mrs K. a goldfish, standing for a baby.

Richard seemed much less worried on leaving. Mrs K. and he went together a little way, and before coming to a corner of the road he said 'bang-bang'.

*Mrs K.* asked whom he was shooting. Richard replied that there were enemies round the corner, they might be anywhere, and he went on shooting in all directions.

*Notes to Twenty-eighth Session:*

I. Richard's play was at times so varied and one action so quickly followed the other that I could generally select only some of the material for interpretation. For the same reason his drawing material was hardly ever fully interpreted, a fact with which we are familiar in the interpretation of dreams. When the child's play activities are at their richest—which often happens after interpretations by which anxiety is diminished—the abundance of associations appearing simultaneously is expressed by the speed with which they succeed each other. Our adult patients sometimes complain that they have several thoughts at the same time, from which they must select if they want to verbalize. This often means that they also experience a variety of contradictory emotions simultaneously. I have repeatedly expressed the view that one of the features of the complexity of early mental processes is that a variety of them operate at the same time. We are confronted here with problems that await future elucidation.

II. The analysis having revived Richard's early night-time anxieties (which might well have also expressed themselves as *pavor nocturnus*), he remembered that when he was a little boy his nurse had to sit at his bedside until he went to sleep—a fact which he had not forgotten but had not told until then. It is of interest that this memory entered in the context of that particular session in which early anxieties, desires, and impulses had been revived in the analysis. This brings me also to the question of new memories coming up in the analysis. Their full value, in my view, consists in the possibilities they offer to the analyst to explore the experiences and emotions on which that memory is built. If this is not done, the coming-up of memories in the analysis loses in importance. The exploration of deep layers of the mind leads to the very vivid revival of early internal and external situations—a revival which I would describe as memories in feelings. Such revival may follow on the analysis of actual memories. Or, conversely, such concrete memories can come up as the result of the revival of early emotions. It was implied in Freud's concept of cover memories that, in order to get their full significance, we have to uncover the emotions, experiences, and situations that lie behind them.

## TWENTY-NINTH SESSION (Friday)

*Mrs K.* and Richard met on the road. Usually when this happened, Richard would run towards her, but this time he did not do so. All he said was, 'Here we are.' In the playroom he wanted first to make sure whether both he and Mrs K. had been punctual. He remained silent. After a while he said he had not brought the fleet. Mrs K. asked him whether he had forgotten it.

Richard replied no, but he did not feel like bringing it. (He was clearly determined not to cooperate.)

*Mrs K.* asked him after a pause what he was thinking about.

Richard first said, 'Nothing.' Then he said he had a thought, but he did not want to tell it. He walked about in the playroom, exploring and looking round, then went into the kitchen and turned on the tap. He held the plug under the tap and then squirted water in Mrs K's direction by holding a finger under the tap.

*Mrs K.* interpreted that this was like urinating and suggested that he might not wish to talk to her because that would mean to him splashing her with urine.

Richard said that the water looked dirty and added that the thought which he had not wanted to admit to Mrs K. was that he was not going to tell her anything that could make her say more unpleasant things about poison. He did not want to know such thoughts.[1]

*Mrs K.* interpreted that on the previous day he had said the water in the sink looked awful after he had washed his knees in it; the sink stood for Mrs K., who was full of poisonous urine because he had dirtied her, and therefore he felt that only poisonous words could come out of her. The same applied to Mummy when he distrusted her words and was afraid of them, because she and Mrs K. represented to him also what went on in his own mind—unpleasant worrying thoughts that he wished to ignore.

Richard went out, asking Mrs K. to pull out the plug in the sink because he wanted to see where the water would run to. . . .

*Mrs K.*, after a while, asked Richard whether his mother had left.

Richard said very angrily, turning quite red in the face, that she had—she had gone to Paul. He was grinding his teeth and made a noise almost like growling. He added that he was rebellious and would leave Mrs K. when he felt like doing so; the work with her was too unpleasant and he wasn't going to be stopped from going away when he wanted to. He then settled down to draw (Drawing 19) and after a little while he said, 'I don't want to go just now.' He began with the usual starfish shape (*a*). Then he wrote, 'Nasty Paul, yah, yah, yah',[2] and explained that 'Yah' was German for 'yes' and that Paul was a nasty German. Again he was very angry, flushing and opening and shutting his mouth, although he no doubt also exaggerated and over-dramatized his feelings. Having expressed his hatred of Paul, he suddenly said, 'But I also like him, he is nice.' Meanwhile he was drawing (*b*), a shape half fish, half snake, which he blackened out. Then he made the dividing line (*c*) and drew (*d*). While colouring the face and body green he said this was Mummy and she was sick, this was why she was green. He vigorously blackened the figure's legs and feet and made the 'cock and hen' noises, getting more and more angry. He said that her legs were black because she had been stamping on the black Daddy. Then he made the green body red and pressing hard on his pencil wrote beside it 'Sweet Mummy'. He looked amused and ironic, clearly aware that this was a lie.

---

[1] I believe that his anxiety lest he would hurt me by his aggression had been diminished by the analytic work done. It is noticeable that during the more recent part of his analysis, both his aggression and his resistance had become more outspoken. At the same time he was more capable of expressing conscious thoughts that he had been withholding.

[2] I have blacked over the actual name on the drawing and put dots above it. I have also marked the drawing with the letters (*a*), (*b*), (*c*), and (*d*).

*Mrs K.* asked him what was happening now between the cock and hen.

Richard said : 'She killed him'—adding, after a pause, 'because she is so bad.' Meanwhile he had been writing (*e*) : 'Mrs K. is a brute', but had at once angrily and anxiously blackened it out.

*Mrs K.* interpreted that he felt that both the sweet Mummy and the brute Mrs K. were bad. Mummy was felt to be dangerous and he suspected her of killing and devouring Daddy. She became sick and therefore was first green. Then her body became red because Richard felt that she contained the red octopus-Daddy who was devouring her inside. But she was also stamping on Daddy and devouring him, and black because Richard felt that she was furious, urinating and defæcating, as Richard was doing himself. That was the cause of his fear of Mrs K. and Mummy poisoning him [Persecutory anxiety and projection].

Richard had meanwhile been colouring (*a*). He said that there were only two people there, fighting over the empire : the black Daddy and he himself. They both wanted the coast parts (pointing at the outside sections). Then, indicating the top black sections, he sand that Daddy's genital was rather funny, it was so pointed. He, Richard, was clever and quickly grabbed most of the coast parts. Mummy had only something in the centre. But while saying this, he gave her a bit of the coast and remarked that he still kept most of it.

*Mrs K.* interpreted that the red coast parts standing for himself were supposed to be a bigger and more powerful genital than Daddy's, which was funny and pointed. But red had previously been the octopus-Daddy. The red parts also represented Daddy's genital which he, Richard, had eaten up and therefore the red parts were now his genital which, as he had felt, had been cut off when he was operated on. Red might also refer to his genital when he was excited and played with it. Actually he knew that his penis was much smaller than his father's. It was also represented by the two small sections at the right-hand lower corner of the starfish. He seemed to have given Mummy a penis as well, after having said that she had only got some parts in the centre—which meant she had no penis. But then he seemed to have decided unconsciously that she should after all have one.

Richard did not disagree with this interpretation. Although he had not admitted that he had ever seen a girl's or a woman's genital, he seemed to be well aware of the difference between the female and the male genital.

*Mrs K.* also interpreted that Richard was not only furious with Paul and jealous of him and had excluded him from the empire, which meant ejecting him from home, but that here he seemed mainly jealous of and angry with Daddy. The empire he had drawn today also represented Richard's inside : he had taken into himself, so he felt, a sick, poisoned, and angry Mummy with a bad or dead father. Mrs K. reminded him that on the previous day the 'carcasses', which were to be buried, were linked with his fear that dead people would come back ; also that the movements of his jaws when he was angry and opening and shutting his mouth, before and while drawing, showed that he had eaten his family in anger.

Richard, during Mrs K.'s interpretations, scribbled on the pad with quick and vehement movements. In the middle was a human figure and various letters which he quickly blackened over.

*Mrs K.* interpreted his wishing to attack her and Mummy with his 'big job'.

Richard then made dots on the paper, crumpled it up, and threw it away—very angrily and anxiously.

*Mrs K.* interpreted that he was throwing the blackened, injured, and therefore angry Mrs K. and Mummy away, but also attempting to throw them out of himself.

Richard then drew on another page, but at once jumped up and wanted to go outside. He asked Mrs K. to come with him, adding, 'Let's go out of this awful place.'

*Mrs K.* interpreted that this awful place represented his inside which he felt to be awful because it was full of dead and angry people and poison—his own and their poison. Wishing to take Mrs K. with him out of the room meant taking the good and protective Mummy out of his own inside, to save her and have her in the external world.

Richard admired the country, the hills, and the sunshine. He asked Mrs K. not to interpret in the garden as people would be able to hear her. But he did not stop her when she interpreted in a low voice that he did not want her interpretations because they stood for the bad things she would give him in contrast to the good external Mrs K. and the beautiful countryside.

Richard attempted to dig up weeds from the flower-beds, but stopped when Mrs K. asked him not to do it. He had, however, pulled out one plant and wondered whether it was a weed or a flower. Then he picked up stones from between the flowers and threw them angrily against the wall.

*Mrs K.* interpreted that he was exploring Mrs K.'s and Mummy's inside and pulling out their babies. (At that moment the voices of a woman and children were heard.)

Richard said : 'They are nasty children.'

*Mrs K.* interpreted that Richard's attacks on Mummy's inside were partly due to jealousy, partly to his fear that she contained nasty—that is to say, dangerous—starfish babies who had devoured her and whom he should, therefore, take out in order to protect her. Mrs K. reminded him that this was expressed in former drawings.

Richard went on throwing stones against the wall and said, 'This is Mummy's breast.'

*Mrs K.* reminded him that when he had squirted water at her earlier, he had first let the water run over the round plug which represented her breast. This meant that he felt he was urinating at and poisoning the breast, as he felt he had done as a baby, and this had to to do with his fear that Cook, who stood for Mummy, would retaliate by poisoning his food; for any food was suspected of being poisonous. At present his attacks on the breast were also due to his anger and jealousy about the babies which Mummy might have and would feed. This was what he felt about Mrs K. when she was seeing John and other patients; and this anger was much stronger because she was going to London and see her family and patients.

Richard had again and again expressed his admiration of the view. He now sat down fairly peacefully with Mrs K. on the doorstep and said he wanted to climb one of the higher hills. How long would it take? Could Mrs K. do it too? This question he repeated several times during the following actions. He had found a stick and pushed it deep into the ground, very close to the flower-beds, saying that he was now pushing it into Mummy's breast. He pulled it out again, found some earth and filled up the hole.

*Mrs K.* interpreted that the stick stood for his teeth and his penis and that he was attacking the breast by biting it and pushing his penis into it.

Richard again said he wanted to climb the hill with Mrs K.

*Mrs K.* interpreted Richard's desire to have a grown-up penis. His wish to climb the hill with her expressed his wish for a grown-up sexual intercourse with her (standing for Mummy), which would not be dangerous and biting but loving; this linked with his admiration of the country and of the hills. Through this 'good' sexual intercourse he also wished to repair all the damage done to Mummy, first of all to her breast.

Richard, before going back into the house, tried to find out whether the side door could be left ajar so that he could get into the playroom when he arrived earlier than Mrs K.[1]

[1] As I have pointed out, he could only get in at the appointed time when I arrived with the key.

*Mrs K.* interpreted his desire always to have access to the breast and Mummy, then he would never feel frustrated and would not destroy Mummy's breast and body. (This whole interlude in the garden and on the doorstep had lasted for fifteen to twenty minutes.)

Richard sat down at the table, looking at the drawings.

*Mrs K.* asked him what the last one meant.

Richard said that the two planes on top were colliding. He was the smaller, British plane, the other was Mummy. Here he looked at Mrs K. in a frightened way and said that then they would both be dead. He wondered whether the big British plane on one side was Paul.

This was the end of the session, and when leaving with Mrs K., which by then had become part of the analytic situation, he said with relief, 'Now we have finished.' On the way he remarked, looking at his cap, that it was so small that he must stretch it, and he pulled it with both hands. He told Mrs K. that he would meet Nurse, and would Mrs K. talk to her? Nurse had said she was anxious to see Mrs K. At that moment Nurse appeared, and Richard looked very pleased while Mrs K. exchanged a few words with her.

(There was a break of several days after this session, because on the day after the twenty-ninth session Richard went to bed with a cold. He had expressed his wish to come and see Mrs K. but Nurse would not let him. He was to be taken home by car.)

## THIRTIETH SESSION (Thursday)

Richard looked anxious when he and Mrs K. met. He gave a detailed account of his illness. He had had laryngitis and only a slight temperature and was kept in bed; he had been unhappy because he could not go out with his father and Paul when it was such lovely weather.[1] He said how nice Paul was. Yesterday they had had a very good time going fishing together. He described how they cast the fly. There were lots of little fishes about, but they did not catch any. But Daddy and Paul had gone fishing by themselves and Daddy had caught a very big salmon; since he had no permit for salmon-fishing, he had to break the line. It was a wonderful

---

[1] Richard's mother had told me that he also worried a good deal lest I might be angry because he did not come back and wanted his mother to reassure him that I would not be angry.

fish. Richard wondered whether the salmon got rid of the fly, or would it die because the hook stuck in its throat? When Richard went fishing with Paul, the weather was very good and everything was pleasant. He had said to Paul that it would be nice if 'Melanie' were there with them; after all, she could have come by car. Here he asked whether Mrs K. minded him calling her Melanie.

*Mrs K.* said that she did not mind. About his wish to have her with him, she reminded him of one weekend when he had wanted to see her come into their garden and had felt that she 'was about' (Seventh Session). This also stood for having a good Mummy inside him and therefore always with him. Now he had wished to share Mrs K. with Paul, which meant sharing the good mother with him.

Richard had so far scarcely looked at Mrs K., or round the room, which was unusual. He asked her what she generally did at this time of the day (Mrs K. had arranged an afternoon session for him as he had only come back that morning).

*Mrs K.* replied that he knew she had other patients, but that while he had been away he might have wondered who was with her during his usual times; that he was jealous as well as anxious about what might have happened to her, since before leaving her had expressed his aggression so strongly.

Richard asked, did Mrs K. not mind if he said nasty things to her? Would she mind if he swore?

*Mrs K.* repeated that he was free to say what was in his mind and to use any words that occurred to him.

Richard spoke about a film in which a German naval officer was saying about Germany, 'It is a bloody awful country.' He looked anxiously at Mrs K., obviously enjoying using these words and yet terrified of swearing, which he knew his parents would object to. While telling about the film, he had begun to draw (Drawing 20). Meanwhile he had been watching the road intently. Some children were passing; a few men were standing about and Richard said they were 'nasty men' and about a woman with a baby in her arms, he remarked, 'Dirty people.' However, watching the way the baby was leaning on its mother's shoulder, he added, 'The baby is not so dirty.' He kept his voice down to a whisper and asked Mrs K. that she should also whisper, so that the people outside should not hear and attack them. When referring to the 'nasty men', he kept on moving his arm and said 'bang-bang'. He also asked Mrs K., after using the word 'bloody', what sort of things he was not allowed to do to her, and seemed a little reassured when Mrs K. reminded him that she had mentioned before that he was not supposed to attack her physically. . . . Then Richard again spoke about fishing with Paul, and became very angry that he had not been allowed to go out with Daddy and Paul. He had felt that he hated them both, that he wished they should not catch anything and that the fly should stick in their throats. He had mentioned something like that to his mother. He became flushed with anger, kept on opening and shutting his mouth and grinding his teeth, and then became more and more outspokenly angry with Mrs K., as well as frightened of her. He said he thought she was a brute. Then he asked whether it did not hurt her to be told that. He kept watch on the people outside and hid when the group of children he was most afraid of —among them the red-haired girl—passed by. He was clearly trying hard to keep down his anger as well as his hatred and fear of Mrs K. He said he had wondered whether she would be angry with him because he did not come back. Had she been angry? Was she angry now? What was she like when she was angry? She must look terrible—like Hitler. Then, showing what Mrs K. would be like— but without looking at her—he made faces, moving his jaws up and down, grinding his teeth. Although he was no doubt also dramatizing, he actually shuddered when he said that Mrs K. resembled Hitler. He avoided looking at her, moved away from her, and said he would like to run away, to go to the bus and go home. What would Mrs K. do if he did that—would she let him go?

*Mrs K.* reminded him that she had already told him that she would not stop him. She interpreted that he wanted to run away at this moment because he was also frightened of the terrifying Hitler-parents, now Mr and Mrs K., inside him.

Richard returned to his drawing and explained that it all started with black, which was Daddy. There were only four people there. Paul was Belgium; Norway was not there; and Mummy was Greece. Richard himself was British and Daddy German. Now he mentioned the loss of Crete and expressed his worry about the war situation, but at once changed the subject.[1]

*Mrs K.* interpreted his great fear about the war, which contributed to his concern about her and Mummy being injured and about his own inside.[2] Because he was so frightened both about Crete and about the bad Mummy, he had tried to separate the bad Hitler-Mummy (Mrs K.) from the good one, the injured Greece; therefore he had said that there were only four people in the empire drawing, and this meant that Mrs K. was not among them.

Richard, looking at his drawing again, said that Paul helped him

[1] After the fall of Crete Richard's mother told me that he had said that if Britain lost the war he would commit suicide. He had never used that expression before to her, and had not said anything about it to me.

[2] As I have said before, fears derived from external sources increase anxieties about internal dangers, and the other way round.

to keep Daddy away from Mummy; but then he noticed that a bit of Daddy had gone into her. He also found that a bit of Daddy had got into his own country. He was surprised to discover this. Then he became aware that a bit of himself had gone into Paul [Mutual projective identification]. That, he said, was nice; they were kissing. When he noticed that everybody had bits in each other's territory, he became increasingly depressed and hopeless. He said in a thoughtful and apologetic way, would it hurt Mrs K. if he said that he really did not see the effect of her work with him? Was it going to help and when would it help?

*Mrs K.* interpreted that he despaired because he could not believe that Mrs K., even when she was good and helpful, could put all these people who were inside him in bits and mixed up with each other together again, nor could she help Britain in her precarious situation.

Richard, while Mrs K. was speaking, fetched a broom and began to sweep the floor.

*Mrs K.* went on to say that he also doubted whether she could clean and cure his inside which he felt was full of bits of people. Referring again to the drawing, she said that Richard had expressed that his genital had gone into Paul and that he was making love to Paul. The bad Daddy, Paul, and Richard were all making love to Mummy, putting their genitals into her. But they also ate each other and therefore they were all in bits. He had shown previously that Mummy contained Daddy's dangerous octopus-genital, which was devouring her.

Richard ran into the kitchen and called Mrs K. and showed her that he had found a spider in the sink; he drowned it with evident pleasure. After that he went back to the drawing.

*Mrs K.* continued her interpretation. She said that to begin with he had tried not to be angry; he had referred to the good weather, had said how nice Paul was, how pleasant everything was, and had spoken of Mrs K. in a friendly way. But soon he had become more and more angry when he told her that he had not been able to go fishing with his father and brother. Then he had been opening and shutting his mouth as if he were eating, and grinding his teeth. He had also expressed his death wishes against Paul and Daddy; something bad was to stick in their throats. All this was at the bottom of Richard's fear of bad, angry, fighting, dirty people inside him who devoured each other.

Richard suddenly said, 'I have a pain in my tummy.'

*Mrs K.* asked him where the pain was.

Richard said, 'Just there where one feels one's food.'

*Mrs K.* interpreted that he felt he had the frightening and dangerous people inside him.

Richard said he wanted to go; he was fed up with psychoanalysis.

*Mrs K.* pointed out that he had used the expression 'fed up',[1] because that was what he felt at that moment: it seemed to him that he had actually eaten up everybody, and that Mrs K. was feeding him with frightening words. Mrs K. also linked his suspicion of her putting awful food into him—poison—with his suspicion of Mrs K. and Mr K. as foreigners, because he had not seen her for a few days and she seemed in his mind to have become worse and worse. He hated her all the more because she had frustrated him: although it was he who had had to stay away from her because of his illness, he nevertheless felt that she had deprived him (Note I). The day before leaving Mrs K. he had experienced strong hatred against Paul and Mummy. He felt that Mummy was frustrating him by preferring Paul to him. He suspected that Mrs K. would see somebody else during the times when he usually came to her, and so she was like Mummy who preferred Daddy and Paul to him. He was also afraid of her being harmed by them, as he often felt when he did not see Mummy and Daddy. Mrs K. reminded him of the cock and hen noises when the hen was killed (Twenty-eighth Session).

Richard corrected Mrs K. and said no, it was Daddy who was killed by Mummy.

*Mrs K.* interpreted his uncertainty at night about the outcome of the fight between the parents. Since he felt he had taken these fighting parents into himself, his uncertainty was greater still, for he could not find out what went on inside him. The 'bloody awful country' represented his inside. All these fears had increased, and every one of these people inside him was felt to be more dangerous, dirty, and poisonous because he himself was becoming more and more angry and more frightened; therefore his attacks became worse. This also accounted for his increased fear of the children outside.

Richard replied that these children were in fact dirty and smelled like 'big job'. He had repeatedly interrupted Mrs K. He protested when she interpreted the 'bloody awful country' as his inside. But at

[1] It is, of course, well known that in analysis great attention is to be paid to the words in which a patient expresses his feelings. In my experience this applies also to quite familiar expressions, such as being 'fed up'. It depends on the context, and in particular on the specific dominant anxiety situation, whether the interpretation should include reference to the actual expression used, however familiar. See Twenty-eighth Session when Richard stated he was 'sick' of what I was saying.

the same time he had filled in some of the countries with red, and while doing so he sang 'God save the King'.

*Mrs K.* interpreted that he was now protecting the king and queen (standing for Daddy and Mummy).

Richard replied, yes, he was protecting them against attacks.

*Mrs K.* interpreted that he was guarding them against his own aggression, feeling that he was devouring them, and therefore the red represented his own 'bloody' inside. . . .

Richard mentioned that Cook and Bessie often said 'vulgar things', and he added half humorously that when they did that he was very haughty, as if he were Lord Haw-Haw. (When saying this, Richard made faces as he had done when he was showing what the Hitler-Mrs K. was like; he also marched up and down and did the goose-step.)

*Mrs K.* interpreted that Richard thought she was vulgar because in her interpretations she had used his swear-word. She also interpreted that Lord Haw-Haw and Hitler were the same to him, as he had shown by making faces and marching; but since he felt that he contained the hated Hitler-parents, he in his mind turned into Hitler or Lord Haw-Haw.

Towards the end of the session there was an interruption. A few of the Girl Guides, who used the house at other times, wanted to come in. Mrs K. sent them away without any difficulty. Richard was terrified; even after he and Mrs K. had left the house he did not look at her, and remained silent on the road.

*Note to Thirtieth Session:*

I. Such accusations for any frustration derive from babyhood. This is due not only to the baby being actually frustrated by his mother at times, but also to the feeling that everything good is given to him by the good breast and everything bad—such as internal discomfort—by the bad breast.

## THIRTY-FIRST SESSION (Friday)

Richard looked carefully round the room. He wondered if the Girl Guides had altered anything when they came after Mrs K. and he had left on the previous day. He thought that a few things had been moved; some photographs were changed round and a new stool had been brought in. But then he found with relief that the little robin-postcard was still where it had been.

*Mrs K.* interpreted that he had been afraid on the previous day of the children being hostile—the intruding babies—but felt reassured that they did not take away his genital, represented by the robin-postcard.

Richard sat down and began to draw; he looked straight at Mrs K., in contrast to the previous day when he had scarcely glanced at her or at the room. He sneezed and said smilingly that a balloon had gone out of him, and wasn't the balloon very glad to get away from him. He began another empire drawing (not reproduced). He asked Mrs K. whether she had been to the cinema last night and wished she had been. He had enjoyed it and would have liked Mrs K. to have been there too. He asked her to pick out the crayons in the colours which represented Daddy, Mummy, Paul, and himself, pushed the toys aside and said he did not like them. He started colouring the drawing and pointed out to Mrs K. that each one had his own country and that Daddy, although black, was very nice and there was no fight. (There was a striking change of mood in comparison to the preceding session; he was now much less tense and anxious.)

*Mrs K.* interpreted that in contrast to the previous session's drawing where everyone was in bits, this time they all had their own country and none of them had bits in other people's territories. She also pointed out that yesterday's fears referring to the eaten-up bits of the family were increased by the anxieties he felt when he was ill and his throat was sore as well as by his mother's concern about his cold.

Richard had listened attentively and was also looking at Mrs K. while she interpreted. He said he had had some pain in his tummy during the cold and his throat had hurt him.

*Mrs K.* reminded him that at the moment when she had interpreted his feeling that he had eaten up the hostile family, and in particular Paul and Daddy, he had felt a pain in his tummy. The pain in his throat might also have something to do with his wish that the fly (or hook) should stick in his father's and brother's throats.

Richard protested; he did not want Mrs K. to tell him such unpleasant thoughts and he wanted to go away. (He was, however, not very anxious while he said this and did not stop drawing.) He then asked if Mrs K. could help him not to be so frightened of children. He also said that Daddy really was nice, not only in the drawing but actually; he was the nicest possible Daddy and Richard was very fond of him. Suddenly beginning Drawing 21, he said he had had an unpleasant dream. *HMS* Nelson *was sunk, and sunk in the same way as the* Bismarck. (He became very sad while he told this.) It must have been in a naval battle near Crete. We had just lost a few cruisers and our navy was much less strong. . . . There was a long pause. . . .

*Mrs K.* interpreted that Richard was actually very worried about the war and afraid that there soon might be more battles and possibly more defeats. She added that recently, since he had become more and more worried about the war, he had spoken less and less about it.

Richard agreed that he was very worried and did not like to think about it at all. (He was obviously afraid that the Allies might lose the war but was incapable of saying so.)

*Mrs K.* asked what did he think—who could have sunk *Nelson* in the dream?

Richard said he did not know and showed strong resistance.

*Mrs K.* interpreted that in all his drawings *Nelson* had represented his father, whom—as he had just said—he loved very much. However, when he was jealous of his father he hated him, and at such times Daddy turned into the black Hitler-father. But Richard felt guilty because in his anger and hate he attacked the good and loved father [Attacks on the loved object, bound up with depressive anxiety and guilt], and he also felt guilty because in his jealousy and hatred he had blackened him and made him bad; moreover, he had wished that Daddy should be a Hitler with Mummy. Mrs K. linked his remark about the balloon being glad to get out of him with the feeling that the good Daddy should be rescued out of him because he was in danger of being destroyed in the internal fighting. Being ill with a cold had contributed to his feeling that awful things were going on in his inside. This was shown by the dream in which the sunk *Nelson* stood for the dead father inside him. He felt responsible for *Nelson* being sunk, and all his fears about the war and a possible defeat were increased.

Richard asked Mrs K. to help him draw the curtains and darken the room. He turned on the electric fire and again spoke about something moving inside it (see Ninth Session). He said, 'It is a ghost.' He was worried and frightened and drew the curtains back, again asking Mrs K. to help him. He had become restless, did not finish the drawing, but said that the fish baby was calling for help.

*Mrs K.* asked who was attacking it—was it the *Salmon*?

Richard did not reply. He had become very anxious and said he wanted to look at Mrs K.'s clock; he asked her to set the alarm.

*Mrs K.* linked the ghost with his fear of the dead father, mother, and Mrs K. She reminded him that turning off the electric fire had formerly meant attacking the babies and Daddy inside Mummy, which also implied killing her. Turning on the fire stood for reviving them all. Also, the 'ghost' inside the fire stood for the dead father and babies who might come back and harm him. But the injured 'ghost' children were also his enemies—the children on the road. He was particularly afraid of ghosts at night. Then he hated his father and was jealous of him because he could put his genital into Mummy and make babies grow inside her. This made Richard afraid that by his jealousy he had killed Daddy and Mummy's babies. His sudden wish to hear the alarm meant not only a warning but also a sign that the clock, standing for Mrs K. and Mummy, was still alive. He had just shown his jealousy about Mrs K. when he had asked whether she saw patients on Sundays, when he was usually away from 'X'.[1]

Richard said that the playroom was awful; he could not stand it and must go out. He tried again whether he could get back into the house if the side door was left unlocked. He revelled once more in the beauty of the countryside; but when he looked at the flower-beds, he pointed out to Mrs K. that there was a footmark which he said had surely been made on the previous day by one of the Girl Guides.

*Mrs K.* interpreted his fear of the bad children breaking into the house—standing for Mrs K.'s and Mummy's body—and injuring it. If the door were kept open for him, he need not break into the house and would not attack his mother's inside, and then he could protect her. Mrs K. reminded him of his fear of the dangerous starfish babies and the octopus-Daddy injuring Mummy's inside. This added to his desire to get into Mummy in order to protect her.

Richard had meanwhile been picking up stones from the ground and found a bit of a broken bottle. He was very indignant, threw it away, and said that it should not be there. . . . He went back into the house and looked at the toys; he picked out the 'slum house' (the little house which in his play he had described as the station with a slum behind it). He also picked up a damaged figure (a man with one arm missing), squeezed it in his hand, and broke off the second arm. Then he asked Mrs K. whether she was angry.

*Mrs K.* interpreted that he would expect her to be angry—on the previous day she had even been terrifying—if he injured her babies and her husband. He had been afraid that his mother would hate him if he attacked his father and Paul, as well as her babies.

Richard asked whether Mrs K.'s grandson spoke Austrian or English.

[1] I have no note of when he put this question but it must have been in connection with the fact that, as an exception, he was going to stay over the weekend in 'X', and I had agreed to see him on the Sunday.

*Mrs K.* reminded him that he had asked this and similar questions on previous occasions, but her answers did not seem to reassure him. He distrusted not only Mrs K.'s son and grandson but the hostile 'foreign' babies and the 'foreign' Daddy inside Mummy. The more he distrusted them, the more he wished to attack them. Also he could not find out anything about them. Pointing at Drawing 21 Mrs K. suggested that the starfish baby was very near the plant, which meant that it was greedy and dangerous to Mummy; the greedy baby had often represented himself and therefore he felt very guilty.

Richard at first did not wish to look at the drawing, but after this interpretation he became interested. He agreed to what Mrs K. had said and, looking at her entreatingly (almost with tears in his eyes), he asked if she would do something for him. He was deep in thought.

*Mrs K.* asked what he wanted her to do.

Richard (obviously not knowing what he wanted) thought it over and then asked her to colour the drawing for him and finish it.

*Mrs K.* asked what colours she should use.

Richard first suggested that she should use what colours she liked, but soon began to direct her. The funnels of *Rodney* were to be light blue, the body and the flag red. Then he suddenly took over and vigorously blackened *Salmon*'s funnel, gave it a red body, and coloured the fish. While doing so he became much livelier and happier.[1] He said the fish was Mrs K. and then, pointing at her dress, he added that there actually was a bit of green in its pattern.

*Mrs K.* interpreted that she—the fish—also had some of the colours which represented Mummy, Paul, and himself; he was reviving Mrs K., giving her babies, and had asked her help in doing so; she was to put the breasts right—the light blue standing for the good feeding Mummy—because he felt that he had been greedy and destroyed them (the starfish by the plant who had also stood for himself); the dead father, the sunk *Nelson,* was to be revived as well; the body of the ship filled in with red stood for his father's genital and for the whole father (Note I). However, as soon as he felt that the parents were revived and reunited, he—the *Salmon*—became angry and jealous, and with the black funnel (his 'big job') he attacked the ship (the parents in sexual intercourse). Mrs K. further pointed out that the fish baby had changed into Mrs K. who was also standing for Mummy [Reversal].

Richard had been drawing during these interpretations. When Mrs K. rose at the end of the session he was disappointed that time was up. As he was leaving the house, he looked back and said

[1] Cf. Fifteenth Session.

affectionately, 'The old playroom looks quite nice, doesn't it?' On the way to the corner Richard suddenly told Mrs K. (obviously wanting to use every minute) that he had been stung by a wasp when he was two years old. He had caught it because he thought it was a fly. It stung him in the palm and died of that.[1]

During the session as a whole he was quieter; there was less tension and anxiety; he had listened more attentively to Mrs K.'s interpretations. In the later part of the session he was more sad and less persecuted, both in regard to people passing on the road and to Mrs K.

*Note to Thirty-first Session:*

I. The change in Richard's attitude from anxiety, listlessness, and despair to liveliness and activity, which occurred when I had interpreted his attacks on the father and babies inside mother, was impressive. When I pointed out to him that in his drawing the starfish near the plant expressed his guilt about his greed, as we had seen repeatedly in previous material, his anxiety diminished sufficiently to give way to interest and to the desire to make reparation. It is quite clear that when he asked me to help him he did not know what he wanted. But the unconscious meaning of his urge to revive and repair (the depressive position), and his longing for me to support his desires to make reparation, came out clearly in the activity that followed—colouring the drawing. This is an instance of my experience that it is essential to interpret the anxiety contents which are activated most acutely, and of the effect such interpretations produce. The contrast between Richard's depression and despair about dead people inside his mother, and correspondingly inside himself, and a setting-in of liveliness and hope after my interpretations of these anxieties is very striking; but I have observed this over and over again. The change in his attitude was also illustrated by the fact that, while earlier in the session the room had become so frightening that he said he must get out of the awful place, at the end of the session he spoke of it with great affection.

# THIRTY-SECOND SESSION (Saturday)

Richard was very pleased when he met Mrs K. at the corner of the road; inside the playroom he seemed friendly and at ease. He turned on the electric fire and remarked that the room was cosy and

[1] I do not know whether this was an actual memory or something he had heard afterwards.

looked nice. He shut the windows, saying that it was nice inside but nasty outside (although the sun was not shining, the weather was not bad). Richard sat down and looked at Mrs K. expectantly.

*Mrs K.* interpreted that the room, which had appeared so terrible to him at one point yesterday, had improved during that session and still looked pleasant today; it had become cosy, warm—that is to say, alive—for him. This happened when he felt that he could revive dead babies and parents, as well as Mrs K., and he had expressed that feeling by colouring Drawing 21, which meant to him that he made it alive. The fish stood for Mrs K. and Mummy and their babies; as he had written on the drawing, they had all been calling for help. Mrs K. also reminded him that even on the previous day, when he had been so unhappy and frightened, he had become happier when he thought that Mrs A.'s hens had had chicks,[1] because they also stood for the babies he wished to give his mother.

Richard agreed and said that he would very much like to give babies to his mother. He added that Mummy had five sons: Paul, himself, Bobby, and the two canaries, who were both boys.

*Mrs K.* interpreted that since Bobby and the canaries belonged to Richard, he felt he had given Mummy three sons.

Richard agreed, but became anxious. He said that the canaries quarrelled a lot and he was sure that if one had a wife the other would be jealous and they would quarrel still more.

*Mrs K.* interpreted his jealousy because Mummy was Daddy's wife; Richard got on better with Paul than with his father, since Paul, like himself, had no wife. But he thought he and Paul were not good sons because they quarrelled. Mrs K. also referred to Richard's jealousy of her patients and of her husband.

Richard, with some hesitation, said that he liked chasing hens—not when their chicks were just about to come, because that would be cruel, but at other times. Nowadays he did it less, though. He added that he would not do it any more, and wrote out, 'I shall not chase hens', and pinned the piece of paper on to the wall. He then discovered that instead of 'signed, Richard' he had written 'singed, Richard'.

*Mrs K.* pointed out that this mistake seemed to show that he wished not only to chase the hens but to singe them, and that while he tried not to chase them when their chicks were about to be hatched, this was exactly what he wanted to do, because these hens represented Mummy about to have babies. The word 'singe' would, moreover, apply to preparing the bird for the table, and his

[1] I have no record of when he exactly said this, but feel quite sure that it was in the first part of the thirty-first session.

mistake therefore also expressed his wish to eat Mummy with the babies inside. His resolution not to chase the hens indicated how guilty he felt, not only about the hens but also about his mother and her babies.

Richard had listened quietly and with interest and began to draw (Drawing 22).[1] While doing so he said, 'I am happy.' Then, 'Daddy is nice'; then he corrected himself and said Daddy was not nice. But it did not matter because Mummy was going to have most of the countries. She had a lot of them in the centre and also a good part of the coast. Richard would have liked to come near Mummy, but Daddy had already taken some countries near her. However, Richard managed to get a few countries close to her after all. It turned out that Paul had only one country near Mummy. At that moment Richard discovered that at the bottom left-hand corner there was still a vacant country (an uncoloured section). He said that Daddy intended to take that too, but Richard marched in quickly.[2] Then Richard repeated that he was happy. He was looking forward to going home on Sunday.

*Mrs K.* suggested that he might be sorry not to be going on Saturday, as he usually did.

Richard replied yes, he was a little sorry, but he would still have most of Sunday left to be at home after coming to Mrs K. in the morning.

*Mrs K.* pointed out that when he was feeling happy about going home, it had also to do with Paul having left. In today's drawing Richard had most of Mummy, Daddy was second, and Paul had least of her because Richard expressed his pleasure that Paul had already left home. Mrs K. also suggested that Richard had a pointed section inside Paul's and reminded him of Drawing 20 about which he had said that they all had bits in each other's territory and that he and Paul were kissing. Today he might feel that, since he took Mummy away from Paul, he should make love to him to make up for his loss (Note I).

Richard put various questions to Mrs K. Would she also see John on Sunday? Did she perhaps see him every Sunday? And if so, why not himself?

*Mrs K.* pointed out that his mother wanted him to come home for weekends, and although he himself wished to go home, this did not alter the fact that he felt jealous and deprived because he thought others were receiving from Mrs K. what he might have got.

[1] Here again I have blacked over the names of his brother and of himself.
[2] As I pointed out at the beginning, Richard drew and coloured these empires without any deliberate plan and therefore was often surprised to see how they turned out.

Richard compulsively asked further questions about Mrs K.'s patients, and could she at least tell him whether there were ladies among them, and was he the youngest child? A little later he suddenly asked whether Mr K. was dead.

*Mrs K.* replied that he had repeatedly asked these questions and that he knew Mr K. was dead. In his jealousy of Paul being older, more clever and—as Richard felt—more admired and loved by Mummy, and of Father who had more of Mummy than he, Richard, his greatest comfort was that he was after all the youngest and therefore Mummy's baby. He also wanted to confirm this—as far as Mrs. K. was concerned—by asking whether he was the youngest child patient and by making sure again that Mr K. was actually dead

Richard, a little later, wished to look at all the drawings. (At the end of the previous session he had particularly asked Mrs K. to bring *all* the drawings, though she did that in any case). He looked through them and remarked that one of them (described in the Twenty-third Session, not reproduced) was 'all teeth', and pushed it away with dislike. Then he looked to see whether the drawings were all dated and said he liked them.

*Mrs K.* interpreted that while Richard disliked some of the drawings, such as the one which was 'all teeth', he also liked them because they represented his gifts to Mrs K., standing for good 'big job' as well as babies; because Mrs K. kept them and dated them, this proved to him that she valued them.

Richard replied that Mrs K. was not so young—fifty-nine—but might still have babies. Turning again to the drawings, Richard asked whether it needed much experience and study to become a psycho-analyst.

*Mrs K.* interpreted that he might want to become one.

Richard said doubtfully, perhaps. No, he would prefer Mrs K. to psycho-analyse him.

*Mrs K.* pointed out that to become a psycho-analyst meant to him being adult, potent, and creative, and able to produce babies with Mrs K. But he doubted his capacity to achieve this. Being psycho-analysed by Mrs K. meant that she should help him and then he could produce drawings, standing for babies.

*Mrs K.*, after a pause, asked Richard whether he happened to have had a dream (Note II).

Richard at once replied that he had had a dream but had forgotten it. Suddenly he remembered bits of it. *There had been lots of water, boiling—no, not boiling—but the water came rushing down like the Niagara falls, pipes were bursting; he was in his room at the hotel. A little man was there: he looked like Charles, an elderly cousin of his mother's whom Richard did not like; but his cousin Peter whom Richard liked was also there.* Richard told this dream with great resistance. He had no associations but repeatedly said it had not been frightening. It was rather funny when the water rushed down like that.

*Mrs K.* interpreted that if he were in a room which was actually flooded by boiling water from bursting pipes, this would be a terrifying situation. She suggested that Richard was trying to avoid feeling frightened by maintaining that it was only funny, and this was also why he had forgotten the dream and found it so difficult to report it. She asked him what Charles did.

Richard answered, nothing, he just sat there. He repeated that Charles was unpleasant.

*Mrs K.* suggested that Charles might stand for Richard's father, who he felt would become nasty if the flooding were Richard's fault. Mrs K. reminded him that recently his urinating had stood for flooding and that he had feared it to be dangerous to her and Mummy. He had now for the first time implied that urine could be boiling; but that was also what he might have felt when he was ill as a baby. She also referred to his illness a few days ago, and how uncomfortable he felt inside. The bursting pipes in some way might represent what he felt went on inside him through his own urine flooding him (Note III).

Richard had been glancing at some drawings, particularly at 21, but quickly pushed it away.

*Mrs K.* reminded him that on the previous day he at first said that the fish was a baby calling for help, but later found that the fish represented her. She suggested that *Salmon*—Richard—was also calling Mrs K. for help. Richard had vigorously blackened the funnel of *Salmon*, and this black funnel was just underneath *Rodney*—Mummy. Mrs K. suggested that Richard was terrified that with his dangerous 'big job' he would not only injure the bad Daddy but would attack and harm Mummy; he would shoot his black 'big job' into his mother's bottom; and also the starfish baby was near the plant which previously (Twelfth Session) represented Mummy's breast and genital, and he felt that he was in danger of devouring her. He therefore called for help to Mrs K. so that her work should make it easier for him to control his greed and dangerous attacks on Mummy (Note IV). He had repeatedly asked Mrs K. to help him with his fear of boys, and on the previous day he had begged her to do something for him, though he did not know what he wanted. This turned out to be her help in preserving, restoring, and reviving herself, Mummy, and the babies.

Richard wholeheartedly agreed that he wished her to help him not to be destructive, so that he could keep Mummy alive. . . . A little later, looking at Mrs K.'s necklace, he touched it swiftly, obviously wishing to touch Mrs K.'s breast, and said that her beads were nice; Mummy had some beads like them. . . . At the end of the session he clearly wished to stay longer; he was very slow in getting his things together. Before leaving, he looked carefully to see whether all the windows were closed, whether the garden door was locked, and after having left the house he again made sure that the windows were shut.

*Mrs K.* interpreted, when still in the room, his wish to keep the playroom, standing for her and Mummy, intact. Touching and liking the beads, which were similar to his mother's, expressed his wish to keep Mummy's breast safe and undamaged, and to make sure it was there; the playroom also should be kept safe against intruders, which meant that Mummy and Mrs K. should be protected against the intruding and dangerous father, Paul, and himself.

During the session Richard had made a drawing of a fish, accompanied by two starfishes, swimming at a good distance from the plant; above the line a British plane hovered near *Salmon*. This drawing seemed to express that the whole family was at peace. (However, I did not find any reference to this drawing in my notes.)

In this session Richard's emotions were very different from those of the last few sessions. He was much quieter and happier, less sad and relatively little persecuted. He looked out a few times at passersby, but much less than recently. It was, however, clear that he avoided saying anything which could bring up anxiety or sadness, and this was also shown by his repeated remarks that he felt happy.

*Notes to Thirty-second Session:*

I. The desire to rob father of mother, and the corresponding feeling of sympathy with the father who would then be lonely and deserted, is a strong stimulus towards homosexuality (see *Psycho-Analysis of Children,* Chapter XII).

II. Both in adult and child analyses I sometimes ask a patient whether he had a dream, and in most cases I find that this question does elicit a dream report. It is not easy to define what suggests to me at a certain point in an analytic session that the patient might have had a dream but has not mentioned it. But to take the instance of Richard, it was clear that he was withholding unconscious material, though he was cooperative on one level. I believe that such a situation often indicates the fact that the patient is trying to avoid a conflict which the dream would reveal. I do not, however, as a rule ask for a dream—except in the circumstances just described—and I try to avoid giving the patient the impression that dreams are more important than other material. Nevertheless, it cannot be a coincidence that most of my patients dream frequently and bring the dreams without my asking for them.

III. This is an instance of the type of material which led me to conclusions regarding the feelings of persecution in babies when they feel physical descomfort of any kind, and also regarding the root of hypochondriasis in infancy.

IV. In my *Envy and Gratitude* (1957, *Writings*, 3) I pointed out that the infant's desire for an inexhaustible and ever-present breast—to which I had often referred in the past—has another and very important element besides the wish for food: the breast should do away with or control the infant's destructive impulses and in this way protect the infant's good object as well as safeguard him against persecutory anxieties. This actually means that the baby even at a very early stage experiences the need for a protective and helpful super-ego (cf. my paper 'On the Development of Mental Functioning', 1958, *Writings*, 3.)

## THIRTY-THIRD SESSION (Sunday)

Richard was in a very good mood and said he was pleased to be with Mrs K. on a Sunday; clearly this represented to him a special privilege. . . . After a while he said that 'X' was very quiet on a Sunday morning—like a grave; but he was glad that there were no children about. At the same time he was on the look-out for people to pass and expressed regret that there were so few of them. He said that when he woke up that morning he felt very happy in spite of not being at home on a Sunday. He thought that the work was doing him good after all. He felt so much more brave. He said all this with conviction. He added that he would like to tell Mrs K. about the battles he used to fight at home with other boys. This morning, feeling bolder, he made up his mind that when the war was over and they moved back to their home (in 'Z'), he would not be afraid to fight his enemy Oliver. (He had mentioned this boy earlier—Twentieth Session—and on some occasion had told Mrs K. that Oliver's mother had died a month before.)

*Mrs K.* suggested that it was a relief to Richard to think he would be able to fight and need not pretend to be friendly while he was afraid of being attacked.

Richard strongly agreed, and added that he had also decided to fight another boy, Jimmy, an eight-year-old who was in his gang but had told something about him to Oliver and was a traitor. Meanwhile Richard had taken the pencil—which he had put beside the pad in front of him—into his mouth, biting it so hard that he left tooth marks; and he went on biting it while he talked. He said that after the war he was planning to take Oliver prisoner. There was an untidy corner in the garden with bushes and lots of bees and wasps. It was not actually filthy but was certainly not a clean place. There Oliver would be kept. He would be guarded so that he could not escape, and the bees and wasps would sting him.

*Mrs K.* pointed out that during this account he had been biting his pencil hard, and this meant biting off Oliver's penis as well as eating him up. The prison where Oliver was guarded was not only the garden but also Richard's inside, which he seemed to think was an awful place. Richard was very frightened of bees and wasps; here they represented his dangerous 'big job' and the destructive part of himself, which contained the bad Hitler-Daddy. He felt he could not protect the good Mummy against such dangers inside him. But his present feeling that he contained more of the good Mummy (and Mrs K.)—owing to the analysis which he found helpful—gave him greater security and made him better able to fight his internal as well as his external enemies.

Richard then described what he called a 'minor' battle against Oliver and his gang, in which he and Jimmy had been victorious. He added rather boastfully that he nearly broke Oliver's bones; they also threw stones at each other, and Oliver 'got a good one'. Richard would have liked to kill him; he added, no, not really, but he hated him very much. In another battle a piece of glass hit Richard's nose. It only hurt a little, and he went on fighting in spite of it and would have done so even with one arm in a sling. But his mother had come into the garden and driven the boys away. (There was no doubt that Richard had been relieved when his mother came, because he certainly had been terrified of the cut on his nose.) Meanwhile Richard had been making another empire drawing. While telling Mrs K. that Mummy had protected him, Richard without noticing it had put the blue and red crayons together end to end with the points outwards. He also mentioned, while drawing, that Mummy had now got a lot of countries and so had Paul.

*Mrs K.* pointed out that on the drawing Richard nearly surrounded his mother; while talking to Mrs K., he had without realizing it filled in the section at the bottom with black. This was because, however much he did not want Daddy to touch Mummy, he still felt that Daddy's genital was inside her, and also that his own genital was inside Paul. Nevertheless, he (the red sections) nearly encircled Mummy (the blue sections). In this way he expressed his hope that he could protect her against the bad Daddy and give her babies. This greater hope that he could restore Mummy, which also implied becoming a man, increased both his wish and his power to fight. Mrs K. referred to his fear about injury to his genital, for which his wounded nose and incapacitated arm would stand. She reminded him of what he had felt after the operation on his genital and ever since. But he had just expressed his hope that his genital would not be so badly injured that it could not be used to attack his enemy, standing for the bad Hitler-Daddy.

Richard, when Mrs K. mentioned his circumcision, replied that he had hated the doctor ever since.

*Mrs K.* interpreted that the doctor, as had appeared previously, stood for the bad father; but that Richard had been afraid of Daddy attacking his penis because when Richard was jealous of him and Paul, he wished to attack their genitals. During this session, while he was enraged about his enemies, he bit the pencil hard and this also expressed his attack on their genitals, which meant attacking Father and Paul as well.

Richard looked at Mrs K. with interest and asked whether she thought that this might be the reason why he hated Oliver so much. He also told Mrs K. that, although Oliver often asked him to tea, Richard would not go; but when they were not fighting, Richard was on quite friendly terms with Oliver and did not show that he hated him and planned to fight him.

*Mrs K.* pointed out that this seemed very much like his relation with Paul, with whom at times he was very friendly, at other times hostile, therefore he could never fully trust him as an ally. But Richard knew that he himself was very unreliable because he often concealed his hostility towards Paul.

Richard said sadly that he liked Paul but always fell out with him. . . . Then he spoke about Jimmy, who had told Oliver that Richard was secretly planning to attack him. Since then Richard had become still more afraid of Oliver. He wanted to kill Jimmy because he was a traitor. After a little while he added that he liked Jimmy's two little brothers, who were very sweet babies.

*Mrs K.* pointed out what mixed feelings he had about babies: he was very fond of them, but was also afraid that they could be like rats, bees, and wasps; this was so because he felt he had attacked them inside Mummy when he was jealous.

Richard repeated that he had felt cheerful and hopeful when he woke up that morning, and had decided that he would fight Oliver openly and might be able to win. It had made him feel happier and he also thought that the work with Mrs K. helped him a lot.

*Mrs K.* interpreted, referring to the empire drawing, that this meant that he had the good light-blue Mummy inside himself, and that she would help him to put his genital right. Then he could give her babies, revive her, and protect her against the bad Hitler-Daddy.

Richard got up, looked round the room, and said he had not had any dream. He went into the kitchen and looked into the sink to see whether there were any spiders in it.

*Mrs K.* reminded him of his fear of the octopus, and said that he might feel similarly about spiders; in one of his drawings (6) the octopus had a human face, was red with anger, and represented Daddy (see Fifteenth Session). Therefore the spider which he had recently drowned, and which he thought might still be there, also represented his father.

Richard then asked Mrs K. to let the water run out when he called from outside; he wanted to see where this Niagara would flow.

*Mrs K.* reminded him of his recent dream. Richard did not wish to have another one because the Niagara dream had been very frightening, although he did not seem aware of that. She connected the sink, in his mind now containing the spider (standing for Daddy's eaten genital), with the dream in which, as Mrs K. had suggested, his inside was overflowing and he and Mummy had been in danger through broken pipes, and in which the unpleasant Charles was present as well (Thirty-second Session). Mrs K. added that this also represented the danger she was in through Mr K. (now the spider), who Richard could not believe was dead.

Richard had been making a drawing with aeroplanes and guns during these interpretations. He said the ack-ack gun was Mummy and the British fighter was himself; the German plane, which was shot down, was Daddy. . . . Richard went out into the garden and showed Mrs K. some flowers which he liked. Suddenly he threw stones at them, but did not hit them.

*Mrs K.* pointed out that he seemed to be testing the damage he had done or might do to Mummy's babies, both loved and hated.

Richard again said that it was nice that there were so few people about, but he did not like it to be too quiet. He spoke about his journey home that afternoon. He would like the bus to be empty so that he would be all by himself. Then he wondered whether, if that were so, the bus would go.

*Mrs K.* interpreted that he wished to have Mummy all to himself and also to be alone inside her, and that Daddy—represented by the driver—should agree to that. But his doubts whether the bus would go implied that he wondered whether Mummy would remain alive if she had no more babies. At the beginning of the session he had said that 'X' was very quiet and like a grave because there were so few people about. 'X', like the bus, stood for Mummy's and Mrs K.'s body containing dead babies, but this meant also Mummy's death and everybody's death. He was doubtful whether Daddy, the driver, would agree to Richard's having Mummy all to himself.

Richard was very amused at the idea of his wanting to have Mummy all to himself, and of Daddy, if he were the driver, being outside Mummy (the driver's seat) and yet driving him to her. Towards the end of the session he suggested that Mrs K. should date the drawings made that day. He said that 1941 looked like 1991.

*Mrs K.* interpreted his wish that both he and Mrs K.—but particularly Mrs K.—should live to that time, since he was so afraid of Mrs K.'s and Mummy's death.

In the last two days Richard's mood had changed. He was less sad, manic defences and denial had diminished, and he felt more hope and trust. He was also more responsive to Mrs K.'s intepretations.

A few days later Richard's mother came to see Mrs K. She reported on Richard's progress; she had noticed a striking change in him following this Sunday session. Although he was very aggressive at home, he seemed much more friendly and less tense and easier to get on with. This information was independent of Richard's telling Mrs K. that he was better, for he had not mentioned this to his mother.

## THIRTY-FOURTH SESSION (Monday)

Richard said he had brought Mrs K. a present, handed her a jar, and looked very pleased. He said it was face-cream. When Mrs K. opened it, a green jack-in-the-box jumped out. Richard had watched her carefully and seemed a little disappointed that she was not more startled; nevertheless, he at once asked her if she minded his joke. He fingered the toy, admired its strong springs, and said it was lively; when it was suddenly released it looked as if it would bite. (He obviously liked it very much.) He told Mrs K. that he had put six pennies into a slot machine that was full of tricks and toys. Inside there was a crane that was like a claw. He demonstrated this by forming his hand into a claw, and showed how the crane came down. It caught the jar, lifted it and then it came out. As he so often did, he gave a very dramatic description; he had thought the claw would take the box away, but no, it brought it up and handed it out to him. Then Richard marched up and down the room and stamped his feet. He said the Allied soldiers were marching into Syria and that was good. He was also pleased that the R.A.F. had bombed so many objectives. Then he sat down and drew the usual starfish shape (Drawing 23). While making the outline, and before crayoning it, he announced that it had nothing to do with an empire; it was only a design.

*Mrs K.* pointed out, when he had finished crayoning, that he had now introduced new colours—green and orange.

Richard first insisted that they did not represent anybody and that he had no particular reason for introducing new colours. But after a moment he added that green was Cook and orange was Bessie. He said that Cook wore a green apron. He became silent; then he announced that he had had no dream. When he had finished the drawing, he handed it over to Mrs K. and said, 'Here is a starfish baby for you.'

*Mrs K.* connected the jack-in-the-box with the way he might finger his genital [Masturbation], the jack-in-the-box representing his genital. She suggested to him that he probably touched and played with his genital.

Richard blushed and did not look up. After a while he said, 'Sometimes.'

*Mrs K.* reminded him that, after describing the jack-in-the-box and how he got it, he had spoken of the soldiers marching into Syria, and he himself had been marching and stamping his feet; he might have such thoughts and desires when playing with his genital. Syria would mean Mrs K.'s, Mummy's, or the maids' inside into which he would march with his penis. Inside Mummy he would meet Daddy's penis, clawing and biting his penis; this meant that he was afraid of having his genital injured by a dangerous father inside Mummy. Mrs K. also suggested that the drawing represented hers and Mummy's genitals into which he had deeply penetrated, and where the three men—Daddy, Paul, and himself—were fighting with each other; he had introduced new colours but announced that they had no meaning and that the drawing had nothing to do with an empire, because he was so afraid of the fight inside Mummy and Mrs K. and did not wish to know about it. Mrs K. added that the green in the drawing represented not only Cook but also the jack-in-the-box, which was green and stood for his own penis.

Richard had become very anxious and restless during these interpretations. He got up, marched up and down, and stood by the window farthest away from Mrs K.; he protested that he did not want to hear what she said and he could not see how such things could help.

*Mrs K.* interpreted that her words represented to him an attack on his genital. In this session the fear which he had felt about the circumcision had been revived. He had felt that the claw which would take away the jack-in-the-box stood for the doctor's hand which would take away his penis. She reminded him that the doctor also stood for the bad Hitler-father. If Richard wished to put his genital into Mummy where it would bite Daddy's penis and fight with it—like the jack-in-the-box which looked as if it would bite when it was suddenly released—then he would be terrified of both Father and Mother attacking him. Quite recently Richard had felt that Mrs K., too, was terrible and like Hitler. When she was interpreting to him just now, she was the Hitler-brute-Mummy who was attacking him.

Richard suddenly put his hand into Mrs K.'s bag, rummaged in it, but did not take anything out. Then he ran into the kitchen, turned the tap full on, and watched the water flow away; he said, 'He is attacking.'

*Mrs K.* asked who was attacking whom.

Richard did not reply.

*Mrs K.* suggested that it was Daddy's penis which was attacking —Britain's soldiers attacking Syria—and that the sink represented Mrs K.'s (Mummy's) inside and genital into which they were penetrating. The tap now stood for the father's powerful penis violently attacking Mummy's inside, which Richard wished to do as well; he also longed to have such a powerful genital. He showed this when he was marching like the soldiers into Syria.

Richard went outside and called Mrs K. to let the water out of the sink so that he could see where it went.

*Mrs K.* suggested that because Richard thought of his father's penis and the fluid it contained as dangerous, he wished again and again to see it run out from the drainpipe—Mummy's inside. Mrs K. reminded him of the Niagara dream (Thirty-second Session).

Richard went outside, sat on the doorstep, and asked Mrs K. to sit beside him. He picked up stones and dug in the earth with his fingers.

*Mrs K.* suggested that he was investigating her inside and at the same time using his hand like a claw—the dangerous penis; that he had also investigated her bag, trying to find Mr K.'s genital there.

Richard asked what Mrs K. would say if he put a hedgehog or a mouse secretly into her bed.

*Mrs K.* interpreted that the hedgehog stood for Daddy's bad genital which, when he was angry about Mummy and Daddy being together in bed, he wished should bite and injure Mummy. But this anger had led to his fear that Mummy contained the octopus, the dangerous biting genital of the father.

Richard after a while returned to the room and began to scribble; first green and orange, then other colours were used, and he was scribbling more and more furiously. He said that Cook (green) was quarrelling with Bessie (orange) and the rest of the family had come in. He got up, marched up and down, goose-stepping and giving the Hitler salute. He looked round the room, kicked some little stools, stamped on them, picked them up, and threw them down. He put three on top of each other, was angry when they toppled over, and asked Mrs K. to put one on top of the other for him. Then he tried again to put three stools on top of each other and spoke of the Crystal Palace tower which had had to be dynamited because it had become dangerous.

*Mrs K.* again interpreted his wish to get hold of Daddy's and Paul's penises by clawing and biting them off; he needed them in order to make his penis as powerful and aggressive as Daddy's. This was why he became so angry when his repeated attempts to put the stools on top of each other did not succeed. When the stools tumbled down, they reminded him of his own injured genital which, particularly after the operation, he had felt had gone. He also seemed to have experienced such anxiety when he had rubbed his genital and played with it. He had asked Mrs K. to pick up the stools and that expressed his wish that she should help him to get back his genital. At the same time the tower which had to be dynamited stood for the father's big genital which he admired but wished to destroy in anger and jealousy, as well as because he was so afraid of it. The dynamite represented his dangerous and explosive 'big job'.

Richard was playing with a ball; it rolled under the cupboard and back again. Richard said he thought it was lost but it returned. Then he asked Mrs K. to play ball with him.

*Mrs K.* interpreted his hope that his genital, which he thought he had lost through the operation and also through masturbation, would return. If it did, he might be able to have sexual intercourse with Mrs K. or Mummy—a hope which he had just expressed by asking to play ball with Mrs K.

Earlier in this session, after an interpretation about Richard's wish to castrate his father and his fear of being castrated by him, Richard had strongly protested; he had emphasized how very nice his father was and mentioned that he often played with him. Last Sunday his father pretended to be a German spy and Richard was the policeman chasing him round on a bicycle. Daddy was hiding, but of course Richard caught him in the end.

*Mrs K.* interpreted that in this game Richard had among other things also expressed his suspicion that his father was dangerous and was the Hitler-Daddy. Because the game was enjoyable and his father so nice when playing with him, he could take this as a proof that his father was not dangerous and not the Hitler-Daddy, and this added to his enjoyment.

My notes on this session are shorter than usual. The strong resistance which came up during the session expressed itself in long silences and in many details of behaviour, such as walking about the room, looking out of the window, picking things up and putting them down again—details which are difficult to report in full (Note I). To some extent this difficulty applies also to reports of other sessions, and accounts for the fact that Richard's associations seem sometimes outweighed by the interpretations.

*Note to Thirty-fourth Session:*

I. During this session Richard showed acute anxiety and strong resistance. He particularly objected to my interpretations about his desire to castrate his father and Paul and about his fear of being castrated by them. (Such interpretations are always a cause for great resistance both in boys and men.) This session illustrates the experience which is familiar in psycho-analytic work, that when some relief of anxiety has been obtained, other anxiety situations come to the fore. In the preceding sessions, no doubt Richard's anxieties relating to internal dangers (internal persecutors, threat of being poisoned) had diminished. In this way the repression of his genital and heterosexual desires was partially lifted, and his feelings of potency, together with aggression against the father and his substitutes, came more to the fore. This progress expressed itself also in his conviction that the analysis was helpful and that he would dare to fight his enemy openly. Bound up with this in the present session, castration fear (relating also to masturbation) came up with full strength as did anxieties characteristic of an increase of heterosexual genital desires, such as fears about the inside of his mother's body, in particular the fight with his father's penis inside the mother and in her vagina. I wish to draw attention in this connection to the fact that the emergence of sexual desires towards the mother, the ensuing strong castration fear, and the anxiety relating to masturbation had come up as a sequel to the analysis of intense internal persecution. There had been some material for castration fear and for the interpretation of it earlier on, but this fear and the particular anxieties relating to masturbation came up much more fully and acutely after internal anxiety situations had up to a point been analysed. Generally speaking, I found that in many cases impotence in men could only be diminished after some persecutory anxiety had been reduced, and that progress in this direction went along with the successful analysis of paranoid and hypochondriacal fears, particularly of internal persecution.

## THIRTY-FIFTH SESSION (Tuesday)

Richard appeared friendly, but reserved and anxious. He told Mrs K. that he had brought the fleet again, and put it out on the table. The German battleship *Prinz Eugen* (which had been in the news because the British fleet was chasing it) was represented in his play by a destroyer; the other ships surrounding it represented the British. First Richard intended to have the *Prinz Eugen* sunk, but then took pity on the 'brave but solitary' ship, and it was taken prisoner by the British and steamed 'beaten but proud' between two British destroyers into a British port.

*Mrs K.* interpreted, referring to the material of the previous day (the claw taking the jack-in-the-box away, the doctor's hand performing the circumcision, and the stools tumbling down), that the *Prinz Eugen* represented himself, the British ships Daddy and Paul, who would attack him and injure or cut off his genital. She linked this with Richard's feeling during the circumcision that hundreds or thousands of hostile people were present. He might then have felt that he would die, and was glad to come round and find that he was still alive and that his family, who, during the operation, had seemed to be hostile and to threaten his life, were now no longer dangerous (the *Prinz Eugen* who was not sunk but just taken prisoner). Yet his first feeling on coming round after the operation was that he had lost his genital. Mrs K. added that he was so frightened about the Navy's actual losses and about Britain being defeated, that he did not want to be reminded of it; therefore he had not brought the fleet for some days. For the same reason he could hardly make himself mention Crete.

Richard strongly objected to most of these interpretations. To the one about his fears during the operation and about the loss of his genital he replied that what Mrs K. was saying was horrid, and he did not wish her to speak about it. He also denied that he could ever have thought that Britain could be beaten and maintained that this could never happen. He agreed, however, that Crete and the naval losses worried him very much.

*Mrs K.* interpreted that the British port which the *Prinz Eugen* had been entering was Mummy's genital, and he feared that his penis would remain imprisoned inside Mummy and then might be watched and attacked by the frightening Daddy and Paul (the two escorting destroyers).

Richard got up at this point, went away from Mrs K., and looked out of the window, which he had asked her to keep open. He inquired whether she had been to the cinema the previous evening. It was a murder film but it was good. Then he said he wanted to go out, took the keys, and half jokingly said he was going to lock Mrs K. in (which was not possible because it was a Yale lock). He tried it but at once called Mrs K. to come out. He was obviously pleased that she had remained unperturbed and friendly. He said that in any case she could have got out by the other door. He returned to the room and went on with his fleet play.

*Mrs K.* explained that he had walked away from her and even left the room when she interpreted that he was afraid of his genital being attacked and imprisoned. At that moment this dangerous situation had become as real as if he were still being operated on, and Mrs K. had turned into the treacherous Mummy who had not protected him against the dangerous doctor-Daddy; also when Mrs K. explained that in his play he (*Prinz Eugen*) wished to get into Mummy's (Mrs K.'s) inside (the British port) between Daddy and Paul (the British destroyers), he became very frightened that these two men inside Mummy would attack him, that his genital would be imprisoned, and he would be robbed of it. The playroom had turned into both the place where he was operated on and into Mrs K.'s inside where his genital would be attacked. In contrast to his usual wish he had asked Mrs K. to keep the windows open today and he had not been watching out for people on the road, because from the beginning of this session he was afraid of being imprisoned with Mrs K. and inside her. This fear he had already felt strongly in the previous session. Therefore it was the room and Mrs K. who were dangerous and not the people outside, who might help him if the windows were open (Note I). Yesterday he had also spoken of dynamiting the big tower which stood for his father's genital, and therefore was frightened of his genital being attacked by his father inside Mummy.

Richard again strongly protested against this interpretation, looking pained and frightened; but he went on playing with the fleet. Speaking under his breath and moving *Nelson* out of the harbour, he whispered, 'Here goes the unprotected *Nelson*.' He added, speaking more audibly, 'No, he only goes on patrol.'

*Mrs K.* interpreted that the unprotected *Nelson* was his father when he was either unwell or friendly and patient with Richard. Richard felt that when Daddy was unprotected, which also meant unsuspecting, Richard could attack and castrate him. Mrs K. also reminded Richard that he had been very sorry for the sunk *Nelson* and guilty in the dream (Twenty-first Session), since he loved his father. Because of his wish to attack Daddy, which he imagined was actually damaging Daddy, he felt guilty whenever he noticed that his father was unwell, or ageing and growing bald.

Richard put the two long pencils near each other, making what he called 'harbour gates'. The opening formed by the two pencils was so narrow that only one ship could pass at a time. First *Rodney* steamed out, then *Nelson*, and when Richard noticed that *Nelson* was touching *Rodney*, he moved *Nelson* away a little. Two destroyers followed, and they and *Nelson* were then arranged round *Rodney* but not touching her.

*Mrs K.* interpreted that he had established peace by surrounding Mummy by Daddy, Paul, and himself; but nobody was to be too close to her, which meant that no one should have sexual intercourse with her: when *Nelson* (Daddy) first touched her, Richard had at once moved him away.

Richard made various movements with the fleet. One destroyer, with a submarine on each side, moved through the gate. Here Richard laughed, being reminded of a film where several pigs had tried to get into the pigsty at the same time.

*Mrs K.* reminded him of her earlier interpretation that the *Prinz Eugen* steaming into the harbour, escorted by two destroyers, meant that Richard, Paul, and Daddy were getting into Mummy's genital together; that they were now represented by pigs, because Richard thought of sexual intercourse as something piggish, greedy, and dirty.

Richard pointed out that Daddy (*Nelson*) was further away and was not one of the three ships trying to enter the gate.

*Mrs K.* suggested that while Daddy was *Nelson*, his penis was represented by the destroyer, and that the submarines stood for

Richard's and Paul's genitals. The two pencils forming the gate were also the two parents, as often before.

Richard described with some amusement how he had once frightened a cock and a hen whose heads were together inside the henhouse and their bodies still outside; their tummies shook when he threatened them.

*Mrs K.* interpreted that the cock and hen which stood with their heads together represented his parents in sexual intercourse and he wanted to frighten and disturb them. She reminded him of the cock and hen noises in connection with the football (Twenty-fourth Session). Mrs K. suggested that he might have seen his parents together in one bed and that this would have confirmed that they were doing sexual things together.

Richard replied that he sometimes slept in his parents' bedroom; but he maintained that they had separate beds and that they never slept in one bed, therefore they could not do such things together. He mentioned that once, when he had slept with Daddy—not in the same bed but in the same room—he had had an awful dream about big crows flying overhead and colliding with the planet Jupiter.

*Mrs K.* interpreted that Richard might have assumed that his parents would get into one bed together and have sexual intercourse, but he hated the thought of this so much that he clung to the knowledge that they had separate beds.

Richard meanwhile made shadows with his hands on the table, on which the sun was shining. He made what he said was a duck's beak, then a man's cap, then something like a duck's head, but the body was only a dark and indistinct shape. Perhaps it was two ducks together, he explained. At that moment he became very uncertain. Then he made a unicorn and exclaimed, 'How clever a hand can be!'

*Mrs K.* interpreted the varied shadow play and his uncertainty about it, particularly about the two ducks together, as expressing his feelings about his parents' sexual intercourse. He might have seen his parents together in one bed, possibly when the room was dark, and was uncertain what was actually going on, or he might have imagined what they did in bed together. The 'clever hand' referred to his masturbation which gave him the feeling of being powerful (the unicorn) and able to destroy his parents or to separate them; then again to revive them and bring them together.

Richard again played with the fleet. He suddenly said with much feeling and tears in his eyes: 'I am doing my bit for the country.' He said he had saved up fifteen shillings and put them into National

Savings; also he had been digging up his part of the allotment in the garden, and after leaving Mrs K. he was going to buy vegetable seeds to plant as soon as he got home.

*Mrs K.* interpreted that doing his bit meant not only helping the country but also—though his penis was still small—keeping his mother alive by giving her babies. He felt that his penis might grow and become capable of giving babies to his mother (planting the seeds).

Richard looked very contented, but seemed relieved when the session finished. He carefully put the table and chairs against the wall.

*Mrs K.* interpreted that this also meant putting the playroom, standing for her, in order and doing his bit for her. She then told him that her nine days' trip to London would begin the following week.

Richard asked whether this was to be a holiday.

*Mrs K.* agreed.[1] At that moment Richard did not seem to be upset by this news.

During this session there was no sign of manic defence. His anxiety came out strongly but much more directly. His resistance, too, was strongly and openly expressed. His attention wandered, as often when resistance came up, but he seemed to hear everything that Mrs K. said and repeatedly voiced his disagreement. The greater capacity to experience and express his aggression had been noticeable in the Thirty-third Session. (Richard had been very relieved because he felt he could fight his enemy Oliver.) In the present hour this was shown in the way in which Richard openly stated his disagreement with Mrs K.'s interpretations. At the same time he was more able to pay attention to them although they were obviously painful to him (Note II).

*Notes to Thirty-fifth Session:*

I. This is an instance of an anxiety situation centred particularly on an internal situation. As can be seen from my interpretations, internal here meant both the room in which he was enclosed with me and my inside. I would go farther still : in my view the anxiety relating to his own inside in which all these dangerous fights were going on, and which had come up very clearly in the preceding sessions, had also

[1] For some time I had intended to give Richard particulars about the break in the analysis, so as to give him time for working through the anxiety which this was bound to stir up. However, his anxiety had been so acute during the last week that there had been no suitable opportunity to tell him. After this session, in which anxiety had been greatly relieved, realizing that I could no longer postpone it, I informed him of the proposed date.

been stirred up. In contrast, the fear of persecution by outsiders—passers-by, etc.—had diminished. This change from external to internal is one of the criteria by which we can detect whether internal anxiety has become predominant.

II. During this session I had given interpretations of a number of anxiety contents. Doubts have often been expressed whether a child—and for that matter an adult—can understand such apparently complicated interpretations. My experience has shown me that there are occasions, not at all infrequent, in which it is essential to bring together in the interpretation several anxiety contents in order to deal with the accumulated anxiety operative at the time. Richard had been in such an anxious state that at an earlier point in the session he had even left the room. After the interpretation in which I linked various anxiety contents (in particular those relating to his mother's genital), he strongly objected and looked pained and frightened; but he continued his fleet play, which produced further material and confirmed my interpretation. This diminution of anxiety was also shown by his changed attitude, for after this particular interpretation an element of humour entered into his associations. By the end of the session his anxiety was clearly relieved.

## THIRTY-SIXTH SESSION (Wednesday)

Richard was in a thoughtful but friendly mood. He showed Mrs K. his new cap and asked whether she liked it. He had mentioned once before that his old cap was too small and that the peak was broken. He also asked what she thought about his 'mixture'—his blazer, grey shorts, and tie. His mother did not think it was too good.

*Mrs K.* interpreted that the broken peak of his cap meant his damaged genital, that he hoped it was improving and growing, but that he wondered how the more grown-up penis would fit in with the rest of him, with his whole person; hence the 'mixture'. He wished Mrs K., standing for the good Mummy, to reassure him about his growing up, which implied permitting him to become an adult and have sexual desires, while he felt that his own mother did not trust him.

Richard replied that he had thought, while he was speaking to Mrs K., that she would explain it the way she did.

*Mrs K.* asked whether he thought the explanation was correct.

Richard said with conviction, 'Oh yes.' Then he added, with

embarrassment, but obviously determined to speak out, that last night his genital had been very red and that he had been annoyed about this.

*Mrs K.* asked if he had done anything to make it red.

Richard replied that he scratched it, but that it was sometimes red, in any case.

*Mrs K.* interpreted that in one of his earlier drawings (14), red had already represented himself in the empire drawings. She suggested that red had also meant his injured and broken genital, damaged by his masturbation; he was very worried about this, not only annoyed. She asked what he thought about when touching or scratching his genital.

Richard did not reply to this, but did not deny that he had been masturbating. . . . He then spoke about yesterday's exploits of the R.A.F., about which he was pleased. He also referred with amusement to Mussolini's remark that he felt it in his bones that Britain was going to lose. . . . Richard took out the fleet from his pocket, handling it with particular care. He put down *Nelson* and *Rodney*, with one destroyer between them, followed by another destroyer immediately behind, at the back of which he put three other ships. A cruiser which he called the largest was to the left of *Rodney*, a little distance away, and followed by three destroyers. He told Mrs K. that Mummy had arranged that while Mrs. K. was on holiday they too would have a holiday at home, and that he would be back in 'X' the day Mrs K. returned. Then he said that the fleet was out for a trip, no—it was on patrol.

*Mrs K.* suggested that the family seemed to go on a holiday.

Richard agreed and at once pointed out whom the ships represented. Daddy and Mummy, with Richard between them, were followed by Paul with the two canaries and Bobby. Then, pointing at the 'largest' cruiser, he said that this was Mrs K., followed by her children and her grandchild. The grandson was a submarine. He was guarded by the two destroyers—her children—on each side.

*Mrs K.* asked whether the two families were going on their holiday together.

Richard seemed very pleased with this idea and agreed. He said it would be very nice. He told Mrs K. what he was going to do on his holiday. (He was clearly attempting to stress the pleasant side in order to deny his fear of parting from Mrs K.) Soon he said that Mrs K.'s family group and his family were parting ways. Paul also went away separately. Richard explained that Paul went away because he did not like it any more; but he corrected himself by saying that Paul's leave was up. Meanwhile he turned the clock round and laughed as he had done previously when the back of the clock stood for Mrs K.'s bottom (Seventh Session). Suddenly he put his cap over the clock.

*Mrs K*. reminded him that the clock had often stood for her, and that by putting his cap on it he expressed his wish to remain with her and also to have sexual intercourse with her. She then interpreted the last part of the fleet play. He had first very much wished the two families to go on holiday together, but then he had separated them because he felt that he would quarrel with Mrs K.'s children and attack them, particularly her grandson. Therefore the grandson had to be guarded and in the end Richard had moved Mrs K. and her family away to protect them.

Richard rearranged the fleet; in a line one behind the other were *Rodney* and one destoyer touching her, then a gap and five 'small' destroyers all touch each other; farther away *Nelson* alone, and at that end of the table, side by side, one pair of destroyers, two pairs of submarines, and a single submarine.

*Mrs K*. suggested that Mummy was followed by Richard who was touching her, which also meant sexual intercourse with her.

Richard suggested that the five little ones were their babies.

*Mrs. K*. interpreted that the 'large' destroyer, standing for Richard, also expressed his wish for a grown-up genital which could make babies. However, then he would have to fight his father or keep him away. . . . She asked him whom the other group represented.

Richard pointed out that the two destroyers side by side were Paul and himself, being equal in size. He also said that when he was alone with Mummy—the 'large' destroyer by *Rodney*—he had grown. He added that one pair of submarines were the canaries, the other pair Cook and Bessie, the one by itself Bobby.

*Mrs K*. pointed out that now only Bobby and Daddy were by themselves.

Richard said with feeling, 'Poor Daddy,' and agreed with this interpretation. He put Bobby near Daddy, and soon *Rodney* and the others joined them. Richard said that Mummy had come back and that *Nelson* was very surprised but very pleased. He put *Rodney* and *Nelson* close to one another, but quickly made a different arrangement, explaining that now Paul and Daddy were together and Mummy and Richard were by themselves.

*Mrs K*. interpreted his strong wish to bring his parents together, but jealousy and fear again and again made him separate them. She suggested that the different ways of arranging the fleet expressed his thoughts of fighting Daddy, of having sexual intercourse with Mummy or with his brother; these various possibilities, shown in his play, were going through his mind while he masturbated; in

this play the canaries and Bobby were also standing for genitals—
his own, his father's and brother's—as he had shown on the previous day when some of the ships represented genitals.

Richard listened to this interpretation but remained silent.

*Mrs K.* pointed out that when she had asked him a little earlier
what he was thinking about when he was masturbating, he had not
replied in words, but had shown it to her by his play.

Richard had stopped playing and was deep in thought. He looked
into Mrs K.'s eyes very affectionately and said warmly that there
was something very nice about her eyes; he liked them. He added
that they had little brown spots in them. After a pause he said, 'I
am fond of you.' . . . He returned to the fleet play. *Rodney*, the
destroyer, and the smaller vessels went off. Richard pointed out
that the end of the table in the shade was quite different from the
other part on which the sun was shining (and where *Rodney* and
her group were at that moment). Then he moved *Rodney* a little
farther away, out of the sun, touched her, and put her back into the
sunshine.

*Mrs K.* asked why she had come back again.

Richard said that it was not so good for her to be out of the sun.
After a little while *Rodney* and her group of ships moved back to
the shade. Before doing so, however, Richard had touched *Rodney*'s
mast and asked Mrs K. to touch it because it was 'as hot as a red-
hot poker'.

*Mrs K.* suggested that this meant that somebody had put a red-
hot poker into Mummy.

Richard replied that the sun had done it.

*Mrs K.* interpreted that the *sun* might also stand for the *son*, and
that this expressed Richard's doubts as to whether his penis was
dangerous or not. If he put it into Mummy (or Mrs K.) it might be
good for her or it might be as dangerous as a red-hot poker. He had
also expressed this by burning some grass on the bar of the electric
fire.[1] Mrs K. linked this with his red penis and suggested that he
was frightened that his penis was burning and damaged.

Richard, on leaving, asked how long the analysis of other children usually went on. His was going to last only three months,
wasn't it?

*Mrs K.* asked him why he thought it would be three months, but
Richard did not reply.[2] She told him that it was still uncertain

[1] I have no other reference to this in my notes.

[2] Actually he must have been told by his mother. I had said to her that I
would have to stop the analysis in three to four months. The fact that Richard
did not reply to my question was mainly due to his fear—so characteristic of
the latency period—that his mother's and my statements on that point might
be contradictory.

whether his analysis would last three or four months, since she could not yet decide about the date of her departure, but she expressed the hope that his analysis might be continued in the future.

On the road Richard was quiet and in thought. He asked if Mrs K. was going to stay in London, and did she go there every two months?

*Mrs K.* replied that she was going to stay in London, but in a suburb.

Richard was very serious; he was obviously worried both about the danger to Mrs K. and the premature end of his analysis.

During this session Richard showed less anxiety, was very co-operative, responsive, and at times very affectionate. He was not at all manic. It was also significant that he had at the beginning of the session suggested that they should not open the windows because it was cold. The fact that anxiety relating to being alone with Mrs K., and as it were imprisoned by her, had diminished, was shown throughout this session.

## THIRTY-SEVENTH SESSION (Thursday)

Richard seemed in a friendly and not very anxious mood. He said he had not brought his fleet as he wanted it to have a rest. He had had a very happy day with three Polish soldiers who were staying at the hotel. He had been for a long walk with them in the evening. They had invited him to visit them in Warsaw. Two of them did not know what had happened to their families; one of them had a child of four; it was all very sad. They also told him about their experiences in bombed Warsaw. He was very sorry for them and talked at length about it to Mrs K. Two of them had left 'X', but the third was staying on and had promised to teach Richard to play croquet in the Polish way. He then spoke about the plans for his holiday and said he was looking forward to it.

*Mrs K.* pointed out that this sounded only partly true. She reminded Richard that at the end of yesterday's session he had been worried about her going away and staying in London.

Richard replied that he did not like to think she would stay in London, but then he quickly returned to the subject of his holiday plans and how he was looking forward to them.

*Mrs K.* pointed out that he was trying to turn his thoughts away from what he felt to be the injured Mummy whom he could not save (Mrs K. in London), and referred to the time when he had in his play buried the injured toy Mummy, but soon decided to revive her by carrying bandages and food to her on the train (Twenty-first Session); Mrs K. added that he was also very worried about his analysis coming to an end because he feared that he would not have completed it by then.

While Richard was talking he had begun to draw (Drawing 24).[1] He again called the drawing an empire. He said he was going to bring in somebody else (which meant a new colour besides the usual ones).

*Mrs K.* asked who that other person would be.

Richard answered it was to have been green and to stand for Bobby, but he decided not to do so. When he had finished colouring he counted how many countries each person had and found out that he had most of them;[2] therefore, he said, he was entitled to make the line under the drawing in his own colour. Looking at the empire, Richard explained that Mummy had only three countries, but they were good ones because two of them had coastlines. Paul had four, Daddy had eight, and Richard had eleven (he included the smaller sub-divisions as separate countries). While still drawing he spoke about the war, and said he was pleased about the R.A.F. again bombing Brest and wished they could hit the German cruiser *Prinz Eugen*. He wondered how the Allies were getting on in Syria. Then he went to look at the map, which he had not done for some sessions, and marched up and down the room.

*Mrs K.* reminded him that the empire had repeatedly stood for her and Mummy's inside and genital. The marching, the bombing, the successful soldiers, all this represented his powerful genital controlling that of Daddy and Paul inside Mummy. This seemed to show that he was hoping his penis was, after all, all right, would grow and protect Mummy against the dangerous Daddy and Paul (Note I). Mrs K. suggested that Bobby, who was at first to be included in the drawing, stood for his penis, but his anxiety that it would be too domineering and soon become too destructive made him decide to leave Bobby out (Note II).

Richard, while Mrs K. interpreted, looked anxious and began to yawn; he strongly objected to the last part of the interpretation but soon became more lively and elaborated and confirmed it. He

---

[1] I have blacked out two names on this drawing.

[2] I have repeatedly remarked that his drawings were not done in a premeditated way and expressed very strongly his unconscious thoughts and feelings. In this instance, although he had deliberately decided not to 'bring in' Bobby (green), nevertheless a good deal of the drawing was carried out without plan. This was shown by his surprise when he found how many countries each person possessed.

pointed out that he was protecting Mummy; for one of his countries, the largest one, was between Mummy's countries. So he could defend her against the bad Daddy who was quite close to her. Suddenly, looking straight at Mrs K., he said, 'You look very nice.'

*Mrs K.* interpreted that his largest country was in between two sections of Mummy, and that this large section, together with the red line—his own colour—stood for his genital inside hers. He suddenly thought Mrs K. looked nice, but he thought so at that moment because he felt she was allaying his fear about his injured penis. This meant that she was actually putting it right, allowed him to have one, and did not punish him for his desire to have sexual intercourse with her and Mummy. He therefore felt her to be the good Mummy.

Richard replied that he even had four more genitals on the drawing, and then he counted Daddy's and Paul's and said that in a fight he would win.

*Mrs K.* interpreted that he also feared that if his penis fought Daddy's and Paul's penises inside Mummy, he would injure her— the bombed and destroyed Warsaw, also Syria which he was worried about. But when he was so pleased about the R.A.F. successfully bombing Brest, he was allied with the bad Daddy who attacked Mummy's breast (Seventh Session) and thereby injured her—France standing for Mummy.

Richard replied that he would hate to do that. He looked at the electric fire and remarked on the broken bar. Then he repeatedly turned the fire on and off.

*Mrs K.* reminded him that on the previous day he had burnt some grass on this bar. She referred to the 'red-hot poker'— *Rodney's* mast made hot by the sun—which expressed his fear of injuring Mrs K.'s and Mummy's inside with his burning penis, felt to be burning because of the urine it contained. He was also afraid that his burning urine would destroy his own genital. This was one of the reasons why he was always red in his drawings.

Richard had become restless, he walked over to the map and studied how much there was of occupied and unoccupied France. He again wondered how the Allies were getting on with Syria. Then he went outside and, as usual, called Mrs K. to come too. He looked round and said he did not like seeing the sky overcast. He repeatedly jumped down from the steps, which were fairly high, and said it was fun. He said he was looking forward to playing croquet with the Polish soldier.

*Mrs K.* interpreted that the soldier stood for the nice Daddy who would help him to become potent, would teach him (croquet) and treat him like an equal, which meant that he would also help him to be equal in sexual matters—to have sexual intercourse with Mummy and give her children. His pleasure in jumping well had the same significance.

Richard kept on running up and down the footpath. Suddenly he asked Mrs K. to go quickly back into the room with him; he had seen a wasp. (He was not really very frightened of the wasp, but was dramatizing.)

*Mrs K.* followed him into the room and interpreted that the footpath represented her inside and genital, running up and down and jumping from the steps meant sexual intercourse with her; the dangerous wasp stood for the hostile Daddy and Paul inside Mummy, or Mrs K.'s son or Mr K. inside Mrs K.

Richard played with the stools, piling some of them on top of each other. He pointed out to Mrs K. that he had again made a big tower, and the way he said it plainly showed that he was thinking of the tower which had to be dynamited (Thirty-fourth Session). He knocked the stools down and said, 'Poor Daddy, here is his genital tumbling down.' Then he remarked on a man passing by on the road, said he was nasty and might do him some harm. He watched the man, hiding behind the curtain, until he had disappeared from sight.

*Mrs K.* interpreted that though he was sorry for Daddy if he attacked Daddy's genital, he also felt that Daddy would turn into an attacker and injure Richard's genital [Mixture of depressive and persecutory anxiety]. That was why he was suddenly frightened of the 'nasty' man (the wasp) and had been so afraid of children in previous sessions. The boys not only stood for Daddy and Paul and the attacked babies, but also for Daddy's attacked genital.

Richard had gone back to the table and looked at the drawing, reminding Mrs K. to date it. He said he would like to see all the drawings next day. Then he pointed at the blue section which had no coastline because he had divided it off by a pencil line, and asked Mrs K. whether she knew what this represented. But he answered the question at once himself : it was Mummy's breast. He mentioned for the second time that a lady at the hotel had given him liquorice—she was very nice. He now looked happy and very friendly, and putting his arm lightly round Mrs K.'s shoulder and leaning his head against her, he said, 'I am very fond of you.'

*Mrs K.* interpreted the connection between her, as helpful and protective, and Mummy's feeding breast—the lady's liquorice. Also, by cooperating with Mrs K. and asking her to preserve the drawings he wished to return to Mrs K. what she had given him. Richard particularly felt that she was good to him and fed him with her good breast because the work she was doing with him had made him less frightened about his genital.

Richard replied that he thought so too. He ran into the kitchen and turned on the tap, made the water squirt by putting his finger inside the tap, and listened to the noise it made. He said that this was Daddy's genital and that it sounded very angry. Then, by putting his finger into the tap in a different way, he made the water squirt differently and said that now it was himself—he too was angry.

*Mrs K.* interpreted that he had shown that his and his father's genitals were fighting inside her (the tap); he expected Daddy or Mr K. to be angry with him if he put his genital into Mummy or Mrs K.

Richard went outside and asked Mrs K. to pull the plug out of the sink so that he could see the water running away. Then he found a bit of coal and crushed it with his foot.

*Mrs K.* interpreted that he was destroying his father's black genital.

Richard fetched the broom, swept the floor, and said he would like to clean up the whole place.

*Mrs K.* suggested that he felt if he destroyed Daddy's genital inside Mummy, he would also dirty and injure her, and then would wish to put her right again.

Richard went back to playing with the tap. He said he was thirsty and drank from the tap. Then he asked if Mrs K. knew what he had been drinking, and again without waiting for a reply, he said, 'Little job.'

*Mrs K.* interpreted that he was testing how burning his or Daddy's 'little job' was, and how mixed with 'big job'.

Richard went back into the room, sat down at the table, looked at Mrs K.'s clock and handled it. He discovered that the clock was not quite straight inside the frame and he put it right. He then turned it round and, as usual when he did this, laughed, looking at the back of it and saying, 'It is funny.' After that, in a rather worried tone, he asked what the hands of the clock were made of, they looked so green. (The hands were luminous.) He also discovered that it was foreign made (Swiss).

*Mrs K.* interpreted that his doubts about the foreign clock and the green hands referred to her inside because it was supposed to contain the hostile Mr K.—the Hitler-Daddy. He was afraid that Daddy had a poisonous, dynamiting genital and would harm

Mummy. This linked with his fears about Mrs K. going to London and being in danger there.

Richard closed the clock with the same care with which he always closed the door of the playroom.

*Mrs K.* interpreted that this expressed his wish to keep her safe and that nobody should intrude into her.

Richard had only once during this session watched out for passers-by, when he saw the 'nasty man' and felt persecuted by him. On the whole, this being 'on guard' against possible enemies on the road had consistently decreased.

*Notes to Thirty-seventh Session:*

I. In the last few sessions Richard's hopes to grow up had increased. This is a very important point in the analysis of a neurotic child and, for that matter, also of adults. If the hope to grow up enters, the feeling of impotence in comparison to adults diminishes, which alleviates anxiety and feelings of being inferior and useless. In the adult neurotic, too, we find that his unconscious feeling that he is still a child in comparison to other people plays an important role in his impotence, in both the narrower and the wider sense. Alternatively, he might feel himself to be quite old; there seems nothing between these two extremes.

II. At this stage of his analysis the role of the genital and of heterosexual desires had come much more to the fore. I have no doubt that these desires had been quite strong from infancy onwards, but his castration fear and hopelessness about ever being potent had led to strong repression which prevented even the unconscious expression of his interest in the genital and in his heterosexual desires. With growing hope, his genital desires and his longing to be potent could find expression. I believe, however, that the analysis of his anxieties relating to internal dangers—among others, the threat by the dangerous penis of the father to the mother's inside and to himself inside mother —had contributed much to this development.

## THIRTY-EIGHTH SESSION (Friday)

*Mrs K.* could not open the door of the playroom because something had gone wrong with the lock. She therefore took Richard to her lodgings.

Richard was sad about this. On the way he suggested that if John was due to come soon after him, he would leave as soon as

Mrs K. asked him to, because he did not want to take up John's time.

*Mrs K.* replied that he could have his full session because John was not expected immediately after him.

Richard said very little on the way; once or twice he remarked that the Girl Guides must have done something to the door.

*Mrs K.* answered that she was sorry, but it would be all right tomorrow.

Richard emphatically said that it was a great pity and that it would be nice if it were all right tomorrow. When they arrived at Mrs K.'s lodgings, Richard put out the fleet on the sitting-room table. He did not seem very anxious, but sad and thoughtful. When Mrs K. asked him what he was thinking about, he replied that he was very worried over Mrs K. going to London and afraid that she would be bombed.

*Mrs K.* repeated that the part of London where she was going to stay was not particularly unsafe. (Obviously this reassurance had no effect.) She went on interpreting his fear of Mummy being bombed by the Hitler-Daddy and suggested that the fear of Mummy being destroyed went back long before the war, to the time when he was a small child.

Richard, who was obviously ill at ease, asked in a whisper whether they could be overheard. Where was the 'grumpy old gentleman'? (referring to Mrs K.'s fellow-lodger about whom he had heard from John).

*Mrs K.* told him the lodger was not in, and interpreted that he stood for Daddy and that Richard feared and suspected that Daddy could find out whether Richard wanted to attack him. She reminded him that on the previous day he had been afraid of the 'nasty' man on the street attacking him just when he had smashed up Daddy's big tower genital.

Richard asked whether Mrs K. had been to the hairdresser and whether they put that awful hatlike thing on her head (meaning the drier).

*Mrs K.* interpreted that this awful thing on her head also stood for the dangerous and bombing Hitler-penis.

Richard asked where was Mrs K.'s bedroom and could he see it.

*Mrs K.* took him upstairs into the bedroom (Note I).

Richard looked round, approved of it as nice, glanced at one or two photographs and also had a look into the bathroom. He asked Mrs K. twice whether she minded his wishing to see this part of her lodgings.

*Mrs K.* interpreted his fear of intruding into her private room, which also meant finding out about Mr K. and about her sexual relations (now the 'grumpy' lodger), and looking into her inside; all this was connected with his curiosity about what his parents were doing together.

Richard, back in the sitting-room, settled down to play with the fleet. Destroyers and submarines were arranged in two groups, so placed that the battleship could pass through. *Nelson* went first and was inspecting the ships, and Richard admired the clever way in which *Nelson* turned round. Then *Rodney* appeared and was made to do the same.

Mrs *K.* interpreted that Daddy (the old gentleman and Mr K.) inspected the sons to see whether they were good—not too aggressive, not too jealous, and not claiming too much of Mummy. The gangway he had made represented Mummy's genital, through which the clever, which meant potent, Daddy's genital could go in and out. Inside it the sons—Richard, Paul, and Mrs K.'s son— should keep quiet and not fight Daddy there. Mrs K. reminded Richard of the fights between the genitals which he had arranged yesterday, and that he had afterwards been sorry for Daddy and wished to restore his injured genital.

Richard put the two long pencils with their points against each other to form the harbour entrance. Then he placed a small destroyer very close alongside one of the pencils, but soon decided it should not be there and moved it back into the group of destroyers.

Mrs *K.* interpreted that Richard, in spite of wishing to keep the peace in the family, was running to Mummy, wanting to make love to her, but felt he should not because otherwise he would have to fight with Daddy and Paul, and 'disaster' would ensue.

Richard then moved one large destroyer alongside *Nelson* and they went on patrol together.

Mrs *K.* interpreted that Richard had changed over from making love to Mummy to making love to Daddy, because the destroyer represented himself turning to Daddy—*Nelson.* They had put their genitals together and this was partly because he was afraid and felt guilty if he made love to Mummy [Flight from heterosexuality to homosexuality].

Richard had meanwhile made various movements with the fleet and asked Mrs K. whether she had seen the imbecile boy who could hardly walk and made noises like a beast. Richard thought that he was awful, but he was sorry for him.

Mrs *K.* interpreted that, when he masturbated and became excited, he was afraid he would injure his genital and turn into a mad person like that boy.

Richard quickly changed the whole arrangement. He put *Nelson* at one end of the table, saying that an admiral had come on the *Prince of Wales* to inspect the fleet. *Rodney* was moved to the opposite end; she was not needed yet. *Nelson*—now the *Prince of Wales*—being the admiral's ship, passed through groups of destroyers and submarines, arranged as before all round the table, and then moved away. Next, *Rodney*, which was now commanded by another admiral, came along and went through the same movements.

*Mrs K.* interpreted that Richard was supposed to be one of the two admirals and his father the other. This would mean that they would alternately posses the big potent genital as well as Mummy. Then they would avoid any fight, injury, or destruction.

Richard now spoke of the second admiral as Wavell's brother, but then decided that this could not be, since they did not have the same surname : but they were both Scotsmen.

*Mrs K.* interpreted that this mistake meant that Paul too should share command with Richard. Then everyone would be satisfied (Note II).

Richard again spoke about Mrs K. going to London. He had all along been very serious and in thought, but not very tense. He was also particularly friendly and affectionate with Mrs K. He said how he did not like it at all that she was going and asked her to promise him one thing : if she heard the sirens, would she go to a shelter at once?

*Mrs K.* said she would.

Richard seemed a little cheered up by that. He asked whether Mrs K. would be staying with her son, and whether he could have his address as he wanted to write to her.

*Mrs K.* agreed and said she would also send him a postcard.

Richard said that if Mrs K. died he would go to her funeral. Then he remarked very seriously, as if he had made an important decision : would Mrs K. tell his mother who could continue this work with him if Mrs K. died.

*Mrs K.* said she would give his mother the name of another analyst. She interpreted that going to her funeral also meant continuing the work (here Richard interrupted to say he thought the work was good and helped him). It meant taking Mrs K., standing also for the dead Mummy, into himself and keeping her alive inside him. The wish to continue the analysis, which he found helpful, was the same thing as having the good and light-blue Mummy inside him. Mrs K. reminded him how pleased he was whenever he found that in his drawings the light-blue Mummy had more countries, for this meant that the good mother and her breast were expanding inside him.

Richard asked for all the drawings and looked through them. Pointing at one, he said it was done a whole month ago.

*Mrs K.* interpreted that he hoped he and Mrs K. would be together in another month's time, which meant that she would still be alive.

Richard then looked at Drawing 8 which, as he said, was unfinished (it was not coloured). He decided to finish it now. Would Mrs K. write on the back that it was finished on that day? He mentioned the date and made a mistake, making it two days later than it actually was.

*Mrs K.* interpreted his wish for her to be still with him in two days' time, since there was now only one day left before the weekend.

Richard was very eager to finish the colouring as the time was nearly up, and went on working on the drawing. He began with the starfishes and said that three of the babies had already come to life, the others were still jelly. He asked repeatedly whether there was a little time left yet. When crayoning the sky, he said that it was a nice blue sky.

*Mrs K.* suggested that Richard wished that both he and Mrs K. should have good weather while she was away (to which Richard agreed), because bad weather, and particularly rain, also stood for the bad Daddy's genital; sunshine and blue sky meant the warm, alive, and happy Mummy.

Richard asked whether he could still make another drawing, but then at once noticed that his time was up. He asked Mrs K. whether she was coming with him to the garden gate, and looking round he said that the country looked beautiful today.[1]

*Notes to Thirty-eighth Session:*

I. It is debatable whether my acceding to Richard's wish to see my bedroom was right from the point of view of technique. However, I have often found that when children come into my house and wish to

---

[1] On the previous evening Richard's mother had told me on the telephone that she thought Richard was much improved. He was more carefree and happy, and also less tiresome and quite clearly less afraid of children. She had mentioned improvement five days previously, but she found there was further improvement since then. She also said that Richard had told her that if he now went to school, he could tell the teacher, couldn't he, that he was afraid of children. She reported that he had heard a conversation in which the difficulties of the German mentality after the war were discussed. Richard had joined in the conversation and had asked whether Hitler could not be psycho-analysed and made better.

see the other rooms, it is helpful to let them see them once. I do not agree to further inspection of my house. This seems to me a point in which the analysis of children differs from that of adults. The same applies, as I have remarked earlier, to answering, up to a point, some questions which would not be answered to adults. We have to take into account that the child's curiosity expresses itself in a much more impetuous way, and they also expect, as a much more natural thing, to know, for instance, whether the analyst has a husband or children or what her house is like.

II. I would suggest that these various details of the fleet play, making love to mother, being attacked by father, then sharing with father and brother, were the contents of Richard's masturbation phantasies. This was shown by his suddenly thinking of the imbecile boy and his obvious fear that he could lose his sanity by masturbation, a fear often found in adolescence.

## THIRTY-NINTH SESSION (Saturday)

Richard was serious and not talkative, but friendly. He was very relieved that the lock of the playroom door had been repaired. He said, with strong feeling, 'I am so glad we are back.' It was clear how much he had missed the playroom in the last session. (On the previous evening, as she had promised, Mrs K. had rung him at the hotel and told him that they could again meet in front of the playroom, since the lock had been repaired. He asked Mrs K. for her address and telephone number in London. Mrs K. promised to bring it to him and she also mentioned to Richard that he had left a destroyer behind, which she would also bring.)

Richard at once asked whether Mrs K. had brought the address and the destroyer. He read and re-read the address with great interest. He said he had not brought the fleet, he had packed it away. Looking at the destroyer and moving it about slowly, he said in a low voice and sadly, 'It is the last British destroyer left, our whole fleet is sunk.'

*Mrs K.* asked where it had been sunk.

Richard said it had happened around Crete.

*Mrs K.* interpreted that he had now more openly shown his sad feelings about the Allied losses and had avoided this formerly because it was too painful. Now he felt, in spite of his sadness, more hope that Mrs K. would survive, particularly because the light-blue Mummy was more secure inside him. Yesterday he had felt the playroom was lost; but he had regained it, and he also had his fleet complete again.

Richard was silent and sad. He moved the destroyer up and down saying that it had to get out by itself, although some German destroyers were approaching; it might be beaten but it had to try.

*Mrs K.* interpreted that the little destroyer stood for himself who would have to face his enemies alone because he was going to be left by Mrs K., standing for the good Mummy. At the same time, forgetting this destroyer in Mrs K.'s room yesterday meant that one part of himself, including his genital, would stay with Mrs K., and inside her, and protect her in London from Hitler. His urge to save Mummy from the dangerous tramp, even if he were to be killed in the effort, had already been shown quite early on (First Session) (Note I).

Richard had begun to draw (Drawing 25) listlessly and much more slowly than usual. In between he looked up at Mrs K. (which on the whole he had avoided so far during this session) and said very appealingly, 'Must you go? Why must you?'

*Mrs K.* replied that she wished to see her children and also to do some work with patients.

Richard said that he knew he should not be so selfish but he wished Mrs K. would not go. He then asked were there many analysts? How many people were being analysed? Were there millions of them? Was Mrs K.'s son an analyst? He thought that many people should be analysed because it was so very helpful.

*Mrs K.* interpreted that he wished to become an analyst himself so that he might replace Mrs K. if she died, and in this way also keep her alive through the work.

Richard asked whether Mrs K. had told his mother who could continue the work if she died.

*Mrs K.* replied that she had.

Richard repeated that the work was very helpful and that he was no longer afraid of going out by himself. Today a little girl had walked just behind him and he had also met a boy, and it did not matter at all. He was surprised how little it mattered. While saying this he picked up a tiny woman figure (one of those which represented children in his play) and made her walk. Then he picked up a red crayon and moved it round the figure, making the crayon walk as well. It came close to the little girl, pricked her, and threw her from the table.

*Mrs K.* interpreted that this was what he wished to do to little girls, the pricking standing for aggressive sexual relations.

Richard picked up the figure and repeated the performance, but more violently; he also stepped on the figure, but carefully saw to it that it lay under his instep and was not damaged. He said that now he had put his big black boot on her and she was crushed.

*Mrs K*. interpreted that the 'big black boot' was the Hitler boot, and she reminded him of his marching and goose-stepping on earlier occasions. This showed that he felt his sexual desires for little girls were Hitler-like, and that the black Hitler-father in his drawings and thoughts represented himself too. But if his sexual desires were so dangerous, they would be dangerous to Mrs K. and Mummy as well, and the little girl also stood for both them and their genitals (Note II).

Richard turned on the fire, though it was a very warm day, and looked at the bars as they became red. He again burnt a few bits of grass and leaves on them.

*Mrs K*. interpreted that he showed that his genital would be dangerous, red, and burning, if he gave way to his sexual desires. She reminded him that he also had felt it to be devouring.

Richard replied that he had previously called the destroyer which he had left with Mrs K. *Vampire*.

*Mrs K*. interpreted that the British fleet had recently had great losses, and therefore Richard had left his fleet at home in order to protect it. Though he had left one destroyer with Mrs K., which meant remaining with her when she went to London and protecting her, he had also expressed his vampire desires. For Mrs K.'s imminent departure revived the feelings he had as a baby when Mummy took the breast away from him which increased his desire to suck her breast dry and to eat it up. All this contributed to his fear of Mrs K.'s death and to his feelings of guilt.

Richard then replied that *Vampire* was the name of a real destroyer.

*Mrs K*. pointed out that he used this name for the destroyer because he was afraid of losing Mrs K. through his greed.

Richard asked whether a vampire looked like a bat. He ran into the kitchen, turned on the tap, and made the water squirt, sometimes in Mrs K.'s direction, for which he apologized. He found a tiny spider in the sink, picked it up when nearly drowned, and threw it back again into the sink. He clearly enjoyed this and was jeering at the spider; but when he saw that it was dead, he picked it up and looked depressed. He said 'silly little thing' and put it down the sink.

*Mrs K*. interpreted the squirting tap as Richard's penis, which was drowning Mrs K.'s and Mummy's babies (the little spider). He wished to attack Mrs K.'s children and the other patients to whom she was going because he was jealous of them.

Richard returned to the playroom and drew a picture by placing the destroyer on the paper and outlining its shape several times. When he had finished the drawing and written in the names of the ships, he put against three of them 'sunk off Crete'; only two destroyers, including *Vampire,* remained not sunk.

*Mrs K.* interpreted his wish to drown her children but to leave her one son and himself, so that she should be like his mother, who had two sons.

Richard pointed out that the two destroyers were going in opposite directions.

*Mrs K.* asked why this was—had they quarrelled?

Richard again asked whether Mrs K. really had to go away.

*Mrs K.* interpreted that the two destroyers going in opposite directions also stood for himself and Mrs K. parting.

Richard then looked again at Drawing 25 and stated with some surprise that Mummy had actually left a bit of herself in him.

*Mrs K.* suggested that he attributed to Mummy a penis, the bit put into him, and that Mrs K. going to London and being attacked by Hitler made her into Mummy containing and using the Hitler-penis—a figure both injured and bad (Note III).

Richard pointed out that Mummy had got quite a lot of countries, although he had more.

*Mrs K.* interpreted his desire for Mummy (and Mrs K.) to remain inside him, alive, and to expand there. This implied that he would not suck her dry and devour her, nor would he be the vampire destroyer to the internal Mummy. This was also the reason why he had packed away the fleet and not brought it. The fleet represented Mrs K. as well.

Richard became more and more silent towards the end of the session and was very sad. Before leaving he carefully closed all the doors, looked to see if all the windows were shut, and said with strong feelings, 'Goodbye, old playroom, have a rest and a good holiday and I shall see you in ten days' time.' He looked back at the room from the street. Earlier he had inquired whether Mrs K. was also going to the village. Outside he said that Mrs K. was actually going to be away ten days and not nine.

*Mrs K.* replied that she was seeing him today and would again be seeing him in ten days' time and that therefore there were only nine days in between.

Richard was all the time holding Mrs K.'s address in his hand and told her he now knew the telephone number by heart and would not forget it. On parting he said, 'I hope you will have a good time.' He did not look at Mrs K. as usual or wave to her from the other side of the road; he went on his way without looking back.

*Notes to Thirty-ninth Session:*

I. It is part of my technique not to interpret a symptomatic action either made at the end of a previous session or at the beginning of a current one, but to wait until the full meaning of the action appears in the whole context of the material in the course of that session, or perhaps even in a later one.

II. I have mentioned that the repression of his genital desires and of his interest in the genital had to some extent been relieved in recent sessions. The lifting of this repression included also a stronger expression of his relation to part objects, in particular the breast. Together with his repressed strong curiosity about the sexual intercourse of his parents, the phantasies attached to it had come to the fore. This implied that his masturbation phantasies, bound up with genital desires, and also his actual masturbation, were less inhibited. This was in some measure a regression to an earlier stage of development in which the part object—genitals (male and female) and the breast—played an important role. But it is essential for the child to experience fully his relation to part objects and the sexual phantasies and desires this implies, in order to achieve a satisfactory relation to the whole object. We are quite familiar with the the fact than in analysis one has to enable the patient to relive his earliest relations and emotions; but it is a point which I would wish to underline here that a fully experienced relation to part objects at a stage where this would normally be predominant is the foundation for the gradual development of the relation to whole objects.

III. I had interpreted in this session Richard's feeling that he was putting one part of himself (the *Vampire* destroyer) into me; but that this part was not only meant to be bad but also good, because it was going to protect me in London. In the same way I would say that the penis-shaped section of Mummy inside him in Drawing 25 was not only meant to be a penis (possibly a Hitler one) but also the good protective breast. This links with Richard's next association.

# FORTIETH SESSION[1] (Tuesday)

Richard was fifteen minutes late, looked very shy and anxious, and did not remark on his being late. He said he had left the fleet at home. After a pause he asked Mrs K. how she was, but did not look at her or even at the room. He thanked her for her postcard and asked whether she had laughed about his mentioning on the postcard he sent her that he was not looking forward to coming back to 'X'. There was a long silence. . . .

*Mrs K.* interpreted that this remark and his whole attitude showed that she and 'X' and the playroom had turned bad in his mind, because she had been bombed in London.

Richard now put some questions. Did Mrs K. see much of 'battered' London? Was there an air-raid while she was there?

*Mrs K.* said, 'Yes.'

Richard looked for a moment pleased about Mrs K.'s reply, obviously because he had doubted whether she would tell the truth. He at once said, 'I knew this.' Then he asked whether there had also been a thunderstorm in London, and added that he was afraid of thunderstorms (a fact already well-known to Mrs K.). . . . He said he liked his holidays and did not want to come back. He had thought of 'X' as 'pig-sty X' and also as a nightmare (Note I).

*Mrs K.* interpreted that his fears about a soiled and injured Mummy containing a Hitler-father now centred on 'X' and on Mrs K., and that his wish to stay away from them meant running away from his fears. This was also, she suggested, the reason for his coming late.

Richard now explained that he had gone with his mother to the hotel first.[2] He asked whether Mrs K. was cross about his coming late and said again that he had left his fleet at home.

*Mrs K.* interpreted his wish not to return to the work with her because she had turned into the 'pig-sty' Mrs K., the soiled Mummy; he kept the good work and the good Mrs K. safe inside him, and this was represented by the fleet which remained at home.

Richard asked whether Mrs K. had brought the drawings, and for a moment he seemed pleased that she had done so.

---

[1] I have used some material from the sessions following the break in the analysis in my paper 'The Œdipus Complex in the Light of Early Anxieties' (1945, *Writings*, 1), in particular the drawings and the fleet play as well as a number of his associations and my interpretations.

[2] As a rule at the beginning of a week he came straight from the bus to the playroom.

*Mrs K.* interpreted that the drawings—as did the fleet—stood for the helpful analysis and his good relation with the good Mrs K. or the good Mummy.

Richard looked very listlessly at the drawings, put them down again and remained silent for some time. . . . He went into the kitchen, stated that the sink was clean, but disliked the smell of a pot of ink which stood there. He looked unhappy and anxious. When he went outside he was disgusted with the nettles which had grown in the cracks of the steps, and showed Mrs K., with a little shudder, some toadstools which he said were poisonous. He stamped on both the nettles and the toadstools and said that now his shoes would smell of these dirty and poisonous things. Then he returned to the playroom, went to the cupboard, took out a book, saying this was the one he meant to look at, began to read it, and looked at the illustrations. After a time, he pointed out a picture to Mrs K. which he said was 'awful'. It represented a little man fighting against an 'awful monster'.

*Mrs K.* interpreted that his silences and his reading expressed his wish to escape from his fears about the poisonous and dangerous father-genital and the dead babies inside Mummy—the toadstools and nettles which he crushed under his feet. The playroom, the garden, and Mrs K. had turned bad and poisoned in his mind. He also wished to find out about Mrs K.'s inside by looking into the book. This seemed less frightening than looking round the playroom.

Richard then made Drawing 26. While drawing the red sections he said, 'These are the Russians, they are red—no, it is myself.'

*Mrs K.* interpreted that he was suspicious of the Russians, as he had often said, even though they had now become allies; and therefore when he first spoke of the Russians and then of himself as red, he expressed his suspicion of himself. . . .

Richard asked if Mrs K. would keep him a little longer because he had been late, and was disappointed when she said she could not.

He was throughout listless, did not look at Mrs K. or round the playroom. He was a picture of unhappiness. Obviously he found it very difficult to listen to Mrs K.'s interpretations and was clearly glad to go at the end of session, although a little earlier he had shown some disappointment because Mrs K. could not keep him longer (Note II). He was glad, however, to go with Mrs K. as far as the village and he had made sure about that earlier.

*Notes to Fortieth Session:*

I. At this point resistance had reached a climax. It will be seen that the interpretation of the deep anxieties which had been stirred up by the analyst leaving him at a time when his feelings of loss and his distrust were very strong could within a very few sessions diminish his resistance and make full co-operation possible. I found this to be a fundamental part of the analytic procedure. I do not mean to say that every session in which deep anxiety situations and painful emotions are interpreted necessarily finishes with resistance being diminished, though the material and the interpretations referred to in this book show this at many points. There were sessions, however, in which an accumulation of internal and external anxieties made this impossible. But even then the work in the next session was favourably influenced.

It is no surprise for the analyst that resistance to some interpretations comes up again and again, although it had been considerably diminished in former sessions. We are aware that the working-through —a process which Freud found so fundamental for analysis—makes it necessary to go repeatedly over similar material, using the new details which come up and make a fuller analysis of the emotional situation possible. It seems striking that interpretations which are most painful, such as those of destructive impulses directed against the loved object or even—as will be seen in later sessions—of anxieties relating to internal dangers and persecution by dead and hostile objects, can yet lead to great relief. Such sessions in Richard's case repeatedly finished with a greater feeling of hope and security.

As the result of the analytic procedure, the ego confronted with internal and external anxieties becomes able not only to face them but also to regain hope in dealing with them. One factor in this change is the coming up of love, which, together with destructive impulses and persecutory anxieties, had been split off and therefore had been prevented from making itself felt.

I wish to draw attention to the fact that the approach described above makes it possible for the patient to experience simultaneously resistance and some cooperation. This double attitude is the result of splitting processes which lead to different parts of the self and contrasting emotions being operative in the same session. While Richard at times wished to leave the room when anxiety welled up more fully and resistance reached a climax, he never actually left early; also he repeatedly mentioned that he had not wanted to come, but he came every time. What he did on a number of occasions was not to bring his fleet, which usually expressed his feeling that he had left a good part of his self and of his objects at home. The analysis of this splitting often had the effect that he brought the fleet again in the next session, and that he was able to make another step towards integration. With growing insight concerning deeper layers of the mind, the trust in the analyst and in the psycho-analytic procedure increases, and often shows immediately in a change from negative to positive transference.

This brings me to a further point. At a time when it was an established principle in psycho-analysis that psychotic anxieties should not be interpreted because of the danger of bringing psychosis out into the open, I discovered that progress in analysis was bound up with interpreting whichever anxieties were most acute, whether they were of a psychotic nature or not. In this way I found it possible to penetrate to the depths and diminish anxieties at their roots and in relation to primal objects. This approach, which I developed first in the psychoanalysis of young children, also fundamentally influenced my technique with adults. It has, moreover, had further ramifications of an important nature, particularly in the analysis of psychotic patients, which some of my colleagues are carrying out with promising results.

II. As a matter of routine I do not extend the session either with adults or children if the late start has not been caused by me. There could, of course, be reasons why in very exceptional circumstances I would prolong a session, but on the whole I keep to my timetable, so as to avoid disturbance to the analysis because patients try to take advantage of the analyst allowing them to stay longer. Another reason for being firm on this point is the disorganization it would cause in the analyst's timetable and the difficulties this would make with other patients.

# FORTY-FIRST SESSION (Wednesday)

Richard was on time but had been running because he left the hotel late. He said at once that the fleet was there after all; he must have misunderstood his mother's reply to his question as to whether they had brought the fleet back to 'X'. Mummy had asked him whether Mrs K. had been annoyed because he was late yesterday. He again wanted to know if Mrs K. was going to keep him longer to day to make up for it.

*Mrs K.* replied that this was not possible because of her other arrangements.

Richard asked was it because of another patient; had Mrs K. only got men patients now; was he the youngest even among the London patients; how did Mrs K. travel—did she go first-class; was she by herself; was she comfortable, and did she eat on the train? He again asked whether there had been a thunderstorm in London too. (He had told Mrs K. in the previous session that he was afraid of thunderstorms.) Did they all see Mrs K. off? (meaning all her family).

*Mrs K.* replied briefly to some of these questions and interpreted Richard's wish to find out details about her stay in London; he also wanted to know whether she had had the dangerous sexual relation which was represented by thunderstorms and by being bombed. At the same time he wished to be reassured that Mrs K.'s children had seen her off—that is to say, loved her; this would help him not to think of her as the 'pig-sty,' the 'brute' Mrs K., which meant the injured, soiled, and dangerous Mummy.

Richard replied that he was glad to have come back to 'X', though he still did not like the place. . . . He put out the fleet and turned on the fire, asking Mrs K. to allow it although it was not at all a cold day. He moved the ships about listlessly and made a destroyer, *Vampire*, bump into *Rodney*.

*Mrs K.* asked him whether the *Vampire* was himself.

Richard said yes, but at once rearranged the fleet. He put the battleships *Rodney* and *Nelson* side by side, and then in a row lengthwise some ships representing Paul, himself, his two canaries, and Bobby, arranged, as he said, in order of age. He explained that he had been given Bobby later than the canaries and that one of the canaries came earlier than the other; they had to be arranged accordingly.

*Mrs K.* interpreted Richard's desire for peace and order in the family, his giving way to Daddy's and Paul's authority, as a means of restraining his jealousy and hatred. This meant there would be no Hitler-Daddy, and Mummy would not be turned into the 'pig-sty' Mummy, for she would not be injured and bombed by the bad father, and Richard's genital would not be attacked by him.

Richard broke up the arrangement of the fleet. He had become very undecided, listless, and worried, seemed unable to listen to interpretations, and yet was very keen to please Mrs K. and tried to cooperate. He fumbled about with the ships. . . . After a pause he reported a conversation he had had with his mother while Mrs K. was away. He had told Mummy that he was very worried about having babies later on and asked whether it would hurt very much. Mummy had explained that men did not have babies; it was the woman who had the baby and was in pain when it was born (this was not the first time that she had explained this; cf. Twenty-first Session) (Note I). She had told him that the man puts his genital into the woman's genital, to which he had replied that he would not like to do that, that it would frighten him and that the whole thing was a great worry to him. Mummy had said that this did not hurt the man. Richard added that he had also told Mummy that he could not ask Mrs K. these things as easily as he asked her because, though Mrs K. was very nice, she was not his mother. He also said how very fond he was of Mummy. He was 'Mummy's chick' and 'chicks do run after their Mummies'. He added, 'But, then, chicks have to do without them because the hens don't look after them any more and don't care for them.' He appeared very worried while repeating this whole conversation to Mrs K.

*Mrs K.* interpreted that Richard had been afraid that she would die and needed someone to replace her, and that therefore he had tried to do work with Mummy instead. She was still in his mind the good, helping, light-blue, breast Mummy, while Mrs K. had turned into the bombed, poisoned, dead, or dangerous Mummy [Splitting of mother figure into breast and genital mother]. Mrs K. interpreted his fear of sexual intercourse in connection with yesterday's material—the pig-sty 'X', linked with the dirty, soiled, poisoned inside of Mummy. She reminded him of the 'poisonous' toadstools, his disgust at the nettles between the cracks of the step, his fear of even looking round in the playroom and the 'awful monster' standing for the dangerous Hitler-penis inside Mummy. This also linked with what had happened before the break: the dynamited big tower penis, the fight with the stools, standing for Daddy's penis and babies inside Mummy, and his fear of his genital being damaged by the dangerous father inside Mummy—fears which had become connected with Mrs K. and the playroom during the break. He had said that he was Mummy's chick, and when Mrs K. went away he felt that the good Mummy had turned bad and left him, as hens leave their chicks. This repeated his frustration as a baby when he did not get much from the breast; at such times he hated Mummy and then felt that she was injured by him. Now he felt the same about Mrs K.

Richard, during this last interpretation, looked fully at Mrs K. for the first time since her return, smiled, and his eyes brightened (Note II). He fetched the same book as on the previous day and pointed out some pictures, particularly the one of the 'awful monster', against which the little man had to fight. He said the monster was awful to look at, but its meat might be delicious to eat.

*Mrs K.* interpreted that the monster's meat he wished to eat stood for Daddy's attractive penis. His desire to suck and eat it like Mummy's breast made him feel that he had got it inside, but then it turned into the monster penis which would fight him internally. Mrs K. referred to the dream about the fishes (Twenty-second Session) when he put himself into great danger by not wishing to eat the octopus, which earlier (Drawing 6) had represented the attacked, ill-treated, and therefore dangerous penis of the father.

Richard thereupon ran into the kitchen, looked round, tried to open the oven but soon gave it up. He had become very listless, yawned, and said repeatedly that he wanted to go to sleep. He said that last night he could not get to sleep until late.

*Mrs K.* interpreted that looking into the oven stood for looking into his own inside to find out whether the monster was there. He felt so sleepy because he wanted to get away from frightening and worrying thoughts which had come up in connection with Mrs K.'s interpretation.

Richard had begun to draw (Drawing 27), and while drawing asked Mrs K. some questions. Did Mr Evans sell her some cigarettes yesterday? Did Mrs K. mind if he, Richard, said something nasty about Mr Evans; was he a friend of hers? (He had obviously seen Mrs K. go into the confectioner's shop on the previous day.) He thought that Mr Evans should not refuse to sell him sweets as he sometimes did—as long as he had any in the shop he should let Richard have some. But it really did not matter much because Mummy always managed to get some from Mr Evans. Suddenly Richard pointed out to Mrs K. the long red section 'which goes all through Mummy's empire'. He at once tried to take this back by saying, 'It is not Mummy's empire, it is just an empire where all of us have some countries.'

*Mrs K.* interpreted that he was afraid to realize that he meant it to be his mother's empire because this would mean that the red section pierced her inside.

Richard, looking at the drawing again, suggested that this red section looked 'like a genital'.

*Mrs K.* interpreted that he felt that with such a long genital he could take everything good which Mummy had received from Daddy out of her. He expressed this by his resentment about the cigarettes which Mrs K. received from Mr Evans and the sweets which Mummy had from him. They stood for the good penis, the delicious meat, which he felt Mummy contained; but he was afraid of injuring and robbing her, and that was why he did not wish to realize that the long red genital was going 'all through Mummy's empire' (Note III). This was also shown by the *Vampire* bumping into *Rodney*-Mummy at the beginning of the session and was linked with his fear of losing Mrs K. For if he took the *good* penis out of her (and Mummy), she was left with the monster, the Hitler-penis, in her inside and it would destroy her.

Richard had become more alive and interested after this interpretation. He looked at the drawing again and pointed out that the red section (which he had called a genital) divided the empire into two; in the west there were countries belonging to everybody; the part in the east did not contain anything of Mummy but only himself, Daddy, and Paul. In the west, Richard and Mummy had two countries each, and he was between Mummy, Paul, and Daddy.

*Mrs K.* pointed out that Richard's genital, the long red section, dominated the whole empire and was thrust into Mummy from top to bottom. The division of the empire also expressed his wish to keep the dangerous Daddy away from Mummy and to protect her against him; but it also meant that Mummy was divided into a bad Mother, the east, full of dangerous male genitals, and into a good and peaceful Mother. He had also shown these two sides of Mummy in the last sessions when his actual mother was the good Mummy, and the 'pig-sty' Mrs K., who he felt was injured and dying in London, was the bad one.

Richard replied to Mrs K.'s interpretation about the drawing that Mummy in the west was preparing to fight against the people in the east and would regain her countries there.

*Mrs K.* interpreted that he wished Mummy should win in the fight between the bad Daddy and Mummy in his own inside and in hers; but because he doubted whether she would win, he was so afraid of his mother's death and of Mrs K.'s death when she went to London.

Richard, when they were getting ready to go, was very slow in putting on his coat and clearly wished to stay longer. He also asked Mrs K. to leave the electric fire on until the very moment they went out of the door; he himself would switch it off. He said it was so much more lively when the fire was on.

*Mrs K.* interpreted that the fear of death—Mrs K.'s, Mummy's, his own—made him wish to leave the playroom alive as long as possible.

During the session Richard had only twice paid attention to passers-by. His persecutory fear was reduced and depressive anxiety had been predominant.

*Notes to Forty-first Session:*

I. It is of interest that the anxieties about my fate in London had increased his repression. Though his unconscious knowledge and phantasies about sexual intercourse and the birth of children had come up in the analysis, and had been interpreted to him and accepted by him, they now seemed to have been lost. (I am referring, for instance, to the play with the football, when the mother died as a result of sexual intercourse, and to the 'cock and hen' material when at times Mother, at times Father, was destroyed.)

II. Richard's response to this interpretation showed that, though it was lengthy and complicated, it met the need in him to have a number of aspects brought into relation to each other. This unconscious need derives from the urge to achieve synthesis.

III. This instance also exemplifies the contention, put forward in my *Psycho-Analysis of Children* (Chapter XII), that the impulses, and phantasies, in both sexes to attack the mother's body and rob it of its contents greatly contribute to feelings of guilt towards the mother and to disturbance in the relation to women. One aspect of homosexuality which has been stressed in connection with promiscuity is the desire to get hold of the man's penis inside the woman. Such desires derive from the earliest greedy relation to the mother's breast and her body which in the infant's mind contain the penis as well as babies.

# FORTY-SECOND SESSION (Thursday)

Richard was from the beginning in very close contact with Mrs K. He said he was going to make some drawings—at least five of them. . . . He told Mrs K. that a boy of his age was now staying at the hotel and worried him. The boy would not leave him alone, wanted to play with him, and was impudent to him. Mummy said something to the boy which made him go away.

*Mrs K.* asked him in what way the boy was impudent.

Richard seemed unable to explain this. Meanwhile he had been looking at some of the drawings, particularly 27. Then he began to draw 28 and asked whether Mrs K. could advise him what to do about the boy at the hotel who worried him so much.

*Mrs K.* interpreted that Richard had been looking at Drawing 27 when he told her about the boy at the hotel; and that the fight on the drawing between himself, Daddy, and Paul inside Mummy in the east had reminded him of the fight between himself and that boy. The hotel stood for Mummy's inside and the boy for Daddy's hostile genital attacking him.

During this interpretation Richard had taken one of the pencils into his mouth and was sucking and biting it. He said it was nice to suck.

*Mrs K.* interpreted that he not only wanted to suck it (standing for Daddy's or Paul's penis), but to bite it off and eat it, and then he felt that inside himself the good penis turned into the octopus, into the bad, dangerous penis. That again made him all the more keen to eat the *delicious* meat of the monster, the good penis (Note

I). It was delicious while he was eating it, but the monster was felt to be an enemy inside. On the previous day, the long red section—the big genital—which he had taken away from Daddy and thrust into Mummy's and Mrs K.'s inside, was also used to take the good penis and all the good things out of her. The sweets which Mr Evans had given to Mummy, and the cigarettes he had given to Mrs K., stood for that good penis which Richard wanted to get hold of. Mrs K. then pointed to Drawing 26, about which he had not said anything. She suggested that she, as the 'pig-sty' Mummy, injured and dead, was represented on the left-hand side because there was hardly anything of Mummy to be seen there; but when he coloured the red sections he had spoken of the Russians, the Reds, and it had turned out that he also meant himself. He was destructive —the vampire—robbing Mummy of everything good she contained. At the same time he was, together with the bad Hitler-Daddy and the dangerous Paul, thrusting into Mummy, soiling, and destroying her. But on the right-hand side of that drawing the light-blue Mother, with plenty of countries, was alone with him as he had been with his actual Mummy while Mrs K., being the injured and soiled Mummy, was in London [Splitting the Mother figure into the good and bad one].

Richard apparently did not pay any attention to this interpretation. He went on making Drawing 28. He told Mrs K. that he had seen a swan with four 'sweet' cygnets. When he finished this drawing, he did not comment on it and started another (Drawing 29). He first drew the two ships, then the large fish and some of the little ones around it, became more and more eager, and filled in the space with baby fishes. Then he pointed out to Mrs K. that one of the baby fishes was covered by a fin of the Mummy fish and said, 'This is the youngest baby.'

*Mrs K.* interpreted that the drawing seemed to show that the baby fish was being fed by the mother. She also asked whether Richard himself was among the little fishes.

Richard said no, and he did not know where he was. He also said that the starfish between the plants was a grown-up person and the smaller starfish was a half-grown person; it was Paul some time ago. Then he found with surprise that he had named the ship *Rodney* and said, 'But that is Mummy.'

*Mrs K.* asked him who was the *Sunfish*.

Richard said he did not know, but pointed out that the *Sunfish's* periscope was 'sticking into *Rodney*'.

*Mrs K.* interpreted that the *Sunfish* might represent Daddy, as did the grown-up starfish who was between the plants. But the *Sunfish* also stood for Richard when he took away Daddy's genital and made himself into an adult. As an adult he would be able to give Mummy babies, and these were the five drawings which he had said, at the beginning of the session, he would make. The swan and the four 'sweet' cygnets were also babies which he wished to give to Mrs K. In this drawing he had become the father, the *Sunfish*, which was the biggest ship—even bigger than *Rodney*-Mummy. At the same time he was sorry for Daddy and wanted to make reparation by putting the 'grown-up' starfish-Daddy between the plants and making him into a gratified child [Reversal] (Note II).

Richard said that the plane on top was British and was patrolling; he did not know whom it represented.

*Mrs K.* suggested that the patrolling plane represented Daddy watching him when he wished to have sexual relations with Mummy—the periscope sticking into *Rodney*. But this fear was also connected with Richard's desire to watch Daddy while he had sexual intercourse with Mummy.

Richard took the blue and the red crayons and stood them up side by side on the table. Then the black one was made to march towards them and was driven off by the red, while the blue crayon drove off the purple one.

*Mrs K.* pointed out that his suspicion of the hostile Daddy was shown by his play with the crayons. The red one represented himself, the blue one Mummy, and both of them were driving off Daddy and Paul.

Richard was very dreamy and in thought.

*Mrs K.* asked what he was thinking about.

Richard said he was thinking about seeing a model railway at a school fête he was going to that afternoon with Mummy.

*Mrs K.* interpreted that the model railway was Daddy's admired and potent genital. He had been sucking the yellow pencil while he was silent and in thought, and this meant that he had been taking this admired genital into himself. . . .

Richard got up and went into the garden. He said he wanted to climb mountains. . . . He remarked on the clouds in the sky and wondered whether a dangerous storm was gathering. On such days he felt sorry for the mountains, which have a bad time when a storm breaks over them.

*Mrs K.* interpreted that his wish to climb mountains expressed his desire to have sexual relations with his mother (Note III), but he at once became afraid of the bad Daddy who would attack and punish him—the storm which would break over the mountains. Mrs K. reminded him that he had asked her whether there had been a thunderstorm while she was in London, and this was linked with his fear of Hitler bombs dropping on her. . . .

Richard went back into the house and suggested that they should play with the fleet, but not do any work. He allocated one ship to Mrs K. and one to himself. Mrs K. was going on a pleasure trip in her ship, and so was he on his. At first he went away from her but soon brought his ship quite close to Mrs K.'s.

*Mrs K.* pointed out that this touching of ships had repeatedly expressed sexual relations. This he tried to avoid by going away from Mrs K., but soon returned. He wished to have sexual intercourse with her; but even more he wanted to be sure that in the future he would be potent. The five drawings which he had said he was going to give her represented himself (the swan) giving her, or rather Mummy, four children, the cygnets. There were also the many babies on the drawing which he had given to the Mummy fish. He wanted Mrs K. to play with him but not to interpret, and this expressed his wish to be loved by Mrs K. as he was by Mummy, and also his wish not to know about what he had often called 'these unpleasant thoughts'.

Before leaving, Richard again said he wanted to switch off the fire himself, and to do so just before they went.[1]

*Notes to Forty-second Session:*

I. The desire to incorporate a good penis is a strong impetus towards homosexuality. The good penis is to counteract the persecutory internal one. But if the anxieties about the internal persecutors are very strong, the inside is felt to be a bad place, in which nothing remains good. The obsessional need to counteract these internal anxieties persists and remains a factor in homosexuality (cf. *Psycho-Analysis of Children*, Chapter XII).

II. Reversal is a very important mechanism in mental life. The young child, feeling frustrated, deprived, envious, or jealous, expresses hate and feelings of envy by omnipotently reversing the situation so that he will be adult and the parents neglected. In Richard's material in this session reversal is used in a different way. Richard puts himself into his father's place; but in order to avoid destroying the father, he changes him into a child and even into a gratified child. This form of reversal is more influenced by love feelings.

III. The desire for sexual intercourse, combined with jealousy and hate against the father—that is to say, the full manifestations of the Œdipus complex—does not really imply that a child of this age (if not

[1] On that day I had received a letter from Richard's mother that there was a great improvement in Richard which had been maintained all through the holiday and was very noticeable to his father as well as to herself.

seduced by an adult) would actually wish to carry out sexual intercourse. Both in girls and boys such a situation would lead to great
anxiety. What the desire consists in is rather that the phantasies of
being able to have sexual relations should not be too repressed. This
links with the hope that such gratifications will be possible in the
future.


## FORTY-THIRD SESSION (Friday)

Richard met Mrs K. outside the playroom. When in the room,
he at once asked for the drawings and looked at 27 which he had
made on the previous day. He put out his fleet in battle order and
spoke proudly of the 'grand fleet'. . . . He was very pleased with the
R.A.F., which had again 'battered' Germany, and also said that
Russia seemed to be doing well. He arranged the destroyers in one
line in the centre, followed by the submarines; the cruisers, *Nelson*
and *Rodney*, were on the right and left of the destroyers. Looking
at Mrs K., he said that he was very fond of her, he liked her eyes
very much.

*Mrs K.* interpreted that she had again come to stand for the good
Mummy because his fear—which had been so strong in the last
few days—of her injured and horrible inside, the 'pig-sty' Mummy,
had diminished (Note I). Mrs K. also referred to what she had said
yesterday about Drawing 27.

Richard now looked with great interest at this drawing, while on
the previous day he had appeared not to listen to Mrs K.'s interpretation of it. He pointed out that to the left the people were acually
fairly equal and to the right there was plenty of the light-blue
Mummy. Richard was surrounding her, but a little of Paul had also
entered. Then he remarked that in the middle she was full of the
dangerous Hitler-Daddy and of himself (who, as Mrs K. had reminded him, was also the suspect Russians).

*Mrs K.* pointed out that the 'grand fleet' was himself, having the
whole family inside and controlling them. He had now separated
the parents. Therefore there could be no sexual intercourse and no
fight. They were supposed to guard and protect him, being on his
right and left, but also to be commanded by him. Mrs K. reminded
him that on the previous day he had shown, by sucking and biting
the pencil and in other ways, that he felt he had eaten up Daddy's
penis—the delicious meat of the monster; but this implied also that
he could take in his parents and the whole family in a less frighten-

ing way. In his play just now he had done this by keeping them under control.

Richard rearranged the fleet to form one long line with the smallest ship in front. He knelt, half closed his eyes, and carefully checked that the row of ships was quite straight.

*Mrs K.* reminded him of how he had said to Mummy that he was worried about sexual intercourse and that he would never want to do it. One of the reasons was that he felt he would not be capable of it because his penis was too small, not straight and strong enough (Note II). Now the whole fleet stood for his penis, which was made up from Daddy's, Paul's, and other people's genitals—the various ships—and all under his command. When he looked so carefully at the fleet this also meant that he was investigating his own inside and tried to find out whether the people whom he felt he had taken into himself were actually helping him and strengthening his penis or injuring it and persecuting him.

Richard began Drawing 30. Meanwhile he pointed out that his enemies, in particular the red-haired girl, were passing the playroom, and spoke of them as 'these lumps of impudence'. He watched them from behind the curtain, but did not seem frightened and soon went back to his drawing. He told Mrs K. that the fat woman assistant at Mr Evans's shop had sold him plenty of sweets but had asked him to keep it secret. . . . While colouring the blue sections, Richard sang the National Anthem and explained that Mummy was the queen and he was the king. When he had finished the drawing, he looked at it and told Mrs K. that there was 'plenty of Mummy' and of himself in it, and that they 'could really beat Daddy'. He showed Mrs K. that there was little of the German (black) Daddy there. While colouring the purple sections, Richard sang the Norwegian and Belgian anthems and said, 'He's all right.'

*Mrs K.* interpreted that Richard, being the king, had now become Mummy's husband; Paul, the purple, was 'all right', but he had become a baby. There were four babies there, the sections being so much smaller than usual. This corresponded to the previous day's drawing when, after speaking about the four cygnets he had seen and saying that he would give Mrs K. five drawings, he surrounded the fish Mummy with many babies. In the present drawing Mummy also had good babies which Richard had given her; he could only do that by changing his father and brother into children. At the bottom of the drawing, though, Daddy's genital was represented, because Richard felt that whatever he did he could not exclude it from Mummy's inside.

Richard went on singing other anthems as well and then sang melodies by great composers, asking Mrs K. which of them she knew. He also said that his mother played the piano. He told Mrs K. that he used to have music lessons but had now given them up, though he had been doing quite well; his mother had given him the fleet which he liked so much as a reward for passing a music examination.

*Mrs K.* interpreted that he might have given up music because he felt he would never be able to compete with the great composers —the ideal father. But because the fleet had come to him from his mother as a reward for his piano-playing, he was particularly fond of it. Now the fleet was an important part of his work with Mrs K. and, like the drawings, meant giving something to her, which also meant being potent and giving her children.

Richard again began to sing; he seemed happy and his eyes were moist. . . . He went out into the garden to look at the hills and, as so often, admired the view. The sun was shining, which always had an influence on his mood. He came back into the house and again sang various tunes, but he interrupted himself to tell Mrs K. that there was such a sweet little puppy at the hotel, a scotch terrier, four months old. It was so funny—it tried to catch its own tail and turned round and round itself.

*Mrs K.* interpreted that the tunes which he felt he was sharing with her (and with Mummy) also stood for good babies whom he contained and could produce; and that harmony meant to him that the people he had taken into himself were at peace and happy together. In the drawing in which he was king and Mummy was queen, they had nice babies; there was only a little of the 'bad black' there. This was also why he felt more confident about the war and less worried about Russia as an ally.

Another passer-by who attracted Richard's attention during this session was an old, neglected-looking woman. Richard said that she was horrid and that she 'spat out some awful yellow stuff'. Apart from this, he paid little attention to people on the road.

When getting ready to leave, Richard was still singing, and he put his arm lightly round Mrs K.'s shoulder, saying, 'I am very happy and I am very fond of you.'

*Notes to Forty-third Session:*

I. It is important from the point of view of technique that in the transference the change from a very injured and bad object to a good one had come about by the consistent interpretation of his anxieties. After my return from London he was unable, as I have described, even to look at me. The whole material indicated how injured and bad I had become to him. These anxieties were traced back to the primary aggressive feelings towards both parents and the resulting fears of having injured them irreparably. It is my experience that this is the only way of diminishing anxieties at their root and thus helping the patient to gain trust both in himself and in his objects. Attempts to bring about a positive transference by neglecting the analysis of the negative one cannot, I believe, achieve lasting results.

II. In analysing children we find their genital desires and sensations active, but at the same time it is important to consider their fear of being impotent in the future; this fear extends in many directions and inhibits sublimations. Less neurotic children have more confidence in themselves and therefore are more able to realize that they will grow up into men or women. With neurotic—and still more psychotic— patients, this feeling is not sufficiently strong and their early doubts in their fertility or potency persist even when they are grown up. This may contribute to impotence or restricted potency in men, and to frigidity or even sterility in women. The fear in the boy of being impotent, and in the girl of being unable to bear children, is closely connected with anxieties relating to the inside of the body. Whether or not they have taken in good objects which would enhance their trust in themselves and thus support their activities, or whether they feel persecuted from within and their internalized objects are grudging and envious, had a decisive influence on the development of their genitality as well as on their sublimations.

## FORTY-FOURTH SESSION (Saturday)

Richard's mother met Mrs K. and told her that Richard had a sore throat and that he was in bed, with a very slight temperature. She added that he had recently been even more worried about physical illness than previously. Mrs K. suggested that since the weather was fine it would do him no harm to come and she would wait for him.

Richard looked anxious and pale when he came. He had asked his mother to bring him to the door and also made her promise that she would fetch him. He said, 'In any case I've got the fleet with me,' put it on the table, and remained silent. His mood was totally different from that of the previous day—he was listless and depressed, and avoided looking at Mrs K. He told her that he had not wanted to get out of bed, and added that he really would have liked to stay in bed and read and read and would have liked Mrs K. to come and see him there.

*Mrs K.* asked him how he felt now.

Richard replied that his throat was hot but he had no pain. He added that he felt he had some poison behind his nose. When saying this he looked very dejected and anxious.

*Mrs K.* asked him where the poison had come from.

Richard said hesitantly he thought Cook and Bessie were poisoning him. He repeated that though his throat did not hurt, it was hot and red. While saying this he took up one of the 'larger' destroyers, knelt down, and looked at it in the same manner as he had done on the previous day with the line of ships. . . . He moved the ships about in an uncertain and listless way.

*Mrs K.* interpreted that he was looking at the ship in the same way as he had done yesterday, which seemed to show that he was afraid that his penis might after all not be straight—that it was injured; his throat being hot and red might connect with his fear that when he rubbed his penis he injured it. Recently, and particularly in the previous session, his sexual desires and his wish to give Mrs K. and Mummy babies had come up more strongly and he had now become very frightened about that.

Richard asked whether he was likely to give Mrs K. his cold?

*Mrs K.* interpreted that he was afraid of infecting and poisoning her, not only with his cold but because he now felt that his penis was poisonous, like the poisonous toadstools which he had recently destroyed.

Richard said again that he would have liked Mrs K. to come and see him in his room.

*Mrs K.* reminded him that after her return from London he had told her he wanted to be Mummy's chick, which actually meant being cuddled and looked after like a baby. Yesterday he had strongly felt his wish to be a man with Mrs K. and Mummy, and to give them babies. He had become very frightened of this desire and fell ill because he wanted to turn himself again into a baby; this was why he wanted attention while he was in bed. He also did not wish to hear about his genital desires, and therefore did not want to do work but wanted Mrs K. to come and see him in bed and look after him as Mummy did (Note I).

Meanwhile Richard had returned to the fleet. He moved *Nelson* away. After a while he did the same with *Rodney*, and the two met and touched each other. Then Richard put them farther away behind Mrs K.'s bag and said they were hiding there.

*Mrs K.* asked why they were hiding. When Richard did not answer, she suggested that possibly when Daddy and Mummy went to bed and had sexual intercourse they had to hide from their sons. She also suggested that, because he felt he was going to attack his parents when they were together, he was afraid that Daddy would attack him if he went to bed with Mummy.

Richard replied that he was now actually sleeping in the same room with Mummy at the hotel, and that he liked that very much.[1] ... He first brought *Nelson* back and made him inspect and patrol the fleet, and then *Rodney* did the same; but they were kept separate. Suddenly the destroyer which he had so closely examined a little earlier was blown up. He said it was the *Prinz Eugen* being attacked by the British.

*Mrs K.* interpreted that the *Prinz Eugen* had been standing for himself fighting alone and also for his genital, which would be destroyed by Daddy if he found out Richard's wish to have sexual intercourse with Mummy; if Daddy found Richard's genital inside Mummy, Daddy's genital would fight his. But he was particularly afraid of Daddy retaliating because of Richard's attacks on him. He had shown in his play that his parents were hiding because Daddy expected an attack by him.

Richard got up, intending to go outside, but did not, because he noticed two men standing on the other side of the road, talking to each other. He hid behind the door and watched them, and said that he was spying on them and they were spying on him. He went back to the table and began to draw (Drawing 31). The first thing he did was to get hold of the black and purple crayons, saying, 'These are the nasty Daddy and Paul.'

*Mrs K.* interpreted that the two men, as well as the black and purple crayons, stood for the frightening Daddy and Paul who would attack him because he now slept alone with Mummy and was suspected of wishing, or even of having, sexual relations with her. They also stood for the suspect Mr K. and Mrs K.'s son. Richard had said that he was spying on the men, and she suggested that this was the reason why he also felt that they were spying on him. When he was jealous and curious about the sexual relation of his parents, he expected Daddy and even Paul to watch him or to guess his thoughts and felt very suspicious of them as well as of Mummy. He suspected his parents of uniting against him because he spied on them and wished to disturb them in their sexual intercourse. At present he also felt that the 'grumpy old gentleman' and John were watching his relations with Mrs K., since he was so keen to know about their relations with her. . . .

Richard had been humming the British anthem while filling in some sections with blue and red, and went on humming something else. When Mrs K. asked what the tune was, Richard replied it was

---

[1] I had advised Richard's mother against that, but was told by her that owing to war circumstances she could not get two rooms.

a song about 'My darling'; he was thinking of Mummy. Then he showed Mrs K. that on the drawing he and Mummy had encircled the little Paul. But Daddy was also close to Mummy; Paul too was touching her and was even cutting through Richard. While saying this, Richard put the yellow pencil into his mouth, first sucking it; but he suddenly pushed it further into his mouth, nearly into his throat.

*Mrs K.* interpreted his fear of having eaten up the penises of the dangerous Daddy and Paul, and of their spying on him and fighting and poisoning him in his inside. He had said at the beginning of the session that his feeling of having poison behind his nose might come from Cook and Bessie wanting to poison him; but it had turned out that he was afraid of being attacked by the hostile and spying parents—the Hitler-parents, Mrs K. and the foreign husband—or by Daddy and Paul who might also fight between themselves or unite against him. The monster which had delicious meat had formerly turned into a dangerous enemy inside. All the more he would cling to the belief that Daddy had a good penis as well, which Richard could take in and which would help him; and he also held on to the feeling that Mummy was always good and would protect him against all the dangers outside and in his inside [Idealization as a corollary to persecution]. He was also afraid that the sore throat would prevent his being analysed—in other words, that his internal enemies would cut him off from Mrs K. who often stood for the good Mummy.

Richard put his finger very deeply into his mouth and appeared extremely frightened. He said he was looking for germs; he was sure to have some.

*Mrs K.* interpreted that the germs were also meant to be Germans—enemies—poisoning him. She reminded him of his 'red-hot throat' which meant a fight with poisonous enemies going on inside him. . . .

Richard had got up, walked about, stumbled over a stool, and kicked it hard. He looked at Mrs K. in a knowing way (indicating that he understood what he was doing).

*Mrs K.* interpreted that Richard would like to kick out of himself Daddy's hostile penis.

Richard said that he felt his 'mucus was running down into his stomach'. He added that it would worry him very much if he were sick in the playroom, but he could not say why this should worry him so much.

*Mrs K.* interpreted his need to vomit out the fighting parents and all the bad things which she had just interpreted. But he was afraid of harming and soiling Mrs K. with all this poison because, if she were poisoned, there would be no good Mummy left.

Richard had been drawing (32). He said it was the same empire as Drawing 31. Then he started another drawing, putting *Nelson* on the paper, drawing its outline and shading it in.

*Mrs K.* interpreted his wish to know exactly about the internal Daddy and his genital because he was so uncertain about what was going on inside himself. The copying of the *Nelson* also expressed his wish to possess Daddy's genital.

Richard asked whether he could take this drawing home, but then decided he would rather have two empty sheets on which to draw at home.

*Mrs K.* interpreted that the two white pieces of paper also stood for her breasts which were to protect him against his internal and external enemies.

Towards the end of this session Richard had been humming more loudly and had become altogether much more lively. The colour had come back to his face and his eyes were brighter. He said he felt a little better and hoped that he would be able to come the following day.

*Note to Forty-fourth Session:*

I. I have often seen in adults that there was a deep longing to be a child and be looked after, which had very early on been repressed. Dissatisfaction with the breast or the mother, fear of destructive impulses towards her, and the ensuing guilt and depression often increase the normal wish to grow up and might even lead to a precocious independence. When in the analysis this repressed desire to be a baby or a young child reappears, it is frequently linked with intense greed and the need to have the analyst (representing the mother) constantly available, which also means that she should always be internally at the patient's disposal. There is a strong depressive feeling of loss connected with this premature independence, because something which to the adult appears to be irreplaceable has not been made sufficient use of.

# FORTY-FIFTH SESSION (Sunday)

Mrs K. met Richard on the road. He looked quite changed—had more colour in his face, did not seem worried, and was talkative and lively. He told Mrs K. at once that he felt much better, his throat was not hurting any more (Note I). In the playroom he said that in the morning when he woke up he had been very hungry, had actually felt sick with hunger; his stomach had been quite thin and small, drawn in, and the big bones in his stomach had been sticking out. After breakfast he had felt quite all right. He described in detail that the shredded wheat which he had eaten was delicious and how he had munched it up.

*Mrs K.* interpreted that the big bones in his stomach represented the eaten-up enemies, particularly the bad father—the octopus and the monster. She also reminded him of his fears of being spied upon and poisoned by the bad parents and Paul. Therefore his thin and weak stomach meant his inside, unprotected and weak and full of persecutors. The good food which strengthened him represented the good light-blue Mummy protecting and restoring him. Mrs K. reminded him that a few days ago he had compared shredded wheat with a bird's nest and that she had interpreted that it stood for the good mother and her breast.[1]

Richard had been looking round in the playroom and was smiling happily. He remarked that the playroom was not so 'smelly' today as it had been yesterday, and looked much nicer. Yesterday it had been very smelly and awful. He said he had not brought the fleet—he wanted to draw. . . . Mummy had been lovely yesterday; she had bought two books for him and gave him some paints. Looking at Mrs K., he asked what her coat and frock were made of—from a distance they looked as if they were made of silver; they were beautiful and so were her shoes. Had she had her hair done recently? Had she just washed it, because it looked so different, it was so beautiful as if it were made of silver.

*Mrs K.* interpreted that he seemed to feel that his internal world had improved, and therefore the external world, particularly Mummy and Mrs K. and their clothes, appeared to be beautiful. She reminded him that on the previous day he had had very different feelings about her and the playroom. The playroom then stood for Mrs K. and for his own inside containing the dirty, poisoned, and poisonous Mummy; he had even avoided looking at the playroom or at Mrs K. They had both turned into that 'horrid' old woman spitting out 'awful yellow stuff' (Forty-third Session) whom he had watched from the window on the day before his trouble in his throat, and who represented the soiled, poisoned, and injured Mrs K. It seemed that because he had begun to realize his fears about his enemies—particularly about his internal enemies and their poisoning him—he felt less frightened of them and therefore also found the external people and things much better. But even when he had been so frightened about these internal dangers, he

[1] Like a number of his associations, this remark had remained unrecorded.

had tried to hold on to his real Mummy as the light-blue Mummy, whereas Mrs K. had become very bad [Splitting of the mother into good and bad].

Richard said that on the previous day the room had seemed to be dead. He then drew at random and said these were the figures 1, 2, 3, 4, 5, 6, all linked together. Then he made Drawing 33, colouring first the blue part, and said that he, Mummy, Daddy, and Paul were quite peacefully together. When he finished the drawing he said that most of it belonged to Mummy and to him. There was little of Paul and Daddy in between, and they did not do any harm.

*Mrs K.* interpreted that on the lower part of the drawing the different people were not thrust into each other. In earlier drawings thrusting had often stood for pushing dangerous genitals into one another (Note II). Therefore the present arrangement indicated that there was no fighting between the men in the family. Also, in the drawing Daddy was not as black as usual, and both he and Paul were small which meant that they were babies and that now Richard and Mummy were the parents, as recently (Drawing 30) he and Mummy had been king and queen and Daddy and Paul had been babies. Also in the present drawing Richard's big red genital was on top of everything. Peace was therefore achieved by his changing places with his father [Reversal]. Whenever he was afraid of Daddy and Paul—because he wished to attack them— Mummy was also in danger. Now he kept Mummy safe by making Daddy and Paul into babies without fighting them. Mrs K. also pointed out that the shape of the drawing was oblong.

Richard replied without hesitation, 'It is an octopus.'

*Mrs K.* reminded him of the fears expressed on the previous day and suggested that between yesterday and today he had felt that his inside had improved. Nevertheless, he still feared that he contained the octopus and that made him into an octopus,[1] for the drawing represented not only Mummy's inside but also his own. Mrs K. pointed out, moreover, that while she was interpreting he had been sucking the yellow pencil which had often stood for Daddy's genital; even when it was felt to be desirable, like the 'delicious meat' of the monster, it was liable to change into an octopus as soon as it had become part of his inside. This anxiety had lessened, but nevertheless still existed. He had attempted to deal with this by dividing the good part of Mummy from the bad one. Therefore on the previous day the left side of Drawing 31 was all light blue, while the fighting went on on the right side. In today's drawing there was

[1] This is another instance of the variety of unconscious situations, some of them entirely contradictory, which are, I think, often experienced simultaneously.

no such strong division and the genitals were not thrusting into one another, but he still was afraid of the octopus inside himself.

Richard now looked with interest at Drawings 31 and 32. He pointed out that in 32 Paul was small and had a bit in Richard, but Richard had a long bit pointing into Daddy, and Daddy was very close to Mummy.

*Mrs K.* interpreted that on the right-hand side of that drawing Richard was small and surrounded by Daddy and Mummy; in the same way, Paul was surrounded on the left-hand side, as he had shown her.

Richard then added, pointing at Drawing 31, 'It looks like a bird and a very horrid one.' The light blue on top was a crown, the purple bit was the eye, and the beak was 'wide open'. While saying this he again had the pencil in his mouth and was biting it.

*Mrs K.* pointed out to him what he was doing with the pencil and interpreted that the light-blue crown represented the crown of the light-blue Mummy who had recently been the queen; that he had been singing the national anthem when he drew it, and that nevertheless this was part of a horrid bird with the wide-open beak, which was the other aspect of Mummy. But partly the beak also represented Richard and his genital, and Paul and his genital, as was shown by the colours, red and purple. His penis, when it was thrusting and piercing, was also meant to be biting and eating. All that, he felt, was part of the horrid bird-Mummy, who therefore had became as greedy and dangerous as he felt himself to be.

Richard repeatedly said that the bird looked horrid and, glancing at Drawing 32 again, he commented that it, too, looked like a bird, but without a head. The black at the bottom was 'big job' dropping out of it, and that was also 'horrid'.

*Mrs K.* interpreted that Drawing 32 stood for his mutilated inside and for his genital having been cut off. This was what he had felt his inside was like yesterday, when he had the cold. She also reminded him that in the previous session he had said that the two empires were the same and this meant that Drawing 32 represented himself after he had devoured the 'horrid' bird and therefore felt he had become like it. In his mind he had eaten up his mother as a destructive and devouring person. In eating the shredded wheat which he said was like a bird's nest, he had felt that he took into himself the good Mummy who was protecting him against the internal bad Daddy (the bones in his stomach). This showed that when he was more frightened, the bad internal Mummy became more powerful; nevertheless, he also believed in the good Mummy inside him. He felt that the horrid bird-Mummy had allied herself with the monster-Daddy, and these frightening united parents were attacking him from inside and eating him up, as well as attacking him from outside and cutting off his genital (Note III).

Richard had begun another drawing : on top of the dividing line there was a ship with a big British flag and two funnels whose smoke lines were meeting. He wrote 'Atlantic convoy' across the top. Beneath the line there was a fish, three starfishes, and a U-boat which was firing a torpedo. At the bottom of the page were the usual two plants. Richard removed the pencil, which he had just again put into his mouth. He intended to show with the pencil the direction of the torpedo, but brought it so near to Mrs K. that it almost touched her genital region. He explained that the fish was silly not to get out of the way because it might be hurt. The starfishes were trying to intercept the torpedo. The convoy carried goods.

*Mrs K.* interpreted that the U-boat seemed to be Richard, hostile to both parents; but since they were also the ones who gave him good things (the goods), he felt guilty. In attacking the bad Daddy, he tried to ignore that Daddy was also good to him.

Richard very strongly affirmed that Daddy was actually very good and kind.

*Mrs K.* interpreted that when Richard in his mind attacked his parents in sexual intercourse, he was afraid of injuring the good Mummy as well and therefore he feared that Mrs K. and the play-room were dead. The 'silly' fish-Mummy meant that she should not have gone to bed with Daddy and exposed herself to Richard's anger and hatred. The horrid black 'big job' which was dropping out of the mutilated bird (Drawing 32) represented his torpedoes. Mrs K. also suggested that the intercepting starfishes stood for the good Daddy, Paul, and Richard, who tried to protect Mummy.

Richard had asked, while drawing the convoy torpedoed by the U-boat, whether Mrs K. did not get tired of her work.

*Mrs K.* interpreted that he had asked this when he bombed the convoy which was bringing goods. This meant that the help which he felt Mrs K. was giving him in his analysis was like the help, love, and milk he was given as a baby. He had felt that he had exhausted Mummy and attacked her, and now he was afraid not only of tiring but of actually exhausting and attacking Mrs K. He had also almost touched her with the pencil when he spoke of the torpedo bombing the convoy.

Richard went on drawing after Mrs K.'s interpretations and seemed to agree with them ; then he looked at the last drawing, put it aside, and said he would not finish it (by which he meant he would not colour it). He went out of the room to watch an aeroplane and said it was not a fighter but he did not know what else it could be; it was going to fly away over the hills. . . . He showed Mrs K. the place in the garden where he had stamped on the 'poisonous toadstools' some days ago. He pulled out some weeds and said he wanted to tell Mrs K. something about a dream he had had which was very sad, and he also felt very sad. Back in the playroom he began to draw. He drew a house and said it was their home (in 'Z') which they had left when the war broke out. The shape on the right was Oliver's house. At the bottom (indicated by a few lines) was the rose-garden and other parts of the garden. He made a dot to show the point on the wall where the bomb had fallen. A square near by was the greenhouse which had been destroyed. Leading up from the roses to the left he drew a path. On the first floor were his parents' bedroom and to the left his room; on the ground floor the drawing-room, which was little used, and to the right the lounge which was much used. Richard said he liked best the lounge and his bedroom, and he put circles round these windows. He liked his room so much because of his electric train which he missed very much and wished it could have been brought to their present house (in 'Y'). He described the train in detail, with strong feelings of affection. The engine was streamlined, and there was a good stock of goods trucks and passenger carriages. He was very careful about this train and very angry when it was once damaged. The automatic control went wrong because Daddy had left the electricity on and the engine and tender were damaged.

*Mrs K.* interpreted that the goods trucks and the convoy, which on the previous drawing was torpedoed, stood for the good parents. She suggested that the various carriages of his train also represented the family, with Daddy at its head (the engine), and all the pleasant memories of his past were linked with the train and his house. Then Mrs K. asked about the dream.

Richard was very reluctant to speak about it. He said only: 'We were back in our old house.'

*Mrs K.* asked whom he meant by 'we'.

Richard said he and Mummy, and there was also an aunt. In the dream she was living at their house with them. After a pause he said that Mummy had told him that even after the war they would not go back to their old home because she preferred living in the country. Richard was very sad because he loved their house, his room, the lounge, his train—all of it. He had told Mummy that if she did not go back, he would go back by himself and live in the house.

*Mrs K.* interpreted that the now unprotected, deserted house stood for Mummy, left alone at night and unprotected against the tramp-Daddy, and also for Mrs K. when she was in London and exposed to Hitler's bombs. By going back alone to the old house he would leave the healthy Mummy in the country and stay with and protect the injured Mummy. But in the fleet play he had repeatedly shown that he was also worried that Daddy would be deserted if Richard took Mummy away from him. Now that Richard again slept in the same room with Mummy, and Daddy was left alone, he felt that Daddy was thrown out and lonely and that Richard should join him in the old house.

Richard, while Mrs K. had been interpreting his wish to protect the injured Mummy, had been glancing at the earlier drawings. He picked out Drawing 14 and said, with a telling look at Mrs K., 'This is the worst of all.'

*Mrs K.* reminded him that this drawing had represented his injured and bleeding inside, containing the injured and bleeding Mummy.

Richard, after this interpretation, went outside to look at the hills.

Earlier during this session Richard had asked Mrs K. to listen to the singing of the birds. He had added, under his breath and with humid eyes, 'How lovely, I do love this.'

*Mrs K.* had interpreted that the birds and their singing stood for good babies, a good inside, as well as the external world being friendly.

At another point, while Mrs K. was interpreting his attacks, Richard had scribbled on a page and violently made some dots; he asked Mrs K. whether she minded his scribbling.

*Mrs K.* interpreted that the scribbling and the dots stood for his bombing with his fæces.

Richard then drew on the same page a little figure, scribbled over it, made dots on it, and said this was Hitler and he was bombing and killing him.

*Mrs K.* pointed out that when he attacked the Hitler-Daddy he feared he was injuring the good Daddy and Mummy, and now Mrs K., and that was why he asked whether she minded his scribbling. . . .

Richard had been throwing the little stools about; he picked up two of them, threw them on the floor and said, 'These are bombs.' Then he picked up one of the stools which had a furry top and which he liked very much, caressed it, and hugged it.

*Mrs K.* interpreted that the furry top seemed to stand for Daddy's desired genital, which had hair round it, and that he would be sorry to have destroyed it; yet at the same time he wished to bomb it.

Richard replied that he knew Daddy had hair under his arms, but did not know that he also had it round his genital. Glancing at

Mrs K., he added that of course mothers would know this from their sons.

*Mrs K.* interpreted Richard's jealousy about her relation to her husband; he seemed to deny that she and Mummy had anything to do with their husbands' genitals. The light-blue Mummy was to be separated from the tramp-Daddy because he was dangerous, but she was also to be separated from him because Richard was jealous.

During this session Richard paid much more attention to passers-by, mainly children, and he also asked Mrs K. to look and tell him who was going along the road, while he went on drawing. His greater interest in people was in keeping with the material of this session, which was focused on external situations. This was also reflected in his feelings about the lost home and all it implied as regards his early experiences. In the previous session he had been mainly concerned with internal situations (particularly the poison behind his nose, the internal bad figures, his hypochondriacal anxieties).

On the road, Richard said how happy he was about the sun shining. His shoes, too, were shining like gold—no, not quite like gold, but they were shining. It is clear that, together with less persecutory and stronger depressive anxiety, he had also used manic defence during this session.

*Notes to Forty-fifth Session:*

I. The improvement which Richard was reporting consisted not only in a lessening of his hypochondriacal anxiety, but in a disappearance of an actual physical symptom. Considering that this child had been suffering since early infancy from colds, it is interesting to see how psychological factors contributed to these colds. It seems likely that without analysis he might at this point actually have developed a sore throat. Another more general consideration enters here. In my experience, hypochondria, which was very strong in Richard, is not necessarily a preoccupation with non-existent symptoms but can develop around actual physical symptoms by exaggerating and distorting their significance. The question arises whether such symptoms in hypochondriacal people are largely the result of their hypochondriacal anxieties. This would imply a connection between hysterical symptoms and hypochondria, a connection which I have repeatedly suggested (cf. *The Psycho-Analysis of Children*, and 'Some Theoretical Conclusions Regarding the Emotional Life of the Infant', 1952, *Writings*, 3).

II. The recent changes in Richard's material show a greater capacity for ego-integration and synthesis of objects, which was due to a diminution of anxiety relating to internal dangers. However, the process of integration in itself arouses anxieties; for instance, the destructive part of the self may be felt to be endangering the other parts of the self, as well as the object, which may be either destroyed or (by projection) turned into a bad object. For instance, when some integration had occurred, the bird with the crown representing the mother (Drawing 31) had turned into a devouring, horrid object dropping fæces. When trust in one's loving impulses increases—and this goes hand in hand with a lessening of persecutory anxiety relating to internal dangers—integration stirs up fewer anxieties. Furthermore, progress in integration and synthesis implies that parts of the object and of the self come together in a constructive way, whereas it is a failure in this process if, under the urge to diminish splitting, they are brought together in a chaotic way which increases confusion (see my paper, 'A Contribution to the Psychogenesis of Manic-Depressive States', 1935, *Writings*, 1, and 'On Some Schizoid Mechanisms', 1946, *Writings*, 3; also H. Rosenfeld's 'Notes on the Psychopathology of Confusional States in Chronic Schizophrenia', 1950, in his *Psychotic States*, Hogarth, 1965). More successful synthesis and integration were expressed at the bottom of Drawing 33; Richard's internal objects were brought together in a peaceful way, and that linked with the violence of projective identification being lessened; this was why the coloured sections (representing himself and his family) were, in Drawing 33, no longer penetrating into one another. The greater capacity for integration and synthesis was clearly linked with diminution of anxiety, in particular less fear of internalized persecutors and their poisoning him, as well as of his poisoning them.

It is significant that for the first time in his analysis Richard experienced and expressed his love for his home, and spoke about his good early memories; this happened after his anxieties about his internal dangers had been lessened by the analytic work. The diminution of these persecutory anxieties led to a stronger experience of depressive anxiety and guilt, which in time led to greater trust in himself and in the external world, as well as to a more hopeful mood. We must remember that at that time we were living in constant actual danger and that these favourable changes in the child had come about in spite of frightening external circumstances. I have often referred to the interaction between external factors and the anxiety concerning internal processes. In Richard, for instance, such anxieties were always increased when the war news was bad. In this context, however, I wish to draw attention to one aspect of this interaction. The present session illustrates my contention that fears of external dangers are intensified by anxieties arising in the earliest stages and that therefore the anxiety aroused by actual dangers can be diminished by analysis.

I have elsewhere reported on my observations of this fact and in this connection discussed Freud's concept of objective and neurotic anxiety (cf. my paper 'On the Theory of Anxiety and Guilt', 1948, *Writings*, 3).

III. The material of the previous day thus expressed his anxieties about integration, whereas in the present session this anxiety was obviously diminished. This change from one day to another indicated a fluctuation between failure and success in integration; it is such fluctuations which prepare the ground for a more stable capacity for integration.

## FORTY-SIXTH SESSION (Monday)

Richard presented a very different picture. He was lively, but over-excited, and his eyes were very bright. He talked constantly and incoherently, putting many questions without waiting for an answer, was restless, continuously, in a persecuted way, watching passers-by, and apparently quite incapable of listening to any interpretation. When Mrs K. interpreted there was no response. He was clearly in a state of strong manic excitement and much more openly aggressive, even directly towards Mrs K., than he had been for a long time. He said at once that he had brought the fleet and was planning a big battle. The Japanese, the Germans, and the Italians were all going to fight the British (he suddenly looked worried). He asked Mrs K. what she thought about the war situation, but went on talking without waiting for an answer. He said he felt very well indeed, there was nothing more the matter with him. He had been writing to his friend Jimmy, who was the second most important person in his gang—Richard being the most important—about plans for a battle against Oliver. Then he put out the fleet. The British were stronger than all the others together and were stationed behind rocks, represented by Mrs K.'s bag and clock. Suddenly the Italians appeared, but soon turned tail. Other enemies started to fight, but one hostile destroyer after another was blown up. Richard said, while putting them aside, 'They are dead.' A small British destroyer fired at a German battleship and was at first supposed to have sunk her; then Richard decided that she had surrendered and the destroyer brought her back. In between he repeatedly jumped up, looked out of the window, and watched children. He knocked on the window to attract their attention, made faces at them, but quickly withdrew behind the curtain; he behaved similarly towards a dog; he said of a young girl that she looked silly. He was particularly interested in all the men who passed by. . . . He looked at Mrs K., admired the colour of her hair, touched it quickly, also fingered her frock to find out what it was made of. Then he spoke of a 'funny' old woman who had walked past the house. When he had started the fleet play he made, as usual, the noise of engines, something like chug-chug-chug. He interrupted himself and said, 'What is this?—I have now got it in my ear.' . . . After having sunk the enemies' fleets, Richard suddenly became 'tired' of playing and put the fleet aside. He took the pencils out and at once put the yellow pencil into his mouth, biting it hard. Then—which was unusual—he pushed the pencil into his nostril and into his ear, put his finger to one nostril, and made various sounds. At one point he said the noise was like the whirlwind in *The Wizard of Oz* which blew away Dorothy, who was a nice girl; she did not die as a result of the whirlwind. Meanwhile he asked Mrs K. whether she liked his light-blue shirt and his tie, but did not seem to expect an answer. He took out his handkerchief to wipe his nose, although he did not need it, but he looked at it and said, 'My mucous hanky.'

*Mrs K.* interpreted that he particularly wished her to admire his shirt and tie, which also stood for his body and his penis, because he felt that he was mucous, actually had poison inside; with it he meant to attack the internal parents and they would retaliate with poisonous attacks on him. Mrs K. also pointed out that he felt that by biting the pencil he had attacked and taken in Daddy's hostile penis and that the noises Richard had made went on inside him, for he had said that he heard the chug-chug inside his ear. In his mind the fleet battle went on internally and these fights would injure not only himself but the internal good Mummy, just as the whirlwind blew away the nice Dorothy. This meant he was the magician who had arranged all these battles.

Richard had been grimacing, biting the pencil violently, and asked whether Mrs K. would mind if he broke it or bit it through. Not waiting for an answer, he asked whether Mrs K. liked her son. . . . He was scribbling his name all over a page, nearly illegibly, and then covered it up with further scribbles.

*Mrs K.* interpreted that, in the fleet play, the little destroyer fighting the hostile battleship stood for Richard fighting against his mother.

(Richard had got up, was running about, not listening at all, and continuing to make noises.)

*Mrs K.* suggested that the 'silly' Mummy-fish which in the drawing of the previous day had got in the way of the torpedo and stood for Mrs K., who exposed herself to his attacks, was today represented by the 'silly' girl who passed by. He had recently expressed his aggressiveness more openly and had said today that he had written to Jimmy his plans for an attack on Oliver. He wished to be able to have an open and external fight. When he had decided to attack Oliver he had said he was happy (Session Thirty-three) and that he hated his pretence of friendliness when he loathed his enemy. But he nevertheless had expressed his hate by secret attacks by 'big job'—the scribble hiding his name and the fleet battle which he felt was going on internally, as represented by the 'chug-chug' in his ear. His jealousy of his parents, and now of Mrs K. and her husband or her son, again and again stirred up his hate; and since he felt he had taken them into his inside, he could not help feeling that the fight went on internally and not only externally.

Richard had been sniffing and swallowing.

*Mrs K*. reminded him that two days ago he had said that his mucus was running down into his stomach; he felt that he was attacking the enemy parents inside his stomach with poisonous mucus which also stood for poisonous urine and fæces. He expected that they would do the same to him. This internal battle would make him feel that he had dead people inside him whom he could not put aside like the fleet, and he was particularly worried about the injured or dead Mummy inside, represented by the 'silly' fish or by Dorothy in *The Wizard of Oz* blown away by his internal fæcal whirlwind.

Richard, while Mrs K. was interpreting, had begun to draw a battleship, on top of which he wrote *Rodney*; underneath he drew a smaller cruiser, and farther down a submarine. He made this by putting ships of his fleet on a page and tracing their outline, and said the cruiser was 'cutting the water'. On another page he repeatedly wrote his name, but did not scribble over it. He also drew on yet another page three German aeroplanes in different sizes, and underneath a very big British aeroplane and a smaller one. He crossed out the two bigger German planes and the smaller British plane and wrote down as the result of the fight : 'Two German and one British plane shot down.' . . . He went outside and stamped on some nettles, and said it would be a good thing if there were more rain, because everything was dry; it would be good for the plants. Then he came back into the house. He picked up a stick which he had found in a corner and threw it at Mrs K., but without hitting her; contrary to his usual behaviour he did not apologize or ask whether she minded this. He said he was going to break the stick, but did not do so. Then he spoke of breaking the window and throwing the stick out, kicked the stools about, and asked how long Mrs K. had been in England. He said he had met a friend of hers.

It turned out that this was John and he had talked with him about his analysis. He asked Mrs K. whether her grandson was English, again not expecting an answer. . . . White hitting the stools with the stick he murmured the names of Mrs K.'s son and grandson, but at once said loudly that he was beating Hitler and wished to kill him. Several times, when he saw an old man pass, he asked Mrs K. whether this was the grumpy old gentleman (meaning Mrs K.'s fellow-lodger). . . . He asked whether he was nasty to Mrs K., and this time he did wait for an answer.

*Mrs K.* interpreted his last two drawings and said the first of them seemed to represent Richard's attack on his parents by bringing the submarine underneath the ships. On the other hand, he had drawn exactly the shape of these ships, which had the same significance as writing on the other page his name quite clearly and not hidden by scribbles, in contrast to the first drawing of this session, when he had written his name rather indistinctly and scribbled over it. He had tried to make it an open attack, but again and again it turned into a hidden and secret one.

Richard then made and coloured an empire drawing (34), and he remarked that Daddy and Paul were very small.

*Mrs K.* interpreted that in this drawing Richard and Mummy were again the parents, Paul and Daddy were supposed to be their children. She also said that by reversing the family situation he had avoided destroying the parents by his jealousy; moreover, when he took Daddy's place, he possessed the good penis which could create babies—the rain which was necessary for making the plants grow.

Richard looked at the drawing of the aeroplanes, but said nothing about it.

*Mrs K.* interpreted Richard's suspicion of the hostile Mummy united with the bad Daddy—and Mrs K. with her foreign son and grandson whom he had hit (the stools), saying that he was going to kill Hitler. Richard had been attempting to keep Mrs K. as the good Mummy, admiring her hair and frock, but had at once expressed dislike of the old woman in the street. 'Old' seemed also to mean near death: Richard had great fear of Mrs K. dying in London, and of the dying Mummy inside him when he was ill.

Richard was again kicking the stools about. . . . He picked up the stool with the furry top, caressed it, leant it against his cheek, and asked Mrs K. to touch the furry top.

*Mrs K.* interpreted that because he was jealous he hated his father and attacked his genital and wished to destroy it, all of which changed Daddy into an enemy in his mind. At the same time he also loved Daddy, and the rain which made plants grow was now Daddy's good urine, which gave babies to Mummy and created Richard. He even felt unhappy if Mummy turned away from Daddy; he wished her to love him as he wished Mrs K. to caress the soft top of the stool which he had kicked and which had previously (Session Forty-five) represented Daddy's genital.

Richard now said [1] that on the drawing representing the battle of the planes the two German aeroplanes which were shot down were Daddy and Paul, the small German one which was 'alive' was himself; the big British plane was Mummy, the small British plane which was shot down was also himself.

*Mrs K.* interpreted Richard's fear of his own death and of his genital being destroyed as a punishment for his having killed Daddy and Paul. At the same time the bad part of himself, the small German aeroplane (in earlier material the U-boat, Session Twelve), remained alive.

Richard went out and closed the door behind him so that he was locked out. He called for Mrs K. to let him in. When she opened the door he said with relief : 'At least I had the fleet with me.'

*Mrs K.* interpreted that the fleet stood for his good internal people, the good family, similarly as the train had done. She also suggested that Richard's locking himself out of the house expressed his unconscious feeling that he should, or would, be turned out of his home because of his murderous wishes.

Richard had quietened down, and towards the end of the session —particularly after Mrs K.'s interpretation of the last drawing— had become silent and sad. Before leaving he again asked, when an old man passed, whether this was the grumpy old gentleman; then he repeated earnestly and with concern his question whether Mrs K.'s fellow-lodger was really nasty to her, and waited for her to answer his question. He was relieved when she said no, the lodger was not nasty. Shortly before leaving, Richard told Mrs K. that he had not at all wanted to listen to her explanations.

Although Mrs K. parted from Richard at the corner of the road, since she was not going into the village, he did not show any fear of going on by himself; but the anxiety about his external enemies had come out more strongly during this session, together with a greater belief in his being able to fight them (Note I).

[1] I draw attention to the fact that while Richard had not been able to make any association to the drawing of the aeroplanes, he did so after my interpretation referring to his conflict between love and hatred towards his father—between the wish to replace Father with Mother; that is to say, for Mother to discard Father, and his opposite wish that she should love Father.

*Note to Forty-sixth Session:*

I. This session was in striking contrast to the previous one and shows how little stable the feelings expressed in the previous one—love for his parents, the capacity to fight an aggressor openly—had been. It is true that these feelings had gone with a good deal of manic defences against depression. In the present session he had also tried to external-ize his internal danger situations and hostile feelings but had not succeeded. Again and again he reverted to secret attacks, and internal anxieties reappeared. It is to be considered, however, that these anxieties were constantly increased by his fear of my leaving him and exposing myself to what he felt to be my undoing.

## FORTY-SEVENTH SESSION (Tuesday)

Richard was much quieter and looked happy. He said he had not brought his fleet. He went to have a drink from the tap and asked Mrs K. whether she minded this. Without waiting for an answer he had another drink. This time he inquired whether Mrs K. would mind if he exhausted the whole water-supply; he also asked whether she had seen John on that day.

*Mrs K.* interpreted that his asking permission to drink expressed his fear, not of exhausting the water-supply, but of exhausting Mrs K.'s strength and thereby robbing the other patients, particularly John. He experienced again the fear he had as a baby of having exhausted his mother and sucked her dry and thus deprived any babies who might yet be born; the tap also stood for Daddy's good penis, and that meant that he was afraid of robbing Mrs K. of the good penis she was supposed to contain. Mrs K. reminded him that (in the Forty-first Session) he had tried to find out whether Mr Evans had sold her cigarettes and said that his mother had got sweets from him and that on the previous day he had asked whether Mrs K. had sweets from him.[1]

Richard said he wanted to draw and added that he was very happy. He also explained his reasons for feeling happy: he felt much better, actually he was quite all right; the sun was shining; the war news was good; he had no socks on and his legs were bare; the unpleasant boy at the hotel was leaving tomorrow.[2] He repeated

[1] I have no reference to this in my notes of the previous session.
[2] Richard's mother had told me over the telephone that the boy was actually unpleasant.

that he had not brought the fleet because today was different. . . . Then he made Drawing 35. He first drew the boat, which was meant to be a submarine, but turned it into a U-boat by crossing out the British flag. Underneath there were scribbles and Richard explained that he was bombing the U-boat, and that the little figure, which he said was behind the U-boat, was Hitler whom he was bombing as well. Farther down on the page there was also an 'invisible' Hitler whom he bombed. This Hitler was hidden behind scribbles. Richard pointed out where his face was (*a*), his tummy (*b*), and his legs (*c*).[1] He said he had not realized while drawing that these scribbles were meant to be Hitler, but he saw it now. In the bottom corner of the drawing he had made the figure 4 in two ways, but he thought that the 4 drawn in one line was the better way.

*Mrs K.* interpreted that Richard again showed that he felt his scribbles were bombs. She added that he now seemed to attack more openly with his fæces; these attacks were, moreover, more clearly directed against the bad Hitler-father, and in this way he avoided injuring the good Daddy and Mummy. But the 'invisible' Hitler also meant the bad Hitler inside him.

Richard agreed to these interpretations with conviction and said, 'This is true.'

*Mrs K.* suggested that because his cold was better, his fear of poisoning and being poisoned had lessened. He had more hope about Mrs K. and Mummy, and felt he could preserve them inside him and outside. The unpleasant boy who was leaving the hotel was not only a nuisance but also represented to him the Hitler-Daddy as well as the dangerous part of himself, the bombing U-boat part (Twelfth Session) which he hoped to expel from his inside. This went with his feeling that he was more able to fight external enemies and thus preserve the good Mummy and Mrs K. He was much comforted, too, by the good war news. Sunshine, as often before, could mean to him the good, warm, alive Mummy and Daddy being united, like the '4' drawn in one line, and not being disjointed like the bad invisible Hitler and the '4' drawn by separate strokes.

Richard went outside and, looking round, stamped on some nettles; he said he would not like to touch them. He pointed at a large, bushy one, saying it looked horrid, stamped on it and said that at least it would be down for a while.

*Mrs K.* interpreted the nettles as standing for the octopus-Daddy. This meant that though he was more hopeful, Richard doubted

[1] I marked the drawing later with the letters (*a*), (*b*), and (*c*).

whether he could altogether exterminate Daddy's bad penis inside himself and in Mummy and get rid of his own bad feelings.

Richard pulled some weeds from among the plants; he remarked that one should do more of that, but went back into the house. He fetched the book which had interested him before and looked again at the picture of the little man shooting at the monster. He pointed out to Mrs K. that the man was aiming exactly at the monster's eye. The monster had a 'haughty look'. There was something proud about it and 'its meat was delicious'. Richard again put the yellow pencil into his mouth, bit it, and at the same time looked at the drawing of the aeroplane flight made in the previous session. He said that Mummy was a giant in that one.

*Mrs K.* pointed out that the monster was also a giant.

Richard replied yes, but Mummy was a nice monster-giant.

*Mrs K.* interpreted that Mummy contained now a nice monster-Daddy, not the bad octopus- or Hitler-Daddy. She reminded him of his admiration for the big tower (Seventh Session) which was at present to him something like the haughty and proud monster; this expressed his admiration for Daddy's genital.

Richard started to make Drawing 36. While drawing he repeatedly got up, looking for passers-by, and watched two men on a coal-cart with great interest. He said they were very dirty, but it was not their fault; they could not help it and he felt sorry for them. While making this drawing he again repeated that he felt happy. He looked at the other drawings and remarked that No. 34 was quite different from all the others; the end part of the empire on the right was like a fish tail, and there was about as much of him as of Mummy. There were also those very little countries, Daddy and Paul.

*Mrs K.* again interpreted that Richard had made Paul and Daddy into babies and that Mummy, who now contained the good monster-Daddy, and Richard were the parents. In this way he had improved Mummy's inside as well as preserved Daddy and Paul. Mummy contained all of them, because she was the fish with the tail. On the previous day, when Richard had beaten the stools with a stick, he had murmured the names of Mrs K.'s son and grandson, and then he had said aloud that he was beating Hitler—which meant that he was also beating Hitler out of her and out of Mummy.

Richard now readily admitted this.

*Mrs K.* interpreted Richard's fear that in destroying the bad Hitler inside Mummy he would injure her as well as the good people inside her—there was the same danger if he attacked Hitler in Mrs K. and so destroyed her and her son and grandson. . . .

Richard pointed out, as he had done once before, one stool which he hated most; it was a flattened-out soft pouffe; he kicked it again.

*Mrs K.* suggested that Richard in this way expressed his hatred of the injured Daddy with a damaged or destroyed genital, who would retaliate because he had been damaged.

Richard then spoke about Drawing 36. He said that in the centre they all had countries of about the same size.

*Mrs K.* interpreted that Richard felt happy about it—as he had said while drawing—because he had attempted to give all of them almost equal shares of Mummy; if they had equal rights they would not fight each other. There was also less of the black Daddy, and in any case he did not feel as badly about black as he used to do; he had shown this today by his feeling sorry for the coalmen. There were, moreover, a few babies, represented by the small sections; most of them were light blue, but other babies were in Paul's and Daddy's colours, and one in red—his own colour. In this way he admitted that he was not yet adult. This arrangement of both Mummy's and his own inside was the source of the greater happiness and hope he felt today. Yesterday, fighting had been uppermost in his drawings and thoughts, and he felt that he could control both Mrs K.'s son and grandson, and Daddy and Paul inside himself, only by poisoning them; therefore he expected them to persecute and poison him. Even if they were made into children, as in Drawing 34, they would still be attacking him. By contrast, in today's drawing (36) he expressed his hope that there would be less hate and less fight, and therefore less fear, and that Mrs K. and Mummy inside him were safer. But then he had also shown that he was attempting to give the babies a larger share of Mummy.

Richard then decided to draw a town and made Drawing 37. He said he would like to 'construct' it well, but he was so bad at drawing. He mentioned that there would have to be two railway tracks so as to avoid accidents. They joined farther on at the left, as they did at the station in 'X'. Then he drew some houses and the road which he called Albert Road. He said Albert was a name he liked, because it reminded him of Alfred, an older friend of Paul's in the army; a very nice fellow, who was Richard's friend as well as Paul's. At the top left-hand corner of the drawing he wrote 'Buffer'; he said buffers were necessary. There was a level crossing, a bend, which was very dangerous for trains, and a siding to the right.

*Mrs K* pointed out that the meaning of this drawing was similar to that of Drawing 36, namely, equality and agreement between him, Daddy, and Paul about their shares in Mummy's love. This was expressed by the two tracks branching off from the station which was Mummy; the buffers stood for an attempt to avoid collision. The goods yard, as formerly the convoy, was meant to feed all of them. Alfred also represented to him a better brother than Paul, not competing with him. In spite of all this, there was the dangerous bend which meant the dangers inside Mummy, mainly because of the fight between him, Daddy, and Paul. His wish to 'construct' a town well, and his regret that he was not good at drawing, expressed also his desire to rebuild the injured Mummy and give her babies, as well as to restore his own inside and make it safer.

Richard, while making the drawing just described, had been very absorbed and contented, and again said that he was happy. He was sniffing repeatedly although his cold had obviously gone, and remarked that he had not much mucus now.

*Mrs K.* interpreted that he was still concerned with the danger of poison inside him, the mucus represented the poisonous and poisoned stuff and by sniffing he tested whether it was still there.

Richard said he wanted to draw a picture of his present home. He started with the house, made a line which was the road leading to the neighbour who had the chickens, but said there was too little space to put in the neighbour's house. Then he explained the way leading to the station and the position of the station. He started again at the other end and made a line to show which way his father went to the station. He made the way longer by adding, in the middle, a vertical line and then continued in the same direction as the original. He made two little strokes, one representing a pig and the other an ass, which Daddy would pass on the way. Richard then looked at the pencils which Mrs K. had brought a few days ago (because most of the old ones had been used up), to which he had so far paid no attention. He now asked if he could 'make them into pencils', explaining that this meant sharpening them. He was extremely pleased that he managed to do so without breaking any, and also that they had such good points. He touched Mrs K.'s hand with one of the points, carefully, to show how sharp they were. He also decided to sharpen the old green pencil which so far had stood for Mummy, and said that this too should have a good point. He compared them with each other by putting them side by side on the table. Then, taking them all together in his hands, he waved them in the air saying, 'With these I could kill Hitler.'

*Mrs K.* interpreted that he had, in his mind, been restoring the genitals of Daddy, Paul, Mrs K.'s son and grandson ; they were all, he felt, equal and even Mummy (also standing for Mrs K.)—the old green pencil—had now received a penis. So there was no cause for jealousy and envy; more recently he had tried very hard in his drawings (and that meant also in his feelings) to prevent competition and disaster by being fair to everyone. In this way he could unite with all these good men—the new sharpened pencils—to attack the bad Hitler-Daddy.

Richard asked Mrs K., when she was putting away the pencils, to be very careful not to break the points. He had looked repeatedly at the map and said he hoped the Russians would hold out and that the R.A.F. would be successful in bombing Germany. At the end of the session he explained to Mrs K. why he was so glad to be without socks; he wished his legs to get nice and brown—the sun was good for them. He took off his sandals and said he had some sticks in them which he wanted to get rid of. He showed Mrs K. that he had a little corn on one toe.

*Mrs K.* referring to the previous day when he had found a stick and used it to beat the stools, standing for Mrs K.'s relatives as well as for the internal Hitler, interpreted that he wanted to get rid of the stick standing for his bad penis attacking the good people.

Before leaving, Richard found a few leaves on the floor, fetched the broom and swept them up, saying, 'Poor old room, it will do it good.'

Although a manic mood was still discernible during this session, it was much less marked than on the previous day. He was also less on the alert about passers-by. While he was not excessively talkative, he told his thoughts without difficulty, and listened to, and obviously took in, interpretations. He repeatedly said during this session that he was very happy. There was no doubt as to his actual feeling of relief and contentment, together with a manic element.

## FORTY-EIGHTH SESSION (Wednesday)

Richard was a few minutes late but, as Mrs K. could see from the window, he was not running. He seemed quite composed and did not apologize about being late as he had done on former occasions. He said he had brought the fleet and put it out in formation: two battleships ahead, the others following. He told Mrs K. that he had dreamt all night and the dreams had been very unpleasant. He did not want to talk about them and, anyway, he only remembered the one part which had not been unpleasant. He asked whether Mrs K. had seen the nasty children pass before he arrived, particularly the red-haired girl, or had she met them on the way? How did they behave towards her? Then he watched Mr Smith (the ironmonger) standing on the opposite side of the road talking to a man, who was clipping a hedge and whom Richard had occasionally called 'the bear'. Richard said Mr Smith was nice, he was 'sweet', and went to drink water from the tap. On returning he found that Mr Smith was still in the same place. He said he wished Mr Smith would go away, he could not do anything while Mr Smith stood there. At short intervals he kept saying: 'Go away, Mr Smith . . . go to work,' then he asked Mrs K. to say three times 'Go away, Mr Smith' and that would make him go. Mrs K. repeated these words three times, and at his bidding again six times, and again three times. When Mr Smith eventually went—quite a while later— Richard nevertheless attributed this to Mrs K.'s magic powers. Richard watched him go. He also looked at the old man to whom Mr Smith had been talking and said that actually both men looked quite pleasant. He obviously wondered why he had been so upset by Mr Smith being near. During this episode he had been moving the ships about. First *Nelson* went to the other end of the table, soon *Rodney* followed, and they stayed by themselves; a little later the whole fleet followed. Richard said that they were all just waiting for enemies to appear.

*Mrs K.* interpreted that Richard's saying 'Go away, Mr Smith' and at the same time putting *Nelson* to the end of the table meant that he wished his father to be a long way off. On the previous day when he was drawing the road to the station from which Daddy travelled to his office, Richard made this road longer than he first intended, because he wanted his father to be farther away. Mrs K. suggested that the pig and the ass stood for the two bad sons— himself and Paul—who wished their father to be out of the way, to be dead, because they wanted to have Mummy all to themselves. As soon as he felt so hostile towards his father, his father turned into an enemy in his mind.

Richard went outside, stamped on some nettles, looked round, but soon returned into the room and started to draw. While draw- ing he said suddenly: 'When are you at home? I should like to come and see you some time, not for work, but just for a visit.'

*Mrs K.* interpreted Richard's desire to have her as a friend and not as an analyst because he thought that then he could get away from his suspicions and fears about her and Mummy, whom he wanted to keep as the light-blue Mummy. Mrs K. mentioned how he had recently described her as beautiful and her dress looking like silver (Forty-fifth Session), but had soon afterwards spoken of the horrid old woman on the street. He tried not to think of her as the 'wicked brute'-mother united with the Hitler-father and deserting him. Therefore he wanted Mrs K. to be on his side and by magic to remove Mr Smith who stood for Daddy.

Richard replied that he had thought Mrs K. would say this, and when she asked him why, had he perhaps thought so himself, Richard replied yes, he had. Then he asked whether, later on, when the work was finished, he would be allowed to visit her.

*Mrs K.* said that was possible.

Richard asked about Mrs K.'s patients: had she got many in London? He also asked if she was going to the village at the end of the session and if she would call first at the grocer's. He said he did not like her to go there.

*Mrs K.* asked why.

Richard replied that when Mrs K. went to the grocer's she would walk with him for only a very short time, because the grocer was nearer than the other shops in the village. He asked whether Mrs K. had got Player's cigarettes on the previous day from Mr Evans. He said he had seen her go in there. He thought that she might have got some. This made Richard very indignant. He called Mr Evans a cheat and a dirty dog. Mr Evans had told Mummy yesterday that he had no Player's and he often did not let her have any. Then he spoke about the manager of the hotel and said he was nasty and interfering.

*Mrs K.* asked in what way he was nasty.

Richard first replied 'Oh, generally,' but went on to complain about something which had happened on the previous day. He had been told by the manager that he should not pick roses in the hotel garden, yet he had done so.

*Mrs K.* interpreted that Mr Smith, Mr Evans, and the manager were all standing for Mr K. and for Daddy. He was angry for two reasons: Daddy did not give him the good penis which he wished to suck, but gave it to Mummy, who was now represented by Mrs K. When he complained that Mr Evans refused to sell Mummy cigarettes, which also stood for Daddy's penis, but—as he thought —let Mrs K. have some, then Mummy was meant to be his own frustrated self. At the same time Richard wanted to have Mummy to himself and therefore wished his father away, or rather dead. Similarly Mrs K. should have no other patients, or her son or grandson. However, he was also sorry for his father because he not only hated but also loved him. He felt guilty towards both parents and therefore wanted them to be together; in the fleet play he made *Rodney* follow *Nelson*, and the children joined them. They were all on good terms with each other and hostile only towards the Hitler-Daddy. As he had said, the fleet was waiting for the enemies to appear. But the enemy was also the hostile and jealous Richard who wanted to attack his parents and disturb the family peace.

Richard said he distrusted Mr K., who had fought in the last war against the British—but he trusted Mrs K. He once more asked Mrs K. whether she liked her work. He also asked why Mrs K. thought this room more suitable for children : was it because it was quieter?

*Mrs K.* replied that she had already explained that she needed a playroom.

Richard repeated, 'Oh, it is instead of a playroom.' Then he asked whether Mrs K. had rented the room and whether she was paying for it. He inquired about the name of a patient whom he had met (not John) and wondered what a grown-up patient would be afraid of. He could not be afraid of children, could he? Would grown-ups be afraid of other grown-ups—a woman of other women? It would be still worse if it went on in this way, because there are more grown-up people in the world to be afraid of than there are children. He knew that Mrs K. would not tell him any-thing about this patient, but he could not help asking her (Note I). . . . Richard was silent for some time and deep in thought. Then he said he would like to understand what psycho-analysis really was. It seemed such a secret to him. He would like to get to the 'heart of it'.

*Mrs K.* interpreted that while he was actually interested to know all about psycho-analysis, he also wanted to find out all Mrs K.'s secrets. He wished to go into her room when a grown-up patient was there to see what she would do with him. He had had the same wish about his parents' bedroom, and the 'heart' also stood for their secrets and secret thoughts, and for their genitals. It was Richard's chief worry that he often distrusted Mummy, and now Mrs K. His greatest wish was to keep Mummy light blue, good, and reliable. Now he repeated this when he tried to keep Mrs K. silvery and beautiful, but he could not help suspecting her because Mr K. had been in the first world war on the other side. When his parents were by themselves, he suspected they were having sexual intercourse, and because this made him jealous and afraid, he attacked them in his mind. Then he felt they were united against him and that was how Mummy, too, changed into a foreigner, spy, and enemy. Mrs K. reminded him that when he was operated on he felt that Mummy had plotted with the bad doctor.

Richard went out of doors. Looking at Mrs K., he asked what

the colour of her hair had been when she was young. Had it been black? Now it was light, fair—or was it white?

*Mrs K.* interpreted that he did not want to realize that it was white because this meant to him that she was old and he was afraid of her death.

Richard replied that black also reminded him of death. When he said this he was stamping on nettles.

Back in the room, Mrs K. reminded him of his dream and asked him whether he would tell it to her.

Richard, although with evident resistance, reported his dream: *Richard was at a law court. He did not know what he was accused of. He saw the judge, who looked quite nice and did not say anything. Richard went to a cinema, which seemed also to belong to the court. Then all the buildings which were part of the court tumbled down. He seemed to have become a giant and with his enormous black shoe he kicked the tumbled-down buildings and this made them stand up again. So he really put them right.*

During this report he had been drawing (38).

*Mrs K.* interpreted that the judge in the dream had something to do with his having been accused yesterday of picking roses. This stood for his stealing Daddy's genital and also taking Mummy's breast. Mrs K. reminded him that on the previous day he had gone to drink from the tap immediately after saying that Mr Smith was 'sweet'. He had said that the judge was nice and he had described Mr Smith as nice, and had also mentioned the hotel manager on a previous occasion as being nice. The same applied to his father, who nevertheless became very frightening to him if Richard wished to rob him of his genital and of the possession of Mummy's breast. Mrs K. suggested that in the dream Richard, though he did not know what he was accused of, was actually accused of having destroyed the buildings belonging to the court. They stood for his parents whom he felt he had attacked but wished to restore as well. His feeling that he was a giant meant that he contained the giant-Mummy and the monster-father, and therefore was immensely powerful and destructive [Omnipotence of thought]. In the previous session, when he had spoken about the giant-Mummy and the monster, he had shown Mrs K. that when he had all the pointed pencils together in his hand, which meant that he contained the powerful parents, he could fight Hitler. When he kicked the buildings with his big black shoe, that indicated the destruction of which he was really accused. He had not admitted this in the dream, but the black Hitler-shoe showed that he not only restored the buildings with it but had also used it to destroy them and the parents.

Richard, without responding to this interpretation, now drew

Mrs K.'s attention to Drawing 38 and said that people were travelling in different directions on it. Mrs K. was travelling to London by train.

*Mrs K.* asked who was travelling in the opposite direction (*a*).

Richard said Mr K. was. He met Mrs K. at the junction there, they parted and Mr K. went sobbing on his journey.

*Mrs K.* reminded him of the earlier part of the session and of his saying to Mr Smith 'go away', which did not help. Mrs K. had to say 'go away', and then he did go, or so Richard thought. Now she was sending Mr K. away. That also meant it was Mummy who had sent Daddy away. Then Mrs K. asked who was travelling in the other direction (*b*).

Richard said that was himself, travelling to his home town ('Z').

*Mrs K.* interpreted his fear of the end of the analysis, which was shown on the drawing by her going to London.

Richard asked, looking very worried : 'You are not going yet?'

*Mrs K.* said not yet, but in a little less than two months' time, and reminded Richard that he knew this to be so.

Richard said in a low and depressed voice that he might have to go to London too.

*Mrs K.* interpreted that Richard was concerned about the breaking-off of the analysis because of his actual difficulties. He was worried about his future. His query about the fears of grown-ups and his saying they were worse than the fears of children showed this. He had mentioned some time ago his fear of turning out to be a dunce. But he also felt afraid of the good Mummy leaving him, dying, or turning bad, because he had been destructive and dangerous. He had the same feeling about Mrs K. going away.

During Mrs K.'s interpretation, Richard suddenly interrupted her and said he knew what her fees were—his mother had told him.

*Mrs K.* interpreted that he felt hurt that she was taking money for his treatment, for this meant that she was not the good Mummy who fed and helped him because she loved him.

Richard replied that he wanted Mrs K. to be paid because she needed money.

*Mrs K.* said that was also true, but her being paid made him distrustful ; that was one of the reasons why he had wished to come and see her as a friend.

Richard then asked, as often before, whether Mrs K. was going to the cinema that night. She never seemed to go. He was going tonight with Mummy.

*Mrs K.* interpreted his wish for her to go with them, to which Richard at once agreed. He also felt that if she did not go to the cinema, it was he who deprived her.

Richard had meanwhile decided to alter the travelling arrangements in the drawing (38). Originally Mr and Mrs K. were coming from 'X' and parted at the junction. Mrs K. did not meet Richard at all, for he travelled by himself from 'X' to his home town. Now Mrs K. came back from London, passed the junction, and went farther on to another one at which she met Richard coming from 'Z'. Then Mrs K. and Richard went on to 'X' and there she met Mr K. who had returned. In this drawing the name 'Valeing' appeared at several places; Richard said that after all 'they were all in the same district'.

Towards the end of the session, Richard looked at the pencils and asked Mrs K. where she had bought the new ones and how much they had cost.

Mrs K. interpreted Richard's wish that she should spend money on him; he had also asked whether she paid rent for the playroom; he liked to think that she was not greedy in taking money from his mother for his treatment, but also spent some money on him.

At the end of the session Richard noticed, looking out of the window, that his mother was waiting for him. Mrs K. was still packing up her things and asked Richard whether he would rather join his mother straight away. Richard definitely declined. He said he wanted to help Mrs K. pack up, and he also wanted to wait for her. Outside, when he met his mother, he said to her : 'I feel like a new person, or like a new country—I am like an American now' (Note II).

During this session Richard had watched the road much more intently. He was more persecuted and rather upset, but on the whole he was responsive to Mrs K.'s interpretations, except to the one about the dream.

NOTE : I found in my notes a piece of material which I cannot place, though it definitely belonged to this session. At one point I had interpreted Richard's desire to attack Mummy and take babies out of her inside. To this Richard replied that he had eaten a baby that morning. He had found in his egg the bit which would have made it into a chicken. He added that he must have done this hundreds of times without realizing it, but this morning he did not go on eating the egg because he disliked it.

*Notes to Forty-eighth Session:*

I. Both with adults and with children the analyst has to decide, according to his grasp of the situation, which meaning to attribute to a silence. Many patients have difficulties in starting to speak, and it is, I think, advisable to give them time to overcome their difficulty. But if a silence extends, let us say, to fifteen or twenty minutes, I think it is wrong not to try to interpret the reasons for it, which might be found in the material of the previous session. There are other silences which express contentment, the pleasure of being with the analyst, of lying quietly on the couch, which I think one should accept without interrupting them by an interpretation. I have often found it confirmed when the patient began to speak again that he had enjoyed lying there quietly and feeling in silent contact with the analyst, whom he had internalized.

Richard's silence at this juncture in the session was obviously a reflective one—his attempt to find out something in himself—and I did not make any attempt to interrupt that.

II. I have pointed out that the intensity with which Richard experienced internal danger situations (the poisonous internal persecutors and his poisoning them) and the analysis of these anxieties (Forty-fourth Session) was followed by a changed attitude in the Forty-fifth Session—i.e. the concentration of his interests and feelings on the external world, together with memories of the past coming up. In the present session, aggressiveness and hostility were not only externalized but also more directed against what he felt to be an actual bad object in the external world—Hitler. Earlier his feelings about the good and bad father had fluctuated so quickly that none of these relations could be maintained for any length of time, and therefore he was never sure whom he actually attacked. The fight against external foes—that is to say, open aggressiveness which was already expressed when he thought of fighting his enemy Oliver and the hostile gang—brought out persecutory fear of them which he attempted to counteract by manic defences. However, the fact that the fluctuations between what he felt to be good and bad in himself and others were less rapid, was bound up with greater synthesis between the good and bad aspects of the analyst and his mother on the one hand, and of the good and bad father on the other. Such processes of externalization and synthesis of the objects include greater integration of the ego and an increased capacity to differentiate between parts of himself and his objects. Steps in integration and synthesis, however, stir up anxiety although they bring relief. This was shown in the drawing of the aeroplanes (Forty-sixth Session) where he appeared as both the German and the British plane, which implied a greater unconscious insight into his having simultaneously destructive and loving impulses.

Richard was again a few minutes late but did not comment on this. He said that he had an awful cold—it had come back. (It appeared that his only symptom was a slight cough.) He also complained of his legs hurting; he had cramp in them. He then went to drink water from the tap. He described to Mrs K. his visit to the cinema on the previous night. The film had been very sad and he had cried. It all happened in Germany. A very nice old professor—a 'dear old frail creature'—died in a concentration camp; his wife was only seldom allowed to see him. While telling this Richard put out the fleet and began to move the ships.

*Mrs K.* asked was not his father quite soon coming to 'X'? (He had mentioned the date some time ago.)

Richard replied that he was coming the following day.

*Mrs K.* connected his being sad about the old professor who was left alone with the material of the previous session: he had been saying 'Go away, go to work' to Mr Smith when he saw him standing in the road; Mr K., when Richard was describing the drawing, was supposed to be sobbing when he was sent away by Mrs K.; all this was connected with Daddy coming to 'X' for a holiday and with Richard wanting to send him back to 'Y', to work and be alone there. Richard particularly wanted Daddy to go away again because he was jealous of Daddy sharing Mummy's room.

Richard agreed that this was so, but added that Daddy and Mummy would not sleep in one bed. The beds were not side by side in that room. While saying this, Richard had made *Rodney* move away. *Nelson* followed her and the two ships touched by the stern.

*Mrs K.* pointed out that, as before, Richard had expressed his wish that his parents should not have sexual intercourse; but, as he had shown by making *Nelson* touch *Rodney*, he actually believed that they would. This was one reason why he wanted his father to go away. Yet he was also very sorry for the lonely and deserted father, represented by sobbing Mr K.; and in the end he reunited Mr and Mrs K. This was another reason why *Rodney* and *Nelson* were put close together, because he also felt they should be allowed to have sexual intercourse. By biting the yellow pencil and wishing to eat the delicious meat of the monster, and by hearing the chug-chug of the ship representing Daddy (Forty-sixth Session) inside his ears, he had recently again shown that he felt he had eaten up his father. When he hated Daddy, his inside became a prison and concentration camp in which he could torture and and attack Daddy and separate him from Mummy. He felt he was fighting him with his mucus and his 'little' and 'big job' and killing him. Then he was afraid that he also lost the good and loved Daddy. When Richard cried about the professor in the film, he was also sad about the injured and dying father inside himself, as well as the external one deserted by Mrs K. and Mummy. In fact, he knew quite well that Mr K. was dead and he was sorry for him. He was also concerned about his mother being lonely and deprived if Daddy died.

Richard moved the ships about. He told Mrs K. that he now had a new name for one of them—*Cossack*.

*Mrs K.* pointed out that Richard had not spoken about the war in Russia because he felt uncertain and worried about it. She suggested that the *Cossack* was meant to be himself, and that he was trying to help the attacked Russia who now stood for Mummy.

Richard made the *Cossack* move out all by itself, far away from the other ships. He spoke about the *Glow-worm* which had fought gallantly but had been cut in half. He said he was very sorry for the *Glow-worm*. He made the *Cossack* travel all round the table and enter a Norwegian fiord, formed by Mrs K.'s bag and the envelope containing his drawings—which was meant to be the fiord in which the *Altmarck* had been. German ships, too, entered the fiord. British ships joined the *Cossack* and battles developed, which the British won. Outside the fiord, *Nelson* joined *Cossack* and other battles took place. *Rodney* had become the *Bismarck* and was repeatedly attacked on both sides by the united *Cossack* and *Nelson*. However, although the *Bismarck* was in great danger, she was not actually sunk. Sometimes the *Cossack* was joined by another ship of its own size, or by a larger one. During this play Richard said that he was also looking forward to his father coming (he had not disagreed with Mrs K.'s interpretation about wishing Daddy far away), for he was going fishing with him.

*Mrs K.* interpreted Richard's conflict expressed in the play and also referred to what he had said earlier in the session; if he hated his father and wished to keep his mother to himself, this would lead to disaster. The good Daddy would be deserted and lonely, or both parents might turn into enemies and cut him in half—the *Glow-worm* standing for Richard himself. To avoid this he felt he should leave home. The first thing he had done after *Nelson* and *Rodney* had joined each other and were touching at the stern had been to make the *Cossack* go far away by itself. But then Richard (*Cossack*) united with his father (*Nelson*) and together they attacked Mummy, who was changed into the hostile *Bismarck*, because he felt that she would turn hostile if she were attacked. Richard was also sorry for her; in his fleet play she was never sunk, because this would have made him feel too guilty. His fishing with Daddy also stood for his being united with the father. When this failed in his mind, he allied himself with Paul—the *Cossack* at one point joined up with a slightly larger destroyer—and together they could attack either Mummy or both parents.

Richard had begun to draw. . . . He spoke again about the film he had seen on the previous night; there had also been a bit about Austria in it. Then he mentioned a woman they knew who had a German husband, but said so without hostile comment. He asked whether Mrs K. minded his dislike of Germans; she must be fond of them. While saying this, Richard was carefully drawing railway lines in the same way as in Drawing 38. He said that no train could go and that nothing could happen until he had put the sleepers in.

*Mrs K.* interpreted that he wished that his parents and he were asleep at night. Then he would not hurt either of them or Mrs K., and nothing bad would happen. In his play with the fleet he had shown how guilty he felt about both his parents. Mrs K. reminded him of the dream of the previous day in which he was a prisoner about to be judged.

Richard was now very responsive to Mrs K.'s interpretations and said that in that dream he was also being tried for having broken a window. He added that he had not known in the dream how to put the buildings right—it just happened by his putting his enormous foot down—he had grown into a giant.

*Mrs K.* reminded him that a few days ago a window in the playroom had been broken.

Richard replied that it was not he who had broken it—it had been one of the Girl Guides using the room. (This was a fact, but Richard had been very disturbed when he and Mrs K. found that the window was broken.)

*Mrs K.* interpreted that, although he had not broken the window, he seemed to have felt that he had done it because of his aggressive desires experienced in the playroom.

Richard now referred to the drawing he was making. He said that 'all of us'—Mrs and Mr K., Daddy and Mummy, he, the birds and Bobby—were all travelling together. The next-door neighbour who had the chickens was also travelling with them.

*Mrs K.* suggested that this neighbour, whom he had described as elderly, as well as Mrs K., stood for his granny. Richard had been very fond of her and he felt she had been revived in his relation to Mrs K.

Richard said that they were coming from a town where they

stayed and travelling to London, where they would all live together. Later on they would all go back to 'Z'.

*Mrs K.* interpreted that Richard wished his treatment to continue and to follow Mrs K. to London, but with his family.

Richard agreed, but added that Mrs K. had never been to his home town and that he would like her to come and see it.

*Mrs K.* interpreted Richard's wish to reunite and restore the family after having, in his mind, done so much damage to them. This damage, as well as the wish to make reparation, also referred to Mrs K., whom he felt he contained.

During this session Richard had been much less persecuted. He had scarcely paid attention to passers-by. On the other hand, his hypochondriacal fears were stronger. He had been preoccupied with his throat, often clearing it, though he coughed very little. Apart from that, he had been neither extremely worried nor elated, and was very cooperative.

## FIFTIETH SESSION (Friday)

Richard was lively and looked happy. He had come a few minutes early and was waiting. He said he had not brought the fleet—it should have a rest—and mentioned that he had had no dreams. He was eager to draw and started at once. As usual at the beginning of a session, he asked whether Mrs K. had heard anything about an R.A.F. raid. He showed her that on his drawing the station was called 'Roseman'. There were various railway tracks drawn in the same manner as in Drawing 38, leading to different towns, but they all had to pass the station 'Roseman'. One of the towns was his home town. As soon as he had finished the sleepers (represented by vertical lines) the trains would be able to come in. At that moment he noticed Mr Smith passing by, went to the window, waved to him, and Mr Smith waved back. He then spoke of 'nice Mr Smith'. He asked Mrs K. whether 'those girls' had already passed, saw them coming and watched them go by. . . . Richard said his father was arriving this afternoon; he was very glad and was looking forward to it. He was going with his mother to meet Daddy at the station : it would be 'great fun.'

*Mrs K.* interpreted that the station 'Roseman' represented the nice father who had an attractive penis—the rose. Fishing together and the 'great fun' also meant that he wished to have a sexual relation with Daddy and that Daddy's genital was again desirable. The 'Roseman'-father was in contrast to the octopus-Daddy and also to the hotel manager who had forbidden him to pick a rose.

Richard said he thought that if one had eaten an octopus it would certainly give one indigestion, but he felt very well. The cold had gone—it had actually gone after yesterday's session, and he had hardly coughed after leaving Mrs K. He believed that last night he had finished with the octopus for good. He took a knife—no, he just dropped the octopus out of the window and it died. He added that he had not thought of this last night, but it came into his mind now.

*Mrs K.* asked where the octopus had been when he got hold of it.

Richard said the octopus was in his bed, under the sheets. (He spoke of the octopus as 'he'.) Richard must have been lying on the stomach of the octopus. Then he put his hand under the sheet, pulled out the octopus, put his knife into the octopus' heart and threw him out of the window. . . . Meanwhile Richard had gone on busily drawing sleepers and said, referring to the station and the trains, 'It is very complicated.' Then he explained that one train had just arrived. Another—a goods train—was puffing out. He copied the noise which the train made, referred to it as 'the silly old goods train' being now here, now there—pointing at the drawing. After this the noise which the train was supposed to make became sharper and sharper and more hissing—distinctly angry.

*Mrs K.* interpreted that Richard was looking forward to his father coming, but nevertheless he also wanted him not to come. The 'silly old goods train' stood for Daddy, who became more and more angry the more Richard was sending him away to the different towns on the drawing. That was why the train was hissing so angrily.

Richard was amused and laughed at this interpretation.

*Mrs K.* pointed out that when Richard said he was lying on the octopus' stomach, this meant that the octopus-Daddy was inside his own stomach and Richard wanted to kill him and push him out of himself. His remark, 'It is very complicated' applied not so much to the drawing as to his feelings: love for his father, pleasure in seeing him, desires for his penis, fear of the bad octopus in his, Mummy's, and Mrs K.'s inside, jealousy because he wanted Mummy all to himself, fear of the angry Daddy if he turned him out. Mrs K. also reminded Richard that he hated to give up his place in Mummy's room to his father. He had not often had Mummy so much to himself as recently, and he resented being deprived of this.

Richard agreed, but repeated that he did look forward to his father coming; he would have quite a nice room next to his parents.

Meanwhile, some boys on the road had been imitating the barking of dogs. Richard then copied Bobby's barking and said, 'If you could see him when he catches rabbits!' He added that Bobby had never yet eaten a rabbit, he only chased them for the 'fun' of it.

*Mrs K.* interpreted that Richard seemed to have more trust in his being able to love, and felt less frightened that his aggressive wishes and his hatred would really take effect. His saying that Bobby, who so often stood for him, had in fact never actually eaten a rabbit, in spite of enjoying the 'fun' of chasing them, meant that he, Richard, would not actually devour Daddy [Lessening of omnipotence of thought]. Because he was less frightened of inner battles, his cold seemed to have gone and his relations with his family had improved. Since he felt better and happier, he had decided to leave the fleet at home so as to avoid battles. Similarly, when he said that he had had no dream, he wanted to avoid anxieties.

Richard made another train drawing. He was pleased with the name 'Roseman' and kept on looking at both drawings, and former drawings of stations and trains, and made comments on the names he had used. He said that 'Valeing' (Drawing 38) really meant a whale: about the second drawing, which had a station marked 'Halmsville', he said this meant ham: he liked eating ham. He seemed very interested in finding that he had expressed this unconsciously (Note I).

*Mrs K.* reminded him that 'ham' referred also to the big German railway junction Hamm which had so often been bombed and about which he had spoken previously.

Richard agreed and, pointing to the drawing, showed where the goods yards of Hamm were supposed to be.

*Mrs K.* interpreted that eating ham meant taking good things in, which, however, turned out to be very dangerous inside—ham was good food but also the most bombed place at that time. The good penis, and also the good breast, might become mixed with bad ones; he had said about Valeing two days ago (Drawing 38) that the different Valeings were 'in the same district'. He seemed to feel that the whale-Daddy was all over the place in his inside. He was also afraid that the dangerous monster inside would make him, Richard, very dangerous. In the recent dream (Forty-eighth Session) he had become a giant with black Hitler boots who could powerfully restore, but also powerfully destroy. Therefore reparation and destruction were also mixed in his mind.

Richard had begun to make an empire drawing and, when filling in the red section on top, he told Mrs K. that Mummy had been grumpy with him that morning.

*Mrs K.* asked why.

Richard said that he had been rather unpleasant and that he was often so. He was grousing and grumbling, he would not do what he was told, he argued, and he would go on until he got what he wanted.

*Mrs K.* asked what was it he had wanted that morning?

Richard first replied that he had not wanted to get up; then he said he really did not know what he wanted. Should he go on telling what he just thought now? When Mrs K. answered yes, Richard said he would like to break the windows and throw things about.

*Mrs K.* pointed out that while he said this, he had started to colour the sections of his drawing. He, Richard, was on top of everything and had the biggest genital; there was very little of his father in that drawing. She suggested that in spite of his also looking forward, Richard wanted to smash up things because his father was coming. He wanted to be in Daddy's place and on top of everybody in the family. . . .

Richard said in a low voice, and sadly, that he had found a kitten in the hotel garden two days ago. He had been playing with it and was going to take it to the police station, when somebody told him they knew the people to whom the kitten belonged and Richard took it there. Yesterday he had seen the kitten in that house behind the window.

*Mrs K.* suggested that he was very sorry not to be able to keep the kitten.

Richard said he was, but he could not have kept it; anyway, kittens tear up things and are destructive and a nuisance. . . . Richard began to count how many countries everybody had in the empire drawing he had just made. Again, as previously, the one who had most countries determined the colour of the line under the drawing. Richard found that he had 23 countries, Mummy 19, Daddy 4, and Paul 8.

*Mrs K.* interpreted Richard's desire to have babies growing inside himself. In this drawing—after having tried hard to be at peace with everybody—Richard had expressed his desire to have most of everything, the biggest penis, and the most babies; he felt sad that he could not have babies, that they really belonged to Mummy, and that Richard should not rob her, just as he had to return the kitten to its owners. His wish to smash the window was not only to throw things out, but also to break into the place where the kitten was—actually Mummy's body which he thought contained babies. The kitten also represented himself when he was destructive and a nuisance.

Richard looked at some earlier drawings, reckoned out the number of countries Mummy had in them, and wrote that down. He had found out from Mrs K. that she was only going to the corner of the road with him, and he said he was sorry about that but not frightened or worried about going by himself. On the way he told Mrs K. that he was going to have coffee with his mother at Mr Evans's. He had the best coffee and, though Mr Evans was often moody, he seemed to like Richard, for he frequently sold him sweets.

In this session Richard had been in good form, mentally as well as physically. He did not feel persecuted, and only twice—apart from watching Mr Smith and the girls go by—had he paid attention to passers-by; this was when he looked at an old woman and an old man. His hypochondriacal fears had receded; he was not in a manic mood but actually much happier. He talked freely but was also willing to listen and to take in interpretations. While he was on the whole in a friendly and fairly balanced mood during this session, conflicting feelings and desires, and corresponding anxieties and defences, had become very clear and were fully recognized by him (Note II).

*Notes to Fiftieth Session:*

I. It was essentially the same feeling as he had experienced when he became convinced of the existence of the unconscious through drawings and play (cf. particularly the Twelfth and Sixteenth Sessions). I have found with children and adults that gratification about experiencing and recognizing one part of the mind, which until then had been unknown, seems to be both of an intellectual and an emotional nature. The relief of anxiety following an interpretation which conveyed an understanding of unconscious processes is one reason for this gratification. Fundamentally, the fact that the analysis has conveyed something to the patient which he feels is helpful and an enrichment revives the earliest experience of being loved and fed. The feeling of being enriched is bound up with integration of the ego and synthesis of the object. From the earliest stage onwards there is a longing for integration, and one important function of interpretation—ultimately the main aim of analysis—is to help towards integration. The longing for integration and insight is a factor which helps the patient to tolerate the pain and distress of experiencing anxieties and conflicts in the course of the analysis, and even to experience persecutory anxieties aroused by those interpretations which to some extent make the analyst into a persecutory figure. I have repeatedly observed that some patients—children and adults—also experience not only satisfaction but even amusement about some part of their mind, usually felt to be bad or dishonest, being found out by the analyst and by themselves. In my experience these are people who have a sense of humour, and it occurs to me that one root of the sense of humour is the capacity to experience satisfaction about finding out in oneself something which had been repressed.

II. The conclusion presents itself that the lessening of fears about internal dangers, which showed on that day and on the previous one (as a result of the analysis preceding these sessions), enabled Richard to experience and express his anxieties and conflicts more clearly. At the same time his becoming conscious and deeply understanding of his anxieties and conflicts gave him relief, increased his trust in himself and in others, and resulted in a better balance.

## FIFTY-FIRST SESSION (Saturday)

Richard was waiting at the corner of the road, and the first thing he said was that he had 'strained' his ankle when going downstairs to breakfast. In the playroom he mentioned that he would be fishing today with Daddy. He described their plans in detail and said he hoped to catch a trout: they had not yet a permit for salmon-fishing. Daddy had brought Richard's fishing-rod as well as his own. Richard told Mrs K. that he had bought a large scribbling-pad to draw on at home. It was twice the size of the one Mrs K. provided and he got it cheaply. He wondered whether Mrs K. had been overcharged for her pad. At home he had been drawing railway lines and he was eager to go on with this at once. He decided, however, first to reckon out how many countries everyone had in the earlier 'empire' drawings. He put two of the earliest aside, saying that they were not only representing the family, since other colours had been used as well. He was very pleased whenever he found out that Mummy was not badly off, being obviously guilty because in most cases he had more countries than she. After having reckoned this out on a few drawings he gave it up. He also commented on the number of drawings he had made and that the pad had by then been nearly used up. Then he made Drawing 39. While drawing, he told Mrs K. smilingly that something had happened last night in his parents' bedroom. A mouse had eaten two biscuits, but his mother had been too frightened to get out of bed to do something about it, and Richard thought his father, too, had been frightened of the mouse. The mouse had also run up Daddy's fishing-rod. All this he reported with amusement, obviously feeling very superior. If he, Richard, had been there he would have taken his father's slipper and driven the mouse away. He dramatized this report, acting his parents' and his own part in it. He added that he was 'Larry the Lamb' (a well-known character in Children's Hour on the radio). . . . The first thing he drew was the station 'Lundi' and the first line leading to the station 'Valeing'. He at once said that 'Lundi' reminded him of lunatic and associated a 'daft' man who who walked about 'X' without doing any work. He had reddish hair but was nearly bald. Next Richard drew railway lines to 'Roseman' and other places, and said that the line Lundi-Valeing had no siding. A train came roaring out from 'Lundi' to 'Valeing', and Mrs K. was on it travelling to catch whales. He also wished to catch whales, so he went with Mrs K.

*Mrs K.* interpreted that the lunatic stood for his father in his sexual intercourse with Mummy, which Richard assumed had occurred last night. Daddy was also bald and not doing any work at present, like the 'daft' man. The mouse stood for Daddy's genital eating Mummy's breasts (the two biscuits). He wished this attack on Mummy because he felt resentful at being put out of the bedroom, and the mouse also represented Richard and his genital attacking Daddy's genital—the fishing-rod. He was triumphing over his parents and Mrs K. because he thought he could deceive them. He pretended to be as innocent and timid as a lamb. But he wished to have not only his mother attacked but also Mrs K., because she was going to leave him and take care of other people in London. She stood for Mummy when she turned to Daddy or to Paul. He much resented Mrs K. depriving him of his analysis and therefore he had an additional grievance against her. She was also to be in 'Lundi'—London—to be ill-treated there by the bad lunatic Hitler-Daddy. Richard had said that there was no siding on the line Lundi-Valeing. This meant that there was no place there for somebody else's genital—namely, his—to enter; the bad Daddy kept all of Mummy's inside to himself. The train roaring out represented Mrs K. and Mummy, terrified and trying to run away from the lunatic Hitler-Daddy. On the other hand, Richard wished to protect Mrs K. and Mummy and therefore was on the same train as Mrs K., helping her to catch the bad whale—the Hitler-genital. He felt he should get in between the lunatic-Daddy and Mummy in order to protect her, but he was afraid of doing so and rather pretended to be a lamb; in any case there was no place for him to get in between them (no siding). Mrs K. also reminded him of his feelings about the tramp kidnapping and injuring Mummy, and that he was both triumphant and guilty because last night he had wished his father to injure Mummy in sexual intercourse but also felt he should go to her rescue . . . (Note I).

Richard then filled in the railway line with sleepers, repeating again that no train could go before the sleepers were drawn; it was not safe otherwise.

*Mrs K.* interpreted that Richard felt that his parents were in danger because he wished to attack them. They were therefore only safe when he slept—he was the sleeper. But it was safe for him to attack them—the mouse standing for him—only when they were asleep. When they were awake he had to pretend to be a lamb.

Richard said that he was looking forward to the fight.

*Mrs K.* asked him which fight he meant.

Richard replied that he meant fishing, for he was going to fight the fishes as if they were whales. He was going to bait them, to get the fly into their throats; they would bump their noses against stones and then they would be killed and eaten.

*Mrs K.* interpreted Richard's desire to suck and eat the attractive penis of Daddy (the 'Roseman', the trout, the salmon), but he felt that since he also hated the penis and fought it like a whale, it would turn into a whale inside him and be an enemy like the octopus. She also pointed out that Richard had again been biting the yellow pencil.

Richard now showed Mrs K. that, in the drawing, the way from 'Roseman' led to York, saying it sounded like pork, and in between was the way to 'Halmsville', which was ham.

*Mrs K.* interpreted that all the pleasant things were on one side of the drawing and this meant that in one part of his mind Daddy and his penis were good; in another part of his mind they were very dangerous and destructive to Mummy; he felt he contained both the good penis and the fighting parents.

Richard had again put the pencil into his mouth and sucked it; he said he wanted to ask Mrs K. a question, but he would like to have an answer to this one. Was it a rule amongst psycho-analysts that they were never to get cross or impatient? Would it harm the work? He looked searchingly at Mrs K.

*Mrs K.* interpreted that she stood for Mummy and he expected her to become very hostile about his desires to rob her of Daddy's good penis and to devour it. But Richard also hoped that Mrs K. was not actually like Mummy; because she was a psycho-analyst and was doing this work to find out his thoughts and help him with them, she would not be cross and he could speak freely to her. Nevertheless, at this moment he had suddenly become afraid that Mrs K.—like Mummy—would be angry after all because he had deprived them of the 'Roseman'-genital and left them with the lunatic-genital.

Richard had gone back to the drawings, pointed at an empire (Drawing 11) in which all sections were very small, and said that it did not count because it was a child.

*Mrs K.* interpreted that in this drawing all of them were equal and children. This meant that not much harm could come from it, but he doubted whether the children were really harmless.

Richard looked at Drawing 21 and was deeply interested in it. He said : 'Look, here she says "help help" and here pointing at the starfish 'I am going to help her' (Note II). You coloured it, do you remember ?' (Richard had at that time asked Mrs K. to colour it and she did some of it according to his suggestions.)

*Mrs K.* interpreted that this drawing represented Mummy and Mrs K. calling for help against the lunatic black Daddy. Richard now felt that he was coming to her rescue and he was particularly pleased to find this out in this session, in which the fear of having left Mummy to the dangerous Daddy had strongly come up. Richard had repeatedly said that Mrs K. and her work were helping him, and that meant that she also stood for the good and helping Mummy. All the more he felt guilty about leaving her with the lunatic bad Daddy and about his attacks on her.

Richard looked with great interest at the aeroplane drawing made in the Forty-sixth Session. He said that in that one Mummy —the aeroplane afterwards called 'a giant' (Forty-seventh Session) —survived and Bobby too survived, but he added, 'No, it's me.' . . . He then pointed out that the two Germans shot down were Daddy and Cook.

*Mrs K.* interpreted that he had suspected Cook of poisoning him (Twenty-seventh Session); therefore Daddy and Cook, who had been shot down, meant the bad Daddy and the poisoning Mummy, while the good Mummy and he himself survived.

Richard began again to draw trains. The lines now stood for the trains themselves. He accompanied his drawing with noises which the trains were supposed to make. They went in all directions, but no train left from 'Lundi' to 'Valeing'.

*Mrs K.* pointed this out and suggested that it expressed Richard's fear of the dangerous, the lunatic intercourse of the parents and his wish to stop it. He had also shown his wish to help Mrs K. when he went with her to 'Valeing' to catch whales.

Richard returned to Drawing 39 and made a new connection : the train now left 'Lundi' for 'Roseman', and made 'proud' and hissing noises.

*Mrs K.* pointed out that she and Mummy were now angry and wished to take 'Roseman', the good Daddy, away from Richard. She also suggested that Richard's concern about Mummy not hav-

ing enough countries in the empire drawings expressed his wish to
return babies to her, because he felt he had robbed her of babies as
well as of the 'Roseman' genital which would give her babies. The
new writing-pad which Richard had bought and compared with
Mrs K.'s smaller one, thinking that he had made the better bargain,
also meant that he had taken the good penis and the babies away
from her.

Richard held Drawing 39 up sideways, so that 'Lundi' and 'Valeing' were now on top, and said that it was a snake and that was
why some of the trains had been hissing.

*Mrs K.*, turning the drawing upright, asked Richard whether he
thought it looked like the octopus.

Richard very emphatically agreed and added that he thought
Mrs K. was very clever to find this out (Note III).

At the end of the Session, Richard said that today was the birth-
day of an empire builder. His christian name was Cecil. Could Mrs
K. say who he was?

*Mrs K.* replied that it was Cecil Rhodes.

Richard was very pleased about Mrs K.'s answer but added, a
little doubtfully, that an Italian island was also called after him.

*Mrs K.* interpreted Richard's wish to know that Mrs K. and
Mummy were loyal to the good Daddy who built the family and
held it together, and that Richard too wished to be loyal to him. But
he doubted whether Mummy and Mrs K. were reliable; this was
shown by his reference to the Italian island which was a hostile
place. His fears and doubts about the foreign Mrs K.—the Italian
island—applied also to Mummy. He feared that Mummy was
either hostile to him or, if she loved him most, that she would be
disloyal and hostile to Daddy.

*Notes to Fifty-first Session:*

I. The feeling of guilt about having exposed—through sadistic
desires—the mother to the dangerous father in sexual intercourse was
shown in the first session (and in many connections since) by his appre-
hension about the tramp kidnapping his mother. I have often found
in the analysis of children and adults that feelings of guilt about this
specific phantasy situation underlie the self-reproaches of having neglected or not protected the mother in various later situations or of
having harmed her. This is an instance of the importance of guilt derived from very early infantile sadistic phantasies and exemplifies the
urgency to go back in the analysis to these early layers if guilt is to be
diminished at the root.

II. The fact that Richard took a strong interest in former material,
and commented on it with deeper insight and fuller conviction, I take

to be the result of progress in 'working-through'. I have often found that at some stages a patient refers back to earlier material which had obviously been only partly accepted, and links it with present material; this shows progress in the depth of insight, in understanding, and in integration.

III. The material in recent sessions, especially in the previous and in the present one, illustrates some fundamental processes from a particular angle. It is part of my theory (cf., particularly, 'Some Theoretical Conclusions Regarding the Emotional Life of the Infant', 1952, *Writings*, 3) that during earliest infancy the splitting between love and hate, and correspondingly between good and bad—and in some measure between idealized and very dangerous—objects, is the method by which the very young infant maintains a relative stability. In my *Envy and Gratitude* (1957, *Writings*, 3) I have laid particular emphasis on the importance of the earliest splitting processes. If love and hate, and the good and bad objects, can be split in a successful way (which means not so deeply as to inhibit integration, and yet enough to counteract sufficiently the infant's anxiety) the foundation is laid for a growing capacity to distinguish between good and bad. This enables him during the period of the depressive position to synthesize in some measure the various aspects of the object. I suggested that the capacity for such successful primal splitting depends largely on initial persecutory anxiety not being excessive (which in turn depends on internal factors and to some extent on external ones).

To return to my instance, in the Fiftieth Session I had been able to show Richard how closely linked in his mind was the rose, the desired penis of the father (which no doubt also had the meaning of the breast), and the whale-father, the persecuting penis; he had said in the Forty-eighth Session, referring to Drawing 38, that 'Valeing' was 'all in the same district', and this meant that the whale was all over his inside. On the other side of the drawing there were the hated and frightening objects—'Lundi', 'Valeing'—and the train between them represented the dangerous sexual intercourse between the parents. The two sides of the drawing were connected by a single line.

I believe that the division between good and bad objects which was expressed in this session, with only one link between them, indicated a step which Richard had not been sufficiently able to make in early infancy. I also wish to mention here the importance of the process of externalization, a process clearly shown in Richard's material in recent sessions, when he became able to experience his strong emotions and anxieties towards the internal bad objects and to bring them more into the open and direct them towards people whom he actually felt to be bad (Oliver and Hitler). This indicated attempts to deal in a better way with his persecutory anxieties.

In my note to the Forty-fifth Session I drew attention to his more successful attempts towards synthesis of his objects shown by a lessening of the violence of projective identification. (In Drawing 25 his internal and external objects were not thrust into one another but peacefully arranged.) A lessening of projective identification implies a diminution in the strength of the paranoid and schizoid mechanisms and defences and a greater capacity to work through the depressive position. Such greater capacity bound up with progress in ego-integration and synthesis of objects appears to be the consequence of early splitting processes being more successful, which was expressed in the present session. However, this step only partially succeeded, for when he had shown me that the 'bad' side (Lundi-Valeing) looked like a snake—expressing his feeling that here was the bad, snake-like penis of the father—he fully agreed to my suggestion that both sides together looked like an octopus. His attempt to divide altogether the good mother from the bad one, the good father from the bad one, and the parents from each other, had failed. The octopus, which meant the bad father, had become mixed up with the good father on the other side of the drawing and had prevailed.

As in many of these notes, my comments about changes in Richard and the reasons for them indicate steps which are only of interest from the technical and theoretical point of view, although a number of them could not be sustained. My purpose is to show the fluctuations due to the analytic work, without assuming that they necessarily indicated lasting progress. The reason why some of these changes were not lasting lies, as I have mentioned in the Preface, in the fact that the analysis was too short. As we know, the continued repetition of experiences in an analysis, the full working-through (Freud), is a precondition for stable results.

## FIFTY-SECOND SESSION (Sunday)

Richard had gone to meet Mrs K. nearer her lodgings. He at once gave her a piece of the salmon which his father had caught. Richard said that he had 'insisted' that Mrs K. should have a nice piece of it, and he appeared delighted to give it to her. He told Mrs K. that he had not caught any fish, but Daddy caught several, as well as a big salmon.[1] Richard had only once in his life caught a fish; that was all. (He did not, however, appear to be disappointed, but proud of and identified with his father's skill.) He at once began

[1] By then Richard's father had obtained a licence for salmon-fishing.

to draw. While drawing he spoke about the war news : it was good that there were R.A.F. raids, and also the Russians did not seem to be doing badly. He went to the map and looked up two Russian towns mentioned in communiqués. He said he was going to draw railway lines, but this time there would not be any sleepers. To begin with he drew the railway tracks by making only one or two lines, but when the trains were meant to run he drew additional lines, and the pencil became the train. The train was leaving 'Tima' station, running very fast. Along certain stretches it made very loud noises; along others it was quite silent.

*Mrs K.* asked him why that was so.

Richard said he was being chased and was silent at those places where the enemy might hear him. About 'Tima' he said that it reminded him of the name of a place the Allies had conquered in Abyssinia. It also reminded him of Tim, a little boy he knew and liked, but who was tiresome when he became too wild. He was a 'real terror' but nice. While Richard talked about the enemy chasing the train, he made dots on the page, saying, 'Now he is here, now here, now here.'

*Mrs K.* asked whether it was one enemy who was chasing him.

Richard replied no, there were many of them.

*Mrs K.* interpreted that Tim, the nice 'terror', stood for Richard's pleasant side, like Bobbie. He also stood, as did the train, for Richard's genital driving into Mrs K.'s and Mummy's genitals and their insides. That was why it was chased by Daddy and his genital.

Richard said that Daddy was a magician and so he could arrange that there were many of him.

*Mrs K.* interpreted that Richard might have felt that Daddy left his genital inside Mummy every time he had sexual intercourse with her, and that she was full of penises which would be hostile to Richard's genital. Mrs K. reminded him that he had previously shown the fight between Daddy's, Paul's, and his genitals inside Mummy and Mrs K. in play and drawings. She added that the train behaved like Richard did when he was frightened of children. Sometimes he provoked them, at other times he remained silent in order not to attract attention. He also pretended to be the nice and innocent child, yesterday 'Larry the Lamb', today a 'real terror' but nice. In the previous session the sleepers meant that he was safe when his parents were asleep and nothing could happen to them when he was asleep. Today there were no sleepers because he seemed to feel that none of them were safe at night.

Richard, in the meantime, had made the train run more and more quickly and repeated that it was being chased. He made circles where the train was passing at the moment, saying very dramatically, 'Now it is here, now here, quick, quick.' He expressed all the emotions of being pursued as well as the enjoyment of a thrilling adventure. In the end the train got out safely. By then the drawing of the criss-crossed lines looked like a maze, out of which the train had to find its way.

*Mrs K.* interpreted that he had just expressed his fear of Daddy and Daddy's penis attacking him and his genital inside Mummy. Her inside was a maze and he with his penis had to get out of her genital as quickly as possible. Mrs K. reminded him that he had strained his ankle yesterday after his father had arrived. This might have already expressed the same fear, his leg representing also his injured genital (Note I).

Richard suddenly said, pointing at the picture postcard on the wall opposite to him : 'The little robin's breast is quite red.'

*Mrs K.* interpreted this remark as a confirmation of her interpretation. She said that the bleeding robin stood for his injured and bleeding genital which he might not succeed in retrieving safely from Mrs K.'s or Mummy's inside if he were involved in a fight there with Daddy's genital.

Richard, when he had finished this drawing, scribbled all over it.

*Mrs K.* interpreted that Richard as a baby wished to attack both parents with his 'big job'. Now, when he again felt unequal to fighting with Daddy as a rival inside Mummy's genital, he went back to these attacks on both of them by bombing them with 'big job' [Regression].

Richard now made another drawing (40). To the right was a small ship which Richard called the cruiser *Prinz Eugen*, being bombed in the harbour. To the left, inside the harbour, was the much bigger *Gneisenau*. The bombs, drawn as circular shapes, were landing between *Prinz Eugen* and *Gneisenau*. Richard was looking very serious and thoughtful. He said the *Prinz Eugen* was a beautiful ship and wasn't it a pity to bomb it. Meanwhile he had been drawing the *Scharnhorst* outside the harbour and beyond the range of the bombs.

*Mrs K.* interpreted his regret and sorrow about the destruction of the admired Daddy-genital—the *Prinz Eugen*—and his guilt that he was bombing and destroying it in jealousy and anger; he was also afraid of injuring Mummy if he attacked Daddy inside her. In the drawing the bombs were dropping in between the *Prinz Eugen*—Daddy's genital—and *Gneisenau*—Mummy; but he wanted also to save Mummy from these attacks. Therefore he drew another ship (the *Scharnhorst*) outside the harbour which stood for Mummy safely beyond the range of the bombs. In this way he was also preventing the parents' sexual intercourse.

Richard, after this drawing, went outside and looked, as usual, at the mountains, feeling emotional about their beauty. He said that there were some storm clouds over the mountains. . . . He went back to continue his drawing. So far he had not been interested in people on the road, but when he saw the red-haired girl pass with some others, he said they were going to church. He did not show any un-friendly or persecuted feelings. Still looking serious and in deep thought, he began to make another drawing (41). He explained, pointing to the lower part of the drawing, that this was soil and underneath it were two worms. The two vertical lines which he drew through the soil were the way the worms got out. Above the soil the anti-aircraft gun was shelling German aeroplanes. He could not say what the result would be.

*Mrs K.* interpreted that the worms stood for his parents and were kept safely underground.

Richard confirmed this and said that the worms were quite safe there.

*Mrs K.* interpreted that Richard was represented by the anti-aircraft gun attacking the German aeroplanes with his genital and 'big job'. His parents, whom he felt he had attacked in his mind, became enemies and therefore were shown, as so often, as German aeroplanes or German ships; and because he felt they were enemies, he had to go on destroying them. But he also loved his parents, thought that they were good, and wished to protect them. Since he was so divided in his feelings about them, he left the result un-decided. Mrs K. suggested that the worms represented not only his parents but also the babies inside Mummy whom he wished to protect against himself. Mummy had actually had two children.

Richard asked whether Mrs K. was expecting him on other Sun-days, apart from the next one, which had already been arranged, since his parents would still be in 'X' on holiday.

*Mrs K.* replied that that was for him to choose. So far, only the next Sunday had been agreed upon with his mother and with him.[1]

Richard, still serious and in thought, began to draw (42). When he had drawn the German aeroplane on the ground, and the light-ning, he said after a silence that he would like to ask Mrs K. some-thing personal. Would she mind? He knew that she would not answer if she did not wish to do so. Did she go to church? Do psycho-analysts go to church? And at once, even before Mrs K.

[1] As the later material also showed, this was again a question of balancing loyalties, this time between his father and the analyst; since during the week his mother and Richard stayed in 'X' for his analysis, he felt they should be with his father at least on Sundays.

could have replied, he said that she could not go, she was too busy.

*Mrs K.* interpreted his fear that she might answer that she did not go to church, which would confirm Richard's strong doubts of her. Mrs K. asked Richard whether he thought it was wrong not to go to church. Did he and Mummy go usually?

Richard said it was wrong not to go to church, God would not like it. He went sometimes, and his mother used to go in 'Z' but not in 'Y'. While discussing this, Richard had begun to fill in the sky with black.

*Mrs K.* asked was he afraid of punishment by God?

Richard, looking very anxious, got up during Mrs K.'s interpretation and stood farther away from her; obviously he had become agraid of being too close to her. He picked up a rope which lay in a corner and threw it away from himself, so that it made wriggling movements. Richard's mood had changed and he became very lively. He kept on throwing the rope with pleasure, and enjoyed improving his skill. He said the rope was like a snake. He put it between his legs a few times while throwing it. He decided that this was going to be a performance and Mrs K. was to be the audience. He himself was going to be the announcer, and straightway announced that a young boy was going to show some tricks with a rope. He had asked Mrs K. to applaud whenever he appeared and to make appreciative comments. Mrs K. did so and, representing the audience, exchanged remarks with imaginary neighbours, like 'Isn't he good?', 'Very clever boy.' Richard was very pleased and went on for a while; he decided that now he was going to announce Mrs K., who was going to do the same tricks as the young boy had done.

*Mrs K.* threw the rope a few times and then interpreted that when Richard held it between his legs, it represented Daddy's genital, which Richard had taken away and now possessed. Mrs K. performing with the rope meant that Mummy, too, should have a powerful penis which would make them all equal. The rope play— both Richard's and Mrs K.'s—expressed also his wish to have sexual intercourse with her; at the same time this was the wish he had been so afraid of and for which he felt that God, standing for Daddy, would punish him. Mrs K. suggested that the wriggling of the rope, which he had said was like a snake, was similar to the lightning on Drawing 42 which had represented God's—standing for Daddy's—powerful and destructive genital.

Richard repeated that the rope was like a snake and agreed that it looked like the lightning on the drawing. He returned the rope to the corner from where he had taken it and said, 'It must have been lying there for a fairly long while.'

*Mrs K.* interpreted that when Richard returned the rope to the corner where it belonged and said that it had been there for a 'fairly long while', this meant that he had only borrowed it from Daddy.

Richard meanwhile blackened the sky in Drawing 42 further and added a few strokes to the Nazi aeroplane. He explained that the sky was full of clouds and that the lightning had struck the Nazi aeroplane. He had again become very anxious and looked pained, as if he were struggling with his emotions. He got up, looked at various things on the shelves, and walked about the room.

*Mrs K.* interpreted that he was trying to escape from very painful thoughts.

Richard clearly made an effort to listen, though with great difficulty, at the same picking up things from the shelves and moving about restlessly.

*Mrs K.* pointed out his strong doubts in psycho-analysis; he felt it to be very wrong. Because Mrs K. discussed with him matters which he thought improper and which he had even been taught to consider as improper, he felt that she was tempting him and allowed him to experience sexual desires towards his mother and herself. These desires seemed all the more dangerous to him because they were connected with hate, jealousy, and destruction of his parents, whom he also loved. He had always been struggling to get away from such hostile feelings which he felt were 'bad' and wished only to experience love. But Mrs K., when he was afraid of her tempting him, represented Mummy as well, who was tempting him by allowing him to sleep in a room alone with her. He also suspected her, whenever she showed him love, of being disloyal to Daddy, and of encouraging Richard's bad and hostile desires. Although he would not in any case have gone to church, he felt Mrs K. should not have given him this session on Sunday; she and he *should* have gone to church and this also meant that Daddy should have his due share of attention and love. At the same time he did want Mrs K. to give him an additional session.

Richard at this moment interrupted and said with conviction that the analysis was helpful.

*Mrs K.* added that because of that, and because she stood for the good and helpful Mummy, it was so painful to him to suspect that she was also the improper and tempting Mummy. He was afraid that the powerful Daddy—God—would punish Mummy too; the lightning which struck the Nazi aeroplane punished the treacherous and disloyal Mummy as well as Mrs K.; when he had been afraid that a storm would break over the mountains (Forty-second Session), that had also meant an attack on the beautiful and loved Mummy. This had made him move away from Mrs K. when

she had asked him whether he was afraid of being punished by
God.

Richard had become calmer towards the end of the session and
said that before leaving he wanted to look again at the piece of
salmon he had brought for Mrs K. He expressed his satisfaction that
it was a nice large piece. He added that he knew Mrs K. was going
to fetch her Sunday papers, so she would be walking a little farther
with him. When Mrs K. was locking the house he said it would be
good for the playroom to have a rest. From the road he looked
back at it and said, 'It looks nice and it will have a rest.' On the
way he pointed out his father in the distance and was pleased that
Daddy and Mrs K. at least saw each other. He also asked Mrs K.
whether she was going to give any of the salmon to the 'grumpy old
gentleman'. Mrs K. replied that she would give some of it to all the
people in the house, whereupon Richard looked pleased.

*Note to Fifty-second Session:*

I. I had deliberately not remarked on Richard's straining his ankle
(see previous session) immediately after his father had arrived, because
with such symbolic actions I prefer to wait until I can interpret them
in the context of the material.

FIFTY-THIRD SESSION (Monday)

Richard met Mrs K. at the corner of the road. He looked very
worried and at once asked her whether she knew, or could find out,
the name of the red-haired girl. . . . In the room he told Mrs K.
about his and Daddy's fishing expedition in the morning. Richard
had caught a salmon parr. He knew that it was forbidden to catch
baby salmon, but he had not recognized it until he had already
killed it. Three ladies not far away were looking at him, so he
threw the dead fish back into the water, behaving as if it were still
alive. Daddy, too, had caught a baby trout and asked Richard
whether he should kill it. Richard had said, 'No, don't, not the
baby,' but by then Daddy had already killed it. Daddy was not
angry with Richard about his having killed the salmon parr, but
he did say that Richard could be put into gaol for this. While
Richard was talking he was arranging the fleet, which he had not
brought for some time, and said that the fleet had had a rest.

*Mrs K.* interpreted that one of the reasons why he had been
concerned about the Sunday session was that he felt that Mrs K.,

and not only the playroom, should have a rest. She then spoke about the salmon parr and reminded him of the 'hundreds of babies'—the fertile eggs which he had said he 'must have eaten' (Forty-eighth Session) and that she had then interpreted that this meant to him taking the babies out of Mummy's inside, killing, and eating them. The same applied to the salmon parr.

Richard then told Mrs K. cheerfully that he had had a letter from their neighbour, who wrote that they had four more chicks and a new kitten. He was very pleased about this.

*Mrs K.* interpreted that this was a comfort to him because it meant that Mummy, after all, had babies inside her and that Richard had either not destroyed them, or that they could grow again. He was also afraid that he had robbed Mrs K. of her children and had destroyed them as he felt he had done with Mummy's children. He wanted to rob Mummy of her babies because he wished to have babies himself, and he also destroyed them in his mind because he was jealous of them. Therefore he was so afraid of children in the street; they stood for Mummy's babies whom he had attacked, but who had after all been born and were now his enemies. Today he had tried first of all to find out the red-haired girl's name because she stood for those unknown enemies inside Mummy and—since he felt he had eaten them—also inside himself. To know her name would mean that he could really find out something about all these unknown enemies.

Richard suddenly pointed to one destroyer and said, 'This is the biggest destroyer.'

*Mrs K.* interpreted that he felt he was more destructive than anybody else.

Richard compared this destroyer with the others and discovered —what he consciously knew—that actually they were all the same size. He arranged the whole fleet on one side of the table and put only one destroyer at the other end, hidden by Mrs K.'s bag and clock. Then he described the situation dramatically, in words something like the following : The German fleet is in harbour at Brest— the sun is shining—the weather is beautiful—everything is pleasant and peaceful—the enemy seems far away—little do they know that the enemy is getting ready to burst upon them. At this moment Richard appeared to be moved by sympathy for the German fleet, but he made the hidden destroyer come forward and shell the fleet. He soon changed the arrangement. He was obviously overcome with fear about attacking the powerful enemy all by himself, the destroyer clearly representing himself. He moved several of the destroyers and one battleship to the British side. There were now

altogether six British ships, and the battle began. The result seemed
uncertain, since ships were being sunk on both sides.

*Mrs K.* interpreted that the destroyer was himself—the biggest
destroyer—and that he first wished to attack the enemy on his
own : the enemy stood for his whole family, hostile and attacking
him inside. But he became frightened and wished to unite with the
'good' family against external enemies, the Germans. The six ships
represented his parents, Paul, himself, Cook, and Bessie.

Richard, while playing with the fleet, had again mentioned recent
R.A.F. attacks and his hopes about the fighting in Russia. In this
session he was once more very much concerned with passers-by.
He suddenly ran to the window when he saw three women passing
together. He said 'these three silly women' and knocked on the
window to attract their attention, but quickly hid behind the curtain so as to puzzle them about where the noise came from.

*Mrs K.* interpreted that the 'three silly women' stood for the
women he thought had been watching him when he killed the
salmon baby.

Richard was very struck by this interpretation. He said, 'But
these *are* the three women who saw me'; he at once added that
they were not, but for a moment he definitely had thought that they
were the same.

*Mrs K.* interpreted that the three women who had watched him
stood for Mummy, Nurse, and Cook, allying themselves against
him because they felt he was destroying Mummy's babies.

Richard protested that it was not Nurse; it was Mummy with
Cook and Bessie.

*Mrs K.* reminded him that he had suspected the maids of poisoning him, but he had also suspected Mummy of attacking him—the
horrid bird with the crown dropping 'big job' (Forty-fifth Session,
Drawing 31)—if she found out the harm done or intended to her
babies. He had thought that the maids were speaking German
together (Twenty-seventh Session), though he knew for certain that
they could not speak even one word of German. Therefore the
maids also stood for Mrs K. who was felt to be an enemy plotting
against him with the two other hostile women. Mrs K. reminded
him how difficult he had found it to refer to her mother-language
as German, and preferred to call it Austrian, though he knew the
Austrian language was German.

Richard had been watching a man on the road and called him a
silly and nasty man; he abused a group of people passing—men,
women, and children—in the same terms. He also again knocked
on the window and behaved as he had done earlier. He had become

very noisy and was stamping strongly, spoke very loudly, and sang at the top of his voice. He asked Mrs K. whether, if he wished to go away during the session, she would prevent him.

*Mrs K.* replied, as before, that she would not, but she would first try to explain that he was frightened of her, and why. He had been frightened of the men, women, and children who passed by. They stood for his whole family, including Mrs K., and he was frightened of them because he felt he had attacked everybody. Mrs K. also interpreted that by his being so noisy he wanted to avoid hearing what she said, because she had become one of his hostile family and therefore what she said to him was felt as an attack.

Richard said that he had not wanted to come to this session at all; about two hours before he came he thought that he was fed up with all this and did not wish to see Mrs K. any more. (However, he had arrived exactly on time.)

*Mrs K.* interpreted that today he was particularly frightened of Mummy, for whom Mrs K. stood, because of his attacks on her babies (the dead salmon parr). On the previous day Mrs K. had represented Mummy tempting him to rob Daddy of his genital, and to take Daddy's place with her; and therefore Daddy—God—would become his and her enemy. He felt that the whole family —and this really meant to him the whole world—was against him. Even the playroom had become the hostile Mrs K. with her hostile babies inside. This was another reason why he wanted to run away. He may also have been so noisy in order to get help from outside against Mrs K.

Richard had meanwhile been making various letters and scribbles, which were scribbled over again, and among which the only recognizable things were an anti-aircraft gun shooting upwards towards a circle with a dot in the middle (Drawing 43). He added that he did not know at whom they were shooting. He scribbled with brown pencil over the drawing made in the previous session showing himself being the train chased by enemies. Then he scribbled on another page saying that these were guns, but they were not shooting now.

*Mrs K.* interpreted that in the drawing where the anti-aircraft gun was shooting, this represented his attacking with his 'big job' Mummy's and Mrs K.'s breast, the circle with the dot in the middle, because he wanted to have more of it. This also linked with his jealousy about the babies who would be fed by Mummy's breasts (Note I) and about Mrs K. going to look after other patients and being near her grandson in London. The scribbles on the same page represented his mother's body, her inside which contained Daddy's genital, and the babies. Therefore he felt that he was attacking the whole family and would be attacked by them. The noise he made stamping and singing had also expressed his attacks by 'big job' on Mrs K., and therefore he had become frightened of her and wanted to run away.

Richard continued to shout and stamp, but had to some extent been listening to Mrs K.'s last interpretation. It was difficult to know what he had heard or taken in. But he quietened down somewhat and drew 44, explaining while drawing that here was a Mummy-fish, with lots and lots of babies. He said that the baby fish closest to the mother's fin was the youngest baby.

*Mrs K.* pointed out that this baby was feeding at its mother's breast and that was one reason why he was jealous of it and attacked both the baby and the breast in the drawing of the anti-aircraft gun shooting at the circle.

Richard protested, saying that a fish has not got breasts, it has fins (Note II).

*Mrs K.* pointed out that the fish, as often before, stood for Mummy, and Richard desired food from her breasts and wanted to prevent babies from getting it.

Richard had become much calmer and clearly enjoyed drawing more baby fishes. He seemed very uncertain which was to be the youngest. While drawing the one right at the bottom of the page he said that it was a funny baby—this was the youngest. . . . No— there was a still funnier one, pointing at the second in the right-hand column. Then he decided that the first in the right-hand column was the youngest, though it was not the smallest, but it was nearest to the Mummy-fish. He said somebody was fishing and throwing out bait; it was artificial bait just to catch the baby. . . . Richard had become silent.

*Mrs K.* asked who he thought was fishing and catching the baby.

Richard replied at once that it was himself, no, it was Daddy; *he* had caught the baby trout.

*Mrs K.* interpreted his feeling of guilt about having killed the baby salmon; while he was speaking he had been drawing a second fishing-line; this showed that both Daddy and he were destroying the babies.

Richard said, with feeling, that the Mummy-fish was ignoring the bait, but the baby was going to take it.

*Mrs K.* interpreted that he felt both he and Daddy were dangerous; their genitals were used to catch Mummy and to destroy the babies inside her. This contributed to his fear that sexual intercourse was dangerous. Mrs K. reminded him that while she had been in London he had again talked with Mummy about the way babies were made. He had said that 'this matter about babies' worried him (Forty-first Session), and asked whether it hurt. He felt he would use his penis to rob Mummy, to eat the babies secretly out of her. Also, on the previous day, he had shown how frightened he was that if he had sexual relations with Mrs K. or Mummy he would be punished by God, standing for the powerful Daddy; therefore, after he had shared Daddy's powerful genital, the rope, with Mrs. K., he in the end had returned it to Daddy—the place from which he had taken it.

Richard said that women have different genitals from men, haven't they?

*Mrs K.* interpreted that Richard might wish Mummy to have a penis because he thought hers had been taken away and was afraid that the same would happen to him.

Richard continued scribbling on another page. While making some dots, he asked Mrs K. whether she understood Morse.

*Mrs K.* interpreted his fear that his secret attacks by 'big job' on Mummy and on her would be found out, and this was why he asked whether Mrs K. understood what he was doing. At the same time he also wanted Mrs K. to find out his secrets, because then they would be less dangerous.

Richard, when he had finished scribbling, sang 'Rule, Britannia'.

*Mrs K.* interpreted that he wished to protect his parents against his own destructiveness. He had also shown in Drawing 44 that he was concerned about the baby which would take the bait. He himself wanted to be Mummy's baby, and therefore could not decide whether the bigger or smaller—Paul or himself—was the youngest baby.

Richard made an empire drawing (45), asking Mrs K. to take out of her bag all his coloured pencils and referring to the red one as 'me'. When he finished with it, he dropped the red pencil near Mrs K.'s foot and then said that she had put her foot on it.

*Mrs K.* interpreted that Richard felt so guilty about his attacks on her and on his family, the wish to devour and destroy them, that he expected Mrs K. to retaliate by crushing him. He had said that the red pencil was himself and it also stood for his penis [Projection].

Richard had been speaking about attacks on German towns and ships, and showed strong sympathy with them, which had already been noticeable in recent sessions. He asked Mrs K. whether she knew some of the towns bombed on the previous night. Did she think Berlin was beautiful? Did she also know Munich, and was it beautiful, to which Mrs K. said yes.

Richard seemed very moved. . . . He finished Drawing 45, which was the last page on the pad.

*Mrs K.* pointed out that on the drawing he was on top and had the largest share. Nearest to him was Mummy; then followed Paul —purple—much smaller than Richard, and at the bottom, smaller still, was Daddy—black. Richard suggested that Mrs K. should take the cardboard home for salvage. It was a step towards victory. He said in a sad voice, that so many steps towards victory were needed—hundreds and hundreds. It was like going up a hill made of glass, and you keep slipping back; we had slipped back at Crete.[1]

### Notes to Fifty-third Session

I. Richard's wish to have babies, which was already indicated in his desire to keep the kitten, had become much more prominent. I would therefore—though I had not interpreted this to him—conclude that the jealousy of the babies being fed by mother was only one element in his strong feelings of hostility. The other was the envy of mother's capacity to feed—that is to say, the envy of her breast.

II. In retrospect I am struck by the fact that Richard, who usually followed quite closely my interpretations of his symbolic presentation of material, at this point stated that a fish has no breasts. I would now conclude that this was because his envy of the breast led him to deny that his mother ever had breasts. This would show how over-determined were the attacks on the breasts to which I referred a little earlier.

## FIFTY-FOURTH SESSION (Tuesday)

Richard was early and was waiting for Mrs K. outside the house. He at once asked whether she had brought a new pad. He was disappointed that it was not the same kind as the old one. Couldn't she have got the same? Mrs K. replied that she was sorry, but there was nothing else to be had in the shop. Richard regretted that she did not have another in reserve. The new one was yellowish and that reminded him of being sick. He said he was sorry the old pad had gone, but comforted himself by adding, 'Never mind, the new one will soon make a good companion.' He stated that he had not brought the fleet, adding, 'The fleet did not want to see the new pad.' He showed Mrs K. (for the first time) a tiny pink mark on

---

[1] I have no note about the end of this session, but I have no doubt that I did interpret his last sad remark as referring to his analysis as a constant and unsuccessful fight against his destructive impulses.

one finger, much smaller than a pinhead, also a tiny discoloured spot on one of his nails, and said that he had had these ever since he was born. Then he made a drawing (46). Meanwhile he told Mrs K. in detail about the film he had seen the previous night; it was very amusing. Why had Mrs K. not gone? It was a pity to miss it. . . . The R.A.F. had again done good work. . . . He said he wished to come today and also he did not—but it was different from yesterday; he mainly wished to come It was about three-quarters he wanted to, and one-quarter he did not. By then he had finished the drawing and explained that a U-boat had been sunk. On top was a British aeroplane which had bombed the U-boat. He described with some emotion the destruction wrought by the aeroplane. The flag of the U-boat was battered, the periscope shattered, the gun smashed. The fish (which was the first thing he drew after the sunk U-boat) was sorry about the U-boat. Then he added the starfishes. There was a line across the drawing, above which was a still undamaged U-boat, and the sunk U-boat, fish, and starfishes were beneath the line.

*Mrs K.* interpreted that the U-boat stood again for Daddy and particularly Daddy's genital, the aeroplane for the destructive part of his self, and the fish for another part of his self which was sorry for the destruction he had brought about. He had repeatedly shown, and particularly in connection with the *Prinz Eugen* (Fifty-second Session), how guilty he felt about destroying Daddy's genital.

Richard said that the two bigger starfishes, which were close to the U-boat, were Daddy and Mummy, and the smaller one was Paul.

*Mrs K.* interpreted that here Daddy, Mummy, and Paul were alive and they all regretted Richard's—the aeroplane's—destructiveness.

Richard said, looking at Mrs K. that he liked her jacket. It was not red, as he had thought before, it was purple, which was his favourite colour. He looked at her dress (which had a design of white spots) and touching it lightly said it was like the Milky Way. It also reminded him of searchlights. . . . He went to the tap and drank from it.

*Mrs K.* interpreted Richard's desire to keep her, and also Mummy, safe. He should not exhaust her by sucking her breast dry —the finished pad represented her breast. Purple, which had always stood for Paul, now also stood for the good Daddy; and both should be preserved, together with Mummy. In order to keep Mummy safe he must not deprive her or suck out of her Daddy's good genital, nor rob her of babies, and therefore he felt he had to fight his greed. The drawings which he had made on the white pad meant the good relation with Mrs K. and Mummy, her giving him food and love, in return for which he wished to give her babies, as well as love and friendly feelings. On the previous day he had given the fish many babies. Mrs K. also interpreted that the pad with the white pages stood for her good breast, her good milk —the Milky Way on her dress; the yellowish pages which reminded him of being sick made him feel that he had soiled the breast. As a baby he actually was often sick, and then felt that the good, white milk and the breast which he had taken in had changed into something bad inside him, into Mummy's 'bad' breast.

Richard reminded Mrs K. that he had also spoken of the dress being like searchlights and added, 'You search, don't you?'

*Mrs K.* replied that he meant she was searching for his thoughts, but he may also have felt that his parents, too, particularly Mummy, might find out his hatred, jealousy, and bombing 'big job'.

Richard mentioned the fête at which yesterday he had met Mrs K., and told her that he had already drunk two bottles of lemonade.[1] He now thought they were not lemonade but something else. When Mrs K. asked what they were, he showed resistance, but then said they were 'little job'. After that he ran into the kitchen, drank from the tap, looked into a jug, sniffed at it, looked also at a large ink bottle nearby and sniffed at that too.

*Mrs K.* interpreted that the tap, which had often represented Mummy's breast, might have turned in his mind into 'little job', or 'big job'—the ink—because Richard, when he felt angry or dissatisfied, wished to pour urine or 'big job' into the breast, or into the bottle which stood for it. This was how he came to feel that Mummy's breast, and the bottle he was given instead of the breast, became poisonous; Cook, who might poison him with something from a bottle in the kitchen (Twenty-seventh Session), represented the 'bad' Mummy and her 'bad' breast. Mrs K. also reminded him that on the previous day the anti-aircraft gun in Drawing 44 had been shooting at a circle which she suggested was her breast.

Richard, looking sad, announced that he was going to write an essay. The essay was as follows:

*'What I am going to be when I grow up*

[1] I had decided to go to the fête, to which everybody in 'X' went, because otherwise Richard would have felt that I avoided him and deprived myself. I had a few words there with him and his mother, and Richard told me he had already drunk two bottles of lemonade.

What I am going to be when I grow up is this. First of all as Mummy says after the war young boys should have 6 months training in the Army, Navy and Air Force. Mummy says I am to go in for this training if the Government approves of it. I am wanting 6 months training in the Royal Air Force. After that I am either going to be a scientist or an engine driver. I hope! *The End.*'

Richard had nothing to say about his wish to become a scientist. Although very friendly, he showed strong resistance at that moment.

*Mrs K.* pointed out that Richard was sad and felt guilty about his wishes to attack her and her son, as well as his parents and Paul. He wanted very much to be a good and obedient child, to carry out what the Government, standing for his parents, ordered him to do, and to get away from all thoughts and desires which he felt to be dangerous and bad.

Richard agreed with this. But before Mrs K. could continue her interpretation of why he might wish to become a scientist, an interruption occurred. A man carrying a pane of glass knocked at the door. He had come to replace the broken window.

*Mrs K.* went to the door and asked the man whether he could come later, to which he agreed quite amicably.

Richard had got up and looked pale and anxious. He seemed very relieved when the man had gone. He said with strong feeling: 'That *was* a disturbance.' Then he went to the window and followed the man with his eyes and said, as if he were reasoning with himself : 'He is really quite a nice man.'

*Mrs K.* interpreted that the man was felt to be the intruding Daddy who would discover the wished-for sexual relation with Mrs K., standing for Mummy, and would punish him, as Richard had been afraid that God would punish him. Mrs K. also reminded him of the dream that he was being tried in court because of the broken window (Forty-eighth Session). The judge, too, as he had said, looked quite a nice man, yet Richard had clearly been frightened of him.

Richard began to draw (47), paused in between and put his whole thumb into his mouth, doing so again a little later.

*Mrs K.*, pointing this out, interpreted that Richard not only felt the man intruded into the playroom and into Mrs K. and Mummy, but also into Richard's inside. She reminded him that the nice Daddy, the 'Roseman', turned into an enemy—a whale—when Richard felt him to be inside.

Richard explained the drawing to Mrs K. He said it was the

Chinese ambassador [1] leaving Germany in a German aeroplane. . . . He asked Mrs K. whether she had seen Mr Smith pass. He hoped she had not. . . . He said that in the drawing the lightning was striking the plane and also the ambassador when he was just about to get into it.

*Mrs K.* interpreted that the yellow ambassador was so bad because yellow meant to him the 'sick' he contained and vomited, the bad Mummy, the bad Daddy, and also his own 'little' and 'big job' which he felt to be dangerous and treacherous. She referred again to the lightning in Drawing 42, which he thought was God punishing him.

Richard agreed and said that God was punishing the ambassador because he looked a nice man but was really a rascal.

*Mrs K.* interpreted that this also referred to the man with the pane of glass, who looked a nice man but stood for an intruder and judge.

Richard, pointing at the circle in the cockpit of the aeroplane, said that this was himself, he had already got into the plane.

*Mrs K.* interpreted that the German aeroplane stood for her and for her body. In his mind Richard had gone into her [Projective identification], was discovered there, and punished by Mr K.

Richard replied that he was going to bring the lightning down on the bad man, because now Richard had turned into God. He picked up the rope, tied it round his waist, passed it between his legs, and did 'the same actions with the rope as he had done two days before.

*Mrs K.* interpreted that Richard had turned powerful and God-like by taking away the powerful weapon which God had : the lightning. But this stood for Richard taking away Daddy's genital and therefore he was afraid of Daddy injuring his genital. When Richard had shown her the marks on his finger and nail, this meant that he was afraid his genital was injured because he distrusted Daddy who, as he had often said, was nice but who might turn into a powerful and punishing man if Richard attacked him.[2] Daddy was now staying in 'X' and these fears had increased.

Richard looked listless and unhappy; he did not seem to be listening to what Mrs K. said. He picked up the book with the picture of the monster, looked at the illustrations, and also read a story in the book.

*Mrs K.* interpreted Richard's wish not to know about such pain-

[1] Richard, who was well informed about the war situation, failed to differentiate here between the Japanese and Chinese because, I think, he was at that moment so suspicious of everything yellow—the pad.

[2] See Note I to Fifty-second Session.

ful thoughts and also to find, perhaps, some information in the book about the actual relation of his parents to each other and to him.

Richard now pointed at the picture of the monster and said, shuddering a little, that the small man shooting at the monster with his bow and arrow was aiming at the monster's eyes. (When saying this he half covered his own eyes with his hand.) Then, referring to the story which he had been reading, he said how awful it must be to be inside the carcass. (In the story the man, after killing the monster, had gone inside it with a companion to hide from his enemies and complained to his companion how very stuffy it was there.) . . . Richard went into the garden, looked round and came back again.

*Mrs K.* interpreted that the monster also stood for the playroom, inside which he felt imprisoned. Mrs K. had combined with the foreign Mr K., the Chinese ambassador. Richard felt that if he got into Mummy when she was united with the bad Daddy, and Richard killed him inside her, he would be caught there and would be unable to get out again—he would also be unable to breathe. All this expressed his suspicions and fears of Mrs K. and Mummy containing the bad Daddy; which also at times made the playroom bad.

Richard said emphatically that these were very unpleasant things Mrs K. was saying.[1]

This was at the end of the session, and though Richard as usual put the table into place and the chairs at each side of it, he seemed very glad to go. On leaving, he said pleadingly to Mrs K. that he wished she would go to the cinema. When Mrs K. asked why he so much wished that, he replied that she should have a rest and a change. He thought that she was always working.

Outside he was very friendly and sorry that Mrs K. was not going into the village on that day (Note I).

*Note to Fifty-fourth Session:*

I. The increasing sympathy with the attacked enemy, which was shown in the material of that day, as well as of the previous ones, is noteworthy. Love and hate had come closer together, as I have pointed out. The suspect and the light-blue mother, also the good and the bad father, had become more synthesized. It has repeatedly appeared in the material that Richard had become aware of his hostility and that the German aeroplanes and ships came to represent the hated and

[1] I have repeatedly pointed out that Richard had much less difficulty in recognizing suspicion of his father than of his mother, to whom he clung as his good object.

hostile parents. Together with the guilt arising from this insight, to which I have drawn attention, and with the steps in integration and synthesis, the tolerance towards the bad object increased and sympathy with the actual enemy could be experienced—a very important emotional change. Synthesis went with stronger depressive feelings and amounted occasionally to despair and great sorrow. My experience has shown me that when guilt and depression can be borne to some extent and are not warded off by regression to the paranoid-schizoid position with its strong splitting processes, further steps towards ego-integration and synthesis of objects occur. Together with this, hate is more mitigated by love and can also be better canalized. It becomes more directed against what is felt to be bad and harmful to the good object. In so far as hate serves the protection of the good object, sublimation and the trust in the capacity to love increase and the sense of guilt and persecutory anxiety decrease. These changes, in turn, make for better object-relations and allow more scope for sublimations.

## FIFTY-FIFTH SESSION (Wednesday)

Richard, appearing very anxious, at once told Mrs K. two things: his cold had come back and he had again brought the fleet. . . . He looked round and was pleased to find that the broken window-pane had been replaced. He also inspected the playroom and was glad to see it unaltered.

*Mrs K.* interpreted that he felt relieved to find that the intruding Daddy, who was represented yesterday by the man with the window-pane, had in fact not done any harm to Mrs K.—the playroom—which meant also that Mummy had not been injured.

Richard put out the fleet in battle order. He showed Mrs K. that five destroyers were quite alike and also that a group of five smaller ships were alike.

*Mrs K.* reminded him that recently he had suddenly thought that one of the five was the 'biggest destroyer' and that he had said so after she had interpreted that he felt guilty about having destroyed the baby salmon and Mummy's babies.

Richard discovered that Mrs K. had brought a new pad of the same kind as the one which had been used up. He was delighted and asked where she had found it. Mrs K. replied that it had been, after all, among her things. Richard said 'good' and inquired whether Mrs K. had brought the yellow pad as well. When she answered that she had not, Richard again expressed great satisfaction.

*Mrs K.* repeated her interpretation that Richard disliked the yellow pad because it reminded him of feeling sick, and she referred to the meaning of Drawing 47 and his associations to it on the previous day.

Richard listened attentively, though he first said this was a horrible drawing and he would rather not look at it.

*Mrs K.* interpreted that the rascal who seemed nice (the Chinese ambassador, the judge in the dream, Mr Smith, the man with the window-pane), and whom Richard so much distrusted that he felt the lightning would come down on him, stood for Richard as well, since he had gone secretly into the hostile aeroplane and was also going to be struck by lightning. Richard had said that the lightning was God's punishment for the man *seeming* nice but being a rascal; but when Richard had described to her how he would go into his parents' bedroom in connection with the mouse incident (Fifty-first Session), he had added that he was 'Larry the Lamb'. In fact, he was only pretending to be a lamb, for the mouse stood for his wish to attack Daddy's genital, the fishing-rod, and to eat up the two breasts (biscuits). Therefore he would be attacked and struck down by Daddy—God. The German aeroplane into which Richard had secretly gone represented Mrs K., who was suspect and disloyal because she interpreted to him his sexual desires towards her and Mummy. Since Mummy slept in the same room with Daddy, and Richard had to sleep by himself, Richard felt her to be bad and even a spy and allied with Daddy against him. Then he wished that Mrs K. and Mummy should be destroyed—the lightning that struck the aeroplane—and he hated and distrusted himself very much for wishing it; he felt guilty and wanted and expected to be punished.

Richard looked very ashamed and embarrassed when Mrs K. mentioned that he thought of himself as insincere, the 'rascal', pretending to be the innocent 'Larry the Lamb' while he had such hostile desires against his parents. He replied, 'But I am an innocent child'; after a little pause he admitted, 'Maybe you are right.'

*Mrs K.* added that on the previous day Richard had felt it so painful to realize his doubts of himself as well as of Mrs K. and Mummy, and his fears of being attacked by both parents, that he had hardly been able to listen to what she was saying.

Richard looked at Mrs K. for a moment and said in a low voice that he heard her even if he did not seem to do so.

*Mrs K.* asked him whether he even heard her when he kept on interrupting her, making a noise or reading, as he had done on the previous day.

Richard replied that then he did not listen so well, yet he heard most of what Mrs K. said.

*Mrs K.* pointed out that Richard had brought the fleet because he wished to do work with her and felt that the fleet—which so often stood for a good side of himself and of the family—helped him with the work.

Richard said he thought so too. He had already begun to arrange the fleet, putting *Rodney* and *Nelson* together and, farther away, one cruiser and one destroyer. He made *Rodney* move far away on the table, and then he paused.

*Mrs K.* suggested that Richard wished to avoid jealousy and conflicts and in this way to improve his relation to Daddy and Mummy. The cruiser and destroyer stood for Paul and himself being friends, but he could not stop feeling jealous and anxious if his parents—*Rodney* and *Nelson*—were close together; so he wished Mummy—*Rodney*—would go away, and then Daddy, Paul, and he could remain in a friendly relation to each other.

Richard had meanwhile made the *Nelson* join *Rodney*. They steamed round Mrs K.'s bag and were stationed behind it. Richard pointed this out and said, 'Look where Daddy and Mummy are hiding.' He at once contradicted this and said they were making ready for battle; some of the other ships, one cruiser and a few destroyers which had been on the far end of the table, joined *Nelson* and *Rodney*.

*Mrs K.* asked who the destroyers were.

Richard replied they were Paul and himself, and some of the other children, going to help their parents against the enemies; the cruiser was Mrs K. He reminded her that on earlier occasions, too, she was the cruiser and had joined the family.

*Mrs K.* asked him if she was also sometimes among the fleet when he had not actually mentioned it.

Richard replied that he thought she must have been, but he did not know then on which side she was.

*Mrs K.* interpreted that his painful doubts in her and Mummy made him wish not to know that Mrs K. might be among the enemies.

Richard asked Mrs K. which newspaper she read and told her which papers Mummy read; he hoped that Mrs K. read the same. . . . Meanwhile he moved another cruiser (not the Mrs K. cruiser) to the enemy side saying, 'This is Mrs K.,' then, 'No, there she is,' pointing to another group, which were not the Germans. After a moment he added, referring to the Germans, 'This is the bad Mummy with the bad children.' [1] He then pointed to one destroyer and submarine and said that they were Italians. Then he made the British Mrs K. cruiser come forward (while humming a few notes of 'Rule, Britannia') and made her shoot at the two Italians and at one German destroyer.

*Mrs K.* interpreted that Richard so much hated the red-haired girl because she had asked him whether he was Italian.

Richard emphatically said that he would really like to blow up her and her friends.

*Mrs K.* interpreted again that Richard had greatly resented this question because he felt himself to be a traitor to his parents—the British. In the fleet play he had made Mrs K. blow up the bad children and the bad Mummy, and wished her to protect him against his enemies. He had great doubts about Mrs K.'s reliability, as he had again shown by having one British and one German Mrs K., which meant that he could not decide on which side she was. Mrs K. acknowledged that since there was a war with the Germans going on, it was particularly unpleasant for Richard to know that Mrs K. was Austrian, which meant to him German-born, and that he would much prefer her to be British and to be like his mother. That was why he wished that Mrs K. should read the same newspapers as Mummy. Nevertheless, the suspect Mrs K. also stood for the suspect and unreliable Mummy.

Richard agreed to that, but again asked whether it really did not hurt Mrs K. if he spoke of his suspicions. Then he added, did it really not hurt her if he said to her 'wicked brute'?

*Mrs K.* interpreted that when he had said 'wicked brute' (Twenty-third Session) he actually hated her, standing for Mummy who, he felt, was combining with the bad Daddy. He was afraid that he would destroy Mrs K. or Mummy by his hate and hostile desires [Omnipotence of thought], and this he felt was more dangerous still if he actually put his hostility into words.

Richard asked Mrs K., as he often did towards the end of a session, how far she would be walking with him and whether this was her day for going to the grocer's.

*Mrs K.* replied that she was first going to the bank. Richard asked whether he could wait until she came out of the bank; should a boy attack him in the meantime, could he go into the bank and would Mrs K. protect him against his enemy?

*Mrs K.* interpreted that he wanted her to do what she had

---

[1] This was the first time he had explicitly used the expression 'The bad Mummy', thus now acknowledging consciously his doubts in his mother and showing that he had accepted Mrs K.'s interpretations.

actually done in the fleet play when she attacked the Italians. Mrs K. should also protect him against the bad Mummy and Daddy united against him. Maybe this had been the reason why today the Mrs K. cruiser entered directly into the fleet play. She stood for Nurse, who might protect him against the bad parents.

Richard said that he did not mind Mrs K. going to the bank; she only went there once a week, but he very much disliked her going so often to the grocer's.

*Mrs K.* interpreted that the grocer seemed again to represent Mr K. and Daddy who gave Mrs K. and Mummy good things; Richard was jealous, both because he himself could not get the good things—the penis—from Daddy and because he did not wish Daddy to love Mummy. She reminded him of his jealousy over the cigarettes she bought from Mr Evans (Forty-first Session).

Richard had picked up the new pad and looked at it with great pleasure. He made Drawing 48 without saying anything about it.[1] He took up a calendar and looked at the pictures; when replacing it on the shelf he was careful that the picture of the King and Queen should be at the top, and stroked it tenderly.

*Mrs K.* interpreted that looking at the calendar, and yesterday at the book, partly expressed his wish to get information about what his parents were doing.

Richard asked Mrs K. appealingly, 'What *are* your secrets?'

*Mrs K.* interpreted that Richard would wish to know every minute of the night what Mummy was doing with Daddy in bed and what Mrs K. was doing at night. And yet he also wished Mummy and Daddy to be together and happy—he loved the picture of the King and Queen together.

Earlier, while Mrs. K. had been interpreting his dislike of the yellow pad, Richard had been sniffing, and asked Mrs K. whether she minded him doing this.

*Mrs K.* interpreted that on the previous day, after the workman had come and when Richard had been drawing the Chinese ambassador, he had suddenly put his whole thumb into his mouth; and that Mrs K. had suggested to him that the dangerous Daddy and his penis had, he felt, intruded into him. The sniffing meant

[1] I have apparently not given any interpretation of this drawing to Richard, but would like now to say something about it. It is striking how red—Richard—dominates the whole picture. Two parts of him are linked with black—Father; close to him is purple—Paul; but he is also linked with the two small light-blue sections—Mummy. In this session the distrust of his mother had even been consciously expressed—there was a German and a British Mrs K. and he had said he did not know on which side she was. There is a close connection between this distrust and the scarcity of light blue in this drawing.

pouring mucus down into his stomach as well as fighting his 'little' and 'big job', an internal enemy. This internal fight had previously been connected with his cold, and today he had told her when he arrived that his cold had returned.

After leaving the house, Richard told Mrs K. that he felt his cold 'red-hot' inside him, but actually he did not seem to have any pain or trouble.

## FIFTY-SIXTH SESSION (Thursday)

Richard went to meet Mrs K. much nearer to her lodgings than usual. (As a rule when he was early he waited either in front of the playroom, or met Mrs K. at the corner of the road, which meant that he walked for a minute or two with her.) He was very excited because he had brought her a letter from his mother, asking her to make two changes next week, so that he could spend more time at home with his brother, who was coming on leave. He also asked Mrs K. what she had decided about the Sunday hours after the following Sunday, after which his father would have returned home. Richard was delighted when Mrs K. replied that she would change the times and would not see him on Sundays after the next one.[1] He was obviously relieved about Mrs K.'s decision. He put his arm swiftly round her shoulder, saying that he was fond of her. He suddenly remembered that he had left the fleet at home; he said he had meant to bring it. (Usually when he did not bring the fleet he gave definite reasons for having left it behind, or merely said he did not feel like bringing it.) Richard noticed, after a quick glance, that Mr Smith was coming along the road and therefore would have met Mrs K. by herself if Richard had not been with her. Richard pointed this out casually, saying, 'There is Mr Smith,' but went on at once talking about the change of sessions.[2]

[1] I had previously left the decision to Richard, but this turned out to be unsatisfactory since he obviously could not make up his mind.

[2] The place where Richard had met me today was at the corner of the road that was nearer to my lodgings and ran parallel to the one where the playroom was situated; and Richard had previously remarked that some people used this road to get to the shops. A few days before, when Richard did not see Mr Smith pass the playroom, he had asked me whether I had seen him on the road before I met Richard, and had mumbled that he did not like me to meet Mr Smith by myself. This had been the reason why—against his principle not to impose on me—he had met me nearer to my lodgings to prevent my meeting Mr Smith by myself.

*Mrs K.*, when they arrived at the playroom, referred to what Richard had said recently about her meeting Mr Smith, and that Richard, in waiting for her at that corner, might have wanted to find out whether she met Mr Smith sometimes on the way to the playroom. He had repeatedly, and again on the previous day, expressed his jealousy and suspicion about Mrs K. going to the grocer's and to Mr Evans's shop.

Richard looked searchingly at Mrs K. and asked whether Mr Evans was very fond of her and whether he 'gave' her many sweets.

*Mrs K.* interpreted his jealousy of every man whom she met or might have known in the past. He was still jealous of Mr K. although he knew he was dead. But when he referred to him as if he were alive, this not only meant that he felt Mrs K. still contained him, but that Mr K. stood also for all the men with whom Mrs K. in the present might have sexual relations. He also seemed to be very suspicious of Mummy in this respect.

Richard sat down at the table and asked for the pad and pencils. Mrs K. discovered that she had left the pad at home. She said she was sorry, and Richard tried to control his feelings and said he was going to make his drawings on the back of earlier ones. He first drew three flags next to one another—the swastika, the Union Jack, and the Italian flag—and then sang the National Anthem. Then he drew a few musical notes and sang a tune to these notes; he wrote 3 plus 2 equals 5, but did not give any associations. Then he began scribbling on another page, making dots with quick, angry movements, and in between he wrote his name and hid it again under scribbles. Now his anger and sorrow, which he had been trying to restrain, had become quite apparent, both in his movements and in his facial expression. He looked very much changed—white and suffering—and it was clear that his anger about Mrs K. not having brought the pad was coupled with misery.

*Mrs K.* interpreted that her not bringing the pad was felt by Richard as if the good Mummy at that moment had turned into the hostile and bad one who was also allied with the hostile Daddy— now Mr Smith. This was shown in the drawing of the flags; the British flag, representing himself, was squeezed in between the hostile German and Italian flags. Richard also felt that Mrs K. and Mummy had turned hostile towards him because, when he was frustrated and did not get enough milk and love and attention from Mummy, he soiled her secretly with his urine and fæces; therefore in turn he expected her to frustrate him as a punishment.[1] Mrs K.

[1] Joan Riviere (Int. Journal of Psycho-Anal., 1927, Vol. 8) suggested a connection between deprivation and the super-ego mother. Cf. also Ernest Jones, 'Early Development of Female Sexuality', *ibid.*

also suggested that when he was jealous of men in connection with her—Mr Smith, the grocer, Mr Evans—he tried to believe that they were nice. At the same time he suspected them of being insincere and 'rascals' towards her and towards him. The 'nice' Mrs K. and the 'light-blue' Mummy also seemed in his mind to be sweet, but he could not trust them either; as soon as they withheld love and goodness—now the pad—they turned into enemies.

Richard had been scribbling angrily, spoke for a moment like 'Larry the Lamb', but quickly returned to making angry noises. Meanwhile he had been sharpening all the pencils, and swiftly, with a glance to see whether Mrs K. saw him do it, he bit the green pencil which had often stood for Mummy (and which so far he had not bitten or injured) and put its rubber end into the pencil sharpener, thereby damaging the rubber. . . . He scribbled over Drawing 43 which represented an anti-aircraft gun shooting at a round object and which had been interpreted by Mrs K. as Richard shooting at Mummy's breast.

*Mrs K.* interpreted that Richard's biting the pencil and secretly using the sharpener on the rubber end expressed his feeling that he had secretly bitten up and destroyed Mummy's breast as well as soiled it. These feelings came up again every time he felt frustrated. But he also felt every disappointment and deprivation as a punishment for having attacked or destroyed Mummy's breast. Now he had expressed this in relation to Mrs K.—the pencil representing her as well as Mummy; he had been careful that she should not see what he was doing to her.

Richard went outside and noticed a man in the garden on the other side of the road (which was at a distance at which he could not possibly hear what was being said). Richard said anxiously, 'He watches us, don't speak'; then he whispered, 'Please say "go away".' Mrs K. said this, but since of course the man did not go, Richard went back to the playroom. But even there he walked on tiptoe. He found a quoit on a shelf, threw it against the stools and up to the ceiling. He said under his breath, 'Poor old thing.' When it rolled towards the cupboard (which formerly Richard had closed so that the ball would not fall into it), Richard took it quickly away.

*Mrs K.* pointed out that the 'poor old thing' represented her breast and genital, pushed violently against the genitals of various men (the stools)—Mr Smith, Mr Evans, the grocer—of whom he had been jealous. In that way he meant to punish and ill-treat both parents, was suspicious of both, and became very sorry for them (Note I).

Richard was writing something and read it out in a defiant tone:

'I am going back home on Monday to see Paul. Ha-ha-ha-ha, ho-ho-ho-ho, ho-ho-ho-ho, haw-haw-haw-haw.'

*Mrs K.* interpreted that Richard wished to show her that he was pleased to leave her and could turn to Paul, because he felt frustrated by her (not bringing the pad) and jealous, believing that she preferred Mr Smith or Mr Evans to him. But he also wanted to show that he did not care, that he felt triumph and punished her by deserting her. He might also have had such feelings when he allied himself with Paul against Nurse, standing for Mummy. He had just written 'haw-haw-haw', which meant that he was like 'Lord Haw-Haw', of whom he had spoken repeatedly as the worst traitor to this country. Richard felt he was like him if he turned against his parents with secret biting and bombing attacks.

Richard went to the window and looked out. He said under his breath 'Why don't you keep me for two hours every day?' (Note II).

*Mrs K.* asked did he mean twice daily?

Richard replied, 'No, two hours at a time.'

*Mrs K.* interpreted that he had been deeply upset because she did not bring the white pad, which stood for his good relation with her and for her good breast, and yesterday had been linked with the Milky Way. As a baby he had felt that he did not get enough from Mummy's breasts; and might have been angry and disappointed when he was given the bottle, which he disliked and suspected as bad. Now this situation was repeated with Mrs K. when she gave him the yellow pad and, as he felt, took away the white one. In fact, today he had been given neither of them.

Richard made Drawing 49 slowly and carefully. He said, while drawing it, that this was altogether different. When he had finished, he said it was an eagle and he pointed at the lighter sections in the centre, saying that this was its face and beak. Richard pulled up his coat over his ears, leaving only part of his face uncovered, and said this was what the eagle was doing.

*Mrs K.* interpreted that the eagle inside the coat represented Richard inside Mrs K. (and Mummy); he had gone into her, hurting her inside and devouring her. The black eagle also stood for Daddy's devouring genital, blackening and destroying Mummy. At the same time it also meant Richard's inside, into which both Mrs K. and Mummy had entered. Mrs K. reminded him of the queen with the light-blue crown, who had turned out to be a devouring bird with a big beak and 'horrid "big job" dropping from it' (Forty-fifth Session). Richard felt he contained this 'devouring' bird—now represented by the eagle. It was so black because Richard's scribbling meant that with his 'big job' he had blackened the bird-Mummy, and then she blackened his inside with it (Note III).

Richard fetched the calendar and looked at the pictures, admiring landscapes and in particular, as he had done before, some daffodils.

*Mrs K.* interpreted that Richard was trying to get comfort about what he felt to be a bad, dangerous, and dirty inside—his own as well as Mummy's—by looking at the lovely country.

Richard asked Mrs K. had she been to the cinema last night, or what else had she been doing then.

*Mrs K.* reminded him that on the previous day when he had examined the calendar, he had begged her to tell him her secrets. Today he had shown how very much he suspected her of having sexual relations with different men.

Richard, towards the end of the session, climbed up on a wide shelf, opened the first-aid box there, looked into it, shook the shelf above him and wondered if it was going to come down on top of him. . . . He told Mrs K. he had been to the fish-and-chip shop and eaten chips but not fish, which he would have hated to eat in such a dirty nightmare place, full of horrid dirty children—really disgusting.[1] The red-haired girl had not been there, but the imbecile was, a horrible creature; Richard could kill him if the law were not against it.

*Mrs K.* interpreted that Richard, by going to the fish-and-chip shop, where formerly he would never have dared to enter, showed that he was less frightened of children; it was also a sign how very much he wanted to see what the inside of Mummy's body was really like, since he pictured it full of poisonous dirty children who, as he felt, had become dirty because he had bombed and soiled them. She reminded him of the 'slum' in his play, which was supposed to be full of diseases and dirty children (Sixteenth Session).

When Richard and Mrs K. left together, he seemed surprised and upset that she went to her lodgings, although during this session Richard had remarked that he knew Mrs K. did not go to the village on Thursdays, but usually went straight home. This frustration might have also contributed to his going to meet Mrs K. so much nearer her home, which was rather an unusual thing for him to do.

Richard's mother reported to Mrs K. by telephone that on that particular afternoon Richard was very wretched and worried. He said so to her and also retired to bed, which normally he only did

---

[1] Such remarks, full of contempt for poor and dirty children, were frequent with Richard, particularly now in relation to the hated evacuee children. His mother had told me that Richard was contemptuous of people in inferior social positions, like servants, although he never heard such remarks at home.

when he felt ill. He had been most difficult since his father had arrived, irritable and moody, but on that afternoon and evening he was strikingly depressed and unhappy.

*Notes to Fifty-sixth Session:*

I. Paranoid and depressive anxiety alternated more quickly during recent sessions. Richard had come much closer to experiencing the depressive position, which was also shown in his greater sympathy with the enemy which I referred to in an earlier note. I have repeatedly pointed out that the depressive position implies also persecutory anxiety, but is characterized by a prevalence of depressive anxiety and guilt and the tendency to make reparation.

II. There is no doubt that the longing for a fully satisfactory breast-feeding had come up very urgently. (As I have mentioned, Richard's breast-feeding had been unsatisfactory and short.) The fundamental importance of the relation to the mother's breast had already appeared with full strength in the preceding sessions. In the Fifty-fourth Session, the deep disappointment and anxiety aroused by the yellowish pad had shown the longing, never overcome, for the mother's good breast (the white pad, the 'Milky Way' on my dress). However, the white pad also meant that Richard could have confidence in a completely reliable mother; and in bringing the wrong pad I had proved untrustworthy and had revived his early doubts in his mother. In the Fifty-sixth Session, for the first time during his analysis, Richard had asked why I did not give him two sessions consecutively. Clearly at that moment the desire had come up for a fully satisfactory feeding situation—expressed by both breasts giving him all possible gratification. This was, however, not only a regression to babyhood : he was also upset because I seemed to have become unreliable in the present situation. Speaking generally, I would say that such elements of a current situation are, simultaneously with regression, always operative in varying degrees and imply that the more developed ego is still to some extent active in spite of the regression. It is this non-regressed part of the ego with which we make contact in our interpretations and which allows interpretations to be effective. As far as Richard was concerned, I had proved unreliable because I had first given him a yellow pad and then no pad at all. This reinforced his feeling that he could not trust me because I was going to leave him, and confirmed his suspicions about his mother. The analysis of these feelings in the current situation had also made it possible to analyse the earliest dissatisfaction and doubts experienced in babyhood.

The Fifty-sixth Session, when I had forgotten to bring the new white pad with me, started with great jealousy of Mr Smith, and it became clear how very much Richard had suspected me of meeting Mr Smith in his absence. The revived ambivalent breast relation had led to the openly expressed, heightened, and paranoid jealousy of the men he connected with me. I have found that the earliest jealousy and suspicion of the father are based on the baby's feelings that when he is not able to enjoy the breast or is frustrated by it, somebody else—the father—has got hold of it (cf. 'Some Theoretical Conclusions Regarding the Emotional Life of the Infant', 1952, *Writings*, 3; these conclusions had already been foreshadowed in my *Psycho-Analysis of Children*, Chapter VIII). This view is of importance in explaining the nature of the earliest stages of the Œdipus complex which are influenced by such jealousy and suspicion.

I have formerly also expounded my contention that paranoia is based on the distrust and hate of the internalized penis of the father (see in this connection my comments about the 'Wolf man', *Psycho-Analysis of Children*, Chapter IX). Further work has led me to link that distrust and hate of the internalized penis of the father with the relation to the mother's breast, for hate and distrust of the breast are transferred to the penis of the father. All these factors seem to me of importance in the understanding of paranoia.

The link between paranoia and homosexuality is well known. The positive element in homosexuality, as I suggested (and I would here recall Freud's conclusions about Leonardo Da Vinci) lies in transferring love for the breast to the penis and in an equation between these two part-objects. The hostile element in homosexuality, which in some degree is always bound up with lesser or stronger paranoid feelings, derives from the factors described above : the hate and distrust of the breast; the suspicion of the intruding father (penis) and the need to pacify him. There is, therefore, a strong connection between paranoid jealousy, which was illustrated in the material of this session, and a turning towards the man in order to pacify him. There are, of course, a number of other elements in homosexuality, some of which I have referred to in preceding notes and in former writings.

As had appeared repeatedly, Richard was both jealous of Mr Smith and attracted to him, and was very envious of the sweets and cigarettes which Mr Evans gave me. The homosexual component had also become quite clear in these sessions in his relation to his father, at the time when his father was staying in 'X', and was very much influenced by Richard's attempts to cope with his Œdipus jealousy and paranoid suspicions.

III. This is an instance of projective identification which is quickly followed by, and possibly simultaneous with, internalization. The fear of the object attacked by hostile projective identification (such as bad fæces put into it) in turn increases the feeling that the object will intrude into the subject. It is important to distinguish in analysis between this fear of being intruded into by the object with whom projective identification has occurred and the process of introjecting the hostile object. In the former case the ego is the victim of the intruding object, while in introjection it is the ego which sets the process in motion, even though it is bound to lead to persecutory anxiety.

## FIFTY-SEVENTH SESSION (Friday)

Richard again met Mrs K. nearer her home. He knew quite well that he was not supposed to do that, though Mrs K. had not expressly forbidden it. He straight away held out the fleet which he was carrying in his hand (for the first time he did not carry it in his pocket), being keen to show it to Mrs K. at once. He was very friendly and talkative, obviously trying to amuse and pacify her. Very soon he asked whether she had already met Mr Smith. Mrs K.'s answer that she had not did not seem to disperse Richard's doubts, for he kept on looking out for Mr Smith. Soon after they had arrived at the playroom, Richard noticed that Mr Smith was passing by and seemed relieved; but he became worried when Mr Smith stopped by the garden on the other side of the road to talk to the old man there (the one whom Richard had nicknamed 'the bear'). Richard asked whether Mr Smith could hear Mrs K. and him, and began to speak in whispers.

*Mrs K*. interpreted that by meeting her near her lodgings, Richard not only wanted to find out whether she was going to see Mr Smith and what they would do together, but that he also wanted to go into Mrs K.'s bedroom and find out whether perhaps she went to bed with the 'grumpy old gentleman'.

Richard interrupted at this point, asking whether there had been any raids by the R.A.F.

*Mrs K*. added that he would like to watch her movements day and night, as he wished to do with Mummy, but this was not only because he was jealous but also because sexual intercourse meant to him dangerous attacks like the R.A.F. raids, which could kill Mummy as the tramp-Daddy might have done, or Hitler might kill Mrs K. when she returned to London.

Richard, though embarrassed, agreed that he always very closely watched Mummy to find out what she had been doing and was inquisitive about all her movements, and in particular about any letters she received. He added, 'And she watches me all the time— no, she does not.'

*Mrs K*. interpreted that Richard's curiosity was increased by the desire to know what went on in his mother's inside. He was afraid that the 'rascal'-Daddy (and the 'rascal'-Richard), who seemed nice but was treacherous, was injuring and bombing her; and in this way Mummy would be changed into the poisoned 'nightmare' fish shop. Because he constantly watched her, he expected her to watch him all the time [Projection], though he realized that this was not actually true: that was why he had added, 'No, she does not.'

Richard went to the tap, drank from it, and said that all this was very unpleasant to hear and he wished Mrs K. would not say it. . . . He put out the fleet and asked Mrs K. whether she would do something for him.

*Mrs K.* asked what he wanted.

Richard replied, would she help him to darken the room completely? With her help he did so very thoroughly. He said it had to be so dark that he himself could not see the fleet or it would be no good, he would not be able to make a night attack. He made sure by touch which was the *Nelson* (as he had previously shown Mrs K., there was a very slight difference between *Nelson* and *Rodney*, which otherwise were quite alike, the difference being that the mast of the *Rodney* was a little 'injured', it was not quite so pointed).

*Mrs K.* again interpreted that Richard felt that her and Mummy's—and all women's—genitals were injured, that the penis was broken or cut off. He had shown this in earlier drawings, in particular Drawing 3: quite recently he had spoken about this difference (Fifty-third Session).

Richard moved the *Nelson* out with rather loud noises. He commented dramatically: 'There he goes and does not know he might be attacked in the dark.' (As usual, he said 'he' about the *Nelson* and 'she' about the *Rodney*.) Then Richard moved out one destroyer, and made a few more follow it.

Mrs K. asked who was going to attack the *Nelson* at night.

Richard immediately replied, 'Me.' He added, could Mrs K. hear the ghosts who were attacking the *Nelson*, and he made some rather unusual noises.

*Mrs K.* interpreted that Richard felt he would wish to attack Daddy like a ghost in the dark, then Daddy would not realize that it was Richard who was attacking him. Richard might also be afraid that he and Daddy would die in the fight, and then both of them would soon be ghosts. . . .

Richard, a little earlier, had told Mrs K. that he was worried about an 'awful' new boy who had arrived at the hotel. People thought he was nice—perhaps he even was. But Richard knew that the boy was going to suggest to him that they should play together and the boy would also watch Richard. Or was it perhaps he himself who was always looking at other boys and watching them? ... Meanwhile, Richard had repeatedly switched the light on and off and decided to draw back the curtains. He had also looked out from behind the curtain to see whether Mr Smith was still there and remarked with relief that he had gone.

*Mrs K.* interpreted this fleet play as expressing Richard's feelings at night. He wished to attack Daddy and Mummy but was terrified of doing so. Richard's bombs—the R.A.F.—would then, he felt, fall on the bad, hostile parents, but would injure or destroy the good ones as well. Mrs K. also interpreted Richard's fear of being watched and overheard. At the beginning of the session he had wondered whether Mr Smith could hear him and Mrs K., and had begun to whisper. All this connected with Richard's constant wish to spy on his parents and watch their every movement, to find out their hidden thoughts and attack them secretly. But having in his mind eaten them up—the chips in the fish shop, the salmon, the whale, now the black eagle—he also felt that he contained the dangerous Daddy and Mummy who would watch him internally and know all his movements and thoughts. That made him so afraid of being looked at by the 'awful' boy in the hotel, and of being overheard by Mr Smith or the other man (even though they were on the opposite side of the road and could not possibly hear him).

Richard had been listening intently, particularly when Mrs K. spoke about his feelings of persecution by men and boys. He asked, evidently trying to understand, why was this always on his mind and were the thoughts that he and Mrs K. were talking about quite real to him. He went outside and looked round but, though the weather was beautiful, he remained serious and silent. He threw a stone at a cat in the next garden which he thought was spoiling vegetables, and returned to the playroom. He looked round and was glad to see that the Girl Guides who had been there on the previous day had not rearranged anything. ... He decided to sweep the room and particularly to clean the floor under the electric fire. Then he went into the kitchen and cleaned the stove, removing some soot. He asked Mrs K. to replace the axe which had been lying on the stove so that nobody should know that he had moved it.

*Mrs K.* interpreted Richard's fear of the bad babies inside Mrs K. (and Mummy), soiling and poisoning her, and of the bad 'big job' which Richard felt he and the bad Daddy had put into her. The cat which was spoiling the vegetables stood for Richard disturbing the growth of the good babies, and when he was pleased that the Girl Guides had not upset things in the playroom, this expressed the hope that he and the children would after all not harm Mummy's inside, or that it could be put right by him. This was shown by his cleaning the room and stove.

Richard picked up a book, read in it, and looked at the illustrations. His face brightened when he saw a picture of a child playing with a tiny kitten. Another picture at which he looked with interest was of a cat in front of a high wall.

*Mrs K.* interpreted that Richard was so pleased with the picture of the kitten and the child because it represented to him the good baby whom he wanted to give to Mummy, or whom he wanted to have for himself.

Richard was so lost in thought that he did not seem to hear that Mrs K. was speaking to him. Suddenly he looked up as if awakening from a dream, gazed into Mrs K.'s face without apparently taking any notice of what she interpreted, and said with strong feeling. 'You look very nice. You have a nice face. I am very fond of you.'

*Mrs K.* interpreted that when Richard was so anxious about what went on in Mummy's and Mrs K.'s inside, he seemed to feel that they became not only destroyed but angry, and turned into the 'wicked brute'. When through Mrs K.'s interpretations he realized that he was not only afraid of Mrs K. and Mummy but also hoped that they contained good babies and friendly thoughts, Richard could actually look at Mrs K. and found that she appeared as the good, which also meant uninjured and helpful, Mummy and that she looked nice.

As usual, Richard had repeatedly asked whether Mrs K. was going to the village and whether she was going to the grocer's. Although the shoe-shop, where Mrs K. said she was going, was nearer than the grocer's shop and Richard would therefore have less time with her, he seemed quite satisfied. There were only women assistants in the shoe-shop, and this might have reassured him (Note I).

*Note to Fifty-seventh Session:*

I. The stronger paranoid element in his jealousy of Mr Smith and other men in relation to me was clearly the result of his father's presence in 'X'. The analysis of his Œdipus complex helped to bring out to the full the repressed jealousy of his father and the phantasies about the sexual intercourse of the parents. This seems to contradict my observation that the depressive position had come more strongly to the fore. I would suggest, however, that, together with his paranoid and jealous feelings about his father, the conflict between love and hate had also become more accessible to the analysis, and the mixed feelings towards the parents—such as guilt about displacing the father and the pity for him—were more in evidence. Together with his more acute jealousy, he was also more aware of its paranoid character, which was shown by his often being puzzled about his suspicions.

## FIFTY-EIGHTH SESSION (Saturday)

Richard met Mrs K. at the corner of the road near the playroom. He looked very worried. First he asked whether the rearrangement of his sessions (to enable him to go home for his brother's leave) was still all right. Then he said he had some very distressing news. He was going to tell Mrs K. about it, but decided to wait until they were inside the house—it would be better there. He asked Mrs K. whether she had met Mr Smith, and at that moment noticed that he was passing by. He exchanged an extremely friendly greeting with him, but watched the way Mrs K. greeted him. When they were in the playroom, he put out the fleet and told Mrs K. the news. He had had more earache, and the doctor said that both ears were pink inside but that the right one 'was of course the worse of the two'. He did not reply to Mrs K.'s question why this was 'of course the worse', but only added that it hurt more. In fact, at present it did not hurt at all, but what worried him so much was that he might need another operation. He often worried about this. All along Richard had been watching the road from the window and then said, with obvious relief, 'Mr Smith has gone.' (Mr Smith had again had a chat with the man on the other side of the road.)

*Mrs K.* pointed out that Mr Smith (standing for Mr K. and Daddy) was a constant source of persecution to Richard.

Richard looked very puzzled and said that Mr Smith was really quite a nice man. . . . He mentioned that Mr Evans had 'given' him sweets yesterday and praised him very much for that.

When Mrs K. asked whether Mr Evans had sold the sweets to him, Richard agreed, but passed this over very quickly, obviously not wanting to realize that Mr Evans actually took money for the sweets. Suddenly he became angry about Mr Evans and said that he had accepted an order for strawberries and had not delivered them. He said Mr Evans was a cheat. He also complained that on the previous Sunday, when people were queueing up for newspapers, Mr Evans had sent him back to the end of the queue, and Richard could have murdered him. (Mrs K. had been in that queue and Richard was particularly humiliated because she had seen the incident. On the very next day he has asked Mrs K. whether she too had been standing in the queue, knowing quite well that she had, and had tried to hide his anger; Mrs K. had interpreted this. . . .) A little later Richard watched two boys on the road and said he knew them. One of them came from 'Z'. He said they were quite nice. He added that they had not been looking round at him because they did not feel, as he did, that they must watch other boys all the time. Meanwhile he had begun to arrange the fleet. He had—which was quite unusual—put the *Nelson* to his mouth, taking the mast between his teeth. For a little while he chased a bluebottle, calling it 'Mr Bluebottle'. At first he intended to kill it, then he decided that Mr Bluebottle wanted to get out of prison, caught it between his fingers, and set it free.

*Mrs K.* interpreted that the mast of *Nelson* stood, as often before, for Daddy's and now Mr Smith's genital. Mr Bluebottle had the same meaning. Richard wanted to destroy Daddy and his genital, which he felt he had taken into himself. He had just again shown this by biting the mast of *Nelson*. But the bluebottle also represented Daddy, for whom Richard was sorry. Another reason for setting it free was that Richard wanted to get rid of this genital he had desired and taken in, and at the same time was most suspicious and afraid of it. He was constantly expecting retaliation for his own hostile feelings towards Daddy and his genital. If the 'Mr Bluebottle-genital' was imprisoned in Richard's inside, what would Richard feel was happening to him?

Richard went on arranging the fleet. He put out some destroyers; another group was formed by submarines, another by the two cruisers; the ships in each group were side by side and little space was left between the groups. Richard explained that the cruisers were himself and Mrs K. After a little while he made *Nelson* move out, go all round the table, and hide behind the cliffs formed by Mrs K.'s bag and basket.[1] Soon *Rodney* followed, trying to find *Nelson*, who had attempted to return to *Rodney* but missed her because she had gone the other way round. Richard then spoke of 'poor lonely *Nelson*'. Now *Rodney* was hidden behind the cliffs. *Nelson* steamed into the harbour. Meanwhile Richard had put a submarine between the Richard-cruiser and the Mrs K.-cruiser, saying that this was Bobbie. At once he made *Nelson* move towards the Richard- and Mrs K.-cruisers, and made loud noises.

*Mrs K.* asked whether *Nelson* was angry.

Richard said yes, and that *Nelson* was asking what Richard was

[1] As so often before, my bag and basket represented a safe hiding-place.

doing here with Mrs K. But when *Nelson* got alongside the Richard-cruiser, quite close to him and remained there, the noise stopped.

*Mrs K.* interpreted that at the beginning of this session Richard had wished to leave Daddy and Mummy happily together and had chosen Mrs K. instead of Mummy, as he had in the past often turned to Nurse instead of Mummy. But he did not succeed in leaving the parents together; in the play Daddy was pushed out and made lonely. Again, Richard had wanted Mummy to follow Daddy and had tried to reunite them, but felt afraid that he could not make them happy. They did not find each other. Bobbie, who had come between the Richard- and Mrs K.-cruisers, stood for Richard's genital, which he had put into Mrs K.; that was why Daddy became so cross and interfered. Mrs K. and Nurse stood for Mummy as well. Therefore Richard feared that Daddy, who was also now represented by Mr Smith, would come in between and attack and injure Richard's penis. The fear of operation on the ear brought up again the fear of the hated doctor (Sixth Session), the bad Daddy, attacking and destroying Richard's genital. Richard joined up with Daddy in order to make him less hostile; but also because he felt sorry for him, the 'lonely *Nelson*'. Now *Nelson*-Daddy and the Richard-cruiser, standing so close to one another, had put their genitals together.

Richard strongly objected to this interpretation and said he could not have such desires, he would not like to do such things with his genital at all.

*Mrs K.* interpreted that these desires towards Daddy and Mummy were covered up by many fears. One was that Daddy was threatening, deserted, and therefore dangerous. Richard also believed that his genital would not be big enough or good enough for Mummy, that it would be injured inside her, that he could not retrieve it from her; but in spite of all these fears he also wished to be able to be in bed with Mummy and to put his genital into her; in order to take Daddy's place with her, he would have to make him lonely or kill him. There was also a deeply hidden wish to 'make love' with Daddy, now Mr Smith, as he had shown by putting *Nelson* and the Richard-cruiser quite close to one another.

Richard had meanwhile moved *Nelson* away, and *Rodney* came out from behind the cliffs. Although he now left enough space for movements, *Rodney* in turning round touched with her stern the sterns of both *Nelson* and the Richard-cruiser, then came alongside Richard. Richard remarked that Mummy (*Rodney*) too was saying something about what he was doing with Mrs K.; then he quickly removed the Bobbie-submarine, which was still between the

Mrs K.- and Richard-cruisers, and said, 'Now the genital is not there any more. . . .' Suddenly he altered everything. All the ships were lying on their sides in a heap and only one destroyer was left, standing upright and apart. Richard said this was the *Vampire* and it was all that was left of the British navy. Then he quickly put up the fleet again : it was now the German fleet. The *Nelson* had become the *Tirpitz* and steamed out. The *Vampire*, which had been hiding behind the cliffs, came out and attacked the *Tirpitz*, which was now joined by other ships. The battle remained undecided. Richard suddenly asked Mrs K. whether she had a knife, and she gave him her penknife. Richard scratched with the knife on the mast of the *Vampire* and said he had cut off the bad bits of it. The penknife now became an American base where all nationalities could land. He said the U.S.A. were not in the war—yes, they were. Japanese and Russian cruisers and the *Vampire*, which now was also German, went alternately into the harbour, and then various battles took place. It appeared that the Russians were no longer on the side of the British but had joined up with Japan and Germany. In the end some of the fleet had become American who, after all, came to the help of the *Vampire* (which by then was again British) and of the British fleet. Here the play finished. Richard ran to the tap, drank from it, and filled the sink.

*Mrs K.* interpreted that the British navy, representing the whole family, had died. The *Vampire* stood for Richard, as it had previously done, and only a day or two before Richard had described himself as 'the biggest destroyer' (Fifty-third Session) ; but he felt he had eaten the others and taken them in. That was why the *Nelson* had suddenly changed into the German *Tirpitz*. Since Richard was left alone, he was lonely and had no allies. He felt that each member of the family had been attacked, betrayed, and deserted by him and, since he contained them all, he felt not only their anger and their attacks inside him, but also their unhappiness; this increased his own unhappiness and loneliness. In the end of his play he had hoped that he could revive the good parents with the help of the good American fleet, and that was when he drank from the tap and filled the sink, standing for his inside, with the water representing the good milk of the good Mummy.

Richard had been looking at the electric fire, which was not turned on, and asked whether he could burn himself on it, and whether there was any electricity in it when it was switched off. He touched it anxiously and then turned it on and watched it becoming red. He switched it off again, saying it was getting too red.

*Mrs K.* interpreted the connection with his feeling that the 'inside of his ears' was very pink.

Richard said that he would like to take the red (imitation) coals out of the fire. He had become increasingly angry. He said he wished to tear out the broken bar from the fire and asked if Mrs K. would allow this if the stove belonged to her.

*Mrs K.* replied that even then she would not want him to break it.

Richard asked if he could break up the table if it were in Mrs K.'s home.

*Mrs K.* said she would not let him break the table completely, but it would not matter if he scratched or marked it; she would let him have pieces of wood or other things to cut up. She interpreted that all these questions expressed his wish to destroy, as well as his fear of destroying, Mrs K., who contained Mr K., the bar standing for a man's genital inside her; this applied also to his parents. Therefore Richard, however angry, also wished Mrs K. to restrain him from violence; he felt he had to be prevented from destroying his parents and from attacking his own genital; cutting off the bad bits from the mast of the *Vampire* destroyer meant doing this to his penis, the bits he cut off being those which seemed to him to be bad and dangerous. He felt full of persecuting people inside him and bad genitals inside his own. He wanted to get rid of them in the same way as he had wished to get rid of Mr Smith and Mr Blue-bottle. When he had suddenly asked whether he could burn himself on the electric fire, though it was switched off, this expressed his uncertainty about his inside being on fire. The pink ear, the ear-ache, stood for Daddy's burning genital inside him, which would burn him in retaliation for Richard's burning attacks on Daddy's genital.

Richard went again to drink water and on the way he found one of the quoits, picked it up, and bit it hard. He said it had a nasty taste. He drank from the tap and said that *this* was good. Before leaving the kitchen he filled the sink and asked Mrs K. to pull out the plug while he went outside to watch with great interest how the water ran out.

During this session Richard had not asked for the pad, which no doubt was the response to Mrs K.'s not having brought it on the previous day (Note I). He felt less persecuted by passers-by and also by internal figures. When in his play the whole fleet was destroyed and the Richard-ship was the only one left, depression was marked; but it did not persist, and he managed to find a happier solution. The impression he conveyed on the whole, there-fore, was not one of hopelessness (Note II).

SALMON

U6

TRUANT

U 72

SUNFISH

U 102

U 16

U2

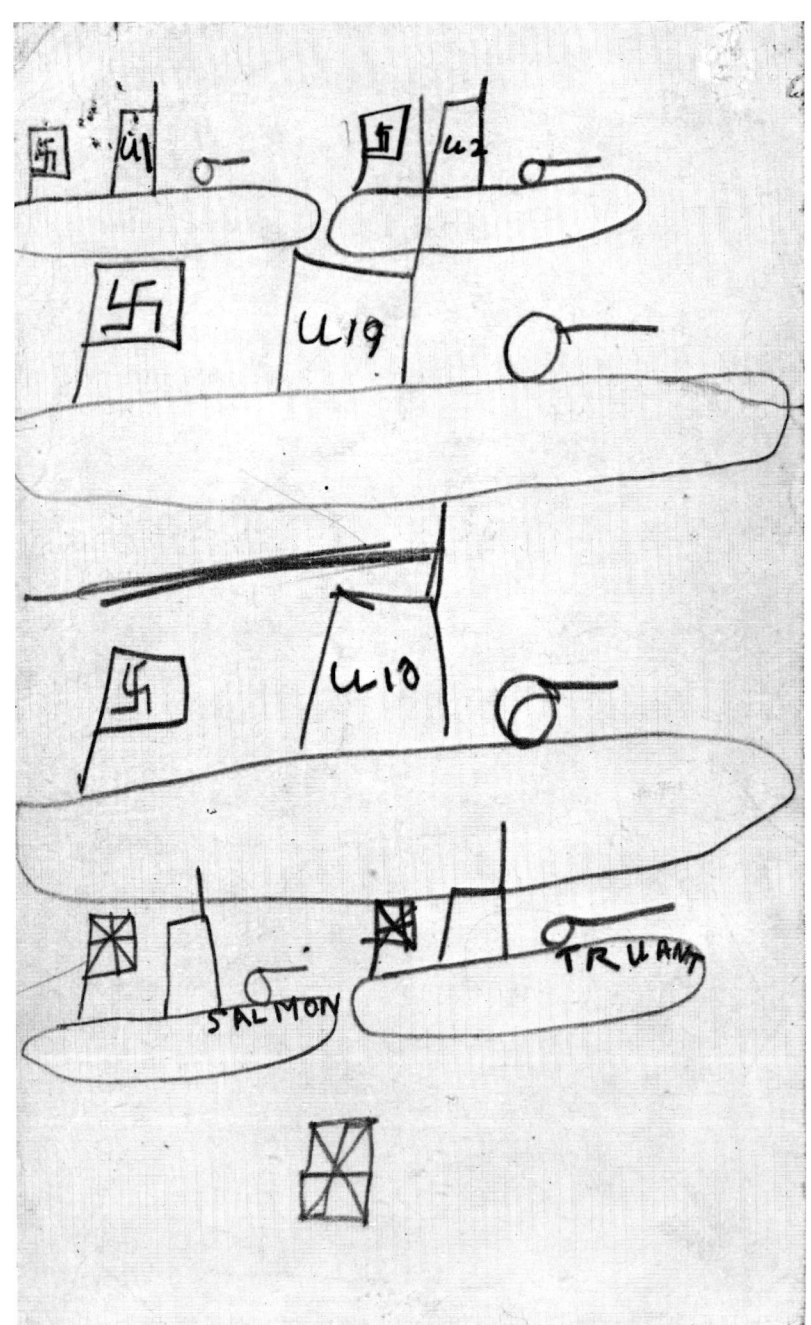

3

4

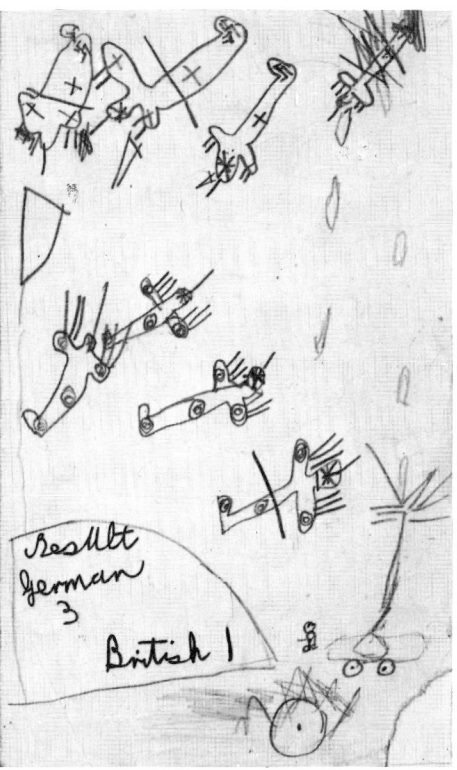

5

6

7

8

9

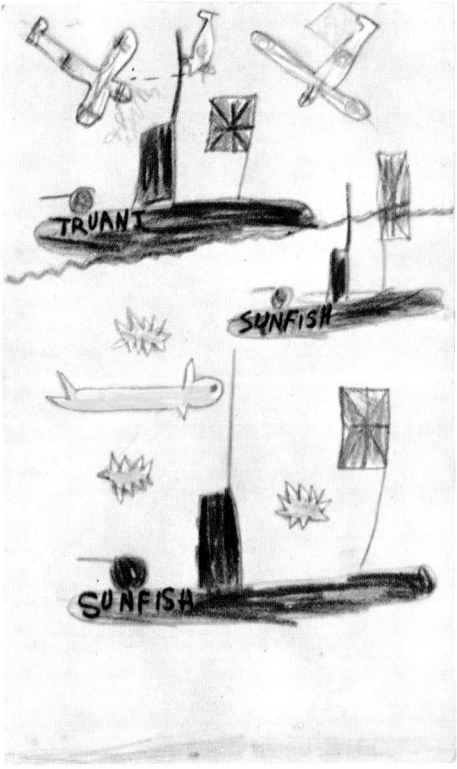

10

11

12　　　　13

14

15

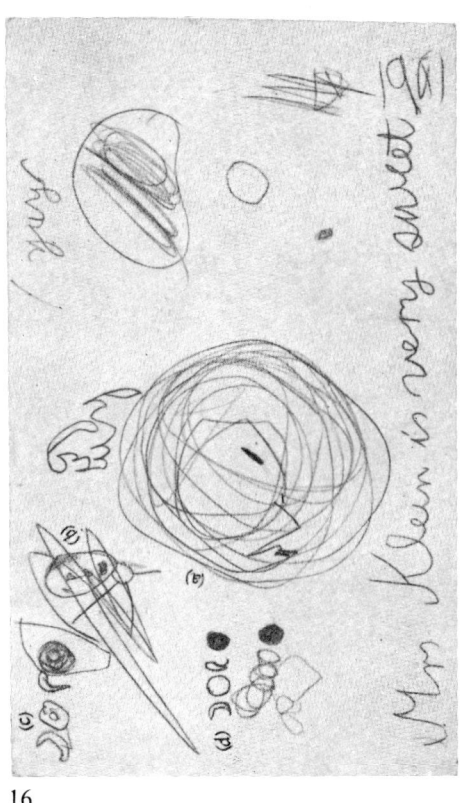

16

17　　　　18

19

20

21

22

23

24

25

26

27

28

29

30

31          32

33

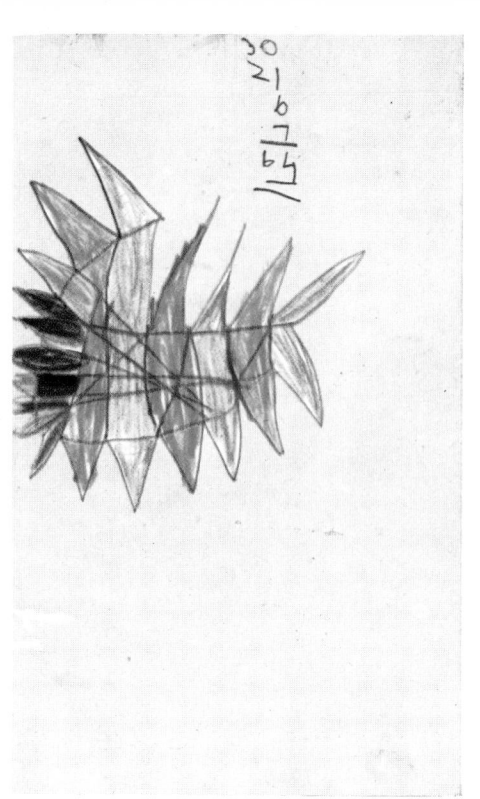

34

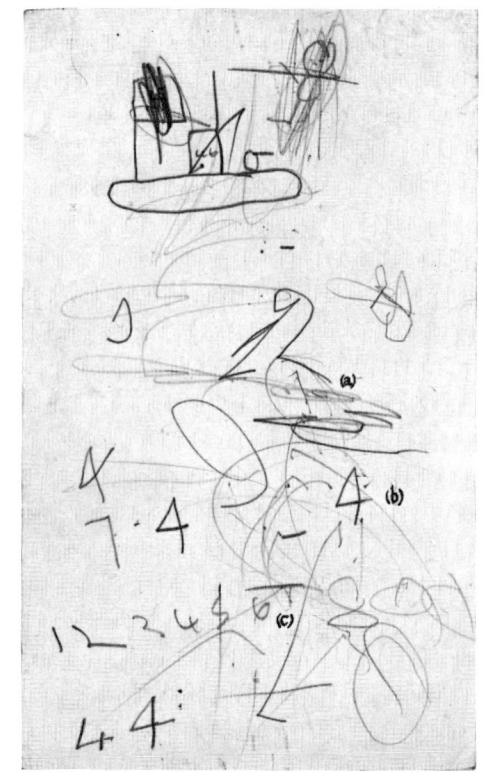

35

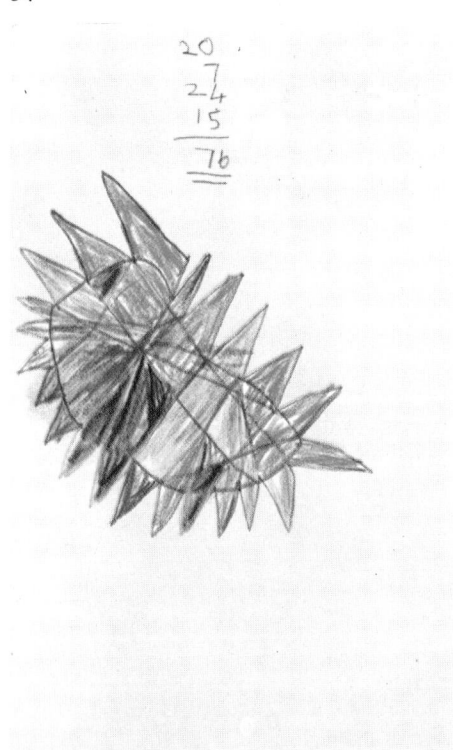

36

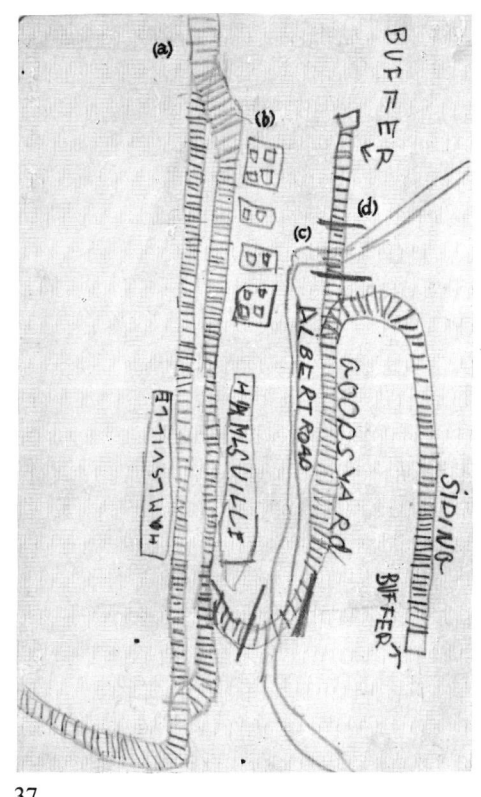

37

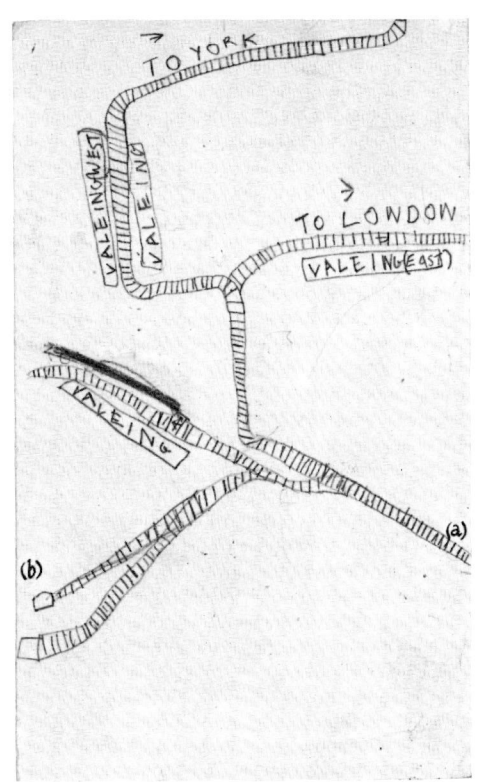

38

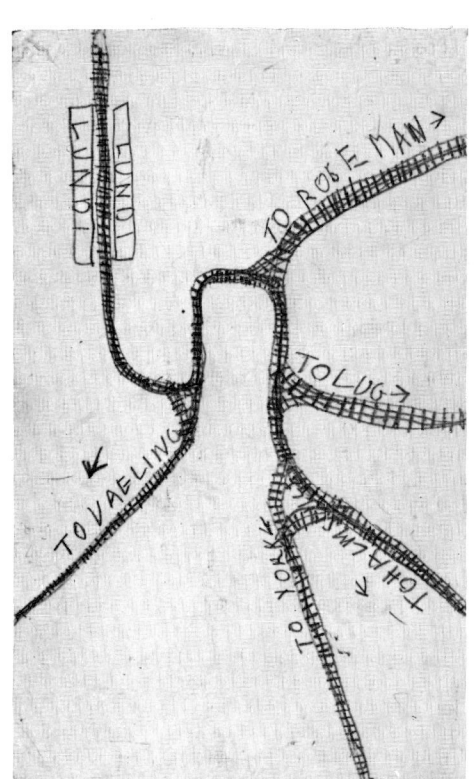

39

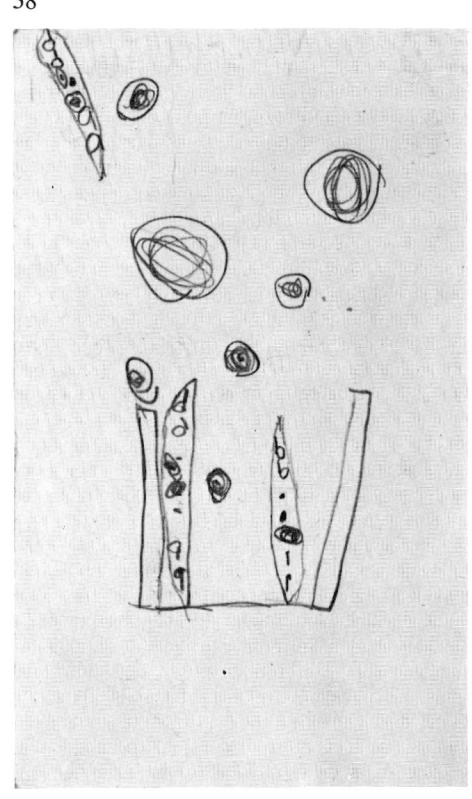

40

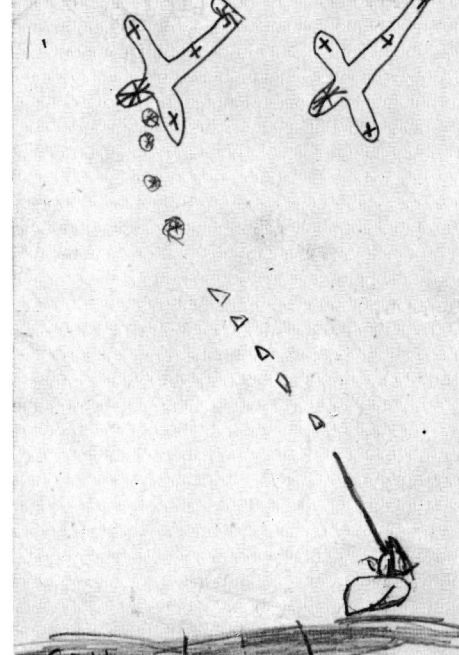

41

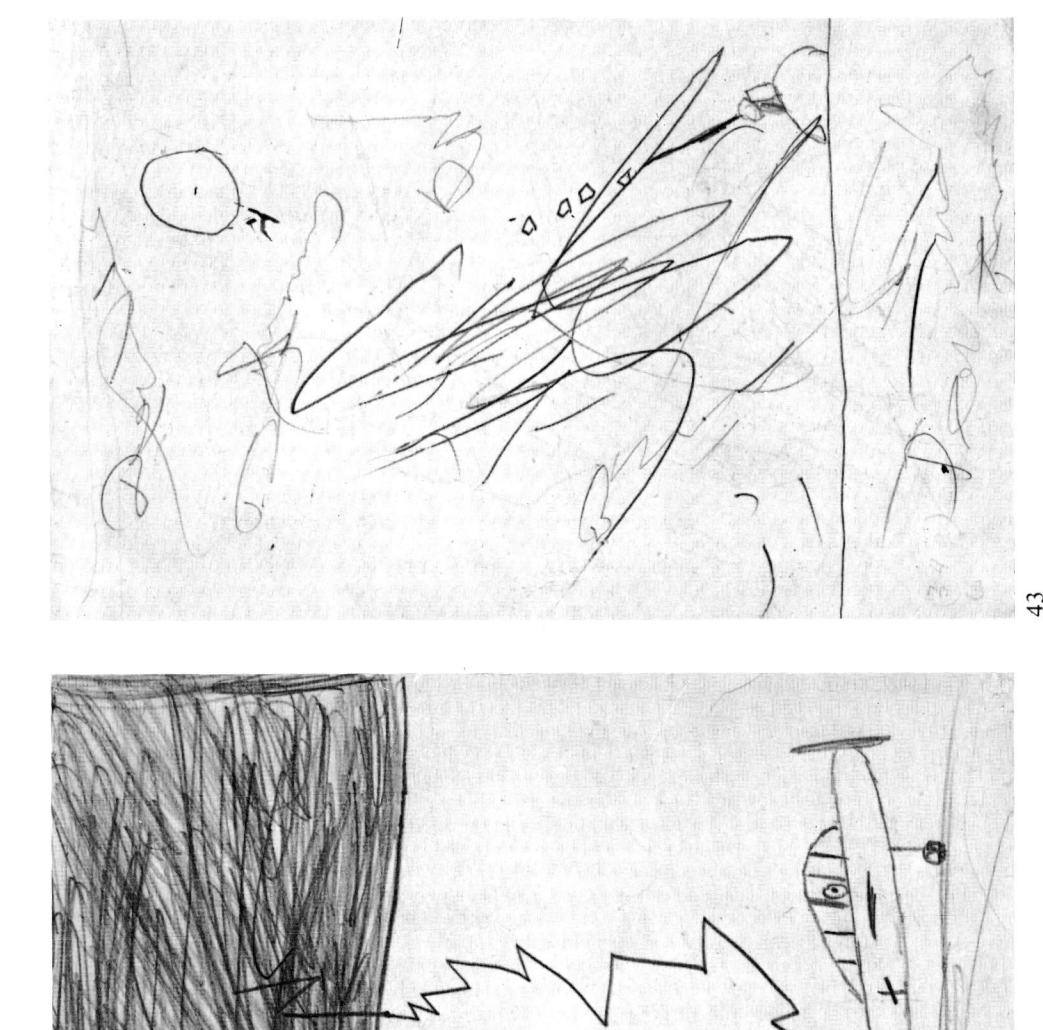

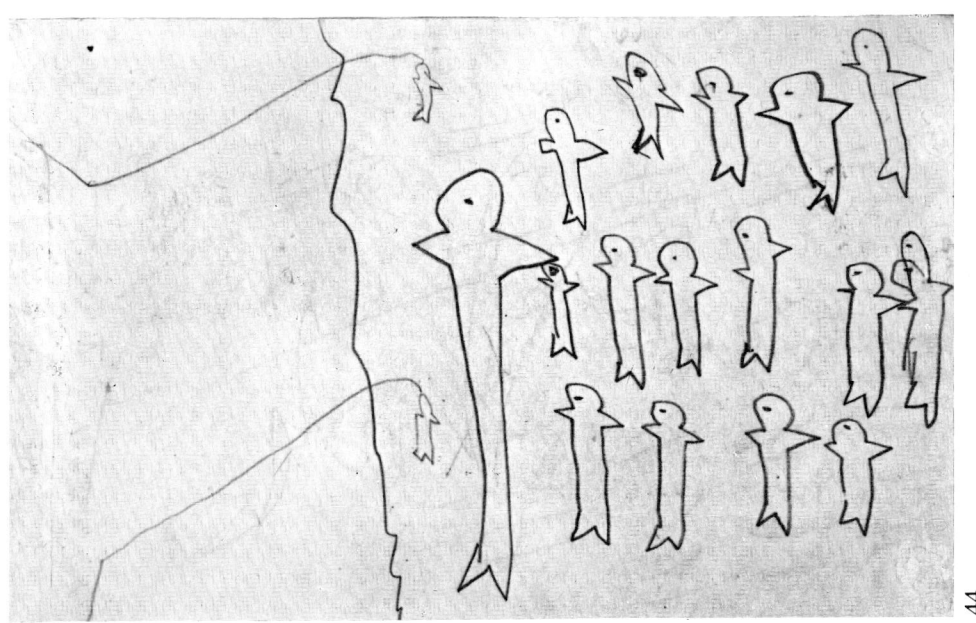

44

45

46

47

48

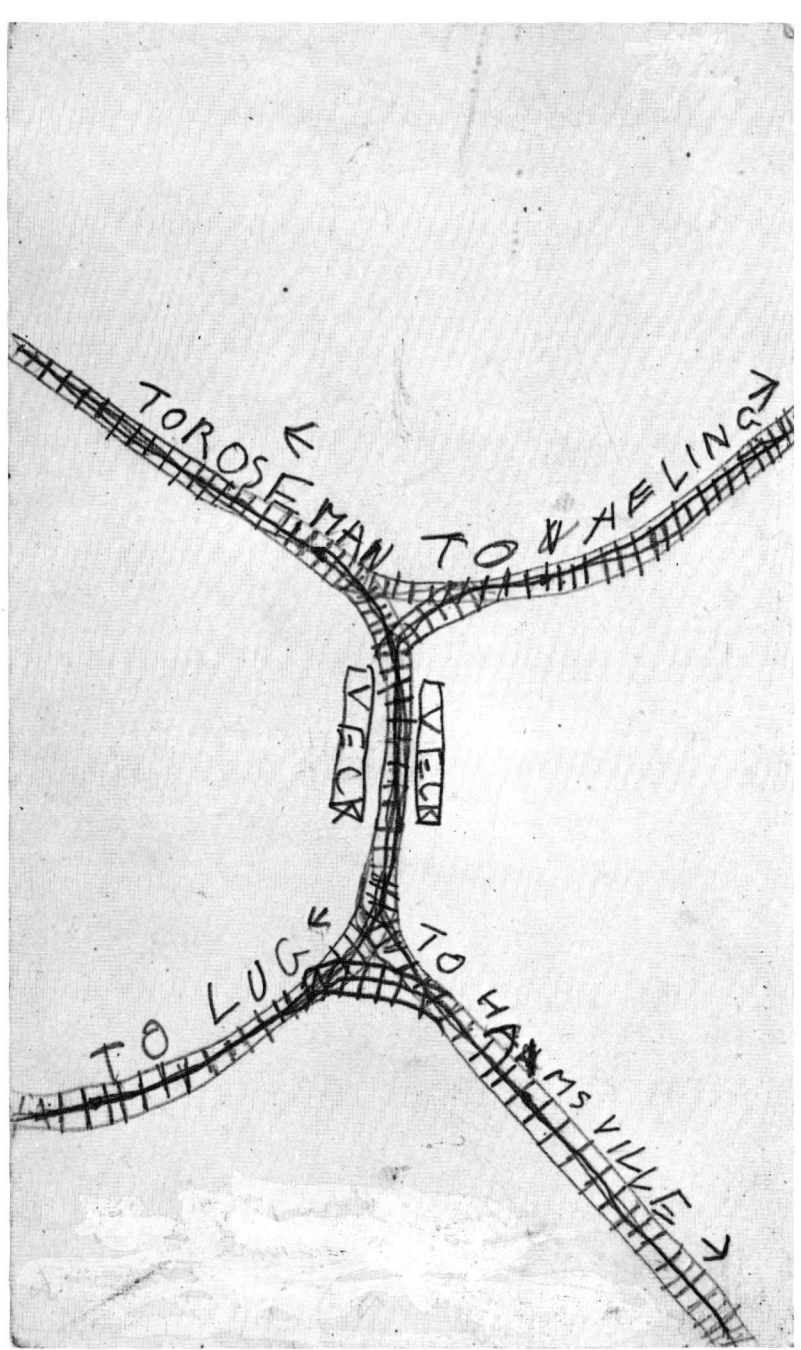

50

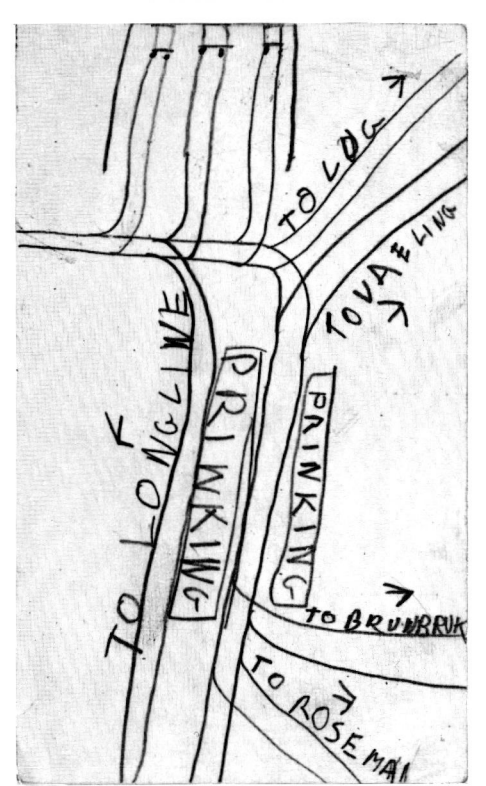

52

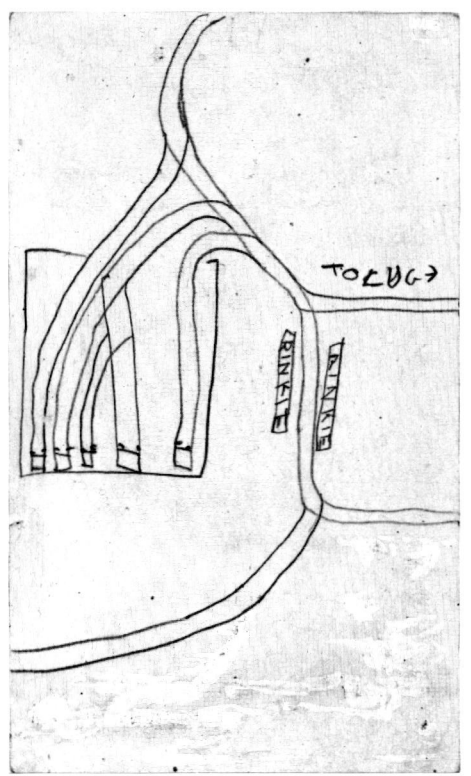

53

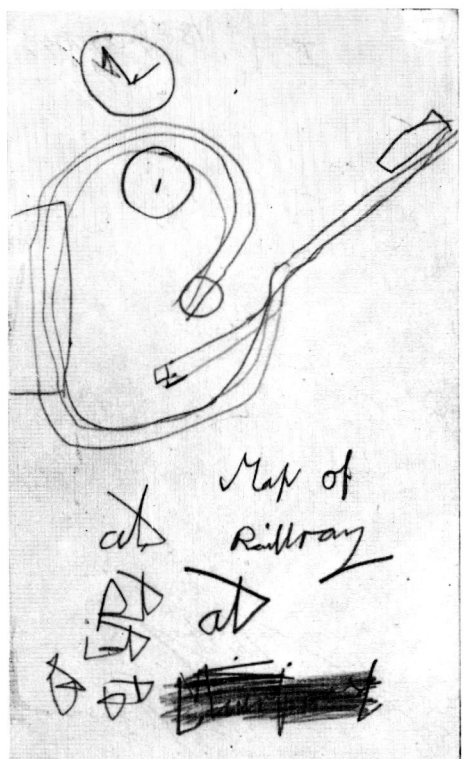

54

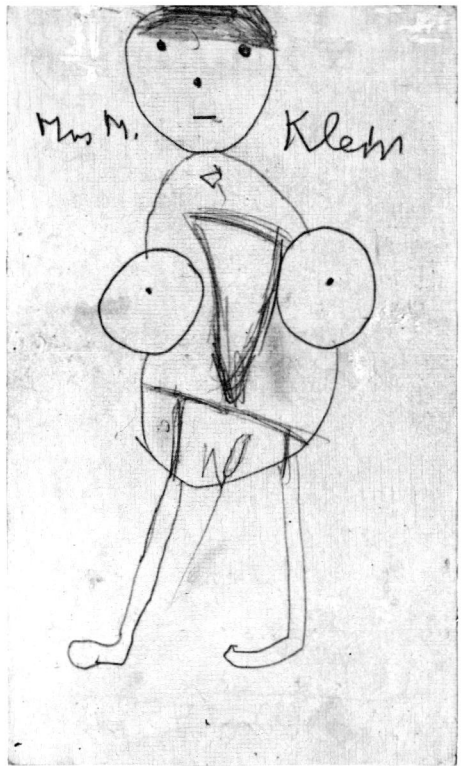

55

H.M.S. SALMON
Mummy
H.M.S. RODNEY
H.M.S. VAMPIRE
H.M.S HOOD.
H.M.S. DELHI
Daddy
H.M.S. EFFINGHAM

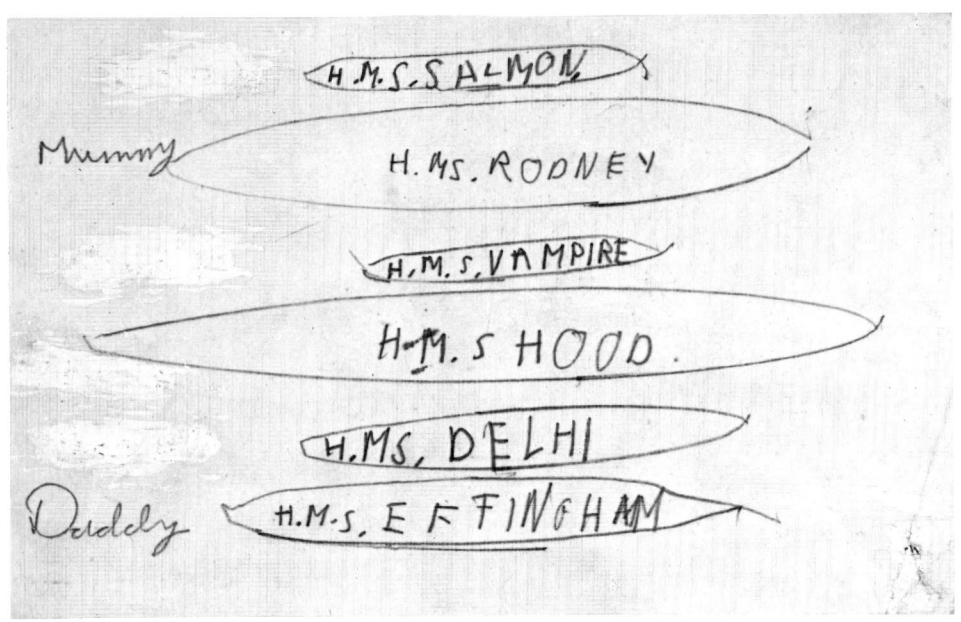

56

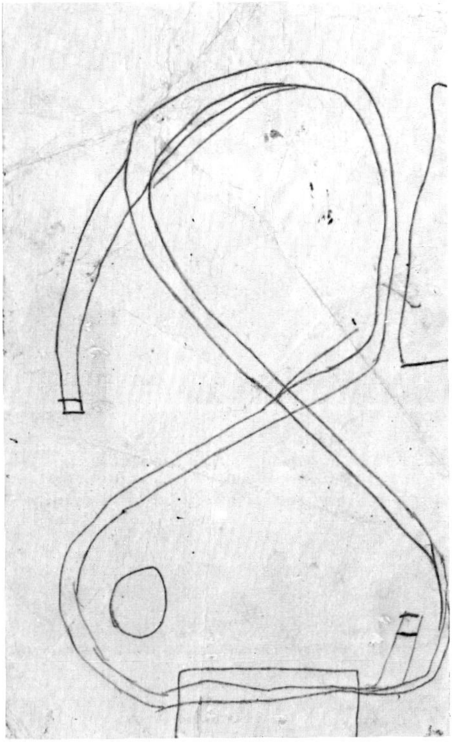

57

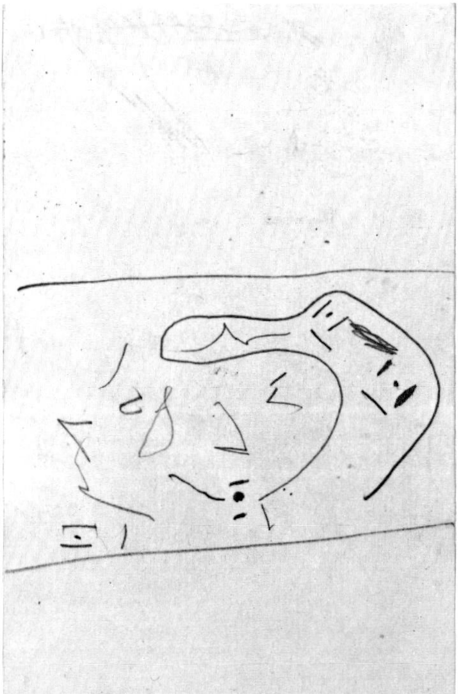

58

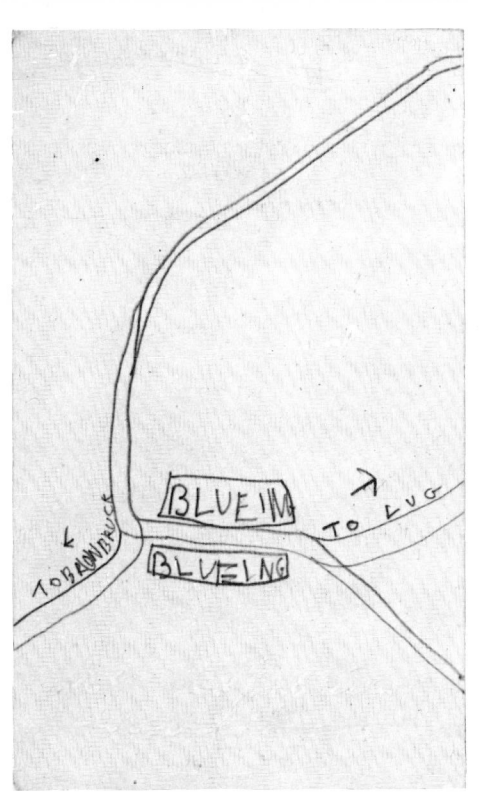

59

60

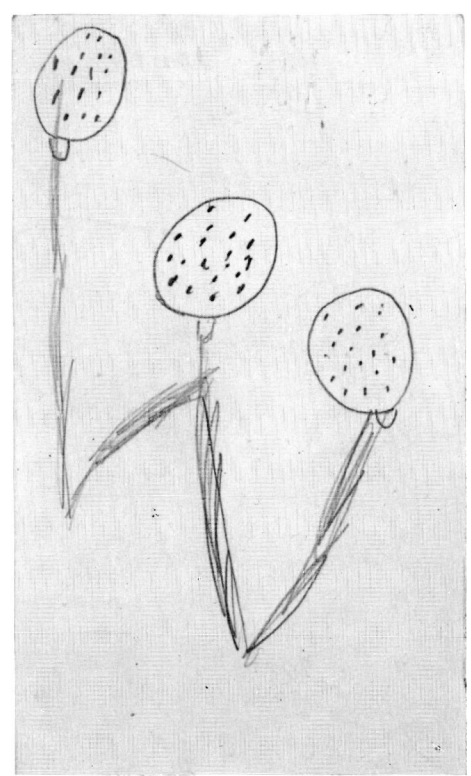

61

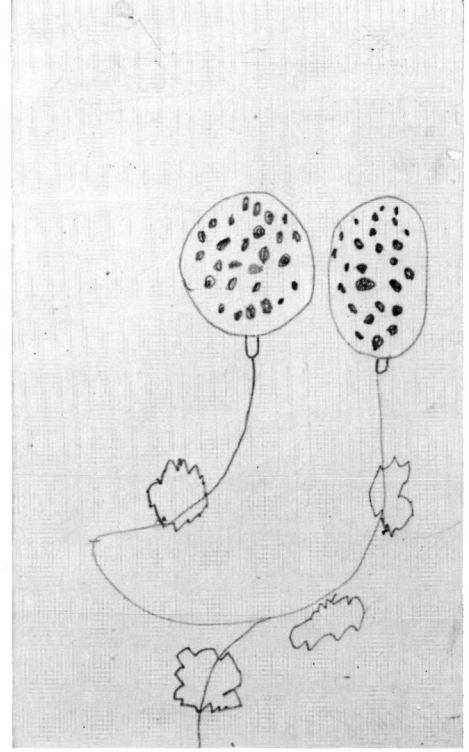

62

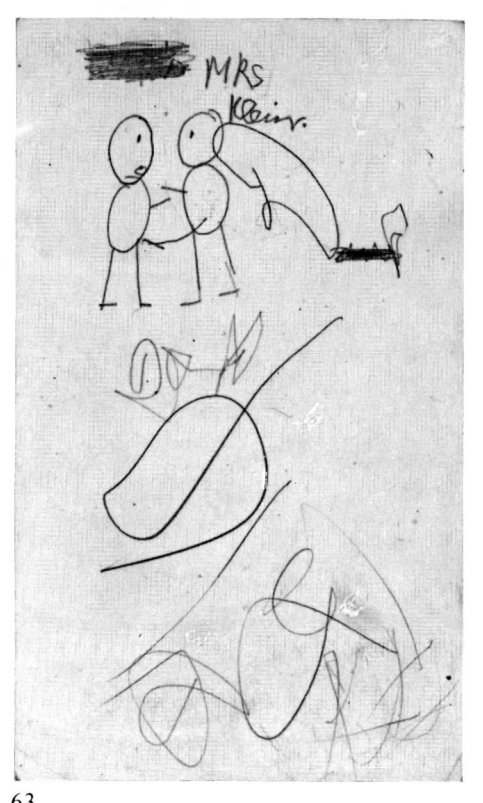

63

64

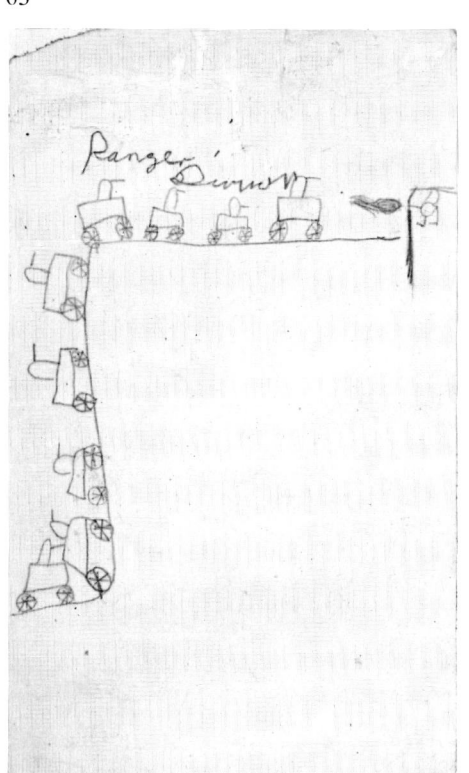

65

66

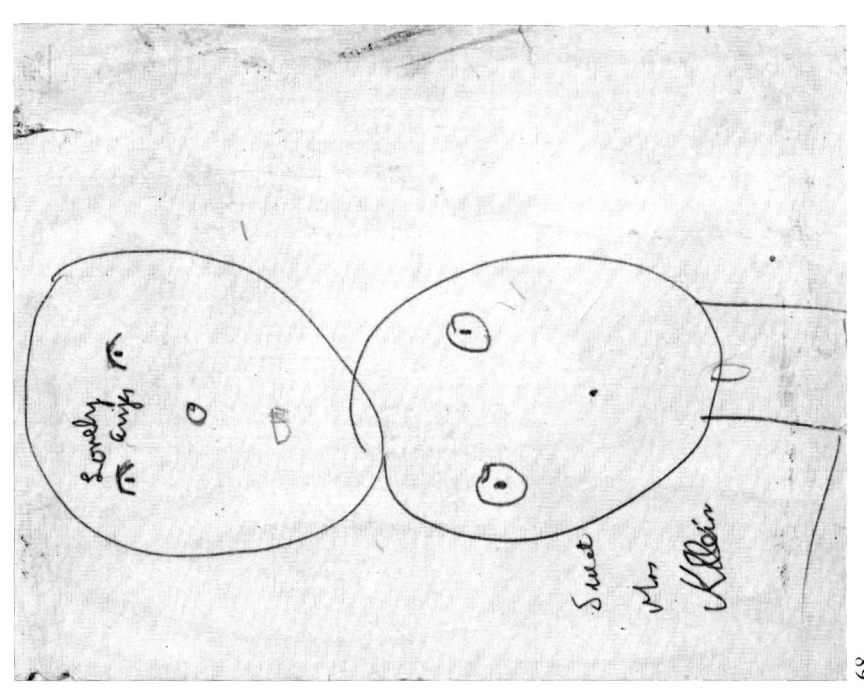

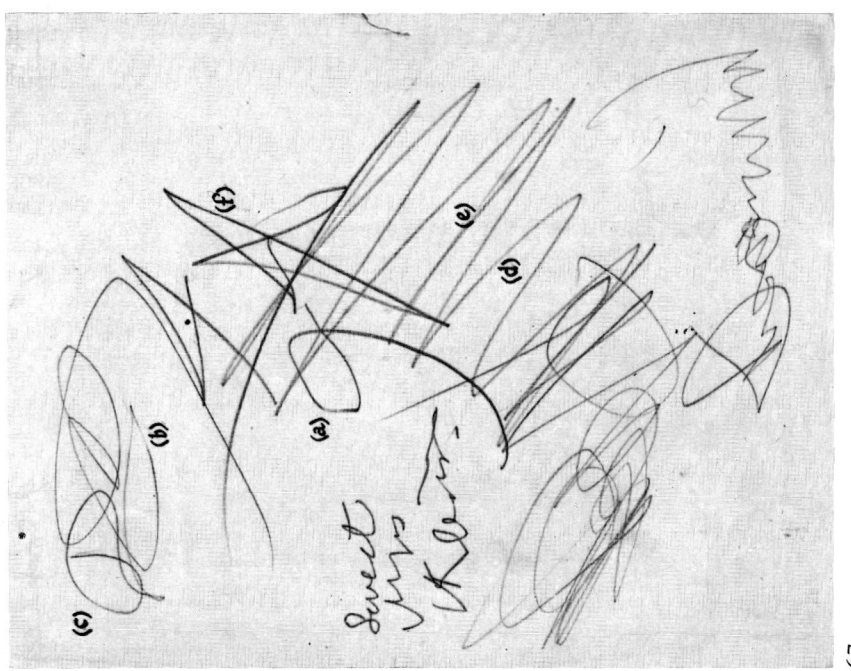

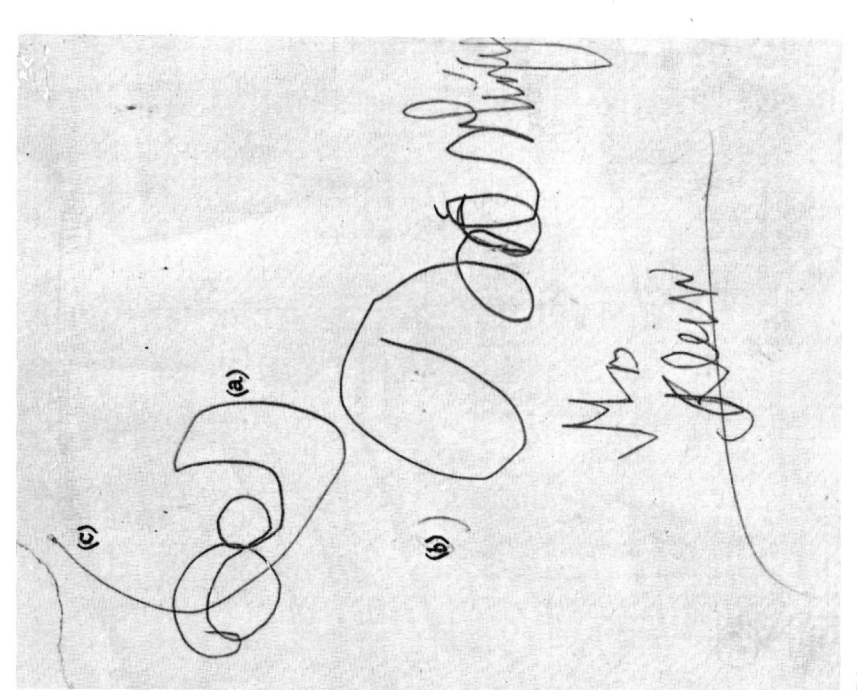

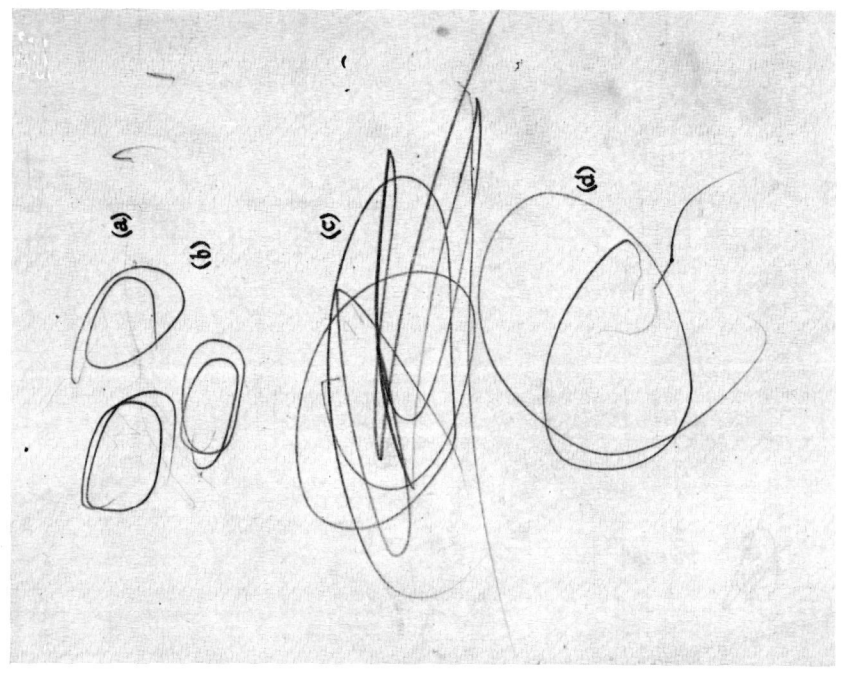

70

69

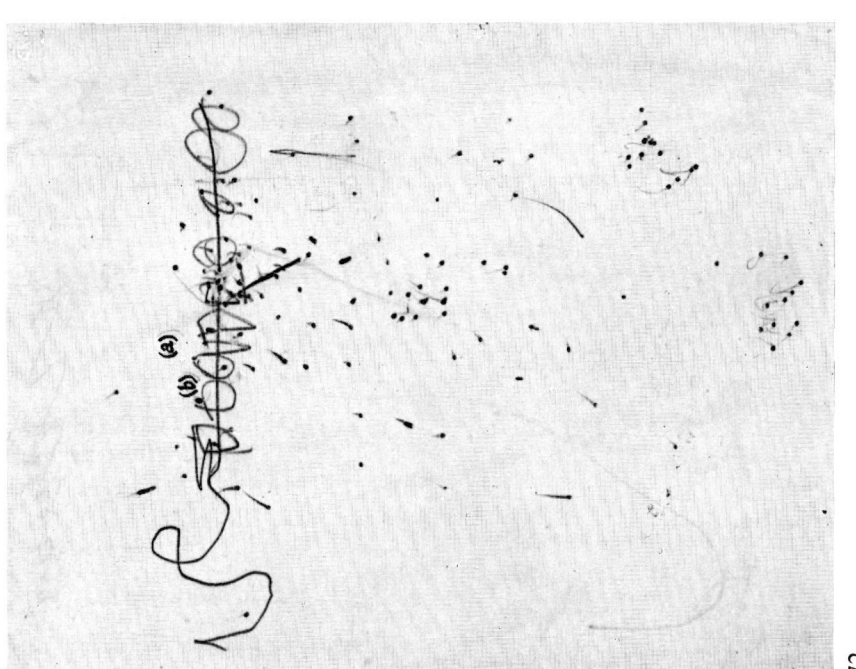

72

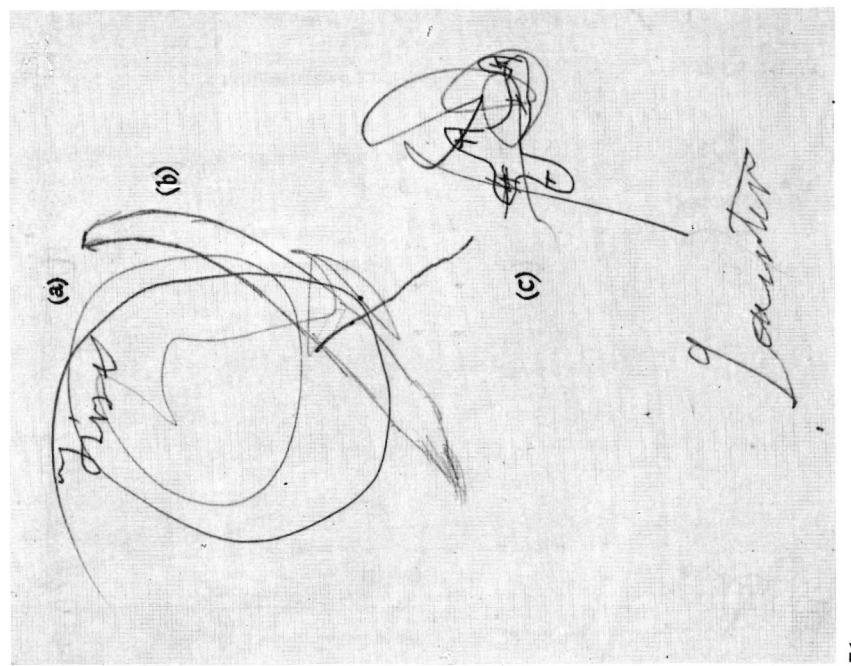

71

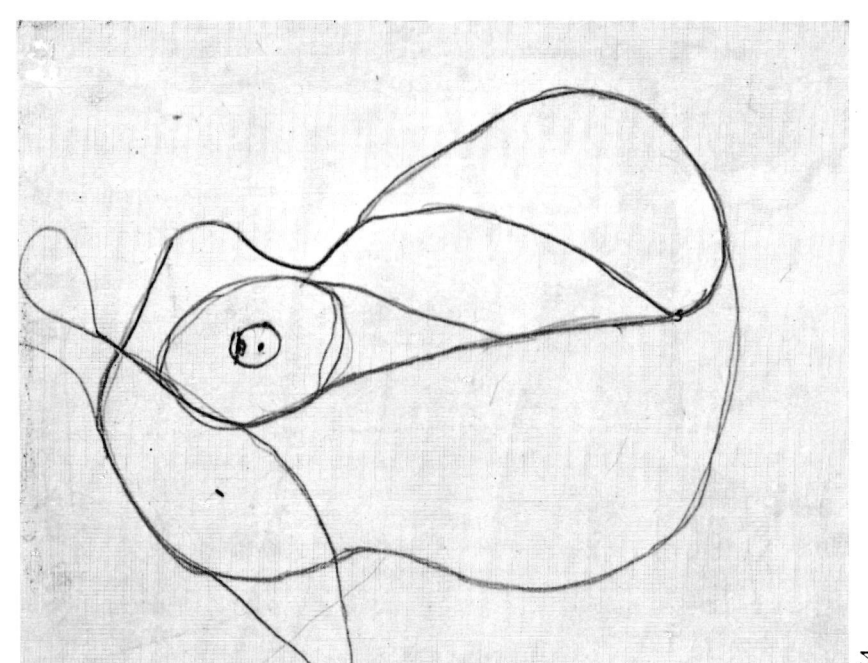

74

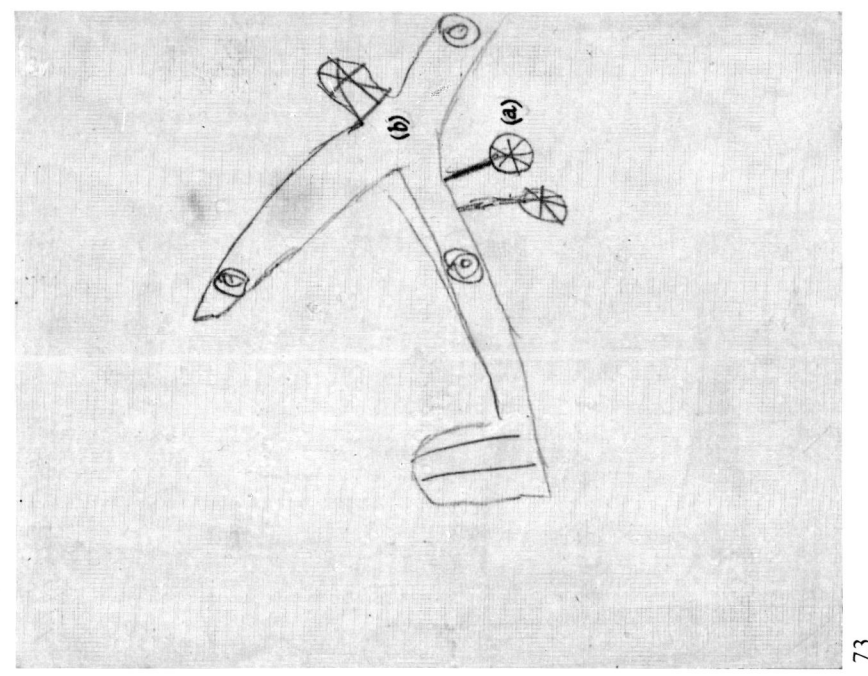

73

*Notes to Fifty-eighth Session:*

I. I believe that Richard was afraid I might again have left the pad at home; but my impression was that it had not at all consciously occurred to him to inquire, i.e. that he had repressed his interest in the pad because of fear of disappointment. The process underlying this attitude seems to have been a turning away from the desired object and a denial of its importance to him, in order to escape from hating and destroying the loved person, which would have led to guilt and depression. This manic defence, however, only partially succeeded. For his hate and resentment led him to sink the entire British fleet, the whole family, and then he experienced guilt, loneliness, and despair. Also his homosexual desires, expressed by turning to the penis of the father (taking the *Nelson* between his teeth), were increased by the frustration by the breast.

As I mentioned, in spite of being deeply depressed at times during this session, he did not on the whole give the impression of complete hopelessness. I have no doubt that the analysis, particularly during the last few sessions, had the effect of diminishing his depressive and persecutory anxieties and making it possible for him to experience hope; I became again the good and loving mother, and he could take in the helpful interpretations, a process symbolized by his drinking the 'good' water from the tap.

The process of deflecting guilt and depression from their focal point, the relation to the primal and unique object, the mother's breast and the mother, and experiencing these emotions in other connections, is a frequent phenomenon which can be considered as a compromise, a partial success of the manic defence against the depressive position. Many patients suffer from a generalized feeling of guilt and depression, or from guilt arising for trivial reasons; but the experience of guilt in the transference situation often meets with great difficulties because all the emotions bound up with the original object are then revived.

II. By this stage of the analysis certain features had become a routine. At the beginning of the session he asked whether there had been raids by the R.A.F. Since he always listened to the early news, he knew the answer, but wanted it confirmed by me. This question also implied wanting to know whether I had had a good night. As was shown in the material of the Fifty-seventh Session, the R.A.F. raids referred also to the dangers threatening the mother and me from a bad intercourse.

It had become a regular routine that he drank water from the tap soon after the beginning of the session, before settling down to play. In this way he began the session by reassuring himself that he would get something good from the analysis. He also usually asked whether I had been to the cinema, or what else had I been doing the previous night. This question had two meanings : in the first place he was concerned that he deprived me of going to the cinema; but he also suspected me of having been with the 'grumpy old gentleman' or Mr Smith, his jealousy having come to a climax during this period when the Œdipus complex had shown itself in full force.

## FIFTY-NINTH SESSION (Sunday)

Richard again met Mrs K. near her home. Since he was well aware that this was taking advantage of her, he coped with his embarrassment by being over-lively and jocular. He asked Mrs K. whether she had wondered who was coming to meet her—was it perhaps Mr K.? He told her that everything was all right, his earache had gone and he was very well; also that he was wearing his new suit. While Mrs K. went to fetch the key of the playroom, Richard waited outside. He asked her whom she had seen, was it only the old lady (with whom the keys were deposited) or was somebody else with her? While on the road with Mrs K. he was alert to everything that was going on and all the people they saw. He often turned round, but even when he did not, he seemed to be aware of what was happening behind him. He said that today they would not meet Mr Smith, since it was Sunday, and pointed out the way Mr Smith went in the morning from his home to his business. He said that today there were not many people on the road, but in any case he was no longer so frightened of meeting people; but he added that one should not become too careless. This last remark he mumbled. . . . On arriving at the playroom he said he had not brought the fleet—he did not want to. He drank water from the tap and asked for the pad. Then he changed his mind and asked for the whole basket (in which Mrs K. carried the toys, the pad, and the pencils). He looked eagerly into it and took things out. He first looked at the little swing and became anxious because he said it was not quite all right—one side was a bit loose. He at once put it back into the basket, which he pushed aside, saying that this was an injured Mummy. He began to draw (Drawing 50). This again consisted of railway lines and the trains were rushing from 'Roseman' to 'Halmsville'. He again spelled it 'Halmsville', and when Mrs K. pointed this out to him he repeated that it was 'Hamsville' he meant and was at first unable to see that he had really spelt it 'Halmsville'. Then he acknowledged the mistake, was surprised, corrected it, but had no further association to 'Halm'. His depression and his incapacity to cooperate were mounting. Moving his pencil along the railway lines, he said that the trains were going from 'Roseman' to 'Hamsville'. But there were also trains crossing them from 'Valeing' to 'Lug'. Meanwhile, he had repeatedly put the yellow pencil into his mouth.

*Mrs K.* interpreted that this drawing showed the danger of the 'Roseman'-penis turning into whales, because the two railway lines adjoined, though he had tried to deny this by making the trains go from 'Roseman' to 'Halmsville'. The reason for his denial was the fear about his ears—'Lug'—which he was afraid might have to be operated on. The whales—the bad internal Daddy-genital—were getting into his ears.

Richard at this moment put on the electric fire and watched the bars becoming red.

*Mrs K.* interpreted that the bars stood for his ears which were becoming red inside.

Richard agreed to this, but turned off the fire and said that now they were getting white again.

*Mrs K.* interpreted that Richard was afraid that in the fight with the internal bad Daddy—the whale—his ears might not become white again. His ears also stood for his genital, and his fear of another operation was linked with the frightening experience of his genital being operated on. On the previous day he had asked whether, if the fire belonged to Mrs K., she would allow him to tear out the broken bar—the dangerous penis of the father. Also, he was afraid that by turning off the fire he killed everything in Mrs K. and himself. She reminded him that switching off the fire had formerly meant stopping life inside Mummy and Mrs K. When he told her about the dream of the black car with the number plates (Ninth Session), which stood for the dead Mummy with the dead babies, this had been linked with his switching the fire on and off, which meant alternately life or death inside Mummy.

Richard, with a very unhappy expression, said that he could not listen to this and he wanted to go outside. He looked round, but did not make his usual comments; then he said it was a shame there were so many weeds in the garden and people should take better care of it. . . . Back in the room, he repeatedly wrote his name on a page, but without scribbling over it as he usually did. . . . He asked whether it would do harm either to the analyst or to the patient if the analyst became really angry.

*Mrs K.* interpreted that Richard could not believe that she would not be angry, because he felt he had done harm to her. He wanted the garden put right by having the weeds pulled out, which meant tearing out the bad babies and genital. Turning off the fire also partly meant the same thing; but he was afraid that it would at the same time result in Mummy's death. By writing his name without covering it up with scribbles, he confessed more openly that, if he became angry or jealous, he would be dangerous to Mrs K. and Mummy.

Richard said that this would not help. When Mrs K. asked him whether he was referring to the work, he said yes; he knew it helped him and yet he felt it could not help him.

*Mrs K.* asked whether Richard thought so because she was going to leave him shortly.

Richard confirmed this and said that he was worried about Mrs K. going away. Could a few more weeks really help him and do something for him?

*Mrs K.* replied that even a few weeks might be of some value.

Richard looked less unhappy, made Drawing 51, but first asked a number of questions: Where had Mrs K. been last night? Was she at home? What language did she speak with Mr K.? Was it Austrian or German? Did Mr K. fight in the last war against the British? Were Hungary and Austria on the German side? Did Mr K. wear the kind of collar and tie that Richard wore now, or was it the old-fashioned type? What was his Christian name? (He looked very anxious and persecuted.)

*Mrs K.* interpreted Richard's distress about her at night, which was increased now that she was going away for a long time. He was afraid she would change into the wicked brute-Mummy who, in his mind, was full of the wicked brute-Daddy. This increased Richard's curiosity about Mr K., standing for Daddy, and about his penis— whether it was poisonous, red-hot, the devouring whale (that is to say, dangerous to Mrs K.), or whether it was the good 'Roseman'. But he had the same fears about Mummy's and his own insides. Mrs K. reminded him of the eagle (Drawing 49) which represented the black poisoned and poisonous Mummy containing the ghost Daddy.

Richard looked at this drawing and shrank from it, saying that it was horrid. He then made the elliptical shape in the lighter section.

*Mrs K.* interpreted that now the devoured and devouring bad parents were represented by an open mouth.

Richard had asked a little before whether Mrs K. could see him later on Tuesday than had been arranged, so that he could come

back to 'X' by train instead of by bus; going by bus was so unpleasant and tiring.[1]

*Mrs K.* said she was sorry but she could not arrange this; she
added that she would ring his mother; perhaps some other arrangement could be made so that he need not go by bus.

Richard, when Mrs K. said that she could not see him earlier,
turned pale and had tears in his eyes. He calmed down a little at
her suggestion that she would discuss it with his mother, but
obviously this frustration had made him very depressed.

*Mrs K.* interpreted that if she did not do whatever he wished, she
seemed at once to turn from the good Mummy into the Hitler-
Mummy who would leave him to his enemies (Note I).

Richard had continued Drawing 51. He asked Mrs K. whether
she could see what it was, and added that it was a Zeppelin; it
dropped bombs from its middle. To the right and left the shells
from the *Nelson* were going up. A British aeroplane was bombing
the Zeppelin; to the right of the aeroplane was a bomb. When he
had finished this part of the drawing, he made the line under the
*Nelson* and there was nothing below it but one fish. By now he had
become extremely depressed.

*Mrs K.* asked whom the fish represented.

Richard said it was himself.

*Mrs K.* interpreted that the Zeppelin represented Mr K. and
Mrs K., about whose relations he had again inquired—the bad or
suspect parents who were destroying the good, the British, parents,
but were in turn killed by Richard who was on top, represented by
the British aeroplane. But Richard felt that if he killed the bad
parents, he was also bound to kill the good ones, because he understood better that the good and bad parents were really the same
people. During this session Richard had again shown that he was
fond of Mrs K. who was to help him. But she also represented the
spy-Mummy speaking in the enemy language to Daddy (Mr K.),
and Richard felt that in the end he had killed everyone and was
quite alone in the world—the fish under the line.

Richard quickly added a second fish, some starfishes, and plants.

*Mrs K.* asked who the second fish was.

Richard replied that it was Paul. Then, looking again at the
picture, he added after a pause that it was Mrs K. and wrote it
down. He said that two of the starfishes were his birds and the third
was Bobbie. Then he quickly began to write lots of numbers, begin-

[1] Richard was presumably going back to 'Y' on Monday with his parents
and had to travel back to 'X' by himself on Tuesday.

ning with 1. When Mrs K. asked him what the numbers were for, Richard replied that he was just filling up the page.

*Mrs K.* suggested that they might stand for people.

Richard, without hesitation, said they were all babies. He looked again at Drawing 51 and said that it was a sad picture.

*Mrs K.* interpreted his despair because the drawing suggested that his family, Mrs K., the whole world, would perish and he would be left alone; on the previous day he had been the only destroyer remaining of the whole British fleet. But he also expressed his hope that he would not be alone any longer. That was shown by the second fish (which was first Paul and then Mrs K.) joining him. On the previous day, in his mind, the United States had after all come to Britain's aid. This meant that despite his fears, he hoped that the analysis would later on be continued and the good Mummy and himself be kept alive.[1]

Richard had looked out of the window a few times, watching passers-by. About a woman, he said that she was funny and looked like an Italian. When a group of children passed, he did not hide as usual, and said, 'Never mind if they see me.' Even when the red-haired girl and her friends—his particular enemies—passed, he did not withdraw from the window, but looked very stern, thrusting his chin forward in an obvious attempt to face them. His depression and guilt were increased by the fact that his father was leaving and was going home on the following day. Richard also had conflicting feelings about the Sunday sessions; he was relieved that he would not have them any more and would be at home at the weekends; yet missing the analysis on Sundays increased his feelings of loss and guilt. He asked Mrs K. during the session whether she was going to see anybody else on Sundays and said he wished she would not, since she was not seeing him on Sundays. He was aware that it depended on him whether he had Sunday sessions or not.

On the way to the village Richard was particularly observant of everything and everybody. He asked Mrs K. if she was going to fetch the Sunday paper from Mr Evans (he had asked this earlier in the session but repeated it now). He said with a note of triumph that today she could not go to the grocer's. He added that there was one shop open, though, and that was the chemist.

During the walk Richard stopped watching people and his ten-

[1] A further interpretation which I do not seem to have given suggests itself. Richard, in order to revive Mummy, would have to give her many babies (the numbers); but he was very much afraid of sexual intercourse—this had been again quite clear in the last few days—and of being attacked and punished by his father. He was also very doubtful of his ever being potent and having a good and creative penis. I have a note about this session to the effect that I had been unable to relieve his depression sufficiently.

sion relaxed when he saw the kitten that he had returned to its owner a few days previously. His face lit up and he asked Mrs K. to come near to the wall on which the kitten was sitting and to look at it. He caressed it and asked Mrs K. whether she did not think it sweet. Then he talked to the kitten, telling it to go home and not to get lost again. It was very striking to see the change, both in his facial expression and in his whole attitude, from a state of depression, persecution, suspicion, and watchfulness, to feelings of love and tenderness.

*Note to Fifty-ninth Session:*

I. In the view of many psycho-analysts frustration is the cause of persecutory anxiety and aggression. While it is true that excessive frustration is apt to increase persecutory anxiety, I wish to stress here, as I have done in many other places, that children—and for that matter adults as well—whose persecutory anxiety is strong are particularly unable to bear frustration because frustration in their mind turns the object into a persecutory one, allied with enemies. I would connect this with the projection of destructive impulses which we may assume is operative from the beginning of life.

## SIXTIETH SESSION (Monday)

Richard waited for Mrs K. at the corner of the road along which Mr Smith might come. He clearly wanted to keep an eye on him. Richard was less excited and persecuted than on the previous day, although a thunderstorm was about to break and, as has been mentioned, Richard was frightened of thunderstorms. Now he said he was only frightened of the lightning, not of the thunder, but soon gave up this pretence. He told Mrs K. that his mother had arranged for him to come back to 'X' next day by car, and therefore he would not have to come alone by bus. In the playroom, Mrs K. and Richard found that various packages and poles (for use by the Girl Guides) had arrived. Richard tried to peep into the packages but gave it up; he made another attempt before leaving. He said there might be a bear in one of the sacks.

*Mrs K.* asked whether it would be a live bear.

Richard said no, but seemed doubtful.

*Mrs K.* suggested that, if he were neither alive nor dead, it might be a ghost bear.

Richard agreed eagerly that this might be so. As usual he drank from the tap and asked Mrs K. whether there had been any R.A.F. raids. Then he asked her if she would do something for him—pick up his coat which had dropped on the floor. He explained that he had cramp in his leg and it hurt him to bend down.

*Mrs K.* picked up the coat, but explained that Richard needed her to do things for him, apart from the analysis, for the same reason as he drank water from the 'good' tap. This meant reassuring himself that Mrs K., for whose breast the tap stood, was not angry and was not the attacked and attacking Hitler-Mummy.

Richard asked Mrs K., when the thunderstorm had come nearer, to darken the room so that he would not see the rain and the lightning and would feel safer. Before Mrs K. had completely darkened the room (Richard did not attempt to help her), he was hunting for bluebottles. He said about two of them, which he saw together in a corner of the window, 'Here are two lusty ones—I shall drive them out.'

*Mrs K.* asked what he meant by 'lusty'.

Richard said, 'Oh just dirty and . . .' Then he showed Mrs K. that there were lots of them on the other window and said that sometimes there were hundreds of them together with their babies.

*Mrs K.* interpreted that lusty and dirty meant sexual. The two lusty ones with their babies stood for his parents in sexual intercourse, whom he wanted to drive out because he was jealous and hated them.

Richard was catching some of the flies between his fingers and addressing them as dirty Mr and Mrs Bluebottle. After that he said regretfully that they would get very wet now, but perhaps they would be able to get home.

*Mrs K.* asked where their home would be.

Richard, after a pause, said sadly, 'I think it is in the playroom.' He put on the electric fire, saying that he felt cold; actually it was quite close. The rain was pouring down and Mrs K. had darkened the room. Richard switched on the electric light and said, 'We are quite cosy here by ourselves, aren't we?' But every few minutes he looked out from behind the curtains and spoke of bucketsful coming down, of torrents, also of the 'nasty, dirty rain'. He said that Mrs K. and he were in more danger because the house stood all by itself and was not in the village (the thunderstorm was not severe and was fairly far away). Richard asked Mrs K. whether she had seen Mr Smith, though this was impossible, since the curtains were drawn over the windows, and Mrs K. could not have met him on the road before she met Richard. Richard also repeatedly asked her what the packages and poles were for, though he realized that she knew as little about this as he did. He frequently peered behind the curtains in order to report on the weather. He said there was less rain now, the sun was coming out, the hills would have less rain; he seemed pleased about this.

*Mrs K.* interpreted that by watching he tried to keep control of the weather and also of Mr Smith, standing for Mr K. and Daddy, who always seemed to be on his mind. Doing away with thunder and lightning meant controlling the powerful penis of the father. Mrs K. reminded him of the play with the rope (Fifty-second Session), and how it linked with the lightning coming down on the Chinese ambassador and himself (Drawing 47). His wish to send Daddy away was not only because he wanted to have Mummy (and, in relation to Mr Smith, Mrs K.) all to himself, but also because of his fear that the dirty rain hurting the hills also stood for Daddy's poisonous genital dangerous to Mummy. Therefore he had constantly to watch both parents and keep them separate. But he was also sorry for his father, because he had thrown him out into the cold and rain like the bluebottles. He felt this particularly because his father had left that very morning, and it seemed as if Richard had made Mummy say 'go away' to him as he had asked Mrs K. some time ago to say about Mr Smith. This was why he felt that his father was going at his command and feared he would be punished by Mrs K. leaving him. Moreover, when Richard got rid of both parents—Mr and Mrs Bluebottle who were driven away from home by him [1]—he felt that they were also the good parents whom he had destroyed. Mrs K. referred to Drawing 51, which Richard had said was a sad one; he had felt that he was quite alone in the world, just as in the fleet play two days before the Richard destroyer was all that was left of the British navy.

Richard said emphatically that the play with the fleet had nothing to do with the drawings.

*Mrs K.* interpreted that Richard often left the fleet at home, saying that it did not want to come, because he seemed to feel that, if he separated the fleet from the other play, in some way he kept the family safe. They would be kept alive through the fleet if he felt that they were destroyed in other ways [Splitting].

Richard replied that the *Nelson* in Drawing 51 was not destroyed; the bombs dropped by the Zeppelin fell outside the ship and did not hurt it. Only the Zeppelin was destroyed and the Zeppelin was Mr K. alone, not Mrs K, for she had been with Richard under the line, where they were the two fishes.

*Mrs K.* interpreted that when Richard was making the drawing

[1] The thrown-out bluebottle babies would also stand for the 'dirty poor slum children' of whom Richard was contemptuous and at the same time afraid, ultimately for Mummy's destroyed unborn babies.

he seemed to have felt that she too was on the Zeppelin and was the spy-Mummy; on the other hand, the *Nelson* with its two funnels stood for the good parents who, when he was making the drawing, also had to die together with the bad ones, the Zeppelin. In that situation only the bombing aeroplane, Richard, seemed to survive. The first fish under the line was supposed to be himself, again as the only survivor. But since that was unbearable to him, he drew the second fish which stood for Mrs K., the good Mummy, and the starfishes standing for the two birds and Bobbie—actually Paul and the parents. In this way he had revived the whole family under the line, insisting that what happened there had nothing to do with the upper part. This meant that in his mind he had kept separate his hostile bombing self and the disaster to which it led—the destroyed family—from his need to love and revive the family, which was shown in the peaceful situation under the line.

Richard had meanwhile been looking at the drawings and did not seem to listen while Mrs K. was interpreting. But suddenly he looked up into her face and said, in a tender voice, 'What are you thinking about?'

*Mrs K.* replied that she had been thinking about what she had just been telling him.

Richard answered that he liked what she had just said.

*Mrs K.* interpreted that while she explained Richard's attacks on the bad parents, he felt that everybody, including Mrs K., was bad and hostile. Therefore he did not listen to that part of the interpretation; but when she showed him that in another section of the drawing, and that meant also in another part of his mind, he had revived the whole family, she became the live, helpful, and feeding Mummy. This was the part of the interpretation which he liked because it proved to him that she also recognized good feelings in him.

Richard went out when the rain had nearly stopped, looked round, and said that the hills had had an awful lot of rain and he felt sorry for them; the rain might also do some good, because some people thought it was needed. He discovered a big moth on the window and was frightened of it. He attacked it with his penknife, wounded it, and, putting it on the table when it was still moving a little, watched it gleefully. He blew the dust off the wings and obviously had to force himself to stop this because he felt guilty and frightened. As often, he dramatized this situation by saying, when he was about to finish off the moth with his knife: 'Now the knife is over him and he is going to die.' He then crushed the moth underfoot. He was very excited, flushed, and in a triumphant voice spoke about the moth's death and his victory. When he looked at it again, he suddenly became anxious and said it was rather like a beetle, and he was afraid of beetles. He was restless and disturbed.

*Mrs K.* interpreted that the moth was to him the same as 'Mr Bluebottle'. Richard's attack on it was meant to be an attack on Daddy and his genital, which he wanted to treat like the moth. Therefore it turned into a frightening beetle in his mind and he was afraid that it would treat him in the same way as he had treated it [Fear of retaliation and persecution].

Richard said: 'Please don't call it a beetle, it makes me frightened.'

*Mrs K.* interpreted that this was so because in his mind the killed moth changed into the more frightening beetle. It became an enemy whom Richard felt he had also eaten up, for he had been grinding his teeth while killing it. At one moment Richard in his thoughts killed the hated Daddy, who then became the bad internal octopus-Daddy; at another moment he wished to save him and Mummy, as he had shown by setting the bluebottles free. The same thing had happened in his drawing, when Richard had first killed the good and bad parents and the bad Mrs K., and then revived her and the whole family.

Richard, when the thunderstorm had completely passed, asked Mrs K. to help him pull the curtains back and enjoyed seeing the sun break through the clouds; he ran out to see what the hills and the garden were like. When he came back he looked for the moth on the floor, and was worried and suspicious because it had disappeared.

*Mrs K.* interpreted that he felt the moth had disappeared into him and become an internal enemy; in fact it might have stuck to the sole of his shoe when he went out of the room.

Richard agreed that this was likely, but nevertheless looked worried and depressed. . . . He drew (52) with evident enjoyment: as can be seen, there were two main lines; over one he wrote 'Longline' and over the other 'Prinking'. The 'Prinking' line led to 'Lug' and 'Valeing' on one side, and 'Brumbruk' and 'Roseman' on the other. When he was told by Mrs K. that the session had come to an end, he was reluctant to go (Note I). He was slow in taking up his things, and said about 'Prinking' that it was a 'proud king'.

*Mrs K.* interpreted that this meant Daddy restored, because 'Longline' stood for the powerful and uninjured genital. Also the second 'n' in 'Longline' looked very much like a 'v', and that meant 'Longli*ve*'.

Richard said 'Brumbruk' was brown.

*Mrs K.* interpreted that the restored Daddy with the 'longline' went from whales to a brown place; this expressed Richard's fear that the 'proud king' Daddy was very dangerous because he was going to attack the brown place which stood for Mummy's bottom, as the brown clock had so often stood for Mrs K.'s bottom.

Richard asked, on leaving, where Mrs K. was going to first. After her reply that she was going to the grocer's, Richard asked whether she had to go there again. He did not mind the grocer's father, who was a very old man—he was all right. But he did not think the grocer himself was all right.

*Mrs K.* interpreted that the grocer stood for the dangerous Daddy and Mr K., and when Mrs K. went to his shop they became together the dirty and sexual bluebottle parents.

*Note to Sixtieth Session:*

I. It has been my experience that when a patient's attention wanders and resistance is very strong, cooperation can be brought about only by interpretations. In this instance, as soon as I had interpreted Richard's desire to revive the family—an interpretation based on the material following the preceding interpretations about destruction and ensuing loss of the family—Richard's full cooperation was established. On the previous day, as mentioned, I had not been able to work through Richard's depression sufficiently. This was because I had not succeeded by my interpretations in establishing adequately the connection between destruction and reparation. Nevertheless, the previous session seemed to have had some effect, for Richard started the current one in a much better frame of mind and was, from the beginning, more capable of cooperation.

The therapeutic importance of linking the different aspects of impulses and situations—in this case of destruction and reparation—cannot be overrated. One of the main purposes of the analytic procedure is to enable the patient to integrate the split-off parts of his mind, so that the effects of the different phantasy situations which arise through splitting may be mitigated. For integration to come about, the analyst has to follow the material closely and give due weight in his interpretations to destructive impulses and their consequences. At the same time he must not neglect indications of the capacity for love and the wish for reparation when they appear in the material. This, however, is very different from reassuring the patient about his destructive impulses.

# SIXTY-FIRST SESSION (Tuesday)

Richard met Mrs K. at the corner of the road; he said that he had very distressing news. At that moment Paul, who had driven him to the hotel, was passing in the car, and Richard pointed him out to Mrs K. Paul and Mrs K. nodded to each other; Richard was very pleased and said he had wanted Mrs K. to see Paul as he was really a very nice boy. Then he told Mrs K. that something awful had happened, but he was not going to talk about it to her until they were inside the house. He even waited until Mrs K. and he were seated (there was already an element of dramatization in that). He told Mrs K. that early in the morning he had found his father lying on the floor, ill and nearly fainting. He had called Mummy, who 'burst into the room' followed by Paul; they carried his father to the bedroom and put him to bed. He made this report dramatically, enjoyed the part he had played and his being able to relate such an important event, but at the same time he was clearly very upset. He added that he hoped his father would recover. The detailed description of how his father was being nursed showed that in his mind his father had turned into a baby and Richard into an adult who would look after the baby.[1] He asked Mrs K. what she thought about all this, and was pleased when she expressed her sympathy. Richard also said that he would talk about what had happened to everybody in the hotel, but corrected himself and said, no, not to everybody, but to some people. He told Mrs K. that he would have to stay by himself in 'X' until the weekend. He added that it was a good thing he was so much better and less frightened and could stay by himself. Richard explained that there were two reasons for his father falling ill: 'X' was a stuffy place and also his father had worked too hard and had had a strenuous winter (here again he appeared genuinely concerned). Daddy was not going to be operated on. Richard had feared that he might be, but he would not; this was a good thing as Daddy might not be able to stand an operation. In between Richard emphasized repeatedly that he had done his best, he could not have carried his father to bed alone because he was so heavy. After he had told Mrs K. all these details a great change took place in Richard. He had been quite emotional, though fairly composed, and his face had been expressive and lively. Now he became restless, turned pale, and looked anxious and perse-

[1] Previous material had shown that by reversing the father-son relation, Richard could combat his jealousy and maintain feelings of love and compassion towards his father.

cuted. He tried to explore the packages which had been left in the playroom on the previous day, and kicked the poles. . . . He returned to the table and again spoke about his father's illness and repeated that it was a good thing he need not be operated on. He took a penknife out of his pocket, saying it was his own and he need not borrow Mrs K.'s this time, opened it, and started scratching the poles with it. Then, standing at the window and turning his back on Mrs K., he hit his teeth with a knife.

*Mrs K.* interpreted that on the previous day there had been in his mind two ways of dealing with the intruding father. He had driven out Mr and Mrs Bluebottle to set them free; but he had recognized that he had, after all, driven them away from their home and out into the rain.

Richard interrupted and asked which was the second way.

*Mrs K.* interpreted that he had operated on and killed the moth which stood for Daddy; and when he had just now tried to cut the poles with his knife, this expressed his fear that he had attacked his father. When his father actually became ill, this had made Richard feel that he was the cause of it [Omnipotence of wishes]. Because he felt guilty and wanted to punish himself, he had turned the knife against himself and hit his teeth.

Richard had become less restless during this interpretation and the colour returned to his face. He looked impressed and understanding. (It appeared to me that this insight must have been almost conscious.) But soon he became very aggressive with his knife. He slashed at the wooden poles, scratched along the window-pane, attempted to cut the table, and nearly cut open the packages. Mrs K. told him that he should not do that. Richard also repeatedly put the blade into his own mouth. Mrs K. warned him that he might hurt himself and he stopped it. Then he walked about with the open knife pointing directly at himself so that if he had slipped he would have hurt himself. Mrs K. warned him again, and Richard closed the knife (Note I).

*Mrs K.* interpreted Richard's feeling that the injured, cut-up, and dead moth-Father was inside him; this feeling was increased by his father's illness and the fear of his death. Richard wanted to remove this ill, dangerous, or dead father out of his inside and therefore turned the knife on himself, which would imply hurting or even killing himself. The pole, which stood for Daddy's big genital, was also felt to be inside him and to be attacked there. Richard's attempt to smash the table, and his cutting at the window, meant the same thing. He felt very guilty about such aggressive wishes and wanted to punish himself.

Richard looked very frightened and miserable and said he wished he were 'not here'.

*Mrs K.* interpreted that the 'stuffy X', which as he had said had made Daddy ill, stood for Mrs K. and the analysis. Mrs K. had changed into the injured Mummy containing the injured and therefore dangerous Daddy. Richard felt so guilty that he attempted to blame Mrs K., representing also the bad Mummy, for Daddy's illness.

Richard explored the playroom. He also went into the kitchen, opened the doors of the kitchen stove, and took out some soot. He hit the draining-board with an axe, though rather cautiously, and showed Mrs K. that some marks had already been there. Then he hit the stovepipe with the axe and said that if it were his own house, he would smash up the whole thing.

*Mrs K.* interpreted Richard's fears about her and Mummy's inside, as well as his own, containing an enormous destroyed Father-genital, now particularly dangerous because he was afraid of his father's death. He felt that there was nothing else to be done but to smash it up inside Mrs K. and inside himself, or to get it out by operation. Richard had been cutting various things with his knife, and he had now attacked the draining-board and stovepipe with the axe. He might also feel that only an operation could remove the illness out of Daddy (Note II).

Richard cleaned out some more soot from the stove. He explored one of the packages and managed to get his hand a little way in, but could not find out what it contained. He again mentioned a bear and asked whether people would mind if he really opened the package or cut it open. Then he swept the floor and said he wanted to make it nice for the others who were using the room. He found a lavatory brush and cleaned the lavatory pan ; he was pleased that it looked much nicer after he had done this. During these hectic activities, Richard had asked only a few things, the last being whether there had been any raids by the R.A.F.

*Mrs K.* interpreted that Richard had now attempted another way of dealing with his fear. If he could clear Mrs K.'s, Mummy's, and his own inside of the dangerous 'big job' which was, in his mind, the same now as the beetle, the moth, and the dangerous genital of the father, then he might make everybody all right again. This implied that he also wished to rid his father's inside of what had made him ill, and this meant that Richard's 'big job', which had so often represented bombs in his mind, might have contributed to his father's illness.

Richard explored the room and the kitchen further and found in a cupboard various things which so far he had never touched. He opened boxes and took out odds and ends, but was as usual very careful to replace everything as he had found it, mainly because he was afraid of the Girl Guides. He picked up a book and looked at the pictures. He had considerably quietened down. Repeatedly he asked Mrs K. whether she was going to the village that day and was pleased when she said she was calling at the post office.

*Mrs K.* asked why he liked this so much better than the grocer's shop, or Mr Smith's shop.

Richard replied that in going to the post office she would walk a longer distance with him (which was not so, since the post office was nearer to the playroom).

*Mrs K.* suggested that he preferred the post office, and the shoe shop, because there were only women there and he need not be so frightened of the 'awful' men—Mr K., Mr Smith, Mr Evans, and the grocer.

It was striking that during this session he only experienced sadness about his father's illness at the beginning. When he mentioned how his father had been put to bed and was being looked after, his father—in his mind—had obviously turned into a baby for whom he felt great compassion. The predominant feelings during this session were of persecution relating to internal dangers, his own as well as his mother's (Note III), and a strong urge to put things right. The fact that his attacks—although they were repeatedly directed against objects in the room—were felt to be against internal persecutors was also illustrated by Richard not watching passers-by with his usual intensity. Later, on the road, he was also not interested in either children or grown-ups; but by then his mood had changed. He had become serious and sad. He was still in deep thought when he took leave of Mrs K. Clearly concern about his father and anxiety about his illness had again come uppermost.

*Notes to Sixty-first Session:*

I. I have already pointed out earlier that the analyst has at times to prevent the child from doing harm to the analyst, and would now add that it is equally important to prevent the child from doing harm to himself.

II. An important impetus towards aggression derives from the need to save the object by tearing out or cutting out something bad it is felt to contain. This mechanism is very important in the understanding of delinquency. To give an instance from my observations : a little boy of four, whose mother was pregnant, felt great anxiety about her pregnancy. Although he was looking forward to the baby, he was also very jealous of it and, I believe, afraid that it was something bad inside his mother because she was often unwell during her pregnancy. He repeatedly cut the sheets on his bed, the covering of a screen, his own pyjamas; and nothing could stop him from doing this except the removal of all scissors from his reach. It was clear that these attacks were meant to be made partly on himself, containing the mother with the baby, and partly in order to save his mother from the bad and dangerous baby she, in his mind, contained. With this child the link between these destructive actions and his mother's pregnancy was quite clear; but with many children whose mother is not pregnant the need to cut up things also arises. I would not doubt that though other anxieties may also enter, the intense need to look into the mother's body and to remove out of it potential babies or the bad penis is always operative, even when the mother is not pregnant.

III. During this session, when I mainly interpreted Richard's feelings of persecution, I wondered whether, in a situation in which no doubt sadness and concern were also present, my interpretations were adequate. But the course of the session, and the obvious relief experienced by Richard at the end of it, suggested that the interpretations had been appropriate. This has in general been my experience. Also the change to sadness and thoughtfulness at the end of the session showed that this side of Richard's emotions had come to the fore as a consequence of the interpretation of persecutory anxiety.

I have in various connections suggested that persecutory anxiety is often reinforced because depression is unendurable. This reinforcement also means that feelings of love, compassion, and guilt are stifled. On the other hand, when persecutory anxiety is very strong from the beginning of life, the infantile depressive position cannot be worked through. Faced with intense persecution, the individual is unable to bring out and experience the pain of depression and guilt. In our clinical work we might, however, be for long periods confronted mainly with persecution and have to interpret accordingly. Our knowledge that guilt and depression are also operative up to a point in everybody sharpens our observation of any indications of these emotions which may appear in the further course of the analysis. Conversely, there are many depressive cases where we might, to begin with, find mainly depressive feelings or the defences against them; we have still to keep in mind, however, that persecutory anxiety is also operative and will, in the course of the analysis, come to the fore.

The conclusion is that we have to focus our attention in the analysis on whatever emotions are prevalent at the moment, while keeping in mind that other anxiety situations are bound to appear.

## SIXTY-SECOND SESSION (Wednesday)

Richard met Mrs K. outside the playroom. He looked serious and sad, and not so persecuted as on the previous day. He told Mrs K. that he had had a telephone call from his mother : she said that Daddy had had a good night and the doctor was satisfied. Richard was very pleased about this. Inside the room, he said that Mummy had asked him to arrange with Mrs K. to have an afternoon hour on Friday so that he could go home on Thursday night and be back in time for his session on Friday. He looked worried while asking this, and although Mrs K. at once agreed, Richard twice asked when she would know whether this arrangement would be possible.

*Mrs* K. pointed out that it *was* possible and that Richard seemed to doubt whether anything he wished for would come true. Richard's face brightened when he realized that Mrs K. had agreed and that he could go home, and also that there was no clash between his mother and Mrs K.

Richard looked round to see whether the Girl Guides who had, as he knew, used the playroom on the previous day, had rearranged anything and was satisfied to find that they had not. Then he discovered that some of the packages and poles had been removed. . . . He repeated with feeling that he was very glad his father was better. He told Mrs K. about what had happened the night before. Paul had stayed with him until after dinner and—as Richard put it—he had told the people at the hotel that they 'should behave themselves'.

*Mrs K.* asked him if he meant that he was glad Paul had stayed with him and that Paul had been kind to him.

Richard said emphatically that Paul had been very kind. He told Mrs K. that the boy at the hotel was now quite all right, he did not bother Richard ; the waitresses were all very friendly. He went to bed soon after Paul had gone and read to comfort himself, but he felt very lonely and cried himself to sleep. He did not cry for long and soon fell asleep. Looking up at Mrs K. he said ; 'I know you are sorry for me.' He added that he would ask Mrs K. something, though he knew she would not agree. He very much wanted to come and see her in the evenings or, if it were possible, to sleep in her house, in the same room with her. He added very doubtfully, did this mean that he would also wish to put his genital into hers? While saying this he put both his little fingers into his mouth (Note I).

*Mrs K.* interpreted that although at times he might wish to put his genital into Mummy, he was also very much afraid of doing so. In any case this was not what he had felt last night when he was lonely and unhappy. Then he had wished to be comforted by Mrs K., standing for Mummy, to be in bed with her, and be loved and cuddled by her. He had also wished to suck her breasts—the two fingers in his mouth standing for the nipples. He wanted to be a baby again, in the arms of the good light-blue Mummy who had comforted him when he was unhappy as a baby. Mrs K. asked him what he had thought about last night before he went to sleep.

Richard replied that he had wished he were at home, and he pictured Daddy and Mummy and also Daddy's nurse. She looked a very nice woman and he wanted to see more of her. . . . Richard had begun to draw (53). Then he looked at Drawing 52 and was amused that 'Brumbruk' meant 'brown'. He remarked on the whales on that drawing. About Drawing 53, he pointed out that on the left there was a yard where trains would go to sleep, dozens of them.

*Mrs K.* interpreted that Richard would have liked to go to sleep with Paul—with dozens of Pauls, good brothers—and then they would put their genitals together; that was what he might have wished as a young child when he felt lonely and deserted by Mummy. Mrs K. pointed out that he had used a brown pencil for this drawing, quite contrary to his usual habit, and that while she had been interpreting he had put this pencil into his mouth. In this drawing the shapes in the yard, indicated by dots on the ends of the trains, stood for his own fæces and his inside and that of Mummy, which he felt he had taken into himself. Eating these brown things out of Mummy also meant that he ate the whales and Daddy's genital as well; while he wished to get hold of the admired Daddy-genital, the 'longline', the king, the 'Roseman', he was frightened and turned to Paul's genital which he felt was better and safer.

Richard protested and said that he had used the brown pencil today because it was the sharpest of all. But he seemed doubtful of this explanation and added '. . . or at least one of the sharpest.' He said about 'Rinkie', the only word on the drawing apart from 'to Lug', that it meant rink (ice-rink) and that 'kie' meant 'key'. He said that the spelling was funny, but he still thought it meant key. . . . During this explanation he had been playing with the quoit, which he had picked up before sitting down at the table. Earlier, when Mrs K. had asked what he had been thinking about when he felt so lonely, he had been squeezing the rubber quoit into the shape of a capital 'B'. Then he spoke again about Daddy's nurse.

*Mrs K.* interpreted Richard's desire for the breast, represented by the 'B' and shown earlier by sucking his two little fingers. He was longing to meet Daddy's nurse; for she also recalled to him his own nurse of whom he had been so fond as a baby. Some time previously, when his mother was in 'Y', his nurse had come to stay with him for a few days in 'X' and he still missed her. His father was now helpless with a nurse looking after him, and this made him into a baby in Richard's mind—the baby he might always have expected Mummy to have. Therefore he was jealous of Daddy, as he would have been of the newborn baby. He was afraid that he would lose both Mummy's and Nurse's love. Further, the feeling that Daddy had become a baby revived his wish to be a baby himself [Regression]. If he could not be that, he turned to Paul both for company and to be loved.

Richard looked very interested and friendly when Mrs K. interpreted this, though he showed sadness when she described his feelings of loneliness. During this particular interpretation he put the rubber quoit on his head and said smilingly, 'I have got a halo on my head,' and then made a very innocent-looking face.

*Mrs K.* interpreted that Richard seemed to feel like a saint. He enjoyed thinking that Mrs K. was sorry for him and tried to win her affection. Therefore he was acting 'Larry the Lamb', the innocent child.

Richard was amused at Mrs K.'s interpretations and at being found out, and he clearly agreed.

*Mrs K.* also interpreted that Daddy stood in his mind for his own baby. Richard was, in fact, fond of nice babies, although afraid of and disgusted with the dirty ones, the slum children, which meant the injured and therefore dangerous babies.

Richard fully responded to this interpretation. He said that his father was having Benger's Food—wasn't that baby-food? . . . Richard had now become more restless and looked out of the window. He saw Mr Smith pass and waved and smiled. Obviously Mr Smith gave him a friendly gesture, and Richard was pleased when he returned to the table. He did not make any remark about Mr Smith, nor had he asked Mrs K. whether she had met him, which was unusual. Then he searched for his penknife and seemed uncertain whether he had brought it, but discovered that he had. He opened it and looking at the trademark said pointedly, 'Made in Germany.' At that moment he looked out of the window and saw a man pass and said he was awful.

*Mrs K.* asked why.

Richard said he had such a horrid big nose. (There was actually nothing striking about the man.) Richard looked round the room and cut slightly into the wooden pole, but soon put his knife away.

He lifted the heavy pole and let it drop, which made a loud noise. . . . He asked Mrs K. whether there had been any raids by the R.A.F., and when Mrs K. said she did not know, he was annoyed and asked why she didn't listen to the news in the morning. . . . He went into the kitchen, took the axe, and hit the stovepipe, gave this up, and again explored all the parts of the stove. He opened the oven, cleaned the soot out, hammered at some of the pipes to get the soot out of them, opened the damper, and discovered how the stove was connected with the tank. After that he drew water from the tap, filled a bucket, and asked Mrs K. to empty it. All these activities led to a mess on the kitchen floor, and Richard was worried about it and very grateful when Mrs K. cleaned it up.

*Mrs K.* asked if he was afraid of the Girl Guides because of the mess he had made.

Richard said no, but he did not want them to become furious with her.

*Mrs K.* interpreted that Richard was searching for the big and frightening Daddy-genital inside himself, represented by the man's big nose and the German knife in Richard's pocket, and also wanted to find out how big it was inside him. He wished to smash it and to cut it out of himself; therefore he had attacked the wooden pole. But again, as on the previous day, he decided instead to clean his inside, represented by the stove. The stove also stood for Mrs K.'s inside; the penknife made in Germany for Mr K., whom he so often felt Mrs K. contained. She therefore had the ill and frightening Daddy inside. Richard also attempted to clean Daddy's inside of the bad bombing fæces which he (when the R.A.F. stood for him) had put into Daddy. He had been frightened that the mess he had made would lead to trouble between the Girl Guides and Mrs K. That meant that his mess—his bad fæces—would cause trouble between other people, particularly between his parents.

Richard, when everything had been cleaned up, picked up the calendar, looked at the pictures, and admired some landscapes. When he saw one representing a cottage with a brown thatched roof—the whole picture being in rather brown shades—he said that he did not like it, passed on quickly, and looked at another admiringly. He seemed annoyed when Mrs K. asked him why he disliked the preceding picture but replied, though reluctantly, that he did not like the roof in it. The picture he liked represented a scene with lambs and sheep and was called 'Solitude', and Richard became emotional over it.

*Mrs K.* interpreted his feeling lonely and his desire to be back with his parents : the lambs with the sheep reminded him of home.

Richard replied that he wished to be back, but he was not really unhappy. Various pictures which he passed over quickly were in sepia.

*Mrs K.* interpreted this again as Richard's dislike of his own fæces; the brown roof of the cottage stood for his parents' home and their bodies, which he felt he had soiled and spoiled.

Richard then showed Mrs K. two pictures which were brown and said he liked them; the sun was shining and made one part of them look golden.

*Mrs K.* reminded Richard that the sun had often, in the analysis, represented the good, warming, and helping Mummy. She could even put the bad 'big job' right and turn it into something good. Richard had once said about his shoes that they shone like gold in the sun.

Richard was getting ready to go. Throwing a quick glance at the drawings, he said (about 49), shuddering a little, 'The horrible eagle is watching you and me.'

*Mrs K.* interpreted that the eagle represented Daddy and Mummy, mixed up and black with bad fæces; the open mouth showed that they would devour him. These bad parents were watching what Richard and Mrs K., who was the good Mummy, were doing and saying. But they had also, in his mind, been eaten up by him and were therefore watching him and his thoughts internally. At present the eagle stood particularly for the ill and injured Daddy, united with the hostile Mummy.[1]

*Note to Sixty-second Session:*

I. Consciously the thought of sexual intercourse had all the time been strongly repressed, but unconscious material provided evidence of it. At the present time oral desires and situations had been reinforced by regression due to his father's illness. This has already been made clear in the note to the Fifty-sixth Session. The anxiety about rivalry in the Œdipus situation with his ill father had become unbearable. Former material had repeatedly shown how Richard in his play with the fleet had attempted—in order to keep the peace within the family—to give up any genital desires and consequent rivalry with his father. His father's illness increased this urge and contributed to the regression to the baby stage. The father had also turned into a baby by having a nurse in whom Richard, as he had said, was very interested. Thus the father also stood for the baby who would take away Mummy's breast. The nearer my departure came, the more his oral desires were reinforced. Moreover, since his anxiety centred so much on the sexual intercourse of the parents, and genitality appeared dan-

[1] I have no note about his response and the way in which he left me.

gerous to him for this and other reasons, the regression to orality was increased. It is significant, however, that the jealousy he wanted to avoid in the Œdipus situation had reappeared in the oral one.

Some of the factors I have mentioned, such as the anxiety about damaging by rivalry the father's genital, fear of retaliation by the father, anxiety about the mother's damaged and dangerous genital—dangerous because it contained the destructive Father-genital—can in general be observed as causes for impotence or reduced potency in men. I would add that the longing for the good feeding breast, expressed in many sublimations, is a feature which persists throughout life and is therefore easily revived when anxieties from inner or outer sources arise. We have, therefore, to consider not only regression but also the influence of early desires which had never been given up and affected the whole development.

## SIXTY-THIRD SESSION (Thursday)

Richard met Mrs K. a few doors from the playroom. He looked fairly happy. He had been leaning against a garden wall and pretending not to see her, making a face and half-closing his eyes: he said jokingly he wondered whether she would recognize him, and that he was pretending to be a 'silly old fool'. He told Mrs K. that his mother had rung up; she, Richard, and Paul were going to 'Z' for a day if his father was well enough to be left with the nurse; if not, they could not go. Inside the room he sat down at the table and told Mrs K. that the fleet had not come, it did not wish to, it said it did not want to see her.

*Mrs K.* interpreted that Richard seemed to have mixed feelings about her; in one way she seemed dangerous. The fleet stood for one part of Richard's mind, as well as for his family, whom he wished to keep safe when he was with her.

Richard accepted Mrs K's interpretation, but said emphatically that he very much wanted to come and was very fond of her. He told her that he had had quite a happy night and slept well. In the evening he went to the cinema, saw a good film, and was lucky to get his favourite seat, which was on the right-hand side, highest up and overlooking all the seats. He also told Mrs K. the number of it. He had been quite by himself on that side of the cinema. There were, of course, plenty of people in the cheaper seats; but he would not have minded if people had sat near to him as long as he had this seat. There were a few boys there who, he thought, were looking at

him, but he just ignored them and then they did not look again. He
went back to the hotel and read a little before going to sleep; he
slept well and felt well now.

*Mrs K.* interpreted the favourite seat on the right as being in the
same position as his chair was in the playroom when he sat with
Mrs K. To sit with her gave him, as he had often said, a feeling of
security and protection against people who might persecute him.
When he felt more secure in his seat at the cinema, he also felt protected by Mrs K. because she seemed to be more safely inside him,
which meant that he was sure of the good internal Mummy. Mrs
K. reminded him of the weekend when he had felt she was with
him (Seventh Session). Last night she was not the horrible eagle
watching him (Sixty-second Session) but the good Mummy inside,
and that was why he had not felt lonely, in spite of being without
his family and by himself at night. It also made him proud that he
could be alone without being unhappy, and proved to him that
Mrs K. and the analysis had helped him; this too made him feel
that he had the good Mummy inside.

Richard looked up at Mrs K. in a warm and affectionate way
and stroked her sleeve; he said that he liked her red jacket and
asked whether ladies on the Continent wore such nice jackets. . . .
He noticed Mr Smith passing; he had nearly missed seeing him because he had not paid attention to the road. Mr Smith seemed in a
hurry and Richard was very disappointed not to catch his eye, but
he knocked on the window-pane and was relieved when, after all,
Mr Smith smiled at him.

*Mrs K.* interpreted that Richard would be worried if Mr Smith
had not smiled at him because he was afraid that the nice father
might easily turn into the bad one. He had to be friendly with men
who stood for Daddy. When Richard had been leaning against the
wall and was a 'silly old fool', he had been making fun of Daddy
and therefore he felt guilty and frightened.

Richard lifted one side of the heavy wooden pole, so that it
could easily have hurt him had he dropped it.

*Mrs K.* interpreted that he showed in this way his fear of Daddy's
big and revengeful genital; he had to find out how dangerous it
was by lifting the pole and, a moment before, by making sure that
Mr Smith was friendly towards him [Reality testing].

Richard went into the kitchen and explored the stove; he did
nothing violent to it, as he had done on the previous day, but only
explored and cleaned it. When he had drawn water from the tank,
which he referred to as the 'baby tank', he pointed out to Mrs K.
that there were microbes round the opening of the pipe and that he
wished he could get them out. He filled the bucket, at first not very

full so that he could pour it out himself, but the second time he asked Mrs K. to do it for him, saying, 'I hate asking a lady to do this, but would you do it?' After Mrs K. had emptied it, he found a brush and cleaned out the stove and removed a lot of soot from it and also from the stovepipe.

*Mrs K.* interpreted that Richard wished to clean her inside from dangerous babies—the microbes—or rather ill babies, and also to make her better by cleaning Mr K.'s soiled and ill genital which could make her soiled and ill. He was in this way also making his father all right again.

Richard had dirtied his hand and his jacket with the soot. He said, looking unperturbed, that if one cleans one must get dirty (Note I).

*Mrs K.* pointed out that by doing this Richard took over some of the dirt, the microbes, which he felt Mrs K. and Mummy had inside them, and that he felt he lessened their trouble by dirtying himself.

Richard now returned to the tank and again drew buckets of water.

*Mrs K.* asked him not to fill the buckets so full, because that made them too heavy for her.

Richard asked what would happen if he left the tap running and the water flooded the house until it was lifted by the water and floated down the river. Then the river would become very shallow and hundreds of people would be short of water.

*Mrs K.* interpreted that her asking him not to fill the bucket completely made him feel that he was stealing the good breast from Mummy and depriving the other babies. Since he should not draw so much water, the tap had changed in his mind from the good breast into Daddy's bad genital, which could flood, destroy, and take Mummy away—the house floating down the river.

Richard again asked (he had done so soon after the beginning of the session) whether Mrs K. was going to the village that day. He knew that on Thursdays John's session followed closely after his, and that Mrs K. therefore went straight back to her lodgings. Richard added appealingly : 'Must you go home?'

*Mrs K.* interpreted that Richard knew that John was coming and wished that Mrs K. would give her time only to him. This might also have been the reason why some days previously (Fifty-sixth Session) he had asked her to give him two consecutive sessions. He was afraid, moreover, that she would again be soiled and injured by being with John. Such feelings increased his jealousy about Mummy now looking after Daddy and Paul, who might also soil and injure her.

Richard repeatedly closed the lid of the tank rather violently.

*Mrs K.* pointed out that he had now closed Mrs K.'s breast and genital to others, in particular to John. Also, when he felt jealous, he was angry and wished that Mr K. and John would hit Mrs K.'s breast and genital hard and hurt her; that was why he felt so much concern about what might happen to Mummy in sexual intercourse. . . . Meanwhile the lid of the tank, which consisted of two sections, had come apart and one of the sections fell into the tank. Mrs K. fished it out; this made her arm and hand dirty, and she washed them.

Richard dried his hands at the same time on the other end of the towel and said that he and Mrs K. were sharing this, weren't they? He also put the lid together with Mrs K.'s help and clearly enjoyed her doing these things for him.

*Mrs K.* interpreted that Richard wished to share things with her and that this meant keeping her externally and internally as the good Mummy.

Richard found a tiny ball and made it roll through the room from one end to the other. He did the same with a little larger one and also made the balls bump each other.

*Mrs K.* interpreted that he seemed to feel that his genital, though small, could go into Mrs K.'s (the room standing for her), and that meant that he could do something for her and be sure of her love. Then he would be more able to share her with John (or Paul in connection with Mummy), the larger ball standing for John and Paul.

Richard then got out of Mrs K.'s bag a still larger ball and played with it in similiar ways.

*Mrs K.* interpreted that Richard was now sharing Mummy with both Paul and Daddy.

Richard, before leaving, inspected his jacket, which was stained with soot. He did not seem perturbed and said that though there would be a row with Mummy over this, it would not be too bad. He parted in a friendly way, neither particularly excited or elated nor persecuted or depressed. Recently his phobia about children on the street had hardly shown, and during this session he paid scarcely any attention to passers-by.

Richard's mother on that day reported that he had behaved reasonably and helpfully when his father fell ill, though he had as usual dramatized the situation. Although he knew that he would have to stay alone at 'X' in the hotel—the first time for him to be by himself at night—he said that though he would rather stay with his mother he thought the best thing he could do was to go back to 'X' and to his analysis. He seemed quite determined. According to his mother, progress was being made and well maintained.

*Notes to Sixty-third Session:*

I. Richard's insight into the need to dirty himself, if he wanted to clean something, seems to me of some significance. His whole development at this stage showed a diminution of idealization, progress in integration, and therefore a greater capacity to acknowledge that a person can be good without being perfect. This would imply that he himself could be dirty to some extent and yet useful, helpful, and valuable. Greater tolerance towards others was bound up with greater tolerance towards himself and therefore with a diminution of guilt. This lessening of depressive and persecutory anxiety also implied a lessening of obsessional trends.

## SIXTY-FOURTH SESSION (Friday)

It was pouring with rain. When Richard arrived, he looked round the playroom with obvious dislike. He did not look at Mrs K. at all. He offered her a local paper from 'Z' which he had previously mentioned, and asked urgently that she should read it; then she would really know something about 'Z' and would like it. . . . He pulled a shilling out of his pocket and asked whether Mrs K. could give him twelve pennies for it.

*Mrs K.* said she had no change.

Richard then sat down at the table. He said he wished he were 'not here'. He made a gesture which he explained was ringing a bell.

*Mrs K.* asked for whom he was ringing the bell.

Richard, without any hesitation, said that it was for the light-blue Mummy to come in and for the dark-blue Mummy to get out. He pointed at Mrs K.'s navy-blue dress and added that she was not quite black, even though she was dark blue; she was something in between. He told her about his trip with Mummy and Paul to 'Z'. Clearly it was very important to him that they had brought back not only various household things, which were largely for his father's convenience, but also his own clockwork train. He showed very strong feelings about this train.[1] Richard then made Drawing

[1] It was not only that he could play with it; the impression he gave was of having found again a lost, loved object. This was reminiscent of the strong emotions shown when he drew his electric train in the Forty-fifth Session and spoke of their house in 'Z', and of early happy memories. The fleet and his birds had come to play a similar part: all of these were bound up with love which was partly displaced from the relation to his parents and home life.

54 which was a map, as he called it, of his clockwork train. One circle represented a chair, round which were lines standing for rails. He did not explain the circle above it. He imitated the noise of the engine and talked with enthusiasm about the strength and speed of the train. Clearly he was trying to overcome fears and depression [Manic defence].

*Mrs K.* interpreted that Richard was very glad to have his train back not only because he liked playing with it, but also because it stood for himself—the little Richard who was alive and feeding from Mummy's breasts—the two circles. He needed this all the more because he was afraid that his father was very ill and might die, and this had very much increased the fear of his own death (Note I).

Richard said, seriously and sadly, 'Daddy is very ill.' He ran into the kitchen, stood on a box, looked out of the window, and saw that the various packages and poles had turned out to be a tent. He called out excitedly for Mrs K. to come and look out with him, and then asked her to hold his hand while he jumped down.

*Mrs K.* interpreted Richard's desire to make her into the good Mummy by getting her to hold his hand and to give him pennies; then he would not be frightened of the bombed, injured Mummy represented by the house in 'Z' or the dead 'eagle' Mummy (Fifty-ninth Session) who was now standing for Mummy containing the ill Daddy.

Richard was marching up and down the room, shouting and stamping and goose-stepping. . . . He went back to the table, and in great haste—looking angry, worried, and persecuted—covered two pages of the pad with his name and scribbles.

*Mrs K.* interpreted the stamping, shouting, and angry scribbling as expressing his feelings that he had bombed and soiled Daddy with his fæces and urine, that he was like Hitler marching and goose-stepping. He was afraid and very worried that he had made Daddy ill and so also injured Mummy, who, he felt, contained Daddy. Therefore he was not only guilty, but also afraid of being attacked by the internal parents, the eagle inside him.

Richard picked his nose (which was quite unusual with him) and asked Mrs K. whether she would stop a child patient from doing something which might hurt him.

*Mrs K.* asked him what, for instance, this might be.

Richard said : 'Eating his nose-pick.'

*Mrs K.* interpreted that it seemed he had eaten it before and was afraid that it was something bad and dangerous, like his bad 'big job', which he felt could harm him as well as his parents.

Richard said, with a look of relief, that he had eaten nose-pick before, but at once ran out of the room and into the kitchen. He looked into the 'baby-tank', saw that the water contained some soot, got hold of a poker and poked about with it in the tank, and said: 'That is what Daddy's heart is like when he is ill.'

*Mrs K.* pointed out that he felt he had attacked Daddy and made him ill by poking about in him. But by moving the poker up and down he also tried to keep his father's heart going so that it should not stop—in the same way as moving the train gave him a feeling of keeping life going in himself and in Daddy.

Richard had been closing the tank by throwing on to it the lid, which again, as previously, fell into the tank, causing the water to splash on to the stove. While Mrs K. was getting the lid out, Richard, who had all the time been looking anxiously at the heavy rain, ran to the side door, opened it, and kept it open, thus allowing the curtain to get wet.

*Mrs K.* suggested shutting the door, and interpreted Richard's fears of rain as the drowning, flooding, and poisoning urine of the ill Daddy[1]; Richard wished to test these dangers by allowing the curtain to get wet.

Richard was running about in the playroom, which had been tidied and cleaned up by the Girl Guides and, looking at some new postcards which had been put up on the screen, murmured the caption of one of them. It was about Donald Duck who had left at home a baby penguin he had adopted, while he went out to find food for it. When he came back he found that the greedy baby had eaten the goldfish. Richard had been chewing and biting a new red pencil so hard that the red paint at the end had come off. He asked if Mrs K. minded that he had been biting the new pencil which she had provided.

*Mrs K.* interpreted Richard's fear that he, the greedy baby, had eaten the goldfish, standing for Daddy's good 'Roseman' genital— now the pencil—and had left Mrs K. and Mummy with the injured or dead Mr K. or Daddy.

Richard made two drawings of postal orders—the first for £1, was made out to himself and signed in the King's name; the second, made out to Mrs K. and also signed in the King's name, was for the amount of eleven pence.

*Mrs K.* interpreted that he had been showing that he also contained good 'big job'—the postal order given to him by the King, standing for Daddy. Mrs K. was given only eleven pennies, and he

[1] There was a good deal of persecutory anxiety. The rain, which, as had been seen during former sessions, was to him a punishment and a threat, represented the dangerous and poisonous urine from the father above, which had at earlier occasions meant a threat by God (Fifty-second Session).

felt he had robbed her; he had the pound, the good Daddy-penis and the babies.

Richard had become more restless. He went to the window to watch the rain, ran up and down the room, and wrote his name among scribbles on other pages.

*Mrs K.* interpreted his fear that, after all, he did not have the good 'big job'—the pound—which he could give to Mrs K. and to Mummy to replace the good goldfish-penis. He felt that he had only bad fæces—the scribbles—and therefore he could do nothing to return to Mummy what he had robbed her of, nor could he help her in her distress about Daddy's illness.

Richard pointed to the red pencil and said: 'It has turned quite brown because I bit it.'

During this session Richard was at times noisy and restless and thus expressed his persecutory anxiety, but it was quite clear that depressive feelings and realization of the actually distressing situation were much more experienced than in the sessions immediately following his father's illness (Note II).

*Notes to Sixty-fourth Session:*

I. It would have been appropriate to add to this interpretation the following, which was not given in this context: Richard, represented by the train, being alive implied that the internal father was also being kept alive. This feeling was bound up with his memories of early childhood, revived by seeing their house again, and stirred up the love and concern for his father and the wish to renew the family life. As had been seen in connection with earlier material, the deserted and bombed house in 'Z' also stood for his deserted mother. By reviving the past and experiencing love, Richard felt that he could undo or counteract his destructive desires and his identification with the Hitler-father. It is significant that at this stage of the analysis feelings of love, which had been stifled by persecutory anxiety, were able to come up more freely and were fully experienced.

We can see here that in the course of the analysis not only were early memories revived, but the emotions and anxieties which influenced his whole development had also come to the fore. In particular I am referring to memories in feelings which went back to earliest infancy and which often underlie a cover memory. Such cover memories are of importance if we are able in the analysis to discover the deeper and earlier emotional situations which are condensed in them.

II. It can be seen from the material following immediately on the sudden illness of Richard's father and his attitude towards it, that first of all persecutory anxiety was predominant. It is after this anxiety had been analysed and diminished to some extent that depressive feelings, guilt, and the wish to make reparation came strongly to the fore. For instance, Richard had shown himself capable of staying by himself in the hotel, an achievement which was, I am sure, due to the analysis; at that particular time he felt that in doing so he was helping his mother as well as protecting his analysis. The fact that persecutory feelings are reinforced as a means of avoiding the pain of experiencing guilt, responsibility and depression, has been referred to in my paper 'A Contribution to the Psychogenesis of Manic-Depressive States' (1935, *Writings*, 1), where I suggested that the incapacity to work through the depressive position may often lead to a regression to the paranoid one. The pain that Richard experienced, and was now more able to bear, was very poignant. His feelings of guilt were bound up with his incapacity to return to his mother the good penis and the babies he had robbed her of in his mind, to undo the harm he felt he had done to his father and to her by his jealousy and omnipotent death wishes, and to help her now in her distress over his father's illness. Not only was anxiety from all sources—oral, anal, and urethral—mobilized, but also conflicts of loyalties in various connections : between his duty to father and to mother, between the analyst and his mother; at the same time he felt jealous of his father because of the attention given to him—particularly by the nurse—and his jealousy conflicted with his feelings that his father should be kept alive. He also felt guilty because his father had been left alone when he, his mother, and Paul went away for the day. He realized now, quite consciously, that family life would be endangered if his father were to die, that his mother would be lonely and deserted, and he felt extremely guilty about his jealous and hostile feelings in the past, which, to some extent, were still operative in the present.

## SIXTY-FIFTH SESSION (Saturday)

Richard had brought his case with him because he was ready to go home by bus after the session. He looked serious, but friendly and determined. He told Mrs K. that this was parting day. He had left the hotel for good.

*Mrs K.* asked whether he felt sorry.

Richard said he *was* sorry. The people at the hotel had been nice to him. On Monday he was going to stay with the Wilsons (who, as mentioned before, were friends of the family and lived in 'X') for three nights a week ; he was to go home on the other nights and at weekends. . . . In the playroom he looked round and then asked

Mrs K. if she would tighten his shoe-laces so that they would last for the whole day, and Mrs K. did so. Sitting down at the table he again made the gesture of ringing a bell. He said he was ringing for Mrs K. to come in, she was the light-blue Mummy today and had also got her lovely jacket on.

*Mrs K.* asked why he rang for her to come in, since she was already there.

Richard was surprised and thoughtful. He replied that this was true—obviously he could not understand it himself.

*Mrs K.* interpreted Richard's desire to have her as a good Mummy, coming not into the playroom but into his inside. The tightening of the laces so that they should last expressed his wish to keep her inside as a good Mummy while he was away for the weekend. His wanting that she should do things for him, as his mother did, such as taking the lid out of the tank, holding his hand when he jumped down from the box, giving him change, tightening his shoe-laces—all this meant that Mrs K. was not only to be the analyst whose help made him feel that she stood for the good Mummy, but also that she should actually replace his mother of whom he saw less now. Moreover, Mrs K. was to give in to all his wishes because he was afraid she might turn bad, as he had felt her to be on the previous day. Mrs K. suggested that with Mummy, too, he often wished to get as much attention as possible because he needed reassurance that she still loved him and had not changed into the injured and hostile Mummy—the eagle—containing an ill and injured Daddy.

Richard agreed that he was asking for more attention from his mother. . . . He went out into the garden with Mrs K., closed the door, and said that he had locked her in.

*Mrs K.* interpreted that although he was with her outside, he wished to lock her into his inside, represented by the house, and he needed this all the more because he was going away for the weekend, and because Mrs K. was soon going to leave him.

Richard, back in the room, asked for the pad and noticed that the drawings were in a new envelope; he was sorry about this. He asked Mrs K. what had happened to the old one (Note I).

*Mrs K.* replied that it had become soaked in the previous day's rain.

Richard said he had liked the old envelope, and he asked whether Mrs K. had burnt it.

*Mrs K.* replied no, she had salvaged it (Note II).

Richard had obviously hoped for this answer; his face brightened and he said he was glad that Mrs K. was patriotic. Looking out of the window he said about a girl who was passing by and had rather curly hair that she was like the monster in the book. Richard had again been sucking and biting the pencil and asked whether Mrs K. minded him sucking 'her' pencil. He added that so far she had not been cross, but she still might get cross. Then he wondered whether she liked the newspaper he had shown her. Suddenly he became worried and said that he had wanted to give this paper also to the head waitress at the hotel and was sorry he could not because he wanted Mrs K. to have it. It did not matter, however, because the waitress had already read it.

*Mrs K.* pointed out that he wished to satisfy both her and the waitress, as he had tried to be loyal to the good mother and nurse. The monster-Mummy was Mummy containing the bad and now ill father, and he wished to keep her apart from the good Mummy. This was shown by his dividing the 'good' Mrs K. from the bad one, who was represented by the little girl who passed by and 'looked like the monster'. Mrs K. linked this with his guilt and fear about the illness of his father. He was also frightened and guilty because he felt his mother contained the injured and therefore dangerous father, having been robbed by Richard of the good Daddy-genital, the goldfish, the 'Roseman', the 'Prinking' and 'Longline' which also meant 'long-live'.[1] He had spoken of Mrs K.'s red pencil and repeatedly inquired whether she minded his sucking and spoiling it. He had never before referred to any of the pencils as belonging to Mrs K.: but he did so now because he feared that he was responsible for her being left with dangerous and bad genitals, since he had sucked out of her—and that also meant out of Mummy—the good Father-genital. The red pencil had turned brown because he had bitten and sucked it. Since it belonged to Mrs K., it also stood for her breast, and Mummy's, which he felt he had bitten and dirtied.

Richard looked round the playroom. He had earlier had a good look at the tent outside and remarked that now he knew what the remaining packages contained—meaning another tent. Richard had not commented, either on the previous day or in this session, on the fact that the playroom and kitchen had been carefully cleaned and tidied.

*Mrs K.* drew his attention to this and suggested that Richard did

[1] Up to a point this interpretation was the same as that given on the previous day, but I was not sure how much of it I had been able to convey to him at the time. Also, as usual, some new details appeared in the new context. Now Richard listened quite attentively; but it became clear that he had in fact taken in then much more of the interpretation than he had seemed to do; this was shown by his attitude, right from the beginning of the session, being very different from that of the preceding day.

not like the Girl Guides cleaning the playroom and kitchen because he would have wished to do it all himself.

Richard, during this interpretation, wrote out another postal order, this time made out to his mother, for the sum of nineteen shillings and twopence.

*Mrs K.* interpreted that Richard felt he was returning the good penis—the good 'big job'—to his mother; in fact he had not only divided the £1 which he had received from the King between Mrs K. and his mother but had added to it. In that way he was also trying to be fair to both Mrs K. and Mummy, as he had often wished to divide his affection and love between mother and nurse, and between mother and father.

Richard had been scribbling : he said it was Chinese writing (in fact, his scribbles had some likeness to Chinese characters) and was a protest, either by General Chiang Kai Shek or to General Chiang Kai Shek—he did not know which.

*Mrs K.* asked what the protest was about.

Richard said he did not know that either. He then drew a tram-line of an unusual shape, starting and finishing at the station 'Rose-man', the whole of which he scribbled over. He repeated the question asked earlier, whether Mrs K. was going to the village after the session. Then he marched up and down the room as on the previous day, making a good deal of noise and goose-stepping. He drew a swastika which extended over the whole page and which he changed into a Union Jack. He then drew a large aeroplane which he emphasized was a British aeroplane.

*Mrs K.* interpreted that this was the same as the swastika changing into a Union Jack. The 'British' aeroplane was actually felt to be German, although trying to be British. He had shown this by the way he stamped and goose-stepped, which he felt was an attack on the playroom and on Mrs K., standing for Mummy ; at the same time he also wanted to protect her.

Richard did not say anything about the other pages which he had covered with scribbles and his name, but remarked that he had used up even more of the pad than on the previous day, and kept on tearing pages out of it.

*Mrs K.* interpreted that he wished to get as much as possible out of her, the pad standing for her, because he would not be there the following day—Sunday—and therefore felt angry and frustrated.

Richard said emphatically that he did want to go home and did not wish to stay in 'X'.

*Mrs K.* interpreted that it was true Richard wanted to go home and be with his mother, but nevertheless he also wanted to be with Mrs K., resented being deprived of the Sunday session, and was jealous and angry that somebody else might have it. She also interpreted that he seemed always to be suspicious when he was away from her and afraid of what she might do in the meantime.

Richard, when Mrs K. interpreted that he wanted to go home and see his mother, replied that this was true, but he also very much wanted to see the train which he had brought back from 'Z'. He enthusiastically described, in detail, at what a tremendous pace the engine could run; it was red; the passenger cars were brown (here he looked at Mrs K. significantly), but they were very nice too. Meanwhile he had been drawing (55). The top line of the triangle and the line leading to the genital were added later. Richard explained that the two sides of the triangle were bones. Before he made the additions, he picked up the drawing suddenly and put his lips to one breast. After having added the line to the genital, he completed the head by drawing the hair.

*Mrs K.* interpreted that his not coming on Sunday this time made him feel as he did as a baby, when he was deprived of Mummy's breast and of the bottle which was to replace the breast. All this was revived because his father now had a nurse as if he were a baby. Mrs K. asked what the uncompleted triangle had meant.

Richard replied it was V for Victory.

*Mrs K.* interpreted that there was also a small V above the right leg, and asked who the bigger victory belonged to.

Richard replied that it was his, and Daddy had the smaller victory.

*Mrs K.* also interpreted that the hair on the head, which he had drawn after making the line to the genital, stood for the hair round the genital.

Richard suddenly became very embarrassed about this drawing, ran into the kitchen, and looked round; he examined the stove and noticed, with distress, that there were rust spots where he had splashed water on it the previous day. As mentioned before, he did not refer to the fact that the kitchen had been cleaned by the Girl Guides, but obviously this added to his distress. He looked worried and depressed and said this was what happened when he splashed such dirty stuff on Mummy; he wanted to know what he and Mrs K. could do about it.

*Mrs K.* found a brush and cleaned the stove.

Richard did not look at it any more. He got hold of a rake and ran into the garden, asking Mrs K. to follow him. He raked up the earth between rows of vegetables and said he wished at least to do a few rows. He added that the earth was brown, but it was nice. He looked very satisfied during this activity and paid hardly any attention to passers-by, nor did he ask Mrs K. to whisper, as he usually did when they were outside. Altogether, during that session, he paid little attention to the road and did not inquire about Mr Smith. Once when a man passed by he made faces and also made biting movements with his jaws. Then he turned to Mrs K. and said affectionately: 'This was not meant for you—only for him.'

*Mrs K.* interpreted that the rake stood for the good penis of the father, as well as his own, and could be used for cleaning and restoring Mummy, which meant also making babies grow—the vegetables. He seemed to feel that his 'big job' was not only bombs but also good, because the postal orders which stood for 'big job' were given as presents to Mummy and Mrs K.

Richard had gone back into the room and again scribbled, using the brown pencil. He broke the point while drawing with it.

*Mrs K.* interpreted that when Richard scribbled with the brown pencil so strongly that he broke it, this showed that he was afraid his 'big job' was soiling and destroying Mrs K. after all; she linked this with the water, standing for urine, which he felt had damaged the stove.

Richard put together the unsharpened ends of the green and yellow pencils. The sharpened end of the yellow pencil was broken and he pushed against it with the broken end of the brown pencil so hard that he moved the green pencil out of place.

*Mrs K.* interpreted that what Richard had now expressed was that his penis—the brown pencil—produced bad urine and 'big job' and broke Daddy's genital, made him ill, and also badly upset Mummy; he felt very guilty about all this. He was, moreover, afraid of doing the same damage to Mrs K. Richard's attacks on Mummy's, Mrs K.'s, and Daddy's genitals were also shown by his having bitten the new red and yellow pencils. He had particularly asked Mrs K. whether she minded his biting these pencils; but the biting meant, too, that Richard had eaten the attacked penis and therefore he felt the fight was going on inside him and not only inside Mrs K., as in Drawing 55. He had said that he had won the bigger victory; but when he represented Hitler by goose-stepping, this meant that Hitler had won the bigger victory and controlled him from inside.

Richard had not, during this session, spoken about his father. When Mrs K. was packing up the play material, he glanced at the drawings and said thoughtfully that it was a long time since he had drawn a starfish.

*Mrs K.* asked him whether he could now say what he thought about the Chinese protest.

Richard, looking fondly at Mrs K., said, 'I love you.'

Mrs K. interpreted that this meant that when he protested in a Chinese manner—that is to say with yellow, angry fæces and secretly—he hated Mrs K. because he felt deprived of the Sunday session. At the same time he was guilty about his hate and also loved her, and therefore did not want to speak about the protest.

Richard agreed to that.

When Mrs K. and Richard had left the house and were closing the door, he said, 'The old room is going to have a rest,' and, looking back from the road, he added, 'Goodbye, nice old house.' . . . He looked serious but not depressed or persecuted. He had again made sure that Mrs K. was going to the village. On the road, Richard said that it was not unpleasant to come by bus. He had been talking to a nice lady who was travelling to 'X'. When Mrs K. exchanged a greeting with a woman she knew, Richard was pleased and said that Mrs K. had many friends here, hadn't she, and that she knew nearly everybody.

*Mrs K.* replied that she had met a few people in 'X'.[1]

*Notes to Sixty-fifth Session:*

I. The old envelope had acquired a particular importance because it was so closely linked with his relation to the analyst and in some sense also represented the analyst herself. These transference feelings were rooted in his deep attachment to his first objects, as was shown by his wish to return by himself to the old deserted house which stood for the lonely and deserted mother and was linked with all his early memories. This strong attachment was evidence of his capacity for love and was strongly reinforced by his depressive anxieties. These over-strong feelings of guilt had the effect of making him cling excessively to his mother and interfered with his forming new relations and finding interests; all of this had been a vital factor in the disturbance of his development and was partially mitigated in the course of his analysis.

II. I have repeatedly remarked that, in spite of not deviating in essentials from my technique, I sometimes answered questions, which had the effect of reassuring Richard. In this particular session I had not only answered a question but had given a very direct reassurance which I on the whole deprecate. What caused me to do this was that the child not only unconsciously feared the end of his analysis but

[1] Richard's remark that I knew everybody was a denial of the fact, quite well known to him, that I had hardly any social contacts in 'X'. His repeated question whether I had been to the cinema had also much to do with his fear that I might be lonely. On that particular day this was increased by his fear of deserting me, as he would not be having a Sunday session. We see here the revival of the strong conflict of loyalties between his mother and Nurse, whom he was actually going to meet on his way home.

consciously realized his urgent need for it. My knowledge that he might not, for years to come, have any opportunity for analysis, and the particular circumstance that his father had fallen seriously ill, no doubt had an influence on my counter-transference.

The question will probably arise how far this affected the course of the analysis. I find it difficult to decide, since at the time I also persistently analysed the negative transference and the child's suspicions of myself and of his parents. But as a matter of principle I wish to repeat that even in this case it would have been more useful to have avoided this occasional reassuring attitude. This is illustrated by the remark which immediately followed on Richard's having stated with pleasure that I was patriotic—that is to say, a very good object—and which indicated that I had at that moment increased the positive transference. His very next remark referred to the girl on the road who, although of quite harmless appearance, looked to him like the monster. That is to say, idealization of the analyst—the patriotic and not foreign and suspect Mrs K.—had not resolved the doubt in her; but this doubt was deflected and transferred to the girl passing by. The only way to diminish such suspicions would have been to interpret them. The very fact that instead of giving an appropriate interpretation I had given him a reassurance, which he quite well understood was outside the psycho-analytic procedure, increased his doubts on another level—his doubts in my honesty and sincerity. We find again and again that mistakes of this kind are unconsciously—and with adults sometimes consciously—resented and criticized; and this is true in spite of patients longing to be loved and reassured.

## SIXTY-SIXTH SESSION (Monday)

Richard was friendly and seemed quite happy. He told Mrs K. that he had had a good bus journey by himself. He referred angrily, however, to other occasions when the bus had been crowded and the conductress had said, 'Half fares stand up,' and Richard had had to give up his seat.

*Mrs K.* interpreted that since Richard wished to compete with Daddy for Mummy, he was very angry at being considered to be only half a man. She asked whether there had been any boys in the bus.

Richard said yes, there were, but they did not pay any attention to him, nor did he to them. . . . He said that his father was doing quite well.

*Mrs K.* pointed out that he was proud and happy that he could now travel by himself and not feel that boys were watching him and would attack him.

Richard said that he was looking forward to staying that night with the Wilsons, particularly as Mrs Wilson had promised him a present. He asked whether Mrs K. was going to the cinema that evening and added very appealingly, 'I insist that you go, Mrs K.' He had read about the film and described it as lovely; it was a story about somebody funny bringing up a baby. He again begged Mrs K. to go.

*Mrs K.* replied that she was sorry but she would rather not go.

Richard said he had a surprise for Mrs K. He slowly opened a box and very dramatically took the fleet out of it. He said that the surprise was that the big battle-cruiser *Hood* had been found by Paul when they were in their house in 'Z'.[1] He asked whether Mrs K. was pleased to see the fleet and said he was sure she was.

*Mrs K.* suggested that Richard might also mean he was sure that Mrs K. was pleased to see him back again.

Richard confirmed this strongly. . . . Then he showed Mrs K. how much bigger *Hood* was than *Nelson* (it was in fact the biggest ship in his fleet). He added, regretfully, that *Hood* had really been sunk, but here he would play that she was not. Poor *Nelson*, who had seemed so big, now looked so small.

*Mrs K.* interpreted that Richard was sorry for Daddy who had been made into a child, all the more since he was actually now helpless and ill. Also, since this reversal made Richard into *Hood*, he would not acknowledge that *Hood* had been sunk. At the same time *Hood* represented Daddy as well, and for that reason too should not be sunk.

Richard was surprised and said that he had actually told Mummy today that now he would be the father of the family. . . . He moved *Nelson* and made it go round Mrs K.'s bag and clock and hide behind them. Then *Hood* steamed out and the two met so close to the edge of the table that they nearly fell off. *Nelson* returned to the other ships and *Hood* disappeared behind the bag and remained there for a while.

*Mrs K.,* referring to Richard's comparison between *Hood* and *Nelson,* pointed out that when Richard was a little boy his father seemed enormous to him and so did his genital.

Richard pondered and asked whether his father's genital was really so big in his mind. He maintained that he had never seen it, but recently he had seen Paul's genital and there was actually hair round it.

[1] I have no record of whether he had previously referred to one ship being missing or whether he had not mentioned this until the present session.

*Mrs K.* referred to her having previously suggested that he might have observed his father's genital hair, or Mummy's, or Nurse's. This had been expressed when on the drawing he made of Mrs K. (Drawing 55) he drew hair at the same time as he made a line to the genital. Mrs K. also pointed out that Richard, having in his play nearly produced a disaster between *Hood* and *Nelson*—himself and Daddy—had made *Hood* safe by putting him behind Mrs K.'s bag and clock, while *Nelson* joined the family.

Richard said in a low voice, 'Poor Daddy.'

*Mrs K.* interpreted his sorrow about Daddy's illness; therefore he had said that *Hood* had been sunk but, in the play, it had come back; this meant that he also wished his father to remain strong and alive and continue to be the head of the family.

Richard repeated in a low voice, and very seriously, that he was sorry for his father and added : 'It is for his sake that I am coming here and travelling all by myself.'

*Mrs K.* asked what he meant by this.

Richard said shyly that this work helped him and then his father would not have to worry about him.

*Mrs K.* interpreted that he might also mean that if the work helped him to be less jealous, then he would not hate and attack his father and harm him.

Richard agreed that this was really what he meant. . . . In the meantime he had moved the *Hood* back to the other ships and put him in a central position, on one side *Rodney* and on the other a cruiser. He had put the destroyer *Vampire* a little farther away.

*Mrs K.* interpreted Richard's intention to restore Daddy to his position as father and husband, and himself to being the youngest of the family—the *Vampire*.

Richard, during this part of the session, had shown Mrs K. a packet of radish seeds which he had bought at Mr Smith's. He said that these were the seeds he liked best and he had wanted them for a long time.

*Mrs K.* pointed out that Richard had just sucked his pencil, and interpreted his desire to suck and eat his father's genital; then Richard would be very powerful and could give Mrs K. and Mummy many babies, and thus put them right.

Richard now made Drawing 56.[1] As he was writing the names he hesitated when he came to the *Hood* and murmured undecidedly : 'Daddy—Richard'; then he wrote down his own name.

*Mrs K.* interpreted the conflict between Richard's desire to take

---

[1] I reproduce this drawing after blacking out some of the actual names which Richard wrote by the side of the ships.

his father's place and to let Daddy keep it; he solved this by putting his father, represented in Drawing 56 by H.M.S. *Effingham*, away from Mummy (*Rodney*) and by making Daddy bigger than the ships usually standing for Richard (*Salmon* and *Vampire*) and for Paul (H.M.S. *Delhi*). In the role of *Vampire* he took his actual place as the youngest but also came between Daddy (now *Hood*) and Mummy (*Rodney*) and separated them. *Salmon*, too, represented the small Richard, but he was now next to his mother. At the same time the *Vampire* stood, as before, for Richard's genital, which he would use with Mummy to produce the baby he wished to give her.

Richard then made Drawing 57. He said that the circle was the chair round which the train was running. He had rearranged it in this way.

*Mrs K.* interpreted that the train represented Richard who was now running between the two breasts, formed by the two loops in the railway line, and that also meant going to and fro between Mrs K. and Mummy.

Richard, while Mrs K. interpreted this, pointed at the two ends of the railway line and said that there were two genitals—a small one (within the loop) and a big one.

*Mrs K.* interpreted that as well as longing to suck her and Mummy's breasts, he wished to put his genital near them. The big genital meant that Daddy was not to be left out.[1]

Richard, looking at Mrs K., said he was very fond of her. He further mentioned that his mother spoke of Mrs K. as 'a dear'. He remarked that he had been very cheeky with Cook. He had called her an 'impudent old fish cadger'. She was so shocked that she could not reply.

*Mrs K.* asked why he had said this.

Richard said he really did not know; he just felt angry and disliked her.

*Mrs K.* reminded him that he had told her previously about Nurse having quarrelled with Cook before she left, and that he had hated Cook ever since. She interpreted that Mummy speaking in a friendly way of Mrs K.—as he had mentioned—also meant Mummy being friendly with Nurse; but the bad cook stood for the bad Mummy whenever she was not friendly with Nurse. He had mentioned the bad cook and how angry he was with her just after he had said how fond he was of Mrs K. But Mrs K. did not do all he demanded and therefore the bad cook also stood for her.

[1] In retrospect, it occurs to me that the smaller genital had, in fact, penetrated inside the breast, while the larger one, standing for the father's genital, though it had come near to the breast, had remained outside. I would assume that both also stood for the mouth—his as well as father's.

Richard went into the kitchen and investigated the 'baby tank'. He said that the water was not so dirty. He drank, as usual, from the tap; then he made a wire spring, which was fitted across the draining-board, hit the board and asked Mrs K. to do so too. Suddenly he began to quarrel with an imaginary man outside the door, calling out 'Go away, go away', and locked the kitchen door against him.[1]

*Mrs K.* reminded Richard that he had asked her to make Mr Smith leave by saying 'Go away' (Forty-eighth Session); and on another occasion he had asked her to do the same to the 'Bear'. Both men represented the persecuting Daddy who might intrude when Richard wished to be alone with Mrs K., actually Mummy, and love her.

Richard, during this session, had been sucking the yellow pencil repeatedly, and still had it in his mouth when saying 'Go away' to the imaginary man.

*Mrs K.* interpreted Richard's wish to have her breasts (and the bottle given by the nurse) undisturbed all to himself, and to throw out his father who, he suspected at the time, took mother's breasts and, now that he had a nurse to himself, was also felt by Richard to be a rival baby.

Richard had gone back to the table and began to sort out from among his money the change he had been given by Mr Smith when he bought the seeds. He showed Mrs K. that a penny was larger than a two-shilling piece. He said he liked pennies. Then he put on his gas-mask (which he carried when travelling) and said that some people made a fuss about it. He quite liked it, and also the rubber smell, he had become used to that when he played with his rubber bricks.

*Mrs K.* interpreted that he wanted to keep separate in his pocket (which meant in his inside) the pennies he received from Mr Smith, standing for Daddy's genital, so that they should not mix with the silver coins which stood for Mummy's good breast. Even though he said he liked the pennies, he was obviously suspicious of them. He also wished to keep the good breast inside him separate from

[1] It seems to me that the anger with the cook was reinforced because Father being nursed had revived Richard's love for his nurse. His mentioning this incident at that moment followed, however, on my interpretation that in Drawing 57 he expressed his wish to suck the breasts and to bring his genital near to them. This would also express his anger about the bad mother—the bad cook—who had given him so little of the breast. The imaginary man whom he wanted to lock out represented the father who was accused of depriving him of the breast and of enjoying it himself. This was stimulated by the fact that father was treated like a baby—looked after by a nurse.

Mummy's soiled breast and from the 'big jòb' for which the pennies stood. The gas-mask which he pretended he quite liked was to save him from poison, which linked with his feelings about the poisonous Daddy-genital.

Richard very quickly put his arm round Mrs K.'s shoulder, and a little later did so again, saying that he loved her.[1] . . . He begged Mrs K. to go to the cinema that night; he would be so glad if she did. He spoke most appealingly.

*Mrs K.* interpreted that if she went, he would feel that she behaved much more like Mummy and he would not miss his mother as much as he did at present. If she took Mummy's place, he would be allowed to caress and kiss her.

Richard went outside and called Mrs K. to come with him. Though for a moment appearing disappointed about Mrs K. not agreeing to go to the cinema, he was very friendly. But looking at the hen next door he said, 'Silly old hen.' He went back to the room and said about an old woman who was passing, 'Nasty old woman.'

*Mrs K.* interpreted that both the hen and the old woman stood for her, and that Richard was angry with her because she would not keep him company as he wanted her to do and he felt frustrated by her.

During this session Richard said that he was quite happy in 'X' and did not much mind being away from home. He had, in fact, given the impression of being contented and had hardly been watching the road (except for the old woman at the end of the session). He had shown relatively few signs of being persecuted. His mother reported that Richard felt very strongly that he was 'playing his part' by undertaking these journeys alone, staying by himself at the hotel and now with friends—all of which were new experiences which formerly would have been impossible for him.

[1] Although Richard sometimes touched or caressed me, he always did it very quickly and it was obvious that he was restraining himself. There is no doubt that if I had not intimated through my whole attitude that such physical caresses were out of place in the analytic situation, he would have hugged and kissed me a good deal. The same applies to my other child patients with whom, on the whole, I could keep up a friendly but reserved attitude, necessary for analysing the transference situation (see *Psycho-Analysis of Children*, Chapter II).

## SIXTY-SEVENTH SESSION (Tuesday)

Richard, although a few minutes late, entered the house without hurry, looking depressed and reserved. He put down his attaché case but did not take the fleet out and walked about the room, kicking the stools and stamping on one or two. He did not look either at Mrs K. or at the clock. Altogether he appeared very disgruntled and uncertain what to do. When he noticed a big moth (the same kind as some days before) he first tried to chase it out, then decided to leave it alone. He also kept on tying up his shoelaces to make them quite tight. . . . After a while he asked whether he had been late, and how many minutes late.

*Mrs K.* said it was two or three minutes.

Richard asked if Mrs K. would keep him those two minutes longer.

*Mrs K.* interpreted that the two minutes seemed to stand for her breasts, which Richard was afraid of losing because he was deserting her by going home for the night.

Richard livened up a little and said : 'You are very clever to find this out. . . .' He had been looking out of the window, then sat down at the table and, stretching out his hand in an appealing way, asked Mrs K. to pass him the pad. He began by sucking the pencil. Then he wrote down a line of 'ice', again and again repeating the word with no space between and said with growing intensity : 'Ice, ice, ice.' Then he made Drawing 58. First it seemed as if he were going to do something like the 'Chinese protest' (Sixty-fifth Session). When Mrs K. asked him whether this was Chinese, Richard at first thought it was; but then he decided that these were scratches on the ice and that some of the darker dots and lines were people on the ice-rink who were scratching the ice while skating.

*Mrs K.* interpreted that his wish for lots of ice-cream was bound up with his need to get all he could, and even more, out of Mrs K. The ice-rink stood for Mrs K.'s (Mummy's) inside where the good milk and the babies and the good genital of the father were to be found. But if he were to intrude into her and rob her, he would scratch and injure her. (At this moment Richard drew the two lines enclosing the ice-rink.[1]) Mrs K. also suggested that, when he was dissatisfied as a baby, he had wished to scratch, bite, and injure the breast, and now he felt that he was doing the same to Mrs K. be-

[1] I have no notes about my having interpreted these two lines but think they might have meant protecting the breast by enclosing it.

cause he could not get what he wanted from her—even though it was he who was going away. This was also why to begin with he had thought that this drawing might again be a Chinese protest.[1] Mrs K. further interpreted that leaving her to go home made him feel that she now stood for the good breast—Mummy—while at other times she represented Nurse, and his own mother was the breast-mother. Mrs K. added that actually his mother had breast-fed him for only a short time, not more than a few weeks, after which Richard had been given bottles, probably by Nurse.

Richard at once said : 'What did Mummy do after that with her breasts—did she give them to Paul?' He considered this, and then said slowly that Paul had already been quite a big boy when Richard was born, so that couldn't have been true. He asked various questions, being obviously impressed and interested by Mrs K.'s information. How did Mrs K. know this about Mummy's breasts? Had Mummy told her, and when? What exactly did she say about it? And why didn't Mummy let him have her breasts any longer?

*Mrs K.* told Richard that when his mother had first come to discuss his treatment, Mrs K. had put some questions to her about Richard's babyhood and how things had gone, and his mother had told her, among other things, that she had had to stop breast-feeding Richard and put him on bottles after a few weeks because her milk gave out (Note I). Mrs K. interpreted that Richard's first thought, when being told about his short breast-feeding, was that Mummy had taken her breasts away from him to give them to Paul; and he might, even as a young baby, have felt that he was being punished by her, and that she was therefore giving her breasts to somebody else—Paul or Daddy. That had made him envious, jealous, and suspicious of Daddy and Paul; now again his father seemed to him to be a baby, since he had a nurse, and Richard was actually jealous of him.

Richard replied that his father even had two nurses (he had mentioned that fact before).

*Mrs K.* interpreted that this seemed to mean that Daddy had now taken not only Mummy's breast but also the nurse away from Richard.

Richard, while Mrs K. had been interpreting this, had put both thumbs into his mouth and sucked them hard, which was quite unusual with him. Then he covered a number of pages with scribbles, among which his name was prominent. While scribbling, he had re-

[1] It is significant that the recent Chinese protest, which I interpreted as being Chinese because it stood for yellow and poisonous urine and fæces, was made on a Saturday, preceding the frustration of not having a Sunday session.

peatedly run to the window and watched passers-by, particularly boys. He made faces at them, mainly by moving his jaws, but was hiding behind the curtain while doing so. He went, which was also unusual, three times to the lavatory, looking embarrassed and explaining that he felt like doing 'little job' but could not do it.

*Mrs K.* pointed out that as soon as he wished to take Mrs K.'s breast (or rather, Mummy's) all to himself, he also in his mind attacked the people who were suspected of having taken it away from him. They were represented by the boys at whom he had just now made faces; they had in his mind turned into enemies because he attacked them for having taken the breasts and Mummy away. He had also done so by trying to make 'little job' at them.

Richard, during this part of the session, kept on asking Mrs K. about her patients and the times when they came, and were they all men, and who was next after him.

*Mrs K.* interpreted Richard's jealousy and fears about Mr K., Mr Smith and Mrs K.'s children.

Richard now made Drawing 59. He said the name of the station 'Blueing' meant light blue, and he pointed at Mrs K.

*Mrs K.* asked him whether he could say anything about the 'ing' in the word 'Blueing'.

Richard said he did not know.

*Mrs K.* suggested it might be ink.

Richard said, half smilingly, this was so and he knew it when Mrs K. asked him what it meant but he did not want to say so.

*Mrs K.* interpreted that this was because Richard, being the train, wished to keep the nice light-blue breast-mother separate from the ink. She reminded him that he had thought the bottle of ink which he found in the kitchen was smelly. When Richard felt angry and dissatisfied he wanted to dirty the loved Mummy and her breasts, and now Mrs K., with his 'little' and 'big job'; he also felt he had done so as a baby and poisoned Mummy. The other two lines leading to 'Lug' and 'Brumbruk' expressed his wish to keep the light-blue Mummy free from the soiling and injuring 'big job', and that was the reason why he was uncertain about the spelling of 'Brumbruk'. His repeatedly trying to urinate had also meant soiling Mrs K. standing for Mummy; while at the same time he was afraid of doing so.

Richard had been scribbling and, as very often, he said that he did not know what he was drawing. He first made an oval outline containing two big circles and one small one, all hanging together. Then he drew two rough circles outside the oval shape and began to cover them furiously with dots. After that he made more dots inside the oval. While doing so his eyes flashed, he ground his teeth, and rage was expressed on his face.

*Mrs K.* suggested that the two circles represented the breasts, hers and earlier Mummy's, and that Richard was attacking them by biting and grinding his teeth; the violence with which he made the dots also meant soiling and blackening the breasts with urine and fæces. The pencil point with which he made the dots stood for his teeth and nails. Then Mrs K. asked him what the shape inside the oval (the three circles together) was meant to be.

Richard replied without hesitation that they were eggs.

*Mrs K.* interpreted that the attacks on his mother were made on the inside of her body and on the babies she contained.[1] The three eggs together suggested the shape of an unborn baby. Richard's jealousy of the babies his mother contained appeared to be linked with his feeling that she fed them internally instead of him (Note II).

Richard now drew on the same page two more rough circles and proceeded to dot them all over. After that he said that here were two new breasts; when he made a dot in the middle of each of these circles he added: 'These are the two things which are on top of the breasts—and now they have gone too.' (He did not know the word 'nipple'.) He then drew two more rough outlines and again dotted them all over and scribbled over them. He said they looked like strawberries. Then he made a number of large V's on the page, repeating that this was 'V for Victory'. While making the dots, he spoke of the raids by the Germans on Moscow. When he tore out this drawing from the pad (and more recently such tearing out of pages was very violent), he looked at the next page and at the one after it and appeared concerned when he noticed the sharp marks left on them by the violent dotting (Note III).

*Mrs K.* interpreted that Richard felt that he was not the 'good R.A.F.' attacking for good purposes, but the bad, the Hitler-Richard, destroying Moscow, standing for the injured mother.

Richard, in between making these scribbles, and during Mrs K.'s interpretations, had repeatedly paused to watch passers-by. Earlier, he had asked Mrs K. whether she had seen Mr Smith. He went on tearing out pages and scribbling over them, but less violently. On the last of these pages he began quietly to make dots where the marks showed, but soon gave that up.

*Mrs K.* suggested this was an attempt to hide the marks and possibly also to heal them. She pointed out that his using up so many more pages than he used to do, and wasting them, was also

---

[1] I have in my *Psycho-Analysis of Children* referred to these attacks in various connections. Unfortunately this drawing has been lost and so cannot be reproduced.

meant to prove to himself that he could take from Mrs K. what he wanted, that she liked him even though he had attacked her breast, and that the breast itself could be replaced if it was destroyed and exhausted—the circles which he had added and which he had said were strawberries.

Richard took some money out of his pocket and said that he would have too little for his bus fare.

*Mrs K.* interpreted Richard's wish to receive a present from her which would stand for the good breast; he also wanted to make sure that after all these attacks on her she still had babies inside and breasts left, and that she still liked him.

Richard then produced more money from his pocket and outlined four coins—2s., 6d., 3d., and 1d.—on the next page. He pointed out that the penny was the one which Mr Smith had given him the day before when he bought the radish seeds from him. He put the penny to his mouth and bit it for a moment. Then he took the packet of seeds out of his case and gloated about having it. He said he would not care for any seeds as much as for radishes; they looked lovely on the picture. He shook the packet to show that it contained 'thousands and millions' of seeds.

*Mrs K.* interpreted that the circles with the nipples which he had drawn were to him like strawberries, and to begin with stood for Mummy's good breast. The brown penny seemed not only to be Daddy's, or Mr Smith's good genital, but to be full of 'big job'. It soiled Mummy's breast and so did he when he was angry. Richard's jealousy about Mrs K. meeting Mr Smith, standing for Mr K., was much increased by his fear that Mr Smith would harm and soil her. He always watched his parents so intently, partly because he was afraid of their sexual relations. His desire for the radishes, and for the 'millions' of seeds contained in the packet which he received from Mr Smith, also meant the babies which Daddy's good penis should give him (Note IV).

Richard was now quiet and composed. He outlined Mrs K.'s india-rubber on the pad and copied the inscription from it. Then he made two horizontal lines across the paper and a vertical line which cut the drawing of the rubber in half, and said that these lines were bars. It was a prison.

*Mrs K.* interpreted that Richard, in his mind, had eaten up the rubber, standing for Mr K.'s or rather Daddy's genital, and kept it imprisoned inside himself. It had changed from the marvellous genital—radishes and strawberries, as Richard would have liked it to be—into something which now was full of 'big job'. It had become dangerous. Because he was so uncertain whether Daddy's genital was good or bad, he wished to make sure about it and therefore he drew the outline and wrote the inscription (Note V). He had put it into prison in his own inside because he wanted to control it internally since he felt it to be dangerous when it was outside [Introjection of the object for the purpose of controlling it and preventing it from doing harm].

Richard now suggested playing noughts and crosses, choosing the cross for himself. He arranged it each time so that Mrs K. should win. In the end, by not keeping to the rules, both he and Mrs K. won.

*Mrs K.* interpreted that this meant giving her the breasts, the genital or the babies back, the 'O' which he had given her standing for them.

Richard now made Drawing 60—first a wavy line which he said represented sands. The figure underneath was Mrs K. lying on the sands. The big circle with dots was a landmine, and the smaller circle just above the wavy line was the same landmine which had come nearer and was exploding; the scribble over them showed the way in which it was exploding. He then put this drawing aside and looked very worried and sad, but at once began to draw again (61). He said these were three nice strawberries growing in a garden and the garden belonged to Mrs K.

*Mrs K.* interpreted that he had doubts about Daddy's nice radish and strawberry genital. The 'rascal' father was only pretending that his genital was good, and therefore Richard was afraid that Mrs K. (and Mummy) might be blown up any moment when she was lying in bed—in the drawing, on the sands. Richard was afraid that he would be blown up as well, since he felt that he had taken into himself Mrs K., Mummy, and Daddy's genital. He thought of himself as a rascal who had soiled the strawberry nipple with his own bad fæces—as well as made Daddy attack and dirty Mummy with his genital. On the previous day he had kept separate in his pocket the change (the penny) which he had received from Mr Smith; it stood for the suspect genital—the rascal which he had taken in; and by keeping it apart he tried to preserve the good breast from being destroyed or attacked by the bad genital inside him.

Richard had been listening attentively while taking a toy out of Mrs K.'s basket. It was the swing: Richard made it move, and was pleased that it was all right. For the first time for weeks he actually played with a toy (Note VI). Very cautiously he took out the electric train, put the two carriages together and made them move, and again was very pleased.

*Mrs K.* interpreted that he was trying to find out whether Mrs K.'s and Mummy's breasts (the two carriages) were all right and also whether he could join Daddy and Mummy together (again the two carriages) in a good way.

Richard then put together the other train, the goods train. The two trains met, and the goods train tumbled over, but not violently (Note VII).

Richard, at the end of the session, looked much less depressed than at the beginning, though rather serious. On the road he watched people, but not intently. He said how would it be if the whole population of 'X' were to crowd on top of Snowdon, or into one bus.

During this session he had asked Mrs K. whether the Tuesday bus would be very crowded. He was early for the bus, and decided to go to the hotel to see the people there. Mrs K. asked him whether there was anybody in particular whom he wanted to see there. Richard said no, all of them. He parted from Mrs K. in a friendly but undemonstrative way (Note VIII).

*Notes to Sixty-seventh Session:*

I. I had pointed out to Richard's mother after that first conversation that it would be helpful if at some suitable moment she would inform Richard about his having been weaned from the breast so early. However, she did not do so, and having only a few more weeks of analysis ahead of me, I thought it advisable to introduce this information myself. I have often found that details mentioned by the parents can be made use of in so far as they appear in the material of the patient. But if, as in this case, I introduce a piece of information directly, I tell the patient frankly where I have got it from. As I have pointed out before, this procedure should be used cautiously and not too often, for it is bound to stir up suspicion about collusion between the parents and the analyst. It should be resorted to only when it is very essential for the analytic work; for what we should rely on is the patient's own material.

II. Feelings of frustration are linked not only, as this instance shows, with the suspicion of the father (in this case also of the brother) getting the breast when the infant was deprived of it; even the imaginary babies mother carries inside, and of whom jealousy exists on various grounds, are suspected of being fed inside mother. I would now suggest that envy of the mother's breast, her capacity to produce babies and to feed them, also entered into Richard's feelings of rage and frustration (cf. my *Envy and Gratitude*, 1957, *Writings*, 3).

III. This is one of the instances of a memory in feelings. The whole weaning situation with its anxieties and emotions was reproduced, stimulated partly by the jealousy of the baby-father and partly by my imminent departure.

IV. The quick change-over from the desire for his mother's breast to receiving father's penis, which would give him children, can be considered here from two angles. The love for the breast is transferred to the father's penis in the boy's feminine position. But the fact that mother's breast, her genital, and her body are felt to be injured and soiled by the infant through his jealousy and hate is an impetus towards transferring the desire on to the penis, i.e. towards homosexuality (see *Psycho-Analysis of Children*, Chapter XII).

V. The urge to make an exact reproduction of the object links with the uncertainty about internal happenings and objects, which contributes to the obsessional need to cling to exact descriptions, be it by writing, drawing, or other means. This uncertainty is a cause of great anxiety and confusion. For instance, an adult patient in a dream experienced strong surprise when she saw an object, which was sticking between the wheels of her car and which was of a very indefinite nature. Her associations, however, showed that this object represented a breast or a penis. In the dream she felt she did not want to look at it; but at the same time she knew it had been there for many years and that it was now time to look at it and to get it out. The surprise that she could now see this object was clearly experienced in the dream. The meaning, as further associations showed, was that she had been able to see that her internal objects about whose nature she had been anxious all her life, and which she was wishing both to see and not to see, had now become clear to her.

VI. For many sessions Richard had not played with the toys, although he used other material. (One of the last occasions he had anything to do with the toys was in the Thirty-first Session, when he looked at the 'slum' house and at a damaged figure of a man, of which he broke another part; but he did not play with them. The last actual play was in the Twenty-first Session, and was fully interpreted in the Twenty-second.) The toys, some of which had been damaged, expressed concretely the harm caused by his own aggressiveness—'the disaster'—and linked with all the deep anxieties about his destructive impulses; they had become the representatives of unchangeable infantile situations. The question arises why he was capable of persisting with other media of expression, such as the fleet, drawings, dreams, associations, and the occasional material shown in relation to the various objects in the house and garden. My suggestion would be that these means of expression allowed more control. The fleet, for instance—to him a very dear toy—was never actually damaged, though at one time he found that something had happened to the mast of one of the ships. He never left the fleet with me, though on one occasion he 'forgot' one of the ships; he often did not bring the fleet and gave reasons why it did not 'want to come'. The drawings, which can in some sense be equated to dreams, were also felt up to a point to be under his control, because—when he had finished one drawing—he could start a new one. The feeling of control applied to all the other means of expression which I have enumerated. This also gave him more hope that he could make a new beginning in his relations to his objects and improve on them. Therefore, at a stage in which he was actually unconsciously and consciously putting his whole effort into both progressing in his analysis and testing his strength in facing pain and depressive and persecutory anxiety, the return to the toys is significant. It finds some parallel in the attitude of patients who, at a certain stage in their analysis, return to earlier dreams and bring out more details about infantile anxiety situations because, being more integrated and their anxieties having lessened, they feel more capable of facing the anxiety situations which at an arlier stage they could not deal with.

It is interesting, too, that the scene where the 'disaster' occurred varied. Sometimes the mess was made in the kitchen; sometimes the disaster occurred among the toys or with the fleet. These variations also implied that the means by which the disaster was expressed, and the place where it happened, were split off when the next presentation of such anxieties was staged. I think that turning away from a completely destroyed object not only means expressing anxiety in another context and setting, and thereby also testing its dangerousness, but makes it possible to restrict the disaster to one aspect of the object and of the self, whereby other sides of the self and of the object are preserved. From the transference point of view, keeping the fleet at home meant that the actual family was to be kept safe and the disaster was only to occur in the substitute family represented by the analyst. In this way Richard sometimes felt he saved his actual mother, at other times the analyst. He had also occasionally felt that, if the fleet had come, it would attack me and therefore he said it did not wish to come. So the splitting in this case extended to separating the destructive part of his self from the loving one, thus preserving the analyst, the mother, or the family. This shows that splitting processes—so long as they are not excessive and therefore integration becomes again and again possible—are of great value. They are part of normal mental functioning. Generally speaking, if the dreaded disaster embraces the whole world, external and internal, then we are confronted with despair, deep depression, and often suicidal tendencies. From the technical point of view, it is very important to interpret all this and not to underrate the fact that, even in deeply depressed patients, somewhere the good object may still be felt to exist, either internally or externally.

VII. I would conclude that the ideal situation of the parents joined happily together could not be maintained. The goods train colliding with the electric train again represented Richard interfering with the parents' sexual intercourse and gratification, but the fact that the train was not violently thrown down shows the diminution in the intensity of his feelings. Degrees in intensity of impulses are of great importance in shaping the course of the Œdipus complex. This change can be considered from two angles. He was all the time, though he spoke little about it, aware of his father's illness and weakness; since he was concerned and guilty about that, his jealousy of his father's relation with his mother and his attacks on him were kept more under control. We have to consider moreover that the analysis had diminished his jealousy and increased his need for reparation as well as his wish to see the parents happy together; all the more as he was concerned about his father's health. To consider this diminution of aggressiveness, envy, and jealousy from the angle of the life and death instincts : there was clearly progress in Richard's capacity to mitigate hatred by love, and I would conclude that this expressed an alteration in the fusion between the two instincts, the life instinct being more dominant.

VIII. The day on which Richard had left the hotel, calling it a 'parting day', he had also had to wait a long time for the bus; although it was raining, he did not wait at the hotel, which was quite close to the bus station. I believe that his defence of turning away from the lost object, the hotel and the people there, which was expressed by his not going back to the hotel, had diminished during the present session; he felt more able to meet the people he had lost, for such was his feeling at every parting. This change of attitude was furthermore shown by his looking at the toys in the basket, which obviously represented to him lost objects about which he felt quite unsafe. All this, in my view, was bound up with facing the internal situation because his fear that his objects were hopelessly destroyed had diminished, and was reflected in his relation to the external world—his going to see his friends at the hotel.

## SIXTY-EIGHTH SESSION (Wednesday)

Richard arrived tired and hot from the journey. He complained about the heat and the crowded bus but did not give the impression that he felt persecuted by the other passengers. He said, half jokingly, that he wanted to give Mrs K. a present and gave her his bus ticket. It soon appeared that Richard was very disturbed because he had just heard that the arrangement which his mother had made for his staying in 'X' for the rest of the week might be upset because one member of the Wilson family was ill. Then he decided that he would ring his mother and get her to make other arrangements, after which he felt somewhat relieved. However, this seemed to be on his mind throughout the session; there were long silences and he was very preoccupied. After having discussed this worry, he told Mrs K. that he was very fond of her. Was she of him?

*Mrs K.* asked him what did he think.

Richard answered that he thought Mrs K. was fond of him, and also that she was very nice. Then he said that his mother was coming to see her to discuss plans for future arrangements, since Mrs K. was going to leave in a month's time. Richard asked whether this was definite; although he had known the date of her departure for some weeks, he only now seemed fully to realize it.

*Mrs K.* replied that she really had to leave in a month's time and interpreted that when he had felt so unhappy last Saturday, that had been connected with his fear of her imminent departure.

Richard looked pale and very depressed. He asked Mrs K. for the pad and said he wanted to draw their house.

*Mrs K.* asked if it was the house they lived in now.

Richard said emphatically that their only house was in 'Z'. Then he drew a square, which stood for the house, and made an outline, which stood for his fort and the garden path. He spoke at length about his fort, saying that the blast of the bomb in the neighbourhood had taken away the step leading into it; but the step had been old and rickety anyway. He said that Hitler would not stop him getting back into his fort, because he was going to make a new step for it; nobody was going to stop him getting back into his fort. After saying this, he made a scribble between the house and the fort. He then drew (62) and while drawing asked Mrs K. whether Mr Evans had strawberries.

*Mrs K.* asked him did he mean by that whether she had bought some from him.

Richard repeated his question as to whether Mrs K. had managed to get some. Mr Evans was rather nasty not to have strawberries, because at other places one could get them. Richard decided that he must buy lots more of the radish seeds, so that he would never run out of them and would have some until the autumn. Then he asked how many weeks there were till the autumn, were there five or six?

*Mrs K.* interpreted that by his being so determined to go back to their house and rebuild his fort, he was showing that he wanted to restore his genital, which he felt was injured, as well as to take care of the good Mummy in spite of the bad Hitler-father attacking her. He wished to give babies to Mrs K. and Mummy to keep them alive, but for that he needed more and more seeds, which Mr Evans, standing for Daddy, would give him. He both wished that Mrs K. should get good strawberries—the good genital—from Mr Evans, standing for Mr K., and was at the same time jealous of her getting them. Mrs K. also referred to the old house as standing for Richard's granny, who had died some years before and whom he had been so sad to lose. He was afraid that Mrs K., who was also a granny, would die when she left him. His sadness about her going away increased all his fears, and that was why he had asked how many weeks there were until autumn. It would practically be autumn when she left. By then he felt he should have built up his own good Mummy, and Mrs K., safely inside himself; and in order to keep them alive, they should be given all the seeds—the babies.

Richard said that he would like to eat the two strawberries on the drawing. Looking at it he said they were Mummy's breasts, and pointing at the leaves he added that these were the babies inside her. He scribbled on two pages and mentioned about one of them that the 'V' signs stood for Victory.

*Mrs K.* interpreted that it was his victory if he could control his destructive wishes and keep Mrs K. (and Mummy) for himself without a fight; on the previous day (the landmine drawing) he had doubted this because of his very strong attacks on her breast, body, and babies.

Richard counted his money, reckoned up what he had spent, and thought he should have more left over. He said he hoped he would not have to telephone home and spend money on that. He picked up a book, looked at the pictures, and was altogether unresponsive and inaccessible. Suddenly, looking up from the book, he asked Mrs K. what she was thinking about. He wanted her to promise him that she would go to the cinema and asked whether she would do so for his sake.

*Mrs K.* interpreted Richard's fear about the way she would spend her evening and which man would be with her. To know her thoughts meant knowing all her secrets and what went on inside her. Richard was jealous, but also terrified that the man about whom he was jealous was bad and would put his dangerous landmine-genital into her. At the same time he was also afraid that she was lonely in the evenings.

Richard then asked a number of questions. Did Mrs K. have patients in the evenings, what did she actually do in the evenings, and why would she never go to the cinema?

*Mrs K.* replied that she preferred reading and going for walks if the weather was nice.

Richard did not seem to believe this explanation. He went on turning the pages of the book, but soon looked up and again asked for Mrs K.'s thoughts.

*Mrs K.* interpreted that Richard resented having to tell her his secrets if she did not tell him hers. There were probably a good many secrets in his mind, expressed in the scribbles he had just made, but he did not want to talk about them.

Richard then scribbled on another page and said that a 'G' there stood for God.

*Mrs K.* interpreted that Richard was afraid of God as a strict Daddy, who might punish him for wishing to give Mrs K. and Mummy babies, and for stopping Daddy from giving babies to Mummy. This was also why he felt guilty about Daddy being ill.

Richard now wrote his name clearly on another page, and asked Mrs K. to write her name underneath and to add a few words in Austrian (he persisted in not calling it German). Mrs K. wrote her name and added in German that the weather was fine. Richard asked Mrs K. to tell him the right pronunciation, and repeated it a few times. When he left the playroom he said he felt much less tired than when he came. 'It was a great help.'

*Mrs K.* asked him what particularly had been such a help.

Richard replied that he thought it was sitting with her. As often before, he made sure about the time he was to come the next day and then said (as he also frequently did) in a tone as if it were a promise, 'I'll be there.'

## SIXTY-NINTH SESSION (Thursday)

Richard came to meet Mrs K. much nearer to her lodgings than he had ever done before and he himself drew Mrs K.'s attention to this. He looked carefully to see if Mr Smith was coming along the first road. In the room, Richard seemed rather serious, but not particularly worried, and said that new arrangements for his stay in 'X' had now been made. He mentioned that Mrs K. would be interested to hear that the fleet had now been put into another box, a stronger one, but he had left it behind at the Wilson's.

*Mrs K.* asked why he had done so.

Richard said the fleet did not wish to come because it might do Mrs K. some harm. . . . He had been listening to the noise which a passing lorry made : he said it sounded like groaning.

*Mrs K.* asked him what this groaning reminded him of.

Richard said it reminded him of a bear—the Russian bear, a nice one, not the German one. He spoke about the Russians doing well and was very pleased about this.

*Mrs K.* reminded him of the bear which he had said might be in one of the packages and of his doubts about the foreign and dangerous bear-father, inside Mrs K., inside Mummy, and inside himself. He had often shown that he was distrustful of the Russians.

Richard asked whether Mrs K. had met Mr Smith that day, and, looking out of the window, he said about a man whom he saw in the distance, 'Oh, there is Mr Smith coming.' When the man came nearer he turned out to be not Mr Smith but a very old man. Richard, watching him from the window, said doubtfully that he was quite a nice old man.

*Mrs K.* interpreted that Richard seemed to like old men better than younger ones; they did not seem to him so dangerous (Note I). She reminded him that he particularly disliked her going to the grocer's but that he had said once (Sixtieth Session) that he did not mind the grocer's father.

Richard replied that this was true, and asked why it should be so.

*Mrs K.* interpreted that possibly the younger man represented to him his father when he was strong and well, and possessed, in Richard's mind, the powerful genital which was also a dangerous landmine.

Richard spoke of pictures of Hitler, Goebbels, and other Nazis he had seen, and said that he disliked Goebbels even more than Hitler because he was such a big rat. He asked whether Mrs K. had heard Hitler on the wireless. He copied Hitler's shouting and making faces, and people calling 'Heil', at the same time stamping his feet.

*Mrs K.* interpreted that Richard thought that the Hitler-father, the noisy and openly bad one, was less dangerous because he did not hide his badness. The deceitful bad father—Goebbels, the rat—was more dangerous; he represented the Chinese ambassador, the 'rascal', the smiling Mr Smith, and even Richard's nice Daddy, whom Mummy and Mrs K. might like, although he might be dangerous to them. Mrs K. reminded him that he felt he himself was the rascal (Fifty-fifth Session).

Richard interrupted Mrs K. to say that there was also something nice about Mr Smith; he had sold him those beautiful radish seeds.

*Mrs K.* interpreted that he had some belief in the good and potent Daddy who could give Mummy babies and would even share his potency—the seeds—with Richard. But he was, as he had often shown, very uncertain about Daddy's goodness. This explained why he was so concerned and jealous about Mrs K. meeting Mr Smith; and expecting him to be always with Mrs K., even though today he knew she could not have met Mr Smith, since Richard had been with her when they passed one of the two roads along which Mr Smith could come; also Richard would have seen him should he have passed the playroom.

Richard said Mr Smith could have met Mrs K. even nearer to her lodgings than Richard had come.

*Mrs K.* pointed out that this meant Mr Smith would have come to fetch her, but when Richard met her she was alone, so how could Mr Smith have gone to his shop without Richard seeing him? Mrs K. interpreted that in Richard's mind Mr Smith again stood for Mr K., whom he still believed to be alive inside Mrs K. and also inside himself, since Mr K. stood for Daddy. This was one of the reasons why he so much wanted Mrs K. to go to the cinema in the evenings, because then she would not be with Mr Smith. His fear about the dead and bad Mr K. inside Mrs K. was increased by his father's illness. He was worried about Daddy; but in his mind the ill Daddy also turned into a bad kind of ghost inside Mummy (Note I1).

Soon after the beginning of the session Richard had asked for the pad. He did this in the urgent and appealing way he had recently adopted, expecting too that Mrs K. should put the pad into his hand. Also, during these last few days he had asked Mrs K. to give him the particular new yellow pencil with a metal end which recently he not only occasionally put into his mouth and sucked or bit, but also kept in his mouth for long periods. In this session he did not even take the pencil out of his mouth while he was talking, and kept sucking it—behaving like a baby with its bottle. . . . He asked whether Mrs K. had another pad left and whether it was exactly the same as the one he was now using.

*Mrs K.* said she had another pad, but it was not quite the same, though it was not a yellow one. She interpreted that his wish to have an unlimited supply of pads of the same kind expressed his wish that Mummy's good breasts, now Mrs K.'s, should always remain the same, good, uninjured, and inexhaustible; and that was why he now kept on sucking the new yellow pencil which stood for Mummy's breast (Note III).

Richard again inquired about Mrs K.'s patients. He always asked obsessionally the same questions, hardly waiting for an answer: were they all men, were there women amongst them, their age, the times at which they came to Mrs K. and so on. But he particularly wanted to know whether he was Mrs K.'s youngest child patient in 'X' and how many children she would analyse in London.

*Mrs K.* interpreted Richard's wish to be the favourite: although he was very jealous because Daddy and Paul were adults, he also felt that to be the youngest and the baby had its advantages; he was given more attention and affection. But Richard might also wish Mrs K. to have child patients in the same way as he wanted Mummy to have babies, because they would keep her alive and give her pleasure and were less dangerous than men.

Richard had started to draw 'Blueing' station, but gave it up, saying that it was no good, and scribbled all over it. Then he drew coins on another page and expressed, as on the previous day, some anxiety over the amount of money he had left; he compared the pennies in size and colour with a shilling. . . . He scribbled on a penny and asked Mrs K. whether it mattered.

*Mrs K.* interpreted that Richard was afraid of not having enough of the good breast and of good 'big job' inside himself, and therefore he would not be able to give the good babies to Mrs K. and Mummy. He was afraid of soiling the penny because he felt that after all he would soil the good breast. 'Blueing' stood for putting ink on the good light-blue breast (Sixty-seventh Session) and doing this to the external Mrs K. and Mummy as well as to the internal breast. He had given up drawing 'Blueing' station and said that it was no good, because he was so worried that he could not keep Mummy, and in particular now Mrs K., safe.

Richard asked Mrs K. to go into the garden with him, and he looked round. The old man (the 'Bear') who lived opposite exchanged a few words with Mrs K. After she had answered him, Richard asked her to go back into the house. He said, without appearing to be frightened, but in a serious way, that the man did not seem to know what an analytic session was and that it should not be disturbed. A little later he again went out into the garden with Mrs K., looked at the mountains, and seemed pleased.

*Mrs K.* interpreted that when he enjoyed the sight of the mountains this also expressed his feeling that the good mother was still alive and unharmed.

Richard, back in the house, drew No 63. First he made the two little figures with their genitals joining. Then he made the various scribbles, some of them containing his name.[1] Richard that that he was putting his genital together with Mrs K.'s, and put his and Mrs K.'s name at the head of the drawing. (Mrs K.'s genital, which was also a penis, was much bigger than Richard's.)

*Mrs K.* asked what the big initial letter of his pet name, which partly overlapped the head of the Mrs K. figure, reminded him of.

[1] I have blacked out his name.

Richard said it reminded him of a banana and it had a squiggle in the middle.

*Mrs K.* interpreted that in the drawing he had a smaller genital than Mrs K., but the banana shape which had gone into her head also stood for his genital and it was a big one. The squiggle which he had mentioned represented something on his genital which he felt was not all right.

Richard agreed that he felt there was something not all right.

*Mrs K.* again referred to his circumcision and interpreted that he had put his big genital into the back of Mrs K.'s head. She pointed out that Richard had been sucking the pencil particularly hard during this interpretation; he wanted to suck Mrs K.'s breast as well as Daddy's big banana- or strawberry-genital : in this way he had this big genital inside and he could use it as his own with Mrs K. She reminded Richard that he had again mentioned a little earlier that there was something nice about Mr Smith, namely his lovely radish seeds. . . . Mrs K. asked Richard what he thought about another shape on the same page.

Richard replied that it was also a banana but it it had a tail.

*Mrs K.* pointed at a capital 'G' written at the bottom of the page and reminded Richard that on the previous day the 'G' had stood for God.

Richard, looking very frightened, said that what Mrs K. was saying worried him.

*Mrs K.* asked whether he was afraid that God would punish him. Richard said he was.

*Mrs K.* interpreted that Richard was afraid of a very powerful father who knew and saw everything, and therefore would also punish him for what he wished to do with Mummy and now with Mrs K. He would be punished for wanting to rob Daddy not only of Mummy but also of the powerful genital, and that would make Daddy ill and powerless.

Richard then drew a face which he said was the face of Mickey Mouse. He put his name at the top of the page, saying that it stood for himself. Then he drew another face and said it was that of Minnie Mouse and stood for Mrs K.

*Mrs K.* pointed out that Minnie Mouse's face was very fat and suggested that her face might stand for her tummy as well.

Richard laughed and said that was so.

*Mrs K.* interpreted that he thought there was another reason for her being fat and that was that she was full of babies—of all the seeds which Richard, having received them from Mr Smith, had put into her.

Richard made Drawing 64, looking happy and obviously enjoying using the coloured pencils again. The fear he had felt during the interpretation referring to God punishing him had clearly been resolved. He showed which was the top of the drawing and which the bottom, and explained that the two big red sections were meant to be at the bottom.

*Mrs K.* suggested that these were now standing for his genital, and Richard agreed.

*Mrs K.* asked him whom the light-blue sections represented.

Richard seemed uncertain, and said he thought they stood for both Mrs K. and Mummy. When he had finished this drawing, he asked Mrs K. what his mother, who was coming to see her in a few days' time, was going to discuss with her. Was she going to speak with Mrs K. about the analysis being continued? And what was going to happen in the autumn? He looked very worried.

*Mrs K.* asked him whether he was worrying about how he would get on without analysis.

Richard confirmed this. He was afraid that his fears that had gone might come back again.

*Mrs K.* inquired which fears he felt had gone.

Richard said he was much less frightened of children. He paused and added that he could not say what other fears had gone, but he felt much better.

*Mrs K.* asked if he meant that he was less worried and happier.

Richard agreed and inquired again what his mother was going to discuss with Mrs K.

*Mrs K.* asked him to tell her why he was so worried about this talk.

Richard replied hesitantly that he wondered whether Mrs K. was going to advise his mother to send him to a big school. He could not stand that. He was still very frightened of bigger boys. He would be ill if he had to be frightened all the time. (He had become very worried.) He asked Mrs K. again whether she was going to give this advice to his mother.

*Mrs K.* asked him what he would wish her to say about school to his mother.

Richard replied that she should tell Mummy to get a tutor for him—not a man but a woman. He had at one time had a horrid man tutor and another time a nice woman teacher.

*Mrs K.* asked whether he would go to a small school.

Richard answered he would prefer a tutor, but he could go to a small school. He added with a melancholy little smile, clearly wishing to be frank with Mrs K., that what he would really like would be not even to have a tutor and not to have to learn at all.

*Mrs K.* asked him what he would like to do instead.

Richard replied, 'Actually nothing. Just a little reading, perhaps the papers.' (He still hardly ever read books except occasionally in bed.) He asked Mrs K. to promise him that she would not advise a big school.

*Mrs K.* replied that in any case she would not be in favour of a big school for him because he was so afraid of it.

Richard, who all during this conversation had been pale with anxiety and worry, brightened up and said that he was very relieved. He asked whether Mrs K. really thought that it was better for him not to go to a big school.

*Mrs K.* repeated that she did not think it would be good at present.

Richard asked whether she thought that a little school would be better for him than a tutor.

*Mrs K.* replied that she thought his mother would probably prefer this because then he would not be so much on his own and would be taught in company with other children.

Richard persisted in finding out whether Mrs K., too, thought that it would be better for him to go to a school.

*Mrs K.* replied yes, she thought so too.

Richard inquired how long he would go to a small school: would it be for about two years? He again looked worried.

*Mrs K.* suggested that he was worried because he felt that at some time he would have to go to an ordinary school.

Richard agreed and said that it was true that in the future he ought to go to an ordinary school. Did Mrs K. think he might be able to do so in a year or two?

*Mrs K.* suggested that he might see how he got on during the next year; he might find that he liked being with children better than he used to do. She would try to arrange, if at all possible, to analyse him again during the next summer; but in any case she would discuss with his mother the possibility of his analysis being continued in the future.

Richard now asked for details of where Mrs K. was going to stay in London: he again looked worried.

*Mrs K.* replied that she would live outside London and work in London, and Richard seemed a little comforted by this.

*Mrs K.* asked Richard why he had not told her earlier about all these thoughts and questions, and why he expected her to advise his mother to arrange something which he himself was so frightened of. She interpreted that his distrust of her came up because she was going to talk with his mother in his absence, and that seemed to turn her into the bad father, plotting with mother.

Richard looked puzzled when Mrs K. pointed out his distrust and said it would not turn her into the bad father, but into the 'brute mummy'.

*Mrs K.* interpreted that because she was going away and, as Richard feared, might be bombed by the bad Hitler-father, she would be turned into the wicked 'brute Mummy'. But the 'brute Mummy' (Twenty-third Session) had turned out to be his mother containing the bad father.

Richard during this talk wrote down exactly what Mrs K. was to tell his mother, namely that he wanted a tutor; as the conversation went on, he altered the tutor to 'a small school'. His facial expression during this conversation showed that he was painfully conscious of the seriousness of his inhibitions and of their implications for his future; no doubt he shared in an adult way his parents' concern about himself.

Before leaving the room, Richard repeated with great relief that he was so glad he had discussed all this with Mrs K. and that he felt very much better for it.

*Notes to Sixty-ninth Session:*

I. Richard had never spoken, as far as my notes go, about his wish for a grandfather. I have not ascertained whether he had ever had any contact with a grandfather; they were both dead at the time. But possibly there was an unconscious memory of one of them and a wish to revive him.

II. One fundamental element in paranoid jealousy in my view is that the strongest jealousy refers to the internalized father who, even after his actual death, might still be felt to be permanently inside the mother and would influence her against the son.

III. I have remarked in an earlier note (Note VII, Sixty-seventh Session) on the change which had come about in Richard's fundamental attitude, i.e. some progress in mitigation of hatred by love. The fact that he so strongly expressed his desire to have the good breast for ever was an essential indication underlying this change. The hope that the breast is uninjured and can be kept relatively safely as an internal object I found to be a pre-condition for dealing more successfully with destructive impulses and ensuing anxiety.

Richard met Mrs K. on the road. He had been hiding behind a gatepost and jumped out at her as she passed. He watched her closely to see whether she was frightened or angry, and seemed reassured by her remaining unconcerned. Referring to a cyclist who was just passing, Richard said that man would think he had been jumping at Mrs K., attacking her, and doing her harm. In the play-room he wanted to know whether Mrs K. had arranged to see his mother; she had expected Mrs K. to ring her and discuss a time when they could meet to have a talk.

*Mrs K.* told him that she had rung his mother and that she was going to see her on the following Monday.

Richard seemed relieved that it was not to be postponed any longer. He asked for the pad and also for the new one Mrs K. had prepared. He was disappointed that the new one was different and said that the paper was not quite the kind he liked, but preferred it to the thin yellowish paper Mrs K. had brought on a previous occasion and which had not been used since. He again outlined some coins on paper. . . . He looked worried and tense and remained silent.

*Mrs K.* referred to Richard's suspicion on the previous day that she would after all advise his mother to send him to a big school, which he thought would be cruel.

Richard agreed that this would be cruel, because Mrs K. must know best how terrified he was of bigger boys. Suddenly he burst out: 'Could you do something for me? Don't do work about it just now. Promise first that you are not going to suggest a big school to Mummy.'

*Mrs K.* reminded him that she had already promised this yesterday, but that this had not reassured him at all about her evil intentions.

Richard said appealingly, 'Please promise it again.'

*Mrs K.* repeated that she did not think it a good plan to send Richard to a large school just now, and that she had told him so. Therefore his distrust of her, even though in some ways he thought of her as helpful and liked her, must have other causes. She repeated her interpretation of the wicked 'brute Mummy' and of Richard's constant fear of the unknown, dangerous Mr K. inside her who either injured her or turned her against Richard. He felt that since Mrs K. was going to desert him to go to London, he would be left to his internal enemies and all his anxieties. These were represented by the dangerous big boys at school.

Richard went to drink water from the tap and then put his thumb into his mouth and sucked it. He was again very much on the look-out for passers-by and called out: 'Here is Mr Smith coming.' He ran to the window and smiled at him, and Mr Smith, noticing first Mrs K. who was sitting at the table, smiled at her and a moment later greeted Richard who was standing at the window. Richard had, of course, noticed that Mr Smith had had a separate greeting for Mrs K. He asked her why Mr Smith particularly smiled at her; did she know him very well? He looked very suspicious as he said this (Note I).

*Mrs K.* said that she had been to his shop a few times, as Richard knew; but Richard did not believe this was all, and thought that Mr Smith came to see her when she was by herself, even went to bed with her in the evenings, and was always with her when Richard was not there. Mr Smith stood for Mr K., who had intruded into Mrs K. and had changed her into the 'brute Mummy', which meant hostile to Richard; this was what Richard felt about his parents when he was suspicious of them because he could not see what they were doing.

Richard, when Mr Smith had passed, asked in a worried tone, what would Mr Smith think that he and Mrs K. were doing together? What would other people think about it?

*Mrs K.* interpreted that since Richard was so curious to find out what his parents were doing, he was afraid that others, particularly his father, were watching him, suspecting him of intruding into Mummy and therefore wishing to punish him. She referred to Drawing 63 and suggested that God's punishment was expected there because God-Daddy had watched Richard having sexual intercourse with Mrs K., standing for Mummy.

Richard had been looking at the envelope addressed to Mrs K. which contained his drawings; he asked once more whose writing it was. He had become very restless and persecuted.

*Mrs K.* pointed out that though Richard knew his mother's friends and relatives better than Mrs K.'s, he was still very inquisitive and suspected everything Mummy did and thought—the letters she received and all her secrets. He had previously admitted spying on her. This was partly because he could not trust her love; he himself loved her but also hated her, and thought her feelings about him would be the same. Moreover, he suspected all the time that his parents were possibly discussing, blaming, or hating him; this suspicion was reinforced by his feeling guilty about attacking them in his mind. Richard realized now that in fact he distrusted Mrs K.

and that a 'wicked brute' Mrs K. existed in his mind. But he found it much more painful to realize that he sometimes felt Mummy was a 'wicked brute'.

Richard agreed with this and said he would hate to think of his mother in that way, but he equally hated to think such things of Mrs K., because he liked her very much. . . . He had been looking at a picture on the wall, representing Neptune and a woman separated from him by a globe. Richard had remarked a day or two before that Neptune looked very nasty. Now, pointing again at this picture, he asked whether this was how Mr K. looked. Then he added, no, it wasn't Mr K. at all, it was Neptune. . . . As usual he asked a number of obsessional questions, among them whether Mrs K. knew Mr Owen, a grocer in 'X'. Why did Mrs K. not buy some groceries from him, since he seemed such a nice man, and why did she always go to the other grocer's?

*Mrs K.* replied that Richard disliked the grocer to whom she went and thought of him as a bad man. That was why Richard did not want her to have anything to do with him. She interpreted that Richard would like her to have a nice man to look after her, a nice husband, and might be worried to think she had none. He was also frightened that his father might die, and then Mummy would not have him to look after her and would miss him. Because his father was ill he became to Richard injured, robbed, and therefore dangerous; and that had increased his wish to separate Mrs K., standing for Mummy, from other suspect men, such as the grocer, in the same way as the 'nasty' Neptune was separated from the woman in the picture by the globe—the whole world—between them.

Richard took the drawings out of the envelope and scattered them over the table. Then he suddenly asked for the bag with the toys and, very cautiously, as if he were frightened of seeing something bad come out of it, took the toys out one by one. He asked Mrs K. to collect all the pencils and crayons, but not to move the drawings, her handbag, or the clock. Having put a few houses and people together, he spoke of a Swiss village as a very friendly place.

*Mrs K.* suggested that he thought Switzerland was safer than Britain.

Richard replied, 'But poor Switzerland is surrounded by enemies.' . . . He placed a little toy bucket (which he had, so far, hardly used) beside the clock and said it was an infirmary. Another bucket became a nursing-home. He quickly discarded into these buckets the few damaged figures, and then turned the bag inside out to remove any dust. He made various groups and put again, as in the past, a man and a woman in the motor-lorry, saying these were Daddy and Mummy together. Both trains were making their way round the table; he arranged a station for them and tried out carefully whether there was enough space in the station for both trains to enter. The danger of collision seemed on his mind all the time. Other groups were a man and a boy, some children by themselves, some grown-ups—arrangements most of which had been analysed previously. He pointed at one of the little women, saying something about her breasts. Then he showed Mrs K. that the other toy woman had breasts (Note II). He referred to the two carriages of the electric train as the two breasts. He put the two woman figures together and then staged an imaginary conversation between them, in an exaggeratedly sweet way. One was saying, 'My dear Henrietta, how are you? . . .' and so on. The other was saying, 'My dear Melanie. . . .' At that moment Richard declared that this was not Henrietta, it was Mrs K. and Mummy talking to each other at the interview they were going to have. A little boy figure which had been placed at some distance from the women now joined them. It stood for Richard watching them closely. Then Richard added a man to the group and said it was Mr Smith taking part in their discussion.

*Mrs K.* again referred to Richard's suspicion about her forthcoming talk with Mummy, and his distrust of their sincerity; although there was no man going to take part in that talk, in Richard's mind the suspect Mr Smith, standing for Mr K. and for Daddy, was there as well. The two women figures were the brute Mrs K., containing the Hitler-Mr K., and the brute Mummy, containing the bad father. Therefore they would be bad and hostile towards Richard.

Richard suddenly ran into the kitchen and carefully inspected the stove. He took off the lid of the 'baby tank' and was disturbed to find that the water was not clean. He drew water from the tank into a bucket which Mrs K. emptied into the lavatory. He drew more water and was worried because, whatever he did, the water in the tank did not become clean. He took the cover off the stove and poured a little water into it, trying to find out where it would run. He opened the damper in the stovepipe, trying to get the soot out from there as well as from underneath the cover. He opened the oven doors and was pleased to find a bright tin cup which he had not seen previously. He first used it for taking the dirty water from the tank, but then decided he would not dirty the cup and would use it only for clean water from the tap over the sink. He poured water out of it into the tank, but spilled a good deal over the side. He went on doing this for a while and watched Mrs K. mopping up the water. He said he was glad it was not the day for the Girl Guides, and that they would not see this awful mess. Mrs K. asked him not to pour so much, since the floor was difficult to dry.[1] Richard, as often before, filled the sink, asked Mrs K. to pull out the plug while he stood outside, and watched the water come out. Then he ran back into the room and went on playing with the toys.

*Mrs K.* interpreted that his fear of Mr Smith, the bad Daddy inside Mummy, and the bad Mr K. inside Mrs K., made him wish to explore the whole inside of Mrs K. as well as his own. He now seemed particularly frightened of Daddy's dirty—which meant poisonous—urine and wished to see how it would get out of Mummy. Mrs K. also interpreted his need to keep the good milk from Mummy's breast, represented by the tap and the bright cup, separate and clean.

Richard made the trains move and arranged various groups so quickly that Mrs K. could not follow the details. The dog, as Richard pointed out to Mrs K., had joined one of the groups and wished to do something 'bad'. Immediately after this the 'disaster' occurred. There was a collision and everything tumbled down. Richard picked up the smallest house from the heap and swiftly put it into his mouth for a moment, saying that this was himself and that he had survived; but he did not seem to believe that the house had actually survived.

*Mrs K.* had only time to interpret—since it was almost the end of the session—that the dog, standing for the biting and greedy Richard and his genital, seemed to have caused the 'disaster'; as Richard had pointed out, the dog wanted to do something 'bad'. The 'disaster' was that his parents and everyone, including himself, were dead. His attempt to survive by picking out one of the houses had failed.

Richard agreed to this interpretation. At the last moment, when the toys were already back in the bag and Mrs K. and he were ready to go, he took the ball out of Mrs K.'s bag and made it bounce once or twice.

*Mrs K.* suggested that the ball stood for Richard and his genital, and for the babies inside her, and that he was expressing his hope that she and Richard were after all still alive and all right.

Richard's anxiety during this session was in some measure influenced by the fact that it was raining heavily. As earlier material had shown, rain meant to him the poisonous and flooding urine of the omnipotent father, and linked with the fear of God who would punish by lightning and thunderstorms. He was always depressed when it rained. Preceding his father's illness, however, he had

[1] Even in a suitably equipped playroom, with lino on the floor, children have at times to be restrained in their play with water if it becomes unmanageable.

begun to see rain in a better light. He had said that it made things grow, a fact which of course had long been known to him intellectually but which he had not been able to acknowledge emotionally until his unconscious anxieties about rain had to some extent been modified. In connection with his father's illness the fear of his father's urine and semen being destructive to his mother had increased. As pointed out earlier, Richard drank from the tap every morning, which meant to him something good, contrasted with the dirty water in the tank. It was meant to be the good tap, i.e. the good breast, the good penis, and was to counteract the paranoid fears of being poisoned (earlier, by the maids standing for the bad mother and father—Twenty-seventh Session). It probably also meant giving something good to the internal mother in order to restore her and to counteract her being poisoned. At one point during this session Richard said something which Mrs K. interpreted as relating to her breasts. At that moment Richard picked up the two trees and put them into his mouth. Mrs K. interpreted that he wanted to suck Mummy's breast and felt this would make him as well as her all right again.

*Notes to Seventieth Session:*

I. It is of interest that the information I had given Richard on the previous day had not essentially alleviated his distrust. In the circumstances I thought it right to let him know what my point of view would be in my forthcoming talk with his mother. No doubt had I not done so, his resentment and suspicion would have been more acute; yet his delusional suspicion and jealousy had persisted in spite of what I had told him. This illustrates the experience, familiar in the treatment of paranoic patients, that reassurance and explanation do not dispel their persecutory anxieties and delusional suspicions.

As I have repeatedly pointed out, Richard lacked in inner security because he had never established his mother firmly as a good internal object and was therefore particularly liable to the fear of her changing into a persecutor and allying herself with the dangerous father. His persecutory anxieties had come to a head because his father's illness and the fear of his father's death seemed to change him into a persistently bad figure; although, split off from this aspect, he also had in his mind a good father figure. The external factors had strong repercussions on his internal situation. Richard's persecutory anxieties and schizoid mechanisms were not only stimulated by them, but they were also reinforced as a defence against his experiencing compassion and depression which would have brought out to the full his very strong feelings of guilt.

II. It is rather striking that Richard should have pointed out (which he had not done previously as far as the toys were concerned) that the two insincere women—his mother and I—had breasts. One suggestion which occurs to me would be that in his state of anxiety about his future schooling, his emphasis on the breasts might have had the significance of a reassurance. He might have felt that even if he suspected his mother and me of insincerity and of threatening his security, we could not be so bad after all because we had breasts. I wonder, however, whether the breast, which had been the first object he had not been able to trust, was at that moment not making the two women seem even more suspect. That would imply that he meant: look at them—they are insincere—there they are with their bad breasts.

## SEVENTY-FIRST SESSION (Saturday)

Richard had been waiting for Mrs K. at the corner of the road and told her that he had met the red-haired girl. He had ignored her and she had not spoken to him, but he was sure she 'choked with rage'. He had not been very afraid of her—no, not afraid at all. (Obviously it was a relief to him that he could deal better with his anxiety and feel more like other children.) Richard had his attaché case with him because he was ready to go home for the weekend after the session. He looked a little depressed, but much less so than on the previous Saturday, and did not seem particularly interested in the people who passed by. Inside the room, he took out two half-crowns, played with them, made them spin round on the table, and was pleased with the way they moved and the noise they made. While playing with the money, he asked whether Mrs K. thought (and at that moment he looked worried) that the bus would be very crowded since the weather was rather bad.

*Mrs K.* interpreted that the two coins represented her breasts, and that when Richard played with the two coins he was like himself as a baby playing with his mother's breasts or wanting to do so. Making them move stood for reviving them; he had been afraid when he was weaned that they had either gone away because he attacked them or that he had eaten them up. When he asked at this moment whether the bus would be crowded, that meant that Mrs K.'s children and patients would all crowd to her breast and attack Richard because he wanted to have her entirely to himself. Mrs K. reminded him of his earlier remark (Sixty-seventh Session) as to what would happen if the whole population of 'X' crowded together on top of the mountain or into the bus. All this related also to his feelings that he had destroyed Mummy's babies, who remained unborn, and whom he at times wished to give back to her.

Richard took the toys out of Mrs K.'s bag. He was pleased to find that she had added a few of the tiny figures that always represented children to him and also a small box into which he could put the damaged figures that on the previous day he had been so keen to keep separate. These additions obviously represented to him a gift and a sign of love.[1] At that moment Mr Smith passed and smiled at both Mrs K. and Richard, who were sitting at the table. Richard wondered whether one could see the toys from the road—he said he would not like this because then he would appear too childish. He went out into the road to find out how much could be seen, came back, and said that one could only see Mrs K. sitting there.

*Mrs K.* interpreted that Richard did not wish the toys to be seen, not only because that made him seem childish, but also because they stood for his thoughts and desires which must not be found out by an external and internal father.

Richard put all the 'children'—the new ones and the old ones—together in two rows. First he put near them the house with the tower, called the 'church', and the children were supposed to go to church. But at once Richard reconsidered this (church and God being clearly a source of conflict) and replaced the church by another house which he had earlier called the school. He said the children were now in the playground outside the school; then he fenced in the playround by putting pencils round it. He had been trying whether one of the tiny boy figures which had come unstuck from its base could still stand up; he found that it could not and asked Mrs K. whether she could repair it, to which Mrs K. said yes; then Richard put this figure into the hospital box.

*Mrs K.* asked whether Richard was among the schoolchildren.

Richard replied that he was not—he was the boy who had to go to hospital.

*Mrs K.* again interpreted Richard's fear of going to school; school with the dangerous big boys represented to him the hospital where he had been operated on. He wanted moreover to stay with Mrs K. and be helped by her, which meant the hospital in which he would be cured. She had brought some new toys and this made him feel that she liked him and wanted to help him. The figure going to hospital until Mrs K. could mend it stood for Richard, who would

[1] Usually I did not replace toys when they were broken, but did so at regular intervals, after holidays. I did, however, replace pencils, paper, and chalks, and so on, when they were used up.

remain ill until she came back to continue his analysis; then he would be able to go to school.

Richard made both the trains go round and round the table, passing the school. He said the children liked to see the trains pass. He had put two animals together in the first truck of the goods train, and one by itself, facing the other two, in the next truck. He said that the two together were Mummy and Paul; then he began to correct this by saying Daddy instead of Paul, but left it at the first statement. The figure facing them was himself. He added with some amusement that he was looking at Mummy and Paul all the time to see what they were doing. . . . He had arranged everything which Mrs K. had brought with her—her handbag, the bag for the toys, the clock, the drawings, and also her umbrella—not wishing her to remove anything from the table (Note I). Between these things he made a small space through which the trains could pass, but mainly they were going round the table, always quite near to the edge. At the end of the table opposite to the school and children he put a few houses, the 'church', and all the other people, saying that this was a Swiss village at the foot of high mountains. He made various groups and acted a variety of scenes with the figures (Note II). One of the most important themes in Richard's play was the activity of the two trains passing the children and only narrowly avoiding a collision, which so often had led to the 'disaster' in the past. Richard had mentioned that there was some danger if one train overtook the other, and he said he wondered which train would enter the station first. Then, in the Swiss village, the man figure, the previous day called Mr Smith, first stood beside a boy, but later on joined a woman figure and other people.

*Mrs K.* interpreted that the arrangement of the figures in the goods train expressed not only Richard's urge to keep watch on Mummy and Paul but also, as often before, on both parents. Because of Daddy's illness Richard tried to avoid feelings of rivalry and aggression towards him. But Daddy had for the moment become one of the children (Note III). The goods train, now standing for Richard, was in danger of colliding with the other train representing Paul and Daddy. When Richard made the trains pass between Mrs K.'s clock and bag, this showed that the trains meant to enter Mrs K., the bag and clock having often stood for her inside. Richard was competing with Paul, as well as with Daddy, both of whom wished to enter Mummy. But Richard was afraid of the collision between him and Daddy, because of Daddy being weak and ill; and he was gratified that he could avert it. Mrs K. further interpreted that when in the Swiss village the bigger figure, the previous day called Mr Smith, stood first next to the boy, this represented Daddy joining Richard; but he was soon reunited with Mummy and the whole family. In this way Richard expressed his wish to make reparation for having separated the parents.

Richard pointed out to Mrs K. the two trees which he put about midway between the school group and the Swiss village, rather near the edge of the table, but protected from the trains by the drawings which were lying in between. Near them he had put the motor-truck with its bonnet partly hidden by the drawings. Richard said that the two trees were his canaries, and the truck was Bobbie burrowing into a rabbit-hole.

*Mrs K.* interpreted that the two trees also stood on the previous day for the breasts, which he wanted to keep to himself and safe. Bobbie represented his genital burrowing into Mrs K.'s genital and into Mrs K.'s mind, for the drawings meant to Richard his relation with Mrs K. and her inside; Richard's penis was also chasing inside Mrs K. and Mummy for Mr K.'s and Daddy's genitals.

Richard made another man figure join a woman, who, he said, was Mrs K.

*Mrs K.* interpreted Richard's feelings yesterday when he wanted her to go to the 'nice' grocer—because, as Mrs K. suggested, she should have a nice man to look after her, standing for her husband.

Richard was very struck by this interpretation. He looked at Mrs K. and it was clear from his expression that this was something he had been consciously thinking about. Then he asked if Mrs K. liked Mr K., and if she was not very sad and lonely without him. In asking this, he repeated the word 'lonely' twice (Note IV). Without waiting for a reply, he begged Mrs K. to tell him, apart from the work, at least one thing which he *must* know, and that was whether she felt lonely and unhappy. He again inquired whether she minded his asking her this and said with signs of anxiety that he would like to be Mrs K.'s husband; after a pause he added, 'When I am grown up.'

*Mrs K.* interpreted Richard's wish to be his mother's husband which had become stronger because he was afraid that she too felt lonely and unhappy now that her husband was so ill, and because he felt guilty, having in his mind deprived her of the 'good' husband. Even in the past he might often have wondered whether Mummy was really fond of Daddy and whether they were actually happy together, since he did not greatly trust appearances or what people said about their feelings. Now he was afraid that if his father died, he would have to replace him and try to make his mother happy, and he dreaded this as too great a responsibility because he was only a child.

Richard went on playing and started talking about train journeys.

He said that a woman (who was not represented by a toy figure) told Mrs K. that she wanted to catch a train ; he made one of the trains move out of the station and said that the woman had missed her train.

*Mrs K.* asked where the train was going to.

Richard replied that it was going to London.

*Mrs K.* interpreted that this woman stood for Mrs K. who wanted to catch her train to London and had missed it.

Richard said with great pleasure that this was so, and that he would make her miss her train every time she wanted to go to London, and then she would not be able to go at all. While saying this he made the other train move out from the station, saying that it too was going to London.

*Mrs K.* suggested that this train contained Richard and his whole family and they were following Mrs K. to London because he was, after all, afraid that he would not be able to stop her. A few sessions previously he had said that he would have to go to London to continue his analysis.

Richard again made a train go to London ; the other one in the opposite direction was going to 'Z' and not, as he emphasized, to his present home.

*Mrs K.* interpreted that if Richard went to London with her, he felt that he would be deserting his mother as well as their house in 'Z', which also stood for the deserted and lonely mother. Therefore he would have to go from London back to 'Z'. She interpreted that he wished to be both with his mother and family and with Mrs K.; he had often felt divided in his loyalties when he was either with Mummy or with Mrs K.

Richard again made the electric train go off to London, and the other train, coming from the opposite direction, met it. He said that now a 'disaster' would happen. This time he did not prevent it: everything, including the schoolchildren and the Swiss village, tumbled down.

*Mrs K.* interpreted that he had shown in his play that she would go to London after all and that he could not prevent it. The next thing was that he and his whole family followed her to London. But he felt that this was impossible and in his jealousy and despair caused the 'disaster'. This also meant that if Mrs K. went to London, she would be destroyed there by bombs, by Mr K. (actually by Hitler); and Richard was afraid and guilty, feeling that this would happen because of his hostile wishes. If she died, this would mean to him a complete disaster because she stood for Mummy ; the whole family, all the babies—in fact, the whole world—would, he felt, be lost. It also meant to him an inner disaster: Mummy, now Mrs K., would be dead inside him.

Richard picked up a boy figure saying that this was himself, the only survivor.

*Mrs K.* interpreted that though he seemed to have saved himself in the end, he had first shown that everybody would die, including himself, if Mummy died.

Richard picked up one of the children lying on the table (it had a red hat) and said that this was the red-haired girl. He put the figure into his mouth and kept it there for a little while. Then he took it out of his mouth and went outside to spit, and said that 'she tasted horrid'.

*Mrs K.* interpreted that Richard had now in his mind eaten up his enemy, the girl of whom he had said that she was choking with rage, and that meant that she would also make him choke internally. In his mind not only was there the dead Mummy, now Mrs K., inside him, but he also felt persecuted by Mummy's babies whom he had eaten up, as he had just shown by taking the red-haired girl into his mouth.

Richard said, in a pensive and rather hesitant way, what a long break there had been during which he had not played with the toys; it had lasted about two months. A little later he said that the R.A.F. had again attacked Berlin, for the first time in two months.

*Mrs K.* interpreted that the destruction which happened among the toys also stood for what the R.A.F. had been doing to Berlin, as he had said, for the first time in two months. But Berlin also stood for Mrs K., for the bad Mummy, either because she was mixed up with the Hitler-father, or because Richard in his jealousy attacked her when she was with Daddy.

Richard now put up another group of people, two women who, as he said, were Mrs K. and Mummy; he staged a conversation between them, not in the affected and exaggeratedly sweet manner of the previous day, but in an ordinary and friendly way. They were joined by two children; one was Richard who came up to his mother, and the other was a little boy who was supposed to be Mrs K.'s grandson. Then the man figure who on the previous day had represented Mr Smith joined the group. Richard said that this was Mr K., who was again alive. The school children remained all in a heap until Richard put up the trains; and then he put some of the children into two trucks of the goods train.

*Mrs K.* interpreted that Richard had now tried to put things right, to make the babies come alive inside Mummy and Mrs K. in the goods train. But Mr K. being made alive also meant that his father should not die, or should come alive again if he died.

Richard asked hesitantly whether he could take some of the 'children' home.

*Mrs K.* replied that, as she had already told him about the drawings, she thought that the toys and the other things should remain with her, and that Richard would find them all together when he came again. She interpreted that taking the toy children home stood for getting Mrs K.'s and Mummy's permission to have a share in their children, the babies whom he felt they carried inside (Note V).

Richard had said, at one moment during the play, under his breath and pointing to a broken figure, 'This is me.' He had repeatedly on previous occasions called this figure the 'imbecile boy', referring to an actual boy in the village.

*Mrs K.* reminded Richard (as she had done previously) of his fear of being a 'dunce' and said that he was deeply worried about his difficulties in learning and going to school, and afraid that he would not be able to get on in life. His being the 'imbecile', however, meant not only being a dunce but also containing bad people whom he had destroyed by his murderous feelings.

Richard had been humming snatches from different composers —something which he only rarely did. He became sad after doing so and said he thought Mummy was angry because he did not play the piano any more. He himself also seemed to feel this as a loss, since he added that he had already passed an examination quite well, which must have meant that he could have played. He became puzzled and said that he did like music very much and yet did not want to play the piano.

*Mrs K.* interpreted that music and harmony had appeared previously to represent the voices of nice, alive babies, being happy together; but Richard's doubts in his own goodness and his feeling that he lacked harmony inside himself prevented him from producing music.

Richard, throughout this session, had been deeply engrossed with the toys, and played with the zest and pleasure usually shown by much younger children. Apart from watching Mr Smith for a moment, he only once went to the window to see a woman with a child go by. He had not been putting the pencil into his mouth, and his finger only once and for a moment only. The lack of interest in people outside and the almost complete absence of sucking in this session were connected with giving full expression to phantasies and emotions connected with his inner life. He seemed contented and peaceful when he left (Note VI).

Mrs K. was to see his mother before the next session.

*Notes to Seventy-first Session:*

I. It is significant from the point of view of transference and transference interpretations that the analyst's personal belongings played such an important role. The whole playroom, as I have often pointed out, was at times loved, at other times hated, by Richard, in closest connection with the transference situation. But the analyst's personal belongings—in this case the bag, the clock, the umbrella, and so on— had a heightened emotional significance. The table on which the play and drawing took place, and the chairs on which he and I sat, were also much more important than the other objects in the room. I have mentioned that before leaving, Richard regularly put the two chairs side by side with their seats under the table. On one occasion he had pointed out that he and I were now going to be together until the next session, and clearly he meant that we would be together in a peaceful way.

II. These simultaneous happenings represented his past and present actual experiences as well as his phantasy experiences, and expressed his rapidly changing emotions. I have already pointed out that it was at times not possible to follow, and still less to interpret, all the details of the material presented; the same applied to drawings, scribbles, and so on, which—if the material were to be fully exhausted—would have occupied hours of analysis. To do this would mean leaving out current material. In my view the main principle when the analyst is confronted with such wealth of material in child analysis—and this also applies to adult analysis—is to select what he considers to be the main emotions and phantasies, the most acute anxiety situations and relevant defences; in other words, to be guided by the transference situation and interpret accordingly.

III. It seems that, as on former occasions, his father was not simply destroyed but was made into one of the children. The ambivalence in that situation is shown by the fact that the goods train was to give pleasure to the children who liked to see it pass. We shall remember that in the previous session the two trees which he sucked stood for the breasts, and that the jealousy of the baby-father looked after by nurses had become a cause for a particular aspect of rivalry. This brought up regressively his infantile suspicions about having been deprived of the breast by his father. When he made two carriages of the goods train, standing for the breast, pass the children who were within the fenced-in school playground, the children (including the father who had been made into one of them) had no access to the breast. I would conclude that Richard's early grievance that he could not get the breast because his father enjoyed it, and his wish for revenge, became the stimulus for this particular phantasy.

IV. Loneliness and the fear of loneliness played a great part in Richard's depressive feelings. He had already told me in the first session that when he went to bed he felt lonely and deserted. He had as a consequence a strong sympathy with lonely people and in particular, now that he was deeply concerned and anxious about his father's possible death, with his mother who would become lonely. This was expressed in the transference in the anxiety about my loneliness, and it was quite clear that he had given much conscious thought to this feeling. In some of his drawings the expelled Mr K. was again to be reunited with me. Even the 'grumpy old gentleman', about whom he was afraid that he would bother me, was also meant to keep me company. In the analysis of adult patients I have found that the sympathy with a lonely or ill woman can play a strong role in the choice of a partner.

V. The need to share the good children with mother also came up in order to counteract the dangerous, 'red-haired', hostile, eaten-up babies who would attack and choke him internally. Moreover, if his mother allowed him to have some of her babies, he would not be driven to eat them up in envy and greed; in other words, her sharing with him would lessen the destructive rivalry with mother, and all its evil consequences, and would imply peace in his inner world—the babies inside harmonizing with him and with his parents inside—internal friends instead of dead and dangerous objects.

VI. It is striking that a session in which such strong external and internal anxieties were activated should finish with the patient being in a contented and peaceful mood. In contrast to earlier psycho-analytic views that interpreting and analysing psychotic anxieties might be dangerous, my experience over the years has shown me that if we analyse psychotic anxieties profoundly, and thus get to their roots, we are more able ultimately to help our patients. There are many reasons for this, but here I can only single out one of them which appears to me to be of particular significance. The analysis of these deep anxieties enables the patient to face his psychic reality and to find expression for it. Thus Richard could in this session experience and express his anxieties about his internal enemies, dead and persecutory, as well as his feelings of guilt about it being himself who had made them so dangerous by his murderous feelings. We shall remember that in this session there was also, together with the facing and expression of these various anxieties, a diminution of the violence of his destructive impulses. The cautious and anxious way in which he took the toys out of the bag and in which he decided that the damaged figures would have to go to hospital—asking me at the same time to mend the boy figure who represented himself—shows how both hope and the urge for reparation were operative side by side with his anxieties. When it came to the 'disaster', it was less uncontrolled than on previous occasions. He laid down some of the toys carefully and was concerned not to break anything or let it drop. At one moment it even appeared as if the Swiss village or the trees would remain standing. Usually after the violent catastrophes he had kept one figure or object as the survivor. No doubt this meant that the feeling of universal death, including his own, was unbearable; and therefore—even though his belief in survival was shaken—he attempted to resuscitate himself. When his anxiety was less severe, he still kept some hope that he himself—and that would include some of his inner objects—would be saved. In this session he resuscitated one figure, the little boy, but only after my interpretation that there was no survivor left. I think that he was able in this session to face the danger of death because he felt less hate and despair and more hope.

Excessive splitting off of destructive impulses, including envy, jealousy, and their consequences, is bound up with their being felt to be so powerful—omnipotent—that they threaten the object and the self with complete destruction. This also leads to splitting off feelings of love and trust in a good object and in a good self. It is only by facing feelings of hate, and thereby gradually bringing them together with other parts of the self, that they become less overwhelming. Facing psychic reality revives good aspects, and makes it possible for the capacity for reparation and feelings of hope to come to the fore. Hope was expressed in this session, for instance, by the little toy figure which was to remain in the hospital till I could mend it; this meant that the day would come when I would continue Richard's analysis and help him further. When destructive impulses and their consequences come closer together with a revived capacity for love and are mitigated by it, they become less overwhelming and reparation becomes possible; in other words, the all-important process of integration takes place.

When these internal processes occur, adaptation to external reality improves and external anxieties are no longer quite so overwhelming. In this session Richard had shown more clearly than in the previous ones the fear of his father's death, with all the loneliness this implied for his mother, and had fully expressed his grief about my supposed loneliness and unhappiness. He was also more able to bear the prospect of his analysis coming to an end.

## SEVENTY-SECOND SESSION (Monday)

Richard said, before entering the playroom, that he had mentioned to his mother before she saw Mrs K. what Mrs K. had said about his future schooling and that she was not in favour of a large school. Richard reported that after the interview his mother had told him that they had also discussed the continuation of his analysis; she thought that at some time it would be continued, and if not sooner, she might go with him to London after the war was over. Obviously Richard had mentioned Mrs K.'s views because he distrusted both her and his mother and also wanted to make quite sure that there would be no difference of opinion between them. Furthermore, he also wanted to let his mother know that he had discussed the matter beforehand with the analyst. . . . In the playroom he took the toys out at once. He put a sitting figure on a chair. Then he got out the swing and was pleased to find that Mrs K. had stuck back the tiny figure which had come off the swing on the previous day, and which Richard had put into the 'hospital' box together with the other damaged figure; he had said that this little child was cut in half (actually the figure consisted only of an upper half which was stuck on to the swing). He moved the swing, saying that the little girl enjoyed herself, but soon asked Mrs K. to put it on the other side of the table. There he also placed the 'hospital' box, the toy-bag, the handbag, and the clock, to be part of the scene he was preparing, leaving again only enough space for the trains to go round. At the end of the table nearest to himself he arranged the station, consisting of two houses placed so that the trains could just go between them. In the station, or rather by the side of each house, in groups facing each other were the smaller figures which always represented the children. Richard said that they were standing there because children like to watch trains. The little boy nearest to the station house was the small figure of which Richard had said in the previous session that it had to go to hospital and was himself. Mrs K. had stuck it on to a base which happened to have originally belonged to a larger figure, since she had no other base left. This, as well as the fact that Mrs K. had repaired it, pleased Richard very much. He made various groups of people on a road which was fenced in by pennies: his mother and Mrs K were represented by the same women as on the previous days. He made them greet each other in a friendly but unaffected way. The man figure, formerly Mr Smith, was put a little farther away, while another woman figure was standing nearer to them. The dog stood among a few figures. The two trees were on one side of the road, some distance from one another. The tractor and the coal lorry were 'about to go out'. The only movements he carried out were with the trains. The electric train stopped in the station and the children were put near to it. Richard said that the train carried milk and that everyone got some of it.

*Mrs K.* reminded him that in the previous session the carriages of the electric train had represented Mrs K.'s and Mummy's breasts.

Richard made the train go round the table and again through the station, and said the children were now being given the breasts to suck. The goods train and the electric train alternately passed through the station, and the children also received milk from the goods train. While putting the children near to the carriages of the electric train, Richard changed his mind and the children stood near to the engine instead.

*Mrs K.* interpreted that the engine represented his father's genital and that it was supposed to feed the babies too, as did mother's breast.

Richard after a little while made the trains, which passed alternately round the table and through the station, follow one another so closely that they nearly collided. At this point he interrupted his play and went into the kitchen, looked into the 'baby tank', and again drew water into the bucket, which he asked Mrs K. to empty. He watched very closely the water getting less in the tank.

*Mrs K.* repeated her previous interpretation about the danger of the bad Daddy-genital getting mixed with mother's breast—the two trains had almost collided. She related this anxiety to the conversation between the toy women—Mummy and Mrs K.—and reminded him that he had put Mr Smith (who a day or two before had joined in the conversation) farther away. This had been an attempt to keep the bad Hitler-father inside Mrs K., and the bad Daddy inside Mummy, away from the two women, in order to make the conversation take the favourable turn which he wanted: that he should not be sent to the big boys, the hostile brothers, at a large school.

Richard threw little bits of paper into the tank and watched what would happen.

*Mrs K.* suggested that the bits of paper stood for babies and that Richard wished to find out what had happened to Mummy's unborn babies, and who had destroyed them—Richard by his bombing attacks or Daddy by his genital being dangerous to Mummy's inside.

Richard made a similar exploration of the stove and tank as on recent occasions and then went back to the room and continued his play. He had surreptitiously removed the sitting man on the chair, and Mrs K. asked where he was. Richard said he had put him into the box; he had no use for him.

*Mrs K.* suggested that the man on the chair represented Daddy who could not move about owing to his illness, and that Richard had put him away because it made him feel sad and guilty to be reminded of his illness.

Richard agreed, but added that his father was getting on well, though he was still very weak. He looked sad and worried while he said this. He asked Mrs K. to bring the swing back from the other end of the table, saying that the little girl there would feel too deserted by herself. He again made the trains move. They stopped in the station and fed the children. Once Richard said that the electric train (the breasts) stayed too long and the driver of the other train had become impatient because he had to wait outside the station. When at last he passed through the station with his train, he did not stop to feed the children because he was so angry.

*Mrs K.* inquired what the people in the other groups were doing.

Richard replied that Mrs K. and Mummy were still going on with their talk and therefore remained together.

*Mrs K.* asked who the woman was whom he had put fairly near to them.

Richard replied, 'Oh, anybody.'

*Mrs K.* suggested that this woman might stand for Richard's nurse. Richard would have greatly liked his mother to be friendly with the nurse, but he was also jealous if they talked too long with each other. Similarly, Richard might wish Mrs K. and Mummy to be friendly with each other and yet he was jealous about their being friendly.

Richard agreed to this.

*Mrs K.* pointed out that Mr Smith, standing also for Mr K., was kept at a distance so that he should not take sides against Richard; this meant, however, that Richard would have liked to take the Hitler-father out of Mummy and Mrs K. because he was afraid that containing the Hitler-father would make Mummy hostile to himself. Earlier he had asked whether Mrs K. had seen the 'grumpy old gentleman' that day; Mrs K. referred back to that question and interpreted it in the same way in relation to herself. She suggested that Richard was still suspicious of the result of her conversation with his mother.

Richard asked Mrs K. what the trees stood for, adding smilingly: 'What are your thoughts about them?'

*Mrs K.* pointed out that Richard now wanted to take her place and be the analyst, but he also wanted Mummy's babies and to take her place with Daddy.

Richard protested and said that he would not want to be a woman.

*Mrs K.* interpreted that he was certainly afraid of being a woman because then he would lose his genital and could no longer be a man; but nevertheless he had a great wish to have babies from his father like Mummy—the radish seeds which he had been so happy about represented the good Daddy-genital which would put babies into him. At the same time he wished to be able to feed the babies; this had been shown in his play with the trains, the carriages of which represented the feeding breasts. In these ways he had expressed his wish to share the babies with Mummy; then he would not be driven to attack her and rob her of them. Nor would he then attack and injure the babies, and that would mean that he need not be frightened of children who stood for Mummy's children, such as the red-haired girl. The inside of the station and the trains going round represented Mrs K.'s and Mummy's inside. The tiny girl on the swing whom he had asked Mrs K. to put away to the other end of the table represented the youngest unborn baby, a sister whom he wished not to be there but brought back because he after all wanted her to be born. By asking Mrs K. to put the swing away, Richard had also wished to save the unborn sister from his own attacks.

Richard made the trains race each other more and more. They no longer stopped at the station and now, coming from opposite directions, they repeatedly nearly collided with each other, until he made them collide in fact inside the station. The children tumbled over each other and Richard made everything fall down. The electric train survived and Richard made it run wildly all over the table, apparently quite out of control. He said under his breath, 'That is me now,' pointing at the electric train which he also described as the 'victor'.

*Mrs K.* interpreted that Richard and Mr K., represented by the 'grumpy old gentleman', were fighting inside Mrs K.'s genital and causing death and destruction to everyone. In the same way he had always expected his fight with Daddy inside Mummy to destroy her and her babies, as well as Daddy and himself.

Richard, for the first time during the session, watched the road. It was the end of the session, and Mrs K. was putting the toys into her bag. Richard said that it was quite a busy road, and asked whether all these people were coming to Mrs K. to be fed by her.

*Mrs K.* reminded him that he had spoken of the whole population of 'X' crowding on top of the mountain or crowding into one bus, and suggested that the mountain and the bus now meant Mrs K., who had to feed them all, as well as Richard's fear that she would be exhausted and his jealousy of anyone near to her.

Richard looked at Mrs K. in a way which showed agreement. He said that his mother was also going back by bus now.

*Mrs K.* interpreted that his mother too, in Richard's mind, was a child wishing to be fed by Mrs K., and Richard wanted her to be fed. This was why he had kept the two toy women together for so long ; but he was also jealous about any contact Mummy had with Mrs K.

Richard had, at the beginning of the session, asked Mrs K. which dress she had been wearing when he saw Mummy; obviously he had wished his mother to see Mrs K. in the jacket he liked, i.e. at her best. But he also felt that if Mrs K. had changed her clothes before seeing him, this might have meant that she was bad when she saw his mother—i.e. had not said what he had wanted her to say to his mother—and had changed again into the good Mrs K. in the nice jacket for his analysis.

A little later on Mrs K. met Richard and his mother on their way to the bus stop. Richard's mother said that he had recognized Mrs K. from a long distance, pointing out that she was wearing his favourite red jacket. She added that Richard had asked her in detail what clothes Mrs K. had been wearing when they had met earlier that day.

## SEVENTY-THIRD SESSION (Tuesday)

Richard had been waiting in front of the house. Inside the room he at once sat down and began to play. He was in a friendly but quiet mood. (Contrary to his usual practice, he did not drink from the tap at the beginning of the session.) He looked at Mrs K.'s hand-bag (which she had brought every day) and asked whether she had got this crocodile bag from her husband.

*Mrs K.* interpreted that he wanted it to be a present from Mr K., because that would show that although the crocodile was obviously a dangerous animal, Mr K. was also a 'good crocodile' who gave Mrs K. something lasting, a lasting and good genital.

Richard arranged a station in the same way as on the previous day, but put it up in a different place, farther away from Mrs K. He also put up various groups of toys between her and the station.

Alongside the station was a long row of toy figures—a woman, the 'Mr Smith' man, all the 'children', the trees, some animals, the tractor, the coal lorry, and at the end of the row the dog. Richard said that the first two were Mummy and Daddy, and that the whole family were going off to 'Z'. In one of the groups nearer to Mrs K. there were two women facing each other, the same ones that had represented Mrs K. and his mother on the previous day. Richard again made them talk to each other; but now they were once more speaking in a rather affected and exaggeratedly friendly manner. A little way from them, with its back to them and clearly not meant to belong to them, was another woman figure who had been interpreted by Mrs K. on the previous day as being Richard's nurse.

*Mrs K.* reminded Richard that she had on a former occasion interpreted that Nurse, of whom he was nearly as fond as of his mother, was socially not her equal and that this gave rise to a conflict of loyalties in him.

Richard made the nurse join Mummy and Mrs K., but very soon Mrs K. was made to walk away from Mummy, and Richard explained that Mummy had now said something rude to her and hurt her feelings, and so she went away by herself. Then he added, 'This is the bad Mummy.' He suddenly took a figure which had often represented himself out of the row of people who were waiting to depart, and put it beside Mrs K., saying, 'I am going off with you.'

*Mrs K.* asked where they were going to—was it London?

Richard said that he supposed so.

*Mrs K.* interpreted again his difficulties over the relation between Mother and Nurse, and referred back to the play when Mummy had hurt Mrs K.'s feelings. Mrs K. had now been standing for the nurse and he had sided with her against the 'bad Mummy' and the rest of the family. It appeared, therefore, that he might have heard or feared that his mother had hurt Nurse, or that Nurse might have felt lonely because she did not belong to the family.

Richard strongly disputed this. He said Nurse ate at the table with the family. He did not remember having heard anything unkind said or done to her by his mother; but he appeared to agree that he felt aware of the conflict which Mrs K. had interpreted (Note I). . . . He made the electric train leave the station and said that now he and Mrs K. were on it. Then he made the whole group of parents and children run after the train in order to bring Richard back. After that he made the goods train, on which now the whole family were supposed to be (though he had not put the actual figures on it), chase the train carrying Mrs K. and himself; and the race between Mrs K. and Richard on the one hand, and the pursuing family on the other, was now only represented by the two trains. The race between the two trains turned out a little later to be particularly a race between his father and himself, for he referred to the goods train as 'Daddy', and the electric train represented himself with Mrs K. At the beginning of this part of the play, the train on which Mrs K. and Richard were getting away had nearly run into the family, but Richard at once took care to move the figures away so that there was space for the train to get through.

*Mrs K.* interpreted that the external Mrs K. and Mummy were now represented by the stations through which the trains passed, the stations also standing for their genitals; and his father (the train) pursued and attacked him externally as well as inside Mummy's genital. She also interpreted his wish to run away with her and to be her husband, as he had said previously (Seventy-first Session). She linked this with his desire to run away with his mother and to have her all to himself; but then Daddy and Paul, and even the unborn babies, who would all be deprived of Mummy, would pursue him. Another reason for running away with Mrs K. was his wish to continue his analysis, which he felt to be essential to him.

Richard continued his play. The trains seemed repeatedly very near to colliding, but then Richard decided that there was another track and therefore he could prevent the collision. This theme was drawn out with variations for quite a long time. . . . At one point at the beginning of the play Richard had held in his hand the little chair and a toy man whom he sat on it, and was obviously wondering whether he should put him on the table or not; but then he had decided to put both toys back into the box. (His painful feelings about his father's illness, like all his emotions and conflicts, were strongly checked and their expression controlled and restrained.) . . . A few times during his play Richard had gone to the window and watched people pass. When a woman and two girls went by, he said that one of the girls was nasty and an enemy because she had looked at him (probably when he had met her in the street on some former occasion). He also mentioned that he had met the red-haired girl but they had ignored each other. Then he asked Mrs K. whether she knew a young man who had just passed. . . . The play finished by the electric train becoming quicker and quicker and running zigzag, which Richard accompanied by loud hissing noises. In the end he made the train collide with the other train, and general disaster ensued. At the beginning Richard had put the 'church' near to Mrs K.'s bag and it remained standing, being out of the way; also he had saved the ill father (the toy man on the chair) and the people in the hospital box by leaving them there and not making them participate in the play. . . . Richard then picked up the swing with the child on it and kept it moving for a while. Another survivor was the electric train. Richard picked it up and held it in his hands, looked at it uneasily, and declared that it was like a whale moving its tail; then he detached the second carriage and put it down. When the electric train had made the goods train fall and had run over it, Richard said under his breath, sadly, 'What if Daddy really died?'

*Mrs K*. interpreted that he himself had been the train travelling with Mrs K., who stood for the good Mummy inside him; but that he also contained the whale—Daddy's dangerous genital—and felt driven by it to do harm, and to destroy the parents and their babies, while at the same time he had been trying to control the whale-Daddy. Mrs K. in addition, interpreted Richard's sadness and guilt about his father's illness and his fear of his death, and she connected this with his hate and jealousy and his wish to attack his father. He had just shown this by the electric train, representing himself, running over the goods train, which he had said was Daddy. At the same time he had wished to save his father by putting him and the 'church' (standing for God) safely out of the way of the 'disaster'. Mrs K. mentioned that in his play he had been in competition with his father, wishing to be Mrs K.'s (Mummy's) husband.[1]

Richard left off playing and went into the kitchen, drew a bucket of water from the 'baby tank', and remarked that the water was cleaner and that the dirt must be getting less in the tank. He did not spend as much time over this as in previous sessions, and seemed less intense. Nor did he fill the bucket so full. Then he drank water from the tap.

*Mrs K*. interpreted that Richard was more hopeful that Mrs K.'s and Mummy's inside, and the babies there, could be restored and that his father might recover. He seemed to feel less anxiety that it was he who had poisoned the 'baby tank'. There had been, however, the 'disaster' on the table; but the last thing that Richard had been doing was to make the child move on the swing, and that meant he was expressing his hope that the baby inside his mother was still alive and safe, and that his father's genital was still able to move.

Richard went outside and asked Mrs K. to go with him. He looked at the hills and was sad.

[1] On the previous day, the feminine identification was clearly presented and analysed, and it is interesting that in the next session the male position came strongly to the fore.

*Mrs K.* asked him whether he found it difficult to part from his mother.[1]

Richard said that he was going to see her only at the weekend. He paused and added that he *was* very sad. Then he jumped from the steps into the garden, attempting to do it without touching the vegetables; he had been able to do this a few days before but could not manage it now. Suddenly he went back to the room, because a woman passed by. He went to the window and watched her and said that she looked 'haughty'. He went outside once more and continued the conversation with Mrs K., though reluctantly. He said that he was going to take his yacht to the swimming-pool. Some time previously he had told Mrs K. that he would be taught to swim at the pool and that he was looking forward to this; but now he explained that his mother did not want him to swim in fresh water, that he himself did not wish it either, and that he preferred to play with his yacht (which was obviously not true).

*Mrs K.* interpreted that Richard seemed to resent his mother's prohibition.

Richard maintained that he did not care for swimming. He again went back into the room and ran to the window to observe a young bus conductress he knew. He said she was very pretty. Then he remarked angrily that she always said, 'Half fares stand up,' but he repeated that she was very pretty. Looking at the clock, he expressed his pleasure that there were still ten minutes of the session left, but asked whether Mrs K. could not finish the session straight away. (It was very unusual for him to put his wish to go in such a direct way.)

*Mrs K.* said that he could go if he wanted to, but she interpreted that he wished to go because he was afraid to recognize that he was really very angry with her since she stood for Mummy, who had forbidden him to swim; this was the same to him as being reminded that he was only a 'half fare'—that is to say, a child. This anger about his mother increased his annoyance with the pretty bus conductress and was linked with his finding that the woman who passed by looked haughty—that is to say, superior to him and contemptuous of him. His not being allowed to swim also meant to him that his genital was not like that of a grown-up person and that he was weak and no good.

Richard no longer seemed to wish to go. He suddenly looked into a cupboard, discovered several balls, and took out Mrs K.'s ball from her bag and threw it very sharply against the cupboard.

[1] The arrangement was after all that Richard was to stay during the week with the Wilsons and to go home only for weekends.

*Mrs K.* interpreted that Richard was angrily attacking his mother, the cupboard standing for her, and that he was at the same time showing that he had a strong genital—the ball.

Richard murmured something about a cannon ball and then asked Mrs K. to play ball with him. He arranged that they should each have two balls and roll them so that they would meet. Sometimes he had the big ball and sometimes Mrs K. had it. Then again he had two balls of the same size, and Richard spoke of twin balls. He had become very friendly and interested in the game.

*Mrs K.* interpreted that her playing with him meant that she was the good Mummy, helping him to get over his anger against the bad Mummy. Otherwise he felt he might shoot her with a cannon. Also, in the course of the play he and Mrs K. had become quite equal, they had both two breasts—the twin balls; both had one penis—the one big ball; both had babies—again represented by the twin balls. There was therefore no cause to be angry and envious of each other (Note II).

Richard at the end of the session put the balls back into the cupboard and helped Mrs K. to put away the toys. Looking at them in the bag, he said with concern, 'Now here are Daddy and Mummy and the children all lying together.' The tone and his facial expression indicated that he meant to say, 'What is going to happen to them in that bag?'

*Mrs K.* interpreted the bag as standing for his inside and containing his parents and their children, destroyed by him or fighting with each other, and that he was afraid and worried about what was going to happen there. He was also worried about what was going to happen overnight to his parents at home, when he did not see them, and to Mrs K. when he did not see her.

Richard, just before leaving, said suddenly that he would after all like to swim; and on the road he glanced back at the hills and said that the country looked very nice. For a moment, when Mrs K. was already outside, he closed the door so that it looked as if she were locked out, and Mrs K. interpreted this again in connection with his anger about his mother preventing his swimming and his wish to throw her out of the home because of that.

It was clear in this session that persecutory anxiety had diminished and that Richard could express his anger more openly. He had at one point asked whether Mrs K. had met Mr Smith; but he asked this only once, when Mrs K. referred to the man figure, whom he usually called Daddy, as also representing Mr Smith. Formerly, as has been seen, he had put this question repeatedly, in an obsessional way, wanting to know whether Mr Smith had passed, when he had passed, when Mrs K. had met him, and so on. This concern had recently diminished, and with this change Richard felt less incentive to meet Mrs K. on her way, for he no longer needed so urgently to find out whether she met Mr Smith and on what terms she was with him. His conflicts over the relations between Mother and Nurse, and his complex feelings about his father, were much more fully recognized; and concurrently with sadness and concern he showed more hope. Yet he had not been able to prevent the 'disaster'.

*Notes to Seventy-third Session:*

I. As usual with Richard (and this applies to children in the latency period in general), interpretations of destructive and sadistic phantasies directed against the parents in babyhood—though painful and at times very frightening—were less painful to him than the realization of conflicts about current situations and relationships. This applied in particular to his divided loyalties towards his mother and nurse, towards his mother and myself, and ultimately towards both his parents. In this session he had clearly more fully experienced and understood this conflict. There was also a growing realization of his distrust of his mother, and of the fact that the 'light-blue' and the 'brute' mother were one and the same in his mind.

II. I wish to draw attention to the fact that my having interpreted his denied anger and criticism of his mother's attitude (not allowing him to swim, which he felt prevented him from developing into a man) had the effect of his dealing with this anger. It also enabled him to revive the picture of the good mother—my playing with him. It has often been doubted whether it is safe to bring out into the open the latent criticism of the mother's actual attitude. I contested this view as early as 1927 ('Symposium on Child Analysis', *Writings*, 1); and my further experiences, and those of my colleagues, have shown the benefit derived from enabling a patient (child or adult) to experience repressed criticism in relation to his parents, as well as his phantasies about them.

## SEVENTY-FOURTH SESSION (Wednesday)

Richard again came to meet Mrs K. on the way to the playroom (recently he had waited for her outside the playroom). He told her that he had been trying to meet her as early as possible and that he was so glad to see her. He appeared to be very depressed and unhappy. Mrs K. asked whether anything had happened and Richard said no; he was apparently determined not to complain.[1] On the way he was puffing like a train and said that he was on a train with Mrs K.

*Mrs K.* asked where the train was going to.

Richard replied that it was going to London. When Mrs K. stepped a little aside, he asked her not to get off the rails or she would not be with him on the train. As soon as they arrived in the playroom, Richard started to play with the toys; but he was very much in thought and silent, and gave the impression of withholding what worried him.

*Mrs K.* suggested that perhaps he did not like staying with the Wilsons, but had made up his mind not to complain. She asked whether this was because he was afraid that she might repeat it to them, or that she would not like to hear anything unpleasant about them.

Richard without hesitation said, 'Both.' Then he explained that there were things he disliked. For instance, he did not want to be made to finish his food if he did not like it. He also said, obviously trying to be fair, that the Wilsons were quite nice in some ways; but it was clear that he was sad and was restraining his criticism. Suddenly he said with strong feeling that he wished he could stay with Mrs K.; that would be so nice and why couldn't he? Then he begged Mrs K. to let him stay with her.

*Mrs K.* asked when this wish had ocurred to him.

Richard replied that he was thinking about it all the time.

*Mrs K.* said that it was not possible for him to stay with her if she was to continue doing this work with him.

Richard had in the meantime arranged the station, this time close to Mrs K. and himself. (In the previous session he had put it as far away from her as possible.) Then he put the electric train into the station and left it standing there. He made a second station, which was unusual, in the same position as in the previous session— i.e. at the other end· of the table. Between the two stations he arranged various groups with the toys, which partly hid the second station from Mrs K. He said it was reserved for the goods train. He explained to Mrs K. that one woman figure was Nurse talking with —he was going to say 'Mummy' but said instead 'the rude woman'; another group consisted of three boys supposed to be talking to each other; two boys stood a little farther away, and farther still one boy

---

[1] Because of the illness of her husband, Richard's mother had arranged that Richard should stay with the Wilsons. Richard, who was in some ways treated like an only child since his brother was so much older, and was used to getting much attention at home, found it difficult to fit into a family circle where he was not made so much fuss of.

by himself. The 'Mr Smith' man was standing alone; another group was Mummy and Mrs K. talking to each other. In this play the main activity occurred between the trains and Richard did not move the figures.

*Mrs K.* asked who the three boys were.

Richard replied they were himself, John, and John's friend.

*Mrs K.* asked who the two boys were, and the one by himself.

Richard showed resistance. He said that he did not know. He asked whether Mrs K. recognized which of the toy children was himself and he looked very pleased when she pointed out the figure which often represented him.

*Mrs K.* interpreted that the electric train standing close to her and remaining all the time inside the station stood for Richard staying in Mrs K.'s house and not wishing to go away from her; to which Richard agreed. She further interpreted that the station also stood for Mrs K.'s bed and her genital, and that when Richard wanted to stay with her this also meant he wanted to put his genital into hers.

Richard in the meantime had made the goods train run through the other station on different lines from the electric train, which he had also set going (after Mrs K.'s interpretation that it stood for himself and that he did not want to move away from her).

*Mrs K.* interpreted that Richard wanted to have Mrs K. all to himself instead of Mummy; then Daddy, the goods train, could have his own station (Mummy) all to himself without Richard having to fight him (Note I).

Richard asked whether he might take a photograph of Mrs K.

*Mrs K.* interpreted that Richard not only would like to have this as a keepsake, but also wished to take Mrs K. into himself, keeping her safely inside him. This was also what he meant when he asked Mrs K. to be close to him on the train, which the road to the playroom had represented, and when in former sessions he wished to travel with her on the train which had so often meant keeping her inside him.

Richard meanwhile made both trains move on different lines, but soon brought them close together. The goods train followed the electric train, and then the electric train followed the goods train. A collision occurred, which actually led to a fight between the two trains; in the end, the goods train had two of its carriages on top of the others.

*Mrs K.* interpreted that if the train were a person, Richard had broken this person's limbs.

Richard laughed and agreed to that.

*Mrs K.* suggested that the goods train now stood for Mr Wilson.

Richard then made the electric train rush about until everything tumbled down. He then went to the window and watched people passing by. He became very restless and persecuted and asked whether Mr K. (again speaking in the present tense) wanted Mrs K. to be a psycho-analyst and how long had she been one. Did she start on this when she was already married?

*Mrs K.* interpreted that Richard thought Mr K., whom he still felt to be alive, would dislike Mrs K. being together with Richard and talking with him and other people about such things as genitals. Richard thought that Mr K. would be jealous and angry and would attack Richard, as he thought that Mr Smith was watching Mrs K.'s and Richard's play to find out what they were doing together. He had just shown that the goods train, now representing Mr Wilson, and standing for the bad Daddy and Mr K., was attacking the electric train, Richard, because he wanted to run away with Mrs K.

Richard said that he thought Mr K. would be cross. He then ran into the kitchen and inspected the 'baby tank'. He drew one bucket of water and watched Mrs K. empty it into the lavatory; then he ran to the window and watched people and again asked Mrs K., when a young man passed, who he was. He put this question as if Mrs K. would definitely know him. Then he asked her to go outside with him, and went back himself, shutting the door, so that she was locked out. But very soon he let her in.

*Mrs K.* interpreted that when Richard watched the people on the road and assumed that every man who passed by was known to Mrs K., this showed his fear of the jealous and angry Mr K. and his distrust of Mrs K. who, he feared was allied with Mr K., Mr Wilson, Mr Smith, and ultimately with Daddy. She stood also for Mummy who contained the bad Daddy and was influenced by him against Richard. He was therefore suspicious of all men and connected them with Mrs K.

Richard had collected the balls and, from one end of the playroom, threw them violently through the door into the little corridor leading to the kitchen, aiming in such a way that they rolled from the corridor into the adjoining lavatory. When starting this game he spoke of his cannon balls, then he threw the balls from the opposite end towards where Mrs K. was sitting. One of the balls hit her bag which was hanging over her chair. Richard apologized, but asked whether he had unconsciously meant to hit Mrs K.'s bag and Mrs K.

*Mrs K.* interpreted that she thought he had meant that. She added that the bag, the corridor, and the door through which the 'cannon balls' were thrown stood for her genital and bottom. Richard had particularly wanted to attack with his genital and with his 'big job' (the 'cannon balls') Mrs K.'s inside, because he felt she contained all the bad men (and at that moment all men seemed bad to him) standing for Daddy inside Mummy. She reminded him that this 'bad' Daddy inside Mummy had changed her and Mrs K. into the 'wicked brute'. This was also why Richard wanted to throw Mrs K. and Mummy, whom he had taken into himself, out of himself again when he was angry and distrustful.

During this session Mrs K. found out that Richard had felt very hurt because John did not take him with him when he went to see a friend; then she interpreted that the two boy figures by themselves represented John and his friend and the figure left standing by itself was Richard, who was lonely because he felt excluded. She interpreted that whereas Richard so much hated other children and wished to get away from them, he was at the same time very keen to get on with them and longing to be loved by them; and that it caused him great pain that he did not get on with other children.

In this session the wish to make friends and the sorrow about this failure (which had made him formerly express his fear about becoming a 'dunce'), first of all in his relation with his brother and later with contemporaries, now came more fully to the fore. This explains why Richard had shown particular resistance when Mrs K. had asked him who the two boys and the boy by himself were.

*Note to Seventy-fourth Session:*

I. His arranging two stations on that day, giving one to his father (the goods train) and keeping the other close to Mrs K. and himself, was also an attempt—characteristic of pre-adolescence—to detach himself from the mother and find a substitute. In this way, too, the dangerous rivalry with the father would be diminished. This process of detachment is one which is of great importance in normal development. It makes it possible for the man to free himself to some extent from the dependence on the mother.

## SEVENTY-FIFTH SESSION (Thursday)

Richard was waiting outside the playroom. Before entering the house he pointed to one of the hills and told Mrs K. that he had climbed up there the previous afternoon. It took him an hour and he had been tired. In the room he continued to speak about this. He was not boastful but quietly satisfied. He added, 'But it was not even half as difficult as climbing up Snowdon.'

*Mrs K.* reminded him of another attempt at climbing, which he had mentioned some time ago, and which went back to the time before his analysis; she asked whether that climb had been more difficult than the one on the previous day.

Richard said no, it had been much easier, in fact he had only gone up a little way because another boy chased him.[1] . . . He spoke again, but this time spontaneously and freely, about his difficulties in staying with the Wilsons. He did not much like Mr Wilson and he felt particularly hurt because John was not very friendly with him. He did not think that John actually disliked him, but he wished John would like him more. He went on to say that he realized his own tendency to be provocative; he liked to tease other boys but could not bear it if they teased him. He said that he had more enemies now among the girls in the village. One of them had said to him that he was 'dopey'. Could Mrs K. cure dopey boys? He had been very unhappy the day before when John went to see a friend and would not take Richard with him. But afterwards he had gone out by himself, climbed the hill, and then felt all right; and now he was no longer unhappy.

*Mrs K.* interpreted that today Richard did not seem afraid of telling her his opinion of Mr Wilson; probably he was less afraid that she would dislike his criticism. In the previous session he might have felt that Mr Wilson, whom Mrs K. knew, stood for Mr K. and therefore she would resent any criticism of him. She reminded him that after speaking about his being unhappy at the Wilsons, he had explored the stove and the tank and had used the 'cannon balls', and that she had interpreted that his fears and his distrust referred to the relation between his parents allied against him.

Richard did not disagree, but emphatically said that Daddy was nice and was never unfriendly with anybody in the family.

*Mrs K.* reminded him of the 'tramp-Daddy', the man who might have attacked Mummy, and that Richard had even wished him to attack Mummy when he was angry and jealous. At the same time he wanted to protect and guard her against any injury and harm. Now Mr Wilson stood for the nasty Daddy.

Richard did not reply to this, but he announced that the fleet

[1] This admission was in contrast to his tendency to boast. Richard's mother had told Mrs K. that he was very boastful: for instance, he told people in the hotel, when his father had caught a salmon, that he had caught it himself, and often behaved as if he knew everything. This boastfulness was much controlled in the analysis, since he was so set on being truthful with me.

had come. He was not sure whether the fleet had wanted to come but he had made it come. One ship was missing; however, he hoped he would find it. He asked Mrs K. to take all the toys out of the bag and he helped her to do so. He picked up the little sitting man and looked at him, but put him back into the bag.

*Mrs K.* interpreted that he again wished to keep his father (the little man sitting on the chair) safe by leaving him in the bag. He also did not want to see him so as not to think about him and be worried about his illness.

Richard made a seaside town on the side of the table where Mrs K. was sitting, with a railway line running along the coast (Note I). The coast was indicated by pencils, whereas the toys were all used for making the town, except the swing, which he put outside the town. There were again various groups of people. The 'rude' woman stood with four boy figures—two pairs of 'twins' (they had clothes of the same colour); later on he added another pair of boy twins. His mother and Mrs K. were again standing together. A little away from them stood Nurse, but after a moment he put her together with his mother and Mrs K. His father (the 'Mr Smith man') stood a little aside; there were various groups of children— three boys, two boys, and some girls separately—and Richard pointed out that the dog, the tractor, and the coal lorry were also on the coast. Three animals were arranged so that they had their heads together and looked at each other. Richard said that these were Daddy, Mummy, and himself.

*Mrs K.* pointed out that they were very close to one another so that they could watch each other well and would give each other no reason for jealousy.

Richard put up the trains. The goods train followed the electric one. Then he arranged the fleet and said that now the whole town was watching and admiring it. The *Hood* steamed out, the *Rodney* and *Nelson* followed, and they moved to and fro; sometimes *Rodney* was near the *Hood*, sometimes near *Nelson*, and destroyers followed them. Richard said that *Nelson* was the nice Daddy.

*Mrs K.* interpreted that he seemed to feel that the big *Hood* (actually by then the *Hood* had been sunk) was Daddy, who had died and become a ghost. He was afraid of this 'bad' Daddy-ghost in Mrs K.'s, or rather in his mother's inside.

Richard looked at the peaceful scene on the table and, after repeating that they were all watching the fleet, he suddenly declared that the town was now a German town and the fleet was going to attack it. He said that the toys were actually made in Germany (which was true) and asked what nationality Mrs K.'s father had been, but at once added, 'Austrian, wasn't he?', as if he were afraid

Mrs K. might say German. Then he asked whether Mrs K. really did not mind his referring to her nationality, and said, as often before, that he could not believe Mrs K. would not be hurt if he said such things. He made the bombardment start and the whole town fell down. While this was happening, Richard had put the swing with the child back into the scene of disaster and it also fell. The only survivor was the boy figure representing Richard. Then he declared that the fleet was now German and there was only one single destroyer left, which attacked and sank the German fleet one by one. In the end the only survivor was the British destroyer, which Richard said was himself. . . . Then he asked Mrs K. to put the toys away.

*Mrs K.* interpreted that he wished to get rid of the injured or dead people. She also reminded him that because 'German' meant to him being bad and hostile, he could not believe that Mrs K. would not be hurt if he said that she was not British.

Richard said that he often asked his mother whether he hurt her feelings by things he said to her.

*Mrs K.* interpreted that his fear of hurting was so great because he felt all the time that peace could not last, that he was going to attack Mrs K. or Mummy with his guns, standing for his genital, urine, and 'big job', and would injure or kill them with all their babies inside. He had given the 'rude' woman, who had previously been the 'bad' Mummy, six children (the three pairs of twins) to make up for the injured babies, because he felt that his attacks on her had made her angry and rude and he wanted to change her back into the nice Mummy. The fleet did not want to come, as he had said, because he was afraid of attacking with it the enemy Mrs K. and the enemy Mummy; but at the same time he also wanted to express to Mrs K. what he felt and to do work about it with her. The fleet had first represented the British, the good family which survived, while the bad family, the German town, was destroyed; and the play showed his uncertainty about the good parents who so easily changed in his mind into the bad and attacking parents because, as soon as anger, jealousy, and feelings of deprivation came up, he attacked them in his mind. Therefore there could be no peace; since they so easily changed into the bad parents, he had to go on destroying them for fear that they would attack him. It was the same with the babies whom he felt Mrs K. and Mummy contained. This was why any girls who looked at him, or said something to him, at once turned in his mind into enemies and Richard had to test this by provoking them, making faces, or saying something unfriendly to them, as he had repeatedly told Mrs K. that he was in the habit of doing. When John did not want to take him to meet his friend, Richard felt that this was because Richard was 'dopey' or a 'dunce', which meant to him that he was bad and destructive. Mrs K. reminded him that he would really like to have his brother and other boys, now John, as friends; but he was afraid of them because in his mind they all stood for the attacked and injured babies.

Richard said, pointing to the toy children, that he liked them and also liked babies because they were harmless. At the same time he seemed impressed with Mrs K.'s interpretation that he would have wanted to meet John's friend and would also enjoy being in the company of other boys, if he were not afraid of them. This puzzled him because he used to feel so strongly that he wanted other children to leave him alone and did not want to have anything to do with them. . . . At one stage during the play with the toys Richard had gone into the kitchen. He drew a bucket of water from the 'baby tank' and said, 'Let us milk the cow.' He added that Mrs K. was the dairymaid and he was the dairyman. When Mrs K. emptied the bucket, Richard mentioned that it was a good thing that nothing was spilt, for on that day the playroom would be used by the Girl Guides. He listened to the noises in the pipes, which were quite loud, and said smilingly, 'The cow says, "I want to be milked".' Then he remarked with satisfaction that the tank and the water were almost clean. He went outside and asked Mrs K. to come with him. He jumped about on the steps and said that he might fall with his back on the vegetables. In jumping down he touched, though quite lightly, Mrs K.'s face and was at once very worried about this.

*Mrs K.* interpreted that falling with his back on the vegetables was felt to be an attack by his 'big job' on the babies who also wanted to be fed by the cow (Mummy and Mrs K.). But Richard wished to take for himself all the milk Mummy had and thus would starve as well as injure the babies. When previously the water in the 'baby tank' had been dirty, he had felt that it was his fault and that he had made the babies ill.

Richard said, pointing at the vegetables, 'They feed us.' Then, looking at the hills, he said longingly that he wished he could see the mountains behind them and added that one could see only the lower part of them, the higher parts were hidden. . . . During the fleet play he had gone repeatedly to the window, particularly to watch children. He was observing them intently, not in his usual persecuted and hostile way but rather as if he were interested in finding out what they were actually like. Once, when a girl was passing, he said that he liked her, she looked nice and pretty. He parted from Mrs K. at the corner of the road. Since he was now staying with the Wilsons, he was not going down to the village; but before he left he inquired whether Mrs K. was going to Mr Evans, and when Mrs K. said 'yes', he made a disapproving sound. But he did not actually seem very worried. Moreover, in this session, he put no questions about Mr Smith.

*Note to Seventy-fifth Session:*

I. Since  the Twenty-first Session Richard had not been playing with the fleet and the toys simultaneously. I have pointed out in an earlier note that by sometimes changing the media of expression he used splitting in such a way that he was able to preserve the good family and the good part of his self. Though we can see how quickly his belief in good objects was disturbed even at this stage, the fact that he could bring two important means of presenting his unconscious— the toys and the fleet—together again showed progress in integration. It is true that to begin with he had used them simultaneously, but had then discarded the toys because they had come to represent the injured and hostile objects. Now, since persecutory and depressive anxieties had been analysed to some extent, his present use of the fleet and toys together was carried out on a different basis.

# SEVENTY-SIXTH SESSION (Friday)

Richard looked very depressed and was a few minutes late, which was somewhat unusual. It was obvious that he was unhappy and that something was the matter with him; but when asked by Mrs K. whether this was so, he did not reply. He sat down and said that he had not brought the fleet. Suddenly he discovered that Mrs K. had in her shopping basket a parcel to be posted.[1] Richard at once got hold of it, looked at the address, and saw that it was to go to Mrs K.'s grandson. Holding it to his nose, he said that it seemed to contain fruit, it smelt like oranges, was this true? Mrs K. agreed and Richard wanted to know where she had got the oranges from.

*Mrs K.* replied that on the previous day the grocer had distributed two oranges to each of his customers.

---

[1] Usually I avoided bringing with me anything which did not belong to the analysis, but on that day I had not been able to go to the post office earlier. As it turned out, the stimulus for envy, jealousy, and persecution which bringing this parcel produced, proved that bringing it had been a technical mistake.

Richard looked white with anger and envy, but said that he did not like oranges.

*Mrs K.* reminded him that he did not like milk either.

Richard said no, he did not.

*Mrs K.* interpreted that he would now dislike the idea of his mother giving him the breast, or Nurse giving him the bottle, but at the same time he still felt the same anger and frustration he had felt as a baby when he had wanted the breast or bottle and did not get it. Now he experienced envy of other people who might get whatever stood for the bottle and breast. The oranges at present represented Mrs K.'s breast and milk, as well as her love for her grandson. This also meant that Mrs K., and in the past Mummy, would give her love and attention to another baby.

Richard still looked very dejected and disturbed. He said that he wished he had a net to catch fish, but he had hardly any money left because he had spent most of it. (He received a good deal of money, but spent it quickly.) How could he get some more money now?

*Mrs K.* interpreted that he wanted her to give him either the net or the money, but that was mainly to reassure him that she, as well as Mummy, loved him in spite of his being jealous and wanting to rob her babies of the milk.

Richard took the toys out of the bag, first of all the electric train, handled it, took the two carriages apart and joined them together again. Then he asked if Mrs K. knew that some bombs had been dropped—no, there had been a tornado raging—in 'Z' last night. Two houses were razed to the ground. One was the house where Oliver lived, and the other was the one where Jimmie lived. (Oliver was usually his enemy, and Jimmie was at one time his friend but had changed into a 'traitor'.) While talking about this, the colour had come back into his face and some light into his eyes (which were very dull when he was depressed). His expression also showed some satisfaction or amusement. He added at once that this was only a story; he had seen the tornado in a film.

*Mrs K.* asked whether Oliver's and Jimmie's houses were not near to his own home.

Richard said that Oliver actually lived next door, and he looked as if he had drawn the inference at once. He had put the electric train between two houses (usually called the stations), picked up both houses, turned them round, put his little fingers into his mouth and took them out again. He was a picture of restlessness and despair.

*Mrs K.* interpreted that the two houses stood for her breasts, and sucking his fingers had expressed his desire to stay with her.

Richard, looking very miserable, asked why did Mrs K. not take him with her; and he begged her again to let him stay with her.

*Mrs K.* asked where he would sleep in her lodgings.

Richard replied, 'With you in your bed.'

*Mrs K.* interpreted that Richard felt that because Mrs K. did not let him stay with her, give him the oranges, and love him, she had become the ally of Mr Wilson, who was now felt to be the bad Daddy. This made his need for reassurance and love from her all the greater.

Richard expressed his feeling of anger and dislike for Mr. Wilson. The main complaint was that the Wilsons were strict about rationing out sweets, which seemed to him quite unbearable. (At home he was not much restricted about sweets.) He also appeared to be very disappointed about John, who obviously could not be bothered with him.

*Mrs K.* interpreted that this was all the more disappointing to him because he now felt he would actually like to make friends and yet he could not. It made him lose hope about getting on with other children, which also meant to him that he was different from other children—a 'dunce'.

Richard said that this was very unpleasant and he did not want to hear it, but he asked Mrs K. passionately if she could not stop the village children saying such nasty things to him. The previous night, when he was at the cinema, a boy had called him 'nuts'.... For some time he had been watching passers-by from the window. He said about all children who passed that they were 'awful' and spoke of them as his enemies. He was restless, jumped up, went to the window, sat down again, and was clearly feeling very persecuted. At one point he set the train going towards Mrs K. and then away from her, round and round the bag containing the toys. He went into the kitchen and drew some buckets of water, stopping only when Mrs K. asked him not to draw any more.

*Mrs K.* interpreted that he wanted to use up the whole water-supply, which stood also for the milk in the breast, so that Mrs K.'s children could not get any. On that day, as he well knew, the Girl Guides were going to use the playroom and they now stood for Mrs K.'s children and grandchild; therefore he wanted to empty out all the water.

Richard at once agreed.

*Mrs K.* also interpreted that Richard liked to draw the water because when Mrs K. emptied the buckets this was to him a sign of love and attention; but it was also protection he wanted because of his fear of the persecuting Daddy and Paul. Mrs K. also stood for Nurse, who had been doing so many things for him and at times had protected him from Paul.

Richard returned to the room but played very little. He only took up the two trains, compared them with each other, and made them run, and the electric train threw down the goods train.

*Mrs K.* interpreted his feelings of depression and persecution in connection with her going away, his jealousy of her grandchild and children and of the patients whom she would see when she returned to London. He had shown this by his desire to rage like a tornado and to raze his parents' house to the ground. He also wanted to do this to Mrs K.'s house and to her children, because he was angry about her going to leave him. Therefore his fear of losing her for ever was very great. It was because of his anger and envy of the grandchild, in connection with the oranges, that all the children in the street had become much worse enemies. Razing his parents' and Mrs K.'s houses to the ground implied destroying Mrs K.'s and Mummy's unborn babies. All the unknown children and the children in the street stood for unborn babies, for his brother, and for Mrs K.'s children, whom he felt he had attacked and was continuing to attack.

Richard begged Mrs K. not to go to London. Must she? She should not. He wanted to go with her to London, but where would he stay there? Could he stay with her? No, he would not want to go to London. When was Mrs K. coming back?

*Mrs K.* repeated that she intended to remain in London and not to return, but she hoped and would do her best, and so would his mother, to arrange for him to continue his analysis some time later on.[1]

Richard asked whether Mrs K. would keep her house in 'X'. She would not sell it, would she?

*Mrs K.* interpreted that although Richard knew quite well that she had only rented rooms there, had seen the landlady, and also knew about the fellow-lodger, yet he maintained in his mind, and seemed fully convinced at that moment, that Mrs K. owned the house and would keep it. She further interpreted that the house in the village now stood for his parents' house in 'Z', to which Richard was so attached, and to which he wanted to return, even by himself, should his parents, as they intended, sell it.

[1] By that time I had come to the conclusion that my suggestion that I might return to 'X' in the following summer and continue Richard's analysis could not be carried out. I have no doubt that I had explained this to Richard so that he should not entertain this hope. But I have no note as to when I told him.

Richard then urgently repeated his question whether he would go to London in the coming winter.

*Mrs K*. said that she did not think his mother could arrange this, but she might later on. She interpreted that Richard so much wanted to keep Mrs K., not only because he strongly felt that he needed the work, but also because when she helped him, she stood for the light-blue Mummy. He felt that she was putting into him good milk and love and in this way she was protecting him against his internal enemies and his own anger, as well as against the many hostile children and the bad Daddy.

Richard again took up the parcel, smelt it, and asked how old Mrs K.'s grandson was (a question which he had asked very often before and to which he knew the answer). Then he looked at the envelope containing the drawings (which happened to be one addressed to Mrs K.) and asked who had written the address and suggested that it might have been Mrs K.'s son. That, too, was a question which he had asked on previous occasions; he had been told that it had come from a friend. Richard again wanted to hear whether it was a man or a woman friend, and what the Christian name was.[1]

Mrs K. repeated the name.

Richard at once thought of a sunk ship, but then remembered that there was no British ship of that name. Was there perhaps a German ship so named? (The name Mrs K. had given was English). Then he mentioned the names of Italian ships called after Italian towns. Was not Italy in the last war on the Allies' side? He had now begun to draw (65).[2] While drawing, he asked Mrs K. whether she was glad, in the last war, when Britain had won and Austria lost?

*Mrs K*. asked what he would feel about her being glad that her country had lost.

Richard said he would not like it at all if she had felt that way; but *now* she would be glad, wouldn't she, when Britain won? Looking at Mrs K. he begged her to tell him, apart from the work, that she would be glad and wished Britain to win.

*Mrs K*. said he knew this quite well, and he also knew that Hitler had been an enemy of her native country, having taken possession of it by force.

Richard said that Hitler himself was born in Austria.

*Mrs K*. replied that this made him, in his mind, belong to Mrs K., as the bad Daddy belonged to Mummy. When Mummy and

---

[1] This exemplifies how careful the analyst has to be about every detail which he introduces into the playroom, and therefore into the analysis.

[2] I have blacked out Oliver's real name on the drawing.

Daddy were together at night, Richard suspected them of doing something together with their genitals which made him feel that Daddy was 'bad'—the 'Hitler'-Daddy, the 'tramp'. This also made Mummy 'bad' in his mind : it turned her into the 'wicked brute' allied with the 'bad' Daddy against him. His suspicions of Mummy made him want to get sweets and love all the time, and therefore he could not bear anything to be withheld from him.

Richard finished the drawing and hid it quickly among the others, but Mrs K. took it out of the envelope and suggested looking at it with him. Richard agreed reluctantly, but said that he did not want to hear what it meant. However, he began to explain it. He said that his enemy Oliver was leading a panzer division against him, and the little man on the right was Richard himself. He was protected by a wall and was just throwing a bomb against the tanks of the panzer division.

*Mrs K.* pointed out that Richard was very small and would be powerless and unprotected against a whole division.

Richard said that there was a wall to protect him and also that he had a bomb he could throw, but he now looked very anxious and counted the tanks he had drawn and said there were nine of them.

*Mrs K.* interpreted that the threat of an invasion had been much talked about, as he well knew, and this was a great cause for anxiety to him. Oliver, his enemy, represented the dangerous Hitler-father leading the panzer division against Britain—Daddy's enormous powerful genital attacking and destroying Richard's genital, which was represented by the bomb. Mrs K. reminded him of the earlier material when his genital and Daddy's genital had been fighting. The 'bad' Oliver and Hitler invading Britain also represented his own hate, envy, and jealousy which would be destructive to Mrs K. and her family. This bad part of himself should be destroyed by another part of his self.

Richard, towards the end of the session, wanted to discuss with Mrs K. a change in arrangements. He did not want to stay on with the Wilsons. Could Mrs K., for these three weeks, not come to 'Y' where his parents were staying ?

*Mrs K.* said that this was not possible and interpreted that Richard also wanted to have her all to himself for these three weeks and take her away from her other patients in 'X', whom he felt to be his enemies and rivals.

Richard replied that then he would try once more to get a room in the hotel, or he would rather travel to and fro. Would Mrs K. again give him alternative morning and evening times ?

*Mrs K.* replied that she would.

Richard, before leaving the playroom, quickly picked up the parcel and said, half jokingly, that he could really bite it through, but that he would not do so.

*Mrs K.* interpreted that, since the oranges she was sending to her grandson represented hers and Mummy's breasts, which no other child should ever have, his biting them meant that he would rather destroy the good breasts than leave them for another child; but he had also strong wishes not to hurt either Mrs K. or Mummy or their children, and therefore restrained his biting.

Richard left in a much less unhappy mood and obviously pondering about the steps to take. He had again been sucking the yellow pencil a good deal; this pencil very often stood for his father's penis, and I think at that moment stood for his mother's breast as well. In the second half of the session he had felt less persecuted and watched the passers-by less, though still more than he had done in recent sessions (Note I).

*Note to Seventy-sixth Session:*

I. At this stage, so shortly before my leaving him, Richard's fear of loss as well as all his anxieties and his need to be loved were strongly operative. Nevertheless I think that the specific factor of the two oranges to be sent to my grandson brought out in full force his earliest feelings about the loss of the breast, his envy and jealousy, as well as persecutory anxiety connected with this loss. The whole course of the session shows how these early emotions extended through all his relationships and influenced his persecutory anxieties relating to the Œdipus situation. At the same time the need to restrain his hostile feelings, which was characteristic of Richard's mental life, came fully into play.

# SEVENTY-SEVENTH SESSION (Saturday)

Richard arrived a few minutes late, but seemed unperturbed. He mentioned that he was going home by bus, and the bus ride played a large part in this session. His mood was very different from that of the previous day. This was partly due to his going home; he had been very homesick during that week. Also, as he told Mrs K., he had written to his mother and asked her to make different arrangements and felt that she would do so. Then he spoke a good deal about the chances of the bus being overcrowded. He said he had made inquiries and knew that he would travel with the pretty conductress, the one who always said 'half fares stand up' when the bus was crowded. The other conductress he liked was not so pretty, 'though by no means ugly', and did not say 'half fares stand up'; but she was due to go with the later bus. Obviously, in spite of his anxiety that he might have to stand, he also liked the idea of travelling with the pretty conductress, for he said repeatedly that she was very pretty and that he enjoyed looking at her.

*Mrs K.* interpreted that he liked her, although she was not altogether 'light blue' like the 'good' Mummy.

Richard repeated that she was very pretty and added, with amusement, no, she was not 'light blue', she was 'dark blue'. Her uniform was actually dark blue. What a pity it was that such a pretty girl should go about with a cap and collar and a tie (Note I). He had seen her once in girl's clothes and she looked so pretty. Then he added that he knew what Mrs K. meant about her not being altogether 'light blue'. It meant that she was not quite good and not quite bad. He went and drank some water from the tap and sat down at the table.

*Mrs K.* interpreted that his fears about the crowded bus, with the attractive conductress in it, also referred to the loved but suspect Mrs K. Recently he had felt that all the people on the busy road came to her and made her 'overcrowded' like the bus. He feared the same about Mummy, whom he also thought to be pretty and who would be overcrowded by the babies inside her. On the previous day he had been extremely jealous of Mrs K.'s grandson and felt that he had attacked and destroyed him in his jealousy. Immediately all the children on the street had turned into enemies. They stood for Mrs K.'s grandson and for Mummy's babies inside her.

Richard remarked that actually he did not at all care for oranges. There had been some at the Wilsons' and he might have had one had he wished.

*Mrs K.* again interpreted the particular importance of the two oranges she was sending to her grandson in connection with Richard's love for her and his jealousy of other people, which was very much increased by her preparing to go away and leave him; therefore he felt she would give her love and attention to other patients and to her children. He was not only frustrated by her, but suspicious as well, for he thought, as he did about Mummy, that if she did not love him enough she would ally herself with the hostile men who became so frightening in his mind because he was very jealous and hostile towards them. In the previous session he had felt that because he so much hated Mrs K.'s grandson, he had destroyed him and Mrs K., and this made him despair. He also feared that because of his jealousy he had destroyed Mrs K.'s friend who had written the address on the envelope with the drawings, for he had at once thought of a sunk battleship, only to remember that no ship of that name existed.

Richard was responsive on that day. He listened intently and it was clear that he could now absorb much more of the interpretations which on the previous day he had not been able to take in (Note II). He had been watching two girls from the window, the ones who had called him 'dopey' and of whom he had said that they were his enemies.

*Mrs K.* interpreted that Richard, by provoking their hostility, was testing out who were his enemies and what they would do to him : the more frightened he was, the more he was driven to find this out. Though he was afraid of doing so, he felt some relief because they did not retaliate by injuring or attacking him. Just now he also felt protected by Mrs K. while he was provoking them.

Richard returned to the table and said very seriously, 'Do you know what happened yesterday? My nurse died.'

*Mrs K.* for a moment believed this and asked, 'Your nurse?'

Richard repeated, still quite seriously, 'My nurse.' After a moment he said that this was not true.

*Mrs K.* asked what would she have died from.

Richard, without any hesitation, answered, 'From pneumonia.[1] She got quite cold inside. Her milk went all cold and drowned her.'

*Mrs K.* interpreted that this was a fear which went back to the time when Mummy had stopped feeding him. When he felt deprived and hated her, in his mind he spoilt and dirtied her milk ; and it had been shown in the previous session that he wanted to bite through the oranges, representing Mrs K.'s breast, so that it should be damaged and destroyed—then nobody else could have it. Mrs K. had also been standing for Nurse, and he had in the past been very jealous because Nurse looked after Paul as well. This jealousy had been revived because his father now had a nurse to attend to him ; therefore Richard was jealous of his father not only because he was Mummy's husband, but also because in his mind Daddy had become a rival baby. At the same time he was very guilty and frightened about Daddy being an ill baby because Richard had poisoned, by 'big' and 'small jobs', the milk in Mummy's breast; on the previous day he had wished to bite the oranges which stood for the breast (Note III).

Richard made no attempt to play or draw on that day. He sat at the table and talked with Mrs K., getting up from time to time to look at passers-by, but less often and with much less tension and

[1] His father's illness was not pneumonia.

anxiety than previously. He also walked about the playroom, looked at the pictures, and drew Mrs K.'s attention to a postcard showing a baby penguin eating a goldfish, while Donald Duck was supposed to be away fetching food for it.[1]

*Mrs K.* interpreted that the baby penguin represented Richard. He was eating the goldfish—one of Mummy's babies—even though Mummy was going to feed him. This made Richard feel guilty.

Richard suddenly asked Mrs K. whether she would do him a favour; would she now talk German (contrary to his usual custom, he did not call it Austrian) with Mr K., as if he were sitting at the table?

*Mrs K.* asked what would he suggest she should say in German.

Richard protested that he wanted Mrs K to say what she would say if Mr K. were actually there.

*Mrs K.* then said a few non-committal sentences in German.

Richard, who had been listening with amusement to the foreign sounds, at the same time watching with great interest the expression on Mrs K.'s face and her whole demeanour, asked her to translate what she had said. When she did so, Richard looked pleased.

*Mrs K.* interpreted Richard's wish to find out about her relation to Mr K. in the past. Richard had asked her once before whether she liked Mr K., but had at once added, surely she must have done so. Even more he wished to find out what her relation to the internal Mr K. was like; if it were a good one, it would mean to him that she did not contain the bad Hitler-Daddy, that she was at peace within herself and that she did not feel poisoned and persecuted. It would also mean that she would not be turned into the 'wicked brute'—hostile to Richard—by a bad Mr K. inside. Mrs K. suggested that Richard had similar fears and suspicions about his parents, in spite of his knowing that his Daddy was a kind man.

Richard was deeply in thought and looked at Mrs K. affectionately. Suddenly he stretched himself and asked her to take his hand so as to help him stretch.

*Mrs K.* asked why he wished to hold her hand just then.

Richard (looking for a moment disappointed) said, 'Why not?' He added that he had expected Mrs K. to answer as she did; then he quickly put his hand on her hand, which was lying on the table. He said that he could feel her and he wondered whether she could feel him. After a pause he asked what would he do with Mrs K. if he were in bed with her?

[1] As mentioned previously, a great number of picture postcards were stuck on the wall, or distributed about the room, and it is significant that Richard picked on that one.

*Mrs K.* suggested that he should say what he thought he would do.

Richard (shyly) said that he would put his arms around her, he would cuddle her and get quite close to her. After a pause, he said he did not think he would wish to do anything with his genital with her. From the expression on his face it was obvious that this thought was predominantly unpleasant and frightening to him.[1] Then he ran into the kitchen and drew water from the 'baby' tank, which in his associations had recently turned into a cow's udder and had actually been called 'breast' by him. He filled two buckets and, looking at them, said that one was dirty and the other clean. (One was a little rusty, but there was hardly any difference between the water in the one and that in the other.)

*Mrs K.* interpreted that this meant one breast was the clean, 'light-blue' and the other was the dirty, 'bad' breast.

Richard at once accepted this interpretation and asked how this breast had become so dirty. He caught a fly between his fingers and put it into the 'dirty' bucket. The fly repeatedly escaped and Richard caught it again and again, threatening it (in a dramatic way) with a 'cruel death'. In the end he squashed it in the bucket. Then he caught other flies and put them into the 'baby' tank, watching whether they would go through into the bucket. He was consciously enjoying his cruelty.

*Mrs K.* interpreted that Richard's attacks on the flies stood for attacks on the babies inside her. But he also showed how Mrs K.'s, and that meant also Mummy's, breast and inside had become poisoned and dirty. If Mrs K. and Mummy contained dead babies, then they too would die. He had expressed this by saying that Nurse had died from the cold milk inside her. Also, because he wished to kill the babies and Daddy inside Mummy, he was so frightened that the babies—now the children on the street—would revenge themselves. By keeping one breast good and one bad, he was attempting to keep one part of Mummy all right. When he admired the pretty conductress, she was partly good, but she was also bad because she said, 'Half fares stand up.' Mrs K. added that the black, injured, or soiled part of her and of Mummy was her genital and her inside. The 'light-blue' Mummy was actually meant to be the upper part of Mummy's body—the breast-Mummy; the 'wicked brute' Mummy was meant to be the lower part of her body. Richard wished to cuddle Mrs K., but he felt afraid of her genital and her inside, because it was soiled and poisoned by the dirty and dead babies (the squashed flies) and by the Hitler-Daddy. Richard might, therefore, be terrified—even if he were grown up—of

[1] See Note III to Forty-second Session.

putting his genital into such a dangerous place, in spite of also wishing to do so.

Richard asked Mrs K. to empty the buckets. When she did so, Richard was, as always, embarrassed as well as pleased about it. . . . He went on catching flies, but now he put them out of the window and set them free. Having done this with a bigger and a smaller fly, he said that he had put Daddy and Paul outside. A little later he spoke of a fly as the red-haired girl. He added that he himself had killed only two flies; the others had been killed by the pipe. (Pause.) Was this Daddy's genital? (He was referring to the pipe inside the 'baby tank' through which the water was drawn into the tap.)

*Mrs K.* interpreted Richard's guilt and the wish to undo the harm done to the flies because they also stood for babies, as well as for Daddy and Paul. Therefore he had set some flies free; he felt guilty, but he also put the blame on to Daddy's genital inside Mummy. Yet Richard still felt that it had been his fault, for it was he who had put the flies into the tank and therefore caused them to be drowned in the pipe.

Richard called Mrs K. to come outside with him. He repeatedly jumped down from the steps. He looked up at the hills and at the sky and said that he would like to write a big 'V' on the sky, adding that this meant, of course, victory for the Russians over the Germans. During this session Richard had repeatedly mentioned that he had bought radish seeds from Mr Smith.

*Mrs K.* interpreted that now Mr Smith was standing for the good Daddy who gave Richard good seed—good babies—which Richard could put into Mummy. He also wished to pacify Mr Smith because he felt so suspicious of him.

Richard had at one point hammered the floor very violently with a hammer. He said he wanted to know what was underneath it.

*Mrs K.* interpreted his wish to break into her to find out whether she contained the dangerous Mr K.'s genital or the good Daddy's genital which put the good seeds (the babies) into her.

*Notes to Seventy-seventh Session:*

I. His regret that the pretty conductress wore a uniform also expressed his wish that his mother, and now the analyst, should remain feminine, that is to say not containing her husband (Daddy), the male uniform standing for the internal male object. In his mind only the breast-mother could give him the feeling that she was by herself, unmixed with the father. His fear and dislike of the female genital connected with the feeling that the male genital was inside it. Such feelings play an important role in impotence and in disturbance of potency.

II. This instance has a bearing on technique. We know that interpretations are often repeated when the same material reappears with new details; but there may also be other reasons to go over the same ground again. On the previous day, although no doubt Richard had taken in some of the points I had interpreted, he had been, because of his extreme anxiety and despair, unable to get a full insight. Moreover, in addition to his anxieties about my leaving him shortly and about his father's serious illness—anxieties which were now always present— he was also very disturbed about finding himself in new and uncongenial surroundings. He felt expelled from home, especially since he h.;d never before left home without his mother. Therefore the incident with the oranges had taken on a particular significance.

For all these reasons, although no doubt Richard had understood some of my interpretations on the previous day and they had had some effect, he had been unable to get a full insight into what I said. In the present session he was responsive and both keen and able to understand more fully the important material with which we were dealing. This was because the interpretations given had to some extent diminished his anxiety; but he had also gained some reassurance from the fact that I had agreed to change his hours so that he could live at home, and this in turn meant to him that I cared for him, and I became less suspect. It was also very important that he had been able to express to his mother the wish to make different arrangements and had reason to believe that she would do so.

Therefore I went again and in more detail over the ground of the previous session. Some new material, such as his mixed feelings about the bus conductress and the crowded bus, had entered, so that my interpretations were not a mere repetition of those given in the previous session. But I wish to emphasize that in certain circumstances, such as the ones I have mentioned, even if there are only a few new details, a repetition of the previous interpretations is essential.

III. In my *Envy and Gratitude* (1957, *Writings*, 3) I went a step farther than I did in this interpretation. I suggested there that the envy of the mother's breast and of her creative role stirs up envy in the baby and leads to attacks on the breast and the wish to deprive the mother of it. This I believe to be true in spite of the infant being fed by the breast. There would accordingly be a difference between being fed and possessing the source of all satisfaction which a possession of the breast would imply.

## SEVENTY-EIGHTH SESSION (Monday)

Richard arrived just on time at the playroom. He looked composed, and was obviously determined to cooperate in the analysis as well as possible. He put a chocolate box on the table and said that he had brought something for Mrs K., and asked her to guess what it was.

*Mrs K.* guessed that it was the fleet.

Richard said he wanted to know how she could have guessed this straight away. He was wondering about this and suggested that she perhaps heard a slight rattling when he put the box down on the table.

*Mrs K.* agreed that she possibly did, but added that Richard had also told her recently that he had put the fleet into a box and was keeping it there. Did Richard, by saying that he had brought the fleet for her, also mean that he wanted to cooperate in the analysis for her sake? Some time before he had said that he did it for his parents' sake.

Richard strongly maintained that it was also for her sake.

*Mrs K.* suggested that he might be doing it for his own sake as well.

Richard said that this was not so. (This is striking since he was obviously convinced that the analysis was helpful and necessary for him.) He took the fleet out and put it in battle order. He said that *Nelson* was leading, though the *Hood* was the largest. Then he stopped and said that Mrs K. had not asked him a question which she should ask, and he was not going to say which question—she should think it out herself.

*Mrs K.* suggested that the question (which she always asked when Richard returned from the weekend) was about his father's health.

Richard said that was right; but why had she not asked it?

*Mrs K.* explained that she had rung his mother the previous night, as Richard well knew, about altering the times of the sessions; and she had heard that his father was getting on satisfactorily.

Richard asked with a smile whether Mrs K. also knew why Mummy had had to interrupt the talk. He explained that he had come into the room and Mummy had to get rid of him. Did Mrs K. also hear the banging of the door? It was he who banged it. He looked rather pleased with himself, rebellious and defiant.

*Mrs K.* interpreted his curiosity about her conversation with his mother, his distrust of what they might say about him, and reminded him of the repeated play situation when the Mummy-figure and the Mrs K.-figure were talking to each other. He always felt that they were talking about him.

Richard again interrupted his play with the fleet to compare his watch—which had been away for repairs—with Mrs K.'s, saying his was louder. He asked Mrs K. to adjust her clock, which differed slightly in time from his and Mrs K.'s watch, so that they should all show exactly the same time. As often before, he inspected the clock to see whether it was of foreign make (he knew that it was Swiss) and again compared his watch with Mrs K.'s. Then he moved out some of his ships. They toured round the table, first hiding behind Mrs K.'s bag, then took up positions beside her clock. He said it was the North Sea and a battle was developing. At first when the ships moved out, Richard sang 'God Save the King', and the ships were supposed to be British; but as soon as they had taken up positions at the side of the clock, they became German ships and others came to fight them.

*Mrs K.* interpreted his fear of her inside and genital as bad and dangerous—the foreign clock. She referred to the material of the previous session: Mrs K., or rather Mummy, containing the dead father, Paul, and the babies—the flies killed by Richard. He had expressed his wish to be in bed with Mrs K. and to cuddle her, at the same time being very frightened of her genital. She pointed out that when Richard compared his watch with hers, that expressed his wish that his and Mrs K.'s genitals should be the same, that she should also have a penis, because her genital and inside were so terrifying to him; or that both he and she should have no penis. The 'foreign clock', as he knew (for instance, Eleventh Session), stood for Mrs K.'s inside; and his opening and closing its case meant looking into her inside. When he had put the ships beside the foreign clock, they had become German—that it to say, Mrs K.'s inside was dangerous because it contained enemies. It was Daddy's or Mr K.'s hostile genitals which were being fought inside Mrs K. and Mummy by the British, by himself and the good brother and Daddy.

Richard spoke of the R.A.F. which had made (and here he interrupted himself, looking for a moment terrified) a particularly heavy raid on Berlin. He got up and made loud noises like an aeroplane, pretended that he was bombing the fleet from the stratosphere, and spoke of the *Scharnhorst* and *Gneisenau*. The *Bismarck* (now Daddy) and the *Prinz Eugen* (now Paul) were injured in the bombing but were saved in the end; the *Hood* (now Mother) was sunk. Here the play changed very quickly because at one moment he represented the British and at another the Germans; sometimes he was on Mother's (*Hood*) side, and sometimes on Father's (*Bismarck*), and therefore deeply sorry about the *Bismarck*. At times one destroyer was up against all the rest and represented Richard (or Daddy) persecuted by the whole family. Sometimes he saved Daddy and killed himself, or the other way round. Because these fluctuations were so rapid, Mrs K. could not always follow what happened.[1] During the play Richard repeatedly said that he had bought something from Mr Smith. He saw the red-haired girl pass and pointed out that she was eating a green apple and how very red her hair was. He said that she was choking with rage.

*Mrs K.* interpreted his feelings that women and girls had red, injured genitals, because they did not possess a penis; that would make them furious and would make them wish to eat the man's genital, the apple; they would choke with rage in doing so. Mrs K. added that in his fear of Mummy's inside and genital, he made the *Hood* (standing for her) sink, and was allied with Daddy, who in the fleet play had been fighting Mummy. His concern for his father's health contributed to his anxiety about the *Bismarck*, which in the fleet play represented Daddy. At the next moment, however, he felt sorry and frightened about having lost Mummy, and he tried to make her win. Then again he was on Daddy's side; these changes were re-enacted again and again.

Richard declared that he did not remember ever having seen a woman's or girl's genital, but he seemed not to doubt that it was different from a man's.[2]

*Mrs K.* repeated her interpretation that Richard felt the female genital was injured and that therefore the girls—not only the red-haired one—hated him because they wanted to have a penis. The girls might also represent the injured, and therefore retaliating, mother's genital.

Richard took up two buckets which stood in the kitchen and first said that he was the dairymaid. He corrected himself quickly and said that he was the dairyman and that Mrs K. was the dairymaid and that they were going to milk the 'baby tank'. When drawing water, he noticed bubbles on it and said that it was lovely milk and

[1] The rapidity of the changes and fluctuations from one position to another indicated his insecurity, instability and illness, which were reinforced by my imminent departure and his worry about his father's health.

[2] As I said before, it is most unlikely that he had never seen his nurse, who slept in his room, or his mother undressed. The material had also repeatedly shown his unconscious knowledge of the difference between the sexes. For instance, he had shown me the difference on the masts between the *Rodney* (mother) and the *Nelson* (father), which was so slight that it was difficult to see, the *Rodney*'s mast having a little bit at the top broken off.

that there was froth on it, ignoring the bits of dead flies which he had killed in the previous session and thrown into the tank. Then he wanted to find out how the water got into the tank and made sure about this. He said he could go on all the time drawing water and milking the cow, and that he was angry because the water ran slowly—the cow was giving so little milk.

*Mrs K.* asked him whether he wanted to drink such quantities of milk.

Richard was a little surprised and said no, he drank only very little milk and even then did not like it much.

*Mrs K.* interpreted that whereas he did not like milk at present, Mummy who gave him milk when he was a baby—the breast-Mummy—remained in his mind as the wonderful 'light-blue' Mummy; he clung so strongly to the breast-Mummy because he was terrified of the lower part of Mummy's body, of her injured genital and her inside with the dead and frightening babies—the bits of flies. He wished to be the dairymaid, as he had said first, because this meant that he would have Mummy's breast and that he also contained the good breast-Mummy. If he as well as Mrs K. were the dairymaid, he would also get rid altogether of the male genital, because neither he nor Mummy would have it and neither he nor she would contain Daddy's genital.

Richard went back to the table and played. He moved a small destroyer, saying that it was the *Vampire*, along the table, bent down so that his eyes were level with the table, and screwed them up to see whether the ship was going straight. He said it was, and that it moved by itself. (The *Vampire* usually stood for Richard.) The *Vampire* had moved alongside the *Nelson* and the sterns touched. Richard mentioned again that he had seen Mr Smith. In between, he took the *Nelson* into his mouth.

*Mrs K.* interpreted that the *Vampire* going straight and moving by itself showed Richard's wish that his genital should be uninjured. It also showed that he was playing with his genital and watching what it was like. By making the *Vampire*'s and *Nelson*'s sterns touch each other, he expressed his desire to touch his father's penis and to suck it, since during this play he had picked up the *Nelson* and sucked it. Mr Smith had recently stood for the good father who gave him good seeds; Richard liked to go into his shop because he wanted to see Daddy's genital and to receive babies from it. Then he would be the dairymaid taking Mummy's place. These wishes were increased by the fear of Daddy's and Mummy's bad genitals.

Richard said that a few days before he had had a dream and that he wanted to tell it to Mrs K. but was afraid to hurt her feelings. However, he at once proceeded to tell the dream : *He broke off the*

*analysis with Mrs K. and went to another analyst.* (He spoke with
great difficulty and Mrs K. had to ask him questions.) He said *the
other analyst had a dark-blue suit and reminded him of a woman
in the hotel who had a very nice spaniel. He liked the dog but he did
not at all like the woman and was not interested in her. The dog
was called James.*

Mrs K. asked what the woman looked like.

Richard said emphatically, 'Oh, she wasn't as pretty as you.'
Then he again spoke about the beauty of Mrs K.'s eyes, trying to
look into her eyes while saying so.[1] He also begged very appealingly
that Mrs K. should not be hurt and asked whether she was hurt.
Then he asked seriously whether someone else could continue his
analysis, could a man do so?

Mrs K. returned to the dream and asked where this second
analysis took place, was it also in the playroom?

Richard said it was funny, it was not in the playroom; it seemed
to start at the bend of the road.[2]

Mrs K. interpreted that in his fear of Mummy's genital and inside, he turned away from her to the attractive Daddy-genital. She
also mentioned Richard's play with the fleet in this session and the
rapid changes which showed his conflict as to whom he should
choose, Daddy or Mummy. He was not so much interested in the
other woman analyst to whom he would go in the dream, but she
owned the attractive dog—Daddy's genital inside Mummy (the
bend of the road). She drew his attention to the fact that while she
had been interpreting, Richard had pushed the *Vampire* destroyer
under her key-ring so that it touched the key, something which he
had never done before. That, too, expressed Richard's desire to
touch the good male genital inside Mrs K. This desire for the good
penis was increased by his fear of the bad Hitler-genital inside Mrs
K. and Mummy. Leaving Mrs K. to go to the other analyst meant
giving up the good breast-Mummy and turning to the attractive
Daddy-genital (the dog). Therefore, he was so concerned about
hurting Mrs K.; for he also felt guilty because he wanted to leave
her, as a punishment for her leaving him. All this was very painful
to him. Mrs K. added that Richard was particularly thinking about
the need to go to another analyst because his analysis was soon to

[1] He behaved very much like a man who confesses unfaithfulness and tries
to make the other woman appear unimportant by praising the lover's charms.

[2] Richard was particularly interested when he saw people or cars appearing
or disappearing round this bend, which could be seen from the playroom.
This was shown, for instance, by his interest in the horse's head which he had
watched on one occasion (Eighth Session), the rest of the horse being hidden
by the bend. The horse's head then stood for Richard's genital inside Mrs K.

end. She repeated that it was quite possible, should the occasion arise, that he could continue his analysis with another analyst.

Richard had meanwhile got up; he went outside, looked round, and pointed out that some potatoes had been dug up. He remarked that the sky was very light blue. Actually it was full of clouds.

*Mrs K.* interpreted that Richard denied that the sky was cloudy, since clouds, as so often before, meant to him rain attacking and damaging the mountains. He also wanted to deny the danger to Mrs K. from the bombs in London.

Richard, back in the playroom, spoke about her dress, which had lines of white dots on a blue ground; he said, referring to the lower part of the dress, where the lines went in different directions, that they could be put into a soap-flakes advertisement.

*Mrs K.* interpreted that he was now stressing the cleanliness of her genital and inside of her body, represented by the lower part of her dress, to cover up his fears of the dirt and dangers which he attributed to that part of the body, and also to make up for having thought and spoken of it in such disparaging terms.

Richard had obviously brought the fleet as a present for the analyst and was determined to do his best in the analysis, partly to overcome his guilt about his unfaithfulness which came up in this session. It had appeared that coming to Mrs K. for his analysis, and his relation with her, implied to him being unfaithful to his mother, and he felt the same conflict when he left Mrs K. to go home. He also felt guilty because he was actually less dependent now on his mother and she therefore had become less important to him. His identification with his mother, based on his feminine position, was so strong that he was convinced that it was painful for her to be needed less. This identification also increased his guilt about his homosexual wishes. During the whole session his mood had been genuinely affectionate and loving. He was serious, at times depressed, but not feeling so persecuted by the people outside.

## SEVENTY-NINTH SESSION (Tuesday)

Richard arrived with his suitcase, ready to go home after the session. He compared his watch with Mrs K.'s and again expressed the wish that they should both show exactly the same time. He remarked that his was a little behind Mrs K.'s, but comforted himself by saying that the difference was very slight. He spoke at some length about his watch. He said it was nearly 'starved' last night; it badly needed winding up. When he had wound it up, it went quietly to sleep.

*Mrs K.* suggested that the watch stood for himself, who needed the analysis from Mrs K. and felt starved last night because he could not get it. This was what he had felt as a baby, when he wanted to be fed and loved by Mummy and she was not there. His wish that his and Mrs K.'s watches should show exactly the same time meant that she and he should think and feel alike and that Mrs K. should remain inside him and be all at one with him (Note I). The watch also stood for his genital, and he wished that he and Mrs K. should have the same genitals; then there would be no difference between them. Winding his watch, moreover, meant feeding the genital by rubbing it. But at the same time he was afraid that by playing with his genital he would injure it; in the last session the destroyer *Vampire* had represented his genital, and when he made sure that it was going straight and said that it moved by itself, this meant that his penis was all right.

Richard was very embarrassed during Mrs K.'s interpretation of his masturbation and first denied that he played with his genital. After a little pause, he said that he sometimes did so. Then he announced that the fleet had come; it was in his suitcase. He had not intended to use it, but would do so after all. He took it out of the case and put it on the table.

*Mrs K.* interpreted that Richard might have felt hurt in the previous session because she had not paid much attention to the fleet. (The material had been so abundant and there were more urgent interpretations to be given; consequently she had not been able to follow the movements of the fleet as closely as on other occasions.)

Richard agreed. He showed her the contents of his suitcase, and amongst them his identity card. Had Mrs K. got the same water-proof case for her identity card? Slowly putting the card into the case, he showed that it was now half in, now more than half, now completely inside the case. He took his bus ticket out of his pocket and wondered whether it was damaged and likely to break. (It was actually quite intact.) He was worried because he needed it for the return journey, and carefully put it back into his pocket. Then he showed Mrs K. his diary and said that she was mentioned in it every day: nobody had ever read it—she was the first to do so. Thereupon he read out his entries to her over and over again. There were references to the cook and to everyday happenings. He asked Mrs K. to read the diary herself. The impression he gave was of complete trust in her.

*Mrs K.* interpreted that by showing her his secret diary he meant that he trusted her with his secret worries about his genital and that he had understood, and felt relieved by, her interpretations about what he was doing with it. This was also the reason why he had decided after all to use the fleet. The thought that the ticket, which he needed for his return home, might break expressed the fear that his penis was injured and that he would be unable to use it. When he made the identity card disappear slowly into its case, he expressed what he felt when he played with his genital. For at such times he might think of putting it into Mrs K. or Mummy. At the same time, the identity card disappearing—together with the possible damage to the bus ticket—also showed his fear of losing his genital as a consequence of playing with it.

Richard had meanwhile taken up the fleet, and the manœuvres were extremely complicated and very swiftly carried out. At the beginning of the fleet play, Richard was humming a tune, and then the National Anthem. He said very dramatically, 'At dawn the fleet crept out slowly.' First the *Hood* appeared and Richard said that it was himself; then *Nelson* and *Rodney* came out, and the *Hood* was placed on the right-hand side of *Nelson*. Richard said that *Nelson* was the leader. Several destroyers followed *Nelson*. Richard pointed at one, saying, 'This is the leader of the smaller destroyers.' Then he showed the leader of the 'bigger' destroyers. He had put between *Nelson* and *Rodney* a 'small' destroyer and said that this too was himself (Note II). . . . At one point Richard said, 'Never has there been such a battle before.' The noises which he made, to represent the ships' engines and the bombs, grew louder and louder as the play went on, and he became increasingly excited. He was completely engrossed in what he was doing and hardly looked out of the window; only once, at the beginning of the session, he had looked at an old man outside and asked, 'Is this the grumpy old gentleman?'; but he added that he might actually never see him.

*Mrs K.* interpreted Richard's attempt to give his father (*Nelson*) his due. He also gave him possession of Mummy (*Rodney*), for the destroyer he had placed between *Nelson* and *Rodney* stood for his father's genital, as on previous occasions. He allowed his parents to be together and have sexual relations on condition that Daddy to some extent shared his rights with Richard; for Richard (*Hood*) was on the right-hand side of *Nelson*. He was also the leader of the 'small' destroyers—that is to say, the leader of the children. This expressed his wish for younger brothers and friends whom he could lead. Richard also wanted to give Paul his rightful place, making him the leader of what he called the 'bigger' destroyers (Note III). However, the wish to separate his parents and come between them

was also shown in so far as the destroyer which Richard put between *Rodney* and *Nelson* not only stood for father's genital but
also for himself.

Richard's mood suddenly changed, and so did the scenes which
he enacted. So far, in spite of being excited, he had also been somewhat restrained, serious, and reflective, as if he were trying to find
a solution to his conflict; but at this point one of the destroyers, the
*Vampire*, being himself as Richard said, went off round the table,
hiding first behind Mrs K.'s bag and then reappearing. It was
joined by three more destroyers which Richard led. They were now
German and were getting into battle with some British ships. Then
they fled, but were brought to battle by other British ships. They
hid and were trapped. They were alternately fighting with
bravado, then again hiding and biding their time. The three accompanying destroyers were sunk. Then Richard (*Vampire*) went on
fighting the British by himself, later on joined by another destroyer
who fought on his side. The fight developed more and more
between the *Vampire* and *Rodney* (mother). *Vampire* was, as
Richard said, 'firing at her like hell' and she fired 'with all her
guns' at him. In the end *Vampire* (Richard) was sunk, but the other
destroyer went on firing at the British fleet until they were all sunk,
and remained the only survivor. All this was done with great excitement and loud noises, in a defiant, manic, and rebellious mood.

*Mrs K.* interpreted that the surviving destroyer, which had killed
everybody, represented Richard's genital because he now felt it to
be powerful and destructive. The *Vampire*-Richard had been firing
at *Rodney*-Mummy 'like hell'; it was Richard fighting the dangerous Mummy containing the bad Daddy, and Mrs K. containing
the bad Mr K. This bad Mummy, the 'wicked brute', firing back
'with all her guns' at him, attacked him with all the bad Daddy-
genitals which she contained. Richard now felt that he actually
possessed a genital, but that it was most destructive and was even
treacherous because it had turned into the German destroyer
attacking the British family.

Richard went into the kitchen; he drew a bucket of water and
said it was milk; all this happened very quickly. He went out into
the garden, asking Mrs K. to come with him. Looking at the sky, he
said that it was going to clear up. Actually there were more clouds
than on many days when Richard had complained that they would
not lift.

After the end of the session, when Richard was walking back
with Mrs K., he asked her to guess who tied his tie. It was still all

right, wasn't it? He then disclosed that the maid at the Wilsons, whom he had gone to see, had tied it.

The hopefulness that the clouds would lift and that his tie was all right after having been tied by the maid, who stood for the helpful Mrs K., expressed his greater belief that she would restore his penis, actually would cure him. Richard's mother reported that, at the weekend, she had found Richard much more active, less neurotic, but much more disobedient and rebellious than usual (Note IV).

### Notes to Seventy-ninth Session:

I. I would go farther now. I have observed in some adult patients that the intense but deeply unconscious infantile wish to control the object in such a way that it would think, feel, and even look like the subject, may persist and make it impossible for them ever to be fully satisfied with any relation. This wish extends to the introjective identification as well as to the projective one. For such a strong urge to control implies taking in the object—the analyst—as well as intruding into him and making object and subject identical. These processes may go on in individuals whose personality is in some ways well developed and who do not give the impression of a wish for domination, lack of consideration for others, and so on. To some extent the urge to control and possess the object is part of infantile emotional life and of infantile narcissistic states.

II. As on many other occasions, Richard enacted several roles at the same time—a process well known in children's play. We can find such fluctuations in the personality of people who have not the strength to identify with one particular figure and to maintain a particular aspect of their development. These two failures interact. I have referred to splitting processes which weaken the ego in 'Notes on Some Schizoid Mechanisms' (1946, *Writings*, 3) and in my chapter 'On Identification' (1955, *ibid.*). The indiscriminate introjection of various figures is in my view complementary to the strength of projective identification which leads to the feeling that parts of the self are distributed— a feeling which in turn reinforces such indiscriminate identifications. Normally we find such changes of role in dreams, and some of the relief which dreams provide derives from the fact that psychotic processes find expression in them.

III. It is of interest that these steps towards better social relations, which implied a willingness to acknowledge his father's and brother's authority, were closely connected in Richard with more confidence in his own potency, or rather hope of full potency in the future. As the material of the previous sessions showed, his fears about his masturbation had been to some extent lessened by the analytic work; he was therefore better able to accept his role as a male and the possession of a penis, though a very aggressive one. In the play the destroyer standing for his penis had been the only survivor. The connection between greater trust in one's own potency and a capacity to acknowledge the leadership of father, brother, and ultimately of father-substitutes, has general applications. My experiences in the analyses of men have shown me that the fear of castration and of impotence greatly contributes to the hostile and envious attitude towards teachers and other father-substitutes. When such fears are lessened, the superiority and authority of other men are accepted more easily.

Castration fear and feelings of impotence do not always have the effect of making people rebellious and defiant, but may result in complete and indiscriminate submission to anyone in authority. With such men, the diminution of these anxieties brings about a greater capacity to assert themselves and to prove themselves equal to others.

IV. The connection between this change of attitude, his being more openly aggressive, but at the same time more active and less inhibited, was in keeping with recent material, particularly that of this session. It was clear that Richard was asserting himself because he felt less castration fear and a greater belief in possessing a penis. But the fact that his genital could, in his mind, become so dangerous, destroy the whole family, and rouse persecutors all round, had been in the past one of the reasons why he had felt compelled to deny its possession and had felt impotent. The analysis had enabled him, at the present juncture, to face what was to him still a potentially dangerous possession, but one which he nevertheless was able to value because it implied also initiative, strength, the power to defend himself, and—above all —to create. The anxiety which had come up during this session illustrates some of the factors which inhibit potency in men. The fear that the penis might turn out to be destructive and result in dangers to the mother and to the man himself can make him shrink from being potent. I have observed that these anxieties may increase the identification with the mother and reinforce the feminine position. As one patient put it to me : 'I prefer to be the victim rather than the victimizer.'

## EIGHTIETH SESSION (Wednesday)

Richard met Mrs K. at the corner of the road on the way to the playroom. He was humming a tune and said that it was 'If I were a Tiny Bird'. Almost at once he told her that he had had bad news the day before : his canary Dicky had died. It could not be helped, birds die easily. (He was obviously trying to be casual in order to deny his grief, since he was very fond of his birds.) In the playroom he said that Mrs K. should from now on bring only one tree with the toys. (The two trees had often stood in his play for his two birds.)[1] He was going to give a wife to Arthur (the other canary) who would now feel lonely; but it must not be a budgie because she would tear him up.

*Mrs K.* interpreted that Richard's song expressed his wish to be a bird, so that he could be company for the lonely bird. The bird also stood for Mummy, who would feel lonely if Daddy died; or he wanted to keep Daddy company if Mummy died. Mrs K. reminded him that his two birds had very often stood for his parents. He had frequently been very frightened of the dangerous sexual relation between his parents, and that had been one reason why he felt that they should have the same kind of genital. This meant denying the difference between the genitals of men and women, just as he had done over the watches. He was also very much afraid that his own genital was dangerous and that Mummy's genital and inside were frightening. The budgerigar was different from the canary, and that meant that the parents' genitals were after all different. He had often said that both his canaries were boys; at the same time they also stood for his parents. The budgerigar moreover represented the dangerous Mummy (*Rodney*) firing at him with all her guns (see previous session) and the bad Mummy who could kill Daddy. This was connected with his worry about his father's illness and the fear of his death.

Richard now looked sad. He said that he was very upset because the bird had died and that he was going to miss it. He made a drawing of a railway track, singing meanwhile various national anthems, and associated to it that he had altered the railway track of his train at home. He was tired of it; he was altogether tired of trains. He now looked very depressed.

*Mrs K.* interpreted that he was unhappy about losing her and wished to prevent her going away by train. She referred to the previous day's fight against *Rodney*—Mummy and also Mrs K. His powerful, dangerous genital (the victorious destroyer) had killed the whole family and he was afraid that his wishes would come true.

Richard after this interpretation made a big scribble on the drawing.

*Mrs K.* interpreted that he was now bombing the train because she was going to leave him; but if he did that, she would also be the dead bird.

---

[1] His asking me to bring one tree only meant that in spite of denying his grief, he wanted me to share it. I, too, would have only one tree.

Richard then wrote a note addressed to Mrs K.: 'Dear Mrs Klein, I have enjoyed the work and I shall miss you very much. Love from Richard.' He held his hand over the writing so that Mrs K. should not see it, but he showed it to her as soon as he had finished. He said that the crosses at the end meant kisses. He was going to write to Mrs K. while she was away. Then he scribbled something on another page and showed it to Mrs K., saying, as he had done formerly, that it was easy to change a swastika into a Union Jack.

*Mrs K.* interpreted that the bombing German was Richard killing Mrs K. because she was leaving him, but that he could turn himself into the loving Richard who would write friendly letters to her. That was meant by the quick change from the swastika into the Union Jack. In the previous session the Richard-destroyer, which stood for his dangerous genital, had also been meant to be German, but was now felt to be British. Because as a baby he experienced strong hate when left alone by Mummy, he was always afraid of her death, as he was now in fear of Mrs K.'s death.

Richard scribbled on another page, and was now singing loudly and angrily.

*Mrs K.* interpreted that he was bombing her with sounds and that was how he felt when he made 'big job' and was angry and full of hate. She also showed him that on the scribble he had included an indistinct 23, which was the day of her departure.

Richard then made Drawing 66, and when he had finished and looked at it, he called out that the 's' in 'school' at the bottom of the page was a 3, and that the figure preceding it was a 2; so there was the 23 again, this time more distinctly.

*Mrs K.* interpreted Richard's struggle between his loving and hating her. He was trying to think that she was nice; beside the drawing representing her at the top of the page he had written 'lovely Mrs K.' Nevertheless, he did not actually think that she was lovely, and therefore drew her without arms and hair, and evidently had no intention of making her look nice. He hated her for leaving him and joining other patients and her son and grandson.

Richard insisted that Mrs K. was lovely on the drawing because her tummy was heart-shaped and the arrow in the middle of it meant love. (His face was flushed and he often put his finger into his mouth; the struggle between hate and the wish to control it, and the mixture of persecutory and depressive anxiety, were expressed on his face.) He asked whether Mrs K. was sorry to go away. Was she going to stay with her son? She was not going to live in the heart of London, was she? Richard suddenly became aware of the word 'heart', looked surprised, and pointing at the drawing said, 'But here is the heart.'

*Mrs K.* interpreted that her heart stood for the bombed London and was not only injured by love (the arrow) but also by bombs. Richard, who wished to love Mrs K., was afraid that, because she was leaving him, he might turn into Hitler who was going to bomb her (Note I). This increased his fear of her death, his loneliness, and his sadness about her departure.

Richard said he was going to get some milk. He drew water from the tank, but he was careful not to fill the bucket completely, obviously keeping in mind that Mrs K. had pointed out that a full bucket was too heavy for her to lift. He made a big mess on the kitchen floor. (It was very difficult on that day for Mrs K. to exercise any control over him.) He killed many flies, catching them on the window between his fingers and throwing them into the 'baby tank', setting them free and catching them again. He poured water in and out of the 'baby tank' and insisted on filling all the vessels, though not to the brim. When he killed the first two flies, he mentioned the names of his boy enemies in 'Z'.

*Mrs K.* interpreted that when he said he was going to get milk from the tank—her breast—he wanted to get something good from her and take it into himself. At the same time, because of his jealousy, he killed in his mind Mrs K.'s son and grandson (the flies). The flies stood for her babies and her patients as well. Filling the vessels had another meaning, too: he was trying to feed Mrs K.'s babies (her patients and children) and Mummy's babies (including Paul). She reminded him of his wish to have friends, which also meant to have more brothers. On the previous day the destroyer was accompanied by three ships of its own size, which meant having friends and brothers. This was in contrast to Richard's jealousy and his attacks on Mummy's bad babies, which made him distrust and fear other children and increased his wish to destroy them. Mrs K. further interpreted that Richard made such a mess in order to punish her for leaving him. The mess also stood for poisonous 'big job' and 'little job', expressing his hate, as did the angry sounds earlier. At the same time he wished to get proof that she did not resent the mess. If she did not become angry, that would show that she did not hate him; and if she managed to clean up, that would prove that he had not injured her after all.

Richard, before he left, again got hold of the hammer and hammered the floor so hard that Mrs K. had to restrain him.

*Mrs K.* interpreted that Richard was trying to break into her inside, to take out the poisonous and dead babies and Mr K. in order to keep her alive, as he wished to take all the bad things out of Mummy's body.

This session was remarkable : rage and despair were clearly expressed in Richard's face and in his actions. He often ground his teeth, then again put his finger into his mouth. While he was scribbling, he broke the point of the pencil. At the same time he again and again tried to restrain himself, and feelings of love and concern about Mrs K. appeared together with hate and resentment.

*Note to Eightieth Session:*

I. People who feel very insecure cannot trust their love because any external influence, or internal pressure, may mobilize destructive impulses against a loved person. This arouses the fear that they might injure their object. I have found it useful to interpret this feeling of insecurity. But this is different from the anxiety of having destroyed or being in the process of destroying the object under the impact of rage and hate. By contrast, people who have established their good object more securely are less liable to be shaken by such fears. They have a stronger feeling that they can control their destructive impulses.

# EIGHTY-FIRST SESSION (Thursday)

Richard was again waiting at the corner of the road. He asked whether it was sixteen days until Mrs K.'s departure. In the playroom he adjusted his watch to her clock. He opened the clock, inspected it, set the alarm going, and went on opening and closing the leather case, also caressing it with his hands. He said that even if his watch was a little slower than others, yet it was 'going its way', and he drew his finger round the face of the watch. He said that nobody, and certainly no other watch, could command that it should stop. . . . He quickly looked round the kitchen, glanced uneasily at the 'baby tank', and was disturbed because he saw some rust on it. He tried to scrape it off and seemed grateful when Mrs K. removed the rust with a brush. He quickly went back to the table and again looked into the clock to see whether it was still working. . . . He told Mrs K. that he had a secret which she did not know. He had cycled to the end of the road last evening, and had passed her house. Where did the little path at the end of the road lead to? What was Mrs K. doing at about 8.45 last evening (which was the time when he had passed by her house)? Would Mrs K. have been angry if he had looked in? He did not wait for answers to any of these questions but went on speaking. He explained that he had borrowed the bicycle the day before and had cycled all over the village. Unfortunately it had been too late to go farther out to the next village as he had intended. He went on describing his exploit in detail and said it had been fun and he had enjoyed it very much. When he went downhill he made noises to himself, as if he were a bus (Note I).

*Mrs K.* interpreted, as often before, that when Richard investigated her clock, this meant looking into her inside and reassuring himself about her still being all right. The same applied to his looking around the kitchen. Both were connected with his killing the flies on the previous day, the mess he had made in the kitchen, and his fear of the harm he had done in this way to Mrs K. His cycling tour showed that he was less afraid of other children and also served as a means to satisfy his curiosity. Cycling past Mrs K.'s lodgings meant the exploration of her inside. The little path represented her genital and he wondered where it would lead if he put his penis— the bicycle—into it. He seemed to be less afraid of his penis being a dangerous weapon and therefore could use the bicycle. All this meant that his fear about his hatred and destructive wishes taking effect had lessened. His watch 'going its way', though slowly, stood for the smaller, less potent, but uninjured genital. He seemed to accept that it was only a boy's genital, but he hoped that he would be a man in the future. Making his watch agree with Mrs K.'s clock meant that they would understand each other and he could keep her as a friend, also inside him.

Richard, again manipulating the clock, said with strong emotion, 'Must we two part?' He went outside, looked at the sky, and said under his breath, with feeling, 'It is heavenly.' Back in the room he looked round, found the hammer, and hit the floor hard. While doing so, he mentioned that his canary, the one that was left, was coming home and he was looking forward to that. (The bird had been at his nurse's house, who, as mentioned previously, lived with her husband in the neighbourhood and whom he frequently saw.)

*Mrs K.* interpreted that he had intended by his hammering to open the floor, to take out the dead babies, and to find the live ones, the bird which was coming home.

Richard went to the piano, which had been turned to the wall, and on which a number of things had been put, and said he would like to try to play. In the course of his analysis, Richard had occasionally looked at the piano, but until then he had only once opened it and played a few notes (Fifth Session). Now he attempted to open it and asked whether Mrs K. could help him to move it and to take the things off the lid. She did so. There was a big Union

Jack in the corner by the piano. Richard said that he was going to keep an eye on it, meaning that it might fall down. He first very hesitantly played on the piano with one finger only, then he stopped again. He said it was dusty. Could Mrs K. help him dust it? She did so, and he tried playing again, looking sad, and said that he had forgotten the sonatas he knew; then he tried something else, fetched a chair, sat down and played some harmonies of his own. He said, in a low voice, that he used to do this a lot. After a while he asked whether Mrs K. would play something, and she did so. Richard was very pleased, went back to the piano and, again trying some harmonies, said, under his breath, that this would be a great pleasure when he went home. He opened the top of the piano and asked Mrs K. to touch the keys while he looked 'inside'. He suddenly became aware of the word he had used and, glancing at Mrs K. significantly, said, 'Again the inside'. Then he hit the keyboard with his elbow and trod hard on the pedals. He seized the Union Jack, enveloped himself in it and noisily sang the National Anthem. His face was flushed, he was shouting and was trying to counteract anger and hostility by loyalty. He looked out of the window, saw the old man opposite, and said, 'There is the Bear.' After a pause he asked whether Mr Smith had passed. So far he had paid hardly any attention to passers-by, but now tension and suspicion had set in and he began to watch out for them.

*Mrs K.* interpreted the piano as standing for her inside, as Richard himself had recognized, and his playing on it stood for putting his genital into hers and for caressing her with his hands, as he had done earlier with the clock. In this way he felt he was reviving the killed babies—the black flies, which were now represented by the black keys of the piano. The nice sounds stood for the voices of the babies whom Richard liked, the 'sweet' babies he had occasionally spoken of. The fact that the clock and his watch were going meant that Mrs K. and Mummy were alive, together with their babies, inside himself. He soon became afraid of Mr K., Mr Smith, and the 'Bear' across the road, actually the bad Daddy on whom he had kept an eye, as he had said about the Union Jack when he began to play; at the same time he felt watched by the hostile external Daddy and the Daddy inside Mummy. That was why at one point he stopped playing and began to hit the piano with his elbow; then the fight inside Mummy and inside Mrs K. had begun again. (After Mrs K. had interpreted this, Richard's restlessness diminished and he seemed less anxious to watch the passers-by.) Mrs K. continued her interpretation. She said that Richard was also afraid of having painful feelings stirred up when he played. The piano, which he actually loved—he had said it would be a great pleasure to play again when he got home—stood for the loved but silenced Mummy. He was constantly afraid that she might die (Note II). This fear was increased by the dangers of the war, and the fear of bombs which might destroy Mrs K. when she went to London.

Richard asked Mrs K. to help him move back the piano. He opened his suitcase and wrote in his diary the usual few short notes: that he had been to Mrs K., that he had played with her, that the R.A.F. had made an attack. He showed her what he had written.

*Mrs K.* interpreted that in making these notes he had left out two things which meant much to him. One was that he had cycled past Mrs K.'s lodgings the previous night and that he had enjoyed cycling; the second was that he had, after a long time, again tried to play the piano and this had given him pleasure and hope. He had not mentioned these events in his diary because, though they meant much to him, he was also very much afraid that they might turn out to be bad since he did not trust the goodness of his feelings. Although he treated his diary as secret and showed it only to Mrs K., he did not in fact write anything private in it; but he would have liked to do so and therefore he spoke of it as being secret.

Richard showed Mrs K. some photographs he had taken. Among them was a landscape taken at sunset with a cloudy sky. Richard particularly stressed that he liked this photograph and that the clouds came out well in it.[1] Then he said that he would like to take a snapshot of Mrs K., and she agreed to it. Suddenly he came across a negative of what he called a 'failure'. He asked for Mrs K.'s pen-knife and—becoming more and more aggressive—cut up the negative into tiny bits, took some of them into his mouth, spat them out and wondered whether they were poisoned. He had also made a little mark on the table with the knife.

*Mrs K.* interpreted the 'failure' as his fear that by taking a snapshot of her he might be taking her into himself not as a friend but as an enemy because she contained the bad and poisonous Daddy-genital. Moreover, his cutting up the negative into little bits showed that he was afraid of his own devouring and greedy wishes. Therefore he might not be able to preserve her. The snapshot meant taking her into his inside; this was shown by his taking some of the cut-up negative into his mouth and then trying to get rid of it by spitting it out. The 'failure' had been in the same envelope as the

[1] As I have mentioned earlier, Richard had begun to like clouds, whereas formerly he had only liked a cloudless sky. I attach particular significance to the fact that his idealization—the light-blue Mummy, the cloudless sky—had diminished and that he was more able to recognize both in his mother and in nature features which were not only pleasant.

snapshot of the landscape which he liked so much and which represented the good Mummy. He was afraid that if he cut up and destroyed Daddy's genital inside Mummy, and the bad Hitler-genital inside Mrs K., then he would injure them too. When he marked the table (which often had stood for Mrs K.) this showed that he felt doubtful about being able to keep Mrs K. unhurt. . . .

During this session Richard had repeatedly hammered the floor very hard and also poured a good deal of water over the kitchen floor. Before leaving he asked Mrs K. if she was going to the grocer's and seemed relieved that she was not. He was quiet on the road but did not appear unhappy. He mentioned that he had made inquiries as to which conductress was going to be on his bus that day (he was going home) and was pleased that it would not be the one who made him stand up; nevertheless, this seemed to him less worrying than it had been previously.[1]

*Notes to Eighty-first Session:*

I. Considering that the approaching end of the analysis, together with his father's illness, put Richard under very great strain, it is remarkable that he managed to deal with it in the way he did. At the beginning of his analysis he had been afraid of going out by himself, even in day-time. Now he was enterprising enough to borrow a bicycle and go about on it in the evening. It also shows great restraint that he was able to pass my house without attempting to see me.

II. It had become clear that Richard's inhibition in playing the piano was the result of the piano having come to stand symbolically for his mother's inside and his sexual relation with her; I would not doubt that it linked with his masturbation phantasies. His regret about having given up music, which he loved, was connected also with his concern about the 'silent piano'; the piano which he neglected standing for the neglected and silent—i.e. dead—mother. By playing the piano he would revive her; but at the same time he felt in danger of expressing his wish for sexual relations with her and therefore of being punished by his father. This instance throws some light on the inhibition of sublimations.

---

[1] He was always looking out for protective women and, as mentioned before, he always managed to find them. No doubt the fear of injuring his mother and me, which he had experienced strongly during this session, increased his need for a friendly woman—the good conductress.

## EIGHTY-SECOND SESSION (Friday)

Detailed notes for this session are missing. It was possible to a certain extent to reconstruct the essence of what happened on that day, partly by relying on memory, and partly by deductions from the material of the sessions following and preceding it.

Richard was in a state of strong anxiety and very difficult to control. He hammered the floor forcefully and spilled a lot of water in the kitchen; he had also been cutting the table with his knife. There had already been a good deal of this in the Eighty-first Session, but his obviously violent feelings following the piano-playing had still been up to a point restrained. Now they were much more strongly expressed. In the present session he again asked for a change of times, which Mrs K. could not arrange. This aroused a great sense of grievance in him, as well as rage and despair. He became so violent that Mrs K. had to restrain him and also, at one point, became impatient with him which, being unusual, frightened him very much.

The contents of his suitcase played an important role. He had bought a lobster to take home, and this lobster appeared as a doubtful object in the analysis. First he spoke of it as a delectable food, looking forward to eating it, but soon he seemed to get angry with it and attacked it violently with his knife.

*Mrs K.* interpreted that the lobster was linked with the octopus of the earlier sessions which he (the suitcase representing his inside) as well as Mrs K. and Mummy contained. When he forcefully hammered the floor, that meant breaking it open and taking out from his mother his father's bad penis; it also expressed his distrust and anger towards the analyst who had turned into the 'brute'-Mummy—particularly after having shown impatience.

## EIGHTY-THIRD SESSION (Saturday)

Richard was again waiting at the corner of the road. He glanced furtively at Mrs K. She said that she had been able after all to re-arrange his times. Richard seemed pleased, but still did not look at her. He said he had planned an 'excursion' and was going to climb one of the higher hills with John Wilson and John's friend. In the playroom, Richard opened his suitcase and said that the lobster had disappeared, but at once added that this was only a story, the lobster was still in the case, together with the photographs, his camera, and the other things.

*Mrs K.* pointed out that Richard hardly dared to look at her. He seemed to be terrified because of the previous session. Probably he felt that she had changed into the 'wicked brute' by being impatient with him.

Richard said sarcastically, 'Hitler said, "My patience is exhausted." '

*Mrs K.* interpreted that she had, in his mind, completely changed into Hitler. He felt that she contained Hitler, therefore he was attempting all the more to break up the floor and cut the table, in order to cut out Hitler. What he had said about the lobster on the previous day had shown that he felt it was inside himself and Mrs K. and was linked with the octopus-Daddy, while at the same time he wished it to be a good and edible genital. But he had great doubts of its goodness and therefore he had just now said that it had disappeared, though it actually was in his suitcase. The lobster being in the case together with the nice photograph of the landscape meant that Richard contained both the good Mummy and the bad Daddy-genital. When Richard compared Mrs K. with Hitler, he meant that she was only pretending to be 'sweet' and 'light blue' by keeping calm and not showing anger; but he had always suspected this and expected her, as he did with his mother, to feel angry when he himself felt furious, biting and attacking her. Therefore, he had so often asked her, as he asked his mother, whether he had hurt her feelings.

Richard said he now wished to take Mrs K.'s photograph in the garden, as had been arranged. He asked her to smile, and looked at her in a friendly way. After he had taken the photograph, he asked Mrs K. to look at his shoelaces, to make sure they were tight and would not come undone. At this point he had become distinctly and genuinely friendly with Mrs K. and mentioned with some concern that aliens had now to register. (He had never accepted the fact that Mrs K. was a British subject, although this was well known to him.) He added that this could not apply to Mrs K. since she was over age; then he said seriously and with feeling that she had important work to do anyhow, she had to take care of her patients.

*Mrs K.* had a look at Richard's shoelaces and interpreted that he wanted to take the smiling, 'sweet', 'light-blue' Mrs K. into himself and to keep her safe there for ever; but he needed her assurance that he could really keep her as a friend.

Richard began to scribble (Drawing 67).[1] While scribbling, he spoke of the sweet Mrs K. and said that she was underneath the scribble.

*Mrs K.* asked where; she seemed to be in little bits (Note I).

Richard said yes, she was, and he unhesitatingly pointed out Mrs K.'s face (*a*), her breasts (*b* and *c*), her legs (*d* and *e*) and 'V' for Victory (*f*). Suddenly looking at Mrs K.'s finger, he asked whether it was bleeding. (It was neither hurt nor bleeding.) Then he asked whether there had been any raids by the R.A.F.

*Mrs K.* interpreted that Richard himself represented the R.A.F. and that he had bombed and torn the German Hitler-Mrs K. to pieces. He was pretending that he liked her and that she was sweet, but he triumphed over her being destroyed—hence 'V' for Victory. He had expressed his rage about Mrs K. not having agreed in the previous session to give him the change of times he wanted. He felt about that as he did when Mummy took away the breast and he suspected her of giving it to Paul or to Daddy. Richard's sudden idea that Mrs K.'s finger was bleeding expressed his fear that her breasts had been bleeding because he had destroyed them by biting.

Richard had meanwhile been drawing (68). He leaned forward, looking into Mrs K.'s eyes, and said that she had such lovely eyes. (This sounded entirely false and artificial.) After saying this, Richard added the penis on the drawing and asked Mrs K. what the 'tops of the breasts' (meaning the nipples) were called.

*Mrs K.* interpreted that her tummy was also a face—actually Hitler's—inside her, and that the penis he had added seemed to be Hitler's.

Richard was surprised; he said he had not realized this at all, but he agreed. He then scribbled on three more pages (of which I am reproducing only one, Drawing 69); his rage was increasing, his face was red and his eyes flashing; from time to time he ground his teeth and bit the pencil hard, particularly when talking about breasts or drawing circles representing them. He tore one page after another from the pad. A few times he asked whether Mrs K. had seen the 'nice' Mr Smith; then he put the same questions about Mrs K.'s son and grandson that he had asked so often before. He also asked her whether she could speak Austrian—another of his frequent questions. About one of the scribbles he said that it was also Mrs K. and that she was in bits. In Drawing 69 he pointed out that (*a*) was Mrs K.'s 'lovely eyes', (*b*) her nose, (*c*) her tummy and her breast, and (*d*) the other breast. The third scribble he described as a code letter from Bomber Command, thanking Fighter Command

[1] In this and the following drawings I have indicated the parts referred to by inserting (*a*), (*b*), (*c*), and so on.

for having won the Battle of Britain. This letter consisted of dots and dashes, and had a number of 'V's for Victory.

*Mrs K.* interpreted that Richard was thanking somebody for helping him to beat and destroy Mrs K., the foreign, hostile 'brute'-Mummy.

Richard did not reply but drew 70 and said the line at the top (*c*) was directed against Mrs K.

*Mrs K.* reminded Richard that he had previously drawn (63) a similar shape which he had called a banana and which represented the big genital (his own and Daddy's); in the present drawing, the line which came out of the banana-shaped genital (*a*) and was directed against Mrs K. meant an attack on her with the genital. In the 'darling' (*b*) there was also a banana-shape, which meant the dangerous Daddy-genital inside Mrs K. and Mummy. The lobster which Richard kept in his case, standing for his inside, was used to fight the bad Mummy containing Hitler. The powerful lobster- and octopus-genital in his inside which he used in his fight was the same as Fighter Command, which was thanked by Bomber Command, standing for another part of Richard, for its help.

Richard made another drawing and said that it was 'X'. He pointed to a small square and said that it was Mr Evans's shop. There were other squares next to it which also represented shops. He mentioned that Mr Evans had given him some sweets and they were very nice. A railway, indicated by lines, ran past the shop.

*Mrs K.* asked about some rounded scribbles by the side of the train.

Richard made no reply.

*Mrs K.* suggested that these were the bombs dropped by him on the train in which Mrs K. was leaving, taking away the sweets—her work with him—which stood for the first sweets, Mummy's breast, which he had also lost. When Richard had been deprived of Mummy's breast, and on later occasions whenever he felt dissatisfied, he turned to the 'nice' Mr Smith, the 'nice' Mr Evans, who stood for Daddy's attractive genital. He had felt attracted to it as he did to the lovely lobster. But since he also hated and envied Daddy's genital, it turned in his mind into an enemy inside him and he used it as a hostile weapon against Mummy (Note II). Therefore he felt that his love for Mummy and for Mrs K., and his love for Daddy and his genital, was insincere and that he was a 'rascal'.

Richard now made Drawing 71 and said that there was a full moon (*a*), a quarter moon (*b*), and an aeroplane (*c*), from which he was shooting at the moon.

*Mrs K.* interpreted that the full moon was herself and the quarter moon was Mr K.'s genital inside her. The full moon was also her breast and tummy, and Richard was shooting at both her and Mr K. together.

Richard had been scribbling and said that it was a train going through a station.

*Mrs K.* interpreted the train as Daddy's genital inside Mummy. Richard's anger was all the time directed against the treacherous and dangerous alliance between Mummy and Daddy. He felt that she contained Daddy and in the same way he felt that Mrs K. contained Hitler (Note III).

Richard made another scribble and said, 'This is the train on which Mrs K. is going to travel.' His growing rage and despair were expressed in his face and movements, and while scribbling he violently made some dots. Then he made Drawing 72 and said that (*a*) was again the train on which Mrs K. was going to travel; the shapes of which the train was made up were compartments. He showed the one Mrs K. was in (*b*) and said that he was bombing the train. For a little while he was careful, when making the dots, to avoid the compartment in which Mrs K. was travelling, but he did not manage this and in the end, getting into a real frenzy, said the whole train was bombed and destroyed. He jumped up and kicked and trampled on the stools. When stamping on one he said it was Mrs K. He took up one end of a long, heavy tent-pole, let it fall on the floor, hammered the stools with the hammer, again took up the pole, said that he was shooting Mr Smith with it, and spoke of shooting Hitler.

*Mrs K.* asked where Hitler was standing when Richard shot him.

Richard, without hesitation, said Hitler was where Mrs K. was standing now.

*Mrs K.* interpreted the stools as her son and grandson and patients, whom Richard was shooting and bombing because Mrs K. was joining them. She also said that Richard was in such despair because he was afraid of Mrs K. actually being bombed in London and of his being unable to prevent it. Since he felt that he could not save her, he had to attack and destroy her (Note IV), actually the bad Daddy-genital inside her.

At this point Richard's attitude changed strikingly. He went into the kitchen, chose the two white buckets, drew water, and said that he was getting his milk and it looked very nice. He watched Mrs K. empty the buckets, which had not been quite filled, and asked her to go outside with him. He looked round, jumped from the steps into the middle of the vegetable bed without damaging the plants, and now seemed quite composed and friendly. On leaving, he spoke about the conductress who was going to be on the bus; it was the one he liked, who did not say 'half fares stand up'. He mentioned that the bus might be crowded, but did not seem very worried about it. Then he asked whether the old man on the other side of the road (the 'Bear') was the 'grumpy old gentleman' whom he would so much like to see. Earlier on, when Richard had been in a state of rage, he had hardly looked outside.

*Notes to Eighty-third Session:*

I. The reasons for putting that question were twofold : looking at the drawing, it occurred to me that if I was underneath, I could only be there in bits. Moreover, Richard's state of mind in the last two sessions, in which the need to tear out bits of me was expressed in his attempts to break open the floor—and his increased urethral attacks were shown by pouring much more water than he used to—had given me the feeling that he had regressed to the attempts of young children who are unable to draw a complete figure, for complex reasons, such as lack of skill, lack of integration, and feelings of guilt about having torn to bits the mother's breast and the mother.

But there was more to it. Both persecutory feelings and resentment contributed very strongly to Richard's attacks on me. As can be seen from his reply, he also triumphed over me because the 'V' for Victory in this case was the victory over me, whom he had torn into bits. The regression to early attacks by tearing, biting up, and the corresponding persecutory anxieties, were therefore used in order to get away from depression and despair. I have pointed out generally speaking that the incapacity to cope with the depressive position often leads to a regression to the earlier paranoid-schizoid one.

II. This is an issue which is of great importance in normal and abnormal development. The infant turns his desires from the breast to some extent to the father's penis. If hate and envy of the mother's breast and resentment against it are very strong, the attraction to the father's penis leads to a failure both in homosexuality and heterosexuality. For the hate and envy against the mother are transferred on to the father's penis, and thus the relation to him is disturbed, and homosexuality becomes partly a means of fighting the mother in alliance with a hostile father. If the turning away from the mother's breast to the father's penis occurs with less hate and resentment, the relation to the father and to the mother develops more favourably and the adult is later able to have good relations with men as well as with women (see my *Psycho-Analysis of Children,* Chapter XII).

III. I have pointed out the importance of the combined parent figure, operative in the earliest stages of development, in *The Psycho-Analysis of Children* (see also Note I to Twenty-fifth Session). This figure had remained very strong in Richard's mind, indicating the persistence of his earliest anxieties and phantasies, and proved to be a very important source of his distrust of both his parents and of men and women in general. There is a connection between the strength of the combined parent figure in the child's phantasy and the strength of his internalization of a dangerous and treacherous father-genital which leads to the feeling of an alliance against the mother.

IV. The previous night there had been a B.B.C. broadcast about the Battle of Britain : Richard's letter from one Command thanking the other was stimulated by this. His fear and concern about the dangers awaiting me in London were obviously much increased by the news of renewed air activity. It became very clear that his incapacity to put right or revive his injured or dead loved objects changed them into persecutors. His strong sense of guilt about his dangerous hate and jealousy made him feel completely responsible for the analyst's expected death; the sorrow about this, together with his guilt, were unbearable, and therefore his feelings of hate and persecution were increased. At the same time, he tried to build up and preserve internally the good mother—the photograph of me which he had taken. It was striking how this hope, relating to the internalized good object, was split off from the attitude towards me as an external object when he began to scribble and his rage increased. (In my 'Contribution to the Psychogenesis of Manic-Depressive States', 1935, *Writings*, 1, I came to the conclusion that aggression and persecutory anxiety can be increased in order to avoid depression—a regression from the depressive position to the paranoid-schizoid one.)

His concern about my having to register was quite genuine. But immediately afterwards he gave full vent in his drawings to his aggressiveness and attacks on me, my family, and my patients, and to the rage about my leaving him. The equivalent of the emotions expressed in the drawings would have been a tantrum, of which he had had many as a young child. I believe that tantrums always contain despair as well, because, while the rage and attacks go on, the child feels that he is more and more irreparably destroying the loved person, particularly his internalized one. It was striking how, after the material reported, Richard's attitude changed completely. I have remarked on how he split love and hate, internal and external situations, for example in his wish to preserve me internally and the wish to destroy me externally. During the part of the session when he had been drawing in rage and despair, he had also tried to keep up some love for the external me; but it was striking how artificial and insincere the expression of his love feelings had become. While he was speaking of the 'sweet' Mrs K., of my 'lovely eyes', and so on, he was at the same time destroying me in the drawing. He spoke of the 'lovely' lobster, though it had become clear that he thought it to be a dangerous and suspect object. His expression of love for me was very similar to the sarcastic way in which, according to Richard's mother, he behaved towards some women, being most pleasing to them and even flattering, and making fun of them when they were not present. I had never seen Richard so insincere in his professions of love towards me as in this session. This insincerity was bound up with the material referring to the penis internalized by his mother and by himself. Richard first said that the lobster in his suitcase was a good object which he coveted, but he soon suspected and hated it, and it became a dangerous weapon against the hated mother who also contained the bad father, though Richard at the same time pretended to love her. This process is, I think, of importance for character-formation in general. The need to appease the mother, whom the son feels he has robbed of the good father's penis, and the alliance with the internal father against her, are bound to lead to an unconscious dishonesty and insincerity. Richard's love was genuine when his predominant attitude was to protect me against the bad father, or when he himself felt persecuted by the internal father and expected protection from me. He became artificial and insincere when he felt he possessed the powerful penis with which he would ally himself in a hostile and dangerous way against me. In this situation there is also a deep insincerity in connection with the father, for the internalized penis which was coveted as a good object turns bad when the father becomes a hostile ally against the mother.

## EIGHTY-FOURTH SESSION (Monday)

Richard was waiting at the corner of the road. He looked subdued and depressed. He said that there was not going to be an excursion (see previous session), because John Wilson had decided against it. He was very disappointed about this and was silent for some time after he sat down in the playroom. He looked at Mrs K. appealingly, said that he did not wish to hear any more unpleasant things and, glancing at his wrist, discovered that he had not brought his watch. He looked again at Mrs K. and said he liked her very much and liked her eyes. He said, after a pause, that the lobster was horrid; he had eaten a bit of it, but had spat it out; then he repeated that it was horrid. Suddenly he leaned his head for a moment on Mrs K.'s shoulder and said he liked her very much and she had a nice jacket on. He was clearly struggling very strongly against his depression.

*Mrs K*. pointed out that Richard felt very guilty about the attacks on her during the previous session. In his mind they might have had the effect of killing her and thus Richard would have felt he was losing her forever. She reminded him of the train in which she was bombed and destroyed, and of the other drawings, made in a rage, in which she was cut up and in bits. Mrs K. suggested that Richard felt that when she left him, the nice, light-blue Mummy would disappear, and that he would not be able to keep her alive inside himself because of his anger and jealousy. Then all that he would be left with in his inside would be the lobster, which was meant to be attractive and desirable, but which turned out to be bad and dangerous because Richard had attacked it with his knife; eating the lobster made it even more into an internal enemy. The lobster stood, as the octopus had done, for his father's genital, attacked by Richard through biting and eating it. In his mind, Mrs K. too had such an enemy inside her—the nasty Hitler-genital.

Richard went into the kitchen and drew water. He said that there was plenty for all the children. He filled all the buckets but soon made a mess by pouring water over the floor; this time, however, Mrs K. was able to restrain him from flooding the kitchen, and Richard watched her very carefully to see whether she was annoyed or not. He had also opened all the doors of the stove and put his hand into the soot.

*Mrs K.* interpreted that he was exploring her inside to find out whether or not it was full of the bad bombing 'big job' which he felt he had put into her in the previous session. The kitchen, with the mess which he made there, also stood for her body into which he poured his 'little job'. At the same time, he wanted to test whether Mrs K. would remain friendly, in spite of such attacks and in spite of having to clean up the mess.

Richard, after Mrs K. had wiped the floor, went back into the playroom and played with Mrs K.'s bunch of keys, making the smaller key walk and dance with the larger one. He said that it was Mrs K. and himself. He accompanied the dance by humming some pleasant tunes, but followed this by making the keys jump about while he sang noisily and pulled faces. Earlier he had referred to such grimaces, saying they made him look like Hitler. He remarked on two boys on the road and said that they were 'impudent'; one had looked at him in an 'impudent' way when he met him earlier on. Then he picked up the wooden pole and with some effort held it crosswise over his genital, dropped it, and said that he was shooting at Hitler with it.

*Mrs K.* interpreted that he was using here the internalized Hitler-genital which appeared to grow out of his own—the pole put across his genital—to attack the bad external Hitler-genital represented by the impudent boy. He very much wanted to be alone with the nice Mummy and the nice Mrs K. and to love them; the two keys dancing together inside the keyring stood for Richard inside Mrs K. as well as for her inside him. But he felt that the bad Hitler inside Mrs K. and himself would interfere and attack them, and disturb their nice dance and their loving each other. His greatest fear was that he could not control his own hate and anger, and that made him depressed and anxious.

In this session there had been very long breaks in which Richard was silent; sometimes he got up and walked about and then sat down again, struggling all the time with his depression and later on with his anger. He became more lively during the play with the keys which, however, did not last long, since the 'Hitler-faces' he made showed that he felt full of the bad father and of his own aggressiveness, which would interfere with and disturb the relation with Mrs K. and with his mother.

## EIGHTY-FIFTH SESSION (Tuesday)

Richard was in a friendly and responsive mood, much less depressed. He soon got hold of the keys, and various activities with them went on while he was speaking to Mrs K. He made the larger and smaller key walk together within the ring, which moved with them, and again said that this was Mrs K. and himself, going for walks together. Then he spoke of the recent R.A.F. raids. He took the little key off the ring and made it walk by itself.

*Mrs K.* interpreted that she and Richard were together and went off together to London, but he suddenly became afraid of the attacks on London and wanted to get away : that was why he had taken the little key off the ring and made it walk away by itself. Moreover, he took himself out of Mrs K. because the ring also stood for her body, with Richard inside her. But he also felt that it stood for Richard's body with Mrs K. inside him.

Richard mentioned that he had been cycling on the previous evening all over the village and he intended to go climbing with John and his friend next day after all. Could Mrs K. alter his time? He made the two keys, which he had taken off the ring, dance with each other while he hummed snatches of classical music (Note I).

*Mrs K.* interpreted that he had taken the keys off the ring because he wanted to have her company as an external object—the two keys dancing together, which also expressed his desire to put his genital into Mrs K.'s (Note II). This was shown by his increased pleasure in cycling and climbing, which represented a sexual relation; and the melodies he hummed showed that Richard felt more confident that this relation would be a good one and that he would not hurt his genital nor harm Mrs K., because there was no fight involved in it (Note III). Going climbing with other boys also stood for sharing Mrs K. with her family and other patients, and sharing Mummy with Daddy and Paul. Then he would not have to fight his rivals, either externally or within Mummy's genital.

Richard had begun to watch the passers-by and was more tense and on guard. He told Mrs K. that he had nearly had an accident with his bicycle, he was almost run over by a car. One man in the car called out to him to warn him, and there were also other men in the car.

*Mrs K.* interpreted that at the beginning he felt he could have a nice sexual relation with her and with Mummy, and find out all about her inside, but had soon become frightened of Daddy. When in his mind he put his genital into Mrs K. and explored her and Mummy's insides, this had seemed pleasant and without danger a moment ago, but already it appeared to be disturbed by the dangerous Mr K. or Daddy—the man in the car which nearly ran him over.

Richard replied that the men in the car were Mr K., Mr Smith, the 'grumpy old gentleman', Paul, and Daddy. Then he asked where Mrs K. had been going to when he met her the night before —had she been going home and why had she walked along that particular road? (He had met Mrs K. in the village on the previous evening when he was cycling, but had made no attempt to stop her.)

*Mrs K.* asked where he thought she had been going.

Richard wondered whether she might have been to see Mr Smith. Then he remembered that Mr Smith did not live in that direction.

*Mrs K.* interpreted that Richard was always worried that Mummy, whom he wished to have entirely to himself, was not alone with him because in his mind she contained Daddy; and Richard never knew whether it was the bad or the good Daddy. Now, with Mrs K., he did not know whether it was the Hitler-genital or the good Mr K.-genital she contained.

Richard, while Mrs K. was interpreting, had put the two keys back on the ring and made them move inside it.

*Mrs K.* interpreted this as Richard's curiosity about what was inside her and his fear of the dangers he would meet there.

Richard spoke about the bus ride home. He was going to travel with his favourite conductress. It appeared now that all of them had to say 'half fears stand up' if the bus was full, but he still liked this one best. He told Mrs K. their names and described them. There was the pretty one, then the not-so-pretty but not-ugly one—that was the one he liked best. Then there was another one with a 'painted face'.

*Mrs K.* suggested that the conductress he liked stood also for Nurse. When he felt uncertain and suspicious about Mummy, he had turned to Nurse, who at that time was not married, which meant she had no husband as Mummy had. The pretty conductress stood for Mummy, who was prettier than Nurse; but there was a time when Richard loved Nurse more than Mummy, and he felt guilty about that.

Richard said that Nurse was quite pretty—not at all ugly. He had seen her on the previous day when he changed buses on his journey home, and she had given him some sweets. (He now seemed to realize how fond he still was of her.) He said that Mrs K. was not the one with the 'painted face'; she was very pretty too, but not as pretty as Mummy. Then he asked whether Mrs K. felt hurt.

*Mrs K.* suggested that she represented a mixture of Mummy and Nurse.

Richard said that he had had a dream which was frightening but thrilling at the same time. A few nights before he also had a dream about two people putting their genitals together. He greatly enjoyed reporting the more recent dream and described it vividly and dramatically, sounding sinister at the frightening points, while at the climax his eyes were shining, and happiness and hope were expressed on his face. *He saw Mrs K. standing at the bus stop in the village where the bus leaves for 'Y'. But the bus was going to some other place; in the dream it went to 'Y' only once every fortnight. It passed by without stopping.* (Here Richard made vivid noises like the bus passing by.) *Richard ran after it to catch it, but the bus had gone. He went after all, but in a caravan. With him travelled a very happy family. The father and mother were middle-aged; there were quite a lot of children, and all of them were nice. They passed an island. With them was also a very big cat. First the cat bit his dog, but then they got on well together. Then the new cat chased their actual cat, but they also got to like each other. This new cat was not an ordinary cat, but it was very nice. It had teeth like pearls and it was more like a human being.*

*Mrs K.* asked whether it was more like a woman or like a man.

Richard replied it was both like a gentleman and a nice woman. He said *the island was on a river. On the bank of the river the sky was quite black, the trees were black, there was sand which was sand-coloured, but the people were also black. There were all sorts of creatures, birds, animals, scorpions, all black; and all of them, people and creatures, were quite still. It was terrifying.* Richard's face expressed horror and anxiety.

*Mrs K.* asked what the island was like.

Richard said *the island was not quite black, but the water and sky around were. There was a patch of green on the island and the sky over the island showed a little blue. The stillness was terrible. Suddenly Richard called out, 'Ahoy there,' and at that moment everybody and everything became alive. He had broken a spell. They must have been enchanted. People began to sing; the scorpions and other creatures jumped back into the water, everybody was overjoyed, everything turned light, the sky became all blue.*

*Mrs K.* asked what happened to her at the bus stop.

Richard said that she was half hidden behind somebody else.

*Mrs K.* asked what sort of person it was.

Richard at first said he did not know. Then he said he thought Mrs K. was hiding behind a man.

*Mrs K.* asked of whom that man reminded him.

Richard said that he was tall and, after a pause, added that he thought the man looked like Daddy. When he began to explain the situation in the dream, he had started to draw.[1] The picture represented the 'human' cat, Richard's dog, his actual cat, the still, black people, the black trees, the island, and the road along which the caravan travelled. While Richard was telling Mrs K. about the people on the island becoming alive, he asked her to pass him the bag with the toys, opened it, and took out first of all the electric train. He looked at the two carriages, turned them round and fixed them together. Then he took the swing out and set it going; he put the swing on top of the train and moved the train, took the swing off again and kept on moving it. He put the goods train together with all the carriages he could find. . . . Richard asked whether Mrs K. would not, after all, come to see him and his family in 'Y'. She must come and see the place. He wished she were going with him at least part of the way; then he could show her where he changed buses. Wasn't she going to come and see them all? Why not? It would be so nice if she came and also met Daddy. He said this with strong feeling.

*Mrs K.* interpreted that the train, to which he had added all the carriages he could find (something he had never done before), meant that Mrs K. and her children became part of his family. This was represented in the dream by the happy family in the caravan with whom he was travelling; it also meant that he had all his loved people in harmony with each other inside him. This included Nurse,

[1] This drawing is unfortunately missing, and I have to reconstruct its content from my notes.

who had until her marriage been a member of his family. That was why he wanted Mrs K. at least to go as far as the village on the way to 'Y' where Nurse lived, so that they could see each other again before Mrs K. left for London. In the dream there was a happy, united family in one part of his mind, but—divided off in another part of his mind—there were the black people and animals, the black scorpions, standing for poisonous 'big job' and genitals. That meant he kept the good and bad people separate from each other in his inside, and he felt that Mrs K. too had such black people inside her because he had put his 'big job' into her when he was jealous and angry. The stove with the soot in it had often stood for her, and when he tried to clean the stove, this meant taking out of Mrs K. and Mummy all the badness and dangerous 'big job', babies, and the black genital. But in his dream he also brought to life all these bad and dead creatures; they became light and the sky became all blue—the light-blue Mummy. On the previous day, the water he had drawn stood for milk, not only for himself, but also for other children whom he wished to feed, keep alive, and love (Note IV). In his play, as often before, the two carriages of the electric train stood for Mummy's breasts, and when the child on the swing was on top of the train, this meant that the baby was being fed. His wish to bring together Mrs K. and her family with his family also implied that there would be no separation from her and therefore no reason for fear, hate, and jealousy. Then both the external and internal Mrs K. and Mummy could be preserved.

Richard's mood had changed strikingly after he had reported the dream. For a while the feelings experienced in the dream seemed to persist, and he enjoyed the pleasure of having described it so vividly. He said that he was going to tell his dream to everybody, and appeared to have a feeling of achievement. But soon he gave up the play with which he had accompanied his account of the dream; the light went out of his eyes, he looked depressed, absent-minded, and did not appear to listen to the interpretations Mrs K. gave him. He became restless and persecuted.

*Mrs K.* interpreted that he had become afraid that he might, after all, not be able to revive all the black and bad people and make them good, as he had done in the dream, and that he was all the more worried because the session was soon coming to an end and he was going away for the day, and also because Mrs K. was so soon going to leave him. She reminded Richard that he had mentioned another dream at the beginning of the session, and asked what that dream had been about.

Richard had been standing at the window looking out, and now became quite lively again. He seemed pleased to tell his dream.[1] *He saw two people lying together. It was outside 'X', somewhere out of doors. They were quite naked, like Adam and Eve.*

*Mrs K.* asked whether Richard saw their genitals.

Richard said that *he did, they were enormous and it was very unpleasant.*

*Mrs K.* asked what they were like.

Richard said he did not actually know what a woman's genital was like, but in the dream both people's genitals looked like the monster in the book (which was so big that the man in the picture looked like a dwarf in comparison with a giant; Richard had at the time called the monster proud and haughty, and had admired it). Richard did not add anything to this association.

*Mrs K.* interpreted that in his mind the enormous genitals belonging to the parents were equal, and that the little man in the picture, who had been shooting at the monster's eyes, stood for himself, who was trying to attack both the eyes and the genitals of his parents.

Richard, at the end of the session, rolled a little ball from one end of the playroom to the other, saying that this was Mrs K.'s train and she was on it. The ball ran into some parcels which were lying in a corner, and Richard said that this was a buffer, but he seemed doubtful whether the train was harmed or not. He then rolled a big ball after the small one and said that this was Mr Smith following Mrs K.—no, it was himself, following Mrs K. The end of the session had come and he spoke about the arrangements for the excursion on the next day.

*Notes to Eighty-fifth Session:*

I. This illustrates the change from an internal to an external situation, and it is of interest that this change can clearly be recognized if fluctuations in the material are sufficiently understood. Richard's increased interest in climbing and cycling was in keeping with this greater capacity to get away from his constant preoccupation with internal situations and fights. It is significant, as I have pointed out previously, that an external situation often comes into the foreground when internal anxiety situations have been interpreted.

II. Richard had at that point shown a step in development : he was able to feel that he and I, representing his mother, could be together without his internal object or my internal object interfering. A good balance between internal and external situations and relations is of

---

[1] No doubt his having produced a dream meant having been creative and also implied giving a present to the analyst; thereby hope was revived and persecution lessened.

fundamental importance. In Richard's case this meant that the combined parent figure—and his internal persecutors—had at least temporarily lost in power. This was an indication of progress, although I am aware that these changes were not fully established.

III. I have often found that music represents inner harmony, but in the present session this harmony also extended to what Richard felt as a possibility of sexual intercourse without fight. His anxiety that both in the breast relation and in the genital relation he was faced with an internal fight inside the mother's genital, and was watched and persecuted by his own internal persecutor, had diminished; this made for external harmony, represented through a pleasurable and not destructive intercourse. That, too, was expressed by his being able to appreciate music at that moment.

IV. Here we are touching on one of the important anxiety situations inherent in the depressive position. If Richard felt himself to be full of attacked and therefore bad objects (for instance, the dangerous, attacked flies and the lobster) and dangerous excrement, as well as destructive impulses, then the good objects inside him appeared to be endangered. This meant in states of great anxiety that everything inside him was dead. Richard tried to solve this problem by taking out the bad and dangerous elements (the soot). But when he felt more secure, he resorted, as in the dream, to reviving and improving the bad objects. It is interesting that the island had not been altogther black, but that there had been a patch of green and a bit of blue sky in the centre. This centre of goodness, which enabled him to keep hope going, thus represented the good breast, the good analyst, and the good nurse, as well as the good parents, in harmony; and from this core of goodness life and reparation could spread. The play with the train and the baby on the swing had shown that the good baby also stood for regaining and preserving life. (As mentioned before, Richard was extremely fond of young babies and often asked his mother to have a child. When she replied that she was too old, he said that this was nonsense, of course she could have babies, and there is little doubt that he assumed the same of the analyst.)

The good breast as the core of the ego I take to be a fundamental precondition for ego development. Richard had always maintained his belief in the light-blue Mummy. The idealized mother co-existed with the persecutory and suspect one. Nevertheless, idealization was based on a feeling of having internalized the good primal object to some extent, and this was his mainstay in all his anxieties. In the present stage of the analysis, Richard's capacity to integrate the ego and to synthesize the contrasting aspects of his objects had clearly increased and he had become more able, in phantasy, to improve the bad objects and to revive and re-create the dead ones; this, in turn, linked with hate being mitigated by love. In the dream, Richard could also bring the two parents together in a harmonious way.

These processes were, however, not fully successful, as was shown by my being left behind when I was hidden behind the man, which represented Richard's doubts as to whether the union of the parents would actually be good. (This indicated again the combined parent figure.)

## EIGHTY-SIXTH SESSION (Wednesday)

Richard and Mrs K. met at the corner of the road. It was very windy and cold, and Richard remarked on this. He also said that it was a very unusual time to meet. (Mrs K. had arranged to see him rather late in the evening because of the plans he had for the day.) Richard said that they had not gone up the mountain after all because it was raining. Instead, he and John had been to see John's friend. He asked whether Mrs K. minded seeing him at that time; she did not usually see patients at such a late hour, did she? He again did not wait for a reply. Then he said that he had seen the wreckage of a British aeroplane which crashed on the hillside; the pilot was dead.

*Mrs K.* said Richard was more worried about her being inconvenienced because the thought of the wreckage was so much in his mind. He was afraid of the harm which might happen to her and guilty because he felt it to be his doing. When he was angry and frustrated, he had in various ways indicated his wish that Mrs K. should be bombed in London. He was all the more anxious about what might happen to her.

Richard had been sucking and biting the yellow pencil, but now took it out of his mouth. He was silent and sad, and deeply in thought.

*Mrs K.* asked whether Richard was disappointed that the mountain climb had not come off.

Richard replied that it did not matter much; he had had quite a pleasant time even so.

*Mrs K.* asked if they were going to try again another day.

Richard said maybe they were, but he would not go.

*Mrs K.* asked why.

Richard did not reply to that.

*Mrs K.* suggested that it was perhaps because he would have to ask her for another late session.

Richard said no, but it did not sound convincing. He repeated that he did not want to go; it might make him too tired. He had switched on the electric fire and delighted in the warmth it gave out. He said, pointing to it, that this was the good Mummy who was giving such nice warmth.

*Mrs K.* interpreted Richard's desire to keep her, standing for the good Mummy, alive outside and inside; and when she gave out warmth, that proved that she was alive. Mrs K. referred to the dream in the previous session and pointed out that the patch of green on the island and the bit of blue sky meant that he kept some of the good Mummy and the good breast inside him alive. She reminded him of the empire drawings, with the light blue in the centre, and that he had once said that the light blue was spreading and gaining more countries in the empire, which stood for his inside and Mummy's. Such hopes were the reason why the dream had made him so happy.

Richard strongly agreed and seemed very glad about this interpretation. He said that Mrs K. liked him to listen attentively to what she said, didn't she? He added that he was listening very well today and hearing every word she said, and he had done so on the previous day as well. He was again strongly sucking the pencil. He said he wanted to draw something, but began to wonder what he would draw. (This was very unusual since he hardly ever hesitated when he began to draw.) Then he said that he knew what was best to draw, and very deliberately drew the bus going home.

*Mrs K.* then asked after his father, since Richard had not mentioned him.

Richard replied that he was not very well, he was tired; but on the whole he was getting on satisfactorily. Richard looked worried and sad while he told this. In the drawing a little man was ready to get into a bus; the picture also showed the driver, the 'painted face' conductress, and the empty seat in the centre of the bus which was the one Richard was going to occupy. The aeroplane overhead was flying low over the bus. Richard said he thought the bus looked rickety. Then he spoke about the three conductresses. This time he said he liked them all, they were all very nice to him. Then he mentioned the very pretty one and repeated that she too was very nice to him.

*Mrs K.* referred to her former interpretation that the three conductresses stood for Mother, Nurse, and herself. Richard wished to keep them all friendly, and to think of them as nice to him, particularly because he was sad and worried about Mrs K. leaving.

Richard asked how many days were left. (He knew the date quite well.)

*Mrs K.* reminded him of his having described the bus as 'rickety', and she connected this with the wreckage he had seen that morning.

She pointed out Richard's fear that Mrs K. was old and she reminded him of what he had felt about his granny's death.

Richard asked what Mrs K. was going to do in the evening, was
she going to read or play the piano, or was she going to listen to the
wireless?

*Mrs K.* asked what did he want her to do.

Richard replied that he liked to think that she was sitting by the
fire, listening-in or reading; and what was the 'grumpy old gentleman' doing in the evenings? Then he pointed at an old man who
was passing and asked if that was he.

*Mrs K.* said no, and interpreted Richard's concern that she might
not have the kind of quiet evening he had wished her to have, because the 'grumpy old gentleman' stood for a bad Mr K. or Mr
Smith, who might be there with Mrs K. and injure and disturb her,
or worry her inside.

Richard asked what would Mrs K. say if he came to see her in
the evening? Would she speak to him, or would she not like it? If
he were in serious trouble, would Mrs K. mind if he came to see
her?

*Mrs K.* asked what serious trouble he meant.

Richard asked whether, if he had nowhere to go, Mrs K. would
keep him there and help him. He was very insistent on getting a
direct answer and again and again begged Mrs K. to say whether
she would help him.

*Mrs K.* said that his fear that he would have nowhere to go
meant that he was afraid of losing his home; if Daddy turned him
out or died, he wondered if Mummy would be on his side and keep
him. If Daddy died, Mummy would feel lonely, and he wondered
what she would then do in the evenings. It seemed that while he
was sad and worried about his father's illness, he was also beginning
to be afraid of the ill or dead father, because the dead father, as had
often been seen, might turn into a hostile ghost and worry Mummy.
Because of all these fears Richard wanted to make sure that Mrs K.
would help and protect him.

Richard said that he would wish to kill Hitler and that only the
bad German people liked him, and Mrs K. was naturalized so she
was not German any more. He went outside, looking at the clouds
and said the sky was 'wild'. He pulled a scab off on his arm and it
began to bleed. He said that he liked sucking his blood and that he
had tasted it from his hanky. It was healthy red, wasn't it? He
seemed worried at having lost some blood and again wanted to
know whether it was healthy blood.

*Mrs K*. interpreted that he felt that he had killed the Hitler-Daddy inside him and now did not know whether his blood was his own or Hitler's, whether it was good or bad blood he had been losing. Mrs K. referred again to the dream of Adam and Eve and asked about the positions in which they were lying.

Richard replied, 'They were lying on their backs and cuddling; they were nice.'

*Mrs K*. reminded him that he had called it 'awful' on the previous day, and that the thought about what Daddy and Mummy would do with their genitals was so painful and frightening to him that he wanted to think about it as something nice, but had not been able to do so.

Richard protested. He said that his parents could not have sexual relations because they had had no child for so many years. He again went outside, looked round and spoke about the scenery. Back in the room he said about the drawing that the two guns of the aeroplane were pointing upwards and that they were Mummy's breasts, feeding the children.

*Mrs K*. interpreted that this showed he was thinking of the breasts, not as light blue and good, but as dangerous and as being guns.

In this session Richard was continually attempting to keep everything good. He had therefore corrected the Adam and Eve dream. He was at times very silent and deeply in thought; there were long breaks, but his affection and tenderness towards Mrs K., though not expressed in words, came out again and again. His consistent wish to please her showed in the way in which he listened and tried to draw and to cooperate in the analysis as much as possible. He also restrained his concern and his fear about the aeroplane which had crashed, in order not to worry her. During this session he had repeated and strongly expressed his wish to kill Hitler, so as to protect her. He had quite clearly refused to go climbing with the other boys next time, in order not to ask Mrs K. to see him at a later hour. Also, during the whole session, the feeling of something unusual, even uncanny, because of the late time and the storm and rain, seemed present in Richard. He listened again and again to the wind with a mixture of thrill and fear. At one time during this session Richard had made a drawing of himself with very long legs.

## EIGHTY-SEVENTH SESSION (Thursday)

Richard was waiting for Mrs K. at the corner of the road. He repeated that he had decided not to go mountain-climbing with the others as it would make him tired. But he looked disappointed. Suddenly he said that he had a toothache, but at once tried to deny this by adding that it would pass. After a little while he said the tooth was still aching. Would Mrs K. promise not to tell Mummy about it? He was afraid that if she did, his tooth would be pulled out. He was very worried about the toothache, though he said that the pain was quite slight. He touched his gums repeatedly, and tried to comfort himself by telling Mrs K. that it was not an old tooth but a growing one which was hurting him. Then again he said that it must be a tooth decaying; but his second teeth were nice.

*Mrs K.* interpreted that Richard refused to go mountain-climbing, not only because he did not want to ask for a late session, but also because his toothache linked with his fears about his genital. For climbing the mountain meant to him climbing into Mrs K. and Mummy with his genital; he did not feel he could do it because his genital (the tooth) was not all right. Mrs K. referred to what he had said in the previous session about his father being so tired, and that he was sad about it. She interpreted that his father's tiredness also meant that his genital had been injured and broken by Richard and therefore he felt that his own genital would be broken if he put it into Mummy, or even that it *should* be broken because it was wrong to take her away from Daddy. In the previous session Richard had made a drawing of himself with very long legs; this meant that he had become Daddy and had become potent by taking away Daddy's genital. He had, as he often felt, taken into himself his father who was now tired and ill, and therefore he felt tired himself. He had the bad Hitler-father inside him as well. He had very much battered Hitler yesterday, and when he had scratched off the scab and made his arm bleed, his blood and Hitler's blood seemed to have become confused in his mind, which meant that Hitler inside him was injured and bleeding.

Richard said that he would like to get some toffee from Mr Evans. Then he would bite a piece of toffee and the tooth would stick to it and come out. Or he might be rude to his enemy, Oliver, who would hit him on the jaw, and out would come the tooth.

*Mrs K.* interpreted that Richard felt that his own genital, now represented by the tooth, was mixed up with his father's genital—

the toffee which Mr Evans should give him. For, as he had often shown, he wished to suck or eat Daddy's genital (recently the lobster). Then if he lost his tooth in that way, it would really be the sweet's, or rather his father's, doing, which would be responsible for tearing out both genitals together.

Richard began to play with the toys. He put the Mrs K. figure into the tractor and, facing it, the Mummy figure. They were supposed to be talking to each other.

*Mrs K.* asked what they were talking about.

Richard said they were discussing whether his tooth should be pulled out or not. . . . He made the tractor follow closely on the electric train.

*Mrs K.* interpreted that the electric train, which usually stood for himself, was both watching Mummy and Mrs K. and joining them. Mrs K. suggested that the two women inside the tractor also stood for two people inside Richard—either the good Mummy and the bad Mummy, or Daddy and Mummy; and Richard was uncertain whether his internal Mummy and Mrs K., and the internal parents, were friendly towards himself or hostile. This was why at times he so little trusted Mrs K. and feared that she would give away one of his secrets.

Richard made the goods train engine run between the toy bag and Mrs K.'s handbag, saying that it was moving by itself, and asked Mrs K. to hold it up by putting her finger in front of it.

*Mrs K.* interpreted the engine as Richard's genital, now moving by itself, which meant that Richard was not responsible for it, into Mrs K.'s genital, represented by her finger. But he also wished her to touch his genital with her hand. Another meaning was that she should prevent his genital entering her.

Richard put the stools into two lots: one side, he said, consisted of Daddy's, Mr K.'s, Mr Smith's, Hitler's, Goering's, and Paul's genitals, Hitler's being the biggest—a very large wooden block. On the other side was Richard's genital, for which he chose the nicest stool, covered with a furry top, which he particularly liked. With him were three more men's genitals. Richard explained that these belonged to the good Daddy and the good Paul, and he did not know whose the other could be. He threw stools from each group alternately at the other group. Several times the enemies were killed, but seemed to come to life again. In the end Richard said that his side had been victorious.

*Mrs K.* interpreted that these stools not only stood for genitals but for whole people as well. This would mean to him the death of the bad Daddy.

Richard was for a moment very impressed and said, genuinely

afraid, 'It would be awful if Daddy died.' . . . A little later he took up the big pole and threw it among the hostile genitals, saying that this was his secret weapon. During this part of the play he was very aggressive, made a great deal of noise, and came very near to breaking up the stools.

*Mrs K.* interpreted that the 'secret weapon' (which at that time was much discussed) was the internalized powerful Daddy-genital, recently the lobster, and that he used this internal genital against both the external and the internal enemy.

Richard, during the fight with the stools, said 'Poor playroom—it will soon be in ruins.'

*Mrs K.* interpreted that the playroom also meant Mrs K. whom he would destroy because she was going away. She referred to yesterday's wrecked aeroplane and the 'rickety' bus. He would destroy her if he attacked the bad Mr K. inside her, and would destroy Mummy if he attacked the bad Hitler-Daddy inside her; and yet he felt he should destroy these bad men because otherwise they would harm Mrs K. and Mummy.

Richard had become extremely excited and aggressive, looking flushed and sometimes grinding his teeth. He returned to the table and took up the toys. He made the bus stop in the village where Nurse lived. The buses were represented by the tractor, the coal truck, the goods train engine, and the electric train. They were all going in various directions. Richard himself was travelling to and fro in the electric train (now described as a bus). When these various vehicles met, Richard made angry noises, but he avoided collisions. In between he also talked about the different conductresses and said that, even apart from the three in whom he was so particularly interested, they were all very nice, pleasant, and polite.

*Mrs K.* interpreted that the various routes referred to his actually travelling between 'X' and 'Y', but they also stood for the various bus conductresses who had been so much on his mind recently, in addition to Mrs K., Mummy, and Nurse. The bus stop was also Mrs K.'s or Mummy's inside, as well as that of all these women, and the buses now stood for various men—Daddy, Paul, Mr K., Mr Smith—who, though they were still at loggerheads, had become less destructive with each other and avoided collisions. In the former play with the stools they had killed each other. This meant that Richard now took more account of his actual good Daddy, and of the good Paul, who had become more linked with the bad Daddy, the bad Paul, and Mr K. When previously in the play with the stools the two sides were destroying each other, the entirely bad Hitler-father, the rascal Mr Smith, the foreign spy Mr K., had to be exterminated (Note I).

Richard, when he moved the electric train only and the others were put aside, hummed softly some pieces of music. He also took the two keys (which stood for himself and Mrs K.) off the ring and made them dance with each other.

*Mrs K.* interpreted that now he was with the external Mrs K. and quite happy with her, as was shown by the two keys dancing together outside the ring formerly standing for his and Mrs K.'s insides. He was also able to be by himself and happy, and therefore had been singing when the electric train had been moving by itself.

Richard had asked earlier during this session, and did so again before leaving, whether his tie was all right. On the way to the village, when he was still walking with Mrs K., he met Mrs Wilson, who told him that the boys had definitely decided to go up the mountain and were about to start. Richard was for a moment undecided; he wished to join them, but that would have meant postponing going home. So he after all made up his mind to go home, and his decision was no doubt partly influenced by his wanting to see his father.

At the beginning of the session Richard was timid, anxious, and full of hypochondriacal fears. He kept talking about his tooth and was very much concerned about it. In the course of the session, the intepretations led to his becoming increasingly lively and aggressive, and he was very destructive when he played with the stools. During the play with the buses he was still very flushed and sometimes ground his teeth. He remained unresponsive and in a manic state. It was clear that he was restraining his aggressiveness and trying to find a better solution, as appeared, for instance, when he was careful to avoid collisions. This restraining of aggressiveness was partly due, as has been seen also in some recent sessions, to his strong wish to part from Mrs K. in a friendly way; another motive was his great anxiety lest he injured his father. But the internal struggle was very severe and he could cope with it only by putting all his strength into it. It was a sign of the increased strength of his ego that he was nevertheless capable of having the interlude when he was alone with Mrs K. (the two keys dancing together) and happy and relaxed.

*Note to Eighty-seventh Session:*

I. I have already pointed out that recently Richard had become more capable of integrating himself and synthesizing his objects, and that the ideal light-blue Mummy had come closer to the 'wicked brute' Mummy. Now the same appeared to be happening in connection with the father. This meant that hate became mitigated by love, and that the excessively bad and phantastic figures linked more with the realistic ones. It is significant that these developments were bound up with a greater capacity to find substitutes both for the analyst and for the mother, as shown by the great interest in the bus conductresses. Previously he seemed to have nothing but scorn for women, except the ideal Mummy, Mrs K., and Nurse. As I remarked earlier, his being more able to accept substitutes indicated a step towards freeing himself increasingly from his ties to his mother. Another aspect of this development was that, in spite of his aggressiveness and anxieties relating to the ill and possibly dying father, love for him and sorrow about his illness had come out much more.

## EIGHTY-EIGHTH SESSION (Friday)

Richard arrived a little late, sat down, looked at Mrs K. and, taking out of his pocket a small fir cone, said that this was the first he had found that year. He thought it might help the work and had therefore brought it. He obviously wished Mrs K. to praise its shape and also to make use of it for the analysis. The next thing he took out of his pocket was a poppy. He put it beside the fir cone, tasted a bit of it, said it was poisonous and threw both the poppy and the fir cone away. . . . At this point an interruption occurred. A man came to read the electric meter. Richard said in a whisper, while the man was in the kitchen, 'An intruding Daddy'; but his reaction to this disturbance was of a much less persecutory nature than it had been when a man had come to repair the window (Fifty-fourth Session). However, he asked Mrs K., as soon as the man had left, to help him darken the room. He put on the electric light and the fire and said that he felt very cosy here, and he seemed quite happy.

*Mrs K.* interpreted that pulling down the blinds and putting on the lights was partly meant to keep intruders out; but he also intended in that way to avoid seeing the rain which he so much hated. (It was pouring at the time.) She also interpreted Richard's wish to help the analysis as much as possible, which was why he had brought the fir cone and the poppy. The fir cone stood for his genital and he wanted Mrs K. to praise its shape. She suggested that the poisonous poppy stood for the eaten-up Daddy-genital, the attractive but in the end poisonous lobster, the internal 'secret weapon' which had appeared in the previous session. He felt that this internalized Daddy-genital became mixed up with his own. He wanted to spit it out and to satisfy himself with his own small more harmless penis. However, it seemed that he felt that they could not be disentangled, and so he threw away both the poppy and the fir cone (Note I).

Richard looked at the map and spoke for some time about the war situation. He was worried about the Russians, but he hoped they could hold out. It seemed that there would be a winter campaign. Then he followed up with his pencil the route from the British Isles through the Mediterranean to Alexandria. He was a merchantman (and he also made the noises of a ship) carrying goods which he said were food, ammunition, and guns. He made pencil marks on the sea (which he rubbed out at the end of the session). He said he was sweeping mines. It was a pity that he could not go to Russia by way of the Black Sea, because the French had laid mines. It was terrible to think that our former allies had turned against us.

*Mrs K*. interpreted that his clearing mines from the sea meant cleaning Mrs K.'s and Mummy's inside of the dangerous genitals and 'big job' which were put into them by bad allies, namely by Daddy and by himself. After cleaning them of the bad genitals he could put his good genital into them, and this was what the goods which the merchantman was carrying represented. His good genital was to make babies and also to protect Mrs K. and Mummy against the bad Daddy, which was why he carried ammunition among the goods.

Richard had begun to draw. He made a map and drew the merchantman coming down to Alexandria and also the movements of the hostile ships. After making this drawing, Richard was deeply in thought. He said that he had been thinking a lot about the continuation of his analysis and again asked whether, if Mrs K. were to be killed in an air-raid on London, someone else could continue his analysis. (The way in which he spoke indicated that he had approached the problem in a rather mature and rational way.) He said he wished to go to London for that reason; his mother had written a letter to Mrs K., hadn't she? He had seen it lying on the table. What had she written? (His curiosity was much less intense than on previous occasions.)

*Mrs K*. said yes, she had received a letter. Mummy had written about the arrangements for his education, which she had made in accordance with earlier discussions.

Richard said that it was arranged he should have lessons for two hours every day. He was glad that it was no more. He also mentioned music lessons. (His mother had been very doubtful whether he would agree to.music lessons. He had refused French lessons and everything that was additional to the two hours schooling a day.)

*Mrs K.* asked whether he would like to have music lessons.

Richard replied that he thought he might, but he had not had any for quite a long time.

*Mrs K.* reminded him that in a recent session the piano seemed to stand for her and Mummy's inside and that these fears appeared to have lessened following that session. Instead of his fear of the many dead babies (the flies), he felt more hope about the alive babies which the nice sounds stood for; probably also the fear of the terrifying Union Jack, which represented Daddy's octopus-genital jumping out at him, might have lessened.

Richard was deep in thought. He said he would really like not to do anything at all. The greatest fun was to do nothing. But he looked very sad when saying this, and was only pretending to be amused. After a long pause he said, expressing what seemed to be a very considered decision, that he wanted to go to London and continue his analysis with Mrs K. He would also much like to see London, but that was not so important. It was important to go on with the 'work'. He was afraid that otherwise he would not be able to 'keep a grip' on it, which he had now. He felt it was so essential for him that he did not mind the risks of being bombed. Mrs K. would not be living in London itself, would she? Could he not stay where she would be? Or could she make some arrangements for him? Would she please write to Mummy and support his wish? He thought that Mummy would not do it if he said so, but that she would listen to Mrs K. The danger might not after all be so great if the Russians could hold the Germans, and it looked as if they might (Note II).

*Mrs K.* asked whether he had considered that this would mean staying away from his mother for some length of time, and how lonely and homesick he might feel.

Richard replied that he felt he could stand it if Mrs K. helped him by analysis. He did not want to wait until the war was over, and if Mrs K. were bombed or died, he could, couldn't he, continue with the analyst she had suggested? It was also possible that Mummy could come with him if Daddy recovered as rapidly as he was doing just now. Was Mrs K. going to help him? Would she promise to help him?

*Mrs K.* replied that she could not really advise his mother to make such arrangements at present. She had told his mother quite definitely that his analysis should be continued as soon as possible. But just now it seemed out of the question that Richard should come to London because there was too much risk. Mrs K. asked what he was afraid of when he spoke of 'losing his grip'.

Richard said he could not exactly explain what he meant, but he knew that he had gained something which he was afraid to lose. He felt much better than when he had started the work. He enumerated some of the benefits he had derived : he was less worried, he had less fear of children, he was ready to have some schooling, and so on.

*Mrs K.* agreed that these were really benefits which he wanted to keep, but suggested that he was not only referring to these improvements but also to his greater security because he felt he had the good Mummy, the light-blue Mummy, inside him. She was now represented by Mrs K., who in his mind protected him against the bad and injured babies and against the bad Daddy's genital inside. The good Mummy also helped to control his own feelings of hate and jealousy which would destroy him if he destroyed the good Mummy together with the bad one. But he was afraid of losing the good Mummy when the work stopped. Mrs K. also asked when Richard had come to this decision about going to London.

Richard answered that he had been thinking about it for a long time, but he could not make up his mind.

*Mrs K.* said that he had not mentioned these thoughts so directly before.[1]

Richard replied that he liked to think out some things for himself before he spoke about them. He wanted to be sure they would not hurt when he said them. He also liked his thoughts to come out like a flood and not like a trickle. During this conversation he had been looking at the map and had spoken of Kiev being surrounded and holding out like little brave Tobruk.

*Mrs K.* interpreted this as Richard, although a child, protecting Mrs K. in London against the powerful Hitler, and this was one of the reasons why he wanted to go to London with her. Quite early on in his analysis he had felt that he would risk his life to protect his Mummy against the tramp who turned out to be the Hitler-Daddy.

During this session Richard had scarcely paid any attention to people passing by and on the whole his persecutory anxiety had lessened. Even after Mrs K.'s statement that she could not back up his idea of going to London at the moment, which no doubt was a disappointment to him, he did not seem to feel persecuted. One can conclude that in this session his determination to share dangers with Mrs K. and to protect her, to keep her and the analysis— which meant also the possession of his good mother—alive, counteracted and diminished fears of persecution, internal as well as

[1] In his material these thoughts had been quite noticeable, for instance when in his play with the trains he followed Mrs K. to London, or when the electric train, representing himself, and containing Mrs K., went to London.

external. His decision also implied creativeness, as was shown by the merchantman carrying goods—i.e. babies—and facing a great deal of danger for that purpose.

*Notes to Eighty-eighth Session:*

I. This need in Richard to free himself from the internalized penis of the father, which was felt to be mixed up with his own, is significant of a step towards developing an independent personality. This implies achieving a relative freedom from the internalized father (and also mother) who are felt to be either bad or ruling the self. Even the good object, when too demanding and controlling, becomes bad and persecutory, and therefore the need arises to get rid of this formerly good object which has turned bad. I have pointed out in the *Psycho-Analysis of Children* (Chapter XII) that in the man's mind the penis comes to stand for the ego. As regards the good object changing into a persecutory one if it is felt to be too much in control and making too great demands, I have elaborated this in A Contribution to the Psychogenesis of Manic-Depressive States'.

II. I am convinced that Richard's suggestions were quite carefully thought out. I believe he might have come to London to continue his analysis if his mother had agreed and suitable arrangements could have been made. This is striking, considering the extreme anxieties of this very frightened and neurotic child who some months before did not dare to meet other children on the road. In terms of transference, one could say that he had very strong positive transference feelings towards me, although, as the material showed, I had plenty of opportunity to analyse his negative ones (these two factors are, of course, interrelated). However, this strengthening of the positive transference indicated that, in spite of his internal anxieties and distrust and the need to idealize the mother, the good object had been established up to a point and this internal good relation had been considerably reinforced through his analysis. He felt therefore greater inner security. I have remarked elsewhere ('The Origins of Anxiety and Guilt') that during the war even children who were exposed to the greatest dangers could bear them if their relation with their parents (or even with the mother alone if the father was absent) was sufficiently secure. From this observation, among others, I drew the conclusion that external dangers can be borne if a good internal object is securely enough established. I expressed the view—which also applies to Richard—that although one must allow for the fact that children might not fully realize the extent of the external danger, this should not be over-rated. Certainly London children soon became aware of the dangers which they met face to face in their daily lives.

## EIGHTY-NINTH SESSION (Saturday)

My notes on this session are rather short. This is largely due to the fact that Richard brought little material on that day. There were long breaks and he was obviously under the full impact of the depression preceding the parting. No doubt my refusal, in the previous session, to support his intention to go with me to London had increased his depression and anxiety about my leaving him. It was pouring with rain, which in itself was always a cause—though much less at this stage—for Richard to feel depressed. Mrs K. had a waterproof hood on.

Richard said she looked very pretty when he met her outside the playroom. He added that though she looked sweet, it was not like a young lady but sweet in the way an old lady might look. But he at once asked whether she minded his saying that, and whether she felt hurt by it. He inquired whether Mrs K. was going to go down to the village after the session. (This was particularly important to him because this was one of the days when he was going home by bus; when Mrs K. came back from her shopping, she would pass by the bus stop when Richard had already got into the bus and he would be able to wave to her.) . . . Richard said he did not want to see the awful rain and asked Mrs K. to help him pull the curtains. He turned on the light and switched on the fire and said that now it was nice and cosy in the playroom.

*Mrs K.* reminded him that he had on the previous day thrown out the poisonous Daddy-genital (the poppy) and that the 'nasty rain' had often been in his mind connected with the bad urine produced by it. He wanted to keep that bad genital out of himself as well as out of Mrs K., and then he would feel that he could be with her without the bad internal Hitler interfering. He wanted to have Mummy by herself, not mixed up with Daddy inside her, so that he could really trust her fully (Note I).

Richard said that he knew that Mrs K. rang his Mummy the previous night and he asked what she had discussed with her. (His mother had, as usual, told him all about it.)

*Mrs K.* replied that she discussed with her Richard's wish to go on with his analysis as soon as possible, and had supported this wish. Both Mummy and Mrs K. definitely agreed that it would not be possible to continue it during the coming winter.

Richard was obviously disappointed, but it was also a relief to him that this had been so definitely stated by Mrs K. It clearly diminished his doubts as to whether it was right or not to do it.

While Mrs K. explained this to him, he showed manœuvres of the British fleet by tracing them with his pencil on the map which he had made on the previous day and enlarged in this session. One of the events was that a battleship coming from Germany and managing to slip past Gibraltar at night was sunk by mines in the Mediterranean. This description of fleet manœuvres took up a good deal of the session.

*Mrs K.* interpreted that the Mediterranean now stood for London and expressed Richard's fear of what was going to happen to her there. She referred to recent material : Richard had been repeatedly bombing the train in which she was going to travel, and he had thrown the larger ball (standing for the bad Mr Smith) after the little ball representing her train.

Richard mentioned a dream. *He and Mrs K. had got into a bus and found that there was no conductress on it and that the bus was empty. There was also a car in which there were some people, and on the seat a little girl was lying. The car was very flat.*

*Mrs K.* asked about various points but could not get any associations to this dream. She interpreted that the empty bus without a conductress was Richard without his analysis, and without the good internal Mummy; therefore there would be nothing to guide him.

*Note to Eighty-ninth Session:*

I. I have made much in my *Psycho-Analysis of Children* of the combined parent figure which, I suggested, plays a vital part in the early stages of the Œdipus complex (between about four to six months). I concluded there (and elsewhere) that if this combined parent figure is strongly maintained in the infant's mind, this influences both the sexuality and the whole development of the child. One of these phantastic figures is the mother containing the penis of the father, or many of his penises. Further observations suggested that there are even phantasies in the very young child about the mother's breast containing the father's penis, and this phantasy usually contributes to a disturbance of the love for the breast and to a diminished belief in its goodness. One might consider this phantasy relating to part objects as a step in the earliest stages of the Œdipus complex. I came later on to the conclusion that the brief period—varying individually in length—during which the infant feels his relation to the mother and to her breast still as an exclusive one in which no third object enters, is of decisive importance for stability, for object relations in general, and in particular for developing lasting love relations and friendships (cf. *Developments in Psycho-Analysis*, Chapter VII).

Richard was waiting for Mrs K. at the corner of the road and jumped out at her from behind a tree. He said he had wanted to make fun, but could not keep up this attitude. He soon looked very depressed, and his eyes were red; however, he was not actually crying. He said he felt 'wobbly' in his tummy, though he had no indigestion, and did not know where this feeling came from. He added that this was the last week. When was he going to see Mrs K. at her lodgings? Then he explained that he meant they could do work there instead of in the playroom.

*Mrs K.* interpreted Richard's wish to get away from the playroom partly because he wanted to finish with her at a place—her lodgings—where he had not been destructive. It meant starting again anew, so as to keep Mrs K. as a live and good Mummy inside him. His mentioning the last week also expressed the fear of her death.

Richard made Drawing 73. It represented an aeroplane and he said it was flying to London. Mrs K. was on it and so was he. He added that the aeroplane looked like a person. He pointed to the landing wheels which were put one behind the other and said that here were two breasts. Then, pointing at the front part of the aeroplane, he said: 'Here we sit together.' After that he made a drawing of the bus going to 'Y', and asked when Mrs K. was coming to see them. Could she come one day this week when he went home—perhaps on Saturday? He so much wanted her to see the bus into which he changed, and why couldn't she come and see him at his home? He very much appealed to her to come.

*Mrs K.* said that she was sorry she could not come; but she might on her journey to London, when she went through the village where he changed buses, have a look at it.

Richard said about the bus which he had drawn that he had marked the place where he usually sat.

*Mrs K.* inquired about the two empty seats to the right of him, and the one empty seat on his left.

Richard said that to the right each seat was for two people. On one Mummy and Daddy would sit, and on the other Mrs K., and after a pause he added, 'and Mr K.' On the single seat to his left Paul was going to sit.

*Mrs K.* interpreted his desire for harmony within the family and friendly relations with Mrs K. This was also the reason why he so much wanted her to come and see his family before she left. But he wanted this friendly relation to exist in his inside as well; the bus stood for himself.

Richard then worked out on another page the various times when Mrs K. could take the train to the place where she would break her journey and see the bus. He said he would try and arrange to be there as well, but even if she saw the bus without him, that would be a good thing.

*Mrs K*. asked whether that bus was his favourite, more so than the bus from 'X'.

Richard said he liked both buses because they took him home.

*Mrs K*. reminded him that usually, and always on Saturdays, she saw him sitting in the bus before it left 'X', and he felt that he was taking her away with him, inside himself. Now he wanted her at least to look at the other bus, which was nearer to home, and which she had never seen; this would mean that she would come still nearer to him, to Nurse, and to his family.

Richard then made Drawing 74. He said it was a railway line and made his pencil go over it repeatedly; this stood for a train travelling. He mentioned that he would like to become an explorer and to read books about travel.

*Mrs K*. interpreted the exploration of Mummy's (now Mrs K.'s) inside and pointed out that the drawing of the railway line was in the shape of a female body.

Richard kept on making the train (his pencil) travel over the railway line. After Mrs K.'s interpretation he pointed to the circle near the top and said that this was the breast. The smaller circle was the nipple. He suddenly pounced on it with his pencil, making the dot in the centre, but at once restrained himself from making further dots—obviously preventing himself from destroying Mrs K.'s breast and body. Then he made another drawing: two German planes on the ground and one in the air were destroyed by two British aeroplanes. Richard said that the two British aeroplanes were Mrs K. and Richard, together over London. Then he drew a picture[1] of a Japanese battleship being torpedoed by the British *Salmon*. He suddenly decided to draw the sailors and the boiler inside the ship. First he said that the submarine was Mrs K.; then he remembered that the *Salmon* had always been himself. But the fish just above *Salmon* was Mrs K. and she was quite safe where she was. The starfish to the right of the *Salmon* was Mummy. Both Mrs K. and Mummy were helping the *Salmon* against the Japanese. He did not know who the fish in the corner was. It was nearly clawed by the crab, but cut off the crab's claws in time to get away.

*Mrs K*. interpreted that Richard had been terrified of hurting

[1] Some of the drawings made during this session are unfortunately lost.

and destroying her and her breast when exploring her body (as shown in Drawing 74), because he was so angry about losing her. This anger revived the resentment he had felt at the time when Mummy stopped feeding him and when he therefore attacked her breast in his mind. In the drawing of the Japanese battleship he was uniting with Mrs K. and Mummy against the bad Hitler-Daddy, so that Mrs K. should be safe in London. But London was also the attacked Mummy, and protected by the two British aeroplanes, Mrs K. and Richard. The *Salmon* was both Mrs K. and Richard —either Richard inside Mrs K. or Mrs K. inside Richard. The fish in the corner was also Mrs K. and Mummy, clawed by the external and internal bad genital; Richard felt he had attacked them as well. Hence the dots he had begun to make on Drawing 74. This attack was simultaneous with his trying to keep Mrs K. and Mummy safe.

Richard spoke again about the conductress and referred to the pretty one, saying that he 'would not have her, not on my life'. The less pretty one was much nicer.

*Mrs K.* interpreted that he might now like Mrs K. better than Mummy, though he thought her less pretty than Mummy. Formerly he might have loved Nurse more than Mummy, though she too was much less pretty.

Richard first said that this could not be; he did not love Nurse more than Mummy. But after some reflection he added that it might have been so in the past.

*Mrs K.* then asked for some details about yesterday's dream. Why did Richard get out of the bus when he saw there was no conductress on it?

Richard replied that *it was so eerie, so ghostly. The bus slowed down when he rang the bell and Richard jumped out while it was still moving. He was glad that Mrs Wilson was standing there and took him to her house. The people in the car reminded him of some people who stayed at the hotel.*

*Mrs K.* asked if they had been nice to him.

Richard said they were very nice; they liked him and were pleasant to him. They also gave him half a crown before they left.

*Mrs K.* asked whether he thought that they might have looked after him if he had been left alone. In the dream, after finding the bus without the conductress, he felt deserted and was glad to have Mrs Wilson take him home.

Richard said yes, the people in the hotel might have looked after him because they liked him.

*Mrs K.* asked about the little girl—where was she lying?

Richard said she was lying beside the man, but she soon changed into a spaniel; and he added, 'like Bobby'.

*Mrs K.* asked about the car being so flat, but could not get any association to that. She suggested that the people in the car, and even Mrs Wilson, who had taken him home, represented the new family he hoped to find if he lost his own. This early fear of being thrown out of his home, or of losing his family through death, had now come up again in connection with losing Mrs K. The little girl would then represent a sister whom he might want to have. When she changed into Bobby, this meant she would have the same love for him as Bobby had.

During this session Richard had scarcely paid attention to passers-by. He looked very unhappy. Once or twice he put his head on his arm on the table and appeared as if he did not know what to do with himself. His wish to be caressed and cuddled by Mrs K. was very obvious. At one point he said he would wish to cuddle Mrs K. but thought she would not like that. He repeatedly put his hand on Mrs K.'s arm or on her hand. He kept on saying that he did not want Mrs K. to go. Outside the playroom he said wasn't it a shame that she was going to leave.

*Mrs K.* replied that it was and that she was very sorry that she had to go. She would very much have liked to go on with his analysis and those of the other patients.

On one occasion when Mrs K., as she often did, had asked about his father's health (probably in connection with the seating in the bus), he looked up with a real smile and a very warm expression. When Mrs K. said that she was very sorry that she had to leave, he also looked more alive and pleased. He was altogether more lively during the second half of the session.


## NINETY-FIRST SESSION (Tuesday)

Richard again looked better and was more lively when Mrs K. met him in front of the playroom, and was also much less depressed and despairing during this session than on the previous day. He said that the playroom looked familiar and nice. He at once started to play with the toys, taking the electric train out of the bag and setting the swing going (Note I). Then he put the coal lorry and the tractor on top of the carriages of the goods train. He also arranged the station. In between the two houses which represented the station he left sufficient space for the electric or the goods train to pass. At first the goods train was meant to be going to London. Mrs K. was on it, and other people were there as well. The electric train followed it, carrying Richard (the train also represented Richard, as had previously often been seen). But soon he decided to keep the two trains separate and made them run on different lines. The electric train ran all round the table and behind Mrs K.'s bag and her basket. Later on, when the trains came nearer and nearer to a collision, Richard arranged a wider station and suddenly, when the trains were about to collide, he put them both back into the bag. The train was coming from London and going westwards; then it went to and fro. When the trains were about to meet, the sounds by which Richard accompanied these movements became increasingly angry and Richard also looked very aggressive. During this play he had become rather noisy and quite unwilling to listen to Mrs K., struggling hard to control his hate and to avoid the 'disaster'.

*Mrs K.* asked what the tractor and the coal lorry were for.

Richard first said that the tractor and the lorry were ammunition for the R.A.F. But they seemed to annoy him because, when one fell off the train, he appeared pleased.

*Mrs K.* interpreted that the tractor and the coal lorry were Mr K., Mr Smith, Hitler, and the bad people inside Mrs K. whom Richard wished to attack. If he were to do so, he would wreck the goods train which also stood for the good Mrs K.; this was one of the reasons why he had put them on top so that they could be easily removed and why he was pleased when one of them dropped from the train.

Richard saw Mr Smith pass. He went to the window, smiled at him and received a friendly greeting from him. Richard was watching Mr Smith from behind the curtain very intently, as if he wished to make out what Mr Smith was really like. But he was less suspicious and persecuted. When Mr Smith had passed, Richard seized the stool, which had recently stood for Mr Smith's genital, saying: 'I am going to throw his own genital at him,' and threw the stool on the floor.

*Mrs K.* interpreted again the 'secret weapon' (Eighty-seventh Session) as the internal eaten-up Hitler-genital with which Richard would attack the men whom he connected with Mrs K. and London.

Richard said that now the toys represented buses, and lined up the tractor, the engine of the goods train, the electric train, and the coal lorry. The buses were going in various directions. Again he made very angry sounds, but when the electric train arrived at the bus stop, he hummed softly and melodiously.

*Mrs K.* interpreted that he could hardly contain his anger about the various people connected with her—her patients, her friends, her family—who had first been represented by the people on the goods train and then by the various buses coming towards the bus stop which stood for her. Richard intensely desired to be the only one close to her and was angry with all the others and jealous of them. He also wanted to express his anger in order to get rid of it in that way; then he would be able to remain friends with Mrs K. before she went.

Richard appeared not to have listened to Mrs K.'s interpretation. But at this point he again emphatically affirmed that he did not want to hurt Mrs K. in any way. Yet a minute later he threw all the buses, except the 'electric train bus' which stood for himself, down from the table, saying that it was a 'precipice'. His face was flushed and he was very excited. But he was at once concerned when he saw that the two front wheels of the engine had come off, and asked Mrs K. whether she was angry and whether she could mend it.

*Mrs K.* said that she could mend it and interpreted Richard's wish to know whether he had actually done harm to her children and friends, and if so, whether she could make them well again and forgive Richard for his hate.

Richard went into the kitchen, drew several buckets of water, and said that the water was not very clean; but apparently he did not mind this. He added that he wanted to draw all the water so that the tank should become clean. While drawing water, he kept on looking into the tank to see how the water whirled into the pipe and took the dirt with it.

*Mrs K.* interpreted that Richard was expressing his desire to clean her inside and Mummy's inside from bad 'big job', babies, and genitals. His attacks on Mrs K., represented by the goods train, were meant predominantly to free her from the bad Hitler-Daddy—the ammunition which was put on top of the train—and to save and protect her. But he was also jealous of her, just as he was when he thought of Daddy being in bed with Mummy while he was left by himself. This was why he had thrown the buses down the 'precipice'. The rival buses stood for the rival Daddy (also the good one) and for Paul and all the children who he thought might yet be born.

Richard had during the last few minutes played with Mrs K.'s umbrella, which he had opened. He made it spin round and said he liked it. Then he used it as a parachute with which he was supposed to float down. He looked at the trade mark and stated with satisfaction that it was British made. Then, again holding it open, he turned round and round with it and said that he was dizzy, he did not know where it was taking him. He also said over and over again that 'the whole world is turning round'. Then he let the umbrella drop gently; he once more said it was a parachute and that he was not sure whether it would go down the right way. He told Mrs K. that he had completely wrecked Mummy's best umbrella when he used it as a parachute on a windy day. She had been 'speechless with rage'.

*Mrs K.* interpreted the umbrella as her breast; that it was British made meant it was a good breast, and that Mummy's breast was good too. She referred to his doubts about what Mrs K. contained —a good or a bad Mr K. The open umbrella stood for the breast, but the stick in it stood for Mr K.'s genital. Richard did not know whether he could trust this breast when he took it in because it was mixed with Mr K.'s genital, just as in his mind his parents and their genitals were mixed inside him. The question where the umbrella would take him expressed his uncertainty whether they were controlling him inside or not. The world which was turning round was the whole world he had taken into himself when he took in the breast—or rather Mummy mixed with Daddy, and her children, and all she contained. He felt the internalized powerful Daddy-penis—the secret weapon—as something which made him powerful if he used it against an external enemy. But it became dangerous if it attacked and controlled him internally. Nevertheless, he trusted Mummy and Daddy—the umbrella—more than previously, both as external people and inside him. That was also why he now treated Mrs K.'s umbrella more carefully than he had formerly treated Mummy's (Note II).

At the end of the session Richard saw the 'Painted Face' conductress pass by and waved to her from the window. Then he was concerned about what he should tell her if she asked him what he had been doing in that house. He could not explain to her what psycho-analysis was, and he did not want to lie to her because he liked her. He decided that he was going to say that he had met somebody there.

*Notes to Ninety-first Session:*

I. A particular feature of these last sessions, up to the very last one, was Richard's strong conscious and unconscious decision to finish the analysis in a friendly way—one which would not be too hard for the analyst either. The strength with which he controlled his aggressiveness whenever it came up was very striking. This wish to finish the analysis in a good relation with me also influenced his activities, his play and drawing. Right up to the end he continued what he called 'the work' as well as he could. It is significant that in this session he again played with the toys, and that in the previous one he drew a picture with ships and fishes, of the type he had produced early on in his analysis. The wish to deny the end of the analysis must also have played a part, together with the wish to bring the analysis to a good ending.

II. During the present session, apart from watching Mr Smith when he passed, Richard had hardly paid any attention to people on the road. He was deeply concentrated on an internal situation and in that respect he felt more secure than formerly. This more secure internal situation included a stronger belief in the good protective breast, expressed by the parachute which would help him in an emergency. Although it soon appeared that the good breast was mixed in his mind with the penis, nevertheless it seemed more reliable than on former occasions. His distrust of Mr K.'s genital inside Mrs K., and of Daddy's genital inside Mummy, persisted, but it was less strong because he had more faith in the goodness of the father. More recently Richard had become able to direct his aggressiveness more consistently against the bad, the Hitler-father and to unite with the good mother and help her to defend herself. Instead of quickly turning his aggression against the breast when anxiety came up, he could in a relatively more stable way maintain his trust in the breast and in the mother, and face the fight with the father. (This change in attitude was the result of his aggression being canalized in a more 'ego-syntonic' way.) This increased belief in the good internal mother, and the good internal father, had arisen gradually. In the previous session the depression about being left by Mrs K., and the fear of loneliness reviving his early fears of being deserted by his parents, were expressed much more strongly than in the present session. At the same time, in the previous session, too, he had shown a stronger belief in both parents and their good relation, as was indicated, for instance, in the drawing in which they were sitting together in the bus. The change from stronger depression in the previous session to greater security in the present one was also due to a manic element in his mood. He used the stronger belief in the good internal Mrs K. and mother, and the good father, to ward off the fear of parting and his depression.

# NINETY-SECOND SESSION (Wednesday)

Richard was again more depressed and absent-minded to begin with. He said that he had been playing with John Wilson and John's friends. He at once got out the goods train and the electric train and made a station large enough to accommodate both. The electric train went to 'Z' and Richard said that he and Mrs K. were on it. The goods train went out as well, but Richard did not give details of its destination. He made angry sounds representing the trains whenever they came near to each other. The play centred on avoiding collisions between the trains. They were often quite near to colliding, but Richard always prevented the disaster at the last moment, this conflict visibly giving rise to great mental strain in him. During this play Richard had repeatedly made suggestions about changes of times, choosing particularly times at which he knew quite well that Mrs K. saw other patients.

*Mrs K.* said she could not arrange the times he asked for but offered alternatives.

Richard, at one moment when both trains were standing in the station, suddenly said he felt unwell and had a pain in his tummy. He looked pale.

*Mrs K.* interpreted the station as Richard's inside. He expected all the time a collision inside him between the electric train, containing Mrs K. and the good Mummy, and the hostile goods train, standing for all the angry patients and children from whom Richard wanted to take Mrs K. away and run with her to his home town (Note I). Therefore he also wanted to change the time of his sessions, which meant taking Mrs K. away from everybody else. While Richard was striving to avoid a collision between the trains, because he did not wish to hurt Mrs K. and Mummy and their children and wanted to finish the analysis peacefully, he did not seem to believe that he could avoid the collision internally. This meant that he and Mrs K. would be hurt or damaged by his rivals. Therefore he had seemed so tense during this play and had a tummy ache (Note II).

Richard said, looking at Mrs K. in surprise, 'The pain has now quite gone—why?' The colour had come back into his face.

*Mrs K.* interpreted that the pain, like his throat in the earlier sessions, was connected with anxieties about his inside, and that when he understood these anxieties and consciously experienced them, the pain went.

Richard now made the goods train run after the electric train and again at the last moment stopped both of them in order to prevent disaster, moving the goods train to the other end of the table. A little later the engine from the goods train, leaving the carriages behind, ran into the station; although Richard tried to believe that now no disaster could occur, he obviously felt uncertain because he very soon pushed the engine behind Mrs K.'s bag, saying angrily, 'Silly thing.'

*Mrs K.* interpreted that the electric train was now standing for her. Richard took her away from her patients and children, as was shown when the electric train was running away from the goods train but in danger of being damaged by it. Then he expressed the same anxiety in a different way: the goods train engine—now standing for Mrs K. (the 'silly thing' which he had pushed behind Mrs K.'s bag)—ran into the station by itself, which meant that Mrs K. and he were no longer together. The carriages stood for Daddy and the patients and children, now all Richard's rivals (Note III). The engine also represented the external Mrs K., the good Mummy who was his main help and support.

Richard emphatically said that Mrs K. was with him on the electric train, and he showed her that he was one of the carriages, Mrs K. the other. He unhooked the two and joined them together again and then added that she and he were together and had their genitals together as well.

*Mrs K.* interpreted that Richard had felt that he could not prevent the disaster to him and Mrs K. He had suddenly realized that she would not stay with him any more but would join her other patients and her family. Hence he had unhooked the carriages and then joined them together again.

Richard said that if Mrs K. wanted to leave her other patients it had nothing to do with him.

*Mrs K.* interpreted that this was just why Richard had become so angry with her, the engine, the 'silly thing', because he felt that it was not Mrs K. who wanted to leave her children and patients (the carriages) and stay with him, but Richard who wished to separate them.

Richard very soon joined the goods train engine and its carriages together again, and now a collision between the trains occurred. But he did it very carefully. . . . At one moment, while playing with the trains, he had shown distrust of Mrs K., asking her whether she could keep a secret. He said a very important person (whose name he mentioned) had travelled through 'X' that morning. He again asked Mrs K. not to talk about it.

*Mrs K.* interpreted that his distrust of her had increased because she was leaving him and therefore became more the 'wicked brute' mother.

Richard asked whether Mrs K. was a doctor for the mind as others are doctors for the body.

*Mrs K.* said yes, one could say so.

Richard said that the mind was even more important than the body, though he thought that the nose was very important too.

*Mrs K.* interpreted that the nose also stood for Richard's genital, and that he was afraid that something was wrong with it, that it was damaged and would not develop properly, and this was the reason why he was afraid of becoming a 'dunce'. He doubted whether Mrs K. could actually cure the genital as well as the mind.

Richard, soon after the train disaster, put away the toys.

*Mrs K.,* referring back to one of the drawings of the previous session, inquired again about the fish at the bottom, which was in the claws of what Richard called a crab and which was very similar to the octopus of earlier drawings.

Richard again said the fish got away, and then he added that the two claws were the two breasts.

*Mrs K.* interpreted that Richard's anger was represented by the two claws of the crab. At the same time he wished that the breast should be able to save itself and cut off the claws. But having attacked the breast, he felt that now the breast would change into claws and attack him; and then he, in order to save himself—now having turned into the fish—would have to cut off the breast (Note IV).

Richard said that he did not want any more to look under the surface of the drawing (which meant beneath the line). He suggested that they should look instead at what was going on above the water (referring to the ship which he had drawn with pleasure). . . . Then he spoke about having played recently with John Wilson and his friends and said that he, Richard, had bombed the Burma Road in their play.

*Mrs K.* interpreted that if he had bombed the Burma Road, he was Japanese.

Richard, looking puzzled, said that then he must be the Japanese ship.

*Mrs K.* again interpreted the various sides of his personality which were represented by the British *Salmon* and by the Japanese ship; he had expressed this formerly when he was sometimes German and sometimes British. The ship being himself also contained people—the little men—standing for Daddy who, he was afraid, would harm the good Mummy inside him. This was the same as the fear of Hitler's genital being the 'secret weapon' inside him, which would drive him to harm Mrs K. or Mummy. The British submarine stood for his good self containing the good Mrs K. and Mummy.

Richard's mood during this session was on the whole much like that of the Ninetieth Session, with much unhappiness and tension. His increased desire to be cuddled showed repeatedly in his touching Mrs K., and he dropped things so as to be able to touch her legs when picking them up. He was obviously all the time trying to restrain his aggressiveness because of the fear of injuring his loved objects.

*Notes to Ninety-second Session:*

I. The collision between the good objects and what he felt to be the bad ones (because he had attacked them and wanted to deprive them) was also a conflict between one part of himself felt to be good and allied with the good object and the hostile part of himself allied with the objects felt to be bad.

II. It is important to consider the discrepancy between internal and external situations and the fact that while Richard externally tried to put things right, in order to prevent disaster, he could not get rid of the feeling of internal disaster which expressed itself in physical pain and in very noticeable mental strain. Psycho-analytic experience shows that efforts to deal with external situations and relations have several aims : not only is the relation to the external world to be improved— which implies making reparation to the first external objects—but anxieties relating to the internal world are to be assuaged. External relations thus become also the means of testing out internal ones. If a relatively good balance between external and internal is not established, these attempts will be unsuccessful.

III. There is an interpretation from a different angle which my work on the ego would now suggest. I had already interpreted that one part of his self, felt to be good and allied with the good object, was fighting his destructive part combined with the bad objects. But his ego was not strong enough to deal with the impending disaster. I would conclude that the engine which he put behind my bag (which had in his analysis often represented myself) stood for his destructive impulses which he could not himself control and which were to be controlled by the analyst—ultimately by his good object. This good object was also felt to be the restraining and therefore helpful super-ego.

IV. This is an instance which illustrates the fact that attempts at reparation and at control of destructive impulses cannot prevent the projection of the individual's destructive impulses on to the object. Since he had torn my breasts, the breast remained an object he distrusted and which would bite and claw him. This is an instance of the complexity of processes which are simultaneously operative. We see here the expression of destructive impulses and the wish to control them—even to annihilate them, which may mean annihilating a very important part of the self (cf. 'Notes on Some Schizoid Mechanisms'). In this way the good object is to be saved; yet at the same time there is distrust of it because it might retaliate and thus become dangerous.

Richard was silent and sad. This whole session was characterized by long pauses and obvious efforts to speak, still to do some work, and not to give in to his depression—for his own and for Mrs K.'s sake. At the beginning he said that he was very sad about Mrs K. leaving him. . . . He asked if she knew the name of a woman he had heard of in 'Z' who did some kind of work; but he really believed that she did not do the right thing and was a witch. . . . He mentioned that he had made friends with the pretty conductress.

*Mrs K.* interpreted that since he was going to lose her and the analysis, he was trying to make friends wherever he could; in that way he would prevent being attacked by hostile people. The pretty conductress was a mixture to him of good and bad: as pretty, he thought, as his mother and yet bad because she treated him like a child. But he wanted to be on good terms with her before Mrs K. left.

Richard caught a fly and put it out of the window saying that it was flying into the 'Bear's' garden.

*Mrs K.* interpreted that flies had played various roles in former sessions. Sometimes he had killed them (and then they had often stood for bad babies or even for the bad Daddy). At other times he had set them free, as he had done now when he said the fly would go into the 'Bear's' garden. The 'Bear' stood for a fairly harmless Daddy.

Richard said thoughtfully: 'The Bear is the dark-blue Daddy,' but added that his real Daddy was a light-blue Daddy. This was the first time that he used the words 'light blue' about his father—it had always been reserved for the ideal Mummy or Mrs K.

*Mrs K.* interpreted that he now used light blue for Daddy and seemed to express his love for him in this way. It was also a consolation because he was losing Mrs K. to have Daddy as somebody nearly as good as Mummy.

Richard went into the kitchen and drank from the tap.

*Mrs K.* interpreted that if he could not have the good breast, he wanted now to take in the good penis of the father.

Richard played a good deal with the clock during this session. He caressed it, handled it, opened and closed it, wound it, and was deeply engrossed in these activities. When he set the alarm, he said: 'Mrs K. is broadcasting to the world. She is saying, "I shall give the right kind of peace to everybody."' Then he added a little shyly, 'And Richard is a very nice boy, I like him. . . .' He went about killing flies and cutting them in half. He drew water into the bucket, filling it to the brim, and explained that he did this because he wanted as much milk as possible; but also because he wanted to empty and to clean the tank. He also wanted to kill all the flies he could find in the playroom. While killing the flies he spoke of his big 'V for Victory' over them. . . . He went back to the table and, finding Mrs K.'s bag open, he took out her purse quickly, saying, 'You don't mind, do you?', and opened it. He looked at the shillings, putting them on one side, and took out some notes. He remarked that Mrs K. seemed to have a good deal of money, and then asked whether this was all she possessed or whether she had any more in the bank. When he put the shillings apart, he put his hand over them and made a movement as if he wished to keep them for himself.

*Mrs. K.* interpreted that Richard before parting from her wanted to take as much milk and 'big job' (the shillings) as possible out of her. Then he became afraid that he had left her too little and therefore asked whether she had some more at the bank. This showed his fear that he had exhausted her. His killing 'all the flies' was to protect Mrs K.—and Mummy—against the bad babies whom he felt she contained and who would endanger her.

Richard, as in the previous session, used every opportunity to touch Mrs K. and at one moment he asked her whether she would not like to sit on the furry stool which in an earlier session had represented his genital.

*Mrs K.*, after sitting for a moment on the furry stool, interpreted his wish to touch her not only because he would like to caress her, as he did with the clock, but also because it seemed to him as if by touching her he could better take her into himself and keep her there.

Richard kicked the stools and after that threw the rope in the way he had done formerly (Fifty-second Session); he reminded Mrs K. how he had used it previously when it stood for Daddy's penis which he had got hold of. . . . He also played a lot with Mrs K.'s keys. He made the two keys walk together, having taken the smaller key off the ring, and then put it back again on the ring.

*Mrs K.* interpreted his wish to go with her to London, then again the wish to go back to Mummy, and again to rejoin Mrs K. This was expressed by his play with the keys.

Richard asked Mrs K. to put her hand on a piece of paper, and he drew the outlines of it. On the same paper he had previously drawn the outline of his own hand. This piece of paper he took with him.

*Mrs K.* interpreted that this was another way of keeping her inside him.

Richard again played with the clock, nearly closing the frame so that it almost collapsed, and then saying that he was still supporting it; then he actually closed it and quickly opened it again and said, 'Now she is all right again.'

*Mrs K.* interpreted his fear that she would collapse and that she needed Richard's support to keep her going (he wanted to come to London partly in order to protect her there). But it also referred to the internal Mrs K. who, he was afraid, might collapse inside him, and he was determined to keep her alive externally and internally. He was both afraid that he might not succeed in this and yet hopeful that he might.

Richard had become very silent towards the end, but he said that he had decided to continue to work with Mrs K. at some time in the future.

*Mrs K.* went with Richard to the village, but there he quickly took leave of her and said he would rather she did not see him get on the bus.

All throughout the session Richard had been fighting strongly against his depression and trying to make parting not too difficult both for him and, as he seemed to feel, for Mrs K.; and he had tried to rely on the hope that he would see her again and would continue his analysis. His attempts still to cooperate to the last were also shown by the way in which, when he threw the rope, he reminded Mrs K. of what it had meant before.


# FINAL REMARKS

The psycho-analysis I have presented here was in some respects, which I have mentioned in the Introduction, not an entirely typical one. Yet Richard's material and my interpretations throw light on the basic principles of my technique of analysing children, during both latency and pre-adolescence. Therefore I believe that this book, as a continuation of my *Psycho-Analysis of Children*, should prove helpful to the student of analysis, and in particular of child analysis; in fact, this is my main aim in publishing this work.

I have repeatedly pointed out in my notes certain steps in development, some of which proved evanescent. I nevertheless regard them as important because it is part of the analyst's work to study such steps carefully, even when they are not sufficiently established.

The whole process of an analysis, even a much more prolonged one, always implies such changes, and the working-through is made possible only by the analyst following these fluctuations closely and analysing them. This means not only interpreting new details of the material, but also dealing with the changes in content and form which anxiety situations undergo with every new insight achieved.

One angle from which I would consider the effects of this short analysis is the diminution of persecutory anxieties which were bound up with his internalization processes and identifications. I achieved this by again and again analyzing anxieties relating to his internal objects and his destructive impulses. From another angle Richard's progress was bound up with improvement in his relation to his good object; and it is my conviction that this is fundamentally the case in every analysis in which we can bring about some lasting favourable alterations. I have made it clear that for Richard his loved object was the idealized 'light-blue' mother; and his relation to the analyst was on similar lines. As always, idealization necessarily is linked with persecution in varying degrees, and it was a sign of considerable progress in Richard's analysis when the persecutory aspect of the relation to the idealized mother and analyst came to the fore. In the process of analysing both these aspects, it turned out that Richard's relation to his mother was not entirely based on idealization : to some extent, trust and love for his mother had become established. Nevertheless persecutory anxiety and splitting processes had again and again revived his need for idealization. When these anxieties diminished, a much more secure relation to the primary good object—the mother—came about. Also, owing to the analysis of his Œdipus complex, in which the paranoic element had been quite strong, love for the father could be more deeply experienced. This again diminished suspicion and persecutory anxieties with regard to other people, and, together with a better relation to both parents, his object relations in general improved.

These changes implied that Richard had become able to face more fully, as well as to control and counteract, his destructive impulses, his envy, greed, and persecutory anxieties. This development meant that his ego was better able to accept and integrate the super-ego. Another contributory factor in strengthening his ego was the fact that projective and introjective identification, which had been very powerful, diminished in the course of his analysis. His ego was also reinforced by his growing confidence in his gifts and in good aspects of his character. This was linked with more hope about his future potency and allowed a freer play of his genital phantasies.

In the first part of this book we found Richard in a constant struggle between destructive and loving impulses and a prey to both persecutory and depressive anxiety. His complete insecurity was expressed by the 'disaster' which occurred every time he used the toys. This 'disaster' always involved the destruction of his whole external and internal world, including himself. Another indication that he could not control his greed, envy, and competitiveness was found in his empire drawings. For whatever he consciously intended, it always turned out that he had more countries than anybody else.

This situation altered as the analysis progressed. I have already said that his envy, jealousy, and greed, which in my view are expressions of the death instinct, diminished because he became gradually able to face and integrate his destructive impulses. This was bound up with his capacity for love coming more fully into play, which made it possible for hate to be mitigated by love. As a result, greater tolerance towards other people as well as towards his own shortcomings developed. His sense of guilt, which had existed side by side with his persecutory anxieties, had diminished and this implied a greater capacity to make reparation. He had, in fact, become able to some extent to work through the depressive position.

Another sign of the increasing predominance of the life instinct, and with it of the capacity for love, was that he no longer felt impelled to turn away from destroyed objects but could experience compassion for them. I have referred to the fact that Richard, who so strongly hated the enemies threatening Britain's existence at that time, became capable of feeling sympathy for the destroyed enemy. This was shown, for instance, when he regretted the damage done to Berlin and Munich and, at another occasion, when he became identified with the sunk *Prinz Eugen*. The growing predominance of the life instinct in the fusion between the two instincts and the ensuing mitigation of hate by love were the ultimate reason why he could remain hopeful in spite of the very painful experience of breaking off an analysis which he consciously and unconsciously knew to be essential for him.

This hopefulness, and his ability to maintain a good relation to the analyst as an internal and external object, in spite of resentment, feeling of loss, and great anxiety, confirm my view that as the result of his analysis the good internal object was much more securely established in Richard; and this greater inner security reflected the ascendancy of the life instinct. It is my impression that the changes produced by this incomplete analysis were to some extent lasting.

# INDEX

# PREFATORY NOTE TO THE INDEX

This book is written in three distinct languages: the first expresses the child's material, in concrete every-day terms and symbolic meanings; the second, the chapter notes, is written in the terms of an ordinary psycho-analytic book or paper; the third, the interpretations, is somewhere between the two.

An attempt has been made to index the first two. The third, however, seldom appears in the index, and when it does it is usually for the purpose of illustrating the chapter notes.

Bobby (dog), 26, 28, 29, 33, 34, 40, 49, 53, 77, 78–9, 87, 88, 93, 152, 172, 173–4, 176, 194, 241, 247, 251, 285, 286, 293, 298, 360, 453

Bomb-crater, 74

Bomber Command, 421–2

Bombers (*see also* Aeroplanes) : British, 54; German, 41, 74

Bombs, 16, 20, 74, 79, 80, 252, 282, 303, 388, 392, 417

Book, 90, 91, 191, 195

Boot, big black, 187

Bottle, bought from chemist, 133

Bow and arrows, 40

Boy(s), 35, 120, 251, 285, 311, 413; 'awful', at hotel, 281–2, 306; imbecile, 182, 185, 364; impudent, 198, 427–8; un-pleasant, 223, 224

Breast (*see also* Mother; and e.g. Coins; Football; Oranges; Pad; Plant; Strawberries), 195, 259, 260, 335, 357, 438, 451, 460; analysis as feeding, 59, 66, 179, 278, 289; attacks on, 42–4, 140, 259, 262, 275, 399, 451–2; bad, 146, 264, 289, 358, 460; containing penis, 118, 369, 447, 449; controlling de-structive impulses, 157; desire for, 141, 157, 261, 311, 323, 351, 399; desire for, trans-ferred to penis, 279, 339, 424; envy of, 100, 262, 399, 424; exclusive relation to, 449; good, 146, 209, 264, 357; good breast as core of ego, 434; guilt towards, 289; as internal object, 35, 61, 351, 457; love for, 42; love for, transferred to penis, 279; -mother, 195, 398; preservation of, 263; relation-ship to, and Œdipus complex, 279; restoration of, 357; as super-ego, 157

Breast-feeding, 15, 278, 333

Brest, 41, 42, 54, 176, 177, 257

Britain, 28, 45, 49, 113, 115, 144, 167

Broom (*see* Sweeping)

Brother(s) (*see also* Paul), good, 83; relation to child, 26; patient's, 15, 16, 28; mother's preference for, 16

Brown, 124, 125, 259, 299, 300, 307, 309–10, 323

'Brute, wicked', 108, 109, 111, 112, 117, 120, 122, 134, 138, 143, 163, 194, 230, 271, 283, 292, 351, 352, 354, 382, 392, 396, 397, 408, 419, 420, 442, 459

Bucket(s) (*see also* Water, play with), 312–13, 354, 369, 375, 381, 386, 389, 397, 398, 402, 408, 413, 423, 427

Budgerigar, 411

Buffers, 226–7

Burma Road, 460

Burrowing, 53, 60

Bus(es), 160–1, 393–4, 441, 448, 450–1, 454; crowded, 326, 338, 341, 358, 393–4, 399, 424; drawing of, 436, 450; dream of, 430, 449; 'rickety', 436, 441

Bus conductress(es), 376, 394, 397, 398, 418, 423, 429–30, 436, 441, 443, 452, 456, 462

Bus ticket, 406–7

Butterflies, 86

Calendar, 272, 277, 309; picture, 41, 46, 53

Canals, 34

Canaries, 20, 38, 40–1, 62, 63, 131, 152, 172, 173–4, 194, 360, 410–11, 415

Cap, 29–30, 44, 53–4, 141, 171, 173

Cape Matapan, Battle of, 132–3

Captain, of battleship, 53

Car : flat, 449, 453; man in, 429;

Depression/Depressive—(*cont.*)
151; and external situation,
318, 448; and loneliness, 70,
366; and integration, 49–50,
77, 216–17; and manic states,
45, 51–2; and persecutory
anxiety, 178, 278, 289, 318,
340, 425; and premature independence, 209; and reparation, 50, 51–2

Depressive features, predominance in patient of, 67

Depressive position : conflict at
root of, 51; and danger to
good internal object, 75–6,
434; emergence in analysis,
278, 283; manic defence
against, 289; and persecutory
anxiety, 305; and regression,
319; and sympathy with
enemy, 278; working through
of, 249–50, 466

Desertion, feeling of, 82–3, 84

Desires : early, influence of, 311;
genital, expression of, 180;
oral, 75, 310; sexual, 36, 39,
186

Despair, 71, 114, 118, 129, 144,
151, 294, 340, 414, 425

Destroyer(s), 85, 86, 88, 90, 94,
97, 100, 131, 166, 167, 168,
172, 173, 182, 185, 186, 188,
218, 270, 402, 407–8; biggest,
257–8, 268, 287

Destructive impulses/Destruction
(*see also* Attacks; Death; Disaster; Hatred) : 37 n., 76, 288;
analysis as fight against, 262 n.,
461; control of, 72, 76, 157,
414; and distrust of self, 71;
effects of analysis of, 130, 137;
and fear of death, 74 n.; and
good object, 192, 414, 461;
and guilt, 73 n.; insecurity
and, 72; integration of, 217,
466; against mother, 76;
against mother's pregnancy,
305; omnipotent early, 129;

omnipotent split-off, 367;
against parents, 72, 118–19;
projection of, 31; and reparation, 241, 300; and self, 461;
split off, 60; super-ego and, 60;
and suspicion of father, 73 n.

Diary, 406–7, 417

Dicky (*see also* Canaries), 410

Differentiation, of self and object, 235

Dinner with fishes, 102

Dirtying self, need for, 314–15

Disaster (*see also* Collision), 65,
68 n., 71, 78, 98–9, 103–4, 118,
182, 339–40, 356, 360, 362,
367, 375, 378, 454, 458, 461,
465

Discomfort, and persecutory feelings, 157

Discretion, 18

Dislikes, patient's, 379

Disruption of family, 36

Distrust (*see also* Allies; Ambivalence; Fears); of analyst, 36,
111, 248, 326, 350, 352–3, 355,
382, 419; of appearances, 361;
of breast, 278–9, 358, 461; of
father, 346, 357; of love, 414;
of mother, 111, 113, 248, 272,
279, 361, 378, 382; of reassurance, 326, 357; of sexual desires, 36

Doctor : 'bad', 37, 38, 41, 49,
159, 163, 167; fear of, 286;
for mind, 459

Dog(s) (*see also* Bobby), 26, 65,
68 n., 72, 74, 78, 79, 83, 84, 86,
93, 96, 97, 131, 356, 404; barking, 241; growling, 98, 103; in
picture, 31–2, 34, 38

'Doing his bit', 169–70

Donald Duck, 317, 396

Door, 130–1

'Dopey', 383, 386, 395

Dorothy, in *Wizard of Oz*, 219,
220

Dots, 215, 334–5, 451

Dover, 63–5

Hitler—(*continued*)
3, 126, 128, 134, 148, 158–60, 163, 165, 179, 181, 187, 190, 194, 199, 202, 215, 224–5, 230, 318, 342, 345, 351, 363, 370, 392, 396–7, 438–9, 441, 446, 452, 455, 457; -genital/penis, 35, 66, 87, 88, 91, 181, 188, 195–6, 404, 427, 429, 454; internalized and externalized, 427; invisible, 224; -mother, 143, 293; -parents, 208, 293; salute, 87, 164; suggestion of analysing, 184 n.

Hobbies, 16

Holiday, 170, 172, 175

Home : fear of loss of, 437, 453; love for, 214, 217; picture of, 227

Homosexuality : and breast relationship, 198, 289, 339, 424; as flight from heterosexuality, 182; and internalized dangerous penis, 89; obsessional aspect in, 89, 201; and paranoia, 279; and sympathy with father, 156

Homosexual wishes, guilt about, 289, 405

*Hood*, 116, 118, 125–6, 132, 327–9, 384, 400–2, 407

Hope/hopefulness, 100, 180, 226, 289, 351, 367, 378, 408, 433, 466

Hopelessness, 288–9

Horse's head, 44, 46, 47, 404 n.

Hospital, 97–8, 359

'Hospital' Box (for toys), 359, 367–8, 375

Hostility (*see also* Attacks; Destructive impulses; Hatred) : to father, 41; need to restrain, 393; patient's awareness of own, 267

Hotel manager, 230, 240

Hotel, patient's departure from, 319, 341

House(s) : deserted, 214; razing, 388, 390; toy, 388

Humour, sense of, 171, 243–4

Hungary, 292

Hunger, 210

Hypochondria, 15, 16, 34 n., 85, 205, 216, 239

Hypochondriacal fears/anxieties, 216, 239, 243, 442; analysis of, 166; root of, 157

Hypocrisy, 60

Hysterical symptoms and hypochondria, 216

Ice, 332

Ice-rink, 307, 332

Id, and interpretations, 27

Idealization : diminution of, 315, 417; of father, 204; of mother, 434, 447; of parents, 51; and persecution, 208, 326, 465; and positive transference, 326

Identification (*see also* Introjective identification; Projective identification) : change to male, 375 n.; feminine, 100, 375 n., 405, 410

Identity card, 406–7

Impotence (*see also* Potency), 166, 205, 311, 399; fear of, 205, 410; and growing up, 180

Impudence, lumps of, 203

'Impudent' boys (*see* Boy(s))

Incorporation, oral (*see also* Internalization; Introjection), 85, 158, 200

India-rubber, 35, 45

Information, given by parents, use of (*see also* Technique), 39, 338

Inhibition(s) : decrease in, 410; of faculties and interests, 15; of perception, 43; seriousness of, 351; of sublimations, 418

Ink, 46, 264, 335, 347

Insecurity, 85, 414, 465; against internal persecutors, 85

Inside(s) (*see also* Internal situation): anxiety about, 20, 79, 107, 139, 158, 203, 205, 212, 215, 236–7, 416, 418, 434; curiosity about, 35

Insight, 18, 302; analyst's, 12; and changes in defences, 110; longing for, 243; and repetition of interpretations, 399; and resistance, 130; and trust in analyst, 192; unconscious, 235

Insincerity, 60, 92, 157, 269, 358, 421–2, 425–6

Instincts, fusion of, (see also Death instinct; Life instinct), 341

Integration (see also Ego), 216, 235, 250; and adaptation to external reality, 367; anxiety from, 77, 217–18, 235; and differentiation, 235; longing for, 243; steps in, 192, 218, 300, 315, 387, 434, 442; relief from, 77, 235; and return to earlier anxieties, 340; of superego by ego, 465; and tolerance of depression, 267–8

Intensity, of impulses, degrees of, 341, 366

Interaction, of external and internal situations, 105, 171, 266

Internal (see also External; Externalization; Inside(s); Internalization; Internal object): danger situations, 217, 235; and external, 43, 76, 107, 235, 341, 433, 461; interaction with external, 105; situation and impotence, 205; splitting from external, 425

Internalization (see also Incorporation; Internal object; Internal situation), 211, 425; of analyst, 43, 94, 99; anxieties about, 104–5; earliest processes of, 61; of object, 75, 83, 115; of treacherous penis, 425–6; and paranoia, 279; of parents in intercourse, 118; phantasies of, 31; and projective identification, 113, 279

Internal objects (see also e.g. Breast; Father; Good object; Object(s); Mother; Penis): bad, 83, 249; controlling, 449; control, need to, 87; and depressive position, 75; and ego, 60; freedom from control by, 447; improved bad, 434; injured, 215, 341; integration of, 434; nature of, 205; relation to, 83, 85, 115; as persecutors, 304, 434; and projection, 217; and self, 217, 340, 461

Interpretation(s) (see also Technique): acceptance of, 22, 25, 67; and anxiety due to integration, 77, 235; of deep anxiety, 151, 192–3, 204; of details of prevalent anxieties, 305, 465; of early guilt, 248; first in session, 39; interaction between external and internal situations, 105, 171, 216; length of, 23; linking different aspects, 298–300; of painful material, 99, 100, 104; of omissions, 43; reaction to, 47, 55, 135, 197–8, 240, 243, 321, 361; relief from, 54, 99, 104, 151, 160, 180, 234, 243, 283; resistance to, 22, 28, 31, 55, 70, 167, 170, 192, 300; selection of material for, 135, 171, 305, 365; of silence, 234, 235; of symptomatic actions, 189, 256; timing of, 23; of transference, 11, 22–3, 205

Introjection (see also Internalization; Internal object): of hostile object, 280; indiscriminate, 409; of object for control, 337

Introjective identification, 409, 465

Intuition (see Analyst's intuition)